Introduction to Management:

A Contingency Approach

McGraw-Hill Series in Management
Keith Davis, Consulting Editor

Allen   Management and Organization
Allen   The Management Profession
Argyris   Management and Organizational Development: The Path from XA to YB
Beckett   Management Dynamics: The New Synthesis
Benton   Supervision and Management
Bergen and Haney   Organizational Relations and Management Action
Blough   International Business: Environment and Adaptation
Bowman   Management: Organization and Planning
Brown   Judgment in Administration
Campbell, Dunnette, Lawler, and Weick   Managerial Behavior, Performance, and Effectiveness
Cleland and King   Management: A Systems Approach
Cleland and King   Systems Analysis and Project Management
Cleland and King   Systems, Organizations, Analysis, Management: A Book of Readings
Dale   Management: Theory and Practice
Dale   Readings in Management: Landmarks and New Frontiers
Davis   Human Behavior at Work: Human Relations and Organizational Behavior
Davis   Organizational Behavior: A Book of Readings
Davis and Blomstrom   Business and Society: Environment and Responsibility
DeGreene   Systems Psychology
Dunn and Rachel   Wage and Salary Administration: Total Compensation Systems
Dunn and Stephens   Management of Personnel: Manpower Management and Organizational Behavior
Edmunds and Letey   Environmental Administration
Fiedler   A Theory of Leadership Effectiveness
Finch, Jones, and Litterer   Managing for Organizational Effectiveness: An Experiential Approach
Flippo   Principles of Personnel Management
Glueck   Business Policy: Strategy Formation and Management Action
Golembiewski   Men, Management, and Morality
Hicks and Gullett   The Management of Organizations
Hicks and Gullett   Modern Business Management: A Systems and Environmental Approach
Hicks and Gullett   Organizations: Theory and Behavior
Johnson, Kast, and Rosenzweig   The Theory and Management of Systems
Kast and Rosenzweig   Organization and Management: A Systems Approach
Knudson, Woodworth, and Bell   Management: An Experiential Approach
Koontz   Toward a United Theory of Management
Koontz and O'Donnell   Essentials of Management
Koontz and O'Donnell   Management: A Book of Readings
Koontz and O'Donnell   Management: A Systems and Contingency Analysis of Managerial Functions
Levin, McLaughlin, Lamone, and Kottas   Production/Operations Management: Contemporary Policy for Managing Operating Systems
Luthans   Contemporary Readings in Organizational Behavior
Luthans   Introduction to Management: A Contingency Approach
Luthans   Organizational Behavior
McNichols   Policy Making and Executive Action
Maier   Problem-solving Discussions and Conferences: Leadership Methods and Skills

Introduction to Management:
A Contingency Approach

Fred Luthans
University of Nebraska

with contributions by

Richard Schonberger
University of Nebraska

and

Russell Morey
Western Illinois University

McGraw-Hill Book Company
New York / St. Louis / San Francisco
Auckland / Düsseldorf / Johannesburg
Kuala Lumpur / London / Mexico
Montreal / New Delhi / Panama
Paris / São Paulo / Singapore
Sydney / Tokyo / Toronto

Introduction to Management:
A Contingency Approach

1 2 3 4 5 6 7 8 9 0   KPKP   7 9 8 7 6 5

This book was set in Vega Light by Rocappi, Inc.
The editors were William J. Kane and Annette Hall;
the designer was J. Paul Kirouac, A Good Thing, Inc.;
the production supervisor was Sam Ratkewitch.
The drawings were done by ANCO Technical Services.
Kingsport Press, Inc., was printer and binder.

Library of Congress Cataloging in Publication Data

Luthans, Fred.
    Introduction to management.

    (McGraw-Hill series in management)
    1. Management. I. Schonberger, Richard, joint
author. II. Morey, Russell, joint author. III. Title.
HD31.L86   1976   658.4   75-12953
ISBN 0-07-039125-4

**For
my
Family**

Contents

Preface

In the "future shock" environment we are living in today it is almost a cliché to say that "things are changing." Yet that is exactly the best phrase to describe the current field of management. Things indeed are changing in both management theory and practice. Today, most of the pressures for change in management are coming from the external environment. The ability to cope with and keep up with social, technological, economic, and political/legal forces will largely determine how effective management will be. Yet, despite its tremendous impact, the environment has been largely ignored in the theoretical development of management. Universal assumptions, i.e., that management concepts and techniques apply to any situation, have dominated. Traditionally, the environment was either treated as a given or completely ignored. It was not conceptually integrated into management theory. In a simpler time, management could survive with such a deficiency. However, in today's complex, highly turbulent environment such a glaring omission can no longer be tolerated.

Practitioners are finding out, sometimes the hard way, that the universal "principles of management" simply do not always work. They are finding out that the success or failure of particular management concepts and techniques largely depends on the situation. For example, under one set of environmental conditions a particular concept or technique turns out to be effective, and under different environmental circumstances the same concept or technique turns out to be ineffective. To date, when the practitioner has turned to existing management theory for a solution to this problem, no meaningful answers or even a framework for analysis was available.

The purpose of this book is to help correct two of the major deficiencies in the field of management that are suggested above by (1) conceptually integrating the environment as a vital part of management theory and (2) beginning to bridge the existing gap between management theory and practice. A contingency approach is suggested as a way to meet these goals. Part One of the book spells out exactly what is meant by the contingency approach to management and serves as a conceptual framework for the rest of the book. Particular attention is given in this first part to historical development, the contingency framework, and environmental forces. The succeeding parts of the book present the major concepts and techniques from the existing management approaches. The format is eclectic, taking the best from process (chapters on planning, organizing, directing and communicating, and controlling), quantitative (chapters on the quantitative approach and decision models and operations research), behavioral (chapters on learning theory and behavior modification, motivation, and group dynamics), and systems (chapters on general systems theory, systems design and analysis, and management information systems). At the same time, a contingency conceptual framework is used to integrate the environment into management theory and provide specific contingent relationships between the environment and management concepts and techniques that lead to the more effective practice of management. To assist in this latter effort, there are specific concluding contingency chapters in each part (chapters on process variables and contingency management, quantitative variables and contingency management, behavioral variables and contingency management, and systems variables and contingency management). The last chapter pinpoints some problem areas that need to be given attention for the future development of contingency management.

The book is intended for those who wish to take an environment-based contingency approach to the field of management. It does not assume any prior knowledge on the part of the reader. Therefore, the book can be effectively used in the first or only management course in undergraduate or junior colleges or in the management course in an M.B.A. curriculum. Since the book gives attention to all the diverse approaches to management, it should be ideal for use in the prerequisite course to more specialized courses in organizational behavior, operations management, quantitative methods, management policy, and systems management. Finally, the book should certainly appeal to the management practitioner who is confronted with the environment on a daily basis. It is hoped that by reading this book the practitioner will be better able to meet the tremendous challenge of more effective management of today's organizations.

I would like to make the following acknowledgments but certainly take all responsibility for the content of this book. First of all I would like to sincerely thank Professors Richard Schonberger of the University of Nebraska and Russell Morey of Western Illinois University for their help on some of the chapters. Professor Schonberger wrote original drafts for Chapters 4, 16, 17, and 18; and Professor Morey wrote original drafts for Chapters 7, 9, 10, and 11. Next I would like to thank Professors Richard Hodgetts of the University of Nebraska and Edward Knod of Western Illinois University for the unselfish giving of their time and ideas to portions of the manuscript. I would also like to thank Professors William Reif and John Newstrom of Arizona State University for reading the manuscript and giving me their helpful comments. Finally, I would like to sincerely thank my wife and children for giving me the necessary time and support to complete this book.

Fred Luthans

Introduction to Contingency Management

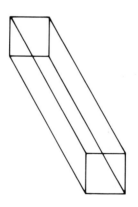

Part One

The Evolving Field of Management

Management is certainly a dominant force in every aspect of modern society. However, like most other important aspects of today's scene, the importance of history, and sometimes the very recognition that there is a history, is often overlooked. The purpose of this introductory chapter is to give recognition to management as an evolving field. Management has a rich heritage and has always been in the forefront of what progress society has made through the years. The first part of the chapter samples some of the many instances of effective management in ancient times. Next, the beginnings of modern management are examined. In particular, feudalism, preindustrialization, and industrialization are given attention. This discussion leads into the major schools of thought in management theory. The discussion traces the development of the process, quantitative, behavioral, and systems approaches that all contribute to the contingency approach to management. Finally, some of the important emerging trends that affect the practice of management are analyzed. Professionalism and the expanding scope of management are given specific attention.

Management in Antiquity

The field of management has a relatively large volume of literature. Some of the writings can be traced as far back as 5,000 B.C. In fact, today's managers are in some ways indebted to managers in antiquity. Managers in the successful civilizations of ancient times were the first to uncover and explain some of the principles and practices most widely used in this century. While time and space limitations preclude acknowledgment of all these contributions, a sampling can give an appreciation of the tremendous managerial feats accomplished by managers in ancient times.

Management in Ancient Egypt

History books are replete with the contributions the Egyptians have made to modern civilization. Perhaps because they are considered one of the seven wonders of the ancient world, the pyramids come quickly to mind. In particular, the Great Pyramid is often singled out for attention. Built with 2,300,000 separate stones, each weighing an average of 2.5 tons, the Great Pyramid covers 13 acres. It is no wonder that the Great Pyramid is viewed with awe. Besides its size, however, is the importance of the managerial feat of putting it together. The giant edifice required the labor of 100,000 workers over a 20-year period. Workers labored in the stone quarries cutting the blocks; others transported them down river during the annual flood season to avoid the need for land transportation; and others dragged them to the construction site, cut them to final size, numbered them, and placed them in position. The management concepts and techniques necessary to build the Great Pyramid, or any of the other giant edifices, illustrate the effectiveness of Egyptian managers. As the management historian Claude George notes,

By using masses of organized labor the Egyptians were able to accomplish tasks that astonish us. While their system of organization may appear unwieldy, cumbersome, and even wasteful, they actually had no reason to economize on labor, since more peasants, mercenaries, and slaves were always available simply for the asking. That they were able to do the job with the available resources is to their credit, and their remaining edifices clearly indicate their managerial effectiveness and sophistication.[1]

Another representative illustration of Egyptian managerial knowhow is found in their use of job descriptions. For example, the vizier or prime minister had a specific list of instructions telling him his duties and providing him guidelines on how to conduct himself before subordinates. Other writings illustrate that the Egyptians encouraged their managers to employ long-range planning, rely on the use of staff advisers, and be honest in their dealings with others. These and many other Egyptian concepts and techniques are very similar to the suggested conduct of a modern management professional.

The Hebrews as Managers

The Hebrews are an example of another ancient group that provided insights into management theories and practices. For instance, it is reported in the book of Exodus that Jethro, who was Moses' father-in-law, counseled the great Jewish leader to delegate minor matters to his subordinates so that he would have more time for handling important decisions: "Every small matter they shall judge, but every great matter they shall bring to thee." This same basic concept of the delegation of authority is employed by modern managers. So, too, is the exception principle which states that managers should devote their time to important matters and allow minor ones to be handled by others.

Another illustration of management practices is found in the Ten Commandments. Moses and the Hebrews used these laws as guidelines for individual and organizational conduct. Today, modern organizations employ rules, procedures, and policies for the same purpose. A final example of the Hebrews' managerial effectiveness is the exodus from Egypt. To accomplish this difficult task, the Hebrews employed many management concepts and techniques.

---

[1] Claude S. George, Jr., *The History of Management Thought*, 2d ed., Prentice-Hall, Englewood Cliffs, N.J., 1972, p. 5.

The Ancient Chinese Managers

Like the Egyptians and Hebrews, the Chinese also used many effective management concepts and techniques. One instance was their use of staff advisers. Early in Chinese history, the emperors realized the value of sound advice and began relying upon their subordinates to provide them with information useful in managing the empire. As a result, the use of advisers, or the staff concept as it is now called, became an integral part of China's government. Thus, when a young emperor named Tai Chai (1753–1721 B.C.) repeatedly ignored the advice of his advisers, the prime minister had him deposed for a period of 3 years. Only when he promised to respect the future counsel of his staff was he allowed to return to his position. Today, of course, advisers often lack the power to force a superior to listen to their counsel. However, when one realizes that most modern organizations utilize a line-staff structure, it is evident that many of today's managers have as high a regard for staff advice as did the ancient Chinese emperors.

Another contribution of the Chinese was their acknowledgment of the need for an overall management system. They believed that there had to be standards of operation which bring together the tools and the workers in some harmonious fashion. Laws or principles of management by themselves were not enough. Everything had to be integrated in a systematic way so that the greatest result for the whole would be obtained. Mencius writing in about 500 B.C. explained the approach this way:

Whoever pursues a business in this world must have a system. A business which has attained success without a system does not exist. From ministers and generals down to the hundreds of craftsmen, everyone of them has a system. The craftsmen employ the ruler to make a square and the compass to make a circle. All of them, both skilled and unskilled, use this system. The skilled may at times accomplish a circle and a square by their own dexterity. But with a system, even the unskilled may achieve the same result, though dexterity they have none. Hence, every craftsman possesses a system as a model. Now, if we govern the empire, or a large state, without a system as a model, are we not even less intelligent than a common craftsman?[2]

Management Contributions from the Greeks

The ancient Greeks should be as famous for their contributions to management as they are for their contributions to philosophy and political science. Perhaps the greatest of their contributions was the recognition of the importance of the division of labor. Plato, the great philosopher, elaborated upon this idea in his famous *Republic*:

Which would be better—that each should ply several trades, or that he should confine himself to his own? He should confine himself to his own. More is done, and better and more easily when one man does one thing according to his capacity and at the right moment. We must not be surprised to find that articles are made better in big cities than in small. In small cities the same workman makes a bed, a door, a plough, a table. . . . In the big cities, on the other hand . . . a man can live by one single trade. . . . One makes men's shoes another women's, one lives entirely by the stitching of the shoe, another by cutting the leather. . . . A man whose work is confined to such a limited task must necessarily excel at it.[3]

---

[2] James Legge, translator, *The Chinese Classics,* Hong Kong University Press, Hong Kong, 1960, p. 226, as found in George, op. cit., p. 13.

[3] Francis Cornford, *The Republic of Plato,* Oxford University Press, New York, 1959, pp. 165–167, as found in George, op. cit., pp. 15–16.

Another interesting managerial innovation of the Greeks was the introduction of music into the work place. On monotonous or repetitive jobs, the work pace was set by music. Flutes or pipes governed the work tempo. Today, of course, not all people work directly to the tempo of music, but many managers and industrial psychologists feel that employees do a better job after a music system is installed. Like the Greeks, modern management is trying to harmonize the physical (division of labor) and psychological (soothing music) aspects of work in attaining greater efficiency.

A third Greek contribution was their belief in the principle of universality of managerial functions. They believed that all managers perform the same basic functions. Socrates, another famous Greek philosopher, pointed out that the duties of a manager, regardless of his field of endeavor, are often very similar. For example, an effective general must choose his subordinates well, maintain morale, demand and obtain satisfactory performance from each, and be prepared to punish incompetent personnel and reward competent ones. This set of guidelines applied to successful leaders in any position. This universality reasoning is still largely depended upon today in much of management theory and practice.

The discussion of the various schools of management thought in this chapter will expand on this universality assumption, and the next chapter will propose an alternate contingency assumption, an assumption that management is not universal but depends on the situation. Since the universality assumption can be traced back to antiquity, the roots are obviously deep, and universality is entrenched in management theory and practice.

The Genesis of Modern Management

Obviously there were many other examples of effective management is antiquity than those cited above. For example, after the Greeks, the Romans made significant contributions to management thought. The Romans had the ability to effectively organize and manage an empire of 100 million people. However, after the fall of the Roman Empire, the world entered the Dark Ages. Initially, during this bleak period of human history, economic, social, and political chaos reigned. The development of management, like everything else, came to a standstill. However, around A.D. 600 order began to be restored, first in the form of feudalism, then preindustrialized commerce, and finally industrialization.

The Age of Feudalism

Feudalism was a period in history which prevailed for almost 900 years. A type of cultural system, feudalism essentially entailed a giant organizational hierarchy headed by a king or emperor who owned all the land in his domain. Keeping the best land for himself, the king invested the highest-ranking nobles with the rest. In return, these nobles or vassals were required to perform financial and military services for the king. Likewise, these vassals had a similar agreement with their subvassals, and the process continued on down the hierarchy to the lowest level. This could be thought of as a type of managerial system. It created order out of the chaos that followed the fall of the Roman Empire.

The feudal system worked hand in hand with the Catholic church, which had a tremendous amount of influence over medieval life. The church became the largest landholder in all Europe and gave a great deal of support to the feudal system. At the same time, domination of life by the Catholic church led to a focus on nonmaterialistic things. As a result, commerce or business was discouraged, and thus development of management became stifled as well.

Preindustrial Commerce

The Crusades changed the cloistered, nonmaterialistic life of the Dark Ages. By opening up new trade routes and exposing feudal, parochial Europe to the wealth of the East, the Crusades stimulated interest in commerce. The populace started turning its attention to economic matters. Eventually, feudalism died out and the power of the church declined. Human history moved into a new era—preindustrialized commerce. This new era was characterized by three dominating ethics which influenced the development of management: the market ethic, the Protestant ethic, and the liberty ethic.[4]

MARKET ETHIC   The market ethic had an economic orientation. With the high interest in commerce, governments began to encourage the formulation of economic trade theories and practices. Concepts of supply and demand were developed, and the father of economics, Adam Smith, popularized management concepts such as division of labor. In *The Wealth of Nations,* Smith described how one unspecialized worker could make 20 pins in a day while a group of specialized workers could produce 48,000 pins in this same time period:

This great increase of the quantity of work which, in consequence of the division of labour, the same number of people are capable of performing, is owing to three different circumstances; first, to the increase of the dexterity in every particular workman; secondly, to the saving of the time which is commonly lost in passing from one species of work to another; and lastly, to the invention of a great number of machines which facilitate and abridge labour, and enable one man to do the work of many.[5]

PROTESTANT ETHIC   The Protestant ethic also supported increased business activity and management. Catholics could receive absolution from a priest for the sins they confessed, thus releasing believers of psychological guilt. In contrasting this Catholic approach with Protestant Calvinism, Max Weber, the pioneering German sociologist, noted:

The God of Calvinism demanded of his believers not single good works, but a life of good works combined into a unified system. There was no place for the very human Catholic cycle of sin, repentance, atonement, release, followed by renewed sin. Nor was there any balance of merit for a life as a whole which could be adjusted by temporal punishments or the Churches' means of grace.[6]

---

[4] Daniel A. Wren, *The Evolution of Management Thought,* Ronald, New York, 1972, pp. 22–34.

[5] Adam Smith, *The Wealth of Nations,* The Modern Library, New York, 1937, p. 7.

[6] Max Weber, *The Protestant Ethic and the Spirit of Capitalism,* translated by Talcott Parsons, Scribner, New York, 1958, p. 117.

In other words, the Calvinist Protestant had to live an entire life of good works characterized by self-discipline, self-control, and asceticism. In so doing, the individual was encouraged to follow the adage "waste not, want not." The gathering of wealth was not sinful unless the person threw it away on life's frivolities. On the other hand, saving and reinvesting the money was perfectly acceptable. By doing this, of course, a person could amass a large fortune. Such wealth was interpreted as a sign that the individual was favored by God and would be rewarded in the next life. The result of this Protestant ethic was hard work, self-denial, and most importantly, capitalism and an entrepreneurial spirit.

LIBERTY ETHIC   The third important ethic in the preindustrial commerce era evolved out of the writings of such famous philosophers as John Locke and Jean Jacques Rousseau. In essence, their works challenged the divine rights of kings and the power of the vassal and manor lord. Under this liberty ethic, people were not felt to be born serfs. Instead, they were felt to be free of arbitrary rules formed by tradition. This new ethic stressed that people should be governed by laws of reason. Such ideas were eventually translated into a famous document, the Declaration of Independence, part of which reads:

We hold these truths to be self-evident, that all men are created equal, that they are endowed by their Creator with certain unalienable Rights, that among these are Life, Liberty, and the pursuit of Happiness.—That to secure these rights, Governments are instituted among Men, drawing their just powers from the consent of the governed,—

It was within this environmental situation (market, Protestant, and liberty) that a significant historical event in the history of modern management thought began—the industrial revolution.

Industrialization: Major Contribution to Modern Management
Changes in the social, economic, and political environment a couple of centuries ago provided the necessary impetus for significant scientific and technological advances. Industrial progress seems to be highly dependent upon such conditions. Of all the countries in Europe in the mid-1700s, the one with the most advantageous conditions for industrial progress was England. First, England's Parliament was sensitive to the desire of businesses for a laissez faire (noninterference, free-enterprise) economic system. Second, England was determined to protect and increase trade with other countries. Third, profit and achievement were socially acceptable values; thus many individuals were encouraged to enter business ventures. Fourth, scientific thinking and practical applications of research were promoted and given direct support.

As a result of the favorable English climate in the eighteenth century, many important inventions were made. In 1763 John Kay mechanized weaving with his flying shuttle. In 1765 James Hargreaves improved the invention by changing the position of the spinning wheel and adding more wheels and power. The resulting spinning jenny was able to weave eighty threads simultaneously. Meanwhile, in 1760 John Smeaton replaced the water-driven bellows in his iron factory with one partially driven by steam and increased his daily iron productivity per furnace by well over 200 percent. During the same decade, Richard Arkwright invented the water frame and within 10 years had over 5,000 workers operating these machines. At the same time, James Watt developed the steam engine and by 1788 was employing the machine in an iron foundry. This use of steam power greatly lowered production costs, which in turn reduced prices and expanded markets. The steam engine replaced human hands in the productive process.

The result of these and other inventions was the emergence of the factory system of work. By bringing everything under one roof, it was found that management could coordinate labor, capital, and machinery in a more efficient manner. For example, management could systematically study such things as machine feed and speed for maximum production. Management became interested in how fast a machine should be run and what was the proper way to feed raw materials into it. The answers to these types of questions dominated management thinking in the early stages of industrialization. Management placed strong emphasis on the economic and mechanical sides of enterprise. Initially, physical things were given precedence over anything else in the factory.

As industrialization began to mature, it soon became evident that in addition to labor, capital, and machinery, there was a fourth important factor of production—management itself. If workers were expected to keep working efficiently, they needed a continuous supply of raw materials. Likewise, if there was an increase in output, a market for these goods had to be found and the product sold. In addition, capital for replacing and buying more machinery and expanding the factory had to be secured; coordination of effort among the workers had to be obtained; and cooperation between and among all levels of the organization had to be achieved. This was management's job.

Industrialization brought not only mechanical but also managerial challenges. The focus on efficiency at the lower levels of the organization soon included middle and upper levels as well. This expanded emphasis led to the emergence of process management theorists. The goal of these theorists was to formulate principles of management that had universal applicability, regardless of the situation. Management by trial and error began to be replaced by a more systematic approach. It became evident that the ability to manage efficiently could be improved through the exchange of information and experience. This marked the beginning of the formalized, academic approach to the field of management as a whole.

During this same period of industrialization when management theory was coming into existence, some practicing managers were also beginning to focus their attention on the human element in the work place. One of the more prominent was Robert Owen, who purchased the New Lanark Mills in Scotland. Upon assuming control, the enlightened Owen introduced reform efforts to improve the housing, sanitation, and education of his workers. He also eliminated corporal punishment of children and saw that the younger ones were taken out of the mills and sent to school. In addition, he instituted a motivation system designed to increase productivity. Under this system, Owen assigned one of four marks to each of his superintendents, each of whom rated their own subordinates.

These marks were translated into color codes of black, blue, yellow, and white in ascending order of merit. A block of wood was mounted on each machine and the four sides painted according to the code. At the end of each day, the marks were recorded, translated, and the appropriate color side of the block turned to face the aisle. Anyone passing, and knowing the code, could immediately assess the workers' last day's effort. This wooden albatross worked to motivate laggards to overcome their deficiency and supposedly to induce the white block "good guys" to maintain theirs. It was most certainly a precursor of modern management's public posting of sales and production data to instill departmental pride or to encourage competition.[7]

While other mills at that time were averaging about a 20 percent return on invested capital, Owen obtained in excess of 50 percent. When asked how he accomplished this, he said that while others were investing money in machinery, he was devoting time and effort to his human resources, which offered a higher return on investment. Owen's attention to the behavioral aspects of management helped account for the success of his operation. Others, such as Matthew Boulton and James Watt, who ran the Soho Engineering Foundry, experienced similar results. They attributed higher productivity to whitewashing walls, having Christmas parties, and designing incentive payment plans for their workers.

During the early stages of industrialization, the seeds were planted for the subsequent emerging schools of management thought. The concern for what types of plant layout and mechanical adaptations led to the greatest productivity evolved into the quantitative school of management thought; the broadened concern for what guidelines or principles the effective manager should use in the management of the overall organization marked the beginning of the process theory of management; and the human concerns of Owen and others was the start of the behavioral approach to management. The next section will give more detailed development of these major historical schools of management thought.

Historical Schools of Management Thought

The discussion so far has shown that management has a long history going as far back as antiquity. However, the genesis of modern management theory did not get underway until the industrial revolution and in comparison with other academic disciplines is very young. As a systematic body of knowledge based on a theoretical foundation, management is almost purely a product of the twentieth century. Yet, in this relatively short period of time several schools of thought have emerged. About 15 years ago, Harold Koontz classified six different schools of management thought: process, empirical, human behavior, social system, decision theory, and mathematical.[8] More recently, four schools have become generally recognized: process, quantitative, behavioral, and systems. Very recently, a fifth approach has emerged.[9] This newest school of management thought and the one which this book uses as its conceptual framework is the contingency theory of management. The following sections discuss the four established approaches (process, quantitative, behavioral, and systems) from a historical perspective, and the next chapter is specifically devoted to the contingency approach to management.

---

[7] Wren, op. cit., p. 65.

[8] Harold Koontz, "The Management Theory Jungle," *Academy of Management Journal*, December 1961, pp. 174–188.

[9] See Fred Luthans, "The Contingency Theory of Management: A Path out of the Jungle," *Business Horizons*, June 1973, pp. 67–72.

Process Approach to Management

Other names attached to the process approach include *operational, functional, universal, traditional,* and *classical.* By whatever name, this school first attempts to identify management functions and then establish fundamental principles. Both the functions and the principles are held to be universal in all managers under all conditions. The Frenchman Henri Fayol is the widely recognized founder of the process school of thought. His career embodied many different phases, including being a practicing mining engineer, a research geologist (he developed a unique theory on the formation of coal-bearing strata), and a practicing executive. In 1888, he became managing director of Comambault, a well-known French industrial combine. At the time of his taking over, a dividend had not been paid for 3 years and bankruptcy seemed inevitable. However, through Fayol's ingenious managerial and organizational methods, the problems were soon corrected, and by the time of World War I the combine was able to make a significant contribution to the French war effort.

Starting at the turn of the century, Fayol began to express his views on management through writing and speaking engagements. In 1900 he gave a paper at the International Mining and Metallurgical Congress and in 1916 put his ideas into a work called *General and Industrial Management.* Unfortunately, this work was not published in English until 1949. In this book he advocated that the successful practicing manager be able to handle men, have considerable energy and courage, have continuity of tenure, and have a great deal of specialized and general experience.[10]

Fayol is probably best known for identifying the five functions of management: planning, organizing, commanding, coordinating, and controlling. Other pioneering process theorists came up with similar functions but sometimes attached different names. For example, in 1937 Luther Gulick used the acronym POSDCORB to represent the functions of management. This stands for planning, organizing, staffing, directing, coordinating, reporting, and budgeting.[11]

The process approach has been the conceptual framework for the traditional principles of management textbooks. For example, George Terry, the author of a widely read principles text, uses planning, organizing, actuating, and controlling, and Koontz and O'Donnell, the authors of another widely read principles text, use planning, organizing, staffing, directing, and controlling.[12] After determining these functions, the next step in the process approach is to formulate universal principles of management. Chapter 5 will cover some of the more common principles, such as unity of command, equal authority and responsibility, limited span of control, and delegation of routine matters. Koontz and O'Donnell cite the value of these universal principles as follows:

When management principles can be developed, proved, and used, managerial efficiency will inevitably improve. Then the conscientious manager can become more effective by using established

---

[10] Henri Fayol, *General and Industrial Management,* translated by Constance Storrs, Sir Isaac Pitman & Sons, London, 1949, p. 50.

[11] Luther Gulick, "Notes on the Theory of Organization," in Luther Gulick and Lyndall Urwick (eds.), *Papers on the Science of Administration,* Institute of Public Administration, New York, 1937, p. 13.

[12] George Terry, *Principles of Management,* 6th ed., Irwin, Homewood, Ill., 1972; and Harold Koontz and Cyril O'Donnell, *Principles of Management,* 5th ed., McGraw-Hill, New York, 1972.

guidelines to help solve his problems, without engaging in original laborious research or the risky practice of trial and error.[13]

The traditional process approach has recently been under severe attack as a conceptual base for management. Critics ask what real progress has been made since Fayol's perceptive analysis at the beginning of the century. Few would question that Fayol made a significant contribution to the development of management thought, but what else has happened? Since Fayol, the process theorists have dickered over semantic problems of what to call the functions (directing or commanding, budgeting or planning, and reporting or controlling). In addition, when the sacred principles have been put to the test of research and even practical experience, they have often failed to prove valid or, especially, universal. This does not mean that there are not functions of management or that there should be no attempt to formulate guidelines or even principles. Management does involve functions such as planning, organizing, directing, communicating, and controlling, but by themselves functions and principles are not an adequate conceptual framework for modern management. The process approach is much to static and does not adequately integrate quantitative, behavioral, and systems concepts and techniques. As far as the principles go, they simply are not and should not be presented as universal in today's complex environment. This will be discussed and analyzed in the next two chapters, and the process functions are covered in detail in the chapters in Part Two of the book.

Quantitative Approach to Management

The quantitative or management science approach has never really claimed to be an overall conceptual base for management theory. Yet, its strong advocates have certainly implied that mathematical models and quantitative processes could serve as the basis for all management.

Frederick W. Taylor's "scientific management" around the turn of the century could be considered the beginning of the quantitative approach to management. A by-product of the industrial revolution, Taylor had actual shop and engineering experience and was directly concerned with increasing productivity through scientific methods. His famous metal-cutting experiments were a case in point. For over 26 years Taylor tested every possible variation in speed, feed, depth of cut, and kind of cutting tool. The outcome of this scientific approach was high-speed steel. It is considered to be a highly significant contribution to the development of large-scale production. In another famous application, Taylor was able to attain about a threefold increase in the productivity of the pig iron and shoveling operations at Bethlehem Steel Company.

Taylor wrote down many of his scientific principles and his management philosophy. He stated that management should consist of (1) science, not rule of thumb; (2) harmony, not discord; (3) cooperation, not individualism; (4) maximum output, in place of restricted

---

[13] Koontz and O'Donnell, op. cit., pp. 14–15.

output; and (5) the development of each person to his greatest efficiency and prosperity.[14] Together, the scientific principles of Taylor and other famous scientific managers such as Frank Gilbreth and Henry L. Gantt formulated a conceptual approach to management as a whole. In the early 1900s "scientific management" became practically synonymous with management itself. The upsurge in popularity was primarily a result of a 1910 railway rate hearing before the Interstate Commerce Commission. Testimony by the efficiency engineer Harrington Emerson dramatically pointed out that the railroads could save "a million dollars a day" by applying scientific management. The newspapers headlined this testimony, and scientific management became practically a household word and renowned throughout American and even foreign industry.

A natural extension of scientific management and more representative of the modern quantitative approach is the operations research movement that got underway during World War II. Operations research, or simply OR, uses model-building techniques to solve managerial decision problems. OR takes a much broader perspective than scientific management and makes more direct and extensive use of mathematics. Mathematically based techniques such as linear programming, economic order quantity, queuing, and simulation are applied to managerial problems such as transportation, inventory levels, optimum allocations, and waiting time. Specific planning and control techniques, such as network and cost benefit analyses, also have a quantitative emphasis.

The stated purpose of the quantitative approach is to provide more and better alternatives for management decision making. When constructing an OR model of the decision problem under consideration, management is forced to make a logical analysis. Goals and measures of effectiveness are stressed. However, it is sometimes forgotten that these quantitative techniques only aid the decision maker. They do not make the decision for the manager. The quantitative approach certainly has an important role to play in modern management. However, similar to the process approach, it cannot stand alone as the theoretical or conceptual base for modern management. The chapters in Part Three of the book present the quantitative approach in detail.

Behavioral Approach to Management

Although there were a few scattered examples in history, such as the work of Robert Owen, of managers giving attention to the human element in work, it was not until around 1930 that the behavioral approach became part of the mainstream of management thought. The Great Depression, the labor movement, and especially the results of pioneering behavioral research were the major precipitating causes.

THE GREAT DEPRESSION   The economy was operating in high gear just before the thundering "crash" occurred in 1929. American industry had achieved amazing results. What went wrong? If production were maximized through scientific management, would

---

[14] Frederick W. Taylor, *The Principles of Scientific Management,* Harper, New York, 1911, p. 140.

not the "invisible hand" of laissez faire economic policy take care of the rest? Obviously, it did not. After the crash, management began to realize that sole reliance on internal production and invisible-hand external economic policies was not enough. The business world was becoming more complex, and the Depression's aftermath of unemployment, discontent, and insecurity brought to the surface many accompanying human problems that managers were now forced to recognize and deal with. Personnel departments were either created or given more emphasis, and all practitioners now began to view the human aspects of management with a new reality. The labor movement gave particular focus to this new awakening.

THE LABOR MOVEMENT Although labor unions were in existence in America as early as 1792 (the Philadelphia Shoemakers), it was not until 1935 that a liberal Congress passed the Wagner Act, which gave organized labor the right to collectively bargain over wages, hours, and conditions of employment. In the past, practicing managers did not properly recognize labor's contribution to the goals of the organization. A "fair wage," decent hours, and adequate working conditions were often sacrificed for more production. Some of the more enlightened pioneers in management, such as Owen, Taylor, Henry Ford, and Alfred P. Sloan of General Motors, openly expressed their sincere desire to give labor its "fair share." However, except for these few exceptions and some scattered paternalistic managers, labor was often exploited. But when the unions became legally entrenched, managers were forced to wake up and take notice. The general reaction was either to fight the union or to realize it was here to stay and might possibly have something to contribute. Although there were often open conflicts in this era, most managers assumed the latter position and formed personnel departments to either deal with the existing union or have such good policies for employees that unions could not get in. In either case, new emphasis was given to the behavioral side of enterprise.

THE HAWTHORNE STUDIES Most important, however, was the beginning of some behavioral research that led to the human relations movement in management. The Hawthorne studies are usually pinpointed as the formal starting point for the behavioral approach to management. They were conducted at the Hawthorne Works of the Western Electric Company, and Elton Mayo and a team of researchers from Harvard began the relay-room phase of the study in 1927. Prior to that, a group of company men had failed to show a relationship between the level of illumination and worker productivity. Mayo and his group attempted to find out the reason. Instead of illumination, with the relay workers they manipulated place of work, place and length of rest pauses, length of working day, length of workweek, methods of payment, and a free midmorning lunch.

As in the illumination experiments, the experimenters could not determine a relationship between these variables and continually increasing performance. What was going on?

Group dynamics and the behavioral element in work was what was going on in the illumination and relay-room experiments at Hawthorne. Through interviews with employees in the plant and through a later study set up to observe the group dynamics of bank wirers, it was shown how powerful, but overlooked, human behavior in organizations actually was. The Hawthorne studies provide an important historical base for the behavioral approach to management because for the first time an intensive, systematic analysis was made of the human factor in management. The studies dramatically pointed out, and the years of controversy surrounding the results substantiate, the extreme complexity of human behavior in organizations. Yet, the early phase of the behavioral approach, the human relations movement, ignored this complexity.

HUMAN RELATIONS APPROACH TO ORGANIZATIONAL BEHAVIOR   The human relations movement essentially revolved around the assumption that if management could make employees happy, maximum performance would result. Moreover, everyone knew that the way to make employees happy was through money, security, and working conditions. Figure 1-1 shows the human relations approach.

Part Four of the book will show that this human relations approach is much too simplistic. Such an approach did not begin to solve the human problems facing management. Similar to the quantitative approach, the behavioral approach began to move away from simplistic assumptions and toward a broader, scientifically based approach. This new behavioral approach is labeled organizational behavior and will be the subject of the chapters in Part Four.

Systems Approach to Management

The systems approach has taken up where the process approach has left off in attempting to unify management theory. Whereas the quantitative and behavioral approaches went off on opposite paths from the process approach, the systems approach has attempted to draw them back together to form an overall theory of management. Today, it is undoubtedly the most widely accepted theoretical base for modern management.

A systems viewpoint has been around for a very long time. Ludwig von Bertalanffy, a biologist-philosopher who is usually credited with being the founder of general systems theory, pointed out that systems thinking goes back as far as ancient times. However, it is von Bertalanffy who first used the terminology and gave meaning to general systems theory in its modern sense. In a 1928 article in German he referred to "the system theory

Figure 1-1   The Human Relations Approach.

of the organism." He talked about general systems theory in the 1930s and in various publications immediately following World War II.[15] In addition to von Bertalanffy, now deceased, a number of other well-known scholars from a wide variety of academic disciplines also contributed to systems thinking. Chapter 16 on general systems theory will trace this development in more detail.

Applied to management, traces of systems thinking can be found in the work of Frederick W. Taylor and even more in the work of operations researchers during World War II. However, as a specific school of thought and a theoretical base, the systems approach to management is relatively new. The first widely recognized systems approach which specifically analyzed and provided a conceptual framework for management was probably the 1963 book by Johnson, Kast, and Rosenzweig.[16] Today, practically all management textbooks incorporate a systems approach.

The systems approach is quite basic in concept. It simply means that all parts are interrelated and interdependent to form the whole. A system is composed of elements or subsystems that are related and dependent upon one another. When these subsystems are in interaction with one another, they form a unitary whole. Thus, by definition, almost any phenomenon can be analyzed or presented from a systems viewpoint. There are biological, physical, economic, and sociocultural systems, and also systems found in organization and management. The next chapter analyzes the systems approach in relation to contingency management, and all the chapters in Part Five of the book deal specifically with systems variables in organization and management.

Historical Schools in Perspective

Harold Koontz's terminology the "Management Theory Jungle" is very descriptive of the divergent and often contradictory schools of management thought. Figure 1-2 attempts to trace the various paths through this jungle and beyond. It shows that the process approach split into two very divergent paths. The simplistic human relations movement in the behavioral approach and the narrow operations research movement in the quantitative approach dominated the decade of the 1950s and into the 1960s. Around a decade ago, however, both the behavioral and quantitative approaches turned back toward a more common conceptual base. The behavioral approach moved toward more broad-based organizational behavior which borrowed heavily from the behavioral sciences and made more complex assumptions. In a parallel development, the quantitative approach became characterized by broader-based management science. In a management science approach, operations research models are still utilized but more complex assumptions are made and more sophisticated mathematical techniques are employed to solve deci-

---

[15] See Ludwig von Bertalanffy, "The History and Status of General Systems Theory," *Academy of Management Journal,* December 1972, pp. 407–426. The article originally appeared in George J. Klir (ed.), *Trends in General Systems Theory,* Wiley-Interscience, New York, 1972.

[16] Richard A. Johnson, Fremont E. Kast, and James E. Rosenzweig, *The Theory and Management of Systems,* McGraw-Hill, New York, 1963.

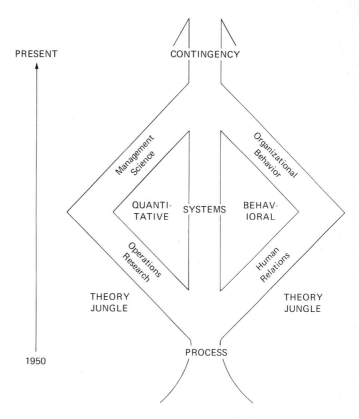

Figure 1-2 Paths through the Management Theory Jungle. *Source:* Fred Luthans, "The Contingency Theory of Management: A Path out of the Jungle," *Business Horizons,* June 1973, p. 69. Used with permission.

sional problems. The figure shows that both the organizational behavior and management science approaches are moving toward a systems base.

By the time the juncture of the process, quantitative, behavioral, and systems approaches are reached, the result may be something entirely different from the sum of the parts. This "something different from the sum of the parts" is the contingency approach to management. This contingency approach is the subject of the next chapter and serves as the conceptual framework for the entire book. Before getting into it, however, some of the important emerging trends that affect the practice of contingency management in particular and management in general are examined.

Emerging Trends in the Practice of Management

Many variables are having an impact on the practice of modern management. Among the more important are management professionalism and the broadened scope of management. Discussion of these vital areas will set the stage for presenting the contingency approach in the next chapter and lend more meaning to Chapter 3 on environmental conditions.

A New Professionalism in Management

In both number and perspective, management is moving toward a new professionalism. In the last census it was revealed that a majority of the people in this country are employed in service industries. This fact makes America in the 1970s the first postindustrial society in the history of the world. For the first time since the industrial revolution, more lower-level employees in organizations were performing specific service functions rather than blue-collar productive-type jobs. Even more important, more managers were performing professional types of activities (staff jobs in engineering, public relations, or research as well as in education, health, and other professional services) than were functioning in a traditional line executive job. The perspective of this new majority of employees in modern organizations is extremely important to the development of meaningful management theory and effective practice.

Over 50 years ago, Mary Parker Follett, a pioneer in the development of modern management thought, stated that management was a profession. However, her basis for such a statement was that management had a foundation of science and a service motive. The requirements for a profession are usually much more exacting than these two broad criteria. Probably the most widely recognized criteria for a profession would include the following:

1 A body of specialized knowledge or techniques
2 Formal, standardized education, training, and experience
3 A representative organization with the purpose of professionalization
4 Fees based on services to clients or customers with priority given to service rather than financial return
5 An ethical code of conduct and broad-based responsibility

Before analyzing the present status of management in relation to the above criteria, a more basic question is whether management should even strive to be a profession. It is generally assumed that professionalization should be the goal of management, but as Peter Drucker, the famous management writer and consultant, pointed out over two decades ago:

Management . . . is a practice, rather than a science or a profession, though containing elements of both. No greater damage could be done to our economy or to our society than to attempt to "professionalize" management by "licensing" managers . . . or by limiting access to management to people with a special academic degree. . . . Any serious attempt to make management "scientific" or a "profession" is bound to lead to the attempt to eliminate those "disturbing nuisances," the unpredictabilities of business life—its risks, its ups and downs, its "wasteful competition," the "irrational choices" of the consumer—and, in the process, the economy's freedom and its ability to grow.[17]

[17] Peter F. Drucker, *The Practice of Management*, Harper & Row, New York, 1954, pp. 9–10.

In other words, Drucker feels that economic performance and achievement, not professionalism, are the goals for management. He sees the two as incompatible. Yet, while such reasoning certainly has some merit, Drucker's concept of professionalization seems much too narrow. There is no reason why a manager cannot be both a professional manager and an economically successful executive. The two go hand in hand rather than working at odds with each other. A professional perspective for management would seem to be in the best interests of the economy's freedom and growth. The following discussion attempts to determine how far management has proceeded in becoming a profession.

BODY OF KNOWLEDGE   At present there is a fairly extensive body of management knowledge. Although it is relatively small compared with that of other academic disciplines, literally hundreds of management books are published every year and scores of management journals are available on monthly, bimonthly, or quarterly bases. Although most of these books and articles are for popular consumption and are not based on sound scientific methodology, there has been an effort in recent years to improve on this score, and the results so far have been quite good. Journals such as the *Academy of Management Journal, Management Science,* and *Journal of Applied Psychology* are representative of journals that report very sophisticated research in the management field. In addition, hundreds of research papers are delivered at national and regional professional meetings across the country. It is probably conservative to estimate that twice as much management research and writing is being conducted today than was done 10 years ago. As a result, the body of knowledge is greatly expanding. This book attempts to incorporate the current body of knowledge in the succeeding chapters.

EDUCATION AND FORMAL TRAINING   The number of managers who have had formal education or training has been increasing dramatically. Today, with very few exceptions, managers have a college education. However, unlike those in the traditional professions, managers as a whole do not yet have a common, standardized educational experience. Yet, because of the increasingly important impact that colleges of business administration are having on the education of executives, the trend is in this direction. A degree of standardization is assured by the close regulation that the American Assembly of Collegiate Schools of Business (AACSB) has over the accredited business schools around the country. The AACSB provides the following guidelines which its member institutions and those striving for accreditation must follow in designing their curriculums:

1 a background of the concepts, processes and institutions in the production and marketing of goods and/or services, and the financing of the business enterprise or other forms of organization;

2 a background of the economic and legal environment as it pertains to profit and/or nonprofit organizations along with consideration of the social and political influences as they affect such organizations;

3 a basic understanding of the concepts and applications of accounting, quantitative methods, and information systems;

4 a study of organization theory, behavior, and interpersonal communications;

5 a study of administrative processes under conditions of uncertainty including integrating analysis and policy determination at the overall management level.[18]

Colleges of business administration closely follow the above guidelines to become or remain accredited. Therefore, it follows that as more and more management positions become staffed with personnel who attend or graduate from these institutions, the more standardized the education of managers becomes.

Besides formal college education, another contributing factor to this criterion of a profession is the widespread attention given to the management training for those already on the job. Sooner or later almost every modern manager becomes exposed to a common body of knowledge through management development programs. These programs are being run "in house" by the companies themselves and/or by outside organizations, such as universities and associations. These programs are both specialized and general in nature and cover a wide variety of topics, but in the end, most managers wind up with about the same amount and type of information.

In addition to these short courses and management development seminars, standardization is also fostered by the many practicing managers who are returning to universities to pursue advanced degrees. Most often their objective is to attain the professional degree of Master of Business Administration (M.B.A.)

In total, it can definitely be said that today's managers have a formal higher education. Not so clear is the form that this education takes. The trend toward more managers being graduates of business administration is a move toward standardization. This is amplified by the very recent trend in many collegiate schools of business to be renamed a college or school of management. This name change gives specific recognition to the professionalization and expanding scope of management instead of the narrow connotation implied by the term *business administration*. Coupled with the ongoing management training programs, there seems to be enough evidence to state that management has or at least is moving toward the educational requirements of a profession.

PROFESSIONAL ORGANIZATION   Unlike the traditional professions, management does not have one unified professional organization for its members. Instead, there are numerous separate professional groups. There are trade associations such as the American Bankers Association, the Automobile Manufacturers Association, and the Steel Service Center Institute. There are also professional/business associations such as the American Management Association, the Academy of Management, and the Society for the Advancement of Management.

These nonprofit organizations provide a number of professional services to their members. They conduct and sponsor research; hold conferences; lobby with federal, state, and local governments; and are a focal point for and disseminate information to the

---

[18] American Assembly of Collegiate Schools of Business, *Policies, Procedures, and Standards*, St. Louis, 1974, p. 28.

membership. The next step would be to have a single, powerful organization. On the academic side of management, the Academy of Management has pretty well done this. By opening up and encouraging membership from practitioners, it may lead to more professionalism in the field of management as a whole.

FEES BASED ON SERVICE   This criterion of a profession is seen in many instances in management. Most obvious has been the rise of management consulting firms in recent years. In 1940 there were approximately 2,000 such firms in the United States. Thirty years later the number had increased 20 times.

In essence, a consultant is an expert brought into an organization to analyze certain management problems. There is a standard joke that a consultant is almost anyone with a briefcase who comes more than 50 miles from home. As an outsider, a consultant can often provide a fresh, objective viewpoint. The style of the consultant may be cathartic (clients get troubles off their chests by openly talking about them with the consultant), catalytic (the consultant indirectly promotes and brings about change but does not directly participate in the change), or prescriptive (the consultant gives direct recommendations and expects them to be carried out by the client).

For such management consulting services, a fee is paid by the client organization. Sometimes this fee is a daily rate plus expenses. Other times it is a contractual fee and includes a set price for a particular job. In either case, it is usually based on a combination of factors such as the magnitude of the job, the capabilities and reputation of the consultants, and the financial strength of the client organization. Today, it is not uncommon to find individual consultant fees running up to $300–$500 a day, and a few of the most famous, nationally prominent consultants can receive up to $2,500 a day for their services. The management consultant represents the fee criterion of a profession but so, at least indirectly, do the high salaries made by most modern managers.

ETHICAL CODE OF CONDUCT AND BROAD RESPONSIBILITY   At the present time there is no overall code of ethics for management similar to, for example, the Hippocratic oath taken by medical doctors. However, there are a number of codes of ethical practice which are subscribed to by various management groups. For example, the Society of Professional Management Consultants has a list of standards, some of which charge the members to (1) conduct their business and private affairs with integrity and high moral purpose, (2) always act in the best interests of the client, (3) be sure that they have the qualifications to fulfill the task before accepting any assignment from the client, (4) regard all client-related information as confidential, and (5) uphold and maintain the dignity of the consulting profession at all times. Other organizations with similar codes include the National Association of Purchasing Agents and the American Association of Advertising Agencies, to name but a few.

Naturally such codes of conduct are only guidelines and are very difficult to enforce. However, the fact that the formulation of various codes is voluntary gives evidence that management is sincere in its effort to be ethical. Furthermore, investigation by writers such as Father Raymond Baumhart reveals that ethics among business leaders are improving and that there seems to be agreement that an industrial code of conduct is desirable.[19]

The strong emphasis currently given social responsibility in modern management is also evidence of a professional perspective. Today's managers realize that a broad-based social concern is a matter of professionalism and pragmatism. The latter raises the question of whether managers have societal responsibility because of a professional attitude or because it has become necessary in order to survive the social revolution that is occurring. If it is purely for pragmatism, then some doubts may be raised when measuring this criterion of a profession. Social responsibilities should be intrinsically motivated to meet the professional standard.

With poverty, civil rights, ecology, and consumerism being the major social issues facing today's organizations, the professional responsibilities of management take on particular significance.[20] There seems to be ample evidence that most managers in the upper echelons of modern organizations already possess a broad responsibility. As yet, this broad viewpoint has not always filtered down to the lower levels or to the grass-roots levels of the large organizations, whether educational, business, governmental, hospitals, military, or religious. However, with the continual input of young, well-educated people into management ranks, there will be a heightened sense of social awareness and sensitivity to social problems.

Chapter 3 gives further insight into the social climate. Overall, it appears to be only a matter of time before management is widely recognized as a legitimate profession. There will always be some criteria such as licensing that will never come about in management. However, when it is realized that profit or other measures of performance, such as patient care in a hospital or public service in a governmental organization, are continually used to measure and evaluate managers, it becomes evident that only the most qualified survive. There is a natural selection and survival process in the management profession. In the long run this may prove to be its strength relative to other professions in modern society.

Expanding Management Horizons
Earlier in the chapter it was pointed out that prior to World War II most attention on management was focused at the lower levels of the organization and much of the literature and writing referred almost solely to industrial or factory management. After the war greater interest in the operations of middle and top management emerged. However, the focus of attention was still heavily on the business/industrial arena, and it was, for the most part, confined to domestic management. However, in the last decade the scope of management has greatly expanded.

---

[19] See Raymond Baumhart, S.J., *Ethics in Business*, Holt, New York, 1968, p. 158.
[20] See Fred Luthans and Richard Hodgetts, *Social Issues in Business*, Macmillan, New York, 1972.

THE IMPORTANCE OF NONBUSINESS ORGANIZATIONS   One of the most noticeable trends in recent years has been interest in the more effective management of nonbusiness organizations. With the increasing importance of service, especially nonprofit, organizations in modern society, there has been an accompanying demand from the public for more efficient management. Hospitals are a prime illustration. While business firms routinely forecast and set objectives, hospitals have generally not. Yet, forecasts of population changes, for example, must be estimated if hospitals are to have the facilities for offering the best possible medical care. Obviously, a hospital with inadequate facilities and equipment cannot possibly attain its goal of maximum patient care. Conversely, a hospital with excess facilities and underutilized equipment will find its costs of operations outrunning its revenues. A balance must be obtained between patient needs and institutional facilities. Effective managerial planning helps the hospital administration accomplish this goal. Furthermore, just as a business is expected to contribute to local charities and provide free services to the community, so are hospitals. Not only do hospitals sometimes provide free care to the poor but they actually operate some of their units at a loss. For instance, many hospitals lose money on their obstetrics units, yet they keep them in operation. However, to remain viable, the hospital administration needs to know its revenues and expenses so that total costs can be controlled. Hospital administration needs to apply process, quantitative, behavioral, and systems concepts and techniques for maximum goal attainment just as the business organization does.

The same holds true for educational organizations. During the 1960s, enrollments in all educational institutions reached an all-time high. However, recently there has been a dip in the number of students, and many of the small private institutions of higher learning are in serious financial trouble. Some of these institutions, however, were able to forecast these changes by systematically analyzing the impact that smaller high school graduating classes and the elimination of the military draft would have on their enrollments. Like their business counterparts, they forecasted future conditions and planned their operations accordingly. In addition, they employed modern management concepts and techniques to help them organize their resources to provide the types of courses and programs (for example, correspondence study, night programs, and internships) which were appealing to the general public. They designed systematic control procedures for evaluating the contribution of these programs and, as a result, have been able to operate profitably.

Analogous illustrations to the hospital and educational cases can be drawn for all types of organizations, public and private alike. As seen in Figure 1-3, management is not restricted to the business arena. For instance, while the term *business policy* has traditionally been used to describe the senior or M.B.A. course in which top-level strategy formulation and implementation are taught in management education, it now appears that the term is going to be replaced by *administrative policy,* indicating that effective managers must not limit their attention solely to the business arena. Many, if not most, college graduates of the 1970s and 1980s will find themselves working in administrative positions

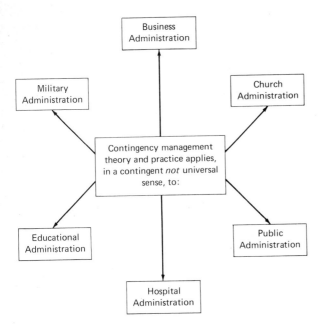

Figure 1-3 The Expanding Scope of Management.

in hospitals, governmental agencies, the military, or educational institutions. Business organizations are and will continue to be a vital force in society, but they no longer dominate, especially in terms of management theory and practice, as they once did. The contents of this book are applicable, in a contingent manner, to all organizations in modern society.

THE IMPORTANCE OF MULTINATIONAL ORGANIZATIONS   In addition to expanding into nonbusiness areas, management is also expanding beyond just domestic applications into international operations. The big American business firms, in particular, are taking their management expertise and applying it on an international scale. Today, multinational corporations dominate and are the rule rather than the exception. Such well-known firms as Ford, IBM, General Motors, and General Electric are all multinational corporations. The problems faced by a manager in the continental United States are usually much different from those encountered on foreign soil. Customs, culture, and traditions often dictate the need for a different management approach. Contingency management becomes especially relevant to this new international situation. For example, in applying cultural differences to interpersonal style, the successful American manager in countries such as Spain or Mexico knows that the most successful type of negotiation requires close, face-to-face discussion. The Japanese, on the other hand, like the Americans, prefer to maintain a discreet distance. Likewise, in the United States a manager who travels to another city to buy machinery, and is invited to the company president's home for dinner, would never belch at the table; however, in many of the Mid-Eastern countries, the belch is considered a compliment for the meal and for the cook. In either case, the American manager would have committed a grievous error. The next chapter will spell out in detail this needed contingency approach not only for the international area but also for all aspects of management theory and practice.

Summary

This chapter provides a historical perspective for modern contingency management. The first part cited representative examples of effective management in ancient times. The purpose was to give an appreciation of the fact that management has been around as long as there have been organized civilizations. However, the genesis for modern management theory and practice can be found in preindustrial commerce characterized by the market, Protestant, and liberty ethics and, more importantly, by industrialization. Soon after the industrial revolution it became evident that management was an important factor in production, and management theory and practice was on its way.

Although some writers recognize several schools of management thought, process, quantitative, behavioral, and systems are the generally recognized approaches. The process approach was founded by Henri Fayol at the turn of the century and attempts to determine the functions of management and then formulate universal principles. The approach is under attack for being too static, and the universal principles have not been generally upheld by research or practice. The quantitative approach is not an overall theory of management but rather an approach to management decision making. Started by Frederick W. Taylor's scientific management, the quantitative approach attempts to use modeling techniques to solve decision problems. Operations research and mathematically based techniques are utilized. The behavioral approach is obviously concerned with the human side of enterprise. The Depression, the labor movement, and especially pioneering behavioral research such as the Hawthorne studies gave impetus to the behavioral approach. At first very simplistic assumptions of human relations were made, but more recently a broader, scientifically based organizational behavior approach is taken. The systems approach took up where the process approach had failed to be a unifying theme for management. Simply defined as the interrelatedness and interdependency of the parts to the whole, the systems approach is probably the most widely accepted theoretical base in the field of management today. Both the divergent quantitative and behavioral approaches have turned the corner and are moving toward a systems base. However, by the time the juncture of the quantitative, behavioral, and systems approaches is reached sometime in the near future, the whole is proposed to be greater than the sum of the parts. This whole is the contingency theory of management, which serves as the conceptual framework for this book.

The last part of the chapter sets the stage for discussing the contingency approach. The new management professionalism and the broadened scope of management are given specific attention. With the reality of a postindustrial society, professionalism becomes especially important. Today's managers generally meet or are moving toward recognized professional criteria. Besides becoming a profession, the whole field of management is greatly expanding its horizons. Accompanying the dominance of service organizations in the postindustrial society is the concern for effective management of these organizations. Management today is not limited to business organizations. The management of church, public, hospital, educational, and military organizations is also important in both theory and practice. The same is true of the expansion into the international sphere. The management of multinational corporations is becoming increasingly important. With this increased diversity, a contingency management framework for theory and practice becomes much more relevant. The next chapter will present such a framework.

Questions for Review and Discussion

1 How long has management been around? Give some examples of management in ancient times.

2 Distinguish some of the major characteristics of feudalism, preindustrialized commerce, and industrialization. How do they contribute to modern management?

3 Briefly summarize the major historical schools of management thought. Trace the development of these approaches from 1950 to the present.

4 Identify the emerging trends in the practice of management. What are the criteria for a profession? How well does management currently measure up to these criteria? Is it important that management be a profession?

References

Albers, Henry H.: *Principles of Management,* 4th ed., Wiley, New York, 1974.
Andrews, Kenneth R.: "Toward Professionalism in Business Management," *Harvard Business Review,* November–December 1969, pp. 49–60.
Barnard, Chester I.: *The Functions of the Executive,* Harvard, Cambridge, Mass., 1962. Original copyright 1938 by the President and Fellows of Harvard College.
Bedelan, Arthur G.: "A Historical Review of Efforts in the Area of Management Semantics," *Academy of Management Journal,* March 1974, pp. 101–114.
———: "Management Theory: A Pediatric Note," *Business Perspectives,* Summer 1973, pp. 2–5.
Duncan, W. Jack: "Management Theory and the Practice of Management," *Business Horizons,* October 1974, pp. 48–54.
———: "The History and Philosophy of Administrative Thought," *Business and Society,* Spring 1971, pp. 24–30.
Fayol, Henri: *General and Industrial Management,* translated by Constance Storrs, Sir Isaac Pitman & Sons, London, 1949.
Fulmer, Robert M.: "Management Models: Yesterday, Today and Tomorrow," *Managerial Planning,* May–June 1970, pp. 9–11.
George, Claude S., Jr.: *The History of Management Thought,* Prentice-Hall, Englewood Cliffs, N.J., 1972.
Koontz, Harold (ed.): *Toward a Unified Theory of Management,* McGraw-Hill, New York, 1964.
Luthans, Fred: "Contingency Theory of Management: A Path out of the Jungle," *Business Horizons,* June 1973, pp. 67–72.
——— **and Richard M. Hodgetts:** *Social Issues in Business,* Macmillan, New York, 1972.

McGuire, Joseph W. (ed.): *Contemporary Management Issues and Viewpoints,* Prentice-Hall, Englewood Cliffs, N.J., 1974.

Mee, John F.: *Management Thought in a Dynamic Economy,* New York University Press, New York, 1963.

Merrill, Harwood F. (ed.): *Classics in Management,* American Management Association, New York, 1960.

Preston, Lee E., and James E. Post: "The Third Managerial Revolution," *Academy of Management Journal,* September 1974, pp. 476–486.

Wortman, Max S., Jr., and Fred Luthans (eds.): *Emerging Concepts in Management,* 2d ed., Macmillan, New York, 1975.

Chapter 2

A Contingency Approach to Management

The last chapter pointed out the need for a new approach to the theory and practice of management. There is a tremendous force of change affecting all organizations in modern society, and as in all academic disciplines, there is a rapidly expanding body of management knowledge. The time has come to meet the challenge of change and harness this knowledge toward the solution of vital managerial problems. The traditional approaches to management were not necessarily wrong, but today they are no longer adequate. The needed breakthrough for management theory and practice can be found in a contingency approach. Contingency management is just starting to emerge and gain stature. The purpose of this chapter, and in fact the entire book, is to develop a conceptual framework for the theory and practice of contingency management.

This chapter specifically defines the contingency approach to management and serves as the framework for the remaining chapters. The first section defines exactly what is meant by contingency management. Next the contingency approach is compared and contrasted with the more traditional approaches and the modern systems approach to management. As with any other "new" approach, a number of examples of contingency management can be found in earlier writings. The third section summarizes some of these studies that contained definite contingency implications. Included are the classic contributions from the Tavistock group, Gouldner, Woodward, and Chandler. In addition, some of the more contemporary contingency contributions are reviewed. Finally, in the last part of the chapter, a specific contingency framework is proposed. A simple two-dimensional matrix is used to depict a contingent (a functional if-then) relationship between environmental variables (both external and internal) and management variables (process, quantitative, behavioral, and systems concepts and techniques). The purpose of this contingency conceptual framework is to organize management knowledge into a meaningful theory that can lead to more effective management practice.

Contingency Management: Meaning and Perspective

By itself, the word *contingency* is very confusing. The biggest problem is that the word has many different meanings to many different people. Even within the academic field of management there is little agreement on exactly what is meant by contingency. One common connotation of the word *contingency* is a chance or accidental occurrence. Such a connotation lends itself to viewing contingency management as an unsystematic, unscientific "seat of the pants" approach. The truth is just the opposite. A contingent relationship is a functional relationship between two or more variables. *Contingency management is concerned with the relationship between relevant environmental variables and appropriate management concepts and techniques that lead to effective goal attainment.*

The following sections elaborate on this definition of contingency management. First, the if-then management contingency is explained and examples are given. Second, the external and internal environmental considerations are analyzed. Third, the distinction between contingency and situational management is made. Fourth, the established contingency approaches are discussed. Finally, the rationale for the need for contingency management serves as a point of departure for the rest of the chapter.

The If-Then Management Contingency

A contingent relationship, as used in this book, can be simply thought of as an if-then functional relationship. The *if* is the independent variable and the *then* is the dependent variable in this functional relationship. For example, if two parts of hydrogen are mixed with one part of oxygen under the proper conditions, then water will be the result. In other words, water (the dependent variable) is a function of the combination of hydrogen and oxygen (the independent variables). An if-then contingency relationship can be applied to management theory and practice. Most often, the environment serves as independent variables, and management concepts and techniques are the dependent variables in the if-then management contingency. For example, if the economy is undergoing a recession and the firm operates in an oligopolistic market structure, then a bureaucratic organization structure would be most appropriate for goal attainment. On the other hand, if the economy is booming and the firm operates in a monopolistically competitive market structure, then a free-form conglomerate organization structure would be most appropriate for goal attainment. Another example of the if-then management contingency would be: if prevailing social values are oriented toward nonmaterialistic free expression and the organization employs professional personnel in a high-technology operation, then a very participative, open leadership style would be most effective for goal attainment. On the other hand, if prevailing social values are oriented toward materialism and obedience to authority and the organization employs unskilled personnel working on routine tasks, then a strict, authoritarian leadership style would be most effective for goal attainment. *Remember, the above and most of the other if-then management contingency relationships that are stated in this and subsequent chapters are only intended to be examples.* They have not necessarily been empirically validated as has the water example. Yet, the examples do indicate possible if-then contingency relationships between the independent environment variables (the economy, the competitive market structure, technology, social values, and the type of personnel in the examples above) and the dependent management variables (organization structure and leadership styles in the examples above). Furthermore, although the environment variables are usually the independent variables and the management concepts and techniques are usually the dependent variables, the reverse can also occur. There are cases where management variables are independent and the environment variables are dependent in the management contingency relationship. For example, _if_ a very participative, open leadership style is instituted by top management, _then_ personnel will respond by exhibiting self-control and responsible social values. Although it is recognized that it is possible for management concepts and techniques to affect the environment in the systems interaction sense, this book will generally treat the environment as independent (the _if_'s) and the management concepts and techniques as dependent (the _then_'s) in the contingency management relationship.

External and Internal Environmental Considerations
The treatment of the environment as independent variables and management concepts and techniques as dependent variables becomes clearer when it is recognized that a distinction is made between external and internal environments. The external environment is discussed at the end of the chapter and consists of general (social, technological, economic, and political/legal) and specific (competitors, customers, and suppliers) variables. Generally, these variables are outside or external to the organization, and management has little, if any, direct control over them. In other words, they are independent of management. The internal environment, on the other hand, consists of the organization structure, managerial processes (decision making, communication, and control), and technology. Generally, these latter variables are inside or internal to the organization, and management can have control over them. In other words, they can be dependent on management.

In the past, most effort in the theory and practice of management has been devoted to the internal environmental factors. The external environment was either ignored or treated as a given. Only recently with open-system analysis has the external environment been given attention in management literature. The internal environment, on the other hand, has played a dominant role in most books and articles written on management. Contingency management must of course give attention to both the external and internal environments. Recognizing both compounds the problem of determining specific contingent relationships but must be dealt with conceptually. This book emphasizes the external environment but also recognizes the importance of the internal environment in contingency management. Although the next chapter is specifically devoted to the external environment, many of the examples, throughout the book and in the contingency chapter at the end of each major section, are internally oriented. The reason for the internal environment examples is that this is where most of the attention in the past has been given.

The external environment variables would almost always be independent, while the internal variables could be either independent or dependent. Technology is a case in point. Technology is treated as both an external and internal environment variable in this book. As an external variable, the overall state of scientific technology largely derived from basic research is usually an independent variable in the contingency relationship for modern management. With a few notable exceptions where organizations are heavily engaged in basic research and development, the management of an individual organization cannot directly influence overall technology. Therefore, this external variable would tend to be an independent variable in the contingency relationship. On the other hand, the internal environmental factor of technology—for example, a particular productive process used by a manufacturing firm—could be either independent or dependent. In other words, the productive process in operation could affect the management concepts and techniques used *or* the management concepts and techniques used could affect the type of technology. For example, if an assembly-line type of productive technology is used, then a bureaucratic structure and an authoritarian leadership climate would lead to effective goal attainment. Or, if a bureaucratic structure with an authoritarian leadership climate exists, then an assembly-line type of productive technology should be used for effective goal attainment. In the first case technology was the independent variable, and in the second it was the dependent variable. Contingency management can deal with both. But because of the tendency for external variables to be independent, which has been largely ignored in management, and because the internal environment variables can generally be considered to be either independent or dependent, the conceptual framework for overall contingency management presented at the end of the chapter treats the environment as independent and the management concepts and techniques as dependent.

Contingency or Situational?

There is a seemingly slight, yet very important, distinction between what has become known as situational management and what is presented in this book as contingency management. The terms, unfortunately, are often used interchangeably. However, the term *contingency* is deliberately used in this book for a valid reason. The major difference between situational and contingency approaches is that a contingency approach implies that there is a *functional* relationship between designated environmental conditions and the appropriate management concepts and techniques for effective goal attainment. As stated in the last section, the environment variables are independent and the management concepts and techniques are dependent variables in the functional relation. In a management context, direct causality between these independent and dependent variables is not inferred. In other words, the environment does *not cause* the management concepts and techniques to occur. Rather there is merely a functional relation between the independent environment variables and the dependent management variables. The goal of contingency management is to determine the if-then functional relationship that will lead to the most effective goal attainment. Again, it should be emphasized that assuming a functional relationship between the independent and dependent variables does not imply that there is a cause-and-effect relationship. Management is *active,* not passively dependent in the practice of contingency management, but the determination of the functional relationships between the independent environment and the dependent techniques and concepts is intended to improve the effectiveness of the practice of contingency management.

Whereas contingency management could be simply labeled the "if-then" approach, situational management could be called the "all depends" approach. A situational approach implies that management must diagnose the situation in order to manage more effectively. Situational management does not attempt to identify functional relationships between situational variables and management variables. For example, Howard Carlisle, who tends to use the term *situational* rather than *contingency,* explains,

Situational theory holds that the principles of organization do not prescribe any specific structure; instead they are guidelines available to the manager after he has analyzed the factors in his particular situation. Organizations are considered not as static structures but as constantly changing entities that, if successfully managed, adapt to internal and external forces.[1]

Robert Mockler, another management writer associated with situational rather than contingency terminology, explains,

Situational theory is based on the premise that business situations usually differ in some way from each other. Managing business situations, therefore, begins with a study or diagnosis of the requirements or characteristics of the specific situation under study. Only then can courses of action be developed to meet the situation's specific requirements.[2]

In other words, both Carlisle and Mockler stress *diagnosing* the situation and *adapting* to it rather than identifying specific functional relationships between situational variables and management variables.

Kast and Rosenzweig, who are closely associated with the systems approach but who have recently advocated contingency management, more closely approximate the approach taken by this book when they state,

The contingency view of organizations and their management suggests that an organization is a system composed of subsystems and delineated by identifiable boundaries from its environmental suprasystem. The contingency view seeks to understand the interrelationships within and among subsystems as well as between the organization and its environment and to define patterns of relationships or configurations of variables. It emphasizes the multivariate nature of organizations and attempts to understand how organizations operate under varying conditions and in specific circumstances. Contingency views are ultimately directed toward suggesting organizational designs and managerial systems most appropriate for specific situations.[3]

Recognizing, diagnosing, and adapting to the situation are certainly important to contingency management, but they are not enough. Specific, identifiable, functional relationships between environmental conditions and management practices also must be established. In contingency management, independent environment factors and dependent management variables are functionally related. This latter emphasis is what separates situational management from the more sophisticated and exacting contingency manage-

---

[1] Howard M. Carlisle, *Situational Management,* AMACOM, American Management Association, New York, 1973, p. 99.

[2] Robert J. Mockler, *Management Decision Making and Action in Behavioral Situations,* Austin Press, Austin, Tex., 1973, p. 3; also see Robert J. Mockler, "Situational Theory of Management," *Harvard Business Review,* May–June 1971, pp. 146–151, 154–155.

[3] Fremont E. Kast and James E. Rosenzweig, "General Systems Theory: Applications for Organization and Management," *Academy of Management Journal,* December 1972, p. 460.

ment approach. Contingency management is based on a very specific conceptual framework which establishes a functional relationship between the variables.

Established Contingency Approaches

As has been pointed out, the word *contingency* is confusing to both lay people and management scholars and practitioners. In management the word has different meanings for different people. The terminology of contingency planning and Pigors and Myers' situational approach to personnel management have been around for a long time. In addittition, all modern management scholars and many management practitioners are familiar with the contingency model of leadership effectiveness and contingency organization designs. Those who study organizational behavior are also familiar with the application of a contingency model to behavioral change. These "established" contingency approaches can be briefly summarized as follows:

1 *Situational Personnel Management*   Paul Pigors and Charles Myers have been associated with a situational approach to personnel management for the past couple of decades. They identify the human element, the technical factor, space-time dimensions and relationships, and organizationwide policies as the major situational variables affecting personnel management.[4] They use case studies to demonstrate the situational impact on the various functions of personnel management.

2 *Contingency Planning*   Contingency plans are those that attempt to plan for unexpected events. For example, a farm implement manufacturer should develop contingency plans in case there is a severe drought. Another example is that during a cold war situation, most military planning is of a contingency nature. Such contingency planning reduces the uncertainties facing management. Chapter 8 will give further attention to contingency planning.

3 *Contingency Model of Leadership*   Based on years of empirical research, Fred Fiedler developed what he called a contingency model of leadership effectiveness.[5] The widely publicized model recognizes the situational impact of leadership but also develops functional relationships between specific situational variables and leadership styles. The three most important situational variables were determined to be position power, acceptance of followers, and task structure. Fiedler found that a task-directed leader is most effective when these situational variables are very favorable and very unfavorable, but a human relations style is most effective when these situational variables are moderately favorable or unfavorable. The Fiedler model will be given more attention in Chapter 8.

4 *Contingency Organization Designs*   Starting with the studies of Paul Lawrence and Jay Lorsch about a decade ago, a relatively great amount of attention has been devoted to contingency approaches to organization theory and structure. The overriding

[4] Paul Pigors and Charles A. Myers, *Personnel Administration,* 7th ed., McGraw-Hill, 1973, pp. 167–168.
[5] Fred E. Fiedler, *A Theory of Leadership Effectiveness,* McGraw-Hill, New York, 1967.

theme of this contingency approach is that there is no one best way to organize. Lawrence and Lorsch introduced the variables of differentiation, which they define as "the difference in cognitive and emotional orientation among managers in different functional departments," and integration, which they define as "the quality of the state of collaboration that exists among departments that are required to achieve unity of effort by the demands of the environment."[6] The degree of differentiation and integration will largely determine the type of organization design that will be most effective. Chapter 8 covers contingency organization designs in more detail.

5 *Behavioral Contingency Model* B. F. Skinner, the well-known behavioral psychologist, extended the classic stimulus-response explanation of behavior into a contingency model consisting of the antecedent, the behavior, and the consequence.[7] The behavioral contingency relationship is based on the premise that behavior is a function of its consequences. The antecedent serves as a cue for the behavior to be emitted, but it is the contingent consequences which largely determine subsequent behavior. To change behavior, the environmental contingencies, antecedent, and/or more especially, consequences must be changed. Behavioral contingency management is given detailed attention in Chapter 15.

The above "established" contingency approaches are found in much of the management literature, and some or all are recognized by management scholars and practitioners. Yet, it must be remembered that they represent only parts of the total contingency management framework presented in this book. The established approaches can serve as prototypes for the development of the overall contingency management approach. They are given further attention in the appropriate places of the book. However, it must be stressed that contingency management is much broader and incorporates not only personnel management, planning, leadership styles, organization design, and behavioral change but all other process, quantitative, behavioral, and systems concepts and techniques as well. In other words, readers should not be misled that any one approach or all five "established" approaches which they may be familiar with are contingency management in total. They are only part of the whole contingency management framework which functionally relates relevant environmental variables with all appropriate management concepts and techniques for effective goal attainment.

Why Contingency Management?
The last chapter pointed out that management has a rich heritage. Like the development of any other discipline, there have been a few benchmark breakthroughs, but generally speaking, the body of knowledge has gradually evolved to its present status. The introductory comments of this chapter suggested that management needs another break-

---

[6] Paul R. Lawrence and Jay W. Lorsch, *Organization and Environment,* Division of Research, Harvard Graduate School of Business Administration, Boston, 1967, p. 11.

[7] B. F. Skinner, *Contingencies of Reinforcement,* Appleton-Century-Crofts, New York, 1969.

through to cope with the rapidity of change and the knowledge explosion. Practitioners have justifiably become baffled by the ever-increasing array of management concepts and techniques. Every concept or technique that comes along is supposedly the answer to all their problems. The advocates of the multitude of process, quantitative, behavioral, and systems concepts and techniques imply that their approaches have universal applicability. Yet practitioners are finding out that a particular concept of technique just does not work in their situation. The advocate most often reacts by assuming that the practitioner is "copping out." It is suggested that the reasons a concept or technique does not work is that practitioners either do not understand it or, more likely, are simply unable or unwilling to implement it properly. The disenchanted practitioner, on the other hand, points an accusing finger at the so-called experts as being entirely unrealistic. Like any such controversy, neither party is entirely right or wrong. There is certainly some truth and some misunderstanding on both parts.

The major problem in the current dilemma is that the parties are operating from different assumptions. The theorists and/or experts assume explicitly or implicitly the universality of their concepts and techniques. Practitioners, on the other hand, often assume universality of their individual style but are highly situational when it comes to applying modern management concepts and techniques. The contingency approach bridges this gap between theory and practice. The modern concepts and techniques are not wrong or necessarily unrealistic. By the same token, the practitioners are not necessarily wrong either. Many of the concepts and techniques do not work in their unique situations. What contingency management attempts to do is functionally *relate* given situational conditions to the appropriate management concepts and techniques for effective goal attainment.

Contingency management deals directly with the situational concern of practitioners and the concepts and techniques advocated by today's management experts. By relating the two in an if-then contingency relationship, both management theorists and practitioners can get on with the extremely important job of more effective goal attainment by organizations in modern society.

Contingency Management: Compared and Contrasted

The last chapter indicated that there were several schools of management thought. This section attempts to compare and contrast a contingency approach with both traditional approaches and the currently popular systems approach to management.

Contingency versus Traditional Views

Starting with the first systematic formulation of management theory at the turn of the century, there has been a search for certain commonalities. The goal of this search has been to develop universally applicable principles of management. Early classical theorists such as Henri Fayol, Luther Gulick, Lyndall Urwick, James Mooney, and Alan Reiley devoted most of their efforts to developing management principles. This approach is perhaps best represented by Urwick, who stated in no uncertain terms:

. . . there are principles which can be arrived at inductively from the study of human experience of organization, which should govern arrangements for human associations of any kind. These principles can be studied as a technical question, irrespective of the purpose of the enterprise, the personnel composing it, or any constitutional, political, or social theory underlying its creation.[8]

Yet, despite statements such as the above, in fairness to the classical writers, they did express some concern for differing circumstances. For example, Fayol qualified his use of the term *principles* by noting:

. . . there is nothing rigid or absolute in management . . . allowance must be made for different changing circumstances.[9]

Gulick, who had a diverse background in academic and public administration, even directly challenged the search for universal principles. At least in reference to departmentation, he noted:

Students of administration have long sought a single principle of effective departmentalization just as alchemists sought the philosophers' stone. But they have sought in vain. There is apparently no one most effective system of departmentalism.[10]

Despite these few exceptions, the general approach taken by the classical writers was that there were universal principles of management that could be applied to any situation. Koontz and O'Donnell, in the latest edition of their widely read management principles text, clearly summarize the classical view when they state:

The principles related to the task of managing apply to any kind of enterprise in any kind of culture. . . . It is true that many of the case examples and techniques used in this book are drawn from business enterprises. In doing so, however, the authors have no intention of overlooking the fact that the same fundamental truths are applicable elsewhere.[11]

The classical assumption of universality had a great deal of logic when it was applied to organizations operating in the relatively stable and homogeneous environment that existed at the time when Fayol in the early 1900s and Urwick in the 1930s and 1940s formulated their principles. However, as the environment became more dynamic, complex, and heterogeneous, it soon became evident, at least to practitioners, that the universality assumption was unrealistic. As Lawrence and Lorsch observed,

Far too many administrators raised in one organizational setting and infused with the theory appropriate to it have wrought havoc by trying to apply it later in quite different settings. A small army of managers, trained and conditioned by classical theory, has tried at great cost to apply it in inappropriate settings.[12]

---

[8] Lyndall F. Urwick, "Organization as a Technical Problem," in Luther Gulick and Lyndall F. Urwick (eds.), *Papers on the Science of Administration,* Institute of Public Administration, New York, 1937, p. 49.

[9] Henri Fayol, *General and Industrial Management,* translated by Constance Storrs, Sir Isaac Pitman & Sons, London, 1949, p. 19.

[10] Luther Gulick, "Notes on the Theory of Organization," in Gulick and Urwick (eds.), op. cit., p. 31.

[11] Harold Koontz and Cyril O'Donnell, *Principles of Management,* 5th ed., McGraw-Hill, New York, 1972, p. viii.

[12] Lawrence and Lorsch, op. cit., pp. 183–184.

Other schools of thought emerged to counter the classical approach and to better understand organization and management. The behavioral approach, in particular, seemed more appropriate for understanding organizations in dynamic, heterogeneous environments. But the behavioral theorists made the same mistake as the classicists—they attempted to present their ideas as being universally true. For example, Douglas McGregor, who formulated the now famous theory X (the traditional assumptions about managing people that employees are basically lazy, need to be threatened, and want to be told what to do) and theory Y (essentially opposite from theory X in that it suggests people will respond to responsibility and self-control), implied that theory Y assumptions would hold for most situations. Although McGregor qualified his statements, as the classical theorists had done before him, the interpretations came out that theory Y should be a universal assumption about organizational participants. The more recent behavior concepts and techniques such as participative management, job enrichment, and team building follow the same pattern. Although most modern behavioral management theorists do make some situational qualifications, when translated to practice, the inference is that the behavioral concepts and techniques are generally applicable to all situations. However, just as in the classical approach, practitioners quickly find out that the behavioral concepts and techniques do not always work out in their particular situations.

The simple fact is that neither the process nor behavioral concepts and techniques worked effectively under all conditions. As the last section pointed out, the traditional approaches are not necessarily wrong per se. Rather the problem is the way the approaches were applied; i.e., the universal assumption precluded the need to apply management concepts and techniques contingent on the environment. This problem became more evident as the environment became increasingly dynamic and complex. Today, the environmental impact is so important that it must be recognized in the theory and practice of management.

Contingency versus Systems Views

As the last chapter indicated, the systems approach is the most recent and has picked up where the process approach left off in unifying management theory and practice. Systems theory, especially open-systems theory which emphasizes environmental input, is very closely related to contingency theory. Some theorists even use the terms *open systems* and *contingency theory* interchangeably. Others argue that contingency is but one part of overall general systems theory (GST). A GST approach attempts to integrate and unify all knowledge. When applied to management, GST would incorporate all schools of thought, including the contingency approach.

Obviously, GST involves a very high level of abstraction and therefore could be thought of as incorporating the contingency approach. In GST all parts of anything are interrelated and interdependent to form the whole. John van Gigch in his recent book, *Applied General Systems Theory,* notes that when applied to organizational analysis, GST "seeks to wed behavioral with strictly mechanistic views, and to consider the organization as an integrated whole, whose goal is to achieve overall system effectiveness while harmonizing the conflicting objectives of its components."[13] This approach certainly rejects a simplistic and mechanistic universality view but tends to be too abstract and all things to all people. The contingency approach is much more pragmatic and applicable to management theory *and* practice. Both systems theory and contingency theory recognize the importance of the external environment and attempt to look at the relationships of the parts to the whole. But depending solely on the systems approach produces a dilemma. As Kast and Rosenzweig point out, "One of the major problems is that the practical need to deal with comprehensive systems of relationships is overrunning our ability to fully understand and predict these relationships. *We vitally need the systems paradigm but we are not sufficiently sophisticated to use it appropriately.*"[14] The contingency approach, on the other hand, strives to develop *specific* functional relationships between identifiable environmental variables and appropriate process, quantitative, behavioral, *and* systems concepts and techniques. Thus, the contingency approach is much more pragmatic and can incorporate systems concepts and techniques as well as the concepts and techniques from the other management schools. Comprehensiveness is not sacrificed for needed pragmatism in the contingency approach.

Just because GST is not yet pragmatic enough should not automatically rule out its present and especially future input into the better understanding of organizations and management. The emphasis given to the whole rather than the parts and the open- (as opposed to closed-) systems concept emphasizing the external environment are especially important. Identifying the systems boundaries, particularly the interface between external and internal systems, and determining the relationships of various external and internal subsystems make a direct contribution to contingency management. In addition, GST concepts such as entropy (a system will become disorganized over time) and equifinality (a system can reach the same final state from different paths of development) and specific systems concepts and techniques found in systems analysis and management information systems are also vital to contingency management. The chapters in Part Five of the book are specifically devoted to the systems concepts and techniques that can make a significant contribution to contingency management.

In the final analysis, it is perhaps more fruitful to recognize systems and contingency views as complementary rather than competing approaches to management. It may be true that the contingency approach is in between the simplistic, mechanistic traditional approach on the one hand and the highly abstract systems approach on the other. However, it is also true that in this case such a middle position does not sacrifice content, logic, accuracy, or applicability. The contingency approach can integrate both the traditional and the systems approaches in a conceptually sound manner. Traditional theoretical approaches were micro-oriented but had trouble being inductively applied to the general practice of management. The systems approach is macro-oriented but has trouble being deductively applied to specific management situations. Like systems theory,

---

[13] John P. van Gigch, *Applied General Systems Theory,* Harper & Row, New York, 1974, p. 36.

[14] Kast and Rosenzweig, op. cit., p. 458.

contingency theory has macroconcerns, but unlike systems theory it can be effectively and pragmatically applied at the microlevel.

The formulation of specific functional relationships between independent environment variables and dependent management variables is what separates contingency from systems theory and practice. All schools of thought, including process, quantitative, behavioral, and systems, have made and it is hoped will continue to make significant contributions to more effective management theory and practice. The contingency approach provides the conceptual framework that relates all these approaches to the environmental situation.

Contributions to Contingency Management

So far the exact meaning of and perspective for contingency management have been given and it has been compared and contrasted with other approaches to management. The reader may be asking, "So what is really new about contingency management?" Like so many of the other "new" approaches in any academic discipline, particularly in management, contingency management has many important historical precedents.

Many of the leading pioneers in the behavioral sciences and management expressed definite contingency views. For example, in 1950 the famed social psychologist George C. Homans astutely noted:

There are no rules for human behavior that apply in every situation without limit or change. . . . In recent years men of practical affairs—industrial executives, for instance—have often come to psychologists and sociologists begging for a plan or set of rules that executives can apply "across the board"—that is, in all circumstances—in dealing with their employees. There are no such rules and if there were, they would be dangerous. [15]

This view is not unique to Homans, but others did not state the contingency premise so clearly.

After World War II, the case method of instruction became popular in schools of business administration. Although the case approach is most closely associated with Harvard, to varying degrees it is currently used in schools of business across the country. The case method definitely has at least a situational if not contingency flavor to it. Each case is considered a unique situation requiring analysis and decision. However, the major thrust is to discover the processes leading to analysis and decision rather than determining contingent relationships between the conditions of the case and appropriate management concepts and techniques. Cases and incidents are incorporated into this book. The incidents are found at the end of most of the chapters, and a longer case is placed at the end of each major section. The contingency framework can be used to analyze the incidents and cases, and they provide a link from the more abstract text material to the actual practice of contingency management.

---

[15] George C. Homans, *The Human Group*, Harcourt, Brace & World, New York, 1950, p. 424.

Besides the precedents of many of the writers in behavioral science and management and the case method, there are also some classic research-based studies that have definite implications for contingency management. Although there are others, probably the most important were those conducted by the Tavistock group, Alvin Gouldner, Joan Woodward, and Alfred Chandler. There are also a relatively large number of more contemporary research-based studies that fall in the realm of contingency management. Most of these latter studies are sociologically oriented and examine two or more variables. Both external and internal environment variables are given attention. The following sections examine some of the more important classic studies and give an overview of some of the findings from the more contemporary multivariate sociological studies of organizations.

The Tavistock Studies

For many years researchers in the Tavistock Institute of Human Relations in London have been engaged in a significant research effort. Primary emphasis has been devoted to the relationship between the technological system and the sociopsychological system and the fit between these two systems. The contingency implications of this sociotechnical system was stated by Rice, one of the Tavistock researchers, as follows: "The technological demands place limits upon the type of work organization possible, but a work organization has social and psychological properties of its own that are independent of technology."[16]

The Tavistock group has conducted a number of field research studies that examined the relationship between the technical and social systems at work, but one of the best known was conducted by Trist and Bamforth.[17] In the coal-mining situation in Britain at that time it was found that very different sociotechnical methods for mining coal were used. Traditionally, the technical system of mining was a very simple operation consisting of small, self-contained work groups. Eventually, however, this single-place method was replaced by the long-wall method of coal mining. This new method was technologically more advanced (it used a new cutter and a face conveyor) and had accompanying reorganization of jobs and social relationships. Each shift under the conventional long-wall method had a specialized task, and each miner had very narrowly defined duties. However, the Tavistock researchers found that not all the mines in Britain had wholly adopted this conventional long-wall approach with its high degrees of specialization. Some mines had carried over the traditional single-place approach to the long-wall method, forming a type of composite long-wall method. Under this latter composite system, work groups rotated through all the specialized tasks required by the new machinery. But significantly, there was variety in the work and no conflicts between shifts in the composite long-wall method.

A systematic comparison made between the conventional long-wall method of operation

[16] A. K. Rice, *Productivity and Social Organization: The Ahmedabad Experiment*, Tavistock Publications, London, 1958, p. 4.
[17] E. L. Trist and K. W. Bamforth, "Some Social and Psychological Consequences of the Long-Wall Method of Coal-getting," *Human Relations*, vol. 4, pp. 3–38, 1951.

and the composite approach yielded some very interesting results. The composite was clearly more effective on almost every dimension measured. The composite method, which recognized the importance of the social relationships and continuity of the task effort, resulted in more productivity, less overtime, less schedule lag, less workforce reinforcement, less absenteeism, and fewer accidents than the conventional method operating in otherwise identical situations. Indirectly at least, the Tavistock researchers had determined some contingency relationships. For example, if there is a change toward more advanced technology, then the work groups should be held intact as much as possible for effective goal attainment. In other words, this research conducted by the Tavistock group was able to determine a functional relationship between the independent environmental variable of technology and the dependent behavioral management concept of cohesive work groups that leads to effective goal attainment. Such research makes an important contribution to contingency management.

Gouldner's Study

Sociologist Alvin Gouldner conducted a classic study of bureaucracy in a gypsum plant which has many contingency implications. The company in the study mined gypsum rock and in a manufacturing operation converted it into wallboard. The company employed 225 workers, 75 in the mining operation and 150 in various departments in the surface plant. The variables given attention in the study were the differeng styles of leadership between the old and the new manager and the differing impact of bureaucracy on the surface and the mining operation.

The old management style was termed by Gouldner to be an indulgency pattern. This leadership pattern operated in a very informal and lenient manner under "Old Doug," the plant manager. He ran a pretty "loose ship," to say the least. During hunting and planting season many of the workers were absent. On Mondays the mines had a high absenteeism rate because of the hangovers of the heavy-drinking miners. The company materials and services were frequently used for personal purposes. In general, the company was a pleasant and comfortable place to work. However, when Old Doug died, the situation drastically changed. A new manager, given the pseudonym of Vincent Peele, took over the plant. The indulgency pattern of leadership died along with Old Doug. Peele operated at the opposite extreme from Old Doug. He was anxious to integrate himself into the existing organization but found much resistance. He was unable to cope with the informal methods and relationships that were part of the indulgency pattern. As a result, Peele cracked down and instituted a very formal bureaucratic approach. Strict rules, formal authority, and discipline replaced the informal methods and leniency of the past. The method of handling absenteeism contrasted the old and the new.

Among other things, Vincent is cracking down on absenteeism. . . . Doug used to go right out and get the men. . . . He would hop into his car, drive down to their house and tell the men that he needed them. . . . Vincent doesn't stand for it, and he has let it be known that any flagrant violations will mean that the man gets his notice.[18]

[18] Alvin W. Gouldner, *Patterns of Industrial Bureaucracy,* Free Press, Glencoe, Ill., 1954, p. 80.

Besides the impact that the change in leadership and bureaucratization had on internal organization variables and personnel, there was also an interesting distinction made between the surface plant and mining situations. In the surface operation, Peele's approach worked out quite well and was even reluctantly accepted by employees. However, it was not effective in the mine. The miners refused to go along with Peele's leadership approach and strict bureaucratic form of organization. Their informal group norms and differing belief system successfully resisted formal bureaucratic structure. The very real threat of physical danger in the mine resulted in a completely different set of attitudes toward work and authority. Often the miner's very life depended on the procedures and rules that existed. Therefore, a miner felt justified in refusing orders from "the top" because "down here we make our own rules and we are our own bosses." Even the head of the mine, "Old Bull," scoffed at Peele's no-absenteeism rule as a bunch of "red tape." Peele attempted to force his brand of leadership and bureaucracy in both situations; it worked in one but not in the other.

The Gouldner research fits very nicely into the contingency framework. Some possible contingency relationships coming out of this research would be: if there is a manufacturing type of technology (as existed in the surface operation), then a bureaucratic organization structure can be successful; or if there are social values of independence and lack of acceptance of authority (as held by the miners), then a lenient style of supervision (like that of Old Doug) is most effective for goal attainment. In the first example, technology is the independent environmental variable and organization structure is the dependent management variable; in the second example, social values are the independent environmental variable and style of supervision is the dependent management variable in the contingency relationship.

Woodward's Study
In the 1950s one of England's leading industrial sociologists, Joan Woodward, directed a research study that proved to be one of the most significant breakthroughs for organization theory. Analogously, the Woodward study is as important to the contingency approach to management as the Hawthorne study is to the behavioral approach to management. It was a pioneering effort that could be considered the beginning of contingency management. Up to the time of the Woodward study, most organization theorists had ignored the role of technology. The formal organization was viewed as a structure and possibly a group of processes. Technology was only recognized as a set of limiting conditions. Woodward, on the other hand, felt that technology played a role in the internal organization equal to if not more important than that of structure and processes. Her research findings tended to support this thesis.

The major study encompassed about 100 British firms (91 percent of the firms in South Essex that had at least 100 employees). They were classified according to three distinct types of productive technology:

1 *Unit and Small Batch*   This type of technology depends upon self-contained units that make products according to customer specifications, prototypes, and fabrication of large equipment in stages.

2 *Large Batch and Mass*   This technology is characterized by mass production of large batches of goods. A moving assembly line is typically employed.

3 *Process*   Under this type of technology there is intermittent production of chemicals or continuous-flow production of substances such as liquids, gases, or crystals.

When the 100 firms studied were classified as to technology, the variables of structure, human relations, and status were analyzed. The results of this analysis are briefly summarized in Figure 2-1. The results clearly show that organization structure, human relations, and status depend greatly on the technology. This finding seemed to be even more true in the successful firms. In other words, there was a definite contingent relationship between certain types of technology (independent environment variables) and certain organization structures and certain human relations techniques (dependent management variables) that lead to effective goal attainment. For example, if the firm has a process manufacturing technology, then a structure with small spans of control and committee management is most effective; or if the firm has a unit manufacturing technology, then a supportive leadership style with opportunities for participation, interpersonal interactions, and job flexibility is most effective. Determining this type of empirically verified functional relationship is the goal of contingency management.

Chandler's Study
A classic study conducted by Alfred D. Chandler also has implications for contingency management. The purpose of his study was to test the thesis that organization structure follows managerial strategy. Although he reviewed numerous major companies, he made an in-depth analysis of four dominant firms in American business: Du Pont, General

Figure 2-1   Summary of Woodward's Findings

Type of Technology	Organization Structure	Human Relationships	High-Status Functions
Unit	Average span of control for first-line supervisor: 21–30; median number reporting to top executive: 4; median levels of management: 3; and top management committees instead of single head: 12%	Small intimate groups; much participation, permissiveness, and flexibility in job interrelationships	Development personnel Skilled workers Draftsmen Experienced managers
Mass or batch	Span for first-line supervisor: 41–50; reporting to top executive: 7; levels of management: 4; and management committees: 32%	Clear-cut duties; line-staff conflict; and generally bad industrial relations	Production personnel (line and staff)
Process	Span for first-line supervisor: 11–20; reporting to top executive: 10; levels of management: 6; and management committees: 80%	Good interpersonal relations like the unit technology, and little conflict or stress	Maintenance personnel Young, technically competent managers

Source: Adapted from Joan Woodward, *Industrial Organization*, Oxford University Press, London, 1965, pp. 50–67.

Motors, Standard Oil (New Jersey), and Sears, Roebuck.[19] Data were obtained from internal company records, correspondence, reports, minutes, and interviews with company executives who actually participated in the changes. Each company eventually evolved into a decentralized organization structure but for different reasons. The four companies evolved as follows:

1 *Du Pont* went from a centralized to a decentralized structure. Decentralization was needed to accommodate a management strategy of product diversification.

2 *General Motors* was a different situation. In the early years of GM there was a lack of centralized control over diverse products and functions. This situation can be attributed to the one-man, authoritative management style practiced by the founder, William C. Durant. In 1920, GM switched to Alfred P. Sloan's plan of organization, which was centralized control over decentralized operations. This strategy put GM back on its feet and was a major contributing factor to its subsequent success.

3 *Standard Oil (New Jersey)* had another experience. It faced many of the same problems as Du Pont and GM but moved toward decentralization on a piecemeal, unsystematic basis. It differed from the other companies studied by Chandler in that its eventual decentralized structure was not the result of a one-shot overall policy change. However, again in accordance with Chandler's thesis, management strategy preceded the changes to decentralization.

4 *Sears, Roebuck* experienced still another pattern. The company started off with a decentralized structure. This proved to be unsuccessful because of unclear channels of authority and communication and inadequate overall planning. Next Sears, Roebuck tried a highly centralized structure, but this also proved to be unworkable. Gradually, the company evolved back into a very successful decentralized structure. As in the other cases, managerial strategy preceded the eventual decentralized structure at Sears, Roebuck.

Although the study was primarily concerned with the relationship between strategy and structure, Chandler makes it clear that some strategies and resulting structures are more effective than others, depending on the situation. For example, Chandler noted:

As long as an enterprise belonged in an industry whose markets, sources of raw materials, and production processes remained relatively unchanged, few entrepreneurial decisions had to be reached. In that situation such a weakness was not critical, but where technology, markets, and sources of supply were changing rapidly, the defects of such a structure became more obvious.[20]

In other words, the contingency relationship would be if the organization operates in a relatively dynamic specific environment (competitors, customers, and suppliers), then a flexible organization structure is most effective. Besides these specific external environmental independent variables, Chandler also recognized internal environmental variables such as territorial expansion, combinations, product diversification, and growth rate as affecting the strategy and structure of the companies he studied.

---

[19] Alfred D. Chandler, Jr., *Strategy and Structure: Chapters in the History of the American Industrial Enterprise*, M.I.T., Cambridge, Mass., 1962.

[20] Ibid., p. 41.

Contemporary Contingency Studies

The studies discussed so far primarily fall in the "classic" category and are mainly of historical significance. A relatively great number of good multivariate research studies have recently emerged that have either direct or indirect implications for contingency management. Most of the studies are of one of two general types. The first type of research is devoted to the already established contingency approaches to organization design, leadership, and behavioral change that were discussed earlier. This research will be expanded upon in Chapter 8, "Process Variables and Contingency Management," and Chapter 15, "Behavioral Variables and Contingency Management." The other general type of contingency research has been devoted to establishing general classification schemes of organizations according to their environments. The work of organizational sociologists Emery and Trist, James D. Thompson, Burns and Stalker, Shirley Terreberry, and Charles Perrow is representative of this approach.[21] Each of these researcher/writers has a somewhat different approach, but they all recognize the importance of the environment. For example, Terreberry stresses that "the selective advantage of one intra- or interorganizational configuration over another cannot be assessed apart from an understanding of the dynamics of the environment itself. It is the environment which exerts selective pressure. 'Survival of the fittest' is a function of the fitness of the environment."[22]

The goal of most organizational sociologists is to determine a classification dichotomy for organizations according to the environment. For example, Burns and Stalker, who are of the Tavistock group, classified organization structures and management systems as mechanistic and organic. The most appropriate system depends on the environment. Generally, the mechanistic system was found to be most appropriate for stable internal conditions (specialized tasks, precise definitions and roles, control and communication from the top down, obedience to superiors, and a local rather than general orientation). The organic system was found to be more suitable for dynamic, unstable internal conditions (unique tasks, unstructured roles and definitions, horizontal communication, consultation rather than direct authority from superiors, and a general professional orientation of personnel). This classification into mechanistic and organic recognizes that there are appropriate systems of organization and management for different sets of internal conditions.

Kast and Rosenzweig extend the Burns and Stalker approach by integrating all the major views into the two classifications of closed/stable/mechanistic and open/adaptive/organic systems. Figure 2-2 shows the results of the Kast and Rosenzweig summary. All the authors represented in Figure 2-2 carefully point out that this should not be viewed as a strict dichotomy but rather as a continuum. Such an approach is very general and abstract. Specific contingency relationships are not inherent in such a one-dimensional continuum, and there is a problem of translating the classifications into practice. What

---

[21] See Fremont E. Kast and James E. Rosenzweig (eds.), *Contingency Views of Organization and Management,* Science Research, Chicago, 1973. This book of readings contains selections written by most of these authors and many others.

[22] Ibid., p. 98.

Figure 2-2   Classification of Contingency Views

Author	Closed/Stable/Mechanistic	Open/Adaptive/Organic
James D. Thompson	Closed system Certain, deterministic, rational	Open system Uncertain, indeterministic, natural
Harold J. Leavitt	Power concentration Combination of relatively independent parts or components	Power equalization Multivariate systems of interacting variables: task, structural, technical, and human variables
Tom Burns and G. M. Stalker	Mechanistic	Organic
Shirley Terreberry	Placid environment	Turbulent environment
Charles Perrow	Routine technology Analyzable search procedures, few exceptions, programmable decisions	Nonroutine technology Unanalyzable search procedures, numerous exceptions, nonprogrammable decisions
Raymond G. Hunt	Performance	Problem solving
D. S. Pugh, D. J. Hickson, and C. R. Hinings	Full bureaucracy: structured, concentrated authority, impersonal control	Implicitly structured organizations: unstructured, dispersed authority, line control
Roger Harrison	"Surface" interventions Low emotional involvement in organization change Emphasis on instrumental relationships	"In-depth" interventions High emotional involvement in organization change Emphasis on interpersonal relationships
William H. Newman	Management design for stable technology	Management design for adaptive technology

Source: Adapted from Fremont E. Kast and James E. Rosenzweig (eds.), *Contingency Views of Organization and Management,* Science Research, Chicago, 1973, pp. 311–312.

often happens is the very thing that these authors are trying to get away from: one classification is clearly superior to another under *all* conditions. Regardless of the warnings, such as that of Burns and Stalker, who state, "we desire to avoid the suggestion that either system is superior under all circumstances,"[23] this is exactly what often occurs. For example, the mechanistic classification often has a "bad" connotation. Organization development activities are often aimed at making the organization more "organic." The assumption is often made that the "organic" organization will be more effective, regardless of the environmental situation.

French and Bell attempt to counter the faulty generalizations made from the classification schemes.[24] Although they do not state the relationships in terms of if-then contingencies, they do point out some contingencies that can be found in Burns and Stalker's classification into mechanistic and organic systems as follows:

1 If the functions are at a high level and are complex, then there is a need for acknowledging expertise, open communication, and goal clarification for effectiveness.

[23] Ibid., p. 79.
[24] Wendell L. French and Cecil H. Bell, Jr., *Organization Development.* Prentice-Hall, Englewood Cliffs, N.J., 1973, pp. 188–190.

2 If there is a great deal of interdependency among personnel, then there is a need for open communication and team leadership styles to be effective.

3 If the human resources have a high degree of cognitive, problem-solving, and interpersonal skills, then an organic system of organization is more effective.

4 If the personnel and leader have basic communication, task, and maintenance skills, then team leadership styles, task forces, and committees are effective.

5 If the organization is operating in a rapidly changing environment, then the organic system is effective.

6 If the organization is faced with an unanticipated crisis situation threatening survival, then the mechanistic system is effective.

7 If personnel have theory X values, then the mechanistic system is effective.

8 If personnel have theory Y values, then the organic system is effective.

These eight if-then contingencies derived from the Burns and Stalker classification scheme point out the environmental conditions where the organic system is more effective and under what conditions the mechanistic system is more effective. Although the environmental variables are mainly internal to the organization, they do demonstrate the potential value that determining contingency relationships can have for effective management. The next chapter will give attention to the work of the other organizational sociologists mentioned (Emery and Trist, James Thompson, and Charles Perrow) who are more concerned with the external environment.

A Contingency Conceptual Framework

Both the classic and more contemporary literature reviewed above does not really provide a conceptual framework for contingency management theory and practice. However, taken as a whole, it can serve as a point of departure for developing such a framework. The introductory section of the chapter spelled out the exact meaning of the contingency relationship and how it is used in this book. To reiterate, contingency management recognizes a functional relationship (not necessarily cause and effect) between external and internal environmental variables which are generally independent and the various process, quantitative, behavioral, and systems management concepts and techniques which are generally dependent. The aim of developing the contingency relationship is to achieve the most effective goal attainment possible. For working purposes, the contingency relationship is translated into if-then terms. The *if*'s represent the independent environment variables and the *then*'s represent the dependent management variables in the functional relationship. In other words, if certain environmental conditions exist, then certain management concepts and techniques are more effective than others for goal attainment.

The three major parts of the conceptual framework for contingency management become the environment, management concepts and techniques, and the contingency relationship between them. Figure 2-3 depicts a general framework for contingency manage-

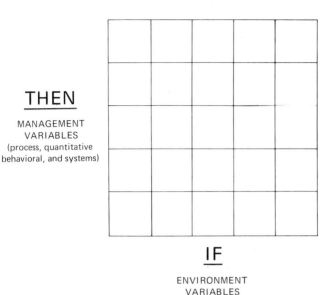

THEN

MANAGEMENT
VARIABLES
(process, quantitative
behavioral, and systems)

IF

ENVIRONMENT
VARIABLES
(external—social, technical, economic, political/legal)
(internal—structure, processes, technology)

Figure 2-3 The Conceptual Framework for Contingency Management.

ment. It is purposely very broad and abstract because at this point in development contingency management can provide only a conceptual framework for theory and practice. A matrix best shows the conceptual framework. The independent *if*'s are along the horizontal axis of the matrix and the dependent *then*'s are along the vertical axis. Remember that a matrix presentation does not intend to imply a cause-and-effect relation between the variables. The goal of contingency management is to fill in the cells of the matrix. For example, in the bottom left-hand cell of the matrix a relevant environmental condition would be identified (one or a combination of the *if*'s) and then be contingently related to an appropriate management variable (one or more of the *then*'s) for the most effective goal attainment possible. Figure 2-3 is only a conceptual model; there are obviously too many variables along each dimension to be specifically identified. Figure 2-4 represents more realistically what will happen in the development and application of contingency management. The cascading submatrices shown in Figure 2-4 recognize that there may be numerous iterations to finally reach a two-dimensional contingent relationship between the relevant environment variable and the appropriate management concept or technique for the goal in question. For example, the environment variable of computer technology as a whole may have to be cascaded down to much more specific numerical control equipment in contingently relating to the most effective management technique for quality control.

In addition to cascading submatrices, contingency management must also depend on the data reduction capability of the mathematical technique of factor analysis. Through factor

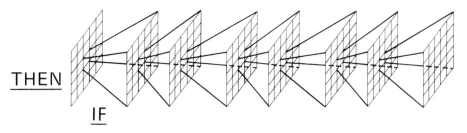

THEN

IF

Figure 2-4 Cascading Submatrices.

analysis, broad environmental data in contingency management could be reduced to smaller sets of factors or underlying components. These reduced sets of environmental variables would account for the interrelations in the broader original set of environmental variables. Potentially, factor analysis could greatly reduce the number of variables involved in the contingency matrix and make it much more realistic and practical.

The content of the cells in the contingency matrix would be the result of empirical investigation. To date, not many of the cells in the matrix are completed. Notwithstanding this lack of research, the if-then contingency matrix can still serve as a viable *conceptual framework* to organize the current body of management knowledge (as it does for this book) and guide the development of future research in the field of management as a whole.

Environmental Variables

The horizontal axis of the contingency matrix represents the *if's*—the independent environment variables. The ideal goal for contingency management is to identify the relevant environmental factors affecting the effective management of a particular business, governmental, military, hospital, religious, or educational organization. In addition, the interrelationships between the external and internal variables and within the external (both general and specific) variables and within the internal variables should be determined. Unfortunately, such a task would be tremendously difficult. The number of environmental variables and their interrelatedness is practically infinite in number and because of rapid change virtually impossible to capture. However, unlike general systems theory, which explains this interrelatedness and interdependency of the environment and lets it drop, contingency management strives to classify the environment, identify as many relevant factors as possible, and determine the specific contingent relationship with the management variables. There is no claim that this is an easy task or that it will be complete in the near future. But it *is* claimed that the contingency approach is better than what currently exists and will lead to improved management theory and practice in the future.

Figure 2-5 gives a very general breakdown of the environment into its major components. The external environment is outside of the formal organization system and is divided into

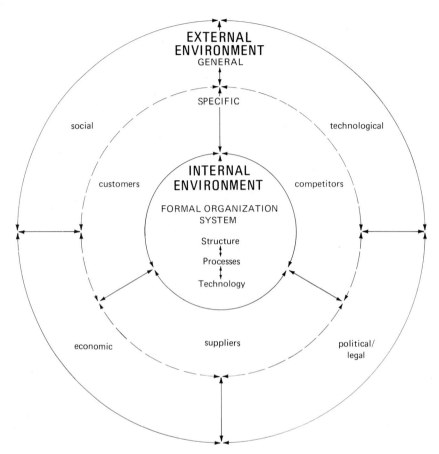

Figure 2-5 Categories of Environment in Contingency Management.

general and specific classifications. The general external environment loosely consists of social, technological, economic, and political/legal forces. They generally do not directly affect the formal organization system but are having an increasingly big impact, at least indirectly. It is now acknowledged that no organization can exist in isolation; all are affected by the surrounding external environment. There are, of course, subcategories within each of the general environmental forces, and the arrowheads in the diagram emphasize that they influence and interact with one another and directly influence the specific environment.

The specific external environment loosely includes suppliers, customers, and competitors. Although they are also external to the formal organization system, they directly affect it. Like the general variables, the specific environment interacts with the external variables, with each other, and with the internal organization variables. The next chapter is specifically devoted to the external environment. Detailed attention is given to all the general and specific variables shown in Figure 2-5.

The internal environment is essentially the formal organization system. Since it is a system, the variables are interrelated and interdependent with one another and with the variables in the external environment. The major internal variables include the organization structure; the processes of decision making, communication, and control; and the organizational state of technology. As was pointed out earlier in the chapter, these internal variables can be dependent; i.e., the external environment can directly affect them. In other words, in the contingency framework, the internal environmental variables can be the dependent *then*'s. For example, if legislation requires increased objectively measured accountability for affirmative action, then the organization should set up a social responsibility accounting system for increased control. In this example an external environment variable (political/legal) was the independent variable, and an internal environment variable (control process) was the dependent variable.

Although the internal environment is extremely important to the theory and practice of contingency management, it is generally not treated as the independent variable in the contingency relationship for two major reasons. First, the internal variables have received most of the attention of management in the past. With the exception of technology, which is also an important external variable, the other two internal variables of organization structure and processes are widely researched and written about. Practically all existing management literature is dominated by discussion and analysis of structure and processes. In contrast, very little attention has been given to the role of the external environment. The second reason for deemphasizing the internal variables as independent is simply that they are for the most part incorporated into the dependent management variables of the contingency framework. Both structure and processes are included under the dependent process management variables. Chapter 5 is devoted to organization structure, and Chapters 4, 6, and 7 give attention to the decision-making, communication, and control process variables.

Management Variables

Obviously, there are not as many possible management variables as there are environmental variables, even when the internal environment is included as management variables. Nevertheless, when all schools of management thought are considered, there are still a multitude of management *then*'s in the contingency matrix. Figure 2-6 identifies the major concepts and techniques that are found in the process, quantitative, behavioral, and systems approaches to management. This figure essentially serves as an outline for Chapters 4 to 19 in the book.

The concepts and techniques listed in Figure 2-6 are not intended to be an exhaustive list. The entire body of management knowledge, now and in the future, can be considered to be the vertical dimension of the contingency matrix. However, just as in the case of the environment, contingency management attempts to classify the management concepts and techniques and to identify and concentrate on those that are especially relevant to the most effective goal attainment. The cascading-matrices concept and factor analysis can also be applied to the management variables in the future.

Figure 2-6 Some Major Management Concepts and Techniques

PROCESS VARIABLES

Planning
  Forecasting
  Strategic plans
  Tactical plans
Organizing
  Classical structures
  Neoclassical concepts
  Behavioral approaches
  Modern structures

Directing
  Leadership styles
Communicating
  Interpersonal
  Organizational
Controlling
  Feedforward
  Feedback
  Standards
  Measures
  Corrective action
  Techniques

QUANTITATIVE VARIABLES

Decision Making
Breakeven Analysis
Present Value
Linear Programming

Economic Order Quantity
Queuing Models
Simulation Models

BEHAVIORAL VARIABLES

Learning
  Classical conditioning
  Operant conditioning
Behavior Modification
  Reinforcement
  Punishment
Motivation
  Expectancy models
  Content models

Group Dynamics
  Group formation
  Conflict
  Laboratory training
Organization Development
  Behavioral contingency management
  Job enrichment

SYSTEMS VARIABLES

General Systems Theory
  Closed, cybernetic systems
  Open systems
Systems Design and Analysis
  PPBS
  Benefit cost analysis
  Cost-effectiveness analysis
  Computer systems design
  Simulation
  Network analysis

Management Information Systems
  Formulation of purpose
  Medium-range decision making
  Short-range decision making
  Computer applications

The classification of management concepts and techniques into process, quantitative, behavioral, and systems categories reflects the development of the field as discussed in the last chapter. It recognizes that all four major schools of management thought can make a significant contribution to contingency management. The chapters in Part Two of this book are devoted to the process management variables (planning, organizing, directing, communicating, and controlling); the chapters in Part Three focus on the quantitative management variables (basic quantitative methods, decision models, and operations research); Part Four contains chapters on the behavioral management variables (learning, behavior modification, motivation, and group dynamics); and, finally, in Part Five are chapters on the systems management variables (general systems theory, systems design and analysis, and management information systems). This approach is eclectic but very comprehensive, and when put into the contingency framework, conceptually sound.

The Contingent Relationship

The third aspect of the contingency management framework is the actual functional relationship between the independent environmental variables and the dependent management variables. This functional relationship is the very heart of contingency management and is what separates it from the other approaches to management. It represents the goal of any scientific pursuit—the determination of functional relationships which lead to improved understanding, prediction, and control. Whether this will *ever* occur in the field of management is subject to debate. But the contingency approach, by its very nature, seems to have a better chance of reaching this goal than the other approaches to management. The complexity cannot be and is not denied, but as Morse and Lorsch state, "The strength of the contingency approach . . . is that it begins to provide a way of thinking about this complexity, rather than ignoring it."[25]

It must be recognized that once a given contingency relationship is empirically established, this is only *one* input into what action management will eventually implement into actual practice. The contingency relationship is usually stated in this book in two-dimensional terms (one environmental variable and one management concept or technique), but, of course, the practice of management consists of multidimensional complexity. The examples of contingency relationships stated in this and subsequent chapters are not intended to be mechanistic solutions to complex management problems. Instead, the intent is to demonstrate that by determining as many empirically derived contingency relationships as possible, there can be an additive input into what action management will take. Again, the two-dimensional examples are only used for illustrative purposes. The future development of contingency management will have a challenge to meet the multidimensional complexity of the practice of management. The last chapter further explores this and other challenges facing the future development of contingency management.

To date, there simply are very few clearly identifiable contingent relationships that have been empirically verified. Some have been discussed in this chapter, and Chapters 8, 11, 15, and 19 attempt to give as many others as exist. Ideally, of course, all cells in the contingency matrix should be meaningfully filled in. Realistically, as Kast and Rosenzweig note, "It will be a slow, painstaking process of trying to analyze the interrelationships and linking the numerous variables together; the contributions of many researchers will be needed to develop a more substantial body of knowledge concerning dual relationships."[26] However, the significant progress that has already been made in the established contingency approaches in organization design, leadership, and behavioral change, plus the contingency research efforts started by the Tavistock group, Woodward, Gouldner, and Chandler that now seems to be really picking up in all fields but especially in the process and behavioral areas of management, gives a great deal of hope for the future of contingency management.

[25] John J. Morse and Jay W. Lorsch, "Beyond Theory Y," *Harvard Business Review*, May–June 1970, p. 68.
[26] Kast and Rosenzweig, *Contingency Views*, p. 314.

Summary

This chapter is the single most important one in the entire book. It outlines exactly what is meant by contingency management (the relationship between relevant environmental variables and appropriate management concepts and techniques that lead to effective goal attainment). The external environment variables are the independent *if*'s, and the management variables are the dependent *then*'s in the contingency relationship.

Contingency management can be compared and contrasted with both traditional and modern systems approaches to management theory and practice. Although the classical theorists may have recognized exceptions, their ideas and principles were largely based on the overriding assumption of universality. The behavioral theorists criticized the classical theories, but their approach also implied universality. The more recent systems approach, on the other hand, recognizes the impact of the environment but is very abstract and tries to be all things to all people. The contingency approach denies the universal assumption and pragmatically relates the environment to appropriate management concepts and techniques.

Like any other "new" approach, there are many important historical precedents and contributions to contingency management. Classic studies by the Tavistock group, Gouldner, Woodward, and Chandler plus more contemporary work by organizational sociologists can serve as an important point of departure for developing a specific conceptual framework of contingency management. A matrix with environmental *if*'s (external social, technical, economic, and political/legal and internal structure, processes, and technology) on the horizontal axis and management *then*'s (process, quantitative, behavioral, and systems) on the vertical is presented as the conceptual framework. It must be remembered that the matrix is only a *conceptual* framework, and the complexity of functionally relating the variables is not denied. But as the subsequent chapters unfold, the value of using this framework for structuring the book should become clear. The contingency conceptual framework can help structure present management knowledge and give direction to future development of the field.

Questions for Review and Discussion

1 Define contingency management. What is a contingent relationship?
2 How does contingency management differ from situation management? Why is there a need for contingency management?
3 Compare and contrast contingency management with the more traditional approaches and with the systems approach.
4 Describe and analyze the conceptual framework for contingency management.

References

Carlisle, Howard M.: "Measuring the Situational Nature of Management," *California Management Review*, Winter 1968, pp. 45–52.
————: *Situational Management*, AMACOM, American Management Association, New York, 1973.

Chandler, Alfred D., Jr.: *Strategy and Structure: Chapters in the History of the American Industrial Enterprise,* M.I.T., Cambridge, Mass., 1970.

Conrad, Robert B.: "The Antithetical Manager and Why He Succeeds," *S.A.M. Advanced Management Journal,* January 1974, pp. 7–15.

Fiedler, Fred E.: *A Theory of Leadership Effectiveness,* McGraw-Hill, New York, 1967.

Gouldner, Alvin W.: *Patterns of Industrial Bureaucracy,* Free Press, Glencoe, Ill., 1954.

Hellriegel, Don, and John W. Slocum, Jr.: *Management: A Contingency Approach,* Addison-Wesley, Reading, Mass., 1974.

—— **and** ——: "Organizational Climate: Measures, Research and Contingencies," *Academy of Management Journal,* June 1974, pp. 255–280.

Kast, Fremont E., and James E. Rosenzweig (eds.): *Contingency Views of Organization and Management,* Science Research, Chicago, 1973.

—— **and** ——: "General Systems Theory: Applications for Organization and Management," *Academy of Management Journal,* December 1972, pp. 447–465.

—— **and** ——: *Organization and Management: A Systems Approach,* 2d ed., McGraw-Hill, New York, 1974.

Katz, Daniel, and Robert L. Kahn: *The Social Psychology of Organizations,* Wiley, New York, 1966.

Lawrence, Paul R., and Jay W. Lorsch: *Organization and Environment,* Division of Research, Harvard Graduate School of Business Administration, Boston, 1967.

Luthans, Fred: "Contingency Theory of Management: A Path out of the Jungle," *Business Horizons,* June 1973, pp. 67–72.

—— **and Robert Kreitner:** "The Management of Behavioral Contingencies," *Personnel,* July–August 1974, pp. 7–16.

McGuire, Joseph W. (ed.): *Contemporary Management Issues and Viewpoints,* Prentice-Hall, Englewood Cliffs, N.J., 1974.

Mitton, Daryl G.: "Entrepreneurial Style and the Situation Ethic," *Business and Society,* Spring 1971, pp. 18–23.

Mockler, Robert J.: *Management Decision Making and Action in Behavioral Situations,* Austin Press, Austin, Tex., 1973.

——: "Situational Theory of Management," *Harvard Business Review,* May–June 1971, pp. 146–151, 154–155.

Morse, John J., and Jay W. Lorsch: "Beyond Theory Y," *Harvard Business Review,* May–June 1970, pp. 61–68.

Narver, John C.: "Rational Management Responses to External Effects," *Academy of Management Journal,* March 1971, pp. 99–115.

Organ, Dennis W.: "Linking Pins between Organizations and Environment," *Business Horizons,* December 1971, pp. 73–80.

Pigors, Paul, and Charles A. Myers: *Personnel Administration,* 7th ed., McGraw-Hill, New York, 1973.

Potter, William J.: "Management in the Ad-hocracy," *S.A.M. Advanced Management Journal,* July 1974, pp. 19–23.

Price, James L.: *Organizational Effectiveness,* Irwin, Homewood, Ill., 1968.

Skinner, B. F.: *Contingencies of Reinforcement,* Appleton-Century-Crofts, New York, 1969.

Thayer, Frederick: "General System(s) Theory: The Promise That Could Not Be Kept," *Academy of Management Journal,* December 1972, pp. 481–493.

Trist, E. L., and K. W. Bamforth: "Some Social and Psychological Consequences of the Long-Wall Method of Coal-getting," *Human Relations,* vol. 4, pp. 3–38, 1951.

Woodward, Joan: *Industrial Organization,* Oxford University Press, London, 1965.

Wortman, Max S., Jr., and Fred Luthans (eds.): *Emerging Concepts in Management,* 2d ed., Macmillan, New York, 1975.

Zwerman, William L.: *New Perspectives on Organization Theory,* Greenwood, Westport, Conn., 1970.

Chapter 3

Environmental Conditions

The impact of the environment has probably been the most neglected aspect of traditional management theory and practice. The last two chapters pointed out that traditionally the environment was felt to be a given; it was not felt to have much of a role in either the understanding or the practice of management. However, the development of open-systems theory for organization and management began to add a new perspective. Whereas traditional theory and practice depended upon "closed" thinking, open-systems theory emphasized that the external environment had a direct input into internal operations. With this open-systems beginning, contingency management then incorporates the environment as a vital aspect of its framework. The last chapter showed that contingency management involves the functional relationship between environmental variables and management variables. The purpose of this chapter is to present and analyze some of the more important general and specific environmental variables that are relevant to contingency management.

Putting the environmental variables relevant to modern contingency management into one chapter is not an easy task. Obviously, the whole book and much, much more could and perhaps should be devoted to the environment. However, for a management book, it seems much more logical, in terms of priorities for space, to devote the greater share of attention to the management variables. The importance of the environment is recognized in this chapter. The chapter concluding each major part will specifically relate the environment to management. The important point to remember is that contingency management must strive to understand the relationship between the environmental variables broadly discussed in this chapter and the management concepts and techniques presented in more detail in the rest of the book. Identifing contingency relationships is the key, not just that management operates in this type of situational environment. The environmental variables represent the *if*'s in contingency management.

There are many ways to classify the environment. Emery and Trist use the currently popular terminology *placid* and *turbulent* to describe the environment surrounding modern organizations.[1] A placid environment is, as the term implies, rather a tranquil, static

---

[1] F. E. Emery and E. L. Trist, "The Causal Texture of Organizational Environments," *Human Relations*, vol. 18, pp. 21–32, February 1965.

situation. The organization is minimally influenced by the external, placid environment and can survive by adapting to local conditions. The turbulent environment, on the other hand, is at the opposite extreme. A turbulent situation is one that is very disruptive and dynamic and greatly influences the internal organization and its management. The turbulent environment is generally recognized to be the most descriptive of modern times. Although some organizations and many subsystems of organizations are and will always be faced with a placid environment, it is the more characteristic turbulent environment that is the major challenge facing contingency management.

This chapter assumes that the environment is relatively turbulent, but for discussion breaks the environment down into two broad categories—general and specific. The general environment consists of social, technological, economic, and political/legal variables. Obviously, one could argue that there are other forces in the general environment, but these were deemed to be the most important and widely recognized and to incorporate other possibilities. After discussing the general environment, the last part of the chapter turns to more specific environmental variables. Particular attention is given to competitors, customers, and suppliers.

The General Environment

The category of general environment that is part of the *if*'s in contingency management is about as general as one can get. In other words, almost everything could be included. To make it a bit more definitive, however, many scholars have recently devoted considerable effort to determine what variables should be included in the general and specific categories.[2] Although there is not complete agreement, social, technological, economic, and political/legal are used in this chapter to represent the most important variables in the general environment affecting contingency management. Figure 3-1 summarizes these general environment forces and how they can be measured. They influence each other, directly influence the specific environment, and indirectly, and in some cases directly, affect a given organization. An understanding of this general environment provides a starting point for more effective contingency management.

The Social Environment

The social environment has become increasingly important and complex in recent years. The social environment prescribes and teaches what human beings learn and accept, and since management is so vitally involved with human beings both internal and external to the organization, its importance is obvious. The social environment largely determines the language, customs, habits, attitudes, and most important for management, the values

[2] See Robert B. Duncan, "Characteristics of Organizational Environments and Perceived Environmental Uncertainty," *Administrative Science Quarterly*, September 1972, pp. 313–327; and Richard H. Hall, *Organizations: Structure and Process*, Prentice-Hall, Englewood Cliffs, N.J., 1972, pp. 297–306.

Figure 3-1 General Environment Variables

Variable	Definition and Objective Measures
Social	The social environment consists of societal values and forces. It is measured by cultural norms and individual, group, and societal expectations.
Technological	The technological environment consists of relatively simple or complex techniques and processes as well as the total body of knowledge. It is normally measured by the status of applied science and engineering.
Economic	The economic environment consists of both the public and private sector with natural resources, monetary capital, and monetary and fiscal policies being some of the most important elements. Some objective measures of the economy include gross national product (GNP), personal income, profits, savings, investments, and unemployment.
Political/legal	The political/legal environment mainly consists of the government and its regulations. Some objective measures include the attitudes and climate of elected public officials (e.g., liberal or conservative) and the various local, state, and federal laws that have been enacted and enforced.

of members of society. Social values have been undergoing drastic change, and there has been a proportionate impact on management.

CHANGING VALUES   Human values are the deeply held convictions that are deemed desirable by an individual within a group, organization, or society. Values largely dictate the way people interpret or perceive stimuli and thus influence their behavior. In recent years, there has been a tremendous change in values of Americans, especially those who are participants in work organizations across the country. However, it should be remembered that not all organizational participants have the same values. For example, the following represent some commonly held, but different, values about work:[3]

"I prefer work of my own choosing that offers continuing challenge, and requires imagination and initiative, even if the pay is low."

"I am responsible for my own success, and I am always on the lookout for new opportunities which will lead to a more responsible position and a greater financial reward."

"I don't like any kind of work that ties me down, but I'll do it if I have to in order to get some money; then I'll quit and do what I want until I have to get another job."

"I have worked hard for what I have, and think I deserve some good breaks. I think others should realize it is their *duty* to be loyal to the organization if they want to get ahead."

"The kind of work I usually do is O.K., as long as it's a steady job and I have a good boss."

"I believe that doing what I like to do, such as working with people toward a common goal, is more important than getting caught up in a materialistic rat race."

The point is that there have always been changing values since the beginning of time. Today, however, management is facing an almost unbelieveable *rate* of changing values in the social environment. For example, most employees several decades ago were gen-

---

[3] See M. Scott Myers and Susan S. Myers, "Toward Understanding the Changing Word Ethic," *California Management Review*, Spring 1974, p. 7.

erally happy with a weekly wage and a steady job. Today, however, most employees want and expect a great deal more. The affluent life style of middle-class America has led to higher and higher expectations. Children brought up during the fifties and sixties who are now in their twenties and thirties "need" a car, a television set, and the latest in stereo equipment. They may put down materialism, but they cannot get along without these "necessities." Their parents and grandparents who were products of the Great Depression have different values toward work and the value of a dollar. The older people tend to be more conservative and, in contrast to the younger generation, more concerned about the future and delayed gratification. What this refers to, of course, is the now famous "generation gap."

A misconception, however, is that when these changing values are taken into the work place, the old and young stereotypes always emerge. In reality, there are many different types of values held by organizational participants. Figure 3-2 gives six different types of value systems that can be found in modern organizations. A major challenge facing contingency management is to determine what behavioral concepts and techniques can be effectively applied to the various values.

Management must change with the times. Managers have done an excellent job keeping up technologically but a poor job keeping up with changing values. For example, one manager deplored the disappearance of what he referred to as the old-style, dynamic leaders like Vince Lombardi. "What we need in our organization," he said, "is a lot of Vince Lombardis who will drive through and achieve organizational objectives." However, what this manager does not realize is that Lombardi's leadership style may have

Figure 3-2 Different Types of Social Values Found in Modern Organizations

Type of Value	Description
Reactive	Not aware of self or others as individuals or human beings. Reacts to basic physiological needs. Mostly restricted to infants.
Tribalistic	Found mostly in primitive societies and ghettos. Lives in a world of magic, witchcraft, and superstition. Strongly influenced by tradition and the power exerted by the boss, tribal chieftain, police officer, schoolteacher, politician, and other authority figures.
Egocentric	Rugged individualism. Selfish, thoughtless, unscrupulous, dishonest. Has not learned to function within the constraints imposed by society. Responds primarily to power.
Conformist	Low tolerance for ambiguity and for people with differing values. Attracted to rigidly defined roles in accounting, engineering, the military. Tends to perpetuate the status quo. Motivated by a cause, philosophy, or religion.
Manipulative	Ambitious to achieve higher status and recognition. Strives to manipulate people and things. May achieve goals through gamesmanship, persuasion, bribery, or official authority.
Existential	High tolerance for ambiguity and people with differing values. Likes to do jobs in own way without constraints of authority or bureaucracy. Goal-oriented but toward a broader arena and longer time perspective.

Source: Clare W. Graves, "Levels of Existence: An Open System Theory of Values," *Journal of Humanistic Psychology,* Fall 1970, pp. 131–155.

been effective for coaching a football team in the 1960s, but would probably be very ineffective dealing with many of today's employees in a complex organization.[4]

THE SOCIAL CLIMATE   Because values are changing at such a rapid rate, it is difficult to present a composite picture of the social climate facing today's manager. Yet, there are enough data available to depict certain trends. One study conducted by General Electric's Business Environment Section reveals some interesting trends that are presently occurring.[5] The views and works of a hundred of the nation's top educators and authors were analyzed and synthesized in this study.

One important finding of the GE study that was particularly relevant to contingency management was the emphasis given to the rights of individuals. Participative management and due process concepts and techniques should become more appropriate. Employees, in many cases, may either accept or reject an organization and gauge their contributions based on whether it provides them with individual freedoms. Another finding was that there will be a trend away from "group think" or conformity and toward diversity of opinion. The stereotyped "organization man" of the 1950s is replaced by a more free-thinking, flexible individual. A third predicted trend is that material wealth will begin to lose its appeal. In particular, as the level of education rises, people will become more interested in self-development and the quality, not material quantity, of life. Living will take on existentialist dimensions, with people searching for a sense of meaning and purpose in their existence. A fourth major conclusion, with special emphasis on the generation gap, was that greater value will be placed on immediate gratification. People will become less concerned with "saving for a rainy day." Instead, the "now" generation will be more interested in solutions to today's problems and live for today and not 10 years from now.

Other more general findings from the GE study followed a similar pattern. For example, ideology and dogma will be replaced by pragmatic, rational reasoning. Only ideas that can stand the test of time will be accepted. Moral absolutes will give way to situation ethics. Rather than judging something right or wrong based on a predetermined code, people will begin evaluating the circumstances of a given situation. This, of course, will mean that organizational participants will no longer blindly accept company policies and procedures. This situation ethic or value, of course, falls in line with and may actually promote the use of contingency management.

THE ROLE OF INCOME AND EDUCATION   At first glance, the above social trends seem to run counter to traditional management thinking. However, the conservative, resistance-to-change stereotype of managers is badly outdated. The fact is that many of the social changes experienced in this country in the last few years have been promoted by well-educated, professional managers. Although it is commonly believed that social change is the direct result of dissatisfied low-income, minority groups, the facts say almost the reverse is true.

---

4 Ibid., p. 14.
5 Ian Wilson, "How Our Values Are Changing," *The Futurist*, February 1970, pp. 5–9.

Figure 3-3 Contrast between Income Groups on Current Social Issues

	Under $5,000 %	$15,000 and over %
CHANGE ISSUES		
Favor Ralph Nader's efforts	37	67
Willing to raise taxes to curb pollution	42	71
Favor women's liberation efforts	48	59
Against student demonstrations	54	38
Favor U.S. Supreme Court school desegregation orders	48	69
Believe blacks asking for more than ready for	56	41
Believe blacks have less native intelligence than whites	59	21
Favor legalized abortions	27	62
Ease criminal penalties for use of marijuana	30	43
Agreeable to coalition government in Saigon with Communists	32	57
Would turn in son or daughter possessing marijuana in room	57	27
Favor United States diplomatic recognition of China	42	68
Support newspapers on publishing of Pentagon Papers	42	56
ECONOMIC-RELATED "GUT" ISSUES		
Favor tax reform with rich paying more	76	73
Favor federal program of productive jobs for unemployed	91	89
Favor return to price-wage freeze	53	53
Favor comprehensive, compulsory federal health insurance program	46	47

Source: Reprinted from *The Anguish of Change,* by Louis Harris. By permission of W. W. Norton & Company, Inc., Copyright © 1973, by W. W. Norton & Company, Inc. The data are drawn from 1971, 1972, and 1973 Harris surveys.

Louis Harris, the famous pollster, has an interesting thesis which he calls "Karl Marx Upside Down."[6] He notes that the traditional pyramid of education and income has been tipped upside down. The forces for change are the dominant highly educated, upper-middle-income professionals in modern society. The low-income group, dominated by older people, actually resists social change. Figure 3-3 contrasts the two groups on the vital issues of the 1970s.

Even more important than income, and of course the two go hand in hand, is education. Harris feels that the vast expansion of college exposure to members of society has been the greatest single stimulus for change. The percentage of persons over eighteen with some college has risen from 12 percent in 1960 to 34 percent in 1973. By 1975 over 40 percent will have been to college, and by 1980 over half the eighteen-and-over population will have attended college. The educated member of society has generalized characteristics such as the following:

1 An inquiring frame of mind to question many of the standard dicta one was raised to believe;
2 a sensitivity to realize there were others in society whose lot and interests were not identical to their own, but who should not suffer by dint of the lack of college exposure; and

[6] See Louis Harris, *The Anguish of Change,* Norton, New York, 1973, pp. 35–52. The facts in the discussion are taken from this source.

3 at least a tinge of guilt about having passed the threshold of potential privilege and, while inclined to reap the material rewards, nonetheless prone still to feel less than self-righteous about it.[7]

Armed with this perspective, the educated person affects societal values and the management of organizations in the society.

The better educated the members of society, the more likely it is that an organization will be able to find highly qualified managerial talent. In addition, as a society becomes better educated, economic conditions usually improve as people find more and better solutions to their problems. This, in turn, leads to increased sophistication which is often reflected in changing priorities. For example, in America this has been accompanied by a reexamination of national priorities and an emphasis on social values, as shown in Figure 3-3. In addition, the educated public begins to expect and demand more from its institutions, both profit and nonprofit. In order to attain new social goals, the level of management expertise must be very high. A contingency approach is very adaptable to such an educated social environment.

Technological Environment
Next to the social environment, the technological environment is probably most important to contingency management. One could reason that technology is even more important than the social environment because it has a more direct, pragmatic impact. However, technology has been a devasting force for enough years for management to finally begin to successfully cope with it. Alvin Toffler's 1970 book *Future Shock* was primarily concerned with the technological impact on society and its organizations. He described future shock as ''the shattering stress and disorientation that we induce in individuals by subjecting them to too much change in too short a time.''[8] As a reaction to this future shock, society has reached a point where people are not asking what technology *can* do but instead what technology *should* do.

Technology is no longer given free rein. Society is now more interested in checking and evaluating technology to make sure that it is contributing to the betterment of humanity. The rejection of the supersonic transport airplane, the cutback in the space program, and the general public outcry against genetic engineering, all technologically feasible, are but representative examples of the new outlook toward technology. Technology is no longer an end in itself for society or, more importantly, for management.

Starting with the Woodward studies, more attention has been devoted to technology than to any other aspect of the environment in contingency approaches. Woodward used mass, batch, and process technologies in her study. Another more comprehensive and conceptual classification is provided by James D. Thompson.[9] His scheme is applicable to a diverse range of technologies found in all complex organizations. First is what he labels *long-linked* technology. This category of technology is characterized by serial

---

[7] Ibid., pp. 43–44.

[8] Alvin Toffler, *Future Shock*, Bantam, New York, 1970, p. 2.

[9] James D. Thompson, *Organizations in Action*, McGraw-Hill, New York, 1967, pp. 15–18.

interdependence between organizational units. The best example is the mass production assembly line in a manufacturing organization. The second category Thompson calls *mediating* technology. Under this technology, there is a joining together of independent persons, such as clients or customers. Examples of organizations utilizing mediating technology include financial institutions, utilities, and the post office. The third and last category of technology he calls *intensive.* Under this type, many diverse technologies are brought together to solve a problem or achieve a change in some object. The general hospital and research and development laboratories in industry are two examples of organizations having intensive technologies.

Charles Perrow also presents an interesting classification of technology.[10] He uses a two-dimensional matrix of four cells to depict the technological variables relevant to various kinds of organizations. Figure 3-4 shows that in a craft type of organization there are few exceptions. For example, personnel in a firm making fine glassware encounter mostly familiar situations and have an unanalyzable search. This latter dimension simply means that the personnel must depend on their experience, judgment, and skill to solve problems rather than depend on bureacratic rules or standard operating procedures. Perrow gives examples of cell 2 being a factory which makes nuclear-propulsion systems, cell 3 being an engineering firm building made-to-order machines such as drill presses or electric motors, and cell 4 being a factory manufacturing a standard product like heating elements for electric stoves. Figure 3-5 shows the same approach to "people-changing" organizations rather than industrial organizations. The nature of the raw material is substituted for the search procedure. Examples of raw material in people-changing organizations are students, delinquents, and mental patients.

Both the Thompson and Perrow frameworks are the type of analyses and classification schemes that are needed in all areas of the environment. This is why the technological environment is ahead of the others in the development of contingency management. However, the ability to diagnose the level of technology of an individual organization now and in the future is also needed. Every type of organization can proudly point to its own remarkable technological feats. Examples are the commercial airline that advertised that one of its jet passenger planes was longer from nose to tail than the total distance flown by the Wright brothers in 1903 and American Telephone and Telegraph, which noted it is about at the point where the revenue from handling long-distance calls for computers is greater than that from handling long-distance calls placed by humans.[11] Another almost unbelievable example of the level of technology in modern organizations is the calculation that if AT&T were to return to the old "number please" noncomputer telephone system, the number of telephone operators required to handle today's volume of calls would be fast approaching the entire population.[12] Chapter 4 will discuss some forecasting techniques that can help management better diagnose and predict the technological environ-

---

[10] Charles Perrow, *Organizational Analysis: A Sociological View,* Wadsworth, Belmont, Calif., 1970, pp. 75–80.

[11] William A. Faunce, *Problems of an Industrial Society,* McGraw-Hill, New York, 1968, p. 39.

[12] David I. Cleland and William R. King, *Systems Analysis and Project Management,* 2d ed., McGraw-Hill, New York, 1975, p. 5.

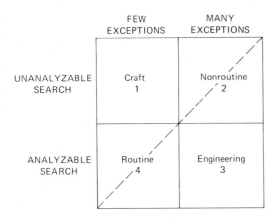

	FEW EXCEPTIONS	MANY EXCEPTIONS
UNANALYZABLE SEARCH	Craft 1	Nonroutine 2
ANALYZABLE SEARCH	Routine 4	Engineering 3

Figure 3-4 Technology Variables. *Source: Organizational Analysis: A Sociological View,* by Charles B. Perrow, Copyright © 1970 by Wadsworth Publishing Company, Inc. Reprinted by permission of the publisher, Brooks/Cole Publishing Company, Monterey, Calif.

	UNIFORM AND STABLE	NONUNIFORM AND UNSTABLE
NOT WELL UNDERSTOOD	Socializing institutions (e.g., some schools) 1	Elite psychiatric agency 2
WELL UNDERSTOOD	Custodial institutions, vocational training 4	Programmed learning school 3

Figure 3-5 Technology Variables in "People Changing" Organizations. *Source: Organizational Analysis: A Sociological View,* by Charles B. Perrow, Copyright © 1970 by Wadsworth Publishing Company, Inc. Reprinted by permission of the publisher, Brooks/Cole Publishing Company, Monterey, Calif.

ment. This in turn will help determine contingent relationships between the environment and appropriate management concepts and techniques.

The Economic Environment

Like the social and technological general environment variables, the economy has a tremendous impact on contingency management. Although the economic environment has always been recognized in the study and analysis of business firms, it has been neglected when applied to other organizations. However, as Richard H. Hall points out, "To most businessmen, this is the crucial variable. In universities and in government work, experience also shows the importance of economic conditions when budgets are being prepared, defended, and appropriated in industrial areas. Changing economic conditions serve as important constraints on any organization."[13] When economic conditions are good, most organizations of any kind operate smoothly. When economic conditions have a downturn, most organizations are adversely affected.

The economy, historically, has run in cycles. Conditions will be good for a while, and then there will be a downturn. During the mid to late 1960s economic conditions in this country were very favorable. However, rising inflation and unemployment halted this trend and resulted in an economic dip during the 1970s. While some organizations attempt to forecast economic fluctuations, they often run into difficulty. Even at a national level, economists rarely agree and are often wrong. However, there are some indications that economic forecasts are improving. The financial editor of the *Philadelphia Bulletin* has since 1955 compared the predictions of sixty professional forecasters with actual economic statistics and has noted improvements over the years.[14]

METHODS OF PREDICTING THE ECONOMY   Among the organizations that elect to consider economic forecast data, some of the larger ones analyze economic data from the national level and make their own predictions. Other organizations obtain economic predictions from trade journals, popular magazines, and subscription services. The main techniques used in forecasting gross national product (GNP) include a piecemeal approach and formula approaches. The piecemeal approach is forecasting each element of GNP—durable goods, residential construction, etc.—separately and then simply adding them together. Formula approaches involve entering available economic statistics in one or more formulas or equations and then solving the equations. The latter approach in its most sophisticated form is referred to as *econometrics*. Econometric models have gradually increased in complexity as more and more influencing variables are added. The best-known econometric models, such as the one developed by the Wharton School of Business, include well over 100 variables and must be processed by a computer.

The other primary method of economic forecasting, which is used to predict economic patterns for given states, regions, sectors, or industries instead of GNP, is called *input/output analysis*. The idea is that the outputs of one industry become the inputs of others. Steel outputs, for example, go to the auto industry, construction industry, appliance industry, and many others. Input/output grids may be constructed to chart the quantities of output, in dollars, moving between industries. Computer analysis reveals what impact a given industry has on other industries.

The reasonableness of this forecasting approach is offset to some extent by the difficulties that exist in keeping the input/output model up to date in a dynamic economy. What

---

[13] Hall, op. cit., p. 302.
[14] George A. Steiner, *Top Management Planning,* Macmillan, New York, 1969, p. 213.

is made from steel today may be made from fiberglass tomorrow and vice versa. The accuracy of input/output forecasting depends on keeping the coefficients for each I/O factor current, for example, having the correct percentage of total aluminum output that goes to the beverage-canning industry. Some of the problems inherent in the economic forecasts point to the complexity of the environment in general. Yet, the understanding of economic variables in the environment can be very helpful to contingency management. Natural resources, capital, and monetary and fiscal policy are particularly relevant. These are discussed next, and some more direct economic variables are also discussed later under the specific environment.

NATURAL RESOURCES   At best, managers have only a limited amount of control over the price of natural resources. Land, for example, has to be purchased at the going rate, which in recent years has often proved prohibitive. One of the major reasons for the high prices is simply that land is a limited resource. As people begin to inhabit more of the earth, the demand for land increases while the supply remains the same. This holds true for other natural resources also. In the last decade the United States has witnessed shortages of all types of natural resources but especially copper, silver, gold, and oil. In the case of oil, costs have mounted dramatically and affected everyone. Car owners know that in the last few years the price of gasoline has risen tremendously. In addition to auto owners, all organizations have been affected by the oil crisis through price increases for heating oil and all petroleum-related products. In such instances, management has been at the virtual mercy of general economic fluctuations.

The future promises more of the past. Natural resources are becoming extremely difficult to obtain, and as a result, prices are being bid up higher and higher. One major reason for the resource crisis in this country in recent years is simply that the United States has only about 7 percent of the world's population but is using approximately 40 percent of all the resources. As a result, price increases are inevitable and are going to get worse instead of better.

CAPITAL   Another general economic factor is capital or money. At one point or another, every organization finds it necessary to raise capital. Sometimes funds are needed for operational purposes; other times they are used for expansion of facilities. Hospitals, churches, or other nonprofit organizations may be short of operating cash during a certain time of the year, such as the summer months, and are in need of a short-term loan to be repaid later in the year. Business firms may find working capital depleted just prior to their big selling season. As a result, they will open a line of credit with a bank to take them through this period. Not all loans, of course, will be short term. A hospital may want to double the number of beds it can service. A church may want to build a house next door for the rector. A business may want to greatly expand its manufacturing facilities. In these cases long-term debt must usually be assumed. In the case of a corporation, the money could also be raised through the sale of stock.

In obtaining the needed capital, organizations have to go into the external financial market and negotiate terms. Quite often, it is the outside financial institution which holds the upper hand. Of course, by shopping around, management may be able to save a minute percentage ($\frac{1}{4}$ of 1 percent) of interest on a loan. However, normally there is little margin for negotiation. Most financial institutions in a local area have a fixed rate of interest which varies only when the large, prestigious Eastern banks, such as Chase Manhattan, change their prime rate. One possible strategy is to renegotiate a loan if the interest rate drops, but to offset this approach most banks charge a penalty for rewriting the note at a lower rate. Thus, in these cases, the prime rate has to drop significantly before renegotiating the loan is advisable.

The alternate approach to raising capital that is open to a corporation also has problems. If a corporation sells stock to raise needed capital, it dilutes ownership and increases the possibility that the shares will be bought by individuals or a group hoping to take over the firm. At the same time, large blocks of stock drive down the price, providing the firm with perhaps only 80 percent of current value per share. Once again, these are conditions over which management has little, if any, control. Yet, by understanding the importance and functioning of the capital markets and by capital budgeting, management can be more effective.

MONETARY AND FISCAL POLICY   In addition to interacting with competitive financial market conditions, management must also be cognizant of the effect of government action on the general economy. Government activities help dictate many of the things that happen in the economic environment. The two major approaches available to the government are monetary and fiscal policy.

Monetary policy affects the money supply. When there are hard times economically, the government urges banks to make loans easier to obtain. To encourage this, the Federal Reserve System can lower the reserve requirements so that banks do not have to keep as much of their deposits on hand at all times. This decreased reserve can free more money for loans. At the same time, this increase in the supply of money will drive interest rates down, and banks will attempt to entice prospective borrowers to take out loans. If they are successful in their efforts, even more money will flow into the economy. In turn, the organizations that borrow these funds will spend them for expansion of facilities or projects designed to increase their operations. The money will be passed on to builders, suppliers, workers, and others, who, in turn, will spend the money. Some of the money will be saved, but the majority will be spent. The result is more jobs, higher salaries, and a greater general level of economic activity.

In turning an economy up, monetary policy on the part of the government is very useful. Conversely, monetary policy can be used to slow up the economy. The Federal Reserve System can raise the reserve requirement, thereby forcing banks to keep more money on hand. This will reduce the total funds available for loans and drive the interest rates up. The effect, of course, is to discourage economic activity and slow down inflation. Organizations attempting to expand under such conditions have to pay a premium price for capital.

Fiscal policy deals with price stability and tax rates. When an economy is faced with inflation, the government attempts to slow down activity through its fiscal policy. One way is to put on a price freeze such as the one instituted by the Nixon administration in the early 1970s. Another approach to curbing inflation through fiscal policy is to increase taxes and then refuse to spend the funds, thereby reducing the amount of money in circulation. This practice is commonly known as "impounding funds." The theory here is that with less to spend, consumers become more discerning in their purchases and often refuse to buy expensive or nonessential items. The result is a cooling off of the economy and a stabilization of inflation. Conversely, to pick up the economy and move it forward, the government needs to do the reverse, cut taxes and spend money. The reduced tax liabilities will eventually be spent, resulting in more economic activity. Government spending will help employment and pump more money into the economy and cause an upturn.

These economic approaches are very tenuous. They do not always work because of the extreme complexities inherent in the nation's economy. Yet, an understanding of the general economic variables is necessary to contingency management. The choice of appropriate management concepts and techniques is often contingent upon the economic environment.

Political/Legal Environment
This last general environmental variable to be discussed is often overlooked, but like the others, the political/legal environment is crucial to contingency management. The political climate, of course, largely dictates what the legal environment will be. For example, the liberal political climate that came about in the aftermath of the Great Depression led to a lot of New Deal legislation that still affects the management of organizations. The more recent Watergate affair and the role of corporate contributions to political campaigns and lobbying also created a political climate that has a definite impact on future management.

Of more direct impact than political climate, however, is the legal environment. Although political and legal matters go hand in hand and are treated as one category in this discussion, the various federal, state, and local laws are a most important environment for contingency management. For example, federal legislation has been enacted to regulate virtually every organization in America. All profit and nonprofit institutions can be audited by the federal Internal Revenue Service. It is possible that a profit-oriented organization may find that it owes the government more taxes than it has paid, and a nonprofit organization may discover that some of its activities do not qualify for nontax status. In either event, it is evident that federal tax regulation extends to everyone. Some of the other more common types of federal regulation include promotion of competition, antidiscrimination, environmental control, and consumer protection. After discussing these federal areas, state, local, and regulated industries are given attention as part of the legal environment.

PROMOTION OF COMPETITION   In 1890, the federal government enacted the Sherman Antitrust Act. In essence this law stated that every contract, combination, or conspiracy designed to restrain interstate commerce was illegal. Furthermore, any person who monopolized or conspired or combined to monopolize would be guilty of a misdemeanor. The penalty for such acts included a stiff fine and/or imprisonment.

Today the antitrust law is still of major concern to many organizations. For example, a few years ago, Ling-Temco-Vought (LTV), a Dallas-based conglomerate, attempted to add Jones, Laughlin Steel Company to its holdings. However, the Antitrust Division of the Justice Department prevented LTV from doing so unless it would divest itself of some other holdings. Otherwise, in the Justice Department's view, LTV would be impeding competition and thus be subject to antitrust action.

Another illustration is found in the case of International Business Machines (IBM). For a number of years smaller computer firms accused IBM of monopolizing the computer industry. Certainly on the basis of size and success, IBM has dominated. Recently, however, the competition has been winning a number of lawsuits in selected areas. Whether or not IBM's grip on the computer market will be loosened through government antitrust is still unclear. However, one thing is certain: IBM proves an often-cited cliché in the legal arena, "Never get too big—it only invites government action." This attitude accounts for why so little has recently been heard about antitrust suits against General Motors. Only about a decade ago, GM held well over half of the automobile market, and American Motors was in serious financial trouble. Today, because of the effect of the energy crisis, small cars are returning to favor, and American Motors is in relatively healthy financial shape. GM's market share, on the other hand, dipped below 50 percent, and there was apparently little chance of any antitrust action. Thus, even though GM was suffering in the market, from the viewpoint of the legal environment it was better off.

ANTIDISCRIMINATION   In recent years laws enacted by Congress have forbidden discrimination on the basis of race, color, creed, sex, and national origin. One of the primary pieces of legislation in this area was the Civil Rights Act of 1964. As a result of this major piece of legislation, many organizations have become very conscious of minority employees. They must have policies and programs to ensure that there is no discrimination in any aspect of employment. In recent years, there has also been a concerted effort to rid organizations of discrimination against women employees. Organizations must pragmatically abide by the civil rights laws in order to head off any suits from either the government or individuals who feel they have been discriminated against.

Not all organizations have successfully implemented antidiscrimination policies, programs, and practices. In particular, women have lately brought successful suits against business, charging that the "equal pay for equal work" clause contained in the Equal Pay Act of 1963 is not being carried out. The results have been dramatic. In the last ten years over 100,000 workers, mostly female, have been awarded over $45 million in back pay. A few representative cases include:

More than 2,000 women glassworkers won $900,000 in back pay and interest from Wheaton Glass Company of New Jersey.

Some 300 female telephone workers won about $500,000 in a decision against Pacific Telephone and Telegraph Company.

Two hundred and seventy-six women won $190,000 from Anaconda Aluminum Company and the right to hold formerly sex-restricted jobs requiring heavy lifting.

When it is remembered that most cases (the Labor Department estimates up to 95 percent) are settled out of court, one can see the tremendous impact that civil rights legislation has on modern management.

ENVIRONMENTAL CONTROL   In the last 10 years, the federal government has stepped up its efforts to ensure a cleaner environment. For example, the Water Quality Act of 1965 gave states the right to set their own water-quality standards or allow the Department of the Interior to do it for them. Five years later the law was toughened, putting emphasis upon eliminating pollution from ocean-going vessels. In 1970 the government passed the National Air Quality Standards Act. This legislation required the use of pollution-control equipment on all new factories and a drastic reduction of auto emissions and nitrogen. Furthermore, the law permitted the federal government to set emission control standards on such pollutants as soot and sulfur dioxide. In addition to these laws prohibiting water and air pollution, there is also legislation regulating solid waste disposal and noise pollution. With the increasing social concern for ecology and the quality of life, these laws are only beginning to scratch the surface. Environmental regulations are going to have a much bigger impact on organizations in the future.

CONSUMER PROTECTION   Ever since 1906, when the Food and Drug Administration was created, the federal government has attempted to provide the consuming public with some form of protection. Initially, the attention was focused on medicines and foods. Today, the concern ranges from toys to automobiles and from labels to warranties.

One of the foremost pieces of consumer legislation has been the Truth in Packaging Act. In essence, this law provides for certain mandatory labeling provisions, including requirements that (1) the identity of the commodity be specified on the label, (2) the net quantity of the contents be spelled out on the package, (3) these contents be expressed in ounces or pounds, and (4) if the package contains a representation of servings, the net quantity of such a serving be stated. Another major piece of consumer legislation was the Truth in Lending Act. According to the provisions of this bill, if a person borrows money, the lender must relate all the charges, both direct and indirect, which are being levied. In addition, on open accounts, such as revolving charges, information about unpaid balances, payments made, finance charges, annual percentage rates, balances upon which finance charges are computed, and the closing date of the billing cycle must all be provided to the consumer. The consumerism movement has surfaced as one of the major challenges facing not only business, but other organizations as well. Like environmental control, there is sure to be more rather than fewer consumer protection laws in the future.

STATE REGULATIONS   Besides the federal regulations discussed so far, there are also many laws at the state level that affect organizations. For example, there are many state laws dealing with labor. Such things as minimum standards for working conditions, sanitary conditions, and adequate protection against unsafe conditions and fire hazards are a few of these. The Occupational Safety and Health Act (OSHA) at the federal level also, of course, deals with these matters and has had a big impact on today's organizations. It is also common to find state legislation related to maximum hours, minimum wages, and overtime pay. Once again the federal government has enacted legislation on these matters in the form of the Federal Fair Labor Standards Act, but state law is used to handle those instances when the act is not in effect, namely for intrastate rather than interstate commerce. Other examples of state labor legislation include regulation of the actual hours women and children can work. For example, in some states children cannot be employed before a particular hour in the morning and must not be allowed to work past a specified time in the evening. In addition, some states have passed what are commonly called "right to work" laws which permit employment without requiring the person to join a union.

Another common area of state legislation is health. In addition to the laws concerned with the health of factory employees are those designed to protect the general public. For example, restaurants must maintain a minimum standard of cleanliness or the operator's license can be withdrawn, in effect shutting the establishment down.

Another major area of regulation primarily coming out of the state level has to do with pricing. Most states have laws similar to that of the federal government forbidding monopolies on trade and pricing practices which tend to reduce or eliminate competition. Some states have established what are called "unfair trade laws." In the twenty-six states which now have such legislation, it is illegal for an organization (producer, wholesaler, or retailer) to sell goods at less than their cost plus, in many of these states, a certain specified percentage markup. In this way minimum price levels are established and cutthroat competition is eliminated. Some of the commodities to which these laws have been specifically applied include alcoholic beverages, gasoline, and cigarettes.

Another version of the above are the so-called fair trade laws. These laws deal with the maintenance of resale prices on brand products. For example, if a druggist buys mouthwash at 59 cents a bottle and, instead of retailing it at 99 cents as suggested by the manufacturer, cuts the price to 85 cents, he or she is selling below the recommended price. Many manufacturers oppose this, demanding that the seller set the price at the level recommended by them. To enforce this, it was common for producers either to make retailers sign contracts agreeing to do so or to sell to them on consignment. However, the latter was expensive and the former was difficult to enforce against nonsigners. Moreover, several state courts have declared that nonsigners were not obligated to adhere to the recommended price.

Still another example of state regulation is found in the usury laws. Many states have legal limits on the maximum rate of interest which can be charged on different types of loans. These laws often regulate the rates on both bank notes and revolving credit accounts. In recent years the inflation rate has led many state legislatures around the country to raise the limit and allow banks and finance companies to charge more for loans. Nevertheless, there are restrictions within which the companies still must operate.

Finally, many states have consumer protection laws. One of the most recent developments in this area has been in liability law. Today, most states have abandoned the old legal interpretation which says that manufacturers are not liable for faulty products. In their place have come strict liability laws which hold that manufacturers have almost unlimited responsibility for any of their products which are deemed to be unsafe and have injured a consumer or user when the product was being used as intended. In fact, negligence does not have to be proved. If it can be established that the product left the factory in a defective or unsafe condition, legal action can be taken. Class action suits involving a group of consumers make an even bigger threat to negligent organizations.

LOCAL LEGISLATION   Besides the federal and state levels, at the local level there are many legal restrictions on organizations. Among the most common are zoning ordinances. Certain areas of a city are zoned for only residential construction, and an organization can build only in specified areas. Building codes are another form of local regulation. These codes specify the minimum requirements for construction. For example, in certain areas only fireproof buildings are allowed. In other locales, all electric and telephone wires have to be installed underground. Still another common local regulatory device is the license. For example, most states require restaurants, movie theaters, and barber shops to be licensed. In addition, individuals who sell autos, firearms, or tobacco are usually licensed. The same is true for liquor store owners. By licensing businesses and individuals, local governments can regulate and monitor these activities to ensure at least a minimum standard of performance.

REGULATED INDUSTRIES   A final area of the legal environment that is especially relevant to contingency management is the regulated industries. Examples include railroads, airlines, public utilities, and motor carriers which are closely regulated by federal and state government. These organizations serve to satisfy a major public need. In order to make the operation economically feasible, the government provides them some form of natural monopoly. For example, it would not be possible to have four competing airlines serving a city when only one can be supported and in some cases none can be supported. The capital outlay required for most of these public services prohibits easy entry and thus prevents competition. In return for the monopoly powers granted to these organizations, the government maintains the right to strictly regulate their activities. For example, utility rates are set to ensure a fair return on investment but no more. This usually means a return of 5 to 8 percent to the privately held company. While this may appear to be low, it must be remembered that the company has little, if any, competition and so there is virtually no risk. The challenge for effective management is to obtain the high side of the range. These organizations in the regulated industries are the extremes of those affected by the legal environment. The contingency management approach attempts to relate the above legal and other general environment variables with appropriate management concepts and techniques that will result in desired goal attainment.

The Specific Environment

So far, the discussion of the environment has been in very general terms. The social, technological, economic, and political/legal environment variables mostly indirectly affect the contingency management of modern organizations. However, just because the discussion was in very general terms does not mean that these environmental variables are not important. They have been badly neglected in the past and must be given increased attention in the future. The general environment plays a vital role in contingency management.

The general environment has a direct effect on the more specific environment affecting modern organizations. The specific environment mainly includes competitors, customers, and suppliers. These three have a direct impact on most individual organizations. Whereas the general environment has an all-pervasive impact on numerous organizations at the same time—for example, the economy affects all organizations—the specific environment is unique for each organization. This is true even for business firms in the same industry or hospitals in the same community or agencies in the same state government.

In contingency management, the specific *if*'s often can and should be identified. The remainder of the chapter gives attention to competitors, customers, and suppliers in the specific environment. Much of the discussion is merely refinements of the general environment. Even though the following deals with the specific environment, the discussion is by necessity broad and general. Chapters 8, 11, 15, and 19 give the reader the opportunity to get much more specific in both the general and specific environments by making a contingency analysis of cases. The following gives only an overall understanding and framework of the specific environment relevant to contingency management.

Competitors in the Specific Environment
In striving to attain objectives, most organizations must compete with others. For example, two hospitals located at opposite ends of a city may offer basically the same services. Yet, they will compete with one another in terms of keeping their beds filled and their facilities fully utilized. In the same manner, two business firms who make similar products and sell them at about the same price must compete for customers. Competitors in the specific environment become a very important input into contingency management.

One of the first things an organization must decide is how it will react to competition. This response greatly depends upon the market structure or the relationship between the various organizations in a particular industry or market. Market structures, applicable to any type of organization, can be depicted on the continuum shown in Figure 3-6.

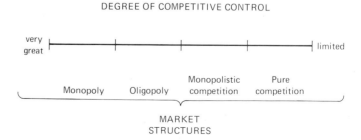

Figure 3-6 The Competitive Environment.

In a monopoly structure there are one or a very few sellers which can affect price and there is limited entry. In an oligopoly there are few sellers and one can affect the price of the other. There is also limited entry in an oligopolistic market. In monopolistic competition there are many sellers who all sell basically the same product or service at about the same price. Organizations operating in a monopolistically competitive market attempt to differentiate their products and services by image building, usually attained through advertising. In a purely competitive market there are numerous sellers, none of which can affect price, and there is easy entry.

The best example of a monopolistic market is the utility industry. Gas, electric, and telephone companies have a monopoly, and that is why they are highly regulated by the government. The automobile and steel industries are the most commonly recognized examples of oligopolistic markets. Yet, a hospital in a large city could also be thought to operate in an oligopolistic market structure. In a large city, where there are several hospitals, each will have an effect on the others' prices. For example, an increase in room rates may decrease the occupancy because prospective patients (or their doctors) choose another hospital. In addition, entry into the hospital business is restricted because of the large financial investment necessary to construct the building and purchase the equipment. This is the same basic environmental situation faced by the auto industry. General Motors, Ford, and Chrysler manufacture most of the cars sold in America. With the addition of American Motors and three or four foreign manufacturers, they account for the whole automobile market. There are a few sellers who affect each other's price, and there is restricted entry because of the high capital outlay required for auto production.

On the other end of the market continuum, organizations operate in a different competitive environment. An example of a firm in a monopolistically competitive environment is Procter and Gamble. Its soaps, detergents, and deodorants have numerous competitors, all basically the same products at about the same price. Differentiation between products to obtain a competitive edge is gained through advertising. Organizations in a purely competitive situation, such as in agriculture, can do little if anything to influence price and can do little to gain a competitive advantage. Yet, if the competitive environment is recognized, there will certainly be some management concepts and techniques that will be more effective than others. Determining such relationships is the goal of contingency management.

Customers in the Specific Environment
Closely related to the competitive environment is the customer environment. Customers or clients have a direct impact on organizations and contingency management. Just as the competitive environment affects management by the number and degree of control that sellers have over price, the customer environment affects management by the number and influence of buyers in the marketplace.

Buyers have varying degrees of demand for the goods and services being offered. Some must have the organization's output and are willing to pay any price for it. In this case there is an inelastic demand. Electricity and medical service are examples of inelastic demand. Other buyers are much more selective. They are very price-conscious, and as the price goes up, the demand goes down. In other words, there is an elastic demand for the goods and services. Figure 3-7 shows a perfectly inelastic, a perfectly elastic, and the most common relatively elastic demand curves.

A monopoly generally has a perfectly inelastic demand for its goods and services. It could charge any price to its customers and they would still buy the same quantity. Organizations in a purely competitive market environment would have a perfectly elastic demand for their goods and services. For example, if an agricultural organization raised its price of grain 1 cent above the market price, it would have no customers. Most organizations fall between these two extremes; they face a relatively elastic demand curve. Their customers are affected by product differentiation and price.

PRODUCT DIFFERENTIATION   Attempts to appeal to customers through product differentiation are common to most organizations. This is especially true in a monopolistic competitive market structure but also occurs in other market environments as well. For example, even though an electric or gas utility has little problem with competitive products and services, it can still push for different uses of its products. Electric heat for homes or gas grills for charcoaling steaks are a couple of current examples. In an oligopoly, differentiation in a product like steel is not important but in automobiles it is very important. Differentiating between a Ford and a Chevrolet is a key strategy for gaining customers. The same is true for hospitals. Two hospitals in the same city offer basically the same services for patient care and treatment. However, one may specialize in the treatment of cancer while the other one has a large cardiac unit. Besides being much more efficient and meeting the goals of comprehensive health planning, by differentiating their services, the organizations are controlling their customers. Product differentiation probably has the least impact on organizations in a purely competitive environment. Yet,

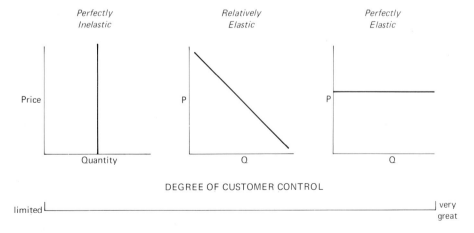

Figure 3-7 The Customer Environment.

even in these cases, an organization could gain a slight competitive edge for customers by stressing higher quality or some other form of differentiation.

PRICING STRATEGIES   Customer demand is largely influenced by price. Under most market conditions the relatively elastic demand curve shown in Figure 3-7 is in effect. There is an inverse relationship between price and demand. When price is low, demand is high; when price is high, demand is low. However, some goods and services are more price-responsive than others. For example, if the price for a gallon of milk rises a couple of cents, there may be virtually no decline in demand. Likewise, if a hospital raises its room rate from $50 to $52 a day, this will have virtually no effect on the number of incoming patients. On the other hand, if a coffee shop increases the price of coffee from $0.15 to $0.20 a cup, there may be a relatively sharp decline in coffee sales. The coffee drinkers start making their own, cut down on consumption, or switch to soda pop or tea.

In any case, price usually plays an important role in determining the amount of control a firm can exercise over its customers. Barring government regulations, some of which were covered in the discussion of the legal environment, an organization can set any price it chooses. However, total revenues will depend upon the elasticity of demand. The economist Richard Leftwich summarizes some of the important factors which can affect the elasticity:

1 The availability of good substitutes for the commodity under consideration
2 The number of uses to which the commodity can be put
3 The price of the commodity relative to consumers' incomes
4 Whether the price established is toward the upper end of the demand curve or toward the lower end of the curve [15]

The organization should understand and, where possible, take advantage of these factors in determining pricing strategies. In order to do this effectively, contingent relationships between the customer environment and the appropriate management concepts and techniques must be established.

Suppliers in the Specific Environment
The third but not any less important aspect of an organization's specific environment is the suppliers. Without adequate supplies of labor, equipment, materials, and parts, an organization cannot transform inputs, which are largely obtained from suppliers, into desired outputs.

One of the most important segments of the supplier environment is labor. The workforce plays an important role in almost every modern organization. In securing and maintaining a labor force, a given organization must compete with others. To effectively staff the organization, attention must be given to workforce planning, recruitment, selection, and

---

[15] Richard H. Leftwich, *The Price System and Resource Allocation,* 3d ed., Holt, Rinehart & Winston, New York, 1966, p. 41.

placement. Management deals specifically with the supply environment in attempting to recruit for labor needs. There are several possible sources.

One is the young person entering the labor force for the first time. Generally, this person has just graduated or dropped out of high school, trade school, junior college, or college. A member of the "now" generation, this person will often have a different set of values and expectations about work than most employees already on the job. Another potential source of labor is the employed but dissatisfied worker or manager. Because of the way jobs have been structured, this is probably the largest source. The majority of employees in all organizations are dissatisfied, but for very pragmatic reasons, remain on the job. Most employees have found out that the grass is *not* greener on the other side of the fence. In addition, they are locked into the seniority and fringe benefit system, and it would be very costly for them to move to another organization and start all over again. A third source of labor is the unemployed person. Such people are usually a poor risk because if they are merely laid off through no fault of their own, they will return to their old jobs at the first opportunity. If the unemployed person was forced from the last job, there is a good chance it will happen again. Lately, however, there has been a growing concern for the "hard-core" unemployable and other overlooked potential employees in the supply environment.

There is a growing movement, especially with increased management professionalism, to understand and more fully utilize the so-called forgotten Americans. Many unemployed workers are minority race members, women, old people, veterans, and the handicapped. For example, blacks, Mexican-Americans, Indians, and Puerto Ricans have traditionally had at least twice the unemployment rate of whites. They have also been badly underemployed. Women, of course, have also been badly discriminated against and overlooked as a source of labor. Although not as vocal, but equally badly treated, have been senior citizens, veterans, especially of the Vietnam war, and the mental and physically handicapped. Recruiting, preparing, and developing these overlooked sources of labor to their full potential can be beneficial to an individual organization and the nation as a whole.

In addition to the labor supply environment, an organization must also purchase the necessary equipment, material, and parts supplies to transform into desired outputs. The economic laws of supply and demand will largely determine the pricing and other strategic factors in this supply environment. As with the other variables in the general and specific environment, the goal is to contingently relate the supply factors of the environment with the appropriate management concepts and techniques that will lead to goal attainment.

Summary

This chapter is concerned with the environmental side of contingency management. The environment represents the *if*'s in the if-then contingency relationship. Obviously, it would be virtually impossible to cover all the environmental variables affecting contingency management, and so the chapter is broken down into two very broad categories—

the general and specific environments. The general environment consists of social, technological, economic, and political/legal variables. The social environment mainly reflects changing societal values. The technological environment has had the biggest impact on management in the past and has been given the most attention in contingency management. For example, Woodward, Thompson, and Perrow have all classified technological impacts on organization structure. The economic environment has been given a great deal of attention but has generally not been contingently applied to management variables. Natural resources, capital, and monetary and fiscal policy all affect management. The same is true of the political/legal environment. The general political climate plus federal legislation involving antitrust, antidiscrimination, environmental control, consumer protection, and various state and local regulations have a tremendous impact on modern management. Except for some important beginnings in the technological environment, the general environmental variables need to be contingently related to the management variables.

The specific environment has a more direct impact on the individual organization than does the general environment. Included in the specific environment are competitors, customers, and suppliers. These specific environmental variables are greatly influenced by their respective market structures (monopoly, oligopoly, monopolistic competition, and pure competition). For example, a monopoly has virtually no competition, while an organization operating in a purely competitive market has severe competition. This competitive environment will affect the management variables. The same is true of the customers and suppliers. A monopoly has perfectly inelastic demand for its goods and services, and a purely competitive organization has a perfectly elastic demand. More realistically, however, are the organizations having a relatively elastic demand where product differentiation and pricing strategies play a role. Suppliers provide the necessary inputs for the organization to transform them into desired outputs. Once again, economic variables such as supply and demand largely determine the strategic factors in the supply environment. Like the general environment, the specific environmental variables must be contingently related to management variables. This task is a major challenge for contingency management in the future.

Questions for Review and Discussion

1 What is the difference between the general and specific environments? What are the major factors in each?

2 What are some of the major dimensions and issues of the social, technological, economic, and political/legal forces in the environment? How can these affect management now and in the future?

3 How do competitors, customers, and suppliers affect management?

4 Does the general or specific environment have more of an impact on management? Explain and defend your answer.

References

Bearinger, Van W.: "Emerging Technologies and Their Impacts," *S.A.M. Advanced Management Journal,* January 1974, pp. 25–28.

Bell, Daniel: "The Coming of Post-Industrial Society," *Business and Society Review/Innovation,* Spring 1973, pp. 5–23.

Bobbitt, H. Randolph, Jr., Robert H. Breinholt, Robert H. Doktor, and James P. McNaul: *Organizational Behavior: Understanding and Prediction,* Prentice-Hall, Englewood Cliffs, N.J. 1974.

Carlisle, Howard M.: *Situational Management,* AMACOM, American Management Association, New York, 1973.

Crockett, William J.: "The Management Conflict with Democratic Values," *Business Horizons,* October 1973, pp. 13–19.

Crover, Michel, Louis C. Gawthrop, Pjotr Hesseling, and Jay W. Lorsch: *Environmental Settings in Organizational Functioning,* The Comparative Administration Research Institute of the Center for Business and Economic Research, College of Business Administration, Kent State University, Kent, Ohio, 1970.

Denning, Basil W.: "Strategic Environmental Appraisal," *Long Range Planning,* March 1973, pp. 22–27.

Douglas, Jack D. (ed.): *The Technological Threat,* Prentice-Hall, Englewood Cliffs, N.J., 1971.

Drucker, Peter F.: *Technology, Management and Society,* Harper & Row, New York, 1970.

Duncan, Robert B.: "Characteristics of Organizational Environments and Perceived Environmental Uncertainty," *Administration Science Quarterly,* September 1972, pp. 313–327.

Dutton, Richard E.: "Science, Cybernation and Human Values," *Journal of Human Relations,* First Quarter 1969, pp. 77–89.

Emery, F. E., and E. L. Trist: "The Causal Texture of Organizational Environments," *Human Relations,* February 1965, pp. 21–32.

Graves, Clare W.: "Levels of Existence: An Open System Theory of Values," *Journal of Humanistic Psychology,* Fall 1970, pp. 131–155.

Hall, Cameron P.: *Technology and People,* Judson Press, Valley Forge, Pa., 1969.

Hall, Richard H.: *Organizations: Structure and Process,* Prentice-Hall, Englewood Cliffs, N.J., 1972.

Hostluck, K. Tim: "Business' Interpenetration of the Political Environment," *Business and Society,* Fall 1973, pp. 19–27.

Hunt, Raymond G.: "Technology and Organization," *Academy of Management Journal,* September 1970, pp. 235–252.

Juricovich, Ray: "A Core Typology of Organizational Environments," *Administrative Science Quarterly,* September 1974, pp. 380–394.

Kast, Fremont E., and James E. Rosenzweig (eds.): *Contingency Views of Organization and Management,* Science Research, Chicago, 1973.

——— **and** ———: *Organization and Management: A Systems Approach,* 2d ed., McGraw-Hill, New York, 1974.

Keller, Robert T.: "A Look at the Sociotechnical System," *California Management Review,* Fall 1972, pp. 86–91.

Lawrence, Paul R., and Jay W. Lorsch: *Organization and Environment,* Division of Research, Harvard Graduate School of Business Administration, Boston, 1967.

Lynch, Beverly P.: "An Empirical Assessment of Perrow's Technology Construct," *Administrative Science Quarterly,* September 1974, pp. 338–356.

Mesthene, Emmanuel G.: *Technological Change,* Harvard, Cambridge, Mass., 1970.

Myers, M. Scott, and Susan S. Myers: "Toward Understanding the Changing Work Ethic," *California Management Review,* Spring 1974, pp. 7–19.

Newstrom, John W.: "Sociotechnical Parallels in Management," *S.A.M. Advanced Management Journal,* July 1973, pp. 57–64.

Osborn, Richard N., and James G. Hunt: "Environment and Organizational Effectiveness," *Administrative Science Quarterly,* June 1974, pp. 231–246.

Perrow, Charles: *Organizational Analysis: A Sociological View,* Wadsworth, Belmont, Calif., 1970.

Peterfreund, Stanley: "The Challenge of the 'New Breed,'" *Michigan Business Review,* January 1974, pp. 26–31.

Post, James E.: "Scanning the Social Environment—A Working Model," *Academy of Management Proceedings,* Aug. 19–22, 1973, pp. 619–625.

Roeber, Richard J. C.: *The Organization in a Changing Environment,* Addison-Wesley, Reading, Mass., 1973.

Sethi, Narendra K.: "The Sociological Impact of Technology," *The Journal of Business,* May 1974, pp. 2–13.

Taylor, James C.: "Some Effects of Technology in Organizational Change," *Human Relations,* April 1971, pp. 105–123.

Thompson, James D.: *Organizations in Action,* McGraw-Hill, New York, 1967.

Wilson, Ian: "How Our Values Are Changing," *The Futurist,* February 1970, pp. 5–9.

———: "Socio-Political Forecasting: A New Dimension to Strategic Planning," *Michigan Business Review,* July 1974, pp. 15–25.

Part Two

Process
Variables

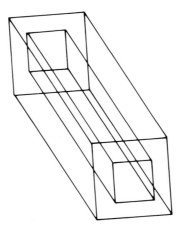

The Planning Process

A dictionary definition of a plan is "any detailed scheme, program, or method worked out beforehand for the accomplishment of an object."[1] This definition points to three important aspects of the managerial planning process:

1 *The Object* Values, purposes, objectives, and goals are the ends toward which the planning process is directed.
2 *The Future* Effective planning is dependent upon accurate assessments of the future.
3 *The Past* Accurate assessments of the future depend upon good experiential and analytical assessment of trends and causal patterns of the past.

Thus, the planning process involves setting objectives and is oriented toward both the future and the past. In today's era of rapid change, assessments of the past do not project very far into the future. In this type of "future shock" situation, there is some question as to whether management can do any more than plan for the short run. On the other hand, it is change that makes planning necessary. Management has to know where it is going before it can devise means of getting there. Were there no changes at all, the planning function would become superficial, humdrum, and eventually nonexistent. With rapid change, planning takes on added importance.

This first chapter in the process variables part of the book concentrates on forecasting, strategic (long-range), and tactical (short-range operational) aspects of the planning process. In the first half of the chapter both technological (trend extrapolation, operational techniques, morphological analysis, and relevance trees) and demand (survey techniques, historical trend analysis, internal demand, and correlational analysis) forecasting are examined. The last half of the chapter is devoted to the methods and problems of strategic, long-range planning and to shorter-range tactical planning for resources, operations, and scheduling.

---

[1] *The American Heritage Dictionary of the English Language,* American Heritage and Houghton Mifflin, Boston, 1969, p. 1001.

Technological Forecasting

Universities and colleges across the country are beginning to offer courses and even majors in futurology. Alvin Toffler, the author of the best-selling book *Future Shock,* advocated assigning science fiction books in schools, and teachers and professors in high schools and colleges have been quick to follow this suggestion.

Futurology applied to management is also becoming very popular. The so-called think tanks at Rand Corporation and the Battelle and Hudson Institutes deal directly with management-type problems. Most closely related to futurology in management are the technological forecasting techniques. Some of the techniques are exploratory or "crystal-ball" in nature; they try to predict what will actually happen. These crystal-ball technological forecasting techniques include trend extrapolation as well as operational techniques (role playing, scenario writing, brainstorming, and Delphi). Other technological forecasting techniques are normative in nature. They try to determine what the future should be and then make it happen. These latter techniques are searching techniques—looking for technological gaps that might be exploited—and include morphological analysis and relevance trees. The following sections discuss these technological forecasting techniques.

Trend Extrapolation Techniques

The exploratory techniques of forecasting assess the technological environment. They try to predict what and when major technological advances are coming. Trend extrapolation is the most common way of doing this. Everybody old enough or knowledgeable enough about history tries their hand at trend extrapolation. Some people are doom sayers and can see trends leading to flood, famine, and war; others are able to extrapolate hopeful trends in the world and forecast peace, plenty, and happiness.

The scientific way to extrapolate should not be affected by personal optimism or pessimism. Instead, the scientific approach involves plotting trends on graph paper, fitting curves, and constructing "envelopes." Initially, it was popular among forecasters to project exponential change and growth. Figure 4-1*a* shows an exponential curve. However, such exponential curves, which plot as straight lines on semilog paper, achieved an unwarranted popularity. Expert forecasters such as Ralph Lenz charge "semilogarithmic graph paper with the possession of occult powers which distort honest data and extort false forecasts."[2]

Trend extrapolation becomes more sophisticated with construction of envelopes. Most forecasting does not follow a clear mathematically projectable pattern as shown by the exponential and logarithmic curves. In enveloping, changing functional characteristics of broad classes of devices are plotted against time on a graph. The major problem facing

---

[2] Ralph C. Lenz, Jr., "Forecasts of Exploding Technologies by Trend Extrapolation," in James R. Bright (ed.), *Technological Forcasting for Industry and Government,* Prentice-Hall, Englewood Cliffs, N.J., 1968, p. 58.

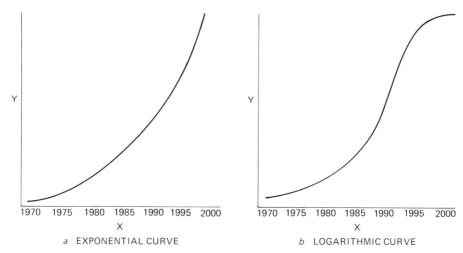

a EXPONENTIAL CURVE   b LOGARITHMIC CURVE

Figure 4-1 Common Forecasting Curves.

this approach is selecting device classes that are broad enough to be realistic but narrow enough to offer useful projective information. Figure 4-2 gives an example of an enveloping projection.

Figure 4-2 shows that the progression of technological advance in vehicle speed produces an envelope that extrapolates upward toward the speed of light. The curve suggests that a vehicle would be developed for interstellar travel. The catch, of course, is that there is no suggestion as to how this could be accomplished. Predicting "how" is, unfortunately, outside the realm of technological forecasting.

Operational Techniques

Exploratory technological forecasting techniques that are heuristic (governed by principles, trial and error) rather than mathematical or graphical include various methods that might be classed as gaming techniques. Role playing is a gaming technique that has mainly been used in human relations training. A trainee acts out an assigned role to gain insights into the role. This approach has also been extended to generating possible futures, including technological change. Opposing teams, for example, representing the firm and a major competitor, may interact in role-playing sessions to generate scenarios (a synopsis or outline) of plausible future actions and reactions of the parties involved.

Besides its use in role playing, scenario writing is a gaming technique by itself. A special type of scenario that has become particularly important to forecasting is the environmental impact statement. Herman Kahn sees two advantages of a scenario approach:

1 Scenarios are an effective tool to counteract "carry-over" thinking, and to force the analyst (or policy-maker) to look at cases other than the straightforward "surprise-free projections."

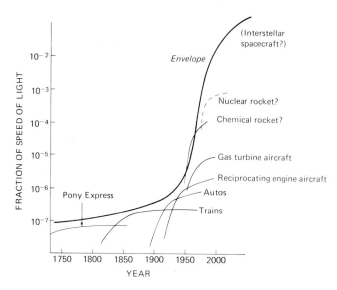

Figure 4-2 Speed Trend Curve. *Source:* D. G. Samaras, USAF, as cited by Robert U. Ayres, *Technological Forecasting and Long-Range Planning,* McGraw-Hill, New York, 1969, p. 21.

2 Scenarios are an antidote for concentrating exclusively on the forest and ignoring the trees: analysts who limit themselves to abstract generalizations may easily overlook crucial details and dynamics (because no single set seems especially worthy of attention), even though looking at some random specific cases can be quite helpful.[3]

Another gaming type of technique is brainstorming. In brainstorming, a group is assembled to generate ideas, perhaps on possible new products or future predictions. Wild, uninhibited thinking is encouraged. One wild idea may trigger another possibly good idea. A brainstorming session at one company is described as follows:

. . . the staff bats around ideas, and scrawls them down on scraps of paper, which are tossed into a huge fishbowl. . . . Any idea goes in it if it has aroused even a glimmer of response from the group. Later on, a two-man team—always one engineer and one industrial designer—cull out the most promising candidates.[4]

Still another type of gaming technique is Delphi. Named after the Greek oracle at Delphi, the technique produces an intuitive and expert consensus through an anonymous process. The Delphi approach avoids some of the shortcomings of typical face-to-face committees, such as dominance by a vigorous member, majority pressures, and pressures to be done and adjourn. With Delphi a coodinator sends written questions to a selected

---

[3] Cited in Robert U. Ayres, *Technological Forecasting and Long-Range Planning,* McGraw-Hill, New York, 1969, p. 146.
[4] *Business Week,* July 2, 1966, p. 54.

group of experts who may be unaware of one another's participation. The written predictions are pooled statistically, and data such as the mean prediction, the interquartile range, and pertinent supporting comments are sent out again to the same group for successive rounds until a consensus is reached. The participants learn what the others are predicting and why and will generally modify their own views. The members of the Delphi group are not identified with a given position and do not have to worry about saving face. So far, the technique has proved to be quite effective in predicting the future.

Morphological Analysis

Whereas trend extrapolation and gaming techniques are exploratory in nature, there are other technological forecasting techniques which attempt to determine what ought to be and then invent or bring about a given future. Morphological analysis is such a normative technique. Morphology is the approach used by various sciences such as biology, physical geography, and linguistics to study structure and form. When applied to technological forecasting, diagrams, lists, tables, and so forth are used.

For example, the morphological analysis of the feasible alternative components to propel an automobile could be structured as found in Figure 4-3. Once the morphology of automobile propulsion is determined, the next step is to develop a list of all possible combinations of the feasible components. The first one, for example, would be a three-wheeler, one of the wheels being powered, with no transmission, and one internal-combustion hydrocarbon-fueled engine. Many of the numerous possible combinations do not make sense and would not be considered. However, among those that are feasible might be ideas that no one has given adequate thought to and that might lead to possible technological breakthroughs.

Relevance Trees

The relevance tree is actually a type of morphological approach. It is especially suitable for descriptive purposes but may also be used for normative technological forecasting. The relevance tree is developed to aid in planning a complex future set of events. For example, a relevance tree is especially suitable to various types of "programming" in the

Figure 4-3 Morphological Analysis of Auto Propulsion

Components	Feasible Alternatives				
Wheels	3	4			
Driven wheels	1	2	3	4	
Engines	1	2	3	4	
Transmission	0	Mechanical	Fluid		
Engine	Internal combustion	External combustion	Turbine	Electric	
Power source	Hydrocarbon fuel	Primary battery	Secondary battery	Fuel cell	Third rail

Source: Adapted from Joseph P. Martino, *Technological Forecasting for Decision Making*, American Elsevier, New York, 1972, p. 305.

government. A government workforce program might be displayed in a relevance tree such as found in Figure 4-4.

The relevance tree is aptly named. As Figure 4-4 shows, the relevance tree simply shows what is relevant for the planning and decision making of future events. These trees may

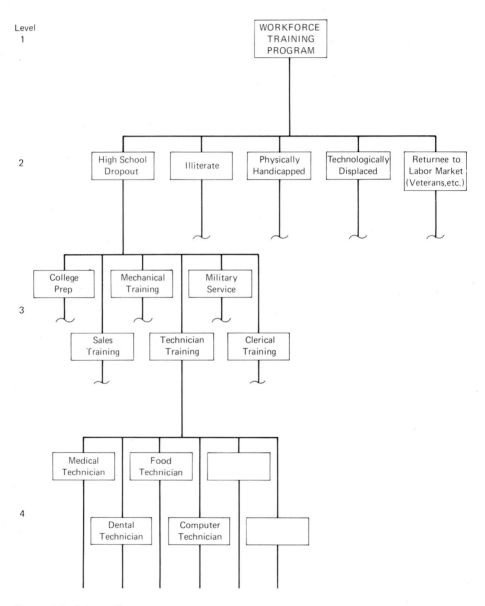

Figure 4-4 Relevance Tree.

be drawn in a wide variety of ways for many different purposes. The morphological example of automobile propulsion could also be constructed as a relevance tree. The tree could be developed to show the component breakdown, alternate propulsion methods, or various propulsion problems. The workforce program could also be drawn differently. For example, instead of showing types of workers at the second level and types of training at the third, these could be reversed. In addition, methods of training could also be displayed at one or more levels. However, as with the other technological forecasting techniques, there is nothing magic about relevance trees. They only assist planning for the future in a systematic way.

Demand or Sales Forecasting

Technological forecasting has the major purpose of predicting and searching for new breakthroughs and opportunities. Demand or sales forecasting, on the other hand, is attempting to predict trends for the existing products or services of an organization. Despite the importance of forecasting, many managers do not do it. At best, they may use intuitive processes, leading to such statements as "We'll probably sell about the same next year as last year."

The primary purpose of demand forecasting is to provide a basis for resource planning and subsequent resource acquisition, disposal, or release. It is essential for effective resource planning. To effectively stock and allocate resources—plant, equipment, tools, people, and materials—there must be some expectation of a future demand for the product or service of those resources. A demand forecast develops these expectations.

Survey Techniques

Perhaps the most widely used technique of demand forecasting is the opinion survey. The purpose is to obtain knowledgeable opinions on product and service demand trends. The management staff, the sales force, and consumers in the market can all be surveyed.

When management staff members are surveyed, they should be given advance notice so that careful thought goes into their opinions; surveying should be done at regular intervals; and the opinions should be systematically weighted according to some formula. The Delphi technique described earlier can be very useful in surveying the management staff.

Surveying the sales force is very common but can be misleading. The major weakness is that salespersons' estimates may be either very optimistic or very pessimistic. The sales force's opinions may vary greatly with the season, recent good or bad luck, the political mood of the country, and the temperaments of each individual. Despite these problems, which any survey has, the salespersons do know their customers well, and the salespersons' estimates are generally well worth soliciting in a demand forecast. The opinions are usually consolidated at the district office level by the sales manager. This individual may be charged with adjusting the figures according to his or her own judgment and knowledge of the thinking patterns of the sales staff. In this manner the forecast may be improved but still remain very subjective.

Probably the most effective survey is directed at customers or clients, the users themselves. Most people have at one time or another participated in marketing surveys and are familiar with the techniques. The surveys ask simple questions about the product or service. To obtain this market information is very costly and time-consuming. The larger firms usually have their own market research staffs, but recently both large and small firms are turning to the burgeoning independent market research industry for demand information.

Historical Trend Analysis

Considerable subjective judgment goes into historical demand data. Consider, for example, the past demand data (sixteen quantities at different points in time) plotted on the time scale of Figure 4-5. Line 1 represents the arithmetic mean, i.e., the sixteen demand quantities added together and divided by 16. Line 2 is a long-term trend line, i.e., the line of best fit for the sixteen points which could be calculated by the least-squares technique of statistics. Line 3 in the figure is a projection of the noticeable trend for the most recent 8 months. Obviously, the three lines of projection give three quite different demand forecasts. Which is best depends on the nature of the product or service being demanded. The shorter-term trend, line 3, looks persuasive; but in some situations such a sharp rise over the past 8 months would be evidence of a degree of saturation and an impending fall in demand. The long-term trend, line 2, also appears reasonable. However, sometimes there is no reason to believe that any up or down trend is believable; in that case the arithmetic mean, line 1 in Figure 4-5, is as good a forecast as any.

Besides the simple arithmetic mean and straight-line trend techniques of demand forecasting are the more sophisticated curve-fitting techniques. For situations where only short-term trends are meaningful (for example, there are many products in the product line that must be forecasted every month), the exponential smoothing or moving-average techniques may be effectively used. Exponential smoothing is a method of forecasting in which next month's estimated demand (E_n) is predicted to be the same as the past month's estimate (E_{n-1}) plus a fraction (α) of the difference between the past month's

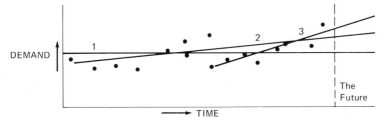

DEMAND

TIME

The Future

Figure 4-5 Methods of Trend Analysis.

actual demand (D_{n-1}) and the past month's estimate (E_{n-1}). The formula for an exponential smoothing forecast is

$$E_n = E_{n-1} + \alpha (D_{n-1} - E_{n-1})$$

The fraction used, (α) (alpha), is the smoothing constant. It is assigned a value between 0.0 and 1.0 and determines how much weight will be given to the forecast error in the most recent past month. The closer the constant is to 1.0, the greater the consideration given to the forecast error. The smoothing constant value is determined by testing different values on past data to see what has worked best in the past.

The moving average is a running arithmetic mean. For example, a 3-month moving average could use the mean of the demand data for the months of January, February, and March as a forecast for April's demand; then January drops off and April is added to compute the mean for the May forecast. This progression is demonstrated below:

Month	Actual Demand Data	3-Month Moving Average	Used as Forecast for Month of:
January	37		
February	19	29	April
March	32	26	May
April	27	29	June
May	29	31	July
June	38		

As shown, the moving average tends to tone down highly variable data. The result is a smoother curve free of much of the unpredictable random influences. A 6-month or even longer moving-average period could be used which would tone down the extremes even more.

Internal Demand Forecasting

A major weakness of many forecasting approaches is that they emphasize only products and services offered to outside customers or clients and ignore facilitating services provided by one department to another within the organization. There is little internal forecasting. In the absense of systematic internal forecasts, department or unit budgets and resources are largely determined by the informal organization (politics, bluffs, and guesstimates).

The forecasts for the organization as a whole may not be accurately extrapolated to each internal unit. To illustrate, consider a firm that manufactures radios and found that a thorough forecasting effort predicted a long-term rise in sales for all its present models.

What would this forecast mean for the design engineering department? It probably does not mean that design workloads would increase directly proportionately. In fact, since current designs are expected to enjoy long periods of increasing sales, this firm might be better off reducing design engineering activities by reassigning, laying off, or reducing by attrition the size of the engineering staff. In a similar manner the activities of the purchasing department would not necessarily increase. Perhaps optimistic sales forecasts for the firm's radios would mean long production runs calling for purchase of components from suppliers already under contract; if so, purchase workloads—and purchasing staff and budget—could decrease. These examples point out the need for separate, internal forecasting.

Correlational Analysis

In the personnel department of the radio manufacturer example, increased radio sales could mean increased hiring activity in order to add workforce to support the increasing demand for radios. In addition, however, the staffing function of this personnel department may also depend on external factors. If there is a surge of job applicants because of external economic conditions, the personnel department is obliged to interview the applicants and process their applications. This increased workload in the personnel department has nothing to do with the sales forecast. It is even mandatory for firms covered by the wage and hour laws to interview applicants—even when there are no vacancies. Thus, for the personnel department, it might be beneficial to find a relationship, or correlation, between its hiring workload and factors that would increase job seekers in the area. Figure 4-6 is an example of such a correlation.

In this example, if the largest company in the area is laying off people, there is a good chance that the laid-off workers will apply for a job at the radio manufacturer. The correlation or degree of relationship appears to be high between the layoffs at Acme and the job applicants in the personnel department. Since the number of layoffs precedes the number of applicants by a month, the correlation should prove to be highly useful to the personnel department in forecasting its needs. By keeping in touch with Acme Corporation on its layoff patterns, the radio manufacturer may get a 1-month head start in resource planning in the hiring unit of the personnel department. With a month's advance notice the required number of interviewers and clerks, desks, application blanks, and so forth may be anticipated.

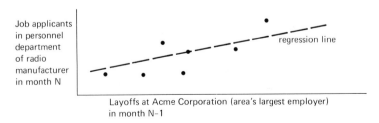

Figure 4-6 Correlational Analysis for Forecasting.

Strategic or Long-Range Planning

Strategic planning attempts to determine long-range courses of action that are consistent with the objectives of the organization. In a general sense probably all organizations do some type of indirect strategic planning. However, systematic, regular, formally staffed programs for strategic planning are relatively new, especially in the private sector. Symptomatic of the new trend is a business journal which changed its title from *Budgeting* to *Managerial Planning* and changed its emphasis from a year-by-year financial planning approach to strategic planning over the longer run. Strategic planning in the government sector has been more commonplace through the years. It has been used in defense, health, welfare, education, and other areas from the federal level on down to the level of local municipalities.

Full understanding of planning in government would require in-depth study of political/ economic issues such as capitalism versus socialism versus totalitarianism. For present purposes, it can be said that the grand experiment in centralized state planning via socialism was tried in Great Britain after World War II and generally failed. The Labour Party took over in July 1946, and was ushered out, by the pressures of serious economic problems, in 1951. Although there were other contributing causes, the British centralized planning experiment failed even though it was carried out by dedicated public servants such as Bevan and Attlee in an atmosphere of open public and Parliamentary debate at each step of the way. The British procedure, of course, is in contrast to the totalitarian brand of centralized planning used by the Soviet Union.

While the British socialist planning was having its problems and the famous 5-year plans of the Soviet Union were also experiencing some difficulties, the American economic machine was grinding ahead impressively seemingly without any planning. In truth, there really was planning in the United States, but it was decentralized to the corporate boardrooms and agency conference rooms. In a private enterprise economy, great dependence is made on the marketplace and public opinion. As Lynn Townsend, former president of Chrysler, commented, "The mistakes will be automatically corrected not by changes in some central plan but by the prompt and effective rebuke of the market. If there is such a thing as a cybernetically sound economy, with built-in feedbacks and corrections, we have it."[5] Undoubtedly, free market planning had a lot to do with the tremendous economic growth of this country. However, there is a growing realization that some of this came from ecological capital borrowed from the future. With the current interest in social responsibility, there is renewed interest in government planning to correct various social, economic, ecological, and consumerism abuses.

Methods of Strategic Planning for Resources

Traditionally, long-range or strategic planning for resources has been more concerned with physical resources—plant, equipment, materials, tools, and information—than with

---

[5] Lynn A. Townsend, in an address before the annual dinner of the Financial Analysts Federation on May 18, 1965; cited in George A. Steiner, *Top Management Planning*, Macmillan, New York, 1969, pp. 83–84.

human resources. However, the hiring of a chief executive would certainly be a very strategic decision because it has long-range implications for the success of the organization. On the other hand, most other staffing tends to be more short-range or tactical in nature. Plans for executive development and employee training, wage and salary schedules, and labor contracts can be considered strategic, whereas selection, job assignments, placements, and on-the-job training programs would tend to be examples of tactical planning for human resources. Planning for the types of human resources to bring into the organization has long-term strategic implications, but in the highly mobile modern society, the hiring of a particular individual is more tactical.

In contrast to human resources, the commitment to plants and major pieces of equipment costing hundreds of thousands or millions of dollars calls for extensive strategic planning. These plans are generally initiated in the operations and engineering areas. Plant and equipment proposals are supported by extensive feasibility studies and careful economic justification. The economic studies may show the payback period and the breakeven (BE) point. The payback period is the total cost divided by the average before- or after-tax profit per year that the proposal is estimated to generate. The BE point is the volume of output (from the new plant or equipment) that must be sold in order for total revenues to exceed the variable plus fixed costs, and the proposal will not be adopted unless projected revenues exceed the BE point. Chapter 9 goes into BE analysis in more detail.

Both the payback and breakeven analyses are only preliminary. Thorough economic analysis of costly capital plant and equipment requires further examination using discounted cash flow techniques, including the equivalent annual cost method (favored at the engineering level) and the net present value and time-adjusted rate of return method (favored by managerial accountants and financial planners). This latter method is given detailed attention in Chapter 9.

Planning for materials is largely tactical rather than strategic. This is especially true for firms that acquire materials mainly on a "hand-to-mouth" basis. Most firms do, however, acquire some types of materials, supplies, and parts on a longer-term basis; i.e., they stock certain commonly used items. The decision to stock an item is a strategic decision that calls for weighing the item's demand frequency against its availability and cost. Once the decision is made to stock an item, the next strategic plans are for determining the quantity per order and the ordering frequency. Quantitative methods such as economic order quantity (EOQ) and economic lot size (ELS) are available for calculating the quantity per order; reorder-point models are also available for determining ordering frequency. EOQ models are given specific attention in Chapter 10. Additional strategic planning for stocked materials concerns establishment of a stock control system involving proper storage facilities, proper stock record keeping, and procedures for conducting periodic physical inventory counting. These latter approaches attempt to discover discrepancies between stock record totals and actual totals.

Strategic planning for tools involves the same kind of variables used in planning for materials plus designing a tool loan and issue system. Most tool rooms operate the tool loan and issue system very much as libraries operate book loan systems. This makes sense because books are to the knowledge worker as mechanical tools are to the machinist and mechanic. Both books and tools are "tools" of the respective trades.

Books, journals, manuals, and other literary materials constitute information resources that, in the emergent era of the knowledge worker, are becoming increasingly important. The specific discussion of strategic planning for information is deferred to Chapter 18 on management information systems.

Problems with Strategic Planning

In recent years many organizations jumped on the strategic planning bandwagon, and 5-year planning began to yield to 10- and even up to 20-year horizons. This long-range planning was necessary where long lead times for major expansion proposals, such as planning and building a petroleum refinery, were increasing to 10 years and beyond. On the other hand, some organizations were caught up in the trend toward longer planning horizons without needing to be. Most organizations are far less capital-intensive than the petrochemical industry and the required lead times for expansion are under 5 years. In addition to capital expansion, the use of modular design techniques, new production technology, and project management techniques has resulted in shorter lead times for new product development. These factors plus the accelerated rate of change (rapid product obsolescence, shorter product life cycles, and proliferation of product styles, models, and colors) resulted in a reexamination of the use of formal strategic planning. Management began to seriously question whether its strategic planning effort was commensurate with the results.

Louis Gerstner recently reported the following reactions of chief executive officers who were questioned about the value of strategic planning:

"Strategic planning is basically just a plaything of staff men."

"It's like a Chinese dinner: I feel full when I get it, but after a little while I wonder whether I've eaten at all!"

"Strategic planning? A staggering waste of time and money."[6]

Gerstner feels that a fundamental weakness in contemporary strategic planning is that appropriate actions do not follow plans. "Nothing really new happens as a result of the plan, except that everyone gets a warm glow of security and satisfaction now that the uncertainty of the future has been contained."[7]

Probably the biggest problem is that strategic plans tend to be unimaginative projections of past trends coupled with overly optimistic expectations of future success. Strategic planners seldom, if ever, plan for cutbacks or failures. Yet, despite the problems mentioned, long-range, strategic planning is absolutely necessary for good management. The problems mentioned merely serve as a caution on the overdependence of strategic plan-

---

[6] Louis V. Gerstner, Jr., "Can Strategic Planning Pay Off?" *Business Horizons,* December 1972, p. 5.
[7] Ibid., p. 7.

ning. Like the other management processes, strategic planning is not the final solution but rather is only an aid for more effective goal attainment.

Tactical or Operational Planning

Tactics follow strategies. That is, once the management of an organization plans for certain strategic courses of action—produce certain goods or services, provide the appropriate plant and equipment, and "stock" the organization with certain kinds of human and physical resources—the courses of action must be translated into specific, shorter-range tactical plans for operational accomplishment.

One of the more significant changes in modern management is the increasing specialization of tactical planning activities. At the turn of the century it was generally line management (especially the first-line supervisor) who planned and executed the hiring and training of employees and the acquisition and care of plant, equipment, tools, and materials. These early line managers often turned out to be "jacks of all trades, masters of none." The modern line manager has had much of this workload reassigned to the point where he or she has practically no specific planning obligations.

With the trend toward relieving line managers of the planning function, where did all the planning go? The answer is in the phenomenal growth of planning staff personnel. Staff planners counsel, advise, and do planning for line management. The purpose is to have specially educated and trained planning specialists devote their effort to effective tactical plans for getting the work done on time, efficiently, and with optimal use of resources. The job of the line manager or supervisor then is to direct and motivate subordinates toward the implementation of the plans. The staff experts often specialize in areas like workforce planning, inventory management, facilities management, maintenance, tool design, plant and office layout, and information management, or in other words, resources, and others specialize in planning and scheduling the operations of the organization.

Tactical Planning for Resources

The demand forecast should trigger decisions to acquire or release some kinds of resources and to retain, maintain, and improve others. Accomplishing resource needs calls for detailed tactical plans of the nature shown in Figure 4-7.

Tactical Planning for Operations[8]

Preparing design specifications, blueprints, bills of materials, menus, prescriptions, quality and reliability standards, and so forth is the first step in tactical planning for operations.

---

[8] For an expanded discussion of this section see Richard J. Schonberger, *Work Planning and Control Systems*, U.S. Army Management Engineering Training Agency, Rock Island, Ill., 1969, chap. 5.

Figure 4-7 Types of Tactical Plans

1 HUMAN RESOURCES

  a *Hiring (Acquisition) and Release Activities*   Developing job descriptions and specifications, pay schedules, and recruiting, selection, and placement plans; revising organizational charts; planning transfers, layoffs, and terminations

  b *Training Activities (Maintaining and Improving Skills)*   Developing training and educational materials, plans, and schedules; developing company policies, instructions, and standard operating procedures (SOPs); planning for promotions, demotions, transfers and reassignments, job rotation, and job enrichment

2 PLANT AND EQUIPMENT

  a *Acquisition and Disposal*   Developing requests for proposals (REPs), design specifications for bidding, engineering drawings and blueprints, and plant layouts; planning for sale, trade-in, or other disposal of excess plant and equipment

  b *Maintenance*   Planning for preventive and breakdown maintenance and relayouts

3 MATERIALS AND TOOLS

  a *Acquisition*   Determining what nonstocked items to buy and when to buy them; designing tools; planning for tool and material deliveries

  b *Maintenance*   Planning for upkeep of inventories and sharpening and care of tools

The next step is to plan for the sequence and required time of operations. The basic methodology originated with the scientific management movement at the turn of the century. Specifically, work measurement and time and motion analysis play a central role in tactical planning for operations.

The motion, methods, and process planning techniques widely use before-and-after flowcharts. The work flow analyst watches the job being performed and records his or her observations on a chart. Then an analysis of the chart is made by using checklists and the principles of motion economy and by asking such questions as: "Can we eliminate?" "Can we combine?" "Can we rearrange?" "Can we simplify?" The result of the analysis is the "after" flowchart. The goal of the after flowchart is a more efficient sequence and arrangement of tasks and generally fewer tasks, delays, storages, and transportations.

Many of the early methods (motion) and time standards analysts were mechanical engineers. They eventually splintered off to found the industrial engineering (IE) field. Before the new IE branch became established, the American Society of Mechanical Engineers (ASME) established a standard set of flowcharting symbols for methods, motion, and process analysis. Figure 4-8 shows these symbols and gives a flowchart example.

Once the optimum sequence of operations has been determined, then a time standard is set. Time standards are important in scheduling, in cost estimating and bidding, in budgeting, in evaluating method and equipment improvement proposals, in determining personnel needs, in evaluating performance, and in acting as an incentive for operating personnel. The common image of a time standard is an analyst with clipboard and stopwatch in hand who times a job repetitively and records time observations on a sheet of paper and then translates the readings into a standard number of minutes per piece or pieces per minute. This traditional approach is just one of several important techniques for setting time standards. Work sampling (formerly known as ratio delay) is another technique which is especially useful for longer-cycle work such as clerical tasks and

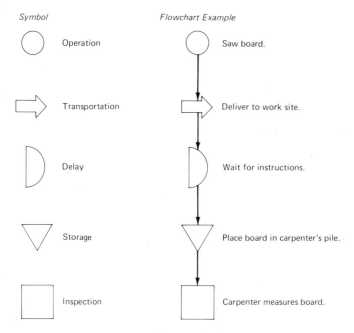

Symbol   *Flowchart Example*

Operation — Saw board.

Transportation — Deliver to work site.

Delay — Wait for instructions.

Storage — Place board in carpenter's pile.

Inspection — Carpenter measures board.

Figure 4-8 Methods, Motion, and Process Symbols.

packing and crating. In a simple form of work sampling, the analyst comes into the work site at random intervals during a working day and simply notes by a tally mark whether the status is "work" or "idle." At the end of the day he or she computes the percentage of tallies in the "work" category and extrapolates it to the number of minutes worked that day. This result is divided by the number of units produced in the same day at the same site and the result is a certain number of minutes per unit, from which comes a time standard for the task. The main advantage of the work sampling technique is that it does not require the continuous presence of the observer.

Another important time standards technique is methods-time-measurement or simply MTM. This approach is an extension of the laboratory work of the scientific management pioneer Frank Gilbreth's work on basic motions. Included in this approach are the micro-motions such as reach, grasp, position, transport empty, and transport loaded. The International MTM Association has produced highly refined and validated tables of data on how long it takes (in fractions of a second) to reach 1 inch, 2 inches, 3 inches; to transport empty 1 inch, 2 inches, 3 inches; etc. A trained MTM analyst can construct or synthesize a time standard by putting together the required time values from the tables to form small jobs or operations. The times for small jobs may then be added together to form time standards for bigger jobs. One advantage of this latter predetermined time system is that it may be applied without the need for actually observing the work being performed. The calculations may be made at the analyst's desk before the decision is even made to go into production.

The MTM approach was first used extensively in machine-shop work and today is also widely used in clerical work. In fact so many MTM analysts developed time standards for routine machine operations such as boring, drilling, turning, milling, and polishing that the standards were eventually published by the MTM Association. Thus, today, standard data (or grouped data) tables are available for many standard machine-shop operations.

Besides the traditional stopwatch, work sampling, and more sophisticated MTM approaches to time standards is the widely used informal unrecorded time estimate. This time estimate may be explicitly stated in an oral exchange between boss and subordinate but more likely the estimate is a vague idea in a planner's mind and not even thought through in numerical terms. For example, a manager may plan the completion of a project without seeming to decide how long it should take. Nevertheless, there is an implied period of time that the manager would consider proper for the task. This implied time or standard, "bogey," norm, or whatever it might be called, is always there. The time standard can serve as an incentive for the worker to get the task completed. It aids in judging when the worker might get to other work and serves as a criterion for self-evaluation.

Scheduling Operations

Time standards can play an important role in performance evaluation or output incentives, but even more vital is the part they play in scheduling. All operations must be scheduled, and scheduling is impossible without a standard or estimate. Figure 4-9 shows the relationship between time standards and scheduling. As shown in the figure, the schedule specifies the planned start time and finish time for a task, and the time standard is the difference between the two. The schedule provides the important linkage between the tactical plans for resources and the tactical plans for operations. Managers who are resource-oriented tend to think of scheduling in terms of resource scheduling, while operations-oriented managers think in terms of operations scheduling. Both are ex-

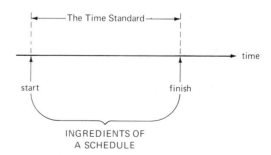

Figure 4-9 Relationship between Time Standards and Scheduling.

tremely important to the success of an organization. Operations cannot be accomplished without scheduling resources. Resource schedules are time assignments of resources to operations.

Figure 4-10 shows different kinds of schedules on a schedule display chart known as a Gantt chart after its developer, Henry Gantt, one of the pioneers of scientific management. Chapter 7 also examines Gantt charts from the perspective of control. In addition to

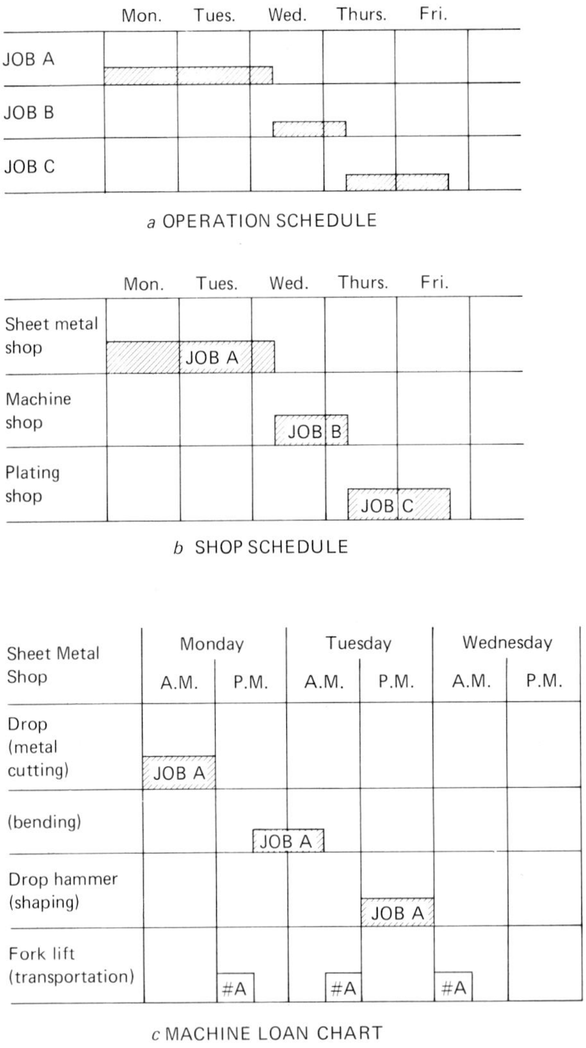

	Mon.	Tues.	Wed.	Thurs.	Fri.
JOB A					
JOB B					
JOB C					

a OPERATION SCHEDULE

	Mon.	Tues.	Wed.	Thurs.	Fri.
Sheet metal shop	JOB A				
Machine shop		JOB B			
Plating shop			JOB C		

b SHOP SCHEDULE

Sheet Metal Shop	Monday		Tuesday		Wednesday	
	A.M.	P.M.	A.M.	P.M.	A.M.	P.M.
Drop (metal cutting)	JOB A					
(bending)		JOB A				
Drop hammer (shaping)			JOB A			
Fork lift (transportation)		#A	#A		#A	

c MACHINE LOAN CHART

Figure 4-10 Use of Gantt Charts in Scheduling Operations and Resources.

the Gantt charts of Figure 4-10, any one or all three of the jobs shown could be portrayed on other Gantt charts, in greater or lesser detail, with persons' names, rooms or buildings, or even tools inserted as row headings. Thus, the plans for a single job may be put in terms of separate schedules for each different type of resource to be used in the job. Network analysis, which is given detailed attention in Chapter 17, is a newer approach to scheduling.

Summary

This chapter introduces the section of the book concerned with the process variables of contingency management by looking at planning. Both past- and future-oriented, the planning process is directed toward accomplishment of an object. The concern for the future is expressed through technological and demand or sales forecasting. The trend extrapolation techniques of technological forecasting plot exponential or logarithmic trends on graph paper or construct envelopes. They try to predict the future based upon the past. Operational techniques such as role playing, scenario writing, brainstorming, and Delphi are heuristic rather than mathematical. These gaming techniques try to trigger ideas for technological breakthroughs. More normative techniques of technological forecasting include morphological analysis (the study of structure and form) and relevance trees. Whereas these technological forecasting techniques are attempting to predict future breakthroughs and opportunities, demand or sales forecasting is more concerned with the future of existing products or services. Surveys of management or sales staff or the consumer or client are one way to make these forecasts. A more mathematical approach is to use simple arithmetic or straight-line trends or more sophisticated techniques such as exponential smoothing or moving average. Internal and correlational techniques of demand forecasting are also useful for effective planning.

Once a forecast is made, the organization must formulate strategic plans aimed at long-range objectives. In particular, strategic plans are developed for the human, plant and equipment, materials, tools, and information resources of the organization. All contribute to the successful accomplishment of long-range objectives. However, strategic planning has not been without its problems. In many instances, managers have been guilty of jumping on the strategic-planning bandwagon without justification or results. With the rapid pace of change and the built-in optimistic bias of long-range, strategic planning, many managers should reexamine their approach. On the other hand, it should be remembered that strategic planning is vital to effective goal attainment. As with any planning, long or short range, management must know where it is going before it can get there.

Tactical, short-range planning has shifted away from line managers or supervisors and has become more of a specialized staff function. Staff planners attempt to meet the resource, operational, and scheduling needs of the organization. Detailed plans for human, plant and equipment, and material resources are made. Techniques for tactical planning for operations include work flow analysis and time standards. The latter have been traditionally set through stopwatch methods, but newer techniques include work sampling and methods-time-measurement. However, the most common way that managers establish time standards is informal estimates used for self-evaluations. Time standards are vital to scheduling which provides the link between the tactical plans for resources and operations. Gantt charts and network analysis are important techniques of scheduling.

☐ Critical Incident

You have recently been hired by the administration of your school as a planning specialist. Your first assignment is to develop a 5-year plan for student housing. Forecasted student enrollment seems to be a major input into your plan. According to the national statistics you have gathered, student enrollment has declined for the past 3 years. Your impression is that student housing should be cut back, but you are not sure.

1 What type of planning are you doing? What are some of the major characteristics of this planning?
2 What forecasting techniques could be used?
3 In light of projected national declines in enrollment, what kind of reasoning might go into a plan to cut back on housing? To have housing remain the same? To increase the housing?

Questions for Review and Discussion

1 Why is technological forecasting important to planning in particular and management in general? Briefly describe some of the major techniques that can be used in technological forecasting.
2 What is the purpose of demand or sales forecasting? Briefly describe some of the major techniques.
3 What are strategic plans? What are some of the methods and problems in strategic planning?
4 How do tactical plans differ from strategic plans? Give examples of tactical plans for resources and for operations.

References

Ackoff, Russell A.: *A Concept of Corporate Planning*, Wiley, New York, 1970.
Anthony, Robert N.: "Closing the Loop between Planning and Performance," *Public Administration Review*, May–June 1971, pp. 388–398.
Ayres, Robert: *Technological Forecasting and Long-Range Forecasting*, McGraw-Hill, New York, 1969.
Bright, James (ed.): *Technological Forecasting for Industry and Government*, Prentice-Hall, Englewood Cliffs, N.J., 1968.

Chambers, John C., Satinder K. Mullick, and David A. Goodman: "Catalytic Agent for Effective Planning," *Harvard Business Review,* January–February 1971, pp. 110–119.

Cleland, David I., and William R. King: "Organizing for Long-Range Planning," *Business Horizons,* August 1974, pp. 25–32.

Gerstenfeld, Arthur: "Technological Forecasting," *Journal of Business,* January 1971, pp. 10–18.

Gerstner, Louis V., Jr.: "Can Strategic Planning Pay Off?" *Business Horizons,* December 1972, pp. 5–16.

Hall, William K.: "Corporate Strategic Planning—Some Perspectives for the Future," *Michigan Business Review,* January 1972, pp. 16–21.

———: "Forecasting Techniques for Use in the Corporate Planning Process," *Managerial Planning,* November–December 1972, pp. 5–10.

Hatten, Kenneth J., and Mary Louise Piccoli: "An Evaluation of a Technological Forecasting Method by Computer-based Simulation," *Academy of Management Proceedings,* August 1973, pp. 60–66.

Herold, David M.: "Long-Range Planning and Organizational Performance: A Cross-Valuation Study," *Academy of Management Journal,* March 1972, pp. 91–102.

Kierulff, Herbert E., Jr.: "Best Estimate Forecasting—A Better Alternative," *California Management Review,* Fall 1972, pp. 79–85.

Kubicek, Thomas: "Organizational Planning: What It Is and How to Do It (Part 1—The Organizational Audit)," *Cost and Management,* January–February 1972, pp. 33–41.

———: "Organizational Planning: What It Is and How to Do It (Part 2—Designing The 'Good Fit')," *Cost and Management,* March–April 1972, pp. 33–42.

Martino, Joseph P.: *Technological Forecasting for Decision-Making,* American Elsevier, New York, 1972.

Meier, Arthur P.: "The Planning Process," *Managerial Planning,* July-August 1974, pp. 1–5, 9.

North, Harper W., and Donald L. Pyke: "Probes of the Technological Future," *Harvard Business Review,* May–June 1969, pp. 68–82.

Roman, Daniel D.: "Technological Forecasting in the Decision Process," *Academy of Management Journal,* June 1970, pp. 126–138.

Rue, Leslie W.: "The How and Who of Long-Range Planning," *Business Horizons,* December 1973, pp. 23–30.

Schoeffler, Sidney, Robert D. Buzzell, and Donald F. Heany: "Impact of Strategic Planning on Profit Performance," *Harvard Business Review,* March–April 1974, pp. 137–145.

Schonberger, Richard J.: *Work Planning and Control Systems,* U.S. Army Management Engineering Training Agency, Rock Island, Ill., 1969.

——— **and Donald Brewer:** "Work Scheduling Techniques," Department of Army Pamphlet 1-54, March 1968.

Sobek, Robert S.: "A Manager's Primer on Forecasting," *Harvard Business Review,* May–June 1973, pp. 6–28, 181–183.

Steiner, George A.: "How to Improve Your Long-Range Planning," *Managerial Planning,* September–October 1974, pp. 13–17, 28.

———: *Top Management Planning,* Macmillan, New York, 1969.

Vandell, Robert F.: "Management Evolution in the Quantitative World," *Harvard Business Review,* January–February 1970, pp. 83–92.

Chapter 5

The Organizing Process

The process of organization has undergone drastic change in recent years. Both the theories and designs of organization are much different today than they were a few short years ago. The purpose of this chapter is to trace this development. In the first part of the chapter various approaches to organization theory are presented. Included is a discussion of bureaucratic and classical theory; the neoclassical concepts of centralization-decentralization, deparmentation, and line-staff; and finally the more behaviorally oriented decision, biological, open-systems, and group and role theories of organization. The last part of the chapter is devoted to specific organization designs. The project, matrix, and free-form designs are given detailed attention.

Bureaucratic Theory of Organization

The logical starting point in the analysis of organization theory is the classical bureaucracy. Starting with the pioneering work of the famous German sociologist Max Weber, there has been a search for an ideal organization structure. Weber called his ideal a bureaucracy. It was a natural extension of his interest in the development and change of Western society. He believed that rationalization was the most persistent cultural value of Western society. On a microlevel, the bureaucracy represented a completely rational form of organization made up of four characteristics:

1 *Specialization and Division of Labor* Weber's bureaucracy contained "A specified sphere of competence. This involves (*a*) a sphere of obligations to perform functions which have been marked off as part of a systematic division of labour. (*b*) The provision of the incumbent with the necessary authority. . . . (*c*) That the necessary means of compulsion are clearly defined and their use is subject to definite conditions."[1] This statement implies that Weber recognized the importance of having the authority and power to carry out assigned duties. In addition, bureaucrats must know the precise limits of their sphere of competence so as not to infringe upon that of others.

---

[1] A. M. Henderson and Talcott Parsons (trans. and eds.), *Max Weber: The Theory of Social and Economic Organization*, Free Press, New York, © 1947 by Oxford University Press, New York, p. 330.

2 *Positions Arranged in a Hierarchy* Weber stated that "The organization of offices follows the principle of hierarchy; that is, each lower office is under the control and supervision of a higher one."[2] This bureaucratic characteristic forces control over every member in the structure. The hierarchy establishes the formal lines for authority and channels of communication.

3 *A System of Abstract Rules* Weber felt a need for "a continuous organization of official functions bound by rules."[3] A rational approach to organization would require a set of formal rules to ensure uniformity and coordination of effort. A well-understood system of regulations would also provide the continuity and stability that Weber felt was so important. Rules persist whereas personnel may frequently change. The rules may range from establishing no-smoking areas to requiring board approval for multithousand dollar capital expenditures.

4 *Impersonal Relationships* It was Weber's belief that the ideal official should be dominated by "a spirit of formalistic impersonality, without hatred or passion, and hence without affection or enthusiasm."[4] Once again Weber was speaking from the viewpoint of ideal rationality and not realistic implementation. He felt that in order for bureaucrats to make completely rational decisions, they must avoid emotional attachment with subordinates and clients.

In total, it must be remembered that the above bureaucratic model was intended to be the ideal; no real world organization exactly follows such an approach. As Blau notes, "Weber dealt with bureaucracy as what he termed an ideal type. This methodological concept does not represent an average of the attributes of all existing bureaucracies (or other social structures), but a pure type, derived by abstracting the most characteristic bureaucratic aspects of all known organizations."[5] Such an ideal is a useful starting point but needs further analysis.

Bureaucracy in Practice

The large size of organizations is undoubtedly the single most important condition that gives rise to bureaucratization. All characteristics of a bureaucracy are built around the framework of large-scale administrative tasks. Bureaucratic adaptability to large size is well documented in history. The administration of the large system of waterways in ancient Egypt, the maintenance of a far-reaching system of roads in the Roman Empire, and the control over millions of people's religious lives by the Roman Catholic Church could probably not have been accomplished without the bureaucratic form of organization. To varying degrees, all large organizations of modern society, regardless of economic or religious orientation, are also bureaucracies. Large business, industrial, governmental, church, military, hospital, union, and educational organizations throughout the contem-

---

[2] Ibid., p. 331.

[3] Ibid., p. 330.

[4] Ibid., p. 340.

[5] Peter M. Blau, *Bureaucracy in Modern Society*, Random House, New York, 1956, p. 34.

porary world are largely bureaucratic in nature. In order to survive and maintain some degree of efficiency in accomplishing goals, most of these large organizations have greatly depended upon specialization, hierarchy, rules, and impersonality.

The relevant question is not whether today's organizations are using the bureaucratic principles, because to a large degree they still are. Rather, the critical question for organizational analysis is whether the functions of bureaucracy outweigh some of the very serious dysfunctions. Weber can be legitimately accused of ignoring this question. He almost completely disregarded or, at least, deemphasized the dysfunctional consequences of the bureaucratic model. A very close reading of Weber does indicate he recognized certain conflicts or dilemmas inherent in bureaucracy. However, he so greatly stressed the functional attributes, either explicitly or implicitly, that the significant dysfunctions were never properly considered in his classic organizational analysis.

Bureaucratic Dysfunctions

The characteristics of bureaucracy can serve equally well in analyzing functional or dysfunctional consequences. The characteristic of specialization is a good illustration. The Weber bureaucratic model stresses that specialization serves as a function for efficiency. The model ignores, but can also be used to point out, the dysfunctional aspects of specialization. Empirical investigation has shown that specialization leads to increased productivity and efficiency but also leads to dysfunctional conflict and boredom. For example, specialization may impede communication between functional units or cause high turnover of hourly personnel. The management team members of a highly specialized unit have their own terminology and have similar interests, attitudes, and personal goals. Because "outsiders" are different, members have a tendency to withdraw into the specialized unit and not fully communicate with units above, below, or horizontally. Boredom caused by high degrees of specialization of jobs at the lower levels of organizations is very costly in human terms.

Besides specialization, dysfunctional consequences result from the other characteristics of bureaucracy as well. The functional attributes of hierarchy are that it maintains unity of command, coordinates activities and personnel, reinforces authority, and serves as a formal system of communication. In theory, the hierarchy has both a downward and an upward orientation, but in practice, it has often turned out to have only a downward emphasis. Thus, individual initiative and participation are often blocked, upward communication is impeded, and there is no formal recognition of horizontal communication. Personnel who only follow the formal hierarchy may waste a great deal of time and energy. Hierarchy can also result in dysfunctional conflict in the manner of specialization.

Bureaucratic rules probably have the most obvious dysfunctional qualities. Contributing to the bureaucratic image of "red tape," rules often become ends in themselves rather than means for more effective goal attainment. Drucker cites the following common misuses of rules that require reports and procedures:

1 First is the mistaken belief that procedural rules are instruments of morality. They should only be used to indicate how something can be done expeditiously, not determine what is right or wrong conduct.

2 Secondly, procedural rules are sometimes mistakenly substituted for judgment. Bureaucrats should not be mesmerized by printed forms; they should only be used in cases where judgment is not required.

3 The third and most common misuse of procedural rules is as a punitive control device from above. Bureaucrats are often required to comply with rules that have nothing to do with their job. An example would be the plant manager who has to accurately fill out numerous forms for staff personnel and corporate management which cannot be used in obtaining the manager's own objectives. [6]

Drucker would like to see every procedural rule put on trial for its life at least every 5 years. He cites one case where all reports and forms were totally done away with for 2 months. At the end of the suspension, only those reports and forms that were deemed to be necessary were allowed to return. Three-fouths of the reports and forms of this organization were eliminated. [7]

The impersonality of the bureaucracy has even more dysfunctional consequences than specialization, hierarchy, and rules. Both internally with personnel in an organization and externally with clients and/or customers of the organization, the impersonality factor has become the dominant dysfunction of bureaucracy. This is what the human resource management (internal) and consumerism (external) movements are all about. If the impersonality factor is not corrected in the near future, it may be the major contributing factor to the demise of bureaucratic organizations.

Classical Organization Theory

Inherent in bureaucratic theory but usually treated separately is classical organization theory. Whereas Weber is usually associated with bureaucracy, Henri Fayol and later Luther Gulick and Lyndall Urwick and James Mooney and Alan Reiley are most closely associated with classical organization theory. These early classical writers concentrated on determining the functions of management and then deriving universal principles for application to organization and management practice. The scientific management movement led by Frederick W. Taylor could also be considered part of classical organization theory.

Henri Fayol, the widely recognized father of classical organization theory, determined five functions of management and fourteen principles. These functions and principles are

---

[6] Peter Drucker, *The Practice of Management*, Harper & Row, New York, 1954, pp. 133–134.
[7] Ibid., p. 135.

Figure 5-1 Fayol's Functions and Principles of Management/Organization

UNIVERSAL FUNCTIONS

1 *Planning* involves assessing the future and making provisions for it. Unity, continuity, flexibility, and precision are the broad features of a good plan of action.

2 *Organizing* provides everything useful to the functioning of an enterprise and can be divided into the material organization and the human organization.

3 *Commanding* gets the organization going. The object is to get the optimum return from all employees in the interest of the whole concern.

4 *Coordinating* harmonizes all activities of a concern so as to facilitate its working and its success. It accords things and actions in their rightful proportions and adapts means to ends.

5 *Controlling* consists of verifying whether everything occurs in conformity with the plan adopted, the instructions issued, and the principles established. The object is to point out weaknesses and errors in order to rectify them and prevent recurrence.

UNIVERSAL PRINCIPLES

1 *Division of Work* Specialization of workers and managers to improve efficiency.

2 *Authority and Responsibility* The right to give orders and the power to exact obedience; responsibility is a natural consequence of authority.

3 *Discipline* Obedience, application, energy, behavior, and respect in accordance with the standing agreements between the organization and its employees.

4 *Unity of Command* An employee should receive orders from one superior only.

5 *Unity of Direction* One head and one plan for a group of activities having the same objective.

6 *Subordination of Individual Interests to the General Interests.*

7 *Remuneration of Personnel* Should be fair and afford satisfaction to both the employees and the organization.

8 *Centralization* A relative concept (to decentralization) which is applied according to the circumstances.

9 *Scalar Chain* The line of authority.

10 *Order* A place for everything (body) and everything (body) in its place.

11 *Equity* Kindliness and justice.

12 *Stability of Tenure of Personnel* Turnover has a negative impact on the efficiency of the organization.

13 *Initiative* The ability to think out a plan and ensure its success.

14 *Esprit de Corps* Harmony and union among personnel are great strength to the organization.

Source: Adapted from Henri Fayol, *General and Industrial Management,* translated by Constance Storrs, Sir Isaac Pitman & Sons, London, 1949.

summarized in Figure 5-1. Gulick and Urwick came up with the POSDCORB conception of management functions (planning, organizing, staffing, directing, coordinating, reporting, and budgeting), and Urwick a little later listed no less than twenty-nine principles.[8] Mooney and Reiley stressed the universal nature of the principles by examining and applying them to religious and military as well as business organizations.[9] Taylor's scientific management philosophy and principles were briefly mentioned in Chapter 1. Basically, Taylor wanted to apply scientific procedures and methods to the physical (not human) aspects of work in order to increase efficiency.[10]

[8] Luther Gulick and Lyndall Urwick (eds.), *Papers on the Science of Administration,* Institute of Public Administration, New York, 1937. Also see Lyndall Urwick, *The Elements of Administration,* Harper & Row, New York, 1943.
[9] James D. Mooney and Alan C. Reiley, *Onward Industry!,* Harper, New York, 1931; and James D. Mooney, *The Principles of Organization,* Harper, New York, 1947.
[10] Frederick W. Taylor, *The Principles of Scientific Management,* Harper, New York, 1911.

Gleaned out of the classical approach to organization are four dominant principles. These are:

1 *Unity of Command* This principle states that each participant in the formal organization should be responsible to and receive orders from only one boss. Fayol stressed this principle above all others. He felt that if it was violated, "authority is undermined, discipline is in jeopardy, order disturbed and stability threatened."[11] The principle is closely associated with military organization and is derived from the bureaucratic concept of hierarchy.

2 *Equal Authority and Responsibility* This time-honored principle of organization simply means that if managers are charged with the responsibility of accomplishing a given task, they must be given the commensurate authority to carry it out. An example would be a supervisor who is given the responsibility of keeping within a given budget. According to the principle, the supervisor should also have the authority to influence every item in the budget. If, for example, the supervisor does not have influence over certain overhead items, then these items should be divorced from his or her responsibility.

3 *Limited Spans of Control* This principle refers to the number of subordinates directly reporting to a superior. The classical theorists were in general agreement that there should be a limited number of subordinates reporting to a superior. They even made the fatal mistake of attaching precise numbers to the optimum span. For example, Urwick concluded, "No superior can supervise directly the work of more than five or, at the most, six subordinates whose work interlocks."[12]

4 *Delegation of Routine Matters* This classical principle of delegation states that decisions should be made as low as possible in the organization. Accordingly, top management should not be making decisions over routine matters that could be effectively handled by first-line supervision. All the classical theorists advocated delegation but recognized that it was not easily accomplished. Mooney and Reiley noted, "One of the tragedies of business experience is the frequency with which men, always efficient in anything they personally can do, will finally be crushed and fail under the weight of accumulated duties that they do not know and cannot learn how to delegate."[13]

The term *classical* was attached to the above concepts mainly because they have been around the longest. It does not intend to imply that they are no longer used or defended. The truth is that the classical principles are still both widely used and staunchly defended. For example, Harold Koontz, among others, still defends the classical principles.[14] Some

---

[11] Henri Fayol, *General and Industrial Management,* translated by Constance Storrs, Sir Isaac Pitman & Sons, London, 1949, p. 24.

[12] Urwick, op. cit., pp. 52–53.

[13] Mooney and Reiley, op. cit., p. 39.

[14] Harold Koontz, "The Management Theory Jungle," *Journal of the Academy of Management,* December 1961, pp. 184–185; and Harold Koontz and Cyril O'Donnell, *Principles of Management,* McGraw-Hill, New York, 1972, pp. viii, 14–19.

of the defense seems completely justified, and some does not. Part of the problem is delineating what is included in classical theory and what is not. A blanket criticism of all classical concepts, merely because they are old and familiar, is neither logical nor desirable. On the other hand, the defenders must also face up to the question of whether the classical principles are universal and still relevant and applicable to organizations today and in the future.

Neoclassical Organization Theory

The neoclassical concepts of organization represent refinements, modifications, and extensions of the classical concepts. Neoclassical organization theorists in the 1950s and 1960s were preoccupied with vertical and horizontal structural manipulations that would lead to greater organizational efficiency and more effective managerial processes. Vertical analysis of structure concentrates on centralization versus decentralization, which is an extension of the classical principle of delegation. Decentralization expands the principle of delegation to the point of an overall philosophy of organization and management. The bureaucratic principle of hierarchy is also closely related to this vertical neoclassical concept. Horizontal structural analysis is concerned with concepts such as departmentation which concentrate on organizing one level of the hierarchy. The third major neoclassical concept of staff attempts to resolve the vertical and horizontal conflicts that often appear. In general, the neoclassical concepts of centralization-decentralization, departmentation, and line-staff carry the classical concepts one step further. They give greater recognition to the importance of the human element and allow for the fact that simple, mechanistic classical structural arrangments are not entirely satisfactory for modern complex organizations.

Centralization and Decentralization

The terms *centralization* and *decentralization* are freely tossed about in both organization theory and practice. Most often, both the scholar and practitioner neglect to define what they mean by the concepts. There are three basic types of centralization-decentralization:

1 *Geographical or Territorial*   This type of centralization-decentralization deals with the concentration (centralization) or dispersion (decentralization) of operations. For example an organization that has all operations under one roof or in one region can be called centralized. On the other hand, an organization with operations spread throughout the country or the world can be called decentralized.

2 *Functional*   Centralization-decentralization can also be broken down functionally. A good example is the maintenance function of a manufacturing organization. If a separate maintenance department performs maintenance functions for the other departments, then maintenance is said to be centralized. However, if, for example, sales maintains its own fleet of automobiles, production maintains its own machines, and the accounting department maintains its computers, then maintenance is considered to be decentralized.

3 *Decision Making* Whereas both geographical and functional centralization and de-centralization are descriptive, this latter type is the most analytical in nature. This third type of centralization and decentralization refers to the retention or delegation of deci-sion-making prerogatives or command. From an organization theory standpoint, this is the most relevant use of centralization and decentralization. They are relative concepts because every organization structure contains both features and differs only in degree.

Neoclassical organization theory implies that decentralization is somehow better than centralization. In truth, neither concept is an ideal or good or bad. Generally speaking, decentralization is much more compatible with the behavioral aspects of management. This is due in part to the lower-level participation in decision making that results from decentralization. Increased motivation is an extremely important by-product. Besides the behavioral benefits, there are other advantages of decentralization. More effective deci-sions are possible because of the speed and first-hand knowledge that decentralization provides. Decentralization also affords invaluable experience in decision making for low-er-level executives. Finally, decentralization allows more time for top management to concentrate on policy making and creative innovations. On the other side of the ledger, centralization also has some distinct advantages. Centralization is generally recognized as more effective for control of operations, consistency of information, and unity of effort toward overall goal attainment. On balance, the answer to the question of what is the optimum degree of centralization-decentralization, as with all the other organization con-cepts discussed so far, is that it depends on the situation.

Departmentation: Functional and Unit
Departmentation deals with organizing one level of the hierarchy and is an extension of the classical principle of specialization. There are two main types: functional and unit. Functional departmentation is found in all types of organizations. For example, in a manu-facturing organization the major functional breakdown would be into production, market-ing, and finance. These are the vital functions that make a manufacturing concern oper-ate and survive. On the other hand, in a hospital organization the major functions might be called nursing, housekeeping, dietetics, and business. Although the titles of the func-tions are different in the hospital example, they are nevertheless analogous to the manu-facturing functions in terms of importance and purpose. The titles of various functional departments may differ between industries and even between companies within the same industry. In addition to industrial organizations and hospitals, universities, governmental agencies, churches, and the military also contain vital functions and are often functionally departmentalized.

The greatest single advantage of functional departmentation is that it incorporates the positive aspects of specialization. Theoretically, functionalism would lead to the greatest efficiency and the most economical utilization of personnel. In practice, however, certain dysfunctions that were discussed under bureaucracy also negate the advantages of func-tional departmentation. For example, functional empires may be created that conflict to the point of detracting from overall goal attainment. A typical case would be the salesperson who operates and is guided by the sales department goal of maximizing the number of units sold. In order to sell 2,000 units to a customer, the salesperson may have had to promise delivery by the end of the week and require no-money-down credit. The production department, on the other hand, has a goal to keep costs as low as possible and therefore does not carry a very large inventory. It cannot possibly supply the customer in question with 2,000 units by the end of the week. Finance has still another goal. It must hold bad-debt expense as low as possible and, thus, require a substantial down payment and thorough credit checks on every customer. In this situation, the sales department is in conflict with production and finance. If the salesperson goes ahead and makes the sale under the specified conditions in the example, the outcome will be that the customer will not receive the order on time and may not be able to pay the bill. In either or both outcomes, the company goals of customer goodwill and bad-debt expense minimization suffer because of the action of the salesperson.

Because the dysfunctions may outweigh the functions of functionalization, many organizations have turned to a unit or product type of departmentation. This type of departmentation is particularly adaptable to large, complex organizations. Unit departmentation goes hand in hand with profit-centered decentralization. It allows the giant corporations, such as General Motors, General Electric, and Du Pont, to be broken down into a group of self-contained smaller organizations. Thus, the unit departmentation allows an organization to take advantage of both large and small size.

Another advantage of organizing on a unit basis is control. Because of their self-contained nature, unit departments are very adaptable to accounting control techniques and management appraisal. Unit department performance, measured according to several different criteria, can be accurately determined. Another advantage is that unit or product departments can be readily added or subtracted with minimum disruption to the rest of the organization.

Many of the conflicts that exist in the upper level under functional departmentation are generally resolved by unit departmentation. However, under unit organization, the functional conflicts may disappear at the upper levels but reappear in the lower levels that are functionalized. Yet, from the standpoint of overall goal attainment, functional conflict at lower levels may be preferable. Besides reducing the potential for conflict, product division lends itself to many of the same behavioral advantages found in decentralization. These include more opportunity for personal development, growth, and self-control. Once again, this does not imply a universal truth because it still depends on many other personal and organizational variables.

The Staff Concept of Organization
The staff organization is the last neoclassical concept that is discussed. It often leads to confusion and problems for the organization. Most of the problems stem from conflicting definitions between line and staff and the hybrid forms of staff that are used by many organizations. The military has escaped some of these problems by precisely defining and successfully implementing a pure staff system. Strictly speaking, line gives orders and represents command while staff only gives advice and provides service to the line.

In contrast to the military, the business, hospital, education, and governmental organizations have not given proper attention to operationally defining the difference between line and staff. In the military, there definitely exists an informal, implied staff authority, but everyone understands the system and realizes that conflicts can be resolved by reverting to pure line-staff relationships. Unfortunately, this is generally not the case in other types of organizations. Usually there is a lack of understanding of the line-staff roles and relationships, which often results in a breakdown of communication and open conflict. A typical example is the business corporation which has a myriad of line-staff roles and relationships. It is not unusual to find many lower and middle managers who do not know if and when they are line or staff. One reason is that they generally wear more than one hat. Normally, managers are line within their own department and become line or staff when dealing with outside departments. The manager's functional authority is often not spelled out in the policies of the organization, and as a result, personal conflicts, role ambiguities, and dual-authority situations run rampant.

Although there are dysfunctions to a hybrid staff concept, it has generally resolved the dilemma of specialization versus unity of command faced by classical organization theory. The larger, more technologically complex organizations have almost been forced to depend greatly on a staff organization to provide the needed specialized expertise. In general, these staff organizations have accomplished their purpose but must be tempered and revised according to the situational variables that also affect the other organization concepts.

Behavioral Organization Theory

Chester Barnard is probably the best-known behaviorally oriented organization theorist. Writing in the 1930s, he considered an organization to be a system of consciously coordinated activities or forces of two or more persons.[15] He emphasized that human beings make up a formal organization, not boxes on an organization chart, and was critical of the existing classical organization theory because it was too descriptive and superficial. For example, the classical view of authority was that it came from the top down. Barnard, utilizing a more analytical approach, maintained that authority came from the bottom up. The view is known as the acceptance theory of authority. Barnard recognized that not every executive order could be consciously analyzed, judged, and either accepted or rejected. Rather, most types of orders fall within a person's "zone of indifference." If an order falls within the zone, the person will respond without question, but if it falls outside the zone, then the person will question and accept or reject. The width of the zone depends upon the degree to which the inducements exceed the burdens and sacrifices.[16] This analysis also represents the beginning of the exchange theory of organization. Based in group dynamics, exchange theory simply contends that in order for a person to

---

[15] Chester Barnard, *The Functions of the Executive,* Harvard, Cambridge, Mass., 1938, p. 73.
[16] Ibid., pp. 168–169.

participate in an organization and pursue its goals, the rewards must be greater than the costs.

Besides authority and exchange theory, Barnard also stressed the cooperative aspects of organization. This concern again reflects the importance which he felt the human element played in the organization. It was Barnard's contention that the existence of a cooperative system was contingent upon the human participants' ability to communicate and willingness to serve and strive toward a common purpose.[17] Under such a premise, the human being plays the most important role in the creation and perpetuation of the organization. Such analysis marks the beginning of behavioral theory of organizations. It has since been refined and extended by decision, biological, systems, and group and role perspectives.

Decision Theories of Organization

Herbert A. Simon is most closely associated with a decision approach to behavioral theory of organization. He felt that an organization consisted of a complex pattern of communication and decision making.[18] He especially felt the decision premise to be the most appropriate analytical unit for the study of organizations.

An outgrowth of the decision premise is the theory of organizational equilibrium or survival. Simon stressed the importance of the human decision to participate in an organization. This concern takes into consideration the decision of participants in joining, remaining in, or withdrawing from the organization and the balance of inducements and contributions for each participant, measured in terms of "utilities."[19] Essentially, this decision analysis is similar to Barnard's ideas and exchange theory.

Biological Theories of Organization

Some behaviorally oriented theorists use biological concepts in analyzing and developing organizations. For example, Waino Suojanen suggests that biology, more than any other science, may provide insights and analogies for the future development of organizations. He uses the DNA molecule (the chemical equivalent of the hereditary gene) as a case in point. DNA provides information, replication, mutation, recombination, and expression. All these DNA characteristics are essential to organized human activity. The DNA, RNA, and protein trinity of biology is also an example for organization because it is adaptable through feedback and control systems.[20]

The ecosystem concept, currently used in the analysis and discussion of environmental protection, is potentially another biological contribution to organization theory. Ecology incorporates general systems theory and is an important conceptual precedent for organizational analysis. Today, of course, systems play a vital role in organization theory and practice.

---

[17] Ibid., p. 82.
[18] Herbert A. Simon, *Administrative Behavior,* 2d ed., Macmillan, New York, 1957, p. xvi.
[19] James G. March and Herbert A. Simon, *Organizations,* Wiley, New York, 1958, p. 84.
[20] Waino W. Suojanen, *The Dynamics of Management,* Holt, New York, 1966, p. 179.

Open-System Theories of Organization

Both the closed- and open-systems approaches are utilized in modern organization theory and practice. In the dramatically changing environment which currently exists, an open-systems approach is becoming more and more important. Organizations of all types are in constant interaction with their environment and are being affected accordingly.

The simplest open system consists of an input, a transformation process, and an output:

$$\text{Inputs} \longrightarrow \underset{\text{processes}}{\text{Transformation}} \longrightarrow \text{Outputs}$$

A system cannot survive without this input, transformation process and output occurring. There are many types of inputs, transformation processes, and outputs. For example, in a manufacturing organization some of the inputs would be material, financial, and human resources. The transformation process consists of a logical network of subsystems which lead to the output and are commonly labeled the operations function. The output is represented as the product, result, outcome, or accomplishment of the system. Specific examples of the outputs of a business organization system that correspond to the inputs of material, financial, and human resources are product sales, profit or loss, and role behaviors.

Besides the simple input-transformation-output conception of an open system, there are other characteristics that should be noted. Katz and Kahn list the following as important to an open system:

1 The *input of energy* from the environment.

2 The *throughput* or transformation of the imported energy into some product form.

3 The *exporting of the product* back into the environment.

4 A *reenergizing of the system* from sources in the environment.

5 The characteristics of *negative entropy* come into play so the system can survive by importing more energy from the environment than is expended.

6 The *feedback* of information which helps the system maintain a steady state or homeostasis.

7 The tendency for *differentiation and elaboration* because of subsystem dynamics and the relationship between growth and survival.

8 The existence of *equifinality* whereby the system can reach the same final state from different initial conditions and by different paths of development.[21]

This open-system concept has general applicability. Any biological, human, social, economic, or technical phenomenon can be conceptualized in open-systems terms. It has probably had the biggest impact on organization theory since bureaucracy.

---

[21] Daniel Katz and Robert L. Kahn, *The Social Psychology of Organizations*, Wiley, New York, 1966, pp. 19–26.

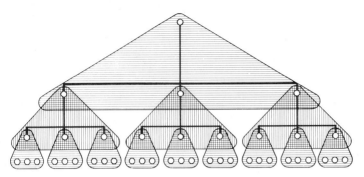

Figure 5-2 Likert's Linking-Pin Model. *Source:* Rensis Likert, *New Patterns of Management,* McGraw-Hill, New York, 1961, p. 105. Used with permission.

Group and Role Theory of Organization

Rensis Likert is best known for his direction of the famous Michigan studies on leadership style. However, he also developed a group model of organization. Figure 5-2 depicts the model.

The model shows that every participant functions as a linking pin for groups in the organization. The individual is the group leader of the lower unit and a group member of the upper unit. In this organization a group-to-group as opposed to a more traditional person-to-person relationship exists.

Likert is very careful to point out the important role that group processes play in the linking-pin organization. All groups must be equally effective because the failure of any group will have adverse consequences for the entire organization. In other words, the linking-pin chain is only as strong as its weakest link. To protect the organization from breaking down, Likert recommends additional staff groups and ad hoc committees. These provide multiple overlapping groups through which linking functions are performed and the organization is bound together.[22]

Another group model of organization is suggested by Robert Kahn and his colleagues.[23] They felt Likert's linking-pin model was closer to reality than the more traditional conceptions but fell short because no distinction was made between different types of groups. Thus, Kahn proposes that organizations should be viewed according to the analytical unit of a role rather than a group. A role is one of the smallest sociological units of analysis and can be defined as the expectations of a position. Applied to organizations, each member would occupy a position with certain expectations, both from self and from others. The organization would be made up of these positions, which interact with others

---

[22] Rensis Likert, *New Patterns of Management,* McGraw-Hill, New York, 1961, p. 115.

[23] R. L. Kahn, D. M. Wolfe, R. P. Quinn, J. D. Snoek, and R. A. Rosenthal, *Organizational Stress: Studies in Role Conflict and Ambiguity,* Wiley, New York, 1964.

to form a role set. Thus, in Kahn's view the organization is made up of overlapping and interlocking role sets which may transcend the boundaries of the traditional organization. Role conflicts and ambiguities become important in organizational analysis. For example, Kahn and his colleagues found that role conflict will be greater if the role set includes insiders and those outside the organizational boundaries and that role conflict and ambiguity tend to be greater the higher the formal rank of the focal person in the role set. This and the other behavioral approaches have stimulated the search for more effective organizational designs for practicing organizations.

Modern Organizational Designs

Along with organization theories, the actual design of practicing organizations is also beginning to change. In fact, this is one case where practice may be running ahead of theory. Many organizations are ahead of the academicians and the textbooks on organization design. Many practitioners realize that the simple solutions offered by the classical hierarchical designs are no longer adequate for many of their complex problems. The needs for flexibility and adaptability to change require new designs. The project, matrix, and free-form designs meet some of these needs.

Project Designs

Project organization designs are utilized by highly technical organizations that require a great deal of planning, research, and coordination. Project designs are commonplace in aerospace companies, but are also becoming widely used in other business, military, and governmental organizations that do contract work or operate on a unit basis. The most salient characteristic of project organizations, and the most radical departure from more traditional organization structures, are the horizontal and diagonal lines of authority, responsibility, and formal communication flows.

There are several varieties of project designs.[24] One is the *individual* project organization. This consists of only the project manager, who has no activities or personnel reporting directly to him or her. A second type is the *staff* project organization, where the project manager is provided staff back-up for project activities, but the primary functional tasks of the organization are performed by the traditional line departments. A third variation is the *intermix* project organization. Under this setup, the project manager has staff personnel and selected primary functional heads reporting directly to him or her. A fourth type is the *aggregate* project organization. The project manager has all personnel necessary for the project, staff and functional line, reporting directly to him or her. Figure 5-3 shows these four types.

[24] See C. J. Middleton, "How to Set Up a Project Organization," *Harvard Business Review,* March–April 1967, p. 78.

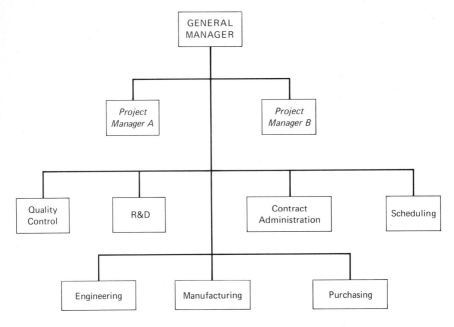

a INDIVIDUAL PROJECT ORGANIZATION

Figure 5-3 Types of project organizations.

Matrix Design

A special case of project organization is the matrix. When a project structure is superimposed on a functional structure, the result is the matrix design. The project overlay provides a formal horizontal structural dimension to the traditional vertical orientation of organization design. Figure 5-4 represents a very simplified matrix organization. In this organization the functional department heads have line authority over the specialists in their departments (vertical structure). The functional specialists are then assigned to given projects (horizontal structure). These assignments are usually made at the beginning of each project by a collaboration between the appropriate functional and project managers.

Matrix organizations flout the traditional organizational principles. The classical principles of hierarchy and unity of command are flagrantly violated. A great deal of conflict is also generated in matrix organizations and can discourage informal groups and the nurturing of supervisor-subordinate relations. On the other side of the coin, however, matrix designs include the positive aspects of both the functional and project organizations. Organizations facing tremendous structural and technical complexity have no choice but to move toward a matrix type of design. They need the horizontal dimension provided by matrix designs.

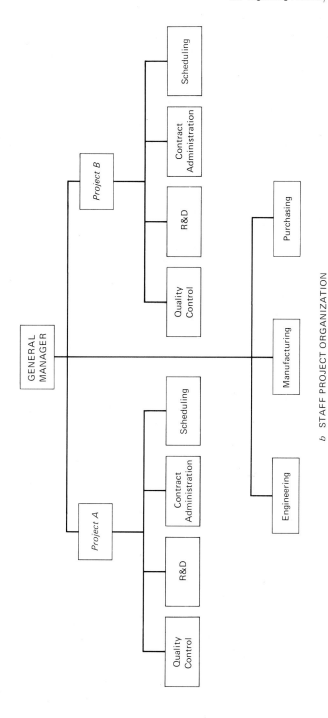

b STAFF PROJECT ORGANIZATION

Figure 5-3 Continued.

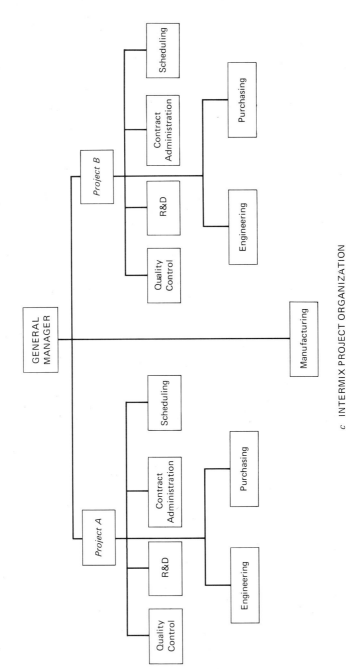

c INTERMIX PROJECT ORGANIZATION

Figure 5-3 Continued.

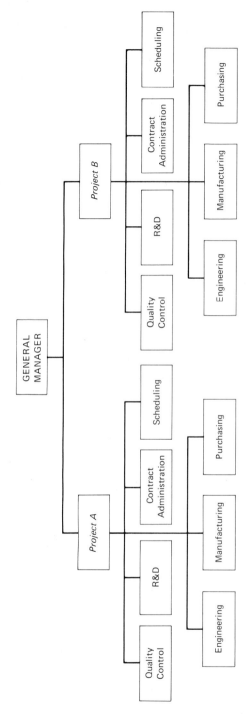

d AGGREGATE PROJECT ORGANIZATION

Figure 5-3 Continued.

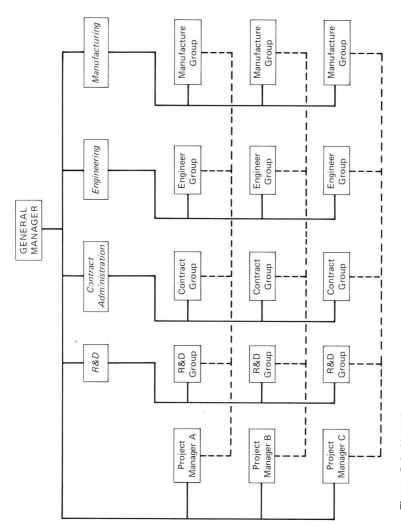

Figure 5-4 Matrix Organization.

Free-Form Designs

In addition to the project and matrix models are the free-form designs, sometimes called the naturalistic or organic designs. The free-form design is based on the premise that the purpose of an organization is to facilitate the management of change. To accomplish this objective, the structural arrangements are highly adaptable and flexible. There are no prescribed or rigid roles, and the internal structure is not allowed to solidify.

It is virtually impossible to draw a free-form design because in most cases there is no organization chart per se. Under the free-form concept, there is no one way of organizing, and organizations that operate under the free-form concept tailor the structure to fit their particular needs at particular times. Usually, the traditional departmentalized functional structure is replaced by self-contained profit centers. These organizational units are results-oriented and are managed as a team. Individual action within a team attempts to incorporate the behavioral approach to management. Participation, self-control, individual initiative, independent judgment, open communication, sensitivity, and teamwork are some of the human factors that are encouraged and facilitated by free-form designs.

There are a couple of other major characteristics common to all free-form designs. First, they make extensive use of computerized information systems, especially to evaluate the performance of various organizational units. Second, free-form organizations are populated by young, dynamic managers who are willing to accept calculated risks. These young executives usually have had previous experience in one of the firms which pioneered the free-form concept, the so-called go-go corporations of the 1960s. The future seems to hold more rather than less of these unorthodox types of organization designs.

Summary

This chapter traced the development of organization theory and design. First bureaucratic theory was examined. Both the functions and dysfunctions of specialization, hierarchy, rules, and impersonalization were given attention. Next, some of the classical and neoclassical organization concepts were discussed. Unity of command (each person should be responsible to only one boss), equal authority and responsibility (if a person is given responsibility, he or she should have the commensurate authority to carry out that responsibility), limited spans of control (limit the number of subordinates directly reporting to a superior), and delegation of routine matters are the classical concepts which are extended and refined by the neoclassical concepts of centralization and decentralization, departmentation, and staff organization. Following this discussion of traditional organization theory was a sampling of more behaviorally oriented organization theories. Included were the decision, biological, system, and group and role theories of organization. The final part of the chapter presented and analyzed specific organization designs. Project (individual, staff, intermix, and aggregate), matrix (a project structure superimposed on a functional structure with vertical and horizontal lines of authority and communication), and free-form (tailor-made, flexible organizations designed to manage change) were given special attention. The future seems to dictate new thinking for both the theory and the design of organizations.

☐ Critical Incident

The Midcontinent Electric Company was founded 50 years ago. The company has experienced an outstanding growth rate in the industry. The company started off with a classical structure, but last year it absorbed the only gas utility in the region and changed its name to Midcontinent Gas and Electric System. Although the company is regulated, Midcontinent top management is convinced that one of the new organization designs will make the utility more effective and responsive to change.

1 Do you agree with the top management of this utility? What are some factors that would contribute to the decision to retain a classical structure? What are some factors that would contribute to the decision to move to a project, matrix, or free-form structure?

2 What neoclassical concepts (centralization-decentralization, departmentation, or line-staff) could apply to the organization of this utility?

Questions for Review and Discussion

1 What are the major characteristics of a bureaucratic form of organization? What are the functions and dysfunctions of each of these characteristics?

2 What are the four dominant principles of classical organization theory? Are these principles still relevant? Defend your answer.

3 The neoclassical concepts refine, modify, and extend the bureaucratic and classical principles; identify and analyze the role of these neoclassical concepts in structuring modern organizations.

4 Describe the components of an open system. What are some of the major characteristics of open systems?

5 Describe some modern organization designs. How does a matrix design differ from a bureaucratic design?

References

Albers, Henry H.: *Principles of Management*, 4th ed., Wiley, New York, 1974, part II.
Aldrich, Howard: "Organizational Boundaries and Inter-Organizational Conflict," *Human Relations*, August 1971, pp. 279–294.
Argyris, Chris: "Personality and Organization Theory, Revisited," *Administrative Science Quarterly*, June 1973, pp. 141–167.
Bennis, Warren: *Beyond Bureaucracy*, McGraw-Hill, New York, 1966.
Blau, Peter M.: *Bureaucracy in Modern Society*, Random House, New York, 1956.
Browne, Philip J., and Robert T. Golembiewski: "The Line-Staff Concept Revisited: An Empirical Study of Organizational Images," *Academy of Management Journal*, September 1974, pp. 406–417.
Butler, Arthur G., Jr.: "Project Management: A Study in Organizational Conflict," *Academy of Management Journal*, March 1973, pp. 84–101.
Davis, Keith: "Trends in Organizational Design," *Arizona Business*, November 1973, pp. 3–7.
Delbecq, Andre, and Alan Filley: *Program and Project Management in a Matrix Organization: A Case Study*, Bureau of Business Research and Service, Graduate School of Business, University of Wisconsin, Madison, Wisc., January 1974.

Drucker, Peter F.: "New Templates for Today's Organizations," *Harvard Business Review,* January–February 1974, pp. 45–53.

Duncan, W. Jack: "Order and Innovation: A New Look at Bureaucracy," *Personnel Journal,* July 1972, pp. 518–523.

Emery, Fred E.: "Bureaucracy and Beyond," *Organizational Dynamics,* Winter 1974, pp. 3–13.

Galbraith, Jay R.: "Matrix Organization Designs: How to Combine Functional and Project Forms," *Business Horizons,* February 1971, pp. 29–40.

Greiner, Larry E.: "Evolution and Revolution as Organizations Grow," *Harvard Business Review,* July–August 1972, pp. 37–46.

Gruber, William H., and John S. Niles: "Put Innovation in the Organization Structure," *California Management Review,* Summer 1972, pp. 29–35.

Hall, Richard H.: *Organizations: Structure and Process,* Prentice-Hall, Englewood Cliffs, N.J., 1972.

Harvey, Donald F.: "Organizational Adaptation and the Matrix Design," *Arizona Business,* August 1972, pp. 19–26.

Henderson, A. M., and Talcott Parsons (trans. and eds.): *Max Weber: The Theory of Social and Economic Organization,* Free Press, New York, © 1947 by Oxford University Press, New York.

Katz, Daniel, and Robert L. Kahn: *The Social Psychology of Organizations,* Wiley, New York, 1966.

Kochen, Manfred, and Karl W. Deutsch: "A Note on Hierarchy and Coordination: An Aspect of Decentralization", *Management Science,* September 1974, pp. 106–114.

Koontz, Harold, and Cyril O'Donnell: *Principles of Management,* 5th ed., McGraw-Hill, New York, 1972, part III.

Levin, Richard I., and Charles A. Kirkpatrick: *Planning and Control with PERT/CPM,* McGraw-Hill, New York, 1966.

Lundstedt, Sven: "Consequences or Reductionism in Organization Theory," *Public Administration Review,* July–August 1972, pp. 328–333.

March, James G., and Herbert A. Simon: *Organizations,* Wiley, New York, 1958.

Middleton, C. J.: "How to Set Up a Project Organization," *Harvard Business Review,* March–April 1967, p. 78.

Miewald, Robert D.: "The Greatly Exaggerated Death of Bureaucracy," *California Management Review,* Winter 1970, pp. 65–69.

Pascucci, John J.: "The Emergence of Free-Form Management," *Personnel Administration,* September–October 1968, pp. 33–41.

Perrow, Charles: *Complex Organizations: A Critical Essay,* Scott, Foresman, Glenview, Ill., 1972.

Potter, William J.: "Management in the Ad-hocracy," *S.A.M. Advanced Management Journal,* July 1974, pp. 19–23.

Scott, William G.: "Organization Theory: A Reassessment," *Academy of Management Journal,* June 1974, pp. 242–254.

Simon, Herbert A.: *Administrative Behavior,* 2d ed., Macmillan, New York, 1957.

Simonds, Rollin H.: "Are Organizational Principles a Thing of the Past?" *Personnel,* January–February 1970, pp. 8–17.

Suojanen, Waino W.: *The Dynamics of Management,* Holt, New York, 1966.

Swinth, Robert: *Organizational Systems for Management: Designing, Planning, and Implementation,* Grid, Columbus, Ohio, 1974.

Waddel, William C., and Paul Zivkovich: "The Care and Feeding of Conglomerates," *S.A.M. Advanced Management Journal,* January 1974, pp. 44–51.

Chapter 6

Directing and Communicating

The process of directing people in organizations (Fayol originally called it "commanding") has always been considered vital to effective management. Even before management per se was written about and discussed from an academic perspective, leadership has been given considerable attention throughout history. In fact, probably more research and writing have been devoted to leadership than any other topic. Most of history, biographies, and autobiographies are directly or indirectly concerned with leadership. Yet, with all this attention, the surface is just beginning to be scratched. Only a good start has been made toward the understanding and successful practice of leadership in general and the directing of employees in organizations in particular. Much remains to be done. The first part of this chapter summarizes the currently accepted theories and techniques of the process of directing. Specific attention is given to the trait theories of leadership and the work of Rensis Likert on leadership styles.

The last half of the chapter is devoted to the communication process. The directing process usually incorporates communication, but it is becoming increasingly important and deserves separate, special attention. By definition, a good leader is an effective communicator and vice versa. Better communication is often cited as the solution to all the problems facing the world and the lack of it as being the root of all evil (lovers' quarrels, ethnic prejudice, war between nations, the generation gap, industrial disputes, and dysfunctional conflict in organizations). After defining communication, the chapter examines the interpersonal and organizational perspectives of communication. Specific attention is devoted to the perceptual and language aspects of interpersonal communication and the downward, horizontal, and upward systems of organizational communication.

The Characteristics of a Good Leader

It is generally recognized that leadership can spell the difference between success and failure, whether in a war, in a basketball game, or especially in attaining the goals of an organization. Yet, despite this recognized importance, the characteristics of a good leader still pretty much remain a mystery. Good leadership is known to exist and have a tremendous influence on organizational performance, but the inner workings and specific traits of an effective leader cannot be precisely spelled out. Yet, a lot of attention has been devoted to the trait approach to leadership.

The earliest leadership theories can be traced back to ancient times. Plato's *Republic* and Confucius's *Analects* talk about leadership. Most of the early theories suggested that leaders were born, not made. This great-man theory of leadership said that a person was born either with or without the necessary traits for leadership. Famous figures in history were used to support the theory. For example, Napoleon was said to have had the "natural" leadership abilities to rise out of any situation to be a great leader.

Eventually the great-man theory gave way to a more realistic trait approach to leadership. Under the influence of the behavioristic school of psychological thought, it became accepted that leadership traits were not completely inborn but could also be acquired through learning and experience. Attention turned to the search for universal traits possessed by leaders. Numerous physical, mental, and personality traits were researched during the period from 1930 to 1950. On the surface, at least, some identifiable traits turned up. For example, in the late 1940s Ralph Stogdill reported on the basis of at least fifteen studies that leaders possess intelligence, scholarship, dependability in exercising responsibilities, activity and social participation, and socioeconomic status. He also found traits such as sociability, persistence, initiative, knowing how to get things done, self-confidence, alertness, insight, cooperativeness, popularity, adaptability, and verbal facility in ten or more leadership studies.[1] However, these findings were so tenuous and nonoperational that they were of little use in predicting or proving leadership effectiveness. Even Stogdill concluded, "A person does not become a leader by virtue of the possession of some combination of traits, but by the pattern of personal characteristics, activities, and goals of the followers. Thus, leadership must be conceived in terms of the interaction of variables which are in constant flux and change."[2] He then went on to stress the importance that the situation plays in leadership. This situational aspect, which is the dominant theme of the modern approach to leadership, is given detailed attention in Chapter 8 of the book.

Recognizing the limitations of a trait approach, Keith Davis has a representative list of four basic traits of a good leader in an organization:[3]

1 *Intelligence*   This trait seems to hold up better than any other. Research generally shows that leaders have higher intelligence than the average of their followers. Interestingly, however, the leader cannot be too intelligent. For instance, political candidates have been defeated because the voters viewed them as being too intelligent.

2 *Social Maturity and Breadth*   Leaders tend to be emotionally stable and mature and have broad-ranging interests and activities. They have an assured, confident, but still respectful self-concept.

---

[1] R. M. Stogdill, "Personal Factors Associated with Leadership: A Survey of the Literature," *Journal of Psychology*, vol. 25, 1948, p. 63.

[2] Ibid., p. 64.

[3] Keith Davis, *Human Behavior at Work*, 4th ed., McGraw-Hill, New York, 1972, pp. 103–104.

3 *Inner Motivation and Achievement Drives* Leaders have relatively intense achievement-type motivational drives. They strive for intrinsic rather than extrinsic material rewards. They are always on the go and work very hard.

4 *Human Relations Attitudes* Successful leaders recognize the worth and dignity of their followers and are able to empathize with them. They are considerate of their followers' needs and are genuinely concerned with their welfare.

These characteristics provide insights but are limited in their ability to improve the directing process in organizations.

Leadership Styles and Techniques

There are many highly publicized leadership studies which are used to support one style or technique over another. The earliest and perhaps most famous is the Lippitt and White study which analyzed the autocratic, democratic, and laissez faire styles of leadership. Hobby clubs consisting of ten-year-old boys were submitted to the three different styles of leadership. Some of the results were fairly definite, and others were not. One clear-cut result was the overwhelming preference the boys had for the democratic style of leadership. The effects of the style on task performance were not as clear. The experiments were set up specifically to examine patterns of aggressive behavior, with performance being only a by-product. It was found that under the autocratic leader the boys reacted either aggressively or apathetically. They seemed to be frustrated by an autocratic leadership style. While the autocratic leader was present, the boys worked diligently at their tasks, but if he left the room, either all hell would break loose or they would drop their tools and become very apathetic. The democratically led groups on the other hand were less aggressive and did not need constant supervision. The laissez faire leadership climate turned out to be no leadership at all. Laissez faire leaders produced the greatest number of aggressive acts from the group.

The direct implications for directing employees in organizations from the pioneering Lippitt and White studies are not clear. Sweeping generalizations are certainly not justified. Young boys performing scout activities under crude experimental conditions are a long way from adults working in a modern, complex organization. Yet, the studies did show that different styles of leadership can produce different, complex reactions from a group. Autocratic leadership led to frustration. The group seemed to produce as long as the autocratic leader was present but became either aggressive or apathetic when he was absent. The democratically led groups did not exhibit such frustration and did not require constant supervision. However, there is a fine line between democratic and laissez faire leadership styles. The laissez faire style was even worse than the autocratic style. It was very unpopular and unproductive. Yet, in practice, many managers who think they are directing according to a democratic style may actually be using a laissez faire style, and the results are disastrous. The democratic and laissez faire styles are so close—but if practiced correctly very far apart—that the democratic style is often unjustly criticized as leading to poor results because of its guilt by association with the very poor laissez faire style.

Besides the Lippitt and White studies, the Michigan studies on leadership styles are also well known. The initial study was conducted on high- and low-producing work groups in the Prudential Life Insurance Company. It was found that most of the high-producing groups were led by supervisors who had a general, employee-centered style, while most of the low-producing groups were led by supervisors who had a close, production-centered style. The effective supervisors did not give detailed instructions and keep a close eye over their employees but instead were concerned with end results and were genuinely concerned with the welfare of their people. In other words, the effective style was ends-oriented rather than means-oriented and gave precedence to the welfare of the employee over task accomplishment.

Four Systems of Leadership Styles

Over the years the Prudential study has been extended by numerous other studies. Most of these follow-up studies, as was the original, have been conducted by the University of Michigan survey research center under the direction of Rensis Likert and are known as the Michigan studies. In 1967, Likert summarized the work of this Michigan group into the now famous four systems of management. Managers who operate according to system 1 are very authoritarian and actually try to exploit their subordinates. The system 2 manager is also authoritarian but in a paternalistic manner. This benevolent autocrat keeps strict control and never delegates to subordinates but "pats them on the head" for "their best interests." In other words, a System 2 manager treats people like children. System 3 managers use a consultative style. They ask for and receive participative input from subordinates, but they maintain the right to make the final decision. System 4 managers use a participative group or democratic style. They give some direction to subordinates, but there is total participation and decision by majority or consensus. In some cases an actual vote may be taken. Figure 6-1 summarizes in more detail Likert's four systems of management style.

Likert has asked hundreds of managers to describe, on an expanded version of the format found in Figure 6-1, the highest and lowest producing work units with which they have had experience. Quite consistently, the high-producing units are described according to systems 3 and 4 while the low-producing units fall between systems 1 and 2. This response occurs irrespective of the field of experience of the managers or whether they are in a line or staff position.[4] Likert is convinced of the value of a system 4 style of leadership and although now retired from the University of Michigan is still actively involved in further researching it and implementing it in practicing organizations.

[4] Rensis Likert, *The Human Organization,* McGraw-Hill, New York, 1967, p. 11.

Figure 6-1 Likert's Systems of Management Leadership

Leadership Variable	System 1 (Exploitive Authoritative)	System 2 (Benevolent Authoritative)	System 3 (Consultative)	System 4 (Participative Group)
1 Superior's confidence and trust in subordinates	Has no confidence and trust in subordinates	Has condescending confidence and trust, such as master has to servant	Has substantial but not complete confidence and trust; still wishes to keep control of decisions	Has complete confidence and trust in all matters
2 Subordinates' feeling of freedom	Subordinates do not feel at all free to discuss things about the job with their superior	Subordinates do not feel very free to discuss things about the job with their superior	Subordinates feel rather free to discuss things about the job with their superior	Subordinates feel completely free to discuss things about the job with their superior
3 Superior's involvement with subordinates	Seldom gets ideas and opinions of subordinates in solving job problems	Sometimes gets ideas and opinions of subordinates in solving job problems	Usually gets ideas and opinions and usually tries to make constructive use of them	Always gets ideas and opinions and always tries to make constructive use of them

Source: Adapted from Rensis Likert, *The Human Organization*, McGraw-Hill, New York, 1967, p. 4. Used by permission.

Other Leadership Styles

Figure 6-2 presents a continuum of possible leadership styles available to the modern manager. Most of the widely known styles of leadership are incorporated into this continuum. Although there are fine distinctions made between the various styles, the following corresponding styles from the Lippitt and White and Michigan studies can be substituted for the boss-centered ←----→ subordinate-centered terminology used in Figure 6-2.

Boss-centered		Subordinate-centered
Autocratic	←——————→	Democratic
Production-centered	←——————→	Employee-centered
Close	←——————→	General
System 1	←——————→	System 4

The verbal descriptions and the relationship between authority and freedom found on the continuum of Figure 6-2 apply to all of the above styles as well. The general conclusion from this traditional approach to leadership styles is that the subordinate-centered (democratic, employee-centered, general, system 4) style is more effective than the boss-centered counterpart (autocratic, production-centered, close, system 1). The newer, contingency-based approach to leadership, which will be discussed in Chapter 8, will indicate that this is not necessarily true. As with the other process variables in management,

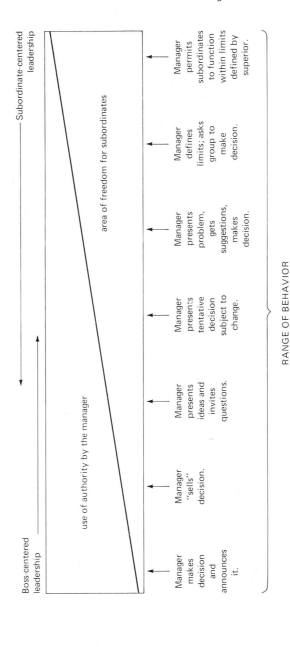

Figure 6-2 Continuum of Leadership Behavior. *Source: Robert Tannenbaum and Warren H. Schmidt, "How to Choose a Leadership Pattern," Harvard Business Review, March–April 1958, p. 96. Used with permission.*

the most effective method or technique of directing employees in organizations depends on the situation.

Communicating Process

The majority of a manager's time is spent in some form of communication. Thus, communicating plays a very important part of all management processes but especially in directing employees. Gellerman compares it to the nervous system of the body as follows:

The process of communication—the flow of facts, ideas, and emotional reactions between people—is to a group what the flow of impulses through the nervous system is to a living body. Communication animates or paralyzes, excites or relaxes, coordinates or confuses a group. The process of supervision cannot really be understood without first understanding communication.[5]

Although there are many slight variations, the best definition of the communication process is the transfer of commonly meaningful information. The ''commonly meaningful'' part of the definition means that mutual understanding must occur before there is communication; merely transferring information is not enough. The transfer can take place from an interpersonal or organizational perspective.

The emphasis of interpersonal communication is on the transfer of information between two or more persons. On the surface this transfer appears very simple and straightforward but in actuality is a very complex process. The interpersonal communication process involves perception and language on the part of both the sender and the receiver. The interactive effects primarily focus on the important concept of feedback, which is probably more important to effective interpersonal communication than is sending or receiving. However, all aspects of interpersonal communication—sending, receiving, and feedback—are closely tied to perception and language.

Perceptual Aspects of Communication

The perceptual process involves a complicated interaction of selection and organization of incoming stimulation. Although depending largely on the senses for raw data, the perceptual process may filter, modify, or completely change these data through its complex interactions. In other words, the perceptual process adds to and subtracts from the ''real'' sensory world. Some organizational examples which point out the difference between sensation and perception are the following:

1 A subordinate's answer to a question is based on what he or she heard the boss say, not on what the boss actually said.

2 The same employee may be rated on the performance appraisal form by one supervisor as very good and by another supervisor as very bad.

---

[5] Saul W. Gellerman, *Management by Motivation*, American Management Association, New York, 1968, p. 41.

3 The same staff report may be viewed by one manager as outlandish and unrealistic and by another manager as interesting and realistic.

These perceptual communication problems can be reduced by a better understanding of the selection and organization aspects of perception.

PERCEPTUAL SELECTIVITY   There are numerous stimuli constantly confronting everyone all the time. With all this stimulation impinging upon the person, one must select out certain stimuli when attempting to communicate. An understanding of the following principles of perceptual selectivity helps determine how this process occurs.

INTENSITY   The intensity principle states that the more intense the stimulus, the more likely it will be perceived. A loud voice will be attended to over a quiet voice. A supervisor may yell loudly at subordinates to gain their attention. However, this last example is also a good one to show that other more complex psychological variables may overcome the simple external variable. By yelling loudly, the supervisor may also turn the subordinates off instead of gaining their attention to communicate.

SIZE   Closely related to intensity is size. The principle of size says that the larger the object, the more likely it will be given attention. A 6 ft 4 in tall, 250-pound supervisor may receive more attention than a 5 ft 10 in tall, 160-pound supervisor. In a staff meeting, a flip-chart presentation with large words is more attention-getting than a few typed lines on a piece of paper.

CONTRAST   The contrast principle states that stimuli which stand out against the background or which change from what people are accustomed to will receive their attention. Plant safety signs which have black lettering on a yellow background or white lettering on a red background are attention-getting. In a similar manner, when the 6 ft 4 in tall, 250-pound supervisor mentioned above is placed next to a 5 ft 4 in tall, 130-pound supervisor, the smaller person will probably receive as much notice in giving orders or directions as the bigger person.

REPETITION   The repetition principle states that a repeated stimulus is more attention-getting than a single one. The explanation is: "A stimulus that is repeated has a better chance of catching us during one of the periods when our attention to a task is waning. In addition, repetition increases our sensitivity or alertness to the stimulus."[6] Thus, a worker will generally "hear" better when directions for a dull task are given more than once. This principle partially explains why supervisors complain that they have to give directions over and over again for even the simplest of tasks. The worker's attention for a boring task is waning, and he or she "hears" directions for the task only if the supervisor repeats them several times.

PERCEPTUAL ORGANIZATION   Perceptual selectivity is concerned with the variables that gain a person's attention in the communication process. Perceptual organization

---

[6] Clifford T. Morgan and Richard A. King, *Introduction to Psychology*, 3d ed., McGraw-Hill, New York, 1966, p. 343.

focuses on what takes place once the information from the situation is received. An individual seldom perceives patches of words or sounds. Instead, the person perceives organized patterns of stimuli. The person's perceptual process organizes the incoming information into a meaningful whole in order for communication to take place.

The figure-ground principle best demonstrates perceptual organization. This principle simply says that perceived objects (figure) stand out as separable from their general background (ground). This principle is operating as one is reading this paragraph. In terms of light wave stimuli, the reader is receiving patches of irregularly shaped blacks and whites. Yet, the reader does not perceive it this way. The reader perceives black letters, words, and sentences printed against a white background. In other words, the reader perceptually organizes incoming stimuli into recognizable figures (words) that are seen against a ground (white page). Another figure-ground illustration is shown in Figure 6-3. At first glance, one probably perceives a jumble of black irregular shapes against a white background. Only when the white letters are perceptually organized against a black background will the words TEA and LET jump out in clarity. How often does one try to read between the lines and ignore the obvious? The opposite, of course, is also true. This important aspect of communication can be better understood and improved by knowledge of organizing principles such as figure-ground.

PERCEPTUAL GROUPING   Another organizing aspect of perception is the grouping principle. There is a tendency to group together several stimuli into a recognizable pattern. This principle is basic to communication. When simple constellations of stimuli are presented in the communication process, the individual will tend to group them according to the principles of closure, continuity, proximity, or similarity.

CLOSURE   The closure principle is related to gestalt ideas of psychology. A basic gestalt principle is that the whole is greater than the sum of the parts and that a whole is sometimes perceived when one does not actually exist. The perceptual process closes

Figure 6-3   Illustration of figure-ground.

gaps which are unfilled from sensory input. In communicating there may be a perceived whole where none exists or a whole that does exist but may not be perceived as such. An example of the first case would be a manager who perceived complete agreement among the members of a department on a course of action when in fact there was opposition from several members. The manager in this situation closed the existing gaps and perceived complete agreement when, in fact, it did not exist. The other side of the coin is expressed in the adage of not being able to see the forest (whole) for the trees (parts). A manager may get so lost in the details that he or she loses sight of the overall objective of the organization. In communicating, often managers cannot join together their part with the other parts to perceive the whole.

CONTINUITY   The principle of continuity is closely related to that of closure, but where closure supplies missing stimuli, continuity says that stimuli are perceived as continuous. This type of continuity may lead to inflexible, static ways of communicating. Only the obvious, continuous patterns or relationships will be perceived. For example, the information system may be limited to obvious flows or continuous lines. New, innovative ways of communicating may not be perceived.

PROXIMITY   The principle of proximity or nearness states that a group of stimuli that are close together will be perceived as a whole pattern belonging together. For example, when communicating to a group, the leader may perceive the group as a single entity because all the members are in physical proximity to one another. In fact, just because the people all come from one department or work in one operation together does not mean that they are similar in other attributes.

SIMILARITY   The principle of similarity states that the greater the similarity of the stimuli, the greater is the tendency to perceive them as a common group. Similarity is conceptually related to proximity but in most cases predominates over proximity. In an organization, all employees who wear a blue (white) collar may be perceived as a common group when in reality each worker is a unique individual. When communicating, this tendency should be recognized.

PERCEPTUAL CONTEXT   The highest, most sophisticated form of perceptual organization is context. It is especially important in communicating because it gives meaning and value to simple stimuli, objects, events, situations, and other persons in the environment. For example, a verbal order or "suggestion," or nonverbal raised eyebrows, or "pats on the back" take on special meaning and value when placed in the context of superior-subordinate relations. The context factors can be looked at from a cognitive or social perspective.

Cognitive context factors are those which are clearly and consciously known and are part of existing knowledge and experience. The modern organization provides many cognitive variables that affect the communication process. Bureaucratic structure and authority and the technological processes of an organization are examples of cognitive variables that affect interpersonal communication. However, of equal importance is the social context of perception. Particularly relevant to the social context are psychological variables.

For example, people's motives, experiences, or group memberships may serve as important social contexts for their perception.

THE PERCEIVER AND THE PERCEIVED   Zalkind and Costello lend better understanding of interpersonal communication by summarizing research findings on some specific characteristics of the perceiver and the perceived. A profile of the perceiver is as follows:

1 Knowing oneself makes it easier to see others accurately.
2 One's own characteristics affect the characteristics he is likely to see in others.
3 The person who accepts himself is more likely to be able to see favorable aspects of other people.
4 Accuracy in perceiving others is not a single skill.[7]

These four characteristics greatly influence how a person interacts with others in the communication process. The same goes for the person being perceived. Research has shown that:

1 The status of the person perceived will greatly influence others' perception of him.
2 The person being perceived is usually placed into categories to simplify the viewer's perceptual activities. Two common categories are status and role.
3 The visible traits of the person perceived will greatly influence the perception of him.[8]

These characteristics of the perceiver and the perceived suggest the extreme complexity found in the perceptual aspects of communicating.

Language Aspects of Communication
Along with perception, language is equally important to the interpersonal communication process. Language is used to transmit meaning in communication. The English language is an obvious example, but accounting, statistics, COBOL, and a lifted eyebrow are also used to transmit meaning and are therefore languages. There are countless problems with the use of language in getting across meaning in the communication process. The infinity of meanings of words and the problem of abstraction and nonverbal language greatly complicate the communication process.

THE MEANING OF WORDS   Although Webster gives several meanings for most words in the English language, this represents only a small percentage of the actual meanings that various words have for people using them. Take the example of the symbol X. The meanings of this one letter range all the way from a kiss at the bottom of a letter to the birth of Christ. The meanings of words also change over time (the word *China* today, 10 years ago, and 35 years ago), according to the context in which they are used (*Jesus* used in a sermon on Sunday morning and used when hitting one's thumb while hanging a picture), and with the person using the word. An example of the latter would be the

[7] Sheldon S. Zalkind and Timothy W. Costello, "Perception: Some Recent Research and Implications for Administration," *Administrative Science Quarterly*, September 1962, pp. 227–229.
[8] Ibid., p. 230.

Figure 6-4 Humorous Definitions of Expressions Commonly Used in Administration

IMPLEMENT:	Hire more people and expand the office.
CONSULTANT:	Almost anyone with a briefcase more than 50 miles from home.
STAR SALESPERSON:	Someone from the home office with a special discount.
NOTE AND INITIAL:	Let's spread the responsibility.
FORWARDED FOR YOUR CONSIDERATION:	You hold the bag for awhile.
IT'S IN THE PROCESS:	We forgot about it until now.
WE'LL LOOK INTO IT:	Meanwhile, you may forget it, too.
TAKE THIS UP AT OUR NEXT MEETING:	That will give you time to forget.
PROJECT:	A word that makes a minor job seem major.
PROGRAM:	A project requiring more than one telephone call.
UNDER CONSIDERATION:	Never heard about it until now.
UNDER ACTIVE CONSIDERATION:	We're trying to locate the correspondence.
WE'RE MAKING A SURVEY:	We need more time to think up an answer.

different meanings attached to the word *fact* as used by union members and managers in a collective bargaining dispute. Stagner and Rosen note that "to a union steward, the 'fact' may be that a change in machine layout has created a safety hazard, whereas the foreman may deny that the safety hazard is a fact. Differences in job duties, calling for a pay increase, may seem obvious to workers, but the plant manager may honestly deny that any differences exist; and, for him, they do not exist."[9] These and other problems with language are closely related to perception, discussed in the last section. Figure 6-4 humorously portrays some different meanings for words that are commonly used in administration. These represent the "language games" people play in an organization.

ABSTRACTION: LEAVING OUT DETAILS   A word, a sentence, a memo, a report, or an entire book is an abstraction of reality. Some of the details in communication are always left out. Statements such as "business is good" or "morale is low" or "production costs are high" are only vague abstractions of the real situation. Including more details in each of these cases would tend to reduce the abstraction and increase the effectiveness of the communication. For example, in "business is good," additional comparative statements on rate of return on investment, market share, and costs in previous time periods would add meaning. In the case of "morale is good," additional comparative statements on turnover and grievance rates and the results of satisfaction questionnaires would give more meaning. The same is true of "production costs are high." Comparative statements on unit costs and percentage of scrap and rejects would reduce the abstraction and add meaning. In the interpersonal communication process that takes place in organizations, between superior and subordinate, between line and staff, between departments, and between management and workers, there should be a concerted effort to get away from the following common use of language:

I know that you believe and understand what you think I said, but I am not sure you realize that what you heard is not what I meant.

[9] Ross Stagner and Hjalmer Rosen, *Psychology of Union Management Relations,* Wadsworth, Belmont, Calif., 1965, p. 19.

NONVERBAL LANGUAGE Verbal languages are spoken or written and receive the greater share of attention in the study and practice of communication. Nonverbal language, dubbed the "silent language" by anthropologist Edward Hall, is equally, if not more, important in transmitting meaning in interpersonal communication. Facial expressions and tone of voice are two good examples. Expressions such as a frown, a smile, tightening the jaw, lifting an eyebrow, or a wink transmit a lot of meaning. Voice inflection, rapidity or slowness of speech, and tonal emphasis on certain words are also extremely important in communicating. Other important nonverbal cues include such things as posture and distance. Hall, through systematic research, has identified four distance zones: (1) intimate distance (the presence of the other person is unmistakable and overwhelming; there are greatly stepped-up sensory inputs), (2) personal distance (a small protective sphere of 1½ to 4 feet; the upper limit keeps someone at "arm's length"), (3) social distance (no touching without special effort, and voice is normal), and (4) public distance (outside the circle of involvement).[10] This type of analysis can be very useful in improving interpersonal communication.

Organizational Communication

Organizational communication is somewhat different in approach and perspective from interpersonal communication. The organization structure functions as a communication system in a downward, horizontal, and upward direction.

DOWNWARD SYSTEM The downward system largely dominates communication in most organizations. Most information flows from the top down, i.e., from superior to subordinate all the way to the bottom level of the organization. This downward orientation promotes an authoritative atmosphere which tends to inhibit the effectiveness of the upward and horizontal systems of communication.

The downward systems rely on many different types of media to disseminate information. Some examples of written media are organizational handbooks, manuals, magazines, newspapers, and letters that may be sent to the home or distributed on the job; bulletin board items, posters, and information displays; and standard reports, written procedures, and memos. Examples of oral media utilized in the downward system are direct verbal orders or instructions from superiors, speeches, meetings, closed-circuit television, public address systems, and telephones. In addition, computerized information systems are greatly contributing to the downward flow of communication.

The numerous types of media give an indication of the avalanche of information that is descending on personnel from the downward communication system. In many cases, quality of information has been sacrificed for quantity. Besides the quantity and quality difficulties, there is also the problem that much of downward communication becomes lost, distorted, misinterpreted, or ignored by organizational participants:

---

[10] Edward T. Hall, *The Hidden Dimension,* Anchor Books, Doubleday, Garden City, N.Y., 1969, pp. 116–125.

HORIZONTAL SYSTEM   The horizontal communication system is required in a coordinated effort to achieve overall organizational goals. This horizontal requirement becomes more apparent as the organization becomes larger, more complex, and subject to accelerated change. The new organization structures presented in the last chapter, e.g., the free-form and matrix, recognize the need by incorporating a horizontal dimension to the structure. Organizations which have not included a formal horizontal structure primarily depend upon the informal system and committees. These latter methods can have positive and negative consequences for the organization. Communication with peers, i.e., those persons of relatively equal status on the same level of an organization, provides needed social support for an individual. The person can more comfortably turn to a peer for social support than to those above or below. This is good if the support is couched in terms of task coordination to achieve overall goals. It is bad if the resulting communication is of a dysfunctional nature. Informal group norms formed through horizontal communication may be detrimental to attaining the formal goals of the organization. In addition, horizontal communication among peers may be at the sacrifice of vertical communication. Persons at each level, giving social support to one another, may freely communicate between themselves but fail to communicate upward or downward. Horizontal communication is also intimately involved with organizational conflict. When one member of a given level of an organization, e.g., a functional department head, isolates himself or herself and does not coordinate his or her efforts with the others on that level, dysfunctional conflict may develop.

UPWARD SYSTEM   The classical organization structure formally provides for vertical communication flows, downward *and* upward. However, in practice, except for feedback controls, the downward system has completely dominated the upward system of communication. Whereas the downward system is highly directive—giving orders, instructions, and procedures—the upward system is nondirective. In other words, the downward system of communication is more compatible with an authoritarian type of leadership climate, and the upward system is more compatible with the participative, democratic leadership climate discussed in the first part of the chapter. Traditionally, the authoritative styles have prevailed over the more participative styles, resulting in upward communication being outwardly stifled, badly misused, and conveniently ignored. To improve upward communication, grievance procedures, open-door policies, counseling, attitude questionnaires, exit interviews, participative decision techniques, and even an ombudsman may be used. The latter technique originated in Scandinavia to provide an outlet for persons who have been treated unfairly or in a depersonalized manner by large, bureaucratic government. The ombudsman has more recently gained popularity in American state governments, military posts, and universities. Although it is just being introduced in a few business organizations, if set up and handled properly, it may work where the open-door policy has failed to provide upward communication.

The purpose of the upward system of communication is to provide personal information about ideas, attitudes, and performance and feedback information about performance that is vital for the control of the organization. Personal information is generated from subordinate to superior from the bottom to the top of the organization. The other type of upward communication directly concerned with organizational performance in the form of feedback control is given attention in the next chapter on the control process.

Summary

This chapter has given an overview of the directing and communication processes of management. Directing is closely related to leadership, which has been given a great deal of attention through the years. However, despite the attention, few practical guidelines for more effective directing of employees in organizations have evolved. Although there are many traits that successful leaders seem to possess, with the possible exception of intelligence, they do not hold up with any consistency when put to the test of research. Intelligence, social maturity and breadth, inner motivation and achievement drives, and human relations attitudes are as good a list of successful leadership traits as any. Much of the same problem of identifying traits has been experienced in determining effective leadership styles. The pioneering Lippitt and White studies analyzed autocratic, democratic, and laissez faire styles, but the results have questionable generalizability to modern management. The Michigan studies under Rensis Likert were able to identify four systems of leadership called exploitive autocratic, benevolent autocratic, consultative, and democratic. Likert infers that system 4 (democratic) leadership climates are more effective than system 1 (exploitive autocratic) climates. He and others supporting a subordinate-centered style (democratic, employee-centered, general, system 4) have some evidence to back them up, but the whole area of leadership in general and the directing process of management in particular is turning toward a contingency approach, which is covered in Chapter 8.

The last half of the chapter was devoted to the communicating process. It is closely connected to directing but was felt to deserve specific attention. Interpersonal communication has two major dimensions—perception and language. Perception is a very complex psychological process that involves selecting (through principles of intensity, size, contrast, and repetition) and organizing (through principles of figure-ground, grouping, and context) incoming stimuli into a meaningful whole for the person. The difficulties of this complicated process are compounded when the interaction with language is used to transmit meaning in the interpersonal communication process. Many different languages are used in communicating meaning. English is obvious, but facial expressions, also a language, are not so obvious. The infinity of the meanings of words, the problem of abstraction, and the many dimensions of the important area of nonverbal language perhaps cause the most problems for effective interpersonal communication. Organizational communication flows downward (is the most extensive, promotes an authoritative climate); horizontal (required for coordinated goal attainment; except in some of the newer organization structures, is largely accomplished by informal organization and committees with good and bad results); and upward (is badly lacking, promotes a more democratic climate). As with the other management processes, directing and communicating are moving toward a contingency-based approach.

☐ Critical Incident

You have been hired for a summer job in the biggest factory in town. The department you have been assigned to assembles small engine parts. Since no one else talks to the supervisor and he seems like a pretty good guy, you have been taking your coffee break with him. During a conversation one day you ask the supervisor why the rest of the workers are so unfriendly toward him. The supervisor says, "Well I guess it is my style of supervision. I believe the best way to both lead and communicate with my workers is to call them in once a month and lay it on the line with them. I tell them in no uncertain terms who is messing up and what will happen to them if they don't shape up. I find they don't like me very much but the job gets done with this approach. You haven't attended one of these monthly sessions yet but you are studying management in college. What do you think?"

1 What would you tell the supervisor?
2 What style of leadership is this supervisor using? What about his method of communicating? How do his workers perceive him? What suggestions do you have to improve communication in this situation?

Questions for Review and Discussion

1 What are the traits of a good leader? Analyze these traits as to their contribution to the directing process of management.
2 Summarize Likert's four systems of management or leadership style. Compare and contrast system 1 with system 4.
3 In the perceptual aspects of communication, what are the major dimensions of selectivity? What are the major dimensions of perceptual organization? What are the major dimensions of perceptual grouping?
4 Analyze the impact that infinity of meanings, abstraction, and nonverbal language has on interpersonal communication.
5 Generally summarize and critically analyze the three major systems of organizational communication.

References

Athanasslades, John C.: "The Distortion of Upward Communication in Hierarchical Organizations," *Academy of Management Journal*, June 1973, pp. 207-226.
Berlo, David K.: *The Process of Communication*, Holt, New York, 1960.
Boyd, Bradford B., and J. Michael Jensen: "Perceptions of the First-Line Supervisor's Authority: A Study in Superior-Subordinate Communication," *Academy of Management Journal*, September 1972, pp. 331-342.
Brenner, Marshall H., and Norman B. Sigband: "Organizational Communication—An Analysis Based on Empirical Data," *Academy of Management Journal*, June 1973, pp. 323-339.
Bromage, Mary C.: "The Management of Communications," *S.A.M. Advanced Management Journal*, April 1973, pp. 42-46.
Davis, Keith: *Human Behavior at Work*, 4th ed., McGraw-Hill, New York, 1972.

Fiedler, Fred E., and Martin M. Chemers: *Leadership and Effective Management,* Scott, Foresman, Glenview, Ill., 1974.

George, Norman, and Thomas J. Von Der Embose: "Six Propositions for Managerial Leadership: Diagnostic Tools for Definition and Focus," *Business Horizons,* December 1971, pp. 33–43.

Graen, George, Fred Dansereau, and Takao Minami: "Dysfunctional Leadership Styles," *Organizational Behavior and Human Performance,* April 1972, pp. 216–236.

Greiner, Larry E.: "What Managers Think of Participative Leadership," *Harvard Business Review,* March–April 1973, pp. 111–117.

Grikscheit, Gary M., and William J. E. Crissy: "Improving Interpersonal Communications Skill," *MSU Business Topics,* Autumn 1973, pp. 63–68.

Hall, Edward T.: *The Silent Language,* Fawcett, Greenwich, Conn., 1959.

Hall, Jay: "Communication Revisited," *California Management Review,* Spring 1973, pp. 56–67.

Haney, William V.: *Communication and Organizational Behavior,* 3d ed., Irwin, Homewood, Ill., 1973.

Harriman, Bruce: "Up and Down the Communications Ladder," *Harvard Business Review,* September–October 1974, pp. 143–151.

Hicks, Herbert G.: *The Management of Organizations,* 2d ed., McGraw-Hill, New York, 1972.

Hollander, E. P.: *Leaders, Groups, and Influence,* Oxford University Press, New York, 1964.

House, Robert J.: "A Path Goal Theory of Leader Effectiveness," *Administrative Science Quarterly,* September 1971, pp. 321–338.

Jacobs, T. O.: *Leadership and Exchange in Formal Organizations,* Human Resources Research Organization, Alexandria, Va., 1971.

Katz, Robert L.: "Skills of an Effective Administrator," *Harvard Business Review,* September–October 1974, pp. 90–102.

Likert, Rensis: *The Human Organization,* McGraw-Hill, New York, 1967.

Negandhi, Anant R., and Bernard C. Reimann: "Correlates of Decentralization: Closed and Open Systems Perspectives," *Academy of Management Journal,* December 1973, pp 570–582

Owens, James: "The Uses of Leadership Theory," *Michigan Business Review,* January 1973, pp. 13–19.

Roberts, Karlene H., and Charles A. O'Reilly, III: "Failures in Upward Communication in Organizations: Three Possible Culprits," *Academy of Management Journal,* June 1974, pp. 205–215.

Tannenbaum, Robert, and Warren H. Schmidt: "How to Choose a Leadership Pattern," *Harvard Business Review,* May–June 1973, pp. 162–180.

Yukul, Gary: "Toward a Behavioral Theory of Leadership," *Organizational Behavior and Human Performance,* July 1971, pp. 414–440.

Zalkind, Sheldon S., and Timothy W. Costello: "Perception: Some Recent Research and Implications for Administration," *Administrative Science Quarterly,* September 1962, pp. 218–235.

The Controlling Process

Control is the last of the process variables that are discussed in this part of the book. Although presented last, control is by no means the least important management process. Once plans are made, the organization designed, directing takes over, and communication begins to flow, then the process of control becomes important. Basically, control is the process which eliminates chaos and provides consistency in an organization in order for goals to be attained. It is absolutely essential to effective management.

The first half of the chapter is concerned with the overall nature of the control process. Specific attention is given to both feedforward and feedback control, the three basic elements of the control process (standards, measures, and corrective action), and answering the question, "Controlling for what?" The last half of the chapter examines specific control techniques. Included are various traditional resource (personnel, material, and money) techniques and newer human resource accounting, planning-programming-budgeting system (PPBS), cost/benefit analysis, network analysis, management by exception, and management by objective techniques.

The Nature of the Control Process

There is a great deal of misunderstanding about the control process. Part of the problem stems from the negative connotation control has in modern society. Control is thought to be the opposite of freedom, and in a democratic society freedom is good and control is bad. Yet everyone's daily life is highly controlled. A person's life is controlled both inside and outside the organization which employs him or her. Outside, the person has to follow the formal rules and informal cultural norms. Inside the organization, the individual also has many rules and norms to follow—where to park, when to punch the time clock or report to the office, safety regulations, codes of dress, and the proper output are just a few examples. In addition, there is the controlling atmosphere inherent in roles such as father or son on the outside and superior or subordinate on the inside.

From the perspective of a management process, the purpose of control is to keep the organization operating within the framework of standards set by the environment, both outside and inside. Control can be simply defined as making sure that performance is going as it should. Control is essential to organizational goal attainment. Koontz and O'Donnell outline four specific principles of control:

1 *Principle of Assurance of Objective* The task of control is to detect potential or actual deviation from plans early enough to permit effective corrective action.

2 *Principle of Efficiency of Controls* Control techniques and approaches are efficient when they detect and illuminate the causes of actual or potential deviations from plans with a minimum of costs or other unsought consequences.

3 *Principle of Control Responsibility* The primary responsibility for the exercise of control rests in the manager charged with the execution of plans.

4 *Principle of Direct Control* The higher the quality of managers and their subordinates, the less will be the need for indirect controls.[1]

These four principles summarize the different dimensions of control.

Ordinarily, control is associated with the overall organization or a specific product or service. Traditionally, performance of the organization or the product or service has been controlled after the fact. The feedback had to sense some error or deviation from desired performance before the control process could initiate corrective action. To get around having only "after the fact" control, the concept of feedforward control has been suggested.[2] Critical inputs as well as output variables are controlled. Figure 7-1 shows this new dual form of control.

Feedforward Control

Evaluating input variables or feedforward control may be accomplished in several ways. In the simplest sense, feedforward follows the simple adage that an organization is no stronger than its weakest link. Anyone who has operated a large piece of equipment knows that if the machine is not functioning properly, the operator will look for certain critical components or strategic factors to see if they are failing. In a similar manner, this logic applies to feedforward control. It is necessary to determine and monitor the critical inputs into any operating system. However, the actual techniques that are used to control these critical points vary from organization to organization. Some examples of feedforward control techniques are preventive maintenance programs, all types of policies, and input checklists. Preventive maintenance is employed to prevent a breakdown in machinery. This maintenance is usually applied to those critical components (such as vital parts that must be greased) which the operator and the maintenance personnel feel will cause the machine to fail. Also, policies are formulated to prevent critical problems from occurring. For example, a policy on absenteeism may be given to a new employee to help prevent potential problems. Last, input checklists can be used for feedforward. For example, a mobile home dealer developed a checklist for all service workers which was kept in

---

[1] Harold Koontz and Cyril O'Donnell, *Essentials of Management,* McGraw-Hill, New York, 1974, p. 414.

[2] Harold Koontz and Robert W. Bradspies, "Managing through Feedforward Control," *Business Horizons,* June 1972, pp. 25–36.

Figure 7-1 Dual Control Model.

the servicing vehicle. After a mobile home was set up, the service worker would use the checklist to check critical points in the home which typically caused problems. This procedure prevented a considerable amount of future customer dissatisfaction.

Feedforward is currently being used successfully in a variety of industries. Koontz and Bradspies report: "Feedforward has had wide application in the chemical and petroleum processing industries. It has been found particularly valuable where constant temperatures of material flow, exact mixtures, and various forms of chemical reactions require the precision that ordinary feedback, with its normal cycling, cannot achieve."[3] In summary, Koontz and Bradspies offer some practical guidelines for applying the feedforward control process:

1 Thorough planning and analysis is required.
2 Careful discrimination must be applied in selecting input variables.
3 The feedforward system must be kept dynamic.
4 A model of the control system should be developed.
5 Data on input variables must be regularly collected.
6 Data on input variables must be regularly assessed.
7 Feedforward control requires action.[4]

Feedback Control
Even though feedback is "after the fact," it is still vital to the control process. Many times input variables are unmeasureable (e.g., the values an employee brings to the job) or are not detected at the feedforward control point. There is always a need for effective feedback control.

Most existing control systems are aimed at output variables. Management often waits until a crisis occurs before taking corrective action. Essentially, in output control the actual performance should be constantly measured against expected performance to determine the necessity of corrective action. This process brings out three essential elements of any control process whether it is feedforward or feedback: (1) setting standards for performance, (2) measuring and comparing performance with the standards, and (3) taking remedial or corrective action.

[3] Ibid., p. 29.
[4] Ibid., pp. 35–36.

Standards for Control

The first step in control is closely linked with and is an integral part of the planning process. The standard, defined as a low-level type of plan, becomes the criterion by which performance is measured in the control process. There are several ways in which standards are determined. They generally reflect the planning goals of an organization and its internal subunits. These standards may be tangible and easily quantified or intangible and very difficult to quantify.

QUANTITATIVE STANDARDS   Standards dealing with physical units, cost, revenues, and capital considerations are generally easy to quantify. Numbers can be attached to physical standards, and dollars can be attached to costs, revenues, and capital investments. In particular, quantitative standards may be set in several ways. One way is to use statistical methods, such as sampling, for determining standards. For example, in quality control, attribute, variable, and/or acceptance sampling is used for setting standards. In attribute and variable sampling, charts (means, ranges, and percentage of defects) are developed with upper and lower control standards. These standards are used for evaluating performance in control. Acceptance sampling determines the number of defects (through an operating characteristic curve) that will be accepted (in a sample) before a lot is rejected. The number of allowable defects in a sample is the standard for comparing performance. In all three sampling cases, the standards depend on the size of the sample and the quality desired for the marketplace demands and the social responsibility management has toward the consumer. With the consumerism movement gaining momentum, modern management is becoming more keenly concerned with its responsibility for quality control.

Besides statistical methods, standards may also be determined from past experience. In most instances, the demand for physical units and cost and revenue figures from past records are used for setting control standards. Finally, standards are also based on industrial or association or similar organization's figures and statistics. For example, industrial figures may show that an automobile dealer needs to average $200 profit for each car sold in order to remain solvent. This standard can be used as an operating guideline by a dealer.

QUALITATIVE STANDARDS   Organizational image is an example of a variable which is difficult to set a standard for and control. Yet, it is these qualitative things which are becoming increasingly important to the success of the modern organization. The following list suggests some ways that the qualitative aspects of an organization may be more effectively controlled:

1 Participative budgeting, in which superiors and subordinates jointly determine targets that will be acceptable to both;
2 Diagnostic rather than purely evaluative or punitive responses by superiors when standards are not met;
3 Executive-performance appraisal programs in which goals are set for each key subordinate on an individual basis, performance is measured against this standard, and a coaching rather than directive role is assumed by the superior;

4 A distribution pattern for control reports in which special emphasis is given to supplying information to the people on the firing line, i.e., to lower-level operating people who use reports to take corrective action rather than to direct and evaluate others;

5 Measurement of employee attitudes by means of such crude indicators as turnover, tardiness, and absenteeism.[5]

Another example of setting qualitative standards can be derived from the expectancy theory of motivation. This theory is given detailed attention in Chapter 13. However, for present purposes, it may be simply said that expectations may be used as a standard for controlling both physical goods and people. In regard to physical goods, Drucker made the following relevant comments for qualitative control: "By comparing the actual course of events against expectations, we can identify in particular two major problem areas: the degenerative disease of the investment in managerial ego and the missed opportunity of the sleeper. Holding performance against expectations is also the best way to find the unjustified specialty."[6] Drucker believed that controlling expectations would lead to successful goal attainment. In regard to the qualitative control of people, Porter and Lawler state: "We assume that managers operate on the basis of some sort of expectancies which, although based upon previous experience, are forward-oriented in a way that does not seem to be as easily handled by the concept of habit strength."[7] Therefore, qualitative standards may often be set by the expectations of a manager for comparing the performance of subordinates. However, Porter and Lawler warn that there may be danger in depending too heavily on expectancy for setting standards because of the vagueness relative to previous learning experiences that produce different expectancies and this approach often does not specify how outcomes require positive or negative qualities for the individuals being controlled.[8] Some of the newer techniques discussed in the latter part of the chapter help in controlling qualitative factors.

Measuring for Control

Management may guess or have a "feeling" that standards are being met or it can objectively measure performance and compare it with standards. Obviously, the latter approach leads to more effective control. In some activities precise measures can be taken, while in others it is virtually impossible to come up with any measurement at all. In any event, to improve the effectiveness of measuring for control, the following guidelines are suggested:

1 Measurements supplant judgment. There is the need not only to measure but also to evaluate what has been measured.

2 Distribute the measurements reasonably among the various key activities. Refrain from having all measurements at the same organization level.

---

[5] Edmund P. Learned and Audrey T. Sproat, *Organization Theory and Policy,* Irwin, Homewood, Ill., 1966, p. 85.

[6] Peter F. Drucker, *Managing for Results,* Harper & Row, New York, 1964, p. 65.

[7] Lyman W. Porter and Edward E. Lawler, III, *Managerial Attitudes and Performance,* Irwin-Dorsey, Homewood, Ill., 1968, pp. 12–13.

[8] Ibid., p. 13.

3 Select measurements to appraise both current and future activities.

4 Measurements applying to a group, as illustrated by an organization unit, can be effective. The unit need not necessarily be an individual employee.[9]

There are many different ways to measure performance. The most common measures are derived from personal observation, statistical data, oral reports, written reports, and accounting information.

PERSONAL OBSERVATION   The simplest, and thus widely used, method for measuring performance is to merely observe whether performance is going according to the standard. It is very easy for a manager to merely observe whether things are going as planned. Although observation can be used effectively, it often is not. The limitations can be summarized as follows:

1 The problems of perception are inherent in this method; e.g., observers see only what they want to see.

2 It is difficult to attach meaningful quantitative values to observations.

3 The observer may be perceived by the person being observed as spying and "breathing down my neck."

4 It is difficult for the observer to put all the bits and pieces together into a meaningful evaluation of overall performance.

5 Left to the observer, standards tend to be very subjective and change frequently.

Despite these limitations, personal observation has and will continue to play an important measurement role in the control process.

STATISTICAL DATA   Statistical data may be used to measure trends, sales, and other types of organizational conditions. Statistical data may be generated to measure the internal performance of the organization. For example, sampling may be used to gather data for measuring the performance of an operating unit. Sampling may be beneficial since it is less costly to inspect only a portion of the goods produced than to have 100 percent inspection, and at least in the case of physical goods, less damage is inflicted by sampling. Such statistical data are not perfect, but they add a dimension of objectivity to measuring performance.

ORAL REPORTS   Oral reports are generally parallel to the personal observation method of measuring performance. This method generally has the same limitations as the observation method. However, unlike the observation method, oral reports can be used when the performance being measured is physically removed from the rest of the organization. For example, salespersons for an equipment manufacturer who did business over a large region had to report each evening by telephone to their superior. They had to orally

[9] George R. Terry, *Principles of Management,* 5th ed., Irwin, Homewood, Ill., 1968, p. 549.

report the number of sales and contacts made during the day. This method of measurement provided faster feedback for control than other means. Corrective action could then be taken immediately; otherwise, a delayed response might have been extremely costly for the organization.

WRITTEN REPORTS   Written reports of all types are widely used for measuring performance in the control process. However, there has been an avalanche of paper in most modern organizations; there is an overuse of written reports. Many managers are so plagued with written reports that they are seldom read and are filed in the wastebasket. Two factors can guide the use of a written report—purpose and timeliness of the information. Written reports can be useful as long as they fulfill a particular purpose and do not become an end in themselves. If a particular report has outlived its purpose, it should be discarded. The criterion of "We have always had this report" should not be justification for continuing its use. Second, information in a written report should be timely and accurate. If information does not pertain to the current situation or is of questionable validity, the report should be done away with.

Drucker cites three common misuses of reports (both oral and written):

1 The first is the all too common belief that procedures are instruments of morality.
2 The second misuse is to consider procedures a substitute for judgement.
3 But the most common misuse of reports and procedures is as an instrument of control from above. [10]

As suggested in Chapter 5, every form or report should be placed on trial for its life at least every 5 years instead of being allowed to continue indefinitely. Most managers would be surprised at the high number of reports that would be condemned if put to this test.

ACCOUNTING INFORMATION   The accounting process has traditionally been used to measure the financial performance of an organization. Common measuring instruments used by accounting are the balance sheet, income statement, and funds flow statement. The balance sheet measures the assets, liabilities, and net worth of a firm at a particular point in time. The income statement reports income, expenses, and resulting profits or losses for a given time period. The funds flow statement shows the inflows and outflows of a company's working capital and cash. Management can use these three financial statements to measure the overall performance of the organization.

Besides the traditional accounting information, there is a newer emphasis on generating information for managerial decision making. This managerial accounting approach is geared more toward helping individual managers control their areas of responsibility. It is internal as opposed to externally oriented information and is closely associated with the management information system, which is the subject of Chapter 18.

[10] Peter F. Drucker, *The Practice of Management,* Harper, New York, 1954, pp. 133–134.

Corrective Action for Control

The third and last element in the control process is to compare the measured performance with the set standards in order to take corrective action or make a control decision. The obvious decision would be to tighten up where a large deviation exists between standard and performance. "Tightening up" implies that some corrective action, usually punitive in nature, is taken. Although this is the type of decision that is usually made, it may not be the best for effective control. Instead, an analysis of the comparison between standards and measured performance by operations factors such as quantity, quality, time use, and cost, which are discussed in the next section, and a diagnosis of the cause for any serious deviations or nondeviations should be conducted by management. Figure 7-2 gives examples of the kinds of questions that could be asked in making the analysis and diagnosis. Such an approach in this vital step would lead to more effective overall control for goal attainment.

Controlling for What?

The control process applies to specific areas or organizational units. However, the discussion so far has not indicated what is being controlled. Each function of an organization has critical areas that need to be controlled. For example, in the marketing function of a business organization, sales volume and expenses, credit, and advertising must be controlled. In the financial and accounting areas, costs, capital expenditures, flow of cash and capital, and liquidity must be controlled; and in the personnel area, labor costs, turnover, absenteeism, tardiness, and safety are controlled. This is certainly not an exhaustive list but gives some idea of what is controlled. At the heart of the control process, however, is the operations function of an organization. Quantity, quality, time use, and cost are vital areas of the operations function that must be effectively controlled. One, a combination, or all of these specific areas for operations control generally apply to the other functions of an organization as well.

Figure 7-2 Control Analysis and Diagnosis

1 Be aware of the employee's needs and social pressures. Controls have a motivating effect in that they answer the employee's questions of "What is expected of me?" and "What does it take to satisfy the manager's work demands?"

2 Develop mutual interest in achieving the objectives. Control efforts are greatly assisted when each member of an enterprise knows the major objectives which are being sought and is thoroughly familiar with the immediate goals of his or her work unit, section, or department—goals which are a reflection and integral part of the overall major objectives of the enterprise.

3 Explain control measurements used—freely supply information about them. The selection and use of measurements in controlling emphasize the need for complete understanding of them by both management and nonmanagement members.

4 Make needed changes automatic. Controlling should take into account specific local factors; that is, some flexibility is necessary, but not to the degree that every gripe results in a change or that sound management practice is evaded.

Adapted from George R. Terry, *Principles of Management,* 5th ed., Irwin, Homewood, Ill., 1968, pp. 559–560.

QUANTITY   Quantity control is usually associated with the amount or the demand for products being sold. For example, in controlling the quantity of sales, the following should be considered:

1 The sales control unit, such as a geographical area to which sales can be identified.
2 The sales potential for this unit. Sales control requires an acceptable sales level or par which sets up the objective of the selling activities.
3 The characteristics of the sales outlet being employed for the distribution of the product or service. Not all outlets are identical in makeup; they differ in regard to size, type of ownership, management methods of purchasing, and, in the case of industrial goods, the use for which products are bought.[11]

Besides sales control, the quantity dimension is important to personnel, inventories, and other inputs. For example, an interviewer may bring in a larger quantity of prospective employees than the firm has jobs available. The control system would set up mechanisms to hire only the best personnel that are needed from the large quantity of applicants. When applied to inventories, the quantity of goods which minimizes costs, both carrying and ordering costs, would be controlled. A quantitative model called the economic order quantity, which is discussed in detail in Chapter 10, could assist in quantity control of inventories.

QUALITY   Quality control, or QC, is generally associated with raw materials that are being either purchased or produced by a firm but can also apply to the quality of any other dimension of organizational performance. Quality control can be broken down into the basic functions of:

1 Meeting customer specifications.
2 Providing interchangeability and fit of parts for manufacture.
3 Meeting legal conditions of contract, warranty, or liability.
4 Maintaining organizational morale and discipline.
5 Reducing the costs of rework and scrap and reducing unnecessary addition of value to rejects.
6 Monitoring the production process for changes.
7 Linking responsibility for errors to specific employees, machines, etc.
8 Providing checks on quantity produced in order to reveal location of waste and spoilage.[12]

These examples of quality control apply to both physical and nonphysical goods and services of an organization.

TIME USE   Time use control is extremely critical to organizational performance. Time use control is most often associated with work scheduling and has depended on tech-

---

[11] Terry, op. cit., pp. 587–593.

[12] Richard I. Levin, Curtis P. McLaughlin, Rudolph P. Lamone, and John F. Kottas, *Production/Operations Management: Contemporary Policy for Managing Operating Systems,* McGraw-Hill, New York, 1972, p. 449.

niques such as network analysis, line of balance, and Gantt charts. However, time use control can and should be applied to the daily conduct of a manager's job. Studies and simple observation have shown that most managers use their time very inefficiently. They spend far too much of their time dealing with minutiae and not enough time in planning, organizing, directing, communicating, and controlling. Managers have to learn how to control their time as much as they control for the quantity, quality, and cost of their physical goods and services.

COST Cost control is generally used to specify where dollars are being expended. Costs can normally be broken down into direct and indirect expenses. Direct costs commonly include labor, material, and sometimes selling expenditures. These direct costs refer to costs that can be specifically identified with a product or that vary closely with the number of products being produced. The two main factors to consider for direct costs are (1) quantity expended (labor or material) and (2) the price per unit of quantity. Indirect costs are usually associated with overhead expenses. They usually include all costs other than direct expenditures. Some of the overhead expenditures are impossible to trace directly to products. Therefore, it becomes necessary to develop one of several methods for allocating these costs for control purposes. Examples of these allocation methods are direct labor hours and direct labor costs. Breakeven analysis incorporates these cost control factors and is examined in detail in Chapter 9.

Control Techniques

Practically all management processes and specific techniques are directly or indirectly concerned with control. Planning sets the standards, organizing provides the framework, and directing and communicating gives life to the control process. As a result, there could be an almost infinite list of control techniques. This section will limit itself to the traditional techniques of controlling the resources of personnel, materials, and money and a sampling of the more modern techniques of human resource accounting, PPBS, cost/benefit analysis, network analysis, management by exception, and management by objectives.

Resource Control Techniques

There are many techniques which are used for controlling the three resources of personnel, material, and money. Two techniques, which are particularly relevant for all three resources and precede the implementation of specific control techniques, are plans and forecasts. These were given detailed attention in Chapter 4. Objectives, policies, rules, procedures, methods, etc., are usually labeled plans but are almost impossible to separate from control. For example, objectives are obviously an inseparable part of management by objectives and programmed budgeting. Objectives are used as standards for comparing performance in the control process. In addition, objectives are important for input and output control of quantity, quality, time use, and cost of goods and services.

Another type of plan which is vital to control is a policy. Policies are developed for controlling personnel, materials, and money. For example, a policy for absenteeism was mentioned earlier for controlling employee performance. Closely related to planning is forecasting, which is used to determine the amount of materials, the number of workers, and the amount of money necessary for maintaining the proper level of efficiency and goal attainment. Forecasts force and assist management to plan and simultaneously to control. Forecasting is particularly relevant for input or feedforward control. It tends to focus management's attention on the critical inputs for future operations. For example, cash forecasting is an excellent technique for controlling critical money resources needed. Management is able to determine the period when additional funds will be needed and give adequate time for obtaining funds before a crisis arises.

Besides general plans and forecasting, there are many specific techniques to control personnel, materials, and money. One that has traditionally been used to control personnel is work measurement. These techniques are used to set standards for an employee's output. Performance is compared with the standards in determining whether the employee met, exceeded, or was below standard. Traditionally, these techniques have only been applied to operating employees. In recent years, output standards are being developed for managers and professional employees as well. A second control technique for personnel is performance evaluation. Several approaches have been used to measure and compare personnel performance with set standards. The oldest and simplest technique is ranking according to an ideal employee or relative to other employees. Since this method did not use well-defined standards, graphical methods were developed, in which traits were used as standards. Variations of these traditional techniques have since been developed, and in recent years appraisal by results is used more frequently. Figure 7-3 summarizes the trends that have occurred in performance appraisal.

Figure 7-3 Trends in Performance Appraisal

Item	Former Emphasis	Present Emphasis
Terminology	Merit rating	Employee appraisal Performance appraisal
Purpose	Determine qualification for wage increase, transfer, promotion, layoff	Development of the individual; improved performance on the job
Application	For hourly paid workers	For technical, professional, and managerial employees
Factors rated	Heavy emphasis upon personal traits	Results, accomplishments, performance
Techniques	Rating scales with emphasis upon scores; statistical manipulation of data for comparison purposes	Management by objectives, mutual goal setting, critical incidents, group appraisal, performance standards, less quantitative
Postappraisal interview	Supervisor communicates rating to employee and tries to sell own evaluation; seeks to have employee conform to supervisor's views	Supervisor stimulates employee to analyze self and set own objectives in line with job requirements; supervisor is helper and counselor

Source: Dale S. Beach, *Personnel,* 3d ed., Macmillan, New York, 1975, p. 336. Used with permission.

Materials resource control is closely tied to the operations function of an organization. In particular, techniques for inventory, quality, and scheduling are considered. For inventory control, the economic order quantity and periodic ordering systems can be used. In quality control, as mentioned earlier, various charts (means, range, and percentage of defects) are employed. Scheduling techniques to control materials include the Gantt chart and newer network models. Figure 7-4 gives an example of a common Gantt chart (see also the discussion in Chapter 4) and the network models are given detailed attention in Chapter 17.

Controlling the money resource is a constant concern of modern management. Several traditional techniques are used for controlling this resource, but budgets are the most common. Budgets control financial resources but can also be applied to personnel and materials. Budgeting, for money, may include revenue, cost, and cash budgets and involves three basic steps: (1) expressing in dollars the results of plans anticipated in a future period, (2) coordinating these dollar estimates into a well-balanced program, and (3) comparing actual performance with the estimated balanced program.[13] This approach to budgeting is analogous with the three basic elements of the entire control process. The first step of budgeting assists in setting the desired standards for performance; the second step emphasizes that coordination between the various control units is needed to ensure attainment of the objectives and goals of the organization; and the third step assists in evaluating performance via appraisal by results. Financial budgeting offers many unique advantages as a method of control but also has been abused and misused. The budget often becomes a straitjacket for human behavior and allows no room for initiative, flexibility, or freedom. From a classic research study conducted by Chris Argyris it is concluded that there were at least four human problems resulting from budgets:

1 Budget pressure tends to unite the employees against management, and tends to place the factory supervisor under tension. This tension may lead to inefficiency, aggression, and perhaps a complete breakdown on the part of the supervisor.
2 The finance staff can obtain feelings of success only by finding fault with factory people. These feelings of failure among factory supervisors lead to many human relations problems.
3 The use of budgets as "needlers" by top management tends to make each factory supervisor see only the problem of his own department.
4 Supervisors use budgets as a way of expressing their own patterns of leadership. When this results in people getting hurt, the budget, in itself a neutral thing, often gets blamed.[14]

To counter these types of problems with budgets, Koontz and O'Donnell suggest that:

1 Budget making and administration receive top management support.
2 All managers who are expected to administer and live under budgets have a part in their preparation.
3 Budgets not be overdone to the extent of seriously compromising the authority of managers.

---

[13] William H. Newman, Charles E. Summer, and E. Kirby Warren, *The Process of Management,* 3d ed., Prentice-Hall, Englewood Cliffs, N.J., 1972, pp. 602–603.
[14] Chris Argyris, "Human Problems with Budgets," *Harvard Business Review,* January–February 1953, p. 108.

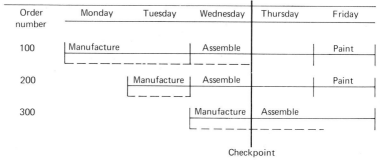

Figure 7-4 A Gantt Chart for Orders. *Source:* Richard J. Hopeman, *Production,* 2d ed., Charles E. Merrill Publishing Company, Columbus, Ohio, 1971, p. 384. Used with permission.

4 Standards be developed and made available by which work can be translated into needs for worker power, operating expenses, capital expenditures, space, and other resources.

5 Managers are provided ready information as to actual and forecast performance under budgets by their departments. [15]

Other techniques besides budgets are used to control money. For example, breakeven analysis and present-value techniques, discussed in Chapter 9, are used to control financial resources. Ratio analysis is another widely used control technique. It uses various relationships such as comparing current assets with current liabilities (current ratio) to control the financial resources of an organization.

Human Resource Accounting

Although human asset measurement has been recognized by economists for years, only recently have conscious attempts been made to measure the value of human assets through the accounting process. The Committee on Human Resource Accounting of the American Accounting Association has defined human resource accounting (HRA) as the process of identifying and measuring data about human resources and communicating this information to interested parties. [16] HRA formally recognizes the monetary value of human resources to the organization. For example, if a good person leaves the organization, the assets of the organization are reduced by a certain dollar amount. The same holds true for a good person joining the organization: the assets will increase by the value of the new person. Rensis Likert suggests that the following types of variables be consid-

[15] Koontz and O'Donnell, op. cit., pp. 376–377.

[16] American Accounting Association, "Report of the Committee on Human Resource Accounting," *The Accounting Review,* vol. 48, p. 169, supplement, 1973.

ered when calculating the value of human resources: (1) level of intelligence and apti-
tudes, (2) level of training, (3) quality of leadership, and (4) quality of decision making,
communication, and control.[17] The dynamic variable of conflict could have both positive
and negative value in calculating the worth of human assets. "If bickering, distrust, and
irreconcilable conflict become greater, the human enterprise is worth less; if the capacity
to use differences constructively and engage in cooperative teamwork improves, the
human organization is a more valuable asset."[18]

At present, human resource accounting does not have any well-established boundaries.
In attempting to give a framework to HRA, the American Accounting Association has
outlined three major objectives:

1 *Measurement*　To develop valid and reliable models and methods for measuring the cost and
value of people to organizations (including both monetary and non-monetary measurements),
2 *Applications*　To design operational systems to apply (implement) these measurement methods in
actual organizations, and
3 *Cognitive and Behavioral Impact*　To determine the behavioral impact of the human resource
accounting measurements and frameworks on human attitudes and behavior (decisions and performance).[19]

Human resource accounting is basically concerned with the measurement aspect of the
control process. Major attention is given to the measurement and quantification of human
assets of an organization. For example, work has been done in using acquisition costs,
replacement costs, opportunity costs, and discounting methods for measuring the value
of human assets. Once a suitable method is determined, and found to be practically
applicable, standards may be established for comparing performance. Then, human asset accounting can get away from being something that is only talked about and become
a useful part of the control process. The success of this approach will greatly depend on
identifying many of the nonmonetary variables as well as the monetary variables in determining the real value of human assets. To date, much work remains to be done in this
effort.

PPBS

Program budgeting, or more specifically, planning-programming-budgeting systems
(PPBS), is relatively new but is becoming more widely used as a control technique. It has
been primarily used and developed in the Department of Defense (DOD) and is discussed
in more detail in Chapter 17. As indicated earlier, traditional vertical, line budgeting techniques have often proved to be inadequate, misleading, and misused. In many cases,
budgets have been inflated and used as a means of getting as much money as possible.
The budget became an end in itself. PPBS tries to change this but is really nothing more
than what traditional budgeting should ideally be.

---

[17] Rensis Likert, *The Human Organization*, McGraw-Hill, New York, 1967, p. 148.
[18] Ibid., p. 149.
[19] American Accounting Association, op. cit., p. 170.

PPBS combines program budgeting with systems analysis. A program is simply a results-oriented plan for the future. A program budget is a financial expression of a future plan. It is not necessarily limited to a specific time period such as a fiscal year. Although in theory there is no direct link between PPBS and systems analysis, "In practice, the basic ideas of systems analysis and the approaches which lead to successful planning, programming, and budgeting are the same."[20] Thus, at least in practice, PPBS turns out to be a systems approach to programmed budgeting. Systems variables are given specific attention in Part Five of the book.

Prior to PPBS, the standard control approach in the Department of Defense was to call for annual budgets from the various departments and agencies. However, with increasingly large and complex space and weapons systems, many agencies were involved and multiyear life-cycle expenditures were required. The result was multiyear budgets for whole space and weapon systems in place of the short-term organizationally fragmented budgets. Under PPBS, plans and budgets are oriented toward long-term missions, ends, objectives, or programs (more or less synonymous terms) as opposed to functions like personnel, engineering, and logistics. In 1961 DOD adopted a programming system to facilitate a PPBS approach to planning and control. The major programs were strategic retaliatory forces, continental air and missile defense forces, general-purpose forces (most of the army and navy), airlift and sealift forces, reserve and national guard forces, research and development, general support, retirement pay, civil defense, and military assistance. However, DOD did *not* realign its organization structure to correspond with these programs. To do so would have meant breaking up the Army, Navy, and Air Force. Staying with the old structure means that tradition is maintained but PPBS is less likely to be fully effective.

Although PPBS is most closely associated with DOD, it has also been adapted to state and local governments. Most governmental operations have long-term programs, for example in education, recreation, health, housing, and transportation, which are adaptable to PPBS. Chapter 17 gives detailed explanations of these PPBS applications.

Cost/Benefit Analysis
In recent years, cost/benefit studies have become an increasingly important control technique, especially with governmental agencies and private industry concerned with water resources, highways, and defense. For example, to gain the necessary approvals to build refineries, mills, strip mines, or nuclear power plants, the firm and appropriate regulatory governmental agencies must prepare environmental impact statements. These reports must often be backed up by cost/benefit analyses in which subjective factors are assigned numerical values. To proceed with a project, the benefit/cost ratio should be greater than 1. In other words, the benefits must be greater than the costs.

---

[20] David I. Cleland and William R. King, *Systems Analysis and Project Management,* McGraw-Hill, New York, 1968, p. 114.

Closely related to cost/benefit analysis is cost-effectiveness study. First developed by Rand Corporation, cost effectiveness has been used primarily by the defense sector but has recently been applied to social welfare analysis in education, poverty, health, crime, and transportation. Whereas cost/benefit analysis attempts to determine if a project should or should not be undertaken, cost-effectiveness analysis attempts to determine which is the best way to achieve a given end. In a cost-effectiveness study, alternatives are examined, but, unlike cost/benefit analysis, all factors are not quantified. Instead, subjective factors are considered ordinally; i.e., rank orders of alternatives are determined. With the public's increasing demand for accountability of defense and social spending of federal, state, and local governments, cost/benefit and cost-effectiveness techniques of control are bound to become more important in the future. Cost/benefit and cost/effectiveness are given more detail in Chapter 17.

Network Analysis
Network analysis, which is discussed in detail in Chapter 17, is an extremely important control technique. It may be applied to all types and sizes of organizations and can be used for controlling both time and cost. The two most common techniques are the program evaluation and review technique (PERT) and the critical path method (CPM). Several organizations have developed variations of these techniques for their particular situations. PERT and CPM can be basically differentiated by two factors:

1 PERT is usually used for research and development, whereas CPM is used where experience exists for handling similar endeavors.
2 PERT uses three time estimates—optimistic, pessimistic, and most likely—for calculating the expected time for each activity. CPM uses one time estimate or assumes time is known to be certain for each activity.

Both PERT and CPM provide a diagrammatical portrayal of interrelationships of all activities in a project. More importantly for control, they focus attention on the critical path or those activities critical for completing the project. All other activities in a project depend on those along the critical path. If problems, such as delays, develop, management is able to allocate resources to the proper activities to speed up the project. Also, PERT and CPM can play a vital part in feedforward control. Network analysis focuses attention on the critical inputs (critical path activities) so that corrective action may be taken before a major problem develops.

Management by Exception
To control every aspect of a complex organization would result in controlling nothing. Therefore, management by exception (MBE) is an effective control technique. MBE is really an integral part of many other control techniques. For example, feedforward techniques such as PERT are really focusing attention on the exceptional activities. As organizations continue to grow in size and complexity, management by exception becomes increasingly relevant. By design or default, management by exception becomes a reality

in the modern organization. Computerization and systems design are also compatible with management by exception. A properly designed system will "red flag" exceptions that require attention in the control process.

In applying MBE, the costs for doing something about the exceptions need to be balanced against the benefits. Martin Starr suggests that the following costs should be considered:

1 The cost of a monitor to observe deviations from standards and to report deviations to a controller unit.
2 The cost of channels for communication between the monitor and the process and between the monitor and the controller.
3 The cost of the controller, including its policy data bank and the facilities (including amplifiers) that enable it to modify the system.
4 The cost of matching the capacities and rates of the monitor and the controller to process transactions with minimum delays resulting from the design specifications.
5 The cost of vertification based on the penalties for Type I and Type II errors—namely, a false signal for management intervention and a missed signal or an unidentified situation that requires managerial attention.[21]

These types of costs need to be balanced with the benefits in order to determine the degree to which the control process concentrates on exceptions.

Management by Objectives
Management by objectives (MBO) can be simply defined as the mutual determination of objectives by superior-subordinate pairs for the subordinate's area of responsibility and then appraisal by results. MBO is a technique of control but in the broader sense is a total philosophy of management. As a technique of control, the subordinate proposes his or her objectives, with review by the superior, and then performance is compared with the goals set. The effectiveness of MBO largely depends on clear and rational goals being determined at the top echelons of the organization which then filter down to each department so that subordinates are able to set their own goals. In turn, MBO unifies the organization in an upward direction toward common, overall goals and objectives. Specifically, MBO assists the planning process by forcing managers to plan by developing objectives; it facilitates organizing by relating the units and individuals by objectives rather than just by strict hierarchy; it helps develop leadership through participative goal setting and objective appraisal by results; it stresses upward as well as downward communication; and it emphasizes objective self-control. However, for the present discussion, MBO is discussed from the perspective of the control process per se. Peter Drucker, who first advocated and used the terminology *management by objectives,* made the following overall comments about control:

It means the ability to direct oneself and one's work. It can also mean domination of one person by another. Objectives are the basis of "control" in the first sense; but they must never become the

---

[21] Martin K. Starr, *Management: A Modern Approach,* Harcourt, Brace, Jovanovich, New York, 1971, pp. 453–454.

basis of "control" in the second, for this would defeat their purpose. Indeed, one of the major contributions of management by objectives is that it enables us to substitute management by self-control for management by domination.[22]

Measurement was said to be the second basic element of the control process. In a similar manner, measurement plays a vital role in MBO. Performance is measured and compared with set objectives. As Drucker notes, a manager "must be able to measure his perform-ance and results against the goal. It should indeed be an invariable practice to supply managers with clear and common measurements in all key areas of a business. These measurements need not be rigidly quantitative; nor need they be exact. But they have to be clear, simple and rational."[23] The third element of the control process, corrective action, also applies to MBO. As Drucker stated, "Each manager should have the informa-tion he needs to measure his own performance and should receive it soon enough to make any changes necessary for the desired results."[24] Thus, Drucker's analysis almost equates MBO with the control process itself.

The true test of MBO, like any other technique, is its application, over time, in a practicing organization. Tosi and Carroll put an MBO program to such a test. They evaluated an MBO program approximately 18 months after it was first initiated in a company, and then in a second phase they tried to improve the program. In the first phase, the following problems with MBO were identified:

1 There was generally a lack of awareness of the rationale and value of the MBO approach.
2 There was insufficient mutual goal setting.
3 There was not enough time spent on periodically reviewing performance during the year.
4 There was a feeling that the MBO program was too rigid and formal.
5 There was inadequate knowledge about top management goals.
6 Superiors and subordinates lacked understanding of how to set goals or targets.[25]

In the second phase the researchers launched into an extensive change effort to improve the MBO program. After evaluating this latter phase, the researchers found that MBO had increased feedback, goals had become more clear, and managers were reported to spend more time on MBO. However, they also concluded that MBO was unlikely to change leadership style in general. More of this type of research is needed on MBO and the other control techniques discussed in this chapter.

Summary

Control is a misunderstood concept. It is often thought of as being the opposite of free-dom and therefore bad. In reality, control is a vital part of everyone's life and is extremely

---

[22] Drucker, *The Practice of Management,* p. 131.

[23] Ibid.

[24] Ibid.

[25] Henry Tosi and Stephen J. Carroll, Jr., "Improving Management by Objectives: A Diagnostic Change Program," *California Management Review,* Fall 1973, p. 58.

important to the goal attainment of an organization. It can be simply defined as making sure performance is going according to plan. The feedforward (monitoring critical inputs) aspects of control have generally been overshadowed by feedback (evaluating output variables) aspects. Both are important to effective control. The control process per se is made up of three basic elements: setting standards (both quantitative and qualitative), measuring performance (personal observation, statistical data, oral reports, written reports, and accounting information), and taking corrective action. This process is applied to all functional areas of an organization but is most directly aimed at controlling quantity, quality, time use, and cost.

The last half of the chapter surveyed the various control techniques available to management. The traditional techniques used to control the personnel, material, and money resources of an organization include plans and forecasts, work measurement, performance appraisal, economic order quantity, charts, budgets, and ratios. Newer control techniques include human resource accounting, PPBS, cost benefit analysis, network analysis, management by exception, and management by objectives. The effective application of these latter control techniques may spell the difference between success and failure of an organization in the future.

☐ Critical Incident

During summer vacation the owner of a small construction firm hired a college student as a laborer in the dry-walling operation of a new apartment complex. On the first morning of the job, the new employee was supplied the essential tools for performing the task, given a few brief instructions, and was told to go to work. During the afternoon of the first day, the owner looked over the work of the new employee and expressed a great deal of dissatisfaction. The owner felt the employee was typical of the younger generation. The owner shouted, "You college guys are all alike. You think the world owes you a living. This is crummy work, and you had better shape up or I'm going to 'can' you."

1 Was the boss in this incident utilizing the process of control? What were the standards of performance? What measures of performance were used? What corrective action was taken? What, if anything, would you do differently in this control process?

2 Many control techniques are discussed in this chapter. Could any of them be applied to the dry-walling operation in this incident?

Questions for Review and Discussion

1 What is the difference between feedforward and feedback control? Is feedforward control really needed? Defend your answer.

2 Identify and discuss the three essential elements of any control process.

3 What are the vital areas that must be controlled in the operations function of an organization?

4 What are the traditional techniques of controlling the resources of personnel, materials, and money? Describe and analyze some of the more modern control techniques.

References

Bittel, Lester R.: *Management by Exception,* McGraw-Hill, New York, 1964.

Dunbar, Roger L. M.: ''Budgeting for Control,'' *Administrative Science Quarterly,* March 1971, pp. 88–96.

Emery, James C.: *Organizational Planning and Control Systems,* Macmillan, New York, 1969.

Flamholtz, Eric G.: ''Human Resources Accounting: Measuring Positional Replacement Costs,'' *Human Resource Management,* Spring 1973, pp. 8–16.

Giglioni, Giovanni B., and Arthur G. Bedelan: ''A Conspectus of Management Control Theory: 1900–1972,'' *Academy of Management Journal,* June 1974, pp. 292–305.

Koontz, Harold, and Robert W. Bradsples: ''Managing through Feedforward Control,'' *Business Horizons,* June 1972, pp. 25–36.

Machin, John: ''Measuring the Effectiveness of an Organization's Management Control Systems,'' *Management Decision,* Winter 1973, pp. 260–279.

McMahon, J. Timothy, and G. W. Perritt: ''The Control Structure of Organizations: An Empirical Examination,'' *Academy of Management Journal,* September 1971, pp. 327–340.

Mockler, Robert J.: ''The Corporate Control Job: Breaking the Mold,'' *Business Horizons,* December 1970, pp. 73–77.

Murdick, Robert G.: ''Managerial Control: Concepts and Practice,'' *S.A.M. Advanced Management Journal,* January 1970, pp. 48–52.

Raia, Anthony P.: *Managing by Objectives,* Scott, Foresman, Glenview, Ill., 1974.

Reimnitz, Charles A.: ''Testing a Planning and Control Model in Nonprofit Organizations,'' *Academy of Management Journal,* March 1972, pp. 77–87.

Sayles, Leonard: ''The Many Dimensions of Control,'' *Organizational Dynamics,* Summer 1972, pp. 21–31.

Schuster, Fred E., and Alva F. Kindall: ''Management by Objectives, Where We Stand—A Survey of the Fortune 500,'' *Human Resource Management,* Spring 1974, pp. 8–11.

Sihler, William H.: ''Toward Better Management Control Systems,'' *California Management Review,* Spring 1971, pp. 33–39.

Stroud, Bill L.: ''Common Fallacies in Monitoring and Control,'' *Managerial Planning,* July/August 1974, pp. 18–21.

Vancil, Richard F.: ''What Kind of Management Control Do You Need?'' *Harvard Business Review,* March–April 1973, pp. 75–86.

Villarreal, John J.: ''Management by Objectives Revisited,'' *S.A.M. Advanced Management Journal,* April 1974, pp. 28–33.

Woodruff, Robert L., Jr.: ''Human Resource Accounting,'' *Training and Development Journal,* November 1973, pp. 3–8.

Process Variables and Contingency Management

More has been done on placing the process variables into a contingency framework than has been done in the quantitative, behavioral, and systems areas. Chapter 2 indicated that there were five established contingency approaches. Three of the five (contingency planning, the contingency model of leadership, and contingency organization designs) are in the process area. The purpose of this chapter is to specifically place the process variables of management discussed in the preceding four chapters into the contingency framework presented in Chapter 2. Specific if-then contingency relationships are attempted whenever possible.

The chapter discusses the four major process functions. The first section examines planning from a contingency perspective. The second section analyzes the contingency implications of the organizing process. Specific attention is devoted to the Lawrence and Lorsch approach to organization design. The third section discusses contingency approaches to directing and communicating. Fiedler's contingency model of leadership effectiveness is given detailed attention. Finally, the last section of the chapter deals with the contingency implications of control. The chapter itself is followed by a realistic case. The purpose of the cases, which are placed at the end of each of the major sections, is to permit and encourage the reader to analyze a realistic situation from the perspective of contingency management. The case contains many of the process variables found in the preceding four chapters.

Planning and Contingency Management

Chapter 4 was devoted to the planning process and the modern techniques of planning. With "future shock" type of change and the input of the external environment, the importance of contingency application of planning concepts and techniques becomes very clear. Most management writers recognize that planning for a changing environment is vital, but they do not give attention to it. Contingency management itself is an effective way of planning for the environment. What better way is there to plan for the environmental impact than through the development of if-then relationships between the environment and appropriate management concepts and techniques. In other words, by planning for contingency relationships, the impact of the environment can be managed more effectively.

Planning may be used as an example of how the management variables are independent and the environmental variables are dependent in a contingency relationship. This simply means that planning can affect the environment as well as the more usual case of environment affecting planning. For example, strategic planning could affect the outcome of legislation, technology, the economy, or even social values. In contingency terms this could be stated as: if lobbying plans are made, then the political/legal climate can be affected; or if an advertising campaign is planned, then social values can be affected. Of more importance, however, is to identify the contingent relationship between independent environment variables and the appropriate dependent planning concepts and techniques that lead to effective goal attainment.

Contingency Planning

Chapter 2 pointed out that contingency planning was one of the "established" contingency approaches in the field of management. The terminology *contingency plan* has been around for many years. Its meaning is simply that management should plan for possible future uncertainties. This past use of contingency planning recognized the need to plan for possible or real environmental changes but did not attempt to build functional relationships between the environment and appropriate management concepts and techniques. Instead, the traditional meaning of contingency planning is more closely related to what was referred to as strategic, or long-range, planning in Chapter 4.

To make strategic planning more effective, more direct attention must be given to the environment. The forecasting techniques discussed in Chapter 4 can help predict environmental impact. Sophisticated techniques are available to predict technological and economic variables in the environment. However, as the discussion in Chapter 4 carefully pointed out, no matter how sophisticated the techniques, the future environment cannot be assessed with complete certainty. Yet, careful assessment of the future environment can be extremely helpful to managerial effectiveness. For example, in attempting to assess the political/legal environment, planners might ask themselves, "What if the political climate is such that competitors from communist countries are allowed to build manufacturing plants in this country?" or "What would happen to our energy supply and its cost if the petroleum industry were nationalized?" With regard to the social environment, planners might ask, "How would we handle a day-care center in our business?" or "What if our employees go on strike to demand meaningful work?" Strategic planning for such external environmental contingencies (technological, economic, political/legal, and social) as well as the specific environment (competitors, customers, and suppliers) is becoming increasingly important to today's management. The external environment must be anticipated by the strategic planning process, and the internal environment (structure, processes, and technology) must be accounted for by the shorter-range, tactical or operational planning process. The development of specific if-then contingency relationships between the environment and appropriate forecasting, strategic, and operational planning concepts and techniques can be very beneficial to effective management.

Contingency Relationships in Planning

Besides doing "contingency planning," some contingency relationships such as the following can be stated for planning: if the technological environment is changing rapidly, then technological forecasting techniques should be employed; or if the economic environment is changing rapidly, then demand or sales forecasting techniques should be used. Other rather obvious contingency relationships could be: if the future environment in general is changing rapidly, then strategic planning should be used; or if the internal environment is undergoing rapid change, then tactical planning should be used.

More specific contingency relationships are needed. About the only specific relationships to date have dealt with the technological environment. For example, William H. Newman classified three general types of technology:

1 *Stable technology,* where there is relatively infrequent need for change and the problems are familiar. Some specific examples of organizations with this type of technology are a paper mill, retirement home, social security office, and telephone operations.
2 *Regulated-flexibility technology,* where there is frequent need for change but the problems are familiar. Examples of organizations with this type of technology are a job shop, hospital, unemployment compensation office, and newspaper office.
3 *Adaptive technology,* where there is frequent need for change and the problems are unfamiliar. Examples of organizations with this type of technology are an aerospace plant, medical research laboratory, training center for the hard-core unemployed, and management consulting firm.

Importantly, Newman relates these three types of technology to organizing, planning, leading, and controlling.[1] If his analysis of technology is adapted to the planning area, the following contingency relationships can be stated:

1 If there is a stable technology, then standing plans should have broad coverage with details specified and single-use plans should have full coverage with details specified and have a weekly or quarterly time dimension, intermediate goals emphasized, and the "how" specified.
2 If there is regulated-flexibility technology, then standing plans should have all main areas covered with details in interlocking activities and single-use plans should be fully planned with detailed schedules and specifications and have a weekly to annual time dimension, intermediate goals emphasized, and results at each step specified.
3 If there is adaptive technology, then standing plans should have coverage that is mostly "local" and self-imposed and cover only the main points and single-use plans should cover the main steps, be able to adjust to feedback, have a time dimension of a month to 3 years or more, emphasize objectives, and stress end results.

The three contingency relationships suggested above can serve as a point of departure for the development of other such relationships between environmental variables and planning variables.

---

[1] William H. Newman, "Strategy and Management Structure," *Journal of Business Policy,* Winter 1971–1972, pp. 56–66.

Organizing and Contingency Management

Starting with the work of Joan Woodward and more recently Lawrence and Lorsch, a relatively great amount of attention has been given to contingency organization designs. The overriding theme of this approach is that there is no one best way to organize. Studies mentioned in Chapters 2 and 3 by the Tavistock group, Gouldner, Woodward, Chandler, Duncan, Hall, Thompson, and Perrow, among others, suggest that the most effective organization design is the one that adjusts to the requirements of the external and internal environment.

The general approach of the work so far has not been to develop specific if-then contingency relationships but rather to classify various aspects of the environment, especially technology, and relate these to certain internal organizational variables and in some cases overall design. Yet, there are certainly some implications for contingency management as defined in this book that are also inherent in the more traditional analyses of organization.

Contingency Analysis of Bureaucracy

At first the criticism of classical organization revolved around the lack of behavioral sensitivity. More recently, with the systems perspective becoming more popular, there is the additional criticism that the classical structures ignore the external environment. In the search for commonalities and universal principles, no attention was devoted to the input of the environment. However, in fairness to the classical theorists, it must be remembered that the environmental impact was not nearly as great when they were formulating their theories and designing the structures as it is today. Weber's bureaucratic structure goes back to nineteenth-century Europe, and the classical theories go back 20 to 50 years. Now it must be recognized that the environment can no longer be ignored in organization theory and design.

The tremendous popular response to recent books such as *The Peter Principle* and *Up the Organization* points to the problems both employees and clients and customers have had with bureaucracies. The following types of experiences are all too common:

Bosses without (and underlings with) technical competence.
Arbitrary and zany rules.
An underworld (or informal) organization which subverts and even replaces the formal apparatus.
Confusion and conflict among roles.
Cruel treatment of subordinates based not on rational or legal grounds but upon inhumanity.[2]

Other common charges leveled against classical structures are that they:

are too mechanistic and ignore major facets of human nature

are too structured to adapt to change

---

[2] Warren Bennis, "Beyond Bureaucracy," *Trans-Action,* July–August 1965, p. 32.

have formal directives and procedures that hinder communication

inhibit innovation

pay the job and not the person

rely on coercion to maintain control

encourage job-defensive behavior and make-work

have goals that are incompatible with those of its members

are simply out of date with the Seventies[3]

Modern social values are becoming more and more intolerant with the above types of problems. In other words, a bureaucratic form of organization may not be compatible with social values which question rather than blindly accept authority, are intolerant of rules and procedures, find a highly specialized job boring and frustrating, and expect personal rather than impersonal treatment. Since contingency relationships are generally stated in the positive rather than the negative, the statement *could* read as follows: if the social environment is one where people accept authority, follow rules and procedures, find satisfaction in a highly specialized job, and tolerate impersonality, then bureaucracy is appropriate. The reader should remember that such contingency statements are only for illustrative purposes. Before being used in actual practice, contingency statements would have to be empirically validated.

Besides the impact of social values, other environmental variables must also be contingently related to bureaucratic structures. As in the other areas of contingency management, the task is difficult. Perrow made the following comment on the difficulty of relating technology to bureaucratic structures: "the rate of change is so rapid, the new techniques so unproven and so uncertain, the number of contingencies so enormous, that the bureaucratic model is only partly applicable. . . . Something else is needed."[4] The "something else" is the alternative organization designs to a bureaucracy.

Despite the difficulty, it does seem possible to develop some meaningful contingency relationships for bureaucracy. For example, using Newman's analysis cited earlier, it could be stated that if there is a stable technology, then a bureaucratic organization could be an appropriate structure.[5] Another relationship could be taken from knowledge of the economic environment. In the middle and late 1960s the "go-go" conglomerates that went with a free-form, nonbureaucratic structure (for example, LTV Corporation, Litton Industries, and Gulf & Western Company) were very effective. However, when the economic pressures began to mount in the 1970s, these companies were hurt badly. Other conglomerates that did not turn to a free-form design (for example, IT&T and TRW) weathered the economic storm of the 1970s relatively better. In other words, if there is an unhealthy economy, then a bureaucratic structure could be appropriate. The same is true

---

[3] Joel E. Ross and Robert G. Murdick, "People, Productivity, and Organizational Structure," *Personnel*, September–October 1973, p. 10.

[4] Charles Perrow, *Organizational Analysis: A Sociological View*, Wadsworth, Belmont, Calif., 1970, p. 60.

[5] Newman, op. cit.

in the political/legal arena. The free-form conglomerates are more susceptible to antitrust action than are the more established bureaucratically structured organizations. In other words, if the political/legal climate is favorable to antitrust action, then a bureaucratic structure is appropriate to meet the goal of survival.

It must be remembered that the above contingency relationships and others that are stated in subsequent chapters are merely guidelines and only one of many inputs into what the final structure or other concept or technique would be. Empirically validated contingency relationships can help improve management practice, but the individual manager must still interpret and translate the contingency model and relationships into action.

Contingency Analysis of Neoclassical Concepts

The neoclassical organizational concepts and techniques of centralization-decentralization, departmentation, and staff were identified in Chapter 5. They are extensions and modifications of the classical principles. Most discussions of these concepts and techniques by management writers have direct implications for contingency management. For example, from Newman's analysis it could be stated that if a stable technology exists, then centralization is appropriate; and if an adaptive technology is present, then the organization should be decentralized.[6] Another technological contingency could be that if there is advanced computerized technology, then centralization should be used.

Relationships could also be determined for the other external environment variables with regard to centralization-decentralization. If social values promote independence and individual initiative, then decentralization would be appropriate. If the economy is strong, then decentralization is appropriate; but if the organization is under severe economic pressure, then centralization is appropriate.

Even the political/legal climate can influence centralization-decentralization. A case in point is the recentralization that took place in General Motors. Traditionally, GM was always the textbook model of decentralization. However, a few years ago GM moved to a centralized operations function. A huge assembly division now puts together the various automobiles that were formerly handled by decentralized product divisions.

The reason for the move toward centralization is extremely interesting. There is strong speculation that GM centralized because of the fear of antitrust action. If its assembly division was decentralized along traditional product lines, the Justice Department could split off one of the divisions relatively easily. For example, GM could be ordered to divest itself of the Chevrolet Division. Under decentralization, such an action would not greatly disrupt the rest of the corporation. On the other hand, if the assembly division was centralized, it might take the company years to separate out the Chevrolet Division from the others and there would be considerable impact on the corporation as a whole. GM could sue the Justice Department for irreparable damages. Thus, in contingency terms

[6] Ibid.

the strategy could be stated: if there is a political/legal climate of antitrust, then a central-ized structure is appropriate for the goal of survival.

The same type of contingency analysis can be made of the other neoclassical concepts and techniques. For example, if there is a stable technology, then functional departmen-tation and a line organization is appropriate; or if there is an adaptive technology, then product departmentation and a strong staff structure is appropriate.[7] The external envi-ronment has as great an effect on departmentation and staff as it does on centralization and decentralization.

Contingency Analysis of Modern Designs

Because of the tremendous pressures for change, mainly coming from the external envi-ronment, new organization structures have surfaced in the last few years. Chapter 5 identified project, matrix, and free-form as being some new organization designs that are alternatives to classical and neoclassical structures. A project organization design is most effective in situations where there is a large, technically complex, closed-ended endeavor such as would be found in research and development or construction. In contingency terms, if there is intensive technology that is self-contained, then a project structure is appropriate.

The matrix organization is very compatible with the discussion of contingency manage-ment. This modern design attempts to take advantage of both the new and the old by superimposing a project structure onto a functional structure. Essentially each unit or individual staff member of the matrix structure has a functional boss and a project boss. This, of course, violates the "universal" principle of unity of command. Sometimes this violation has led to problems of dysfunctional conflict, but in other cases the violation has had very good results.

Jay Galbraith, who is the organization theorist most closely associated with matrix struc-tures, carefully points out that the matrix is not a pure form of organization and that there can be functionally oriented matrix structures and product- (project-) oriented matrix structures. Figure 8–1 shows the range of alternative matrix designs; the appropriate choice largely depends on the environment.

Galbraith cites the case of the aerospace industry to demonstrate environmental impact on organization structure.[8] In the late 1950s and early 1960s the space race and missle gap dominated the environment. Technical performance and technological development were most important to these firms, and a functionally dominated matrix structure was most appropriate (number 1 in Figure 8-1). The contingency statement could be: if there is technological growth and specific application, then a functionally oriented matrix struc-ture is appropriate. However, during the McNamara reign in the Department of Defense

---

[7] Ibid.

[8] Jay R. Galbraith, "Matrix Organization Designs," *Business Horizons,* February 1971, pp. 29–40.

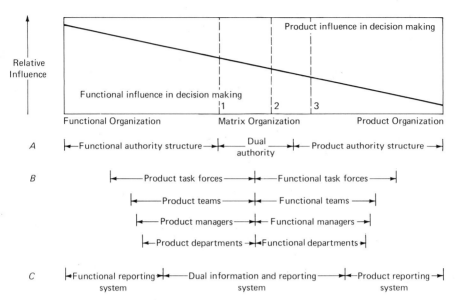

Figure 8-1 The Range of Alternatives in Matrix Designs. *Source:* Jay R. Galbraith, "Matrix Organization Designs," *Business Horizons,* February 1971, p. 37. Used with permission.

(mid-1960s), the political environment faced by the aerospace firms was one of account-ability and managerial efficiency. There was a shift toward a more project-oriented matrix structure (number 2 in Figure 8-1). This could be reflected in a contingency relationship of: if the political environment is one of accountability and efficiency, then a project-oriented matrix structure is appropriate. In the 1970s the environment became character-ized by economically tight times. There was a move toward more project-oriented matrix structures (number 3 in Figure 8-1). In other words, if there are economic pressures, then a project-oriented matrix structure is appropriate.

Galbraith does point out that in some cases where aerospace firms had to cut back on size because of reductions in defense spending (as a result of the social, political, and economic environments), they could no longer justify project structures so they reverted to functional structures. Although this latter change is environmentally induced, it points to the problems facing contingency management. The problems of change and interact-ing variables make it difficult, but not impossible, to determine contingency relationships. Despite these problems, there seems little doubt that contingency analysis and determi-nation of functional relationships can definitely improve understanding and actual imple-mentation of effective organizational designs.

Contingency Organization Designs

Chapters 2 and 3 discussed some of the models and analyses of contingency organization design. The work of Lawrence and Lorsch is best known and makes a significant contribution to contingency management as a whole. By studying ten firms in three industries (plastics, consumer foods, and standardized containers), Lawrence and Lorsch were able to develop a conceptual framework for contingency organization design.[9] The organizations were selected so that there would be different rates of technological change and so that there would be dominant demands from different sectors of the environment.

The Lawrence and Lorsch study provided understanding of the internal organization environment of differentiation (differences among managers in various functional departments according to particular goals, time, interpersonal orientation, and formality of the structure) and integration (the status of interdepartmental relations) and how differences in internal organizations were related to differences in external environments. The study results showed that the internal organizational variables are in complex interrelationship with each other and with the external environment.

The Lawrence and Lorsch study would support the following if-then contingency statements:

1 If the environment is uncertain and heterogeneous, then the organization should be relatively unstructured and have widely shared influence among the management staff.
2 If the environment is stable and homogeneous, then a rigid organization structure is appropriate.
3 If the external environment is very diverse and the internal environment is highly differentiated, then there must be very elaborate integrating mechanisms in the organization structure.

The findings of the study are especially important because they deal with effectiveness. In general they found that if the organization's internal environment was compatible with the external environment, then the organization would be effective. Such an empirically derived conclusion is extremely important to overall contingency management. It documents, at least in this study, that there is in fact a contingent relationship between external environment variables and internal management variables that leads to effective goal attainment.

Directing and Contingency Management

Chapter 6 indicated the important role that directing or leading played in effective management. Essentially two approaches can be taken in the study and determination of effective styles of leadership. The first is the great-man or trait approach, which was

[9] Paul R. Lawrence and Jay W. Lorsch, *Organization and Environment,* Division of Research, Harvard Graduate School of Business Administration, Boston, 1967.

given attention in Chapter 6. The other major approach, which is more modern and directly related to contingency management, is the *Zeitgeist* (spirit of the times) or situational approach. Whereas the first approach emphasizes the traits of leaders themselves, the situational approach puts more emphasis on the situational variables. The assumption is that the effective leadership style (the various styles were discussed in Chapter 6) depends on the situation.

Most of the early research on leadership styles (for example, the Lippitt and White studies discussed in Chapter 6) and even the more contemporary research such as that coming from the Michigan studies inferred that the subordinate-centered (systems 3 and 4 of Likert) styles were more effective than the task-centered (systems 1 and 2 of Likert) styles under *all* conditions. Despite the implications of these widely known studies, few would disagree today that flexibility in leadership style is desirable. Enough studies have shown that the various leadership styles are effective in some situations and not in others. For example, Filley and House in a review of the research literature found the following situational variables to have an impact on leadership effectiveness:

the previous history of the organization, the age of the previous incumbent in the leader's position, the age of the leader and his previous experience;

the community in which the organization operates;

the particular work requirements of the group;

the psychological climate of the group being led;

the kind of job the leader holds;

the size of the group led;

the degree to which group-member co-operation is required;

the cultural expectations of subordinates;

group-member personalities; and

the time required and allowed for decision making.[10]

There seems little doubt that the situation plays a vital role in the directing process of management.

Influence of the External Environment

The list compiled by Filley and House is only representative of some of the situational variables affecting leadership. The list does not contain external environment variables. Yet, there is substantial evidence that the external environment does influence the appropriate leadership styles for effective goal attainment. For example, Woodward's study found that the type of technology affected the human relationships and thus the leadership style that was most effective.[11] In her study technology seemed to dictate the super-

---

[10] Alan C. Filley and Robert J. House, *Managerial Process and Organizational Behavior*, Scott, Foresman, Glenview, Ill., 1969, p. 409.

[11] See Y. K. Shetty, "Leadership and Organization Character," *Personnel Administration*, July–August 1970, pp. 14–20 for a discussion of the leadership implications from the Woodward study.

visory ratio and thus affected the amount of freedom subordinates can be given. A contingency relationship derived from the Woodward study would be: if a unit production technology exists, then a democratic style of leadership is appropriate. Using Newman's classification of stable, regulated flexibility and adaptive technologies that were discussed earlier, the following if-then statements could be made:

1 If there is stable technology, then there should be limited participation, close supervision, cautious sharing of information, and limited emphasis given to job satisfaction.
2 If there is a regulated-flexibility type of technology, then participation should be restricted to one's own tasks, output and quality closely supervised, job information shared, and craftsmanship and professionalism encouraged.
3 If there is an adaptive technology, then there should be a great deal of participation, permissiveness if results are good, general supervision, full project information shared, and opportunity for involvement.[12]

Besides the influence of technology on leadership style, there seems little question that the other external variables have an impact as well. Prevailing social values largely dictate the expectations of followers. If societal values reflect independence and democracy, then a democratic style is appropriate. Even the economic and political/legal environment would seem to influence leadership style. Economic pressures or the threat of antitrust action or compulsory collective bargaining may dictate appropriate styles.

Contingency Model of Leadership
The discussion so far has emphasized the environmental impact on leadership styles and some contingency relationships are suggested. But, as Chapter 2 brought out, a well-established contingency model of leadership effectiveness already exists. From years of extensive research, Fred Fiedler developed a far-reaching contingency model for leadership effectiveness.[13] The model contains a contingency relationship between the favorableness of the situation and leadership style.

Fiedler classified the favorableness of the situation according to three dimensions:

1 *Leader-Member Relations* This is the most important dimension. Leaders who are liked, respected, and trusted have more power and influence than those who do not.
2 *Task Structure* Tasks that are highly structured, spelled out, or programmed give the leader more influence than tasks that are unstructured.
3 *Position Power* The leader who has a great deal of authority over subordinates can have more influence than the leader with no such power.

Using these three dimensions, Fiedler can classify situations along a continuum from very unfavorable to very favorable.

---

[12] Newman, op. cit.
[13] Fred E. Fiedler, *A Theory of Leadership Effectiveness*, McGraw-Hill, New York, 1967.

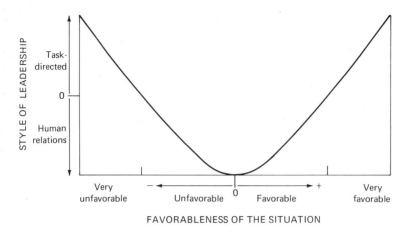

Figure 8-2 Contingency Model of Leadership Effectiveness. *Source:* Adapted from Fred E. Fiedler, *A Theory of Leadership Effectiveness,* McGraw-Hill, New York, 1967, pp. 142–148.

Based on sixty-three analyses using 454 separate groups, Fiedler was able to determine that under very favorable and very unfavorable situations, the task-directed or authoritarian (systems 1 and 2) type of leader (as measured by his instruments) was most effective. However, when the situation was only moderately favorable or unfavorable (the intermediate range of favorableness), then the human relations or democratic (systems 3 and 4) type of leader was most effective. Figure 8-2 graphically depicts Fiedler's contingency model of leadership effectiveness.

Fiedler offers the following examples in explaining why the task-directed leader is effective in very favorable and very unfavorable situations:

In the very favorable conditions in which the leader has power, informal backing, and a relatively well-structured task, the group is ready to be directed, and the group expects to be told what to do. Consider the captain of an airliner in its final landing approach. We would hardly want him to turn to his crew for a discussion on how to land. In the relatively unfavorable situation . . . consider . . . the disliked chairman of a volunteer committee which is asked to plan the office picnic on a beautiful Sunday. If the leader asks too many questions about what the group ought to do or how he should proceed, he is likely to be told that "we ought to go home."[14]

The leader who makes a wrong decision in the latter type of situation is probably better off than the leader who makes no decision at all.

Figure 8-2 shows that the human relations leader is effective in the moderate range of favorableness. Examples of such situations are the typical committees or units staffed by professionals. In these situations, the leader may not be wholly accepted by the other members of the group, the task is generally vague and not completely structured, and little formal authority and power are granted to the leader. Under such circumstances, a human relations, democratic type of leader is most effective.

[14] Ibid., p. 147.

Although there has been some controversy over Fiedler's research methods, the contingency model has generally stood the test of research so far. Fiedler noted, "In all studies that were recently reviewed, 35 of the 44 obtained correlations were in the predicted direction."[15] The way in which the contingency relationships were determined and have since been validated can serve as a prototype for the development of contingency management as a whole. Even though Fiedler's model does not specifically deal with the external environment, many lessons can be learned for contingency management theory and practice.

Communicating and Contingency Management

Directing and communicating were presented in the same chapter, which is indicative of the close relationship between these two management processes. Some of the contingency implications discussed in relation to directing apply equally to communicating. But there are also contingency implications unique to communicating.

Going as far back as 1951, Alex Bavelas, a well-known pioneer in communication research, questioned whether there was one best way to communicate. In one of his papers he stated,

It is not difficult to show, however, that from a given set of specifications one may derive not a single communication pattern but a whole set of them, all logically adequate for the successful performance of the task in question. Which pattern from this set should be chosen? The choice, in practice, is usually made either in terms of a group of assumptions (often quite untenable) about human nature, or in terms of a personal bias on the part of the chooser.[16]

Unfortunately, from this beginning not much has materialized in the way of contingency models for communication effectiveness. Although some attention has been given to areas such as identifying conditions for formal versus informal communication channel selection and the situations when oral or written communication is more effective,[17] the determination of functional relationships between environment variables and communication variables is still in the future. Once again, the challenge for contingency management is clear.

Controlling and Contingency Management

Although most management writers recognize that certain variables must be considered to properly design and implement the control process and its techniques, there is a lack

---

[15] Fred E. Fiedler, "How Do You Make Leaders More Effective? New Answers to an Old Puzzle," *Organizational Dynamics,* Autumn 1972, p. 9.

[16] Alex Bavelas and Dermot Barrett, *Personnel,* March 1951, p. 366.

[17] See Arlyn J. Melcher and Ronald Beller, "Toward a Theory of Organization Communication: Consideration in Channel Selection, "*Journal of the Academy of Management,* March 1967, pp. 39–52; and Dale A. Level, Jr., "Communication Effectiveness: Method and Situation," *The Journal of Business Communication,* Fall 1972, pp. 19–25.

of specific contingency relationships. Just as Chapter 7 was divided into a discussion of the overall aspect of the controlling process and specific control techniques, this final section will follow the same pattern.

Contingency Implications of the Control Process

Similar to the other process variables discussed so far in the chapter, the starting assumption must be that there is no one best control system for all situations. Howard Carlisle stated this position very clearly:

When a manager utilizes a planning and control system or any similar technique, two things are important: he must understand the system or concept, and he must also understand the conditions to which it applies. Too often students and managers gain an understanding of a management tool such as PERT but do not sufficiently appreciate the situational differences that make use of the tool appropriate or inappropriate.[18]

The job of contingency management is to relate environmental variables with various aspects of the control process and with specific control techniques.

In generalizing their results of organizational contingency analysis to "practical affairs" such as control, Lawrence and Lorsch suggest that questions like the following should be asked:

1 Is there a sensible relationship between the time intervals used for data reporting and the time span of feedback from the environment? We have seen that, as we look at progressively higher echelons in the hierarchy, this time span tends to lengthen. Is this reflected in the control reports?
2 We also saw that in most organizations production has a shorter time span than research. Is this reflected in the design of the control system?
3 The degree of uncertainty of information could also be considered in control system design. Are the time interval and the detail of reporting adjusted for variations in certainty?[19]

The first point above may be used to highlight the importance of feedforward in the control process. Since the lag time for environmental feedback tends to increase for top management, input control should be stressed at this level. In short, if there is a lag time for environmental feedback, then feedforward control should be stressed. The second point may be significant for employing various types of control techniques. For example, it may be difficult to implement network analysis or other control techniques because of the operational constraint of short response time. In other situations where there is relatively long response time, then the control techniques would be effective. In reference to the third point, the uncertainty of information received in an organizational unit would affect the effectiveness of control. Certainty and uncertainty are important factors for designing any control system. There is evidence to indicate that tasks that are certain need less control than tasks which are uncertain. John Morse indicates,

---

[18] Howard M. Carlisle, *Situational Management*, AMACOM, American Management Association, New York, 1973, p. 160.
[19] Lawrence and Lorsch, op. cit., pp. 225–226.

Members of organizations doing relatively certain tasks tended to be comfortable in relatively dependent authority relations, preferred structure and highly coordinated work patterns, had a lower ability to cope with rapidly changing and ambiguous situations and preferred to work on uncomplex cognitive problems. Members of organizations doing relatively uncertain tasks tended to prefer autonomy and independence in their authority relations, liked working on individualistic problems independent of others, preferred rapidly changing and ambiguous settings and thrived on tackling complex cognitive problems.[20]

In other words, if the environment is relatively certain, then tight controls are needed; or if the environment is relatively uncertain, then loose controls are appropriate.

Besides the environmental variables suggested by Lawrence and Lorsch and Morse, the technological environment once again seems to have a particularly significant impact on control. The works of Woodward and James Thompson have definite implications for control. For example, Woodward's findings would imply that if there is a unit type of production technology, then loose controls would be appropriate; or if there is a mass or batch production technology, then tight controls should be used. From Thompson's analysis (he identified three types of technology, which were discussed in Chapter 3), the contingency statement could be: if there is intensive technology, then loose controls are appropriate; or if long-linked technology is present, then tight controls are needed. As in the other process areas, Newman's analysis is also relevant to control:

1 If there is stable technology, then efficiency and dependability control standards should be emphasized, there should be frequent control checks with reliability stressed, few mistakes can be tolerated, and central management should initiate corrective control action.

2 If there is regulated flexibility technology, then quality, punctuality, and efficiency control standards should be emphasized; there should be frequent control checks with reliability stressed; few mistakes can be tolerated; and production control and other staff managers should initiate corrective control action.[21]

Contingent Application of Control Techniques
Chapter 7 indicated that there were quite a few specific control techniques available to today's managers. Although these techniques are fairly sophisticated and have a great deal of potential for improving the control of modern organizations, there is little guidance given on which techniques work best in particular situations. About the only statement that can be made at this time is that if there is a complex technological environment, then the newer PPBS, cost/benefit analysis, and network analysis control techniques become more appropriate; or if social values are placing greater emphasis on the human rather than physical variables in the work place, then human resource accounting techniques are appropriate.

[20] John J. Morse, "A Contingency Look at Job Design," *California Management Review*, Fall 1973, p. 72.
[21] Newman, op. cit.

In general, the control area is not up to par with the other process variables in terms of contingency management. Much more work needs to be done in the future to contingently relate environmental variables with control variables for more effective management.

Summary

The purpose of this chapter is to contingently relate environmental variables with process variables. This was done by taking each of the major process variables that were discussed in the preceding four chapters and, where possible, establishing a functional relationship with the environment. In the planning area, "contingency plans" have been around for many years but specific if-then relationships have generally not been developed. Besides some rather obvious relationships between general environmental conditions and forecasting techniques, strategic planning, and tactical planning, most attention was devoted to Newman's analysis. He identified stable, regulated-flexibility, and adaptive technologies which could be placed into contingency if-then relationships for appropriate planning concepts and techniques.

There is little question that the most developed area of contingency management is the organizing area. Many contingency implications can be derived from the analysis of bureaucratic, neoclassical, and modern organization analysis. There is also the "established" contingency organization design literature. The now famous study conducted by Lawrence and Lorsch has made a significant contribution to contingency management. Closely paralleling the development of the organizing process and contingency management is the work done on the directing process. There is general recognition given to the situational impact on leadership. Some general if-then statements can be derived and more specific ones can be taken from Newman's analysis of technological impact on leadership. The work of Fred Fiedler in developing a contingency model of leadership effectiveness is analogous to the work that Lawrence and Lorsch did on contingency organization design. Fiedler's model, although he did not relate to the external environment, is very significant to overall contingency management.

The two remaining process variables, communicating and controlling, were not given as much attention as planning, organizing, and directing simply because very little has been done from a contingency perspective. Although Bavelas recognized the need for a contingency approach to communication a quarter of a century ago, little has been done to date to accomplish this goal. The same is true of control. Most management writers recognize that the control process and techniques should be situationally applied but then do not follow through. The challenge for the future is very clear. Management theory and practice must develop more contingent relationships in all areas but especially in areas such as communication and control. The subsequent contingency-related chapters at the end of the major sections will reiterate this challenge for the future of contingency management.

Questions for Review and Discussion

1 How, if any, does the old approach to contingency planning differ from the contingency approach to planning suggested by this book? What are some possible contingency relationships between the environment and planning?

2 What would be some contingency implications of classical or bureaucratic, neoclassical, and modern organizational designs? Briefly summarize the Lawrence and Lorsch contingency organization design.

3 What influence does the external environment have on leadership? Briefly summarize the Fiedler contingency model of leadership effectiveness.

4 Discuss some of the contingency implications of the control process. What are some specific if-then relationships relevant to control?

References

Carlisle, Howard M.: "A Contingency Approach to Decentralization," *S.A.M. Advanced Management Journal,* July 1974, pp. 9–18.

Cross, Bert S.: "Environmental Impact on Business Planning," *Managerial Planning,* September/October 1973, pp. 9–13.

Fiedler, Fred E.: "How Do You Make Leaders More Effective? New Answers to an Old Puzzle," *Organizational Dynamics,* Autumn 1972, pp. 3–18.

———: *A Theory of Leadership Effectiveness,* McGraw-Hill, New York, 1967.

———, **and Martin M. Chemers:** *Leadership and Effective Management,* Scott, Foresman, Glenview, Ill., 1974.

Galbraith, Jay R.: "Matrix Organization Designs: How to Combine Functional and Project Forms," *Business Horizons,* February 1971, pp. 29–40.

Graen, George, James Burdeane Orris, and Kenneth M. Alvares: "Contingency Model of Leadership Effectiveness: Some Experimental Results," *Journal of Applied Psychology,* June 1971, pp. 196–201.

Hellriegel, Don, and John W. Slocum, Jr.: *Management: A Contingency Approach,* Addison-Wesley, Reading, Mass., 1974.

———, **and** ———: "Organizational Design: A Contingency Approach," *Business Horizons,* April 1973, pp. 59–68.

Hill, Walter: "The Validation and Extension of Fiedler's Theory of Leadership Effectiveness," *Academy of Management Journal,* March 1969, pp. 33–47.

Hollander, Edwin P.: "Style, Structure, and Setting in Organizational Leadership," *Administrative Science Quarterly,* March 1971, pp. 1–9.

Kast, Fremont E., and James E. Rosenzweig: *Organization and Management: A Systems Approach,* 2d ed., McGraw-Hill, New York, 1974.

Lawrence, Paul R., and Jay W. Lorsch: *Developing Organizations: Diagnosis and Action,* Addison-Wesley, Reading, Mass., 1969.

——— **and** ———: *Organization and Environment: Managing Differentiation and Integration,* Division of Research, Harvard Graduate School of Business Administration, Boston, 1967.

Level, Dale A., Jr.: "Communication Effectiveness: Method and Situation," *The Journal of Business Communication,* Fall 1972, pp. 19–25.

Lorsch, Jay W., and Paul R. Lawrence: *Studies in Organization Design,* Dorsey-Irwin, Homewood, Ill., 1970.

McCaskey, Michael B.: "A Contingency Approach to Planning: Planning with Goals and Planning without Goals," *Academy of Management Journal,* June 1974, pp. 281–291.

McMahon, J. Timothy, and G. W. Perritt: "Toward a Contingency Theory of Organizational Control," *Academy of Management Journal,* December 1973, pp. 624–635.

Miner, John B.: *The Management Process: Theory, Research, and Practice,* Macmillan, New York, 1973.

Mockler, Robert J.: "The Corporate Control Job: Breaking the Mold," *Business Horizons,* December 1970, pp. 73–77.

Mohr, Lawrence: "Organizational Technology and Organizational Structure," *Administrative Science Quarterly,* December 1971, pp. 444–459.

Negandhi, Anant R., and Bernard C. Reimann: "A Contingency Theory of Organization Re-examined in the Context of a Developing Country," *Academy of Management Journal,* June 1972, pp. 137–146.

Newman, William H.: "Strategy and Management Structure," *Journal of Business Policy,* Winter 1971–1972, pp. 56–66.

Osborn, Richard N., and James G. Hunt: "Environment and Organizational Effectiveness," *Administrative Science Quarterly,* June 1974, pp. 231–246.

Pastore, Joseph M.: "Organizational Metamorphosis: A Dynamic Model," *Marquette Business Review,* Spring 1971, pp. 17–30.

Reddin, W. J.: *Managerial Effectiveness,* McGraw-Hill, New York, 1970.

———: "What's Wrong with the Style Theories?" *Training and Development Journal,* August 1969, pp. 14–17.

Ross, Joel E., and Robert G. Murdick: "People, Productivity, and Organizational Structure," *Personnel,* September–October 1973, pp. 9–18.

Shetty, Y. K.: "Is There a Best Way to Organize a Business Enterprise?" *S.A.M. Advanced Management Journal,* April 1973, pp. 47–52.

——— **and Howard M. Carlisle:** "A Contingency Model of Organization Design," *California Management Review,* Fall 1972, pp. 38–45.

Simon, Herbert A.: "Applying Information Technology to Organization Design," *Public Administration Review,* May–June 1973, pp. 268–278.

Thomas, Philip S.: "Environmental Analysis for Corporate Planning," *Business Horizons,* October 1974, pp. 27–38.

Van de Ven, Andrew H., and Andre L. Delbecq: "A Task-Contingent Model of Work-Unit Structure," *Administrative Science Quarterly,* June 1974, pp. 183–197.

Case Study for Part Two
Practice What You Preach

Joe Fisher was three-fourths of the way through his first semester as an assistant professor in the College of Business Administration at Western University. Joe had graduated with a Ph.D. degree the previous spring from a prestigious Eastern University. His graduate program concentrated on organization theory and research methodology. His current teaching assignment included undergraduate courses in management and organization behavior. The second week on campus Joe was having coffee with Hank Aims, an associate professor of marketing who had been at Western for 5 years. After discussing the prospects of the coming football season, Joe asked Hank what was expected of an assistant professor in the college. The marketing professor gave a faraway look and said, "Well, no one ever really says, but as far as I can determine, you must attempt to do a good job on teaching, research, and service." Joe said, "In that order?" "Not necessarily," said the marketing professor. "Good teaching is defined as meeting your classes, research means getting out two or three articles a year, and service is anything else such as committee work, community activities, and even consulting work." Joe thanked Hank for buying the cup of coffee and asked if they could do it again.

Joe had a good feeling on how the semester had gone so far. He was covering a lot of good material in his classes, and the students seemed very enthusiastic and were giving him positive feedback. Besides preparing for classes, Joe also was doing some research and writing. He was elated when he received word that an article he had submitted to a leading practitioner-oriented management journal had been accepted for publication. The title of the article was "The Five Keys to Effective Management: Planning, Organizing, Directing, Communicating, and Controlling." This being his first article, he was very proud. The day he received the letter of acceptance from the journal he kiddingly told his management class that their professor was now a famous management author. After Joe relayed the contents of the article to the class, one of the more vocal but bright students, Curt Bradly, raised his hand. Joe called on Curt, who said, "Dr. Fisher, your article sounds really interesting. I would like to get a copy and read it in its entirety when it comes out. From your brief summary it sounds as if the article puts into understandable terms some of the more theoretical things we have discussed in the course so far. However, something has been bothering me lately, and I think this is a good time to bring it up. I am a student representative on the College Academic Planning Committee. It has been a very depressing experience. As far as I can determine, this college does very few, if any, of the things you describe in your article. There are no forecasts made or strategic plans developed. The organization structure is what you label classical. The style of directing is what you have called ineffective and outdated. There is no attempt to obtain upward communication from students or horizontal communication between departments. There seems to be no attempt to evaluate or control performance of faculty or students. These observations, which admittedly come from my limited experience, lead me to the question that is bothering me. Why don't you and your colleagues, who are supposedly experts on effective management, practice what you preach?"

Joe was somewhat startled by the student's question. After stammering around a couple of seconds, Joe finally said, "Well I really don't know if I can answer your question. As you know I'm new here, and I frankly don't know whether what you say is true or not. However, I do think you have raised a legitimate question and I would like to pursue it. I tell you what—give me a couple of weeks to check into exactly what the college is doing with regard to modern management concepts and techniques. I will report back my findings to the class as a whole. This is something we can all relate to and should be able to discuss openly."

Joe was perplexed after class. The student's question really began to bother him. Obviously, he had been so involved in his studies as a graduate student and getting settled into his new job that he had never given any thought to the management of his "own back yard." He decided that he would make a concerted effort in the next couple of weeks to find out what the situation actually was and the reasons for it. After talking with several junior and senior faculty members and one brief discussion with the associate dean, Joe was amazed at the way the college was being managed.

After the two weeks had elapsed, Joe opened up his class by saying, "As promised, I have come back to you with my findings of the status of management concepts and techniques in the college. I am sorry to say that the situation seems even worse than Curt found his experience. To put it simply, I have discovered very little similarity between what I am teaching you about modern management in this class and what is occurring in this college. No forecasts are being conducted on student enrollments, staffing needs, or course offerings. There are no strategic plans to indicate where the college should be 5 years from now or even next year. Sure we submit budget requests each year, but it is a very routine and time-consuming exercise in futility. As far as I can tell, central university administration reacts to legislative pressure and crises and the college in turn reacts to central administration pressures and crises. We don't plan ahead to anticipate problems and needs. We use a classical, bureaucratic structure with functional departmentation. There are numerous styles of leadership. Some department chairmen are autocratic or system 1; some are democratic or system 4; and I would even label one as being laissez faire. The dean apparently tries to use participative management, but everyone is too busy to participate. There is no formal attempt to attain upward or horizontal communication other than the monthly faculty meeting. Finally, there appears to be no concept of control in existence, and most of the old-timers just laughed when I asked what control techniques are used in the college."

After giving this report, Joe slowly shook his head and said, "I still have no real explanation for Curt's original question. I cannot explain why we don't practice what we preach. The associate dean told me that you cannot expect to run an academic organization like a business organization. The objectives are completely different, and you cannot expect professional faculty members to be 'managed' in the traditional sense of the word. He said that the business end of the university is run according to what is taught in a management course but not the academic side of the university. This is about the only answer I can offer you at this time."

Questions for Analysis:

1 Do you think the situation at Western University is as bleak as Curt and Professor Fisher indicate in the case? How do you think academic organizations would compare with other types of organizations in contemporary society in the use of management concepts and techniques?

2 How would you answer Curt's question if you were Professor Fisher?

3 What are some planning, organizing, directing, communicating, and controlling concepts and techniques that could be adapted to an academic organization?

4 What external environmental factors affect an academic organization? What would be some possible contingency relationships (if-then statements) between the environment and appropriate management process concepts and techniques?

Quantitative
Variables

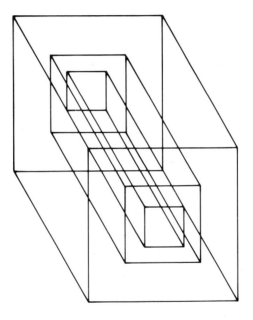

The Quantitative Approach to Management

The managers of all modern organizations are challenged to be more accountable and efficient. This is true in both the public and private sector. Industrial and retail organizations, hospitals, and universities have all experienced a steep escalation in their costs and prices to the client or customer. The public is reacting. People are demanding that the managers of these organizations be more accountable for their decisions and that there be more efficiency in the decisional process. Besides these demands, management is also faced with a shortage of resources. Scarce resources must be allocated more efficiently. These challenges are forcing management to reexamine the theory and practice of decision making. To become more accountable and efficient and be able to allocate scarce resources optimally, management is depending more and more on a quantitative approach to decision making.

This chapter develops an introductory foundation for the quantitative approach to management. Decision making is the focal point of the quantitative approach. The first section examines decision making from a process and a problem perspective. The problem perspective sets the stage for analyzing two traditional quantitative methods (breakeven and present value). After a brief overview, the importance and limitations of these decision techniques are discussed. The last part of the chapter presents a more contemporary approach to quantitative decision making. Decision making under conditions of certainty, risk, and uncertainty are given major attention.

The Decision-making Framework

Decision making may be viewed from two perspectives—process and problem. A process perspective is very general and concentrates on the sequential steps in decision making. The goal for management is to select the best alternative in the decision process. This approach is often criticized for being overly concerned with procedure and not providing any content. The other perspective, the problem approach to decision making, is solution-oriented but lacks sufficient meaning for direct implementation. This deficiency of a problem approach can be overcome when the situations which are appropriate for implementing various models are identified. The following two sections spell out the process and problem approaches in more detail.

Process Approach to Decision Making

Most modern theorists break the decision process down into a series of sequential steps. For the most part, the steps delineate into the very simple three-step problem-solving process of determining what the problem is, what the alternatives are, and which alternative is best. Herbert A. Simon, probably the best-known and most widely quoted decision theorist, expands on these three steps by identifying three distinct phases in the decision-making process. These three phases are:

1 *Intelligence Activity* Borrowing from the military meaning of intelligence, this initial phase consists of searching the environment for conditions calling for decision.
2 *Design Activity* In this second phase, inventing, developing, and analyzing possible courses of action takes place.
3 *Choice Activity* The third and final phase is the actual choice, selecting a particular course of action from those available.[1]

The problem orientation is more concerned with the first two phases (intelligence and design), while the process approach concentrates on the choice activity. Rationality is tied into this choice activity. Why will a decision maker choose one alternative over another; i.e., what is a rational choice? If appropriate means are chosen to reach desired ends, then the decision is usually said to be rational. However, there are many complications to this simple test of rationality. To begin with, it is very difficult to separate means from ends because an apparent end may only be a means for some future end. Simon further warns that a simple means-ends analysis may have inaccurate conclusions. The following three points should probably be recognized to avoid the inherent problems of means-ends analysis:

> *First,* the ends to be attained by the choice of a particular behavior alternative are often incompletely or incorrectly stated through failure to consider the alternative ends that could be reached by selection of another behavior.
>
> *Second,* in actual situations a complete separation of means from ends is usually impossible.
>
> *Third,* the means-ends terminology tends to obscure the role of the time element in decision making.[2]

One way to clarify means-ends rationality is to attach appropriate qualifying adverbs to the various types of rationality. Thus, *objectively rational* could be applied to decisions that maximize given values in a given situation. *Subjectively rational* could be used if the decision maximizes attainment relative to the actual knowledge of the given subject. *Consciously rational* could be applied to decisions where adjustment of means to ends is a conscious process. A decision is *deliberately rational* to the degree that the adjustment of means to ends has been deliberately sought by the individual or organization. A decision is *organizationally rational* to the extent that it is aimed at the organization's goals and *personally rational* if the decision is directed to the individual's goals.[3]

[1] Herbert A. Simon, *The New Science of Management Decision*, Harper & Row, New York, 1960, p. 2.
[2] Herbert A. Simon, *Administrative Behavior*, 2d ed., Macmillan, New York, 1957, p. 65.
[3] Ibid., pp. 76–77.

There are many descriptive models of the rationality of choice behavior. The models attempt to describe theoretically and realistically how practicing managers make decisions. The models range from complete rationality, as in the case of the classical economic person, to complete irrationality, as in the case of the highly emotional, irrational person portrayed in the works of Sigmund Freud. The more realistic model of rationality probably falls somewhere in the middle. By taking a problem approach, the decision maker can apply quantitative methods to make the decision process as rational as possible.

Problem Orientation to Decision Making

In recent years quantification has been playing an increasing role in the theory and practice of decision making. In fact, the term *decision sciences* is becoming more commonplace. Mathematics and statistics are readily being incorporated into management decision making. In addition to traditional math and statistics techniques, numerous innovative quantitative models and techniques for solving particular decisional problems have been developed.

The old and new quantitative decision techniques can all be placed under the label of *management science* or a slightly narrower term, *operations research*. This management science or operations research approach has often been misunderstood. The quantitative analyst often conveyed the false impression that traditional factors in management decisions were discarded and ignored by the new approach. The analyst conveyed the impression of precision and perfect rationality in decision making as opposed to merely improved decision making. In addition, very little attention was devoted to problem identification. Almost all emphasis was given to problem solution.

In the first place, the management science or operations research approach is not anything really new. Many of the quantified decisional techniques have been in existence on a piecemeal basis for decades. The new quantitative approach only systematically quantified the manner in which decisions were made. Secondly, the new quantitative approach is and should be concerned with both problem identification and problem solution. Students of management spend far too much time developing expertise in the mechanics of solving problems. They spend too little time on being able to identify what the problems are and what the solutions mean. The same holds true for management practice. Decision makers must give as much emphasis to problem identification and meaning of solutions as they do to the mechanics of problem solution.

Students and practitioners of management should be receptive and understanding of the new quantitative approach. The emphasis should be placed on both the traditional methods and the logic and inputs associated with the newer management science or operations research decision models. Students and practitioners should not become enraptured with the figures and mechanics of the procedures. There must also be an appreciation and recognition of problems which may be analyzed by quantitative methods and what the answers mean for improved, not necessarily optimum, decisions. This problem-oriented approach is the one used in this and the following two chapters.

Traditional Quantitative Methods

There are many quantitative methods that have been used over the years to help make problem-oriented decisions. Two of the most common are breakeven analysis and present value. These two quantitative methods are primarily oriented toward financial decisions. They are adaptable to cost and revenue relationships and problems.

Breakeven Analysis

Breakeven analysis is used to determine the unit or dollar level at which total revenue equals total costs ($TR = TC$). The basic costs relevant to the analysis are variable and fixed costs. Variable costs are those costs which vary with each unit of output. Examples of variable costs are direct labor and direct materials for producing each unit. For example, if the direct labor and material costs were $1 per unit, then the variable costs would be $10 for 10 units and $100 for 100 units. In other words, the variable costs vary directly with the level of output. Fixed costs refer to costs which remain constant regardless of the level of output. These costs might include building rent and insurance. For example, if these costs were estimated to be $500, this expense would remain constant whether the output was 10 or 100 units.

Even though fixed costs are assumed to remain constant for linear breakeven analysis, this assumption may not be very realistic. If the demand for an organization's product develops beyond the productive capacity, management might be forced to expand facilities. This decision to expand would be complemented with an increase in rent and insurance. Subsequently, the fixed costs would increase. Also during periods of inflation, rent and insurance may increase. This would in turn increase fixed costs. Thus, from these examples, it could be concluded that all costs are variable in the long run. Fixed costs remain constant for only a given range of production. Yet, in linear breakeven analysis, this cost is assumed to be fixed.

The relationship between fixed costs and variable costs and total revenue is shown in Figure 9-1. The fixed costs are represented by the horizontal line extending from the vertical axis. The diagonal line represents total costs (fixed plus variable). The variable costs are the difference between total and fixed costs. Total revenue is represented by the line which begins at the point of origin. The point where total revenue intersects the total cost line is the breakeven point. The area between costs and revenue above the breakeven point represents the amount of profit. The breakeven point determines the output level at which total revenue equals total costs. The simple formula which may be used to determine the breakeven point is total revenue (TR) equals variable costs (VC) plus fixed costs (FC), or $TR = VC + FC$.

EXAMPLE OF BREAKEVEN ANALYSIS An example using breakeven analysis is a mobile home manufacturer that has $100,000 in fixed costs for building and insurance. The manufacturer has also determined the variable costs to be $2,000 per unit with a selling price of $4,000. Using the basic formula of TR = VC + FC, the breakeven point would be fifty units.

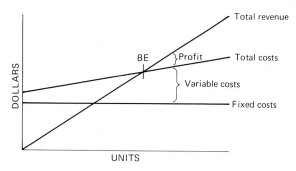

Figure 9-1 Breakeven Chart.

$$4,000x = 2,000x + 100,000$$
$$4,000x - 2,000x = 100,000$$
$$2,000x = 100,000$$
$$x = 100,000/2,000$$
$$x = 50 \text{ units}$$

In the above, x represents the number of units that would have to be sold in order to break even. Total revenue, at the breakeven point, is determined by multiplying the selling price ($4,000) by x. Variable costs, at the breakeven point, are determined by multiplying the variable cost per unit ($2,000) by x. The fixed costs were given as $100,000. A modified formula for determining the breakeven point is the following:

$$\text{BE} = \frac{\text{fixed costs}}{\text{selling price} - \text{variable costs}}_{\text{per unit} \qquad \text{per unit}}$$

It should be noted that since x represents units, the breakeven point is also expressed in units, i.e., fifty units in the mobile home manufacturing example. These units may be converted to dollars by multiplying 50 times the selling price, or 50 × $4,000, which equals $200,000. In this example, for each unit sold, $2,000 went to variable expenses and the remaining $2,000 is a contribution to fixed costs. This contribution to fixed costs continues until fifty units are sold (**BE** point). For each unit beyond fifty units which is sold, the $2,000 becomes a contribution to profit.

To complicate the example, assume that the management of the mobile home manufacturing firm has not yet determined the selling price and variable costs per unit. Instead, management has been presented with the annual figures of $200,000 for total variable costs for gross sales of $400,000. Fixed costs are estimated to be $100,000. These relationships are shown in Figure 9-2. The basic formula for determining the breakeven point may still be used with these different relationships. This time x represents dollars, not units at the breakeven point:

$$TR = VC + FC$$
$$x = 0.5x + 100,000$$
$$x - 0.5x = 100,000$$
$$0.5x = 100,000$$
$$x = 100,000/0.5$$
$$x = \$200,000$$

Since total variable costs are 50 percent of gross sales for the entire year, variable costs would be 50 percent of the revenue $(0.5x)$ at the breakeven point. The breakeven point occurred before the end of the year or before total variable costs and gross sales were accrued. Fixed costs were set at $100,000. Since x is used to represent dollars in this latter example, the breakeven point is also expressed in dollars.

The basic breakeven formula is used in both the unit and dollar problems above. Differences exist in the data presented and in the manner the data are manipulated. The determination of the breakeven point (units or dollars) depends upon the information provided. Both examples deal only with linear relationships. Breakeven analysis can become more sophisticated, and accordingly more realistic, by using nonlinear analysis.

IMPORTANCE AND LIMITATIONS OF BREAKEVEN ANALYSIS   Breakeven analysis is a useful quantitative method for improving management decision making. It is able to show the amount of profit and loss at various levels of output. If market demand indicates a loss or profit less than the expectations of management, appropriate decisions need to be made. The selling price may have to be altered; mechanization or automation may be required to decrease labor costs; physical facilities may have to be modernized to decrease fixed costs; and alternative products may have to be considered. Breakeven analysis may also be useful in detecting a gradual increase in costs, especially in variable costs. One of the biggest advantages of breakeven analysis is its straightforward logic which does not require an extensive knowledge of mathematics or statistics to use or interpret the results. However, there are certain limitations that should be recognized. Linear breakeven models are appropriate for only a given range of output. For example, the fixed costs for the mobile home manufacturer were $100,000. If the productive capacity was 150 coaches, these costs would remain constant. On the other hand, if the manufacturer built additional facilities to produce 250 coaches, the fixed costs might increase to $175,000. Another realistic limitation is that it assumes cost data are easily ascertained. This may not be true, especially for variable costs. For example, the mobile

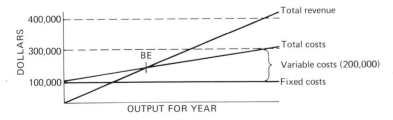

Figure 9-2 Breakeven Chart.

home manufacturer might experience difficulty in allocating power expenses, such as electricity, as a variable cost. Management would need to select an acceptable method for determining and allocating this expense. The final caution about breakeven analysis is that it is sometimes used as the sole means for making a decision. Like the other quantitative methods, this dependence can be dangerous. Breakeven analysis, like the other quantitative methods, is only a tool to help the manager make better decisions.

Present Value

Calculating present value is a common method for aiding the decision maker in the area of financial investments. The future flow of costs and revenues is given attention. The logic of present value is best understood and illustrated through compounding interest. For example, if $0.91 were placed in a savings account which paid 10 percent interest, 1 year later this $0.91 investment would be worth $1. Conversely, the dollar received 1 year from now has a present value of $0.91. If an individual deposited $0.83 in the savings account at 10 percent interest, 1 year later it would be worth $0.91. If this $0.91 was left in the savings account for an additional year, it would be worth $1. Therefore, the present value of $1 received 2 years hence is $0.83.

EXAMPLE OF PRESENT VALUE   The method of present value applied to decision making can be shown in the case of a college student who is purchasing a new automobile. For an additional $100 the student is able to purchase a service contract. The contract applies to the first 2 years of the car and includes free oil changes and tune-ups. The student estimates these expenses to be $50 for the first year and $80 for the second. In order to purchase the contract, the student will need to borrow the money from the local bank at 10 percent interest. Using these figures, the student may use present value to evaluate the investment. Since the present value of $1 received 1 year hence is $0.91, the present value of $50 would be $45.50 (0.91 × 50). Likewise, if the present value of $1 received 2 years hence is $0.83, the present value of $80 would be $66.40 (0.83 × 80). Thus, the present value of the expenses for both years would be $111.90 (45.50 + 66.40). A simple comparison of the investment with the discounted costs shows a savings of $11.90 (111.90 − 100). Therefore, according to present-value analysis the student should make the decision to purchase the service contract.

IMPORTANCE AND LIMITATIONS OF PRESENT VALUE   Just as in the case of the student above, present value can be a useful tool for many management decisions. For example, a manager could use present-value analysis to evaluate alternative capital equipment expenditures. The method is able to predict future flows of costs and earnings. However, this method, like others, is only as good as its inputs. It assumes that variables such as cost of capital are easily ascertained. In the student example this rate was assumed to be 10 percent. In reality this rate may not be easily determined. Such factors as inflation, uncertainty of interest rates, and whether investments are made from cash or borrowed funds may affect cost of the funds. Also, present-value analysis assumes that costs and earnings are accrued at the end of a time period. In the student example, automobile expenses were assumed to occur at the end of each year. In reality, these costs would be incurred throughout the year. This type of occurence distorts the true present value of future costs and earnings. Future revenues and costs are also realistically difficult to estimate. If the student had not previously owned an automobile, i.e., if he or she had no experience to estimate the costs, the yearly expenses would be difficult to derive. The same holds true for management decision makers. They need relevant experience in order to make meaningful estimates or assign probabilities. The next part of the chapter discusses the types of conditions which exist for management to assign these probabilities.

Modern Approach to Quantitative Decision Making

The first part of the chapter viewed decision making from a process and a problem perspective. The contemporary approach to quantitative decision making emphasizes the conditions under which the process and problems of management decision making occur. The most common breakdown is into the conditions of certainty, risk, and uncertainty.

Certainty is the condition where the decision maker can specify exactly the action which will be taken during a given time period to lead to a particular outcome. Risk is the condition where the decision maker can specify a probability distribution of actions leading to different possible outcomes. Uncertainty refers to the condition where the decision maker cannot specify the probability distribution for actions leading to outcomes. The repetitive routine decisions that managers make fall in the realm of certainty. Individually they do not have much of an effect on the goals of the organization but added together, because they make up such a large percentage of the decisions, they have a definite impact on organizational effectiveness. However, especially in middle and top management, the important decisions fall in the risk and uncertainty categories. Managers typically have some experience and knowledge in making vital decisions in areas such as product line or plant location but cannot predict certain outcomes. Yet, it is these risk and uncertain decisions that can spell the difference between success and failure of an organization. Whereas the computer has had a significant impact on decisions under certainty (programmed decisions), the new quantitative decision models have had a big impact on decision making under risk and uncertainty (nonprogrammed decisions).

Controllable Factors in Decision Making

Decision makers are faced with both controllable and uncontrollable factors. Controllable factors are the strategies and tactical alternatives which the decision maker develops in order to achieve desired goals. Such strategies may be developed or based on a searching look within the organization, a broad look around the organization, and a long look ahead.[4] The look within identifies the strengths and limitations of the organization. A look

---

[4] Ewing W. Reilley, "Planning the Strategy of Business," *Advanced Management*, December 1955, pp. 8–12.

around examines the external factors affecting organizational success. Specific consideration is given to the relations with customers or clients, employees, suppliers, and the community at large. The last, a long look ahead, attempts to evaluate the future environment and its impact on the organization. Here is where the planning function becomes especially important. This systematic three-step approach can make decision making more controllable.

Most modern management decision makers are attempting to develop strategies to increase revenue, reduce costs, and improve efficiency in order to attain the goals of their organizations. The appropriate strategy for achieving these types of goals can be developed from three general perspectives: marketing, resource procurement, and efficiency.[5] For example, marketing strategies can help improve a business organization's revenue position. This strategy includes areas such as product line, pricing, advertising, and product and service innovations. Resource procurement strategies, on the other hand, are directly aimed at reducing costs. Resources such as labor, raw materials, and supplies are important to the costs of a business organization. Strategies leading to more effective collective bargaining, recruiting, and training, raw material procurement, inventory control, and location policies would lead to reduced costs. Increases in the overall efficiency of an organization can result from successful implementation of the other two. For example, increased revenues and cost reductions are achieved through an effective design of facilities and equipment, the use of scientific procedures, standardization and simplification, proper utilization of facilities, and proper motivation techniques for employees.

The discussion of strategies so far has been couched in very general terms. Practicing management decision makers would have to translate these general strategies into specific tactical alternatives. These specific tactical alternatives would provide the means for management to achieve its strategic organizational goals. For example, a clothing store owner may develop several tactical alternatives for pricing shirts. These alternatives might include, but not be limited to, (1) using the suggested retail price of the manufacturer, (2) using a markup percentage received from a trade association, or (3) pricing each group of shirts by brand, color, or size. This pricing decision would be of the risk variety if the retailer had some previous experience, e.g., with pants. On the other hand, if instead of shirts, the product was totally new, then the decision would be under uncertainty. This same retailer may be faced with a similar situation in advertising. The retailer may feel there are several possible tactical alternatives for developing an effective promotion effort. For example, the advertising format may be developed by the retailer; the format may be provided by the manufacturer; the retailer may hire an advertising agency to do the layout; or the retailer may decide to copy the basic format used by the major competitor. Each represents a specific tactical alternative to accomplish the marketing strategy. The retail store managers would need to develop similar tactical alternatives for

---

[5] See Henry H. Albers, *Principles of Management: A Modern Approach,* Wiley, New York, 4th ed., 1974, pp. 300–321.

the remaining strategies they have determined are necessary for goal attainment. For the most part management has control over these strategic factors.

Uncontrollable Factors in Decision Making

The uncontrollable factors in decision making are sometimes referred to as states of nature. Examples are consumer demand, legislation, and acts of nature such as the weather. Even though these factors are not directly controllable by management, it can still influence them. For example, management could develop an effective advertising campaign to influence consumer demand and employ a lobbyist to affect legislation. Management may also utilize forecasting techniques to help predict the uncontrollable factors facing it. For example, a large manufacturer of social expression items used a test market for a new pen it was planning to manufacture and sell. The test market was established in the Chicago area. The pen was so successful in the test market that a backlog of orders developed. Later the company marketed the pen nationally with equally successful results. This manufacturer was making a decision under relative uncertainty. However, by using a test market to estimate a relatively uncontrollable consumer demand, the decision was drawn back into the realm of risk rather than uncertainty.

Chapter 4 gave specific attention to various forecasting techniques. They certainly can help predict uncontrollable factors but are not infallible. No technique can perfectly predict the future. This is especially true of the states of nature. For example, a university's administration recently decided to close down a large dormitory because forecasts indicated a trend of decreasing student enrollment. Yet, when the fall quarter started, the university had a 2.5 percent increase in enrollment. Not only were the dorms filled, but students had to temporarily sleep in the lobbies and halls of the residence facilities. In this case, the administration made a wrong decision. Its forecast was completely off base. The administration had relied on general trends and had been dealt a blow by uncontrollable factors that it had not been able to predict.

Both the controllable and uncontrollable factors are relevant inputs into a management decision. The ultimate decision, however, greatly depends on some rule or standard. This rule or standard is known as the decisional criterion. Decisional criteria guide the actions a decision maker will take when certain, risk, or uncertain conditions arise. The decisional criteria are established in deterministic models, probabilistic models, and subjective criteria determined by management. These decisional criteria are illustrated in the following sections on decision making under certainty which primarily uses deterministic quantitative models, risk which depends on probabilistic models, and uncertainty which relies on subjective criteria.

Decisions under Certainty

Decision making under certainty was said to commonly apply to repetitive or routine problems. For example, once a policy is formulated, decisions to carry it out become repetitive and routine. An organization may have a policy on absenteeism for hourly paid personnel such that an employee who is absent for four consecutive days without notifying the company is dismissed. In the case of this policy, the manager knows for certain the action or decision which will be made if absenteeism occurs. The decisional criterion is represented by the absenteeism policy. This does not mean that policies remain static and never change. The policy may change, but the action to be taken is certain for the decision-making period. An example demonstrating this latter situation may be a policy concerning the pregnancy of female employees. Traditionally the policy was that pregnancy would force the woman to resign. Today, societal and governmental pressures have generally altered pregnancy policy. Now pregnancy is treated as a temporary disability. The decision on a pregnant employee is certain. Once the policy has been changed, the decisional action to be taken will be certain until the policy is changed again.

Decisional models which are applied under conditions of certainty are called deterministic or optimizing models. The term *deterministic* means that an exact decision or answer is provided. Many, if not most, of the traditional and contemporary quantitative models used in practice are of this nature. They provide exact solutions or answers. For example, an economic order quantity model determines the optimum quantity to be purchased in order to minimize ordering and carrying costs. The traditional breakeven and present-value approaches discussed earlier are also deterministic. Recently, attempts have been made to evaluate these types of models under the additional conditions of risk and uncertainty. Basically, this is done by changing the simplistic and unrealistic assumptions traditionally made by the deterministic models.

A simple problem may be used to illustrate decision making under certainty. Take the case of a manager of a shoe department in a retail store who is trying to determine the exact number of 20-inch shoelaces which should be ordered for resale. Immediate delivery is available from a nearby wholesaler. The manager has reviewed a previous 200-day period to evaluate demand patterns. This distribution is shown below:

Units Sold per Day	No. of Days	Probability
10	50	.25
11	50	.25
12	100	.50
	200	1.00

During the 200 days, ten boxes were sold 25 percent of the time (50/200), eleven boxes were sold 25 percent of the time(50/200), and twelve boxes were sold 50 percent of the time (100/200). If the manager had perfect information, he or she would know for certain the days in the future when ten, eleven, or twelve units would be sold. This would facilitate the ordering process and allow the manager to determine what the average profit per day would be. This is illustrated below:

Units Sold per Day	No. of Days	Probability	Profit
10	50	.25	$12.50
11	55	.25	13.75
12	60	.50	30.00
			$56.25

The profit per box is set at $5. The average profit per day is $56.25. This analysis assumes the manager knows for *certain* when a particular number of units would be sold. Similar results could be achieved by a simple arithmetic average. This is illustrated below:

Units Sold per Day	No. of Days	Total Units Sold	Profit
10	50	500	$ 2,500
11	50	550	2,750
12	100	1,200	6,000
	200		$11,250

The average profit per day is again $56.25 (11,250/200). This latter arithmetic procedure is simpler, but the probability distribution approach has wider applicability. Probability is especially applicable to conditions of risk.

Decisions under Risk

Decision making under risk was defined as specifying a probability distribution over the possible outcomes. The decision maker does not know for certain which condition will occur, but can select a course of action based on relevant historical data. The ultimate decision still depends on the decisional criteria. A criterion commonly used for risk decisions is probability-based expected monetary value (EMV). The term *expected* is used to denote average. To make the best decision, the tactical alternative which provided the largest EMV would be selected. As indicated earlier, many of the important decisions made by managers fall under the risk category. The key is that historical records must be available for the decision to be of the risk type.

Using the previous example of shoelaces, a matrix for decisions made under risk can be developed. The profit per box is $5 and the cost per box is $4. The decisional criterion is expressed as the largest EMV. This is illustrated below:

Probability	Demand/Buy	10	EMV	11	EMV	12	EMV
.25	10	$50	$12.50	$46	$11.50	$42	$10.50
.25	11	50	12.50	55	13.75	51	12.75
.50	12	50	25.00	55	27.50	60	30.00
			$50.00		$52.75		$53.25

The demand, an uncontrollable factor, is determined from past records to be ten, eleven, or twelve units. Consequently, the manager may consider three alternatives: he or she may buy ten or eleven or twelve boxes. If the manager buys ten boxes and the demand is ten, a profit of $50 is realized. If the demand was eleven or twelve boxes, the profit would still be $50. Applying the probability distribution, the EMV is $50 for the alternative of buying ten boxes. If the manager purchased eleven units and the demand was ten, a profit of $46 (50 − 4) is realized (assuming salvage value is zero). The total revenue is $50 for selling ten boxes, but one unit is left unsold which cost $4. The profit would be $55 for each demand increment of eleven and twelve boxes when eleven boxes were purchased. Applying the probability distribution, the EMV for the second alternative (buying eleven boxes) is $52.75. The same procedure would be applied to purchasing twelve boxes with the EMV being $53.25. The third alternative, buying twelve boxes, should be selected by the manager since it has the largest expected monetary value.

The above example is purposely very simple. It is only meant to show the basic approach to decision making under risk. With limited experience, the application of probability has a great impact on risk decisions. It is a precise mathematical technique that permits the decision maker to calculate possible outcomes and make inferences. The probability calculation is based upon past experience. Tossing a coin provides a clear example of the method and implications of statistical probability. A person tosses an unbiased, balanced coin 100 times. The outcome of the 100 tosses is 50 heads and 50 tails. With this experience, the decision maker will assign a probability of .5 that on the 101st toss of the coin the outcome will be a head (or a tail).

The coin-tossing example represents an ideal situation for the decision maker. Unfortunately, most management decision makers in a modern organization do not have as much or as relevant experience as does the coin tosser. Furthermore, the coin tosser can be pretty sure that half the time the 101st toss will be heads. Yet, if the tosser obtained several tails in a row, it would take little time and effort to toss the coin 100 more times and then he or she would end up with 50 heads. In other words, it may take a great number of outcomes in order for the probability to work itself out. Typically, the management decision maker does not have the time or resources to let the probability work itself out. Albers points out another limitation of probability: "The number of fires or deaths that will occur during a given period can be calculated with a low margin of error if the sample is large enough and randomly distributed. But probability theory cannot determine which house will be destroyed by fire or who will pass through the pearly gates."[6] In short, objective statistical probability has certain realistic constraints which cannot and should not be overlooked. Yet, despite the limitations, if properly applied and interpreted, statistical probability has proved to be a very effective tool in helping managers make risk decisions.

Decisions under Uncertainty

Uncertainty was defined as the inability of specifying the relative likelihood of outcomes. These situations may occur when introducing a new product that does not have any historical or past relevant experience. The ultimate decision is based on subjective criteria developed by the decision maker. Thus, for every decision maker there may be a different set of decisional criteria. The following simple example is used to demonstrate decision making under uncertainty.

Management is planning to introduce a new product in the line. The range of alternatives has been narrowed to product A and product B. The two possible relevant states of nature or uncontrollable factors are a stable economy and an inflationary economy. A profit matrix is developed as follows:

	States of Nature	
Alternatives	Stable Economy	Inflationary Economy
Product A	10	4
Product B	7	6

The two most common criteria used in decision making under uncertainty are the maximax and the maximin. The maximax criterion is optimistic and speculative. The best possible alternative is selected. The decision maker operating under a maximax criterion would proceed to select the greatest payoff for each alternative (product A, 10; and product B, 7). The maximum value of these two alternatives would then be selected (product A, 10). Thus, product A would be selected using the maximax criterion under uncertainty.

The maximin criterion is more pessimistic and conservative than maximax. Operating under maximin, the decision maker selects the worst payoff for each alternative (product

---

[6] Ibid., p. 82.

A, 4; and product B, 6). The maximum of these two values (product B, 6) is then selected for the decision. Thus, under maximin, product B would be selected by the decision maker under uncertainty.

The above example is highly simplified but illustrates the subjectiveness of decisions made under uncertainty. Decisions depend on the decisional criteria which are subjectively derived by the decision maker. The manager may apply any decision rule. However, pragmatically, even under conditions of uncertainty, the decision maker should assign probabilities to the states of nature. Yet, it must be remembered that these are highly subjective probabilities and are not developed from past records. The probabilities are generated from intuitive estimates and are merely attempts by the decision maker to draw decisions under uncertainty back into the realm of risk. This can be dangerous, but uncertain conditions can be bounded by the decision maker so that alternatives can be systematically evaluated as well as possible. A thorough understanding of Bayesian statistics can help the decision maker in this effort.

Summary

Decision making is an important facet of modern management. The present era of accountability, efficiency, and scarce resources requires new decision-making techniques at all levels of management. The quantitative approach seems to be making the biggest inroads. Decision making must be delineated into process and problem perspectives. Management science or operations research techniques have been especially useful in problem-oriented decisions. Traditional breakeven analysis and present value were used to demonstrate how cost and revenue decisions can be aided by quantitative methods. A contemporary framework for decision making was next presented. Both the controllable and uncontrollable factors were previewed for making decisions under conditions of certainty, risk, and uncertainty. Certainty models are primarily deterministic; risk decisions rely on probabilistic models; and uncertainty models are dependent upon subjective decisional criteria. However, both certainty and uncertainty are dependent more and more on probabilistic models for optimum solution.

The simple examples that were used in the chapter to illustrate the quantitative approach to management decision making should not mislead the reader. The purpose of the chapter is not to make the reader competent in the solution mechanics of complex quantitative methods but instead introduce the approach used in quantitative management. Depth and refinements are left to specific books dealing with statistics and quantitative methods. The remaining two chapters in this section of the book give an overview of the major decision models and relate the quantitative variables to the contingency framework of management.

☐ Critical Incident

Green Acres is a real estate company which owns and operates several large apartment complexes. Most of these complexes are located near the university and are largely occupied by students. Consequently, the occupancy level is rather erratic during the year. After experiencing financial problems, the head of the company has asked the accountant to determine the breakeven point for each complex. The accountant is able to obtain last year's figures on total revenue, total variable costs, and fixed costs for each complex.

1 How would the breakeven point be determined? How can this information help the management of this company?

2 Give some examples of certainty, risk, and uncertainty decisions that the management of this company might face.

Questions for Review and Discussion

1 What is the difference between the process and the problem approaches to decision making?

2 What is breakeven analysis used for? Define and give examples of the basic costs relevant to breakeven analysis.

3 What is the logic behind present value? Analyze the importance and limitations of present value.

4 Distinguish between the controllable and uncontrollable factors in decision making. Give examples of each.

5 Distinguish between decision making under certainty, risk, and uncertainty. Give examples of each.

References

Brown, Kenneth S.: "Management Science: Its Role in the Organization," *Managerial Planning,* July–August 1972, pp. 6–10, 38.

Grayson, C. Jackson: "Management Science and Business Practice," *Harvard Business Review,* July–August 1973, pp. 41–48.

Hall, William K.: "The Uncertainty of Uncertainty in Business Planning," *Managerial Planning,* September/October 1974, pp. 7–12.

Heinze, David C.: "The Decision Theory Approach to Managerial Decision-making," *Marquette Business Review,* Fall 1972, pp. 156–162.

Karson, Marvin J., and William J. Wrobleski: "A Manager's Guide to Probability Modeling," *Michigan Business Review,* May 1972, pp. 23–30.

Levin, Richard I., and Charles A. Kirkpatrick: *Quantitative Approaches to Management,* McGraw-Hill, New York, 1971.

————— **and Rudolph P. Lamone:** *Quantitative Disciplines in Management Decisions,* Dickenson, Belmont, Calif., 1969.

Paik, C. M.: *Quantitative Methods for Managerial Decisions,* McGraw-Hill, New York, 1973.

Pokempher, Stanley J.: "Is There a Management Scientist in the House," *The Conference Board Record,* May 1974, pp. 11–15.

Vespar, Karl H., and Yutaka Sayeki: "A Quantitative Approach for Policy Analysis," *California Management Review,* Spring 1973, pp. 119–126.

Decision Models and Operations Research

The preceding chapter developed a foundation for the quantitative approach to management. This chapter builds on that foundation. A discussion of the overall nature and background of decision models and operations research is followed by giving specific attention to the models of linear programming (both the graphic and transportation methods), economic order quantity, queuing or waiting line, and simulation. After the approach is defined and explained, specific examples, diverse uses, and values and limitations are analyzed for each model.

The Nature of Decision Models

The purpose of decision models is to improve management decisions. They provide a viable alternative to simple rule-of-thumb methods. What makes up a good management decision is not as simple as it appears. William Gavett has pointed out four different dimensions of a good decision:

1 A good decision must provide a satisfactory solution to the pertinent problem.
2 A good decision results from a choice from a spectrum of possible alternatives.
3 A good decision considers the economics of the decision-making process itself.
4 If a problem is correctly stated and the list of alternatives is reasonably exhaustive, then a good decision results in satisfactory outcomes.[1]

The goal of quantitative decision models is to provide these types of dimensions to management decision making. The main thrust, however, is the fourth dimension above. Decision models help improve organizational effectiveness and lead to satisfactory outcomes.

The last chapter pointed out that decisions are made under conditions of certainty, risk, and uncertainty. After the states of nature and decisional criteria are determined and the tactical alternatives are established, the decision maker may select and implement an appropriate model for choosing a solution. Models are used so that the decision maker

---

[1] J. William Gavett, *Production and Operations Management.* Harcourt, Brace & World, New York, 1968, pp. 32–33.

can construct boundaries around the decisional problem and make it manageable. Without boundaries, the decision maker is faced with an infinite number of variables and data. Most decisions that managers face could not be made without the use of models. Even though the model may not eliminate all risk and uncertainty, it will reduce the anxiety of working with all possible variables and alternatives. The decision maker will normally make the decision model as simple as possible, as long as it deals with the problem at hand. Simple models are economical in terms of time and thought, can be readily understood by the decision maker, and can be modified quickly and effectively as parameters change.[2]

Although models can help, they are certainly not the magical solution to all decisional problems facing modern management. Decision models have many limitations. For example, there may be a mistake in logic in the process of reasoning from premises to conclusions to solutions. In addition, the model builder may select the wrong variables, select too few variables, or relate them incorrectly.[3] Yet, despite these types of limitations, the use of models has significantly influenced improved decision making. This modeling approach applied to management has generally been labeled operations research.

The Nature of Operations Research

Operations research originated in Britain to solve military problems during World War II. Because of its success there, the United States borrowed the approach during the wartime years of 1942–1945. Operations research, or simply OR, was used in such areas as assigning targets and scheduling bomb strikes and determining the safest way of transporting men and materials across the oceans. Since this beginning, operations research has become a widely used approach to all types of management decision making in all types of organizations. The electronic computer has greatly facilitated the growth of OR by providing high-speed computation capacities.

Operations research is defined many different ways. Definitions range from specific mathematical techniques to the scientific method itself. Most of the definitions include three basic commonalities of an OR approach to management decision making: (1) a systems view of the problem; (2) a commitment to the use of the scientific method in solving the problem; and (3) the use of specific probability, statistical, and mathematical techniques and models to help the decision maker solve the problem.

Characteristics of Operations Research

The systems approach is given detailed attention in Part Five of the book. The OR approach incorporates this systems orientation by recognizing that the internal and external

---

[2] See Harold Bierman, Jr., Charles P. Bonini, and Warren H. Hausman, *Quantitative Analysis for Business Decisions*, 4th ed., Irwin, Homewood, Ill., 1973, p. 4.
[3] Ibid.

variables in decisional problems are interrelated and interdependent. The commitment to scientific methodology is brought out by the following statement by the Operations Research Society of America's Committee on Professional Standards: "Operations research is an experimental and applied science devoted to observing, understanding, and predicting the behavior of purposeful man-machine systems."[4] This statement about OR should not be confused with Frederick Taylor's approach to the scientific method. Taylor, the father of scientific management, was concerned with particular man-machine operations problems. In particular, he attempted to maximize the output/input ratio. Operations research, on the other hand, is concerned with analyzing the operations of a system—not a particular problem.

The specific probability, statistical, and mathematical techniques and models used in OR are most closely associated with this approach. Probability allows the OR approach to deal with decisions under conditions of risk and uncertainty. Statistics permits OR to systematize and analyze data in order to come up with meaningful solutions. For example, statistical sampling may help determine the proper sample size for simulation OR models. Mathematics, such as matrix algebra and differential equations, aids in formulating decisional rules and equations for OR techniques such as linear programming and economic order quantity models. These models are given detailed attention later in the chapter.

Limitations of Operations Research

Before going into some of the common models used in OR, some of its limitations should be mentioned. First of all, it should be remembered that operations research does not and should not make the actual decision. OR is only a tool to aid the decision maker. Other limitations are that many decisional problems cannot be expressed in quantitative terms and some problems are too large to solve by analytical OR techniques, even with the aid of a computer. In these instances, trial and error or rule of thumb may have to be used. This latter type of problem solving can be called heuristic programming. While the heuristic approach may not lead to the best solution in a particular case, experience over time has proved its general usefulness in finding good solutions to recurring problems with a minimum of effort.[5]

One of the biggest problems in operations research has been to know when and where it could be applied successfully. There have been very few effective guidelines offered. Most often, OR is presented as having universal applicability. An exception is a recent analysis by Dr. C. Jackson Grayson, who was chairman of the President's Price Commission. He feels that OR techniques are difficult to implement because of (1) shortage of time, (2) inaccessibility, (3) resistance to change, (4) long response time, and (5) invali-

---

[4] ORSA Committee on Professional Standards, "The Nature of Operations Research," *Operations Research,* September 1971, p. 1138.

[5] See Jerome D. Wiest, "Heuristic Programs for Decision Making," *Harvard Business Review,* September–October 1966, pp. 130–131.

dating simplifications.[6] Time, Grayson believes, has consistently been used as an exogenous variable in the OR approach. For OR models to be applicable, management scientists need to realize the impact of time on decisions and build the time factor into the OR models. His second criticism recognizes the fact that managers use tools and data only if they are both conveniently and speedily accessible. Third, Grayson believes it is a difficult task for managers to introduce the OR approach to others who are not quantitatively oriented and who deliberately resist using and responding to OR techniques. Fourth, few management scientists are prepared to respond to significant management problems in "real time." Most OR personnel have a scientific orientation and think and act in long time intervals. Last, the difficult but real problem areas, such as people, power structures, and political and informal pressures, are simplified out of existence by OR models. These types of limitations should be remembered when interpreting the OR models which follow.

Operations Research Models

At present, there are many effective operations research or decision models used in management decision making. The most important and widely used have been selected for discussion. They are relevant to many types of decisions in many different types of organizations. The discussion of the models is kept at a basic level, and the models are demonstrated by relatively simple examples. However, the reader should be able to gain insights and understanding of OR techniques to be used for application and further study.

Linear Programming

Mathematical programming techniques in general have been used to solve numerous decisional problems. Mathematical programming includes linear programming (linear relationship between the variables), nonlinear programming (nonlinear relationship between the variables), and dynamic programming (dynamic relationship between the variables). This section is limited to the simplest but most widely used linear programming. Linear programming attempts to allocate scarce resources according to a stated objective. The resources may include money, capital, equipment, raw materials, and personnel. The objective may be maximum profit or minimum cost. Both the objective and the environmental constraints which limit the degree of achievement of the objective can be stated in the form of linear equations (the variables are directly proportional) and inequalities (permits more flexibility). There are several specific methods which may be used to solve linear programming problems. These include the graphical, simplex, dual simplex, and modified distribution (MODI) transportation methods. For purposes of simplicity, the graphical and transportation methods are discussed below. The other methods are used to solve the more complex linear programming problems.

---

[6] See C. Jackson Grayson, Jr., "Management Science and Business Practice," *Harvard Business Review,* July–August 1973, pp. 43–45.

GRAPHICAL METHOD   An appreciation of the conceptual basis of linear programming is gained from the graphical method. The following example illustrates this approach.

A small manufacturer is in business to build steps and awnings for mobile home owners. Each of the products has been standardized to be mass-produced. The two tactical alternatives or products, in this case steps and awnings, are constrained by four resources. These constraints include fiberglass, lumber, space, and time. The decisional criterion or objective is to maximize profits. The linear relationship of the products and scarce resources is shown in Figure 10-1.

With the present supply of lumber a maximum of twenty-two awnings could be produced each week or a maximum of twenty-five steps could be produced. Likewise, the available space limits the production of awnings to twenty or the production of steps to thirty-five. The time required by employees to produce the products is also a constraint. There is time available to produce thirty-five awnings or twenty steps. Last, fiberglass is used only for the awnings. This resource does not constrain the production of steps. There is enough fiberglass available to produce twenty-five awnings. The fiberglass constraint is shown by the horizontal line. The shaded area indicates the possible solutions to the problem. This area is represented by the points A, B, C, and D, and the optimal solution for maximizing profits is located at one of these points. Since fiberglass falls beyond the shaded area, it is not a constraint for the optimal solution. In other words, the other three factors will limit the number of units produced before fiberglass will. If the profit is deter-

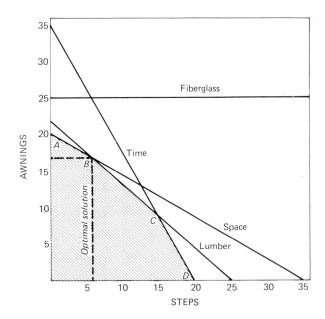

Figure 10-1   Graphic Method of Linear Programming.

mined to be $65 per awning and $40 per step, the optimal solution for the problem can be derived in the following manner:

Graphical Points	Units Produced		Profit per Product		Total Profit
	Awnings	Steps	Awnings	Steps	
A	20	0	$1,300		$1,300
B	16.5	6.5	1,072.50	$260	1,332.50
C	9	15	585	600	1,185
D	0	20	0	800	800

The calculation shows that the decision should be made to produce at point B (16.5 awnings and 6.5 steps) at a total profit of $1,332.50.

THE TRANSPORTATION METHOD   The transportation method of linear programming uses an iterative (repeating) process to develop an optimal solution. The earliest formulation of the basic transportation problem goes back to the early 1940s. Generally, the method attempts to distribute a product from various points of supply to a number of different destinations. The decisional criterion, or objective, is to minimize transportation costs by scheduling the proper quantity from the sources to the destinations. The basic method can be illustrated in the following simple example.

A company has three plants (A, B, C) which transport products to three warehouses (X, Y, Z). Management is trying to determine how many units should be shipped from each plant to each warehouse to minimize transportation costs. The warehouses, plants, unit transportation costs (in the corner of each cell), and capacities are shown below:

Plants	Warehouses			Capacities
	X	Y	Z	
A	.20	.22	.15	1,000
B	.30	.25	.20	4,000
C	.40	.32	.35	3,000
Capacities	2,000	3,000	3,000	8,000 = total capacity

For example, the data above show that the transportation cost of shipping 100 units from plant A to warehouse X is $20. The units may be allocated by using the northwest-corner approach (starting in the upper left-hand corner). Starting in the northwest cell, the allocation totals correspond to the capacities for each plant and warehouse as shown below:

		Warehouses						
Plants		X		Y		Z		Capacities
A	1,000							
		.20		.22		.15	1,000
B	1,000		3,000					
		.30		.25		.20	4,000
C					3,000			
		.40		.32		.35	3,000
Capacities	2,000		3,000		3,000		8,000 = total capacity

For example, 1,000 is allocated in cell A,X because that is the capacity for plant A. In B,X, 1,000 is allocated because warehouse X has a capacity of 2,000. Therefore, the capacity for warehouse X is filled and nothing can be allocated to C,X. The 3,000 allocated to B,Y and C,Z use the same logic. The total transportation costs for the first allocation would be $2,300 (unit costs times units in each cell). However, it must be remembered that each allocation has different total costs. A second allocation (an iteration) is shown below:

		Warehouses						
Plants		D		E		F		Capacities
A	1,000							
		.20		.22		.15	1,000
B	1,000				3,000			
		.30		.25		.20	4,000
C			3,000					
		.40		.32		.35	3,000
Capacities	2,000		3,000		3,000		8,000

In this second allocation the total transportation cost would be $2,060. The decision maker would continue to go through additional iterations until the optimal solution (minimum transportation cost) is determined.

VALUES AND LIMITATIONS   Like other quantitative methods, linear programming can be a valuable tool for the decision maker. First of all, as the examples demonstrated, linear programming can be a tremendous aid to solving simple or complex allocation problems. A sampling of recent literature revealed the following diverse applications:[7]

1 *School Busing*   Linear programming was used to minimize the required routes and mileage for busing students. Extensions of the model were considered useful for school location planning, bus fleet planning, and timing conditions on bus stops.

2 *Academic Administration*   Linear programming was used to allocate faculty effort in an academic department among formal teaching and department service duties and other tasks such as research and student counseling.

3 *Community Development*   A linear programming model was used to determine optimal land needed for the community, maximum revenues, and the optimal division breakdown.

4 *Transistor Production*   Linear programming was applied to the production planning of transistors. The model facilitated the selection of materials processing variables and activity levels.

The above is not intended to be an exhaustive list of linear programming applications. It merely represents a cross section of various organizations where linear programming can be used. Secondly, this OR technique may guarantee to a greater extent that operating-level decisions are being made with reasonable precision; it certainly can provide better solutions to decisional problems, if not necessarily the best solution. Thirdly, the technique, especially with the aid of the computer, relieves busy practitioners from tedious calculations of decision alternatives by enumeration. Last, but by no means least, linear programming can put day-to-day decision making on a more objective basis.[8] By the same token, linear programming is limited by the same factors that hamper other quantitative methods. The technique is only as good as its inputs generated by the functional units of the organization. For example, cost data and market demands have to be accurately determined and forecast by the financial and marketing functions of a business firm. Linear programming only contributes to more effective management; it should not automatically be equated with good management.

Economic Order Quantity Model
Economic order quantity (EOQ) is mainly applied to inventory control. It determines the quantity of goods which should be ordered in order to minimize total costs. The EOQ

---

[7] See R. D. Angel, W. L. Caudle, R. Noonan, and A. Whinston, "Computer Assisted School Bus Scheduling," *Management Science*, February 1972, pp. 279–288; J. S. Dyer, A. Frinberg, and A. M. Geoffrion, "An Interactive Approach for Math-Criterion Optimization, with an Application to the Operation of an Academic Department," *Management Science*, December 1972, pp. 361–362; R. L. Heroux and W. A. Wallace, "Linear Programming and Financial Analysis of New Community Development Process," *Management Science*, April 1973, pp. 857–872; and S. B. Smith, "Planning Transistor Production by Linear Programming," *Operations Research*, September–October 1965, pp. 132–139.

[8] Richard I. Levin and Rudolph P. Lamone, *Linear Programming for Management Decisions*, Irwin, Homewood, Ill., 1969, p. 19.

model is often presented as being brand new but in actuality can be traced back well over a half century to the work of George Babcock:

Babcock recognized that in the case where repeat orders were involved the lowest total unit cost of production was determined by the lot size. He apparently derived a formula for calculating the economical lot size, as he established standard lot sizes in 1912. He did not publish the formula, however, because he felt that the cubic equations used could not be employed by the planning department.[9]

Recognition for developing and introducing the basic EOQ formula has been credited to Ford W. Harris in 1915, when it was used on inventory control in the Westinghouse Electric and Manufacturing Company.

The basic EOQ model considers two costs—carrying and ordering costs. Carrying costs may include such items as insurance and handling expenses, while ordering costs may include the expense of making out an order for purchasing materials. The relationship of these costs is shown in Figure 10-2. The figure shows that as the order size increases to a point, the total ordering costs decrease. This decreasing total cost results from the increase in the number of items purchased each time, which decreases the number of orders placed during a given time period. In addition, as the order size increases, the carrying cost will also increase. The increase of items purchased each time increases the amount of inventory on hand, with a subsequent increase in carrying costs. The point

[9] Roy F. Mennell, "Early History of the Economic Lot Size," in Robert Goodell Brown (ed.), *Source Book in Production Management,* Dryden Press, Hinsdale, Ill., 1970, p. 173.

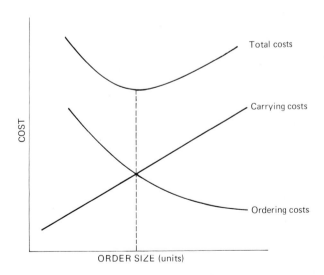

Figure 10-2   Cost Relationships in the Basic Inventory Model.

where the two costs (carrying and order) intersect is where total costs are minimized. At this point, the optimum order size or EOQ may be determined. Setting these two costs (carrying and ordering) equal to each other, the basic formula looks as follows:

$$\text{Carrying cost} = C \frac{Q}{2} \quad \left(\frac{Q}{2} = \text{average inventory}\right)$$

$$\text{Order cost} = S \frac{D}{Q}$$

$$C \frac{Q}{2} = S \frac{D}{Q}$$

$$\frac{Q^2}{2} C = SD$$

$$Q^2 C = 2SD$$

$$Q^2 = \frac{2DS}{C}$$

$$Q = \sqrt{\frac{2DS}{C}}$$

$$EOQ = \sqrt{\frac{2DS}{C}}$$

where Q = quantity ordered
S = order cost
D = yearly demand
C = cost of carrying one unit in inventory

For example, if yearly demand was 16,000 units, the ordering cost was $1, and the per unit carrying costs were $0.20, the EOQ would be 400 units.

$$EOQ = \sqrt{\frac{2 \times 16,000 \times 1}{0.20}} = 400$$

To minimize the total costs, 400 units should be purchased each time or forty orders would be made during a year with a demand of 16,000 units.

USES OF EOQ   The economic order quantity model is best applied to an order point system of inventory control. When inventory levels reach a predetermined point, an order for the economic quantity is placed by the purchasing agent. The time interval between orders would vary, but the quantity ordered would remain constant. This sort of ordering system would largely be used for routine, staple goods which require fewer control dollars than critical goods. A survey of the literature showed that EOQ models have been applied to maintenance materials, general hospital supplies, blood for a blood bank, and greeting cards.[10] In the first three examples, the EOQ was used for purchasing goods from an outside supplier. For greeting cards, the model determined the economic batch quantity. This greeting card company attempted to determine the proper number of cards to produce for its inventory. The company found that present production quantities were too high and that the planned life for card designs needed to be altered for the economic batch quantity to be successful.

The EOQ logic can be applied to very simple supply problems that everyone commonly faces. For example, an individual uses the EOQ and order point system when using personalized checks. The person usually keeps a box which contains several pads of checks; the last pad contains a statement concerning the order point. As the last pad is being used, a new order is sent to the bank for a resupply of checks. This resupply notice also indicates that if the EOQ, which has been used in the past, has lasted more or less than is desirable in terms of handling (storage in the desk drawer) and ordering (convenience), a new EOQ should be used. The EOQ is an attempt to minimize the number of orders a customer makes during a year and the cost of the checks (carrying costs). In this check supply instance, the quantity purchased normally remains constant but the interval between orders may vary depending on how fast checks are being used. Thus, whether dealing with huge supplies in a complex organization or keeping checks supplied to an individual, EOQ can be used to optimize the ordering quantity for inventory control.

VALUE AND LIMITATIONS OF EOQ   As implied above, the economic order quantity model is an important tool for decision making in inventory control. Special-purpose formulas may be developed to meet particular situations. For each situation, the model would reveal and emphasize the significant relationships of relevant variables. Furthermore, the value of EOQ is exemplified in the formula itself. An error in the procurement costs may not greatly affect the total costs.[11] This relative insensitivity is due to the flatness of the total cost curve. Thus, EOQ is fairly flexible, but it must be remembered that the basic formula does not account for quantity discount structures and places considerable emphasis on the subjective acquisition costs of writing orders. Basic information must also be provided for the anticipated monthly and annual usage rates. To compensate for these deficiencies, special-purpose formulas need to be derived.

The EOQ model is mainly used under conditions of certainty. Unfortunately, certainty does not exist in all decisional situations. As with the other models, information may not be easily ascertained and it is dependent on accurate and detailed cost data. The costs are often oversimplified. For example, costs which do not vary with the quantity ordered

---

[10] See R. E. Bley, "Managing Maintenance Materials," *Factory,* November 1972, pp. 32–33; Ronald A. Barnum, Walter C. Griffin, and Thomas A. Rockwell, "Inventory Analysis as Applied to Hospital Whole Blood Supply and Demand," *The Journal of Industrial Engineering,* March–April 1962, p. 114; and S. K. Goyal, "Optimal Decision Rules for Producing Greeting Cards," *Operational Research Quarterly,* September 1973, pp. 391–401.

[11] See Max D. Richards and Paul S. Greenlaw, *Management Decision Making,* 2d ed., Irwin, Homewood, Ill., 1972, p. 546.

are considered irrelevant and have been eliminated; other costs such as inspection have been assumed away; and still other costs have been combined into a single component.[12] These limitations become costs sustained by management in order to implement an EOQ model.

Queuing or Waiting-Line Model

Everyone is confronted daily with problems which the waiting-line or queuing model is designed to solve. Individuals constantly become frustrated with waiting in line to make deposits at a drive-in bank, to be served at restaurants, to pick up supplies, to see the doctor, and to be registered for university courses. The recent success of quick-service hamburger chains is a reflection of successful application of waiting-line theory. A sampling of literature also found queuing models applied to the following diverse situations:[13]

1 *Community Services* The queuing model can be applied to many community problems. In one case it was applied to the emergency service system. The number of emergency units needed on duty, locating the emergency units, designing areas of responsibility, relocating the emergency units, and erecting preventive patrol patterns were problems analyzed by a queuing model.

2 *Airports* There are many waiting lines in a typical large airport. Queuing models can be applied to aircraft waiting for service, aircraft waiting to land, aircraft waiting to take off, and passengers waiting for auto parking, tickets, baggage, boarding, seating, and exiting.

3 *Retail Stores* There are many potential waiting-line problems in a retail establishment. In one case a queuing model was applied to the scheduling of personnel in service activities and variable tasks.

4 *Hospitals* One application of queuing was in the control of hospital inpatient bed occupancy levels. This was mainly accomplished through admissions control.

In a sense, waiting-line theory is an extension of Frederick W. Taylor's scientific management. Taylor was attempting to maximize the output/input ratio through procedural and physical changes, and waiting-line models also emphasize the output/input ratio. The goal of the queuing model is to increase the ratio by having the proper number of servicing units in order to minimize the waiting line. The cost of waiting must be balanced with the cost of adding additional service units. The optimal solution strikes a balance of these two costs. The following example is used to illustrate the approach.

---

[12] William A. Ruch, "Special-Purpose EOQ Formulas," *Journal of Purchasing,* May 1973, p. 35.

[13] See J. M. Chacken and R. C. Larson, "Methods for Allocating Urban Emergency Units: A Survey," *Management Science,* December 1972, pp. 110–130; B. O. Koopman, "Air-Terminal Queues under Time Dependent Conditions," *Operations Research,* November–December 1972, pp. 1089–1114; R. J. Paul, "The Retail Store as a Waiting Line Model," *Journal of Retailing,* Summer 1972, pp. 3–15; and "Stabilization of Inpatient Bed Occupancy through Control of Admissions," *Hospitals,* October 1963, pp. 41–48.

An automobile dealer is trying to determine the proper number of parts workers who should be employed to decrease waiting time of mechanics. The figures below show the total costs of employing one, two, and three parts workers:

	Parts Department Employees		
	1	2	3
Average number of mechanics arriving in an 8-hour day	50	50	50
Average time mechanics wait for parts workers in minutes per wait	10	8	7
Total time lost by mechanics in minutes	500	400	350
Value of mechanics' time at $12 an hour	$100	$80	$70
Value of parts workers' time at $2 an hour	$16	$32	$48
Total value of mechanics' and parts workers' time	$116	$112	$118

In this simple example, the automobile dealer should employ two parts workers. The two parts workers would minimize the combined costs of servicing units and waiting lines ($112).

SINGLE- AND MULTIPLE-CHANNEL APPROACHES   There are basically two types of waiting-line problems: single channel and multiple channel. The two are graphically illustrated in Figure 10-3. In the single-channel problem there is only one servicing facility. For example, a drive-in bank may have only one teller with several customers waiting to make deposits. Multiple-channel problems have more than one servicing facility. For

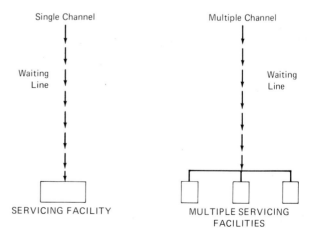

Figure 10-3 Two Types of Queuing Problems.

example, the drive-in bank may have three tellers accepting deposits from waiting customers. The bank would need to balance the cost of adding additional tellers with the cost of customers waiting in line.

CRITERIA FOR ACCEPTING ARRIVALS   To solve a waiting-line problem, consideration needs to be given to the order in which units or arrivals are taken. The criteria for acceptance in establishing a priority list may range from first in–first out (FIFO) to last in–first out (LIFO). In most instances, the FIFO method (first come, first served) would be used for accepting arrivals. For example, the first customers at a drive-in bank will be the first to be served. However, in some situations a priority list may be developed to divide the critical from the noncritical arrivals. For example, the director of medical records in a hospital may have a priority list for processing work. The priority list might run, in order, as follows: (1) history and physicals, (2) consultation, (3) surgical reports, and (4) final discharge summaries. The priority system indicates the work to be processed first when a backlog of medical records exists.

STRATEGIES FOR IMPROVEMENT   Several strategies may be employed for improving the service in a waiting-line problem. Robert Brown has outlined three possible alternatives: (1) provide additional channels, (2) provide parallel channels, and (3) speed up service on the available channels.[14] In the first, the additional channels would need to be compared with the additional costs. In the second alternative, parallel channels would be arranged so there is one common queue or waiting line. This situation commonly occurs during holiday seasons in large retail stores. Customers are asked to take a number which represents their position in a single waiting line. This procedure allows the workload to be better distributed by having one waiting line. The last alternative, increasing output of available channels, may be difficult to achieve, may be at the expense of quality, and may cause frustration of personnel. A fourth strategy may also be added which complements Brown's three. Flexibility could become an integral part of a scheduling and allocation program. For example, a large department store was using the National Cash Register 280 system to record the amount of activity at various departments every 15 minutes. If excessive activity was recorded in a particular area, additional clerks were allocated. This reduced the number of customers waiting to be served when activity had increased in a particular area.

The value and limitations of queuing models are similar to those of the other quantitative models discussed so far.

Simulation Models
Simulation models are used extensively to emulate a real system. These models are used to develop better decision makers or to provide data for developing better decisions.

---

[14] Robert Goodell Brown, *Management Decisions for Production Operations,* Dryden Press, Hinsdale, Ill., 1971, pp. 618–619.

Various alternatives and constraints may be tested by a simulation model before putting the decision into effect. For example, an energy consultant recently simulated the performance of a new federal office building. He tried to determine the effects of incorporating every energy-saving device in existence before the actual building was constructed. In this case, simulation was used to implement change without realizing the negative effects of the change. Other examples of applications of simulation include predicting the operational consequences of alternate systems designs of a hospital; testing the potential managerial succession and recruitment policy of a bank; and judging the impact of police patrol and dispatching units on urban public safety systems.[15]

Simulation models may be divided into the two broad categories of descriptive and normative. These categories are based on degrees of abstraction. The descriptive simulation models describe and categorize data or materials, while the normative models are more mathematically based and give optimal solutions. Like the other quantitative models, decisional criteria are used to determine the optimal solution. Figure 10-4 shows the breakdown of simulation models. It shows that there are iconic, analogue, and quantitative models. An iconic model is a scaled reproduction. For example, city planning commissions many times develop a scaled reproduction of new physical facilities for inner-city development projects. The iconic model would be used to determine the proper arrangement and design of buildings before construction is undertaken. Analogue models use one set of simulated properties to represent a different set of realistic properties. For example, network models (discussed in Chapter 17) and business games are often used for this type of simulation. The participants in the game simulate the management of a company. They are given certain operating, economic, and marketing information. Decisions commonly made by the game participants include the areas of advertising, pricing, plant capacities, and hiring sales persons. These decisions are made within a framework of rules and data which are fed back periodically to the participants. Quantitative models, as the name suggests, are mathematically based. Two common examples are game theory and Monte Carlo. In game theory it is assumed that two rational, reasoning opponents exist. The opponents are competitors, so that the gain of one is a loss to the other. In game theory, abstractions are made of reality and the variables are analytically evaluated. The second approach, Monte Carlo, is usually guided by random numbers to consider the probability of an event occurring. For example, it may be too costly for an individual to observe and collect the arrival and service times for a waiting-line problem. Monte Carlo could be used to simulate these randomly distributed times. Or, Monte Carlo methods may be used to determine the breakdown time of critical components of a machine.

Simulation models, descriptive and normative, are presented as being independent. In actual practice, descriptive models may be used to describe a problem before being

---

[15] R. B. Fetter and J. D. Thompsen, "The Simulation of Hospital Systems," *Operations Research,* September–October 1965, pp. 689–711; R. C. Jones, S. R. Morrisen, and R. P. Whiteman, "Helping to Plan a Bank's Manpower Resources," *Operational Research Quarterly,* September 1973, pp. 365–374; and R. C. Larson, "Decision-aiding Tools in Urban Public Safety Systems," *Sloan Management Review,* Winter 1972–1973, pp. 55–73.

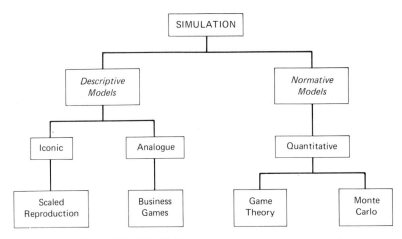

Figure 10-4 Types of Simulation Models.

translated into a quantitative model. Likewise, normative models may be used to determine solutions for descriptive models. In addition, it must be remembered that these models are only used to simulate the real situation or problem. There is a difference between simulation and reality. However, especially with the aid of the computer, simulating a decision via one of the models discussed in this section can be and has been a tremendous help to improved management decision making. Systems simulation is given detailed attention in Chapter 17.

Summary

This chapter was an extension of the last chapter on the quantitative approach to management. Specific attention was devoted to the nature and background of decision models and operations research. A modeling approach allows the decision maker to reduce complex problems to manageable terms for optimal solution. Operations research, or OR, which originated during World War II, depends on a systems view of problems, is committed to the scientific method, and uses specific quantitative techniques. The approach has definite limitations but can be a very effective tool to aid the modern management decision maker.

Linear programming was the first OR technique discussed. It assumes a linear (directly proportional) relationship between the variables. In the graphical method the various resource constraints are plotted. If the objective is to maximize profits, then the point on the graph which yields the highest profit should be used. In the transportation method, iterations are used to arrive at the optimal (minimum transportation costs) way to distribute a product from various points of supply to a number of different destinations. The values and limitations of linear programming are similar to operations research as a whole. The economic order quantity model determines the quantity of goods which should be ordered in order to minimize inventory costs. Both carrying and ordering costs are included in the model. The queuing or waiting-line model generally attempts to balance the cost of waiting with the cost of additional service units. Simulation models attempt to emulate reality. There are both descriptive and normative simulation models. Iconic models (e.g., scaled reproductions) and analogue models (e.g., business games) are examples of descriptive simulations. Quantitative models such as game theory and Monte Carlo are examples of normative simulations. Like the other OR models discussed in this chapter, simulation can greatly improve the management decision-making process.

☐ Critical Incident

You have just been hired by a large hospital as a systems analyst. During your first important conference with the boss, two major problems facing the hospital are presented to you. First is the problem of coordinating the materials management system. There are essentially three purchasing agents—one for dietary, one for pharmaceutical, and one for all other items. This arrangement, in many instances, leads to duplication of effort. Second, the Director of Medical Records is experiencing the problem of doctors being very erratic in dictating their medical reports. Consequently, there is a scheduling problem for the departmental load for medical records. The boss assigns you the task of developing decision models to increase the efficiency of these two areas of the hospital.

1 What quantitative decision models discussed in this chapter would help alleviate the problems described? Briefly describe what would go into these models.
2 What results would you expect from the use of quantitative decision models in this hospital?

Questions for Review and Discussion

1 Discuss the background and characteristics of operations research.
2 How does the graphical method of linear programming differ from the transportation method? Give some examples of the types of problems to which linear programming can be applied.
3 Describe some of the uses of EOQ models. What are some of the limitations of this model?
4 What is the major goal of queuing models? Give examples of strategies that employ additional or parallel channels for improving the service in a waiting-line problem.
5 What is the purpose of simulation models, and how can they be applied? Give some specific examples.

References

Browne, William G.: "Techniques of Operations Research," *Journal of Systems Management*, September 1972, pp. 8–13.

Burack, Elmer H., and Robert Bomi D. Batlivala: "Operations Research: Recent Changes and Future Expectations in Business Organizations," *Business Perspectives*, Fall 1972, pp. 15–22.

Gruber, William H., and John S. Niles: "Problems in the Utilization of Management Science/Operations Research: A State of the Art Survey," *Interfaces*, November 1971, pp. 12–19.

Newman, Joseph W.: *Management Applications of Decision Theory*, Harper & Row, New York, 1971.

ORSA Committee on Professional Standards, "The Nature of Operations Research," *Operations Research*, September 1971, pp. 1138–1148.

Rivett, Patrick: "The Art of Operations Research," *Organizational Dynamics*, Summer 1972, pp. 32–42.

Simmons, Donald M.: *Linear Programming for Operations Research*, Holden-Day, San Francisco, 1972.

Thompson, Gerald E.: *Linear Programming*, Macmillan, New York, 1971.

Van Horn, Richard L.: "Validation of Simulation Results," *Management Science*, January 1971, pp. 247–258.

Wagner, Harvey M.: *Principles of Management Science*, Prentice-Hall, Englewood Cliffs, N.J., 1970.

Wiest, Jerome D.: "Heuristic Programs for Decision Making," *Harvard Business Review*, September–October 1966.

Quantitative Variables and Contingency Management

The last two chapters gave an overview of the major quantitative concepts and techniques found in modern management. These quantitative variables are mainly applied to decision making. The problem is, of course, that they have not been applied contingent upon situational variables. The application of quantitative concepts and techniques has traditionally been based on very narrow and often unrealistic assumptions. The purpose of this concluding chapter in the quantitative part of the book is to place the material in the last two chapters into a contingency framework.

The first part of this chapter presents an overall framework for the use of decision models. The second part discusses the conditional impact on the specific application of economic order quantity, linear programming, queuing, and simulation models. A comprehensive quantitative case follows this chapter. As with the case at the end of Part Two, its purpose is to have the reader analyze the case according to a contingency framework.

A General Framework for Decision Models

There have been only sketchy attempts to determine contingent relationships between environmental *if*'s and appropriate quantitative concepts and techniques (the *then*'s). Although operations research is actually based on a situational premise, through the years the premise was either badly abused or completely ignored. Unrealistic situational assumptions were often cranked into OR models. More recently, management scientists have recognized the importance of the situation but tend to just mention it and not follow through by developing contingent relationships for successful application. Typical would be the following comment by management scientist Stanley Young: "We must know under what conditions it is advisable to move from Linear Programming to rule of thumb and then back to Linear Programming. There is an over-concern with single decision rule, and we must learn how to use different combinations of rules under a variety of operating conditions."[1]

---

[1] Stanley D. Young, "Organization as a Total System," in Fred Luthans (ed.), *Contemporary Readings in Organizational Behavior*, McGraw-Hill, New York, 1972, p. 109.

Contributions from Behavioral Science

Of more value than merely recognizing the importance of the situation, as has occurred in management science, has been the recent work of some behavioral scientists. Scholars such as Robert Duncan have attempted to identify types of environments that contribute to different degrees of uncertainty. Decision making under uncertainty is of course a major challenge of management science. A big step toward contingency management would be the identification of environmental factors that contribute to different degrees of uncertainty as perceived by decision makers. For example, Duncan identified organizational personnel, functional and staff units, and level as important internal environment components, and customers, suppliers, competitors, sociopolitical factors, and technology as important external components.[2] These components affect the degree of uncertainty facing the decision maker. Through empirical research, he found that "individuals in decision units experiencing dynamic-complex environments experience the greatest amount of uncertainty in decision making."[3] In relation to the quantitative techniques, this type of finding could be placed into an if-then contingency framework. For example, if decision makers are faced with a definable "dynamic-complex" environment, then they should use quantitative techniques adaptable to uncertainty. The deterministic and probabilistic models would be of little value in a highly uncertain environment, but models using subjective criteria such as maximax or maximin could be effectively used. Unfortunately, there are very few such contingent relationships that have been verified. The challenge for contingency management is to relate the environmental variables to specific quantitative concepts and techniques.

A Needed Conceptual Framework

Because of the lack of a contingency framework for management science, many organizations are experiencing some real problems. For example, *Business Week* recently reported that companies are running into big and costly troubles because mathematical models cannot handle all the variables that occur in, say, a refinery or a chemical plant.[4] To help meet the challenge of successful application of quantitative concepts and techniques, an overall conceptual framework is needed.

A systems approach can be used to develop a framework for quantitative decision models. The systems approach is selected because the quantitative approach, by itself, does not provide conceptual unity. The quantitative approach is more what Robert Brown has called a "kitbag of tools" rather than a conceptual approach to management.[5] The systems approach also recognizes that organizations are changing from structure to process. As Chapter 9 suggested, a process orientation should be combined with a problem orientation to provide a meaningful base for quantitative analysis.

---

[2] Robert B. Duncan, "Characteristics of Organizational Environments and Perceived Environmental Uncertainty," *Administrative Science Quarterly,* September 1972, p. 315.

[3] Ibid., p. 325.

[4] *Business Week,* Nov. 10, 1973, p. 152.

[5] Robert Goodell Brown, *Management Decisions for Production Operations,* Dryden Press, Hinsdale, Ill., 1971, pp. 535–540

Figure 11-1 represents an overall systems framework to put the quantitative models into their proper perspective. Input, control, decision models, functional subsystems, transformation, feedback, and output are the essential constructs in the framework. The input(s), of course, is where the environments, both general and specific, enter the system and affect the quantitative models. This is where the work of scholars like Robert Duncan, cited earlier, can make a significant contribution. The next section will give some specific examples of how environmental inputs can affect the decision models.

The control aspect of the model incorporates the material from Chapter 7 on the control process and, specifically, quantity, quality, time use, and cost. This control element can directly affect the decision models. For example, a requirement for infallible quality (zero defects) may prohibit the use of a simulation model. A short response time required from the time an input is received until a decision must be made may rule out the use of a quantitative model. The electronic computer, of course, is helping to solve this problem. Many of the quantitative models can and are being stored in computers. These "resident quantitative packages" in computers can give turnaround minutes after receiving the input. Chapters 17 and 18 will discuss computer applications in depth. In addition, the control element would require that the payoff from the use of a particular quantitative model must justify the cost. These are contingency types of relationships.

Functional subsystems as found in the model would include personnel, finance, marketing, and production in an industrial organization. Each of these, in turn, is made up of subsystems. For example, the production function could be further broken down into inventory, scheduling, work measurement, quality, method analysis, maintenance, and facilities planning. Personnel could be broken down into employment, training and development, wage and salary administration, and health, safety, and benefits. Even employment could be broken down further into workforce planning, recruitment, selection, and placement. The same is true of the functions of nonbusiness organizations. For example, a student health clinic has functions such as nursing service, business and finance,

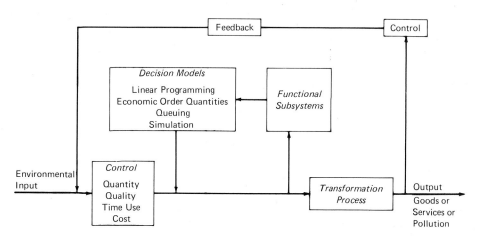

Figure 11-1 The Relationship of Quantitative Decision Models to Other Aspects of the Organizational System.

supportive services (laboratory, radiology, pharmacy, and physical therapy), medical services, and mental health.

The functional subsystems of an organization feed directly into the decision models. Some functional requirements are more adaptable to certain decision models than are others. For example, the production function, in general, would be much more adaptable to decision models than the personnel function. Yet, linear programming and/or simulation could be very helpful to workforce planning in the personnel function. The goal of contingency management is to match up the functional requirements with the appropriate quantitative decision model(s).

Once the decisions are derived with the aid of the quantitative models, the basic raw material is transformed into the output. The basic raw material for the transformation process may be students for a university, patients for a hospital, or physical materials for a manufacturing firm. The functional subsystems play a big role in this transformation process. After being transformed, the output (goods, services, or even pollution) is subjected again to control and feedback. Control, at this point, refers to comparing the actual performance of the functional subsystem with the predetermined expected performance. Both feedback and feedforward controls play a vital role in the system. However, as Koontz and Bradspies note, there is a definite need for better identification of environmental input: "Even the most enthusiastic proponents of feedforward control admit that, if input variables are not known or unmeasureable, the system will not work. Therefore, for the best control, the use of feedback for output variables is also suggested."[6] The comparison of actual performance with expected performance is highlighted in this final control element. Decision models may not give the optimal solution, such as maximization of profits, but only what was expected from the system. If expectations are not met, feedback may be used to change the variables in the quantitative model.

The systems model in Figure 11-1 only attempts to show how quantitative models can fit into the total picture. The contingency goal of relating specific environmental variables with specific quantitative decision techniques cannot be reached with just the aid of this model. However, the model does show that other variables in an organization system such as control, functional subsystems, and the transformation process will also affect the use and application of quantitative techniques. The next section will generally ignore these systems interactions and concentrate on specific conditions which can affect the application of the major quantitative techniques.

Situational Variables Affecting Quantitative Techniques

As indicated in the discussion so far, practically no empirical data or meaningful analysis has been devoted to the situational *if*'s applicable to quantitative techniques. General and

---

[6] Harold Koontz and Robert W. Bradspies, "Managing through Feedforward Control," *Business Horizons*, June 1972, pp. 29–30.

specific environmental variables of the kind discussed in Chapter 3 have not been applied to quantitative analysis or the use of specific techniques for optimal effectiveness. Instead, mathematical assumptions have mainly served as conditional constraints for quantitative techniques. In addition, the categories of certainty, risk, and uncertainty covered in Chapter 9 can also be thought of as situational *if*'s. In this latter sense, if a certainty condition exists, then deterministic quantitative models should be used; if a risk condition exists, then probabilistic models should be used; and finally, if an uncertainty condition exists, then decision models using subjective criteria such as maximax and maximin should be used. Beyond this type of contingent application, little has been done. The first section below attempts to give some general conditions applicable to all the quantitative techniques. This is followed by mention of some specific conditions that management scientists recognize as affecting economic order quantity, linear programming, queuing, and simulation models. However, to date, comprehensive recognition and analysis of the general and specific environmental influence on quantitative models have been ignored.

General Conditions

There are several conditions which are common to all quantitative techniques. These include conditional variables such as cost, management support, availability of data, time, and employee acceptance and expertise. The use of any technique, of course, should be contingent on cost. Management should compare the payoff of using a particular quantitative technique with the costs of developing and implementing it. A meaningful cost-effectiveness analysis may be difficult and, at times, even impossible. However, all efforts should be made to determine cost-effectiveness so that the techniques do not become ends in themselves. Remember, these techniques only help the manager make better decisions; they do not make the decision for the manager.

The second condition, management support, is also relevant for effectively implementing any technique. Managerial understanding and support is necessary to effectively implement quantitative models. This again does not imply that decisional techniques should be thought of as substitutes for good management. In most instances, management must have a clearly thought-through objective before a particular quantitative technique is employed. For application of the technique, the objective should be stated in quantitative terms, such as maximizing profit or minimizing costs. In general, the extent to which quantitative techniques are effective depends on the manager's ability to survey the general and specific environment and be convinced that the technique will help attain organizational goals. Availability of accurate data is also an important condition for the successful application of quantitative techniques. The last section pointed out the importance of the functional subsystems in providing meaningful input for the quantitative models. The outcome of the model is only as good as the data fed into it. For example, the EOQ model depends on the marketing function for data on customer demand and on the purchasing function for data on ordering and carrying costs.

The fourth condition common to all quantitative techniques is time. The lower down the organization hierarchy, the shorter are the time response frames for making decisions.

The first-line supervisor obviously cannot spend 6 months developing an EOQ model for an inventory decision needed tomorrow. On the other hand, the corporate planning department may operate in a very long response time frame. This department may find it highly worthwhile and feasible to develop a simulation for planning new plant facilities 5 years hence. Therefore, the use of quantitative models depends on the availability of response time for a particular decision. As indicated earlier, the computer, especially with the use of remote terminals and time sharing, can help alleviate the timeliness problem.

Employee acceptance and expertise is the final general condition that will be discussed. The use of quantitative models obviously depends upon the ability of experts to develop the models. Management scientists are becoming more prevalent, and all modern practicing managers are becoming more aware of the quantitative tools available to them. Besides management support that has already been mentioned, there must be acceptance of the quantitative techniques by those on the firing line. Many employees resist this type of change and do not accept or appreciate the quantitative techniques' value to the organization. One manager noted, "Our biggest problem is getting older employees to accept statistical and mathematical concepts for decision making." This manager believed that if the staff could be taught to understand and appreciate the quantitative concepts and techniques, problems would be greatly reduced. This observation pretty well summarizes the general conditions for successful application of the quantitative techniques: better understanding and acceptance by all involved.

Conditions for Applying EOQ Models
The formula for the basic economic order quantity model presented in the last chapter was

$$EOQ = \sqrt{\frac{2DS}{C}}$$

This model depends on four major conditions before it can be successfully implemented. The relevant conditions for applying EOQ models include the following:

1 Demand (usage) is relatively stable. Disbursements of materials in the inventory are made at a relatively constant rate.
2 Holding cost is incurred on the basis of the average number of items in the inventory. The more items stockpiled in the inventory, the greater the cost of holding the inventory.
3 An order is received in one shipment and the lead time is known.
4 The cost (price) of an item in the inventory is independent of the size of the order. There are no price breaks.[7]

The first condition of demand stability is one of the few cases that is directly related to the general economic environment and the specific customer and competition environment

---

[7] William A. Ruch, "Special-Purpose EOQ Formulas," *Journal of Purchasing,* May 1973, p. 36.

facing the organization. This condition is definitely adaptable to contingency manage-ment. An expert on EOQ models made the following significant observation:

The first assumption is a matter of degree; few demand situations are perfectly constant. More faith can be placed in the EOQ calculated for a stable demand; if the demand is erratic, the decision maker may have to choose a simple rule-of-thumb or a more complex model than the EOQ.[8]

In other words, if there is a stable demand, then EOQ models will be effective. By the same token, if demand is erratic, then simple rule-of-thumb methods of inventory control will be more effective than EOQ models. All managers with a contingency orientation could identify their various inventories according to whether there was a stable or unsta-ble demand for the items. Those items having a stable demand (most raw materials in a manufacturing organization or undergarments in a large retail clothing store) should use an EOQ technique of inventory control. On the other hand, items with an unstable de-mand (special machine parts in a manufacturing organization or high-fashion goods in the large retail clothing store) should not use an EOQ model for inventory control. For the latter, more subjective methods such as a minimum-maximum system of inventory control should be used.

The other three conditions applicable to EOQ models are not as critical as demand stability to successful implementation. The reason is that the basic model can be changed to account for the variations. Figure 11-2 summarizes how the EOQ formulas may be altered to account for changes in the holding-cost, single-order, and fixed-cost assump-tions. However, even these could be put into the contingency framework. For example, if the holding cost is expressed as a percentage of value and the items are received over time (average calculation), then the EOQ formula should be:

$$Q = \sqrt{\frac{2DA}{IC\left(1 - \dfrac{d}{r}\right)}}$$

The figure actually represents a type of contingency framework for EOQ application. The job of the contingency manager is to refine the environmental inputs that go into holding costs, ordering shipments, and ordering costs.

Conditions for Applying Linear Programming

There are several conditions applicable to the successful implementation of linear pro-gramming. These conditions can be generalized to encompass both the graphical and transportation methods presented in the last chapter. Levin and Lamone note the need for situational application when they state, "Like any other quantitative tool, linear program-ming cannot be used indiscriminately but must be utilized under certain definable condi-

---

[8] Ibid., p. 36.

Figure 11-2 A Contingency Framework for EOQ Formulas
Summary Table of EOQ Formula Variations

Holding Cost Expressed as	Single Price Given				Price Quoted as Fixed + Variable Component			
	Single Shipment		Items Received over Time		Single Shipment		Items Received over Time	
	Average*	Maximum†	Average	Maximum	Average	Maximum	Average	Maximum
Constant per unit	$Q=\sqrt{\dfrac{2DA}{H}}$	$Q=\sqrt{\dfrac{DA}{H}}$	$Q=\sqrt{\dfrac{2DA}{H(1-\frac{d}{r})}}$	$Q=\sqrt{\dfrac{DA}{H(1-\frac{d}{r})}}$	$Q=\sqrt{\dfrac{2D(A+F)}{H}}$	$Q=\sqrt{\dfrac{D(A+F)}{H}}$	$Q=\sqrt{\dfrac{2D(A+F)}{H(1-\frac{d}{r})}}$	$Q=\sqrt{\dfrac{D(A+F)}{H(1-\frac{d}{r})}}$
Percent of value‡	$Q=\sqrt{\dfrac{2DA}{IC}}$	$Q=\sqrt{\dfrac{DA}{IC}}$	$Q=\sqrt{\dfrac{2DA}{IC(1-\frac{d}{r})}}$	$Q=\sqrt{\dfrac{DA}{IC(1-\frac{d}{r})}}$	$Q=\sqrt{\dfrac{2D(A+F)}{IV}}$	$Q=\sqrt{\dfrac{D(A+F)}{IV}}$	$Q=\sqrt{\dfrac{2D(A+F)}{IV(1-\frac{d}{r})}}$	$Q=\sqrt{\dfrac{D(A+F)}{IV(1-\frac{d}{r})}}$
Constant plus percent of value	$Q=\sqrt{\dfrac{2DA}{H+IC}}$	$Q=\sqrt{\dfrac{DA}{H+IC}}$	$Q=\sqrt{\dfrac{2DA}{(H+IC)(1-\frac{d}{r})}}$	$Q=\sqrt{\dfrac{DA}{(H+IC)(1-\frac{d}{r})}}$	$Q=\sqrt{\dfrac{2D(A+F)}{H+IV}}$	$Q=\sqrt{\dfrac{D(A+F)}{H+IV}}$	$Q=\sqrt{\dfrac{2D(A+F)}{(H+IV)(1-\frac{d}{r})}}$	$Q=\sqrt{\dfrac{D(A+F)}{(H+IV)(1-\frac{d}{r})}}$
Constant plus percent of value§	$Q=\sqrt{\dfrac{2DA}{2H+IC}}$		$A=\sqrt{\dfrac{2DA}{(2H+IC)(1-\frac{d}{r})}}$		$Q=\sqrt{\dfrac{2D(A+F)}{2H+IV}}$		$Q=\sqrt{\dfrac{2D(A+F)}{(2H+IV)(1-\frac{d}{r})}}$	

Variables:
Q = quantity ordered
D = annual demand
A = fixed preparation cost per order (may be order cost or set-up cost)
H = holding cost expressed as a constant per unit
I = percentage holding cost

C = value of item in inventory
d = rate of depletion of inventory per time period
r = rate of replenishment of inventory per time period
F = vendor's fixed price component
V = vendor's variable price component

* Holding cost based on average number of units in inventory.
† Holding cost based on maximum number of units in inventory.
‡ Holding cost also could be expressed as a dollar amount per unit of weight, volume, or any other measurable characteristic, or any combination of these.
§ Constant component (H) based on maximum number of units in inventory; percentage component (IC) based on average number of units in inventory.

Source: William A. Ruch, "Special-Purpose EOQ Formulas," *Journal of Purchasing,* May 1973, p. 44. Used with permission.

tions and with certain limitations."[9] They go on to mention the following specific conditions for the application of linear programming techniques:

1 Management must have a definite objective in mind which must be defined or stated mathematically.
2 The resources involved in the problem must be in limited supply and must be statable in quantitative terms.
3 There must be alternative courses of action too numerous for solution by other methods.
4 The variables in the problem must be linearly related.[10]

The choice of which linear programming technique to use, of course, greatly depends on the problem. For example, if the problem is to determine the location of a new plant, then the transportation method can be used most effectively. However, if the problem involves the allocation of materials, then the graphical method is more applicable. But in either situation, the desired objective for linear programming must be stated quantitatively, not qualitatively. A statement suggesting that resources should be allocated to improve the cost and profit picture for a firm is not enough. For example, a manager may state that resources should be better allocated to improve profit for producing steps and awnings. In this case, it is feasible to define the objective as maximizing the total profit contribution of the two products when the per unit contribution of each product is known with some precision. This example was used in the last chapter; profit was known to be $65 per awning and $40 per set of steps. This quantified statement of objective is much more readily adaptable to linear programming.

The resources used for products must be in limited supply for application to linear programming. In fact, if the resources were unlimited, there would not be a problem. Management would have no problem planning in an environment containing unlimited resources. Unfortunately, to expect unlimited resources is very unrealistic for most present-day organizations. The recent energy crisis and its aftermath is a case in point. Today organizations are constrained by scarce resources. This, of course, is a direct reflection of the general environmental impact. Even during times of stable economic conditions, some resources are going to be in limited supply. There are just so many natural resources, and in some cases the drain is irreversible. With the increasing crunch of limited resources, linear programming techniques can become increasingly important to effective management in the future.

The third condition for applying linear programming pertains to the number of alternative methods available for arriving at a solution. For example, if only two products are being produced, such as awnings and steps, then the graphical method is adequate. But if numerous alternatives are being analyzed, then more sophisticated techniques such as

---

[9] Richard I. Levin and Rudolph P. Lamone, *Linear Programming for Management Decisions*, Irwin, Homewood, Ill., 1969, pp. 11–12.
[10] Ibid., pp. 12–18.

the simplex method of linear programming should be employed. Like any other technique in management, the linear programming method should never be used unless it can generate a payoff.

The last condition of linearity is perhaps the most important to the linear programming technique. This simply means that a change in one variable causes an exactly proportionate change in another variable. For example, it may take 2 hours to produce one unit of a product. But if two units are produced, it will take 4 hours. For problems which do not have linear relationships, other quantitative techniques such as nonlinear programming must be used.

In addition to the conditions for application suggested by Levin and Lamone, Gerald Thompson mentions some others. He notes, "Many real situations can arise where linear programming models are of quite limited use. In other instances the model can have very great power."[11] Besides proportionality (linearity), which is discussed above, Thompson also mentions additivity (allows for no interaction effects), divisibility (there are continuous choice variables), certainty (constants in a problem are known), and nonnegativity (only nonnegative activity levels are feasible) as assumptions made by most traditional linear programming models.[12] If these conditions do not exist, then either different variations of the linear programming model must be used (for example, integer linear programming, sensitivity analysis) or the quantitative model cannot be used at all.

Another limiting assumption made by traditional linear programming models is a single objective function or goal, such as maximum profit. More realistically, most conditions would dictate multiple goals, some of which may be competing with one another. Goal programming techniques are currently being developed to handle realistic multiple-goal situations.

The above discussion only gives the very obvious conditions for applying linear programming techniques. About the only point that really reflects the environment is the condition of limited resources. If an organization is faced with limited resources, then a linear programming model can effectively allocate them. Of course, even here, successful application depends on the other more technical conditions mentioned. The challenge for contingency management is to develop more specific if-then relationships for the specific application of linear programming and its variations.

Conditions for the Application of Queuing Models
The two basic types of queuing or waiting-line models, single-channel and multiple-channel, have certain conditions that should be considered. These conditions could be briefly summarized as follows:

1 Arrivals and services that follow a given time schedule

---

[11] Gerald E. Thompson, *Linear Programming,* Macmillan, New York, 1971, p. 19.
[12] Ibid., pp. 19–29.

2 Arrivals that come randomly from an infinite universe

3 Arrivals that come from a finite population[13]

The first condition refers to the problem of scheduling. The criteria for accepting customers, trucks, or whatever the case may be, were outlined in the last chapter as FIFO, LIFO, and a priority list. The solution for the first condition of following a given time schedule is to have the appropriate facilities scheduled to meet the arrivals. The manner in which arrivals are scheduled and costs are determined largely depends on subjective experience. For example, waiting-line costs in a doctor's office are thought to be less costly than the waiting lines at a drive-in bank. Doctors view their time as being more valuable (costly) than that of patients who are waiting. The patient often has little if any alternative but to wait. On the other hand, the bank values the time of customers who are waiting, for fear of losing their business to a competitor. Therefore, the bank is much more willing to add extra servicing facilities and successfully apply a queuing technique.

The second and third conditions refer to the fact that single and multiple facilities may service arrivals from either a finite or infinite population. A finite population would be the patients of doctors who will only see their own patients, whereas the emergency room of the city hospital draws more from an infinite population. These population parameters will definitely affect the application of the queuing model. The infinite population lends itself to more subjective inputs and may not even be appropriate for queuing techniques. Like the other quantitative techniques, there are very few specific contingency relationships that have been developed for queuing techniques.

Conditions for the Application of Simulation Techniques

It should be remembered that simulation may be used with or without actual quantitative techniques. However, in any case there are certain conditions for the successful application of simulation. These conditions can be summarized as follows:

1 A statistically stable system must exist. That is, variations of important parameters of the systems must be within a certain range and vary in a random manner.

2 All of the important parameters of the system must be known.

3 The cost functions must be known.[14]

The first condition above highlights the environmental framework for simulation techniques. If a system operates in an unstable environment, then it becomes very difficult to simulate reality. Quantification becomes especially difficult if the variables are erratic. If the environment (both general and specific) surrounding the organization system or a subsystem is dynamic and/or erratic, then it is difficult to use simulation. On the other hand, if the environment is relatively tranquil and static, then simulation techniques can be very effective.

---

[13] Harold Bierman, Jr., Charles P. Bonini, and Warren H. Hausman, *Quantitative Analysis for Business Decisions,* 4th ed. Irwin, Homewood, Ill., 1973, pp. 360–361.

[14] Arthur W. Gutenberg and Eugene Richman, *Dynamics of Management,* International Textbook, Scranton, Pa., 1968, p. 675.

The second and third conditions for simulation cited above are relevant even without quantification. Gutenberg and Richman note that "the enforced thinking about the nature of the problem can lead to results which are more refined and the uncertainties about the problem may be reduced. Simulation allows one to try many different combinations with various restraints and 'see' what the effect would be, all without actually putting the 'real' system into effect." [15] By knowing the important parameters and cost functions, various alternatives in the simulation may be evaluated for an effective decision.

Simulation can in and of itself prove to be very useful to contingency management. Both general and specific environments can be simulated, and then various management concepts and techniques (process, quantitative, behavioral, and systems) can be applied. The contingent relationships between the simulated *if*'s and the real *then*'s can aid in the development of a contingency management body of knowledge. Besides determining the contingent application of the quantitative techniques, simulation can be used in the development of contingency management as a whole.

Summary

This chapter concludes the part of the book dealing with the quantitative variables in contingency management. There is much less contingency thinking and application in the quantitative area than in the process, behavioral, or systems approaches to management. The first part of the chapter discussed some attempts to classify the environment for decision makers. The work of Robert Duncan was cited as representative of this effort. He found that by classifying the environment according to certain components, the amount of uncertainty for decision makers could be determined. This type of work has at least indirect implications for developing contingent relationships with decision models. The next section of the chapter presented and discussed an overall systems framework. Since the quantitative approach lacks such a framework, it was shown how the quantitative techniques fit in conceptually with the rest of the organization system. The system framework was used to emphasize the integration of process and problem-solving orientations in modern organizations. The inputs are primarily environmental in nature. The control element (both feedforward and feedback) can at least indirectly affect the application of decision models. The most direct influence, however, comes from the functional subsystems of an organization. Once the decisions are made, it is hoped by the aid of the decision models, the transformation process, after a final control check, leads to the output. Again, the purpose of this systems framework was to show how the quantitative techniques fit in and has only indirect implications for contingency management.

The last half of the textual material for this chapter was devoted to the identification and analysis of the situational variables or conditions that directly affect the quantitative techniques. About the best classification of conditional impact is from the widely used catego-

---

[15] Ibid.

ries of certainty, risk, and uncertainty. Some sound if-then contingent relationships can be derived. The following three are particularly useful:

1 If certainty, then deterministic models
2 If risk, then probabilistic models
3 If uncertainty, then subjective criteria decision models

Some general conditions applicable to all quantitative models include cost, management support, availability of data, time, and employee acceptance and expertise. More specific conditions applying to EOQ models include demand, holding costs, number of shipments, and fixed costs. Those conditions directly affecting linear programming include mathematical objectives, limited resources, alternate courses of action, linearity, additivity, divisibility, certainty, and nonnegativity. Multiple-goal problems also must be dealt with. For queuing models, some specific conditions include arrivals on a given time schedule and arrivals drawn from a finite and an infinite population. The specific conditions for simulation techniques include stability, knowledge of parameters, and cost. Most of these specific conditions, with the exception of the demand variable for EOQ models, limited resources for linear programming, and stability of simulation techniques, are not directly related to the general and specific environments in a general contingency management framework. Much remains to be done in developing contingent relationships between environmental variables and quantitative concepts and techniques. Simulation methods may help in this effort and in the development of contingency management as a whole.

Questions for Review and Discussion

1 Briefly describe and analyze the logic of the framework for quantitative models.
2 What are some of the general conditions which are common to all quantitative techniques? Discuss the implications these conditions have for the quantitative techniques.
3 Discuss the conditions specifically applicable to economic order quantity, linear programming, queuing, and simulation.
4 What must be done in the future to make the quantitative approach more applicable to contingency management?

References

Bierman, Harold, Jr., Charles P. Bonini, and Warren H. Hausman: *Quantitative Analysis for Business Decisions,* Irwin, Homewood, Ill., 1969.
Brown, Robert Goodell: *Management Decisions for Production Operations,* Dryden Press, Hinsdale, Ill., 1971.
Brown, William G.: "Techniques of Operations Research," *Journal of Systems Management,* September 1972, pp. 3–13.
Duncan, Robert B.: "Characteristics of Organizational Environments and Environmental Uncertainty," *Administrative Science Quarterly,* September 1972, pp. 313–327.
Koontz, Harold, and Robert W. Bradspies: "Managing through Feedforward Control," *Business Horizons,* June 1972, pp. 25–36

Lee, Sang M.: *Goal Programming for Decision Analysis,* Auerbach Publishers, Philadelphia, 1972.

Levin, Richard I., and Rudolph P. Lamone: *Linear Programming for Management Decisions,* Irwin, Homewood, Ill., 1969.

Ruch, William A.: "Special-Purpose EOQ Formulas," *Journal of Purchasing,* May 1973.

Thompson, Gerald E.: *Linear Programming,* Macmillan, New York, 1971.

Young, Stanley P.: "Organization as a Total System," in Fred Luthans (ed.), *Contemporary Readings in Organization Behavior,* McGraw-Hill, New York, 1972, pp. 97–114.

Case Study for Part Three
Rambling Road

Along with industrial smokestacks, another very visible target for the ecology movement is the numerous highways that crisscross the country. Whenever new highway construction is proposed, a hue and cry usually goes up. Conservationists are justifiably concerned because a new highway often means the clearing of beautiful old trees and the elimination of cover for wildlife. The drainage pattern from a new highway often creates scars, erosion, landsliding, and stream siltation. The highway also creates visual and noise pollution, and the exhaust from the cars leads to air pollution. There is also the problem of land-use conflicts where land is becoming a more limited resource. Owners along the route can also suffer land value depreciation. Despite these problems, with the continued growth of the population and dependence on the automobile for transportation, there is always a crying need for more and better highways. Those responsible for highway construction are in the precarious position of "damned if they do and damned if they don't."

The Midwestern State Highway Department has a section specifically charged with the responsibility of selecting corridors for new highways. The stated objective of this section is twofold: (1) select the most desirable corridors for present and future transportation needs and (2) minimize the negative impact on the community and the environment. A young civil engineer, Jake Sebolt, was in charge of the corridor studies for new highway construction. Jake had previous experience on a survey crew while going to college, and after graduation he was a district construction engineer for the state for 3 years before taking his present job. Jake has been in his present job 3 months.

Jake was generally sympathetic with those expressing concern over the effect that new highways had on the environment. Most of his older coworkers in the highway department were not. Jake felt that in his present position he could possibly indirectly influence policy and attitude in the department about the environment. He felt he could have a direct impact by having greater public input into where highways would be routed. In the short while he had been in the section, he had actively sought out and received as much public input into his corridor studies as possible. His boss, Henry Siss, disagreed with this approach. Mr. Siss finally called Jake into his office and said, "Jake, you are very enthusiastic in your job, and I sympathize with your efforts to obtain public input into the corridor studies. However, believe me when I say it just won't work. You need a more rational approach. Everybody has a different opinion on the route of a new highway. You can't please them all. On the basis of the way you are currently making your studies, I don't see how you or I will ever be able to defend our proposed routes against rational arguments at a public hearing or before the politicians. For example, on the basis of public input, how are you going to explain to the agricultural people that the road should go through farmland instead of wilderness, or, on the other hand, how are you going to explain to the conservationists that the road should go through wilderness instead of farmland? On the basis of public opinion? Whose public opinion? What you need is a quantitative type of model that will give you a rational as opposed to an emotionally based corridor study. Crank your environmental concerns into the model if you want, but also crank in economic and transportation concerns as well. Believe me, the results will be much better. Your proposals will be much more readily acceptable by all concerned. People find it difficult to argue with numbers and with a proposal derived from a quantitative model. We both will be on firmer ground."

Questions for Analysis:

1 Do you think Henry Siss is giving Jake good advice? Why?

2 Can Jake "crank in" his environmental concern into a quantitative model as his boss suggests? How? What would be some of the parameters?

3 What type of quantitative methods and/or decision models that you have studied, if any, could be applied to Jake's corridor studies?

4 Using a contingency framework, what would be some possible *if*'s and *then*'s in the corridor studies? How can Jake be a contingency manager in this case? How can his boss, Henry Siss, be a contingency manager?

Part Four

Behavioral Variables

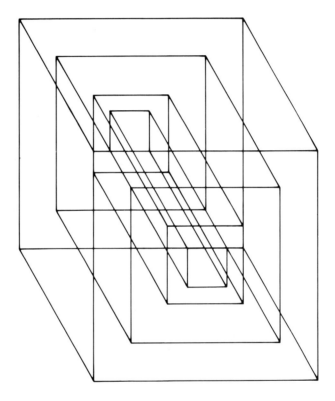

Learning Theory and Behavior Modification

Learning is an extremely important process in human behavior. In fact, learning may be the single most important concept in the study of human behavior. Learning is involved in almost *everything* that *everyone* does. A learning approach to understanding, prediction, and control of human behavior in organizations is particularly relevant. There is little organizational behavior that is not either directly or indirectly affected by learning. For example, a worker's safety record, a manager's knowledge, a supervisor's leadership ability, and a secretary's loyalty all involve learning.

This chapter presents an overview of learning theories and behavior modification principles that apply to the management of human resources. After learning is defined, the major theoretical approaches to learning are briefly summarized. Specific attention is given to classical and operant conditioning. The remainder of the chapter is devoted to behavior modification principles. Reinforcement and punishment are given major attention. Included is a discussion of the law of effect, positive and negative reinforcement, schedules of reinforcement, and the application of punishment. Specific attention is also given to extinction, learning curves, spontaneous recovery, generalization, discrimination, shaping, and modeling.

What Is Learning?

The term *learning* is used by a great number of people in a wide variety of contexts. Yet, despite this diverse use, there is, surprisingly, general agreement on a definition of learning. Although there may be slight variations, the commonly accepted definition is: *Learning is a relatively permanent change in behavior that results from reinforced practice or experience.* However, it should also be stressed that learning is only a concept, a psychological process. No one has ever seen learning. It cannot be examined under a microscope. As McGehee points out:

You have seen people in the process of learning, you have seen people who behave in a particular way as a result of learning, and some of you (in fact, I guess the majority of you) have "learned" at some time in your life. In other words we infer that learning has taken place if an individual behaves, reacts, responds as a result of experience in a manner different from the way he formerly behaved.[1]

In other words, learning is evidenced by observable behaviors.

Applying the definition of learning to the study of human behavior in organizations has direct implications in the following areas:

1 Knowing something intellectually or conceptually one never knew before.
2 Being able to do something one couldn't do before—behavior or skill.
3 Combining two knowns into a new understanding of a skill, piece of knowledge, concept, or behavior.
4 Being able to use or apply a new combination of skills, knowledge, concept, or behavior.
5 Being able to understand and/or apply that which one knows—either skill, knowledge, or behavior.[2]

Knowledge of the definition of learning only serves as a starting point for the theory and behavior modification principles which are covered in the rest of the chapter.

Theoretical Approaches to Learning

The purpose of any theory is understanding, prediction, and control. When theories become perfected, they should have general application. Thus, a perfected theory of learning should explain all aspects of learning, have general application, and predict and control learning situations. Unfortunately, no such learning theory exists. Although there is agreement as to what learning is, there is disagreement on the theory behind it. There have evolved two major approaches: the cognitive and connectionist theories.

Cognitive theories of learning are concerned with various complex cognitions such as attitudes, beliefs, memory, goal seeking, and expectations. Theoretical explanations in this approach assume learning is concerned with the ways in which these cognitions are modified by experience. The ideas of Edward C. Tolman best represent such an approach. In essence, Tolman felt that learning consisted of a relationship between cognitive environmental cues and expectations. Through rigorous experimentation he found that learning took place between the cues and the expectancies. This finding had a big impact on industrial training in the 1940s and 1950s. Programs were set up to strengthen the relationship between cognitive cues (supervision and organizational and job procedures) and worker expectations (incentive payments for good performance). The theory was that the worker would learn to be more productive by building an association between taking orders or following directions and expectancies of monetary reward for this effort. Today, training programs in industry are not as dependent on these assumptions. Yet, the cognitive approach is useful and plays an important role in the expectancy theories of motivation discussed in the next chapter.

[1] William McGehee, "Are We Using What We Know about Training?—Learning Theory and Training," *Personnel Psychology*, Spring 1958, p. 2.
[2] Leslie E. This and Gordon L. Lippitt, "Learning Theories and Training," *Training and Development Journal*, April 1966, p. 3.

The other theoretical approach is termed connectionist. Traditionally, these theories took a very narrow perspective; they were concerned only with the stimulus-response (S-R) connection. The classical conditioning theorists concentrated on this S-R connection. This was a good explanation of respondent (reflexive) behavior but fell short as a theoretical base for learned behavior. The operant conditioning theorists switched emphasis to the response-consequence connection. This latter approach was a much better explanation of learned (operant) behavior. An understanding of both classical and operant conditioning is necessary background to the study of the principles of behavior modification and contingency management of human resources.

Classical Conditioning

The Russian physiologist Ivan Pavlov's work with the gastric secretion of dogs is probably the best-known study in the behavioral sciences. He noticed that when he brought meat to his dogs, they would begin to secrete saliva. Pavlov discovered classical conditioning. The meat (unconditioned stimulus) would automatically elicit saliva (unconditioned response); but his footsteps or opening the door would also elicit the saliva. To test this observation, Pavlov sounded a tuning fork seconds before presenting meat powder to his dogs. After a number of repetitions of this pairing, the ringing produced the saliva by itself. A formerly neutral stimulus (tuning fork) was now able to elicit a response (saliva). Classical conditioning or learning had taken place.

Pavlov's experiment was a major breakthrough and has had a lasting impact on the study and application of learning. He demonstrated that reflex behavior can be learned. Behaviorists term this type of behavior *respondent behavior.* Emotional behaviors such as fear, anger, love, and certain attitudes may be largely the result of classical conditioning. A famous study by Watson and Rayner showed that fear can be learned. They paired a white rat (conditioned stimulus) with a loud noise (unconditioned stimulus) to produce fear in an eleven-month-old boy named Albert. After a few repetitions, Albert was afraid of the formerly neutral rat. He had been conditioned to fear a cuddly white rat. This same type of conditioning is why most people fear snakes.

Classical conditioning experimentation has been a major source of support for the connectionist theories of learning. Since Pavlov's original experiments in the late 1800s and the Watson-Rayner experiment in 1920, psychologists have been able to classically condition many types of behaviors. The overall conclusion from this vast amount of research is stated by Bass and Vaughan as follows: "In all probability, any response in an organism's behavioral repertoire can be conditioned if an unconditioned stimulus can be found that regularly produces the response and if this unconditioned stimulus can be paired in training with a conditioned stimulus."[3]

---

[3] Bernard M. Bass and James A. Vaughan, *Training in Industry: The Management of Learning,* Wadsworth, Belmont, Calif., 1966, p. 15.

Despite the theoretical possibility of the widespread applicability of classical conditioning, most behaviorists would agree that respondent behaviors are not as important as operant behaviors in human learning. This is especially true of human behavior in organizations. The real value of classical conditioning is not that it is descriptive of most of human learning, but that it breaks learning down into very precise analytical units for study. Many of the important principles of behavior modification are partly derived from classical conditioning.

Operant Conditioning

Following the lead of B. F. Skinner, most behaviorists identify two types of behavior: respondent and operant. Respondent behavior is classically conditioned and occurs when a stimulus *elicits* a response. Antecedent stimuli are the critical determinants of respondent behavior. Operant behavior, on the other hand, is a result of operant conditioning and is strengthened or weakened by the consequences of the response. The operant behavior is *emitted* by the organism, not elicited by a prior stimulus. The antecedent stimulus becomes the occasion for the emitted operant behavior, but operant behavior depends on its consequences. Thus, operant behavior is a function of consequences.

The differences between classical and operant conditioning are not always clear. In *classical conditioning,* a change in the stimulus (unconditioned stimulus to conditioned stimulus) will *elicit* a particular response. In *operant conditioning* a particular response from many possible responses is *emitted* in a given stimulus occasion. Subsequent responses will depend on the consequences. If the consequence is reinforcing, the operant behavior will be strengthened; if punishing or neutral, the operant behavior will be weakened. Operant conditioning is more environmentally determined. The organism must *operate* on the environment in order to receive reinforcement. The response is *instrumental* in obtaining the reinforcement.

Operant conditioning has a much greater impact on human learning than does classical conditioning. Operant conditioning also explains much of organizational behavior. The overriding assumption is that behavior depends on its consequences. This significant statement has tremendous implications for the understanding, prediction, and control of organizational behavior. As there is with classical conditioning, there is major value in studying operant conditioning. Operant conditioning, through highly controlled experimentation over the years, has provided a scientifically based behavior technology. This technology is commonly referred to as *behavior modification.*

Principles of Behavior Modification

There are many widely recognized principles of behavior modification. Reinforcement and punishment are probably the most important for predicting and controlling behavior and are directly applicable to the study of organizational behavior. After a detailed look at reinforcement and punishment, the principles of extinction, acquisition or learning curves, spontaneous recovery, generalization, discrimination, shaping, and modeling are briefly examined. These principles are a direct outgrowth of operant conditioning assumptions and empirical research and an indirect result of classical conditioning assumptions and empirical research. They are principles in the real sense of the word. Most behavioral scientists believe that human behavior is subject to scientific investigation. Through the application of scientific methodology, they have established some lawful relationships in human behavior. The following principles reflect this effort.

Reinforcement: The Key to Behavior Modification

The concept of reinforcement is central to operant learning theory and behavior modification. There are three possible consequences of any behavior: reinforcement, punishment, or nothing. A reinforcing consequence is one which tends to increase the strength of the preceding response and induce repetitions. A punishing consequence tends to weaken or, at least, suppress the preceding response and cause it to decrease in frequency. No consequence will tend to extinguish the preceding response in the long run. These three consequences are examined in turn, but reinforcement that strengthens behavior and promotes (not really causes) an increase in its subsequent frequency is the key to behavior modification and given most attention.

Although the importance of reinforcement is universally accepted by behavioral scientists, its theoretical explanation remains controversial. The best explanation of reinforcement still seems to be Edward Thorndike's classic law of effect. After years of experiments, mainly on animal subjects at the turn of the century, he concluded: "Of several responses made to the same situation, those which are accompanied or closely followed by satisfaction [reinforcement] . . . will be more likely to recur; those which are accompanied or closely followed by discomfort [punishment] . . . will be less likely to occur."[4] Modern behaviorists have generally demonstrated the validity of this law through the years. Highly controlled learning experiments and everyday learning experiences have proved the law of effect. Reinforcement will increase the strength of a response and increase its probability of being repeated in the future.

As the law of effect points out, reinforcement is *anything* that strengthens the behavior and tends to induce an increase in subsequent frequency. This is why the commonly interchangeable word *reward* can be misleading. *Reward* has a connotation of something that is good or has universal reinforcing properties. This assumption is not necessarily valid. For example, money and praise are commonly thought of as universally rewarding. Yet, strictly using the definition, money and praise are reinforcing only if they strengthen the behavior and induce its subsequent frequency. Although they are undoubtedly exceptions, some employees in organizations are not reinforced by the common "rewards" of money and praise. The differences between reward and reinforcement point to the need to further clarify various aspects of this most important principle of behavior modification.

---

[4] Edward L. Thorndike, *Animal Intelligence*, Macmillan, New York, 1911, p. 244.

Positive and Negative Reinforcement

There is much confusion over the terms *positive* and *negative reinforcement.* It is important to point out that both positive and negative reinforcement have the same impact on
behavior. Both increase the strength and subsequent frequency of behavior. The difference is that positive reinforcement does this by the presentation of a desirable consequence and negative reinforcement accomplishes the same thing by withdrawing a noxious or aversive consequence. A negative reinforcer strengthens behavior and induces
an increase in subsequent frequency by its termination rather than by its presentation.
Electric shock is often used as a negative reinforcer in learning experiments. Terminating
the shock is reinforcing to the subject. The discussion of punishment will indicate that
there is a difference between punishment and negative reinforcement. But the connotation attached to the word *negative* often leads people to mistakenly equate negative
reinforcement with punishment.

Positive reinforcers may be primary or conditioned in nature. A primary reinforcer is
innately satisfying to the person. Examples are food or water in classical or operant
conditioning. These unconditioned stimuli are unlearned positive reinforcers. They largely
apply to simple learning situations. In more complex human learning situations such as
those found in modern organizations, conditioned reinforcers are much more frequently
used and are more effective than the primary ones.

A conditioned reinforcer results from previous association with a primary reinforcer.
Whereas the primary reinforcer is innately satisfying, the conditioned one must be
learned. Starting in infancy, many neutral stimuli acquire reinforcing properties. A mother
who feeds her infant milk (primary reinforcer), soon becomes a conditioned reinforcer
herself. These conditioned reinforcers play a vital role in understanding the more complex
aspects of human behavior.

Numerous social stimuli serve as conditioned reinforcers.[5] Four of the more common
conditioned reinforcers relevant to organizational behavior include:

1 *Attention*   The mere visual stimulus of a human paying attention by looking at or
   responding to another human is reinforcing. A superior giving full attention to a subordinate's ideas will reinforce participative behavior on the part of the subordinate.
2 *Approval*   A visual stimulus of a human nodding affirmatively or smiling is reinforcing
   to another human. The same is true of a verbal stimulus indicating approval. A superior
   nodding his or her head or voicing approval of a suggestion from a subordinate would
   reinforce the subordinate's behavior.
3 *Affection*   Visual, verbal, or physical expressions of affection are an important form of
   reinforcement for human beings. A superior who expresses genuine affection for a
   subordinate will reinforce the subordinate's efforts to please.
4 *Tokens*   Various tokens are probably the most consciously used type of conditioned

---

[5] See Arthur W. Staats and Carolyn K. Staats, *Complex Human Behavior,* Holt, New York, 1963, p. 54.

reinforcement for human learning. Money is the best example. The adage that a person cannot eat money interestingly points out that money is not a primary reinforcer. Yet, money remains an extremely important reinforcer because many people believe in the other adage that "money will buy everything except possibly happiness." Outstanding performance is reinforced by raises and bonuses in an organization.

A recent study by the author and his colleagues found that social approval, additional responsibilities, rescheduling of breaks, job rotation, special housekeeping or safety duties, positive feedback, and more enjoyable tasks upon the completion of less enjoyable tasks were some of the positive reinforcers supervisors could apply to their workers to improve performance.[6]

Administration of Reinforcement

So far the discussion of reinforcement has been concerned with its definitional basis and the different types of reinforcers. The role that reinforcement plays in predicting and controlling human behavior cannot be overemphasized. In an organizational context it is important in areas such as training, adapting to change, and operational performance. Modification of certain specific aspects of organizational behavior such as tardiness or participation also depends upon reinforcement. Reinforcement will increase the strength of desired organizational behavior and will increase the probability of its being repeated. Costello and Zalkind summarize the research findings on the impact of reinforcement on organizational behavior as follows:

1 Some type of reinforcement (reward or knowledge of successful performance) is necessary to produce change.
2 Some types of rewards are more effective for use in the organization than are others.
3 The speed with which learning takes place and also how lasting its effects will be is determined by the timing of reinforcement.[7]

The last point, in particular, brings out the importance of administering reinforcement.

During the acquisition phase of classical conditioning experiments, every conditioned response is reinforced. This seldom occurs in reality. Human learning situations in everyday life or in organizations are generally reinforced on an intermittent basis. Yet, the exact pattern and timing of the reinforcement has a tremendous impact on the resulting behavior. In other words, how the reward is administered can greatly influence the specific learning that takes place and thus the behavior that occurs. An understanding of administering reinforcement can be gained by examining the four major schedules.

[6] Fred Luthans and David Lyman, "Training Supervisors to Use Organizational Behavior Modification," *Personnel*, September–October 1973, pp. 38–44.
[7] Timothy W. Costello and Sheldon S. Zalkind, *Psychology in Administration*, Prentice-Hall, Englewood Cliffs, N.J., 1963, p. 193.

1 *Fixed Ratio Schedule* A ratio schedule of reinforcement means that reinforcement is given after a certain *number* of responses. A *fixed* ratio schedule specifies the exact number of responses. In basic conditioning experiments and in the beginning of almost every type of learning situation every response is reinforced. However, as learning progresses, it is more effective and convenient to shift to fixed ratios that reinforce after every second or fourth or eighth or even up to the twentieth response. Many everyday behaviors may occur many times before they are reinforced.

Figure 12-1 shows that a fixed ratio schedule of reinforcement tends to produce vigorous and steady behavior. The person soon determines that reinforcement is based on

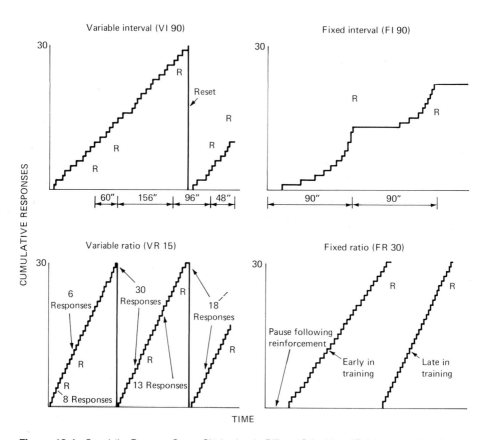

Figure 12-1 Cumulative Response Curves Obtained under Different Schedules of Reinforcement. Hypothetical but fairly typical cumulative response curves obtained under different schedules of reinforcement. Facts to note: (1) The vertical lines marked R mean "reinforcement." (2) Performance under the variable interval schedule is very steady; (3) that under the fixed interval schedule shows a pronounced scallop. (4) There is a pause following reinforcement in the fixed ratio schedule early in training but (5) not later. (6) There is no pause following reinforcement under the variable ratio schedule. *Source:* Gregory A. Kimble, Norman Garmezy, and Edward Zigler, *Principles of General Psychology*, 4th ed., Copyright © 1974, The Ronald Press, New York. Used with permission.

the number of responses and performs accordingly. The piece-rate incentive system is an example of a fixed ratio schedule. In this schedule, production workers are paid (conditioned reinforcement) on the basis of the number of pieces they produce (number of responses). Other things being equal, a worker's performance behaviors should be energetic and steady. In reality, of course, other things are not always equal, and a piece-rate incentive system may not result in this type of behavior.

2 *Fixed Interval Schedule* The other fixed schedule administers reinforcement on an interval basis. Reinforcement is given after a specified period of time and is measured from the last reinforced response. The lengths of time vary. In the beginning of practically any learning situation, a very short interval of reinforcement is required. However, as learning progresses, the interval can stretch out.

Figure 12-1 illustrates that fixed interval schedules of reinforcement result in quite different behavior from that produced under a fixed ratio schedule. Under fixed interval schedules, there is an uneven pattern that varies from very slow, unenergetic behavior immediately following reinforcement to very fast, vigorous behavior immediately preceding reinforcement. This type of behavior pattern is simply explained by the fact that the person soon determines that another reward will not immediately follow the last one. Therefore, the person tends to relax a little until reinforcement time. Most personnel in an organization paid by the hour, week, or month are on a fixed interval schedule. Monetary reinforcement comes at the end of a period of time. In practice, however, even though employees are paid by the hour, they receive paychecks only weekly, biweekly, or even monthly. In many cases the employee never sees the paycheck at all because it is deposited in the checking account. This time interval is generally too long to be an effective form of reinforcement for work-related behavior.

3 *Intermittent Schedules* Both ratio and interval schedules can be administered on a variable or intermittent basis. This simply means that reinforcement is given in an irregular or unsystematic way. In the case of variable ratio, the reward is given after a random number of responses. Each response in a variable ratio schedule has a chance of being reinforced. The variable interval schedule works basically the same way. Under the variable interval schedule, reward is given after a randomly distributed length of time.

Figure 12-1 shows that both variable ratio and variable interval schedules tend to produce stable and vigorous behavior. The variable schedules produce behavior that is similar to the fixed ratio schedule. Under both variable schedules, the person has no idea when reward is coming, so his or her behavior tends to be steady and strong. These intermittent schedules are very resistant to extinction.

Most real life, everyday learning situations are reinforced on intermittent schedules. Although primary reinforcers are administered on a relatively fixed basis, for example, food is given three times a day at meal times, and organization compensation plans are on either a fixed ratio or interval basis, most other human behavior in or out of organizations is reinforced in a random manner. For example, practically all the conditioned social reinforcers are administered on a variable basis. Attention, approval, and affection are generally given on a very random basis.

The fixed and intermittent schedules are not the only methods of administering reinforcement. Many other possible combinations exist. However, these are the most common schedules, and these greatly affect both the modification and extinction of organization behavior. Staats and Staats note, "Not only do these intermittent schedules produce characteristically different rates of maintenance of the response, but, in addition, once reinforcement has been discontinued, different extinction rates are also produced."[8] Much of the behavior of all workers, supervisors, salespersons, engineers, and executives is determined by when and how they are reinforced.

For behavior modification, the timing of reinforcement should be kept as close to the desired behavior as possible, not 2 weeks or a month away as is the case with most formal organizational reinforcers such as the paycheck. In addition, ratio schedules are generally preferable over interval schedules because they tend to produce steady, strong behavior, and intermittent schedules are generally preferable over fixed schedules because they also produce steady, strong behavior and are more resistant to extinction. However, the fixed schedule must generally be initially used before switching to an intermittent schedule. Understanding and then applying what is known about the administration of reinforcement schedules can be of great assistance to the management of human resources. In fact, one of the most important functions of any manager may well be the way he or she administers reinforcement to subordinates. Chapter 15 carries this discussion further by giving specific attention to organizational behavior modification, or O.B. Mod., as a specific technique of contingency management.

Punishment in Behavior Modification

Punishment is one of the most used but least understood and badly administered principles of behavior modification. Whether in child rearing or dealing with subordinates in an organization, parents or supervisors often revert to punishment instead of reinforcement in order to modify or change behavior. Punishment is commonly thought to be opposite from reward and equally effective in changing behavior. Costello and Zalkind explain that this is not the case:

Reward tends to increase the probability of a response's future occurrence; the effect of punishment cannot be said, unequivocally, to decrease its probability. . . . If we are seeking a way to find punishment to be the opposite of reward, perhaps the answer can be found by saying the impact of reward on behavior is simple (it reinforces it); the impact of punishment on behavior is complex.[9]

As a start in understanding punishment, it must be defined operationally. Such an operational definition is: *Punishment is anything which weakens the response and tends to decrease the frequency of the subsequent response rate.* This may occur by applying a noxious or aversive stimulus or by withdrawing a positive reinforcer. In either case, the response must be weakened and decreased in frequency in order for punishment to have

[8] Staats and Staats, op. cit., p. 65.
[9] Costello and Zalkind, op. cit., p. 125.

occurred. This operational definition dispels the false assumptions of what is and what is not punishing. The definition points out that punishment is very personal and individualized. For example, a supervisor cannot automatically assume that verbally reprimanding a subordinate is punishing. Only if behavior for which the supervisor is reprimanding decreases in subsequent frequency was punishment applied. In fact, this may be the only way the individual can receive attention from the supervisor. The reprimand may turn out to be reinforcing because it increases instead of decreases the behavior that preceded the reprimand.

How can punishment be effectively used in the actual practice of management? The answer can be demonstrated by a simple, but realistic, example.[10] One frequently used form of punishment is to dock an employee's pay. However, very often the pay reduction has absolutely no effect on the undesirable behavior in question. Management views pay as a reinforcer for desirable organizational behavior. Yet, the pay is typically far removed in time from the desired behavior. The employee tends to miss the connection between specific pay for specific desirable organizational behavior. The employee certainly knows that work must be performed for money, but he or she does not know which work for which money. Typically, the employee cannot remember which bolt tightened or letter typed or problem solved he or she is being paid for when pay day finally rolls around a week, 2 weeks, or even a month later. The employee only perceives an overall flow of pay in return for an overall flow of work in a specified time. Pay may not be perceived as a direct consequence of anything but opening the pay envelope. The consequence (pay) is too far removed from the response (work) to appreciably affect organizational behavior. The pay does not reinforce the particular behavior for which it was intended.

In the same manner that nonincentive pay often fails as a specific reinforcer, its partial withdrawal also fails as a specific punisher. When management reduces an employee's pay for undesirable behavior, it assumes that the subsequent behavior will improve. Unfortunately, the frequency of the undesirable response may be maintained or even increased. One answer to this dilemma is that pay reduction in this case is not a form of punishment. Docking the employee's pay is not a punishment if it does not reduce the frequency of the undesirable organizational behavior. Instead, the pay reduction may only serve to erode the manager-employee relationship, not modify the undesirable behavior. The employee may simply associate the noxious stimulation with management instead of with his or her own undesirable behavior. Both employee and management lose when punishment is misapplied in this manner.

Constraints such as union contracts notwithstanding, the practice of docking an employee's pay for undesirable behavior can still be made an effective management tool. To begin with, management must reduce, as much as possible, the time between the undesirable organizational behavior and the introduction of the punishing stimulus. Secondly, it is extremely important that the employee understand, and feel capable of adjusting to,

---

[10] The example is drawn from Fred Luthans and Robert Kreitner, "The Role of Punishment in Organizational Behavior Modification," *Public Personnel Management,* May–June, 1973, pp. 159–160.

the desirable alternative behavior. The desirable alternative behavior should be deliberately and systematically reinforced by the manager. If other human and situational variables are favorable, the desirable alternative behavior should replace the undesirable behavior and punishment will have been effectively applied.

Despite its simplicity, the pay-docking illustration points out why many so-called punishments are not effective and what can be done to improve their use. Most often punishment is not an immediate consequence of undesirable behavior and the punishers are associated with the punishing manager and not the undesirable behavior. When using punishment, management must make sure that employees fully understand why they are being punished and then provide the opportunity for and systematically reinforce alternative desirable behaviors.

Opinions on how to administer punishment range all the way from the one extreme of dire warnings *never* to use it to the other extreme that it is the *only* effective way to modify behavior. To date, research has not been able to consistently support either view. The following briefly summarizes what is generally known about the effects of punishment:

1 Punishment is effective in modifying behavior if it forces the person to select a desirable alternative behavior that is then reinforced.
2 If the above doesn't occur, then the behavior will be only temporarily suppressed and will reappear when the punishment is removed. Furthermore, the suppressed behavior may cause the person to become fearful and anxious.
3 Punishment is much more effective when applied at the time the undesirable behavior is actually performed than at a later time.
4 Punishment must be administered with extreme care so that it doesn't become a reward for undesirable behavior. The termination of punishment is reinforcing just as the termination of reinforcement is punishing. [11]

The four points above should be considered when administering punishment in an organization. However, as the pay-docking example showed, the negative side effects can be overcome and punishment can be effectively administered. Despite the potential effective use of punishment, the rule of thumb remains to use reinforcement to accelerate desirable behavior and to extinguish undesirable behavior through nonreinforcement. This extinction principle is clarified next.

Extinction Principle
The behavior modification principle of extinction is closely related to reinforcement and punishment. In classical conditioning, if the conditioned stimulus is not reinforced by the unconditioned stimulus, then the conditioned response will weaken and eventually disappear or become extinct. Similarly, in operant conditioning, if the conditioned response is not reinforced, then the conditioned response will become extinct. For example, in the Pavlov experiment, if the meat powder does not accompany the sound of the tuning fork,

[11] See Howard H. Kendler, *Basic Psychology,* 2d ed., Appleton-Century-Crofts, New York, 1968, pp. 290–291.

then the drops of saliva will slowly decrease and will eventually become extinct with just the sound of the tuning fork. Thus, the extinction principle simply means that if behavior is not reinforced, it will eventually become extinct.

The principle of extinction has important implications for understanding and controlling behavior. For example, workers may be continually reinforced, by bonus and praise, for learning a new skill in a training program. However, when the newly trained workers are placed on the job, they may never receive reinforcement for performing the skill. Their work record may slowly decline, and their newly acquired skill may even become extinct. As pointed out, extinction is generally more effective in eliminating undesirable organizational behavior than is punishment. It does not have the undesirable side effects of punishment. On the other hand, most organizational behavior is intermittently reinforced and thus is very resistant to extinction. Thus, it may take a long time for an extinction strategy to eliminate undesirable organizational behaviors and punishment may have to be used.

Learning Curves

When learning takes place, there is a gradually increasing strength of response for each repeated trial. This increasing strength occurs in both classical and operant conditioning. The relationship can be expressed as an acquisition or learning curve where the vertical axis represents measured performance and the horizontal axis represents the amount of practice or experience. The horizontal is usually expressed in time or number of trials. Figure 12-2 summarizes the four general types of learning curves. Briefly summarized, they are the following:

1 *Decreasing-Returns Curve*   The curve in Figure 12-2*a* is negatively accelerating and is commonly referred to as the decreasing-returns curve. This curve represents the most common way in which acquisition occurs. The learning of most mental and motor tasks follows a decreasing-returns pattern. There is an initial spurt of learning, then the learning begins to slow down, and finally the learning reaches a point where there is practically no progress. Learning to perform most of the specialized, routine jobs found in modern organizations tends to follow a decreasing-returns curve.

2 *Increasing-Returns Curve*   The curve in *b* is basically the opposite of *a*. In *b* there is a positively accelerating learning curve that produces increasing returns. Learning following the pattern in *b* is rarer than that represented by *a*. The *b* curve will usually only occur when a person is learning a completely new and different mental or motor task. Many of the staff and service personnel in an organization, such as engineers and marketing researchers, may experience an increasing return on certain tasks. The same is true of learning very highly skilled lower-level jobs. In both cases, learning may initially progress very slowly but then pick up very fast.

3 *S Learning Curve*   The learning curve in Figure 12-2*c* is commonly known as the S curve. This curve represents a combination of the decreasing- and increasing-returns curves. Theoretically, all learning would probably follow an S pattern if the person brought absolutely no relevant experience to the learning situation. In reality, of course,

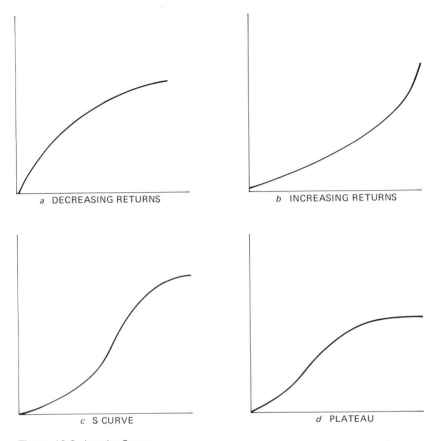

Figure 12-2 Learning Curves.

this is not the case. An S curve will most likely result when a person attempts to learn a relatively difficult, unfamiliar task that requires insight. For example, learning many of the highly skilled jobs in a technical industry might follow an S pattern.

4 *Learning Plateau* The curve in *d* shows the plateau principle of acquisition. Many learning situations seem to progress satisfactorily but then reach a point where nothing new is learned. Increased practice does not lead to increased learning. This leveling off in learning is called a plateau. The learning of many relatively simple tasks follows this pattern. Most lower-level and "dead end" jobs in modern organizations have personnel who are experiencing a learning plateau. Something must spur the persons on to get them on an accelerating path again. New behavioral management techniques are needed to break organizational personnel out of plateau learning situations.

Not all human learning can be neatly fitted into one of the above learning curves. On the other hand, the curves do represent in a general way the major patterns of acquisition. It is important for managers to know that learning of certain types of tasks follows certain types of curves. Kagan and Havemann summarize the applicability of the curves to the learning of specific types of tasks as follows:

1 The more unfamiliar the task to be learned, the more likely it is that progress will be slow at the start and will then increase.
2 In most learning of complicated skills, there is at least one period, short or long, in which each new trial produces an improvement of equal size.
3 As we approach the ultimate limit of learning, progress slows down, and it takes many trials to produce even a small amount of improvement. [12]

Spontaneous Recovery after Rest

Spontaneous recovery is an interesting phenomenon in learning. If a person is experiencing a sequence of nonreinforced responses and then takes a rest, immediately following the break there will be a return to a more intense level of response. This spontaneous recovery occurs even though no reinforcement took place. The jump in response strength following rest occurs in both classical and operant conditioning and suggests that the conditioned response does not totally disappear during extinction but instead is merely suppressed or becomes inhibited.

Following spontaneous recovery, the slope of the learning curve steeply accelerates if the conditioned stimulus in classical or conditioned response in operant conditioning is reinforced. In a parallel manner, the slope of the learning curve steeply decelerates without reinforcement. An example of spontaneous recovery occurring in an organizational situation is a spurt in job performance by an employee immediately following a vacation or layoff. Management could take advantage of spontaneous recovery by making a conscious effort to reinforce desirable responses and nonreinforce undesirable responses. By doing this, managers would be taking advantage of the steep acceleration or deceleration curves following spontaneous recovery.

Generalization of Stimuli and Responses

The common meaning of generalization is applicable to the behavior modification principle by the same name. There is both stimulus and response generalization. In stimulus generalization new, but similar, stimuli or stimulus situations will produce a response that is the same as that produced by the original stimulus. This occurs in classical conditioning when a conditioned response that is elicited by a conditioned stimulus has another stimulus that is similar to the conditioned stimulus and also produces the conditioned response. The more similar the new stimulus is to the conditioned stimulus, the more probable that the new stimulus will produce the same conditioned response. This latter relationship, commonly called the stimulus generalization gradient, is shown in Figure 12-3. In operant conditioning, stimulus generalization occurs when a response is reinforced in the presence of one stimulus occasion and is emitted in a similar stimulus situation.

[12] Jerome Kagan and Ernest Havemann, *Psychology,* Harcourt, Brace & World, New York, 1968, p. 90.

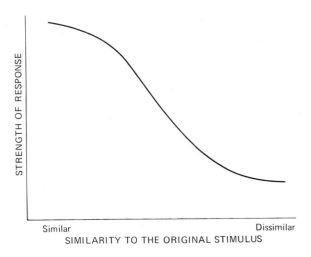

STRENGTH OF RESPONSE

Similar   Dissimilar
SIMILARITY TO THE ORIGINAL STIMULUS

Figure 12-3 A Gradient for Generalization. *Source:* Bernard M. Bass and James A. Vaughan, *Training in Industry; The Management of Learning,* Wadsworth Publishing Company, Inc., Belmont, Calif., 1966, p. 17.

In response generalization, a similar response to one which led to reinforcement in the past will occur. Thus, because of the induction or transfer that takes place, learning in one area of skilled behavior may improve one's ability in another area. Learning how to perform well on one job should transfer to performing well on other similar jobs.

The principle of generalization has important implications for human behavior. Without it, a person would find it extremely difficult to adapt to any new situation. However, because of generalization, a person does not have to completely relearn each new task or situation. In organizations, it allows employees to adapt to overall changing conditions and specific new or modified job assignments. All employees, no matter what their levels in the organization, can borrow from past learning experiences to adjust and make a smoother transition to new learning situations.

Besides the positive contributions to behavior that result from generalization, there are also certain negative implications. Many mistakes are the result of generalization. It may cause a person in an organization to make an error or draw a false conclusion. For example, a programmer may inject a similar, but wrong, bit of data into a management information system. This one error may then lead to the generalization on the part of the user that the entire information system is worthless. Another example of a behavioral problem attributed to generalization could be the case of hiring and training the hard-core unemployed. One or a few bad experiences with hard-core workers may lead management to generalize that "they" are untrainable and poor risks. "They" is a common example of faulty generalization. The one "bad apple" generalizes to the whole barrel.

The word *they* points out the potentially harmful behavioral consequences that may result from generalization.

Discrimination of Stimuli and Responses

In recent times, the word *discrimination* has a negative connotation and is usually associated with race prejudice. Technically, of course, the word has a much broader meaning. Applied to learning, discrimination is essentially the opposite of generalization. Whereas generalization is a reaction to *similar* stimuli or responses, discrimination is a reaction to *differences* in stimuli or responses. The principle of discrimination can be demonstrated by a Pavlovian type of experiment. A light can be added to the experiment of the dog being conditioned to the sound of a tuning fork. If the experiment is set up so that the dog gets food only when the sound occurs *and* the light is on and gets no food when the sound occurs and the light is off, the dog will soon learn to discriminate between the sound–light-on and sound–light-off stimulus. The dog will respond only to the sound–light-on stimulus and not to the sound–light-off stimulus.

Similar to the stimulus discrimination that takes place in classical conditioning is the response discrimination in operant conditioning. This latter type of discrimination is the response discrimination that takes place when behavior is reinforced in the presence of one stimulus situation but not reinforced in the presence of another stimulus situation. This response discrimination is the result of differential reinforcement. Response discrimination allows a person to behave differently in different situations. Without it, human behavior would be in utter chaos.

Being a good supervisor requires effective discrimination. An example is the supervisor who distinguishes between two equally high producing workers. The supervisor responds positively to only one of the high producers because he or she has learned to discriminate between them. One of the workers produces a great quantity of items but pays no attention to quality. The other worker also produces in great quantity, but is quality-conscious and has virtually no rejects. At first the supervisor may respond positively to both workers. However, when the sloppy worker provides no reinforcement to the supervisor's responses, the supervisor soon stops responding. The supervisor discriminates between the two high producers and responds only to the quality-conscious high producer. This discrimination may in turn modify the sloppy worker's behavior. If the worker is not reinforced by the supervisor for high-quantity–low-quality performance, this behavior will eventually decrease in frequency. On the other hand, if no discrimination is made and the supervisor reinforces the high-quantity–low-quality performance, this behavior will continue unabated.

Shaping Behaviors

The principle of shaping is closely related to generalization and discrimination. Shaping allows for new behavior to occur. It consists of reinforcing closer and closer approximations to the targeted new behavior. The effective shaper must carefully select the initial behavior to reinforce. He or she must then determine how long to reinforce each approximation before moving on to the next behavior. This shaping process takes place until the desired behavior is reached. It works because the reinforcement not only strengthens the approximate response given attention, but it also increases the probability that a closer response approximation will occur.

In an organization, shaping allows the manager to "create" new behaviors on the part of employees. The creation can take place in a systematic shaping process. For example, in acquiring a new skill, the worker could be shaped through successive approximations to reach the desired level of competency. Shaping, like the other principles of behavior modification, can be a very powerful tool in training and human resource management in general.

Modeling Behaviors
Modeling is the last principle of behavior modification that will be discussed. Modeling is a type of observational learning and is sometimes called imitation or copying. Its theoretical explanations are still quite controversial. However, there is little doubt that modeling does take place. Most simply, modeling takes place when a learner is given an example of a particular behavior, by a human or symbolic model, and is then reinforced for imitating this behavior. It is similar in concept to shaping but eliminates the busy work of successive approximations.

Modeling can be used to acquire new or novel behaviors, may lead to inhibiting or disinhibiting effects on previously acquired responses, or may lead to a new response that was previously neutral. In other words, modeling can be used to affect almost any type of learned behavior. In organizations, almost all on-the-job training involves modeling. An example of a systematic modeling strategy applied to human resource management would be the following:

1 Identify the target behavior.
2 Select the appropriate model and modeling medium (e.g., live demonstration, training film, video tape).
3 Make sure the employee is capable of satisfying all skill requirements.
4 Structure a favorable learning environment which increases the probability of attentive behavior.
5 Model the desirable behavior.
6 Have the subject attempt the target behavior while employing prompts or cues as necessary.
7 Systematically reinforce any goal-convergent behavior.
8 Systematically extinguish (ignore) any goal-divergent behavior.

9 Maintain and strengthen the target behavior first with continuous reinforcement, later with an intermittent schedule, and finally, with self-reinforcement.[13]

This type of systematic application of behavior modification principles can dramatically improve the practice of human resource management. Chapter 15 will give details on this type of application in terms of behavior contingency management.

Summary

This chapter summarizes the important learning theories and principles of behavior modification. Learning is simply defined as a relatively permanent change in behavior that results from reinforced practice or experience and has two basic theoretical foundations. The cognitive learning theories base learning on cognitions such as attitudes, beliefs, memory, goal seeking, and expectations. Yet, when scientific analysis is applied, the cognitive theories break down because they are dealing with unobservables. On the other hand, the connectionist theories deal with observable behaviors that are amenable to scientific investigation.

The connectionist theories are concerned with the stimulus-response connection (S-R) and, more recently, the response-stimulus connection (R-S). The former is best represented by classical conditioning and the latter by operant conditioning. In classical conditioning, a formerly neutral conditioned stimulus that is paired with (reinforced by) an unconditioned stimulus is able to elicit a conditioned response. In operant conditioning, the stimulus serves only as the occasion or cue for the response to be emitted. The key in operant conditioning is what happens after the response occurs. If it is reinforced, the response will be strengthened and tend to be repeated. If the response is punished, it will be weakened and tend to decrease in subsequent frequency. If there is no consequence of a reinforcing or punishing nature, the response will also weaken and disappear in the long run. In other words, from operant conditioning, the assumption is that behavior depends on its consequences.

Inherent in classical and operant conditioning are insights into human behavior and, more specifically, behavior modification. Through many years of scientific research and study, there have evolved lawful principles of behavior modification. Most important are the reinforcement and punishment principles. Based on the law of effect, reinforcement is operationally defined as any consequence that strengthens the response and tends to increase the subsequent frequency of the response. It may be positive (application of a desirable consequence) or negative (termination of an undesirable consequence), primary or conditioned. How this reinforcement is administered (fixed or intermittent, ratio or interval) will affect the resulting behavior and is vitally important to the application of

---

[13] See Fred Luthans and Robert Kreitner, *Organizational Behavior Modification,* Scott, Foresman, Glenview, Ill., 1975, pp. 140–143.

organizational behavior. The other important principle of behavior modification is punishment. It weakens the behavior and tends to decrease the subsequent frequency. Although there are negative side effects, punishment can be used to modify behaviors.

Besides reinforcement and punishment, extinction (nonreinforcement of a response tends to weaken it and decrease the frequency in the long run), learning curves (decreasing returns, increasing returns, S curves, and plateaus), spontaneous recovery (the jump in the intensity of a nonreinforced response following a rest), generalization (responding to a similar stimulus or having a similar response to one which led to reinforcement in the past), discrimination (reaction to differences in stimuli or responses), shaping (reinforcement of successive approximations), and modeling (observation or imitated learning) are other important principles of behavior modification. These principles play an important role in O.B. Mod. (organizational behavior modification), or more specifically behavioral contingency management, which is discussed in Chapter 15.

☐ **Critical Incident**

You have been designated coach of the Thunderbolts, a softball team in the summer industrial league. You have never coached before but did play shortstop on your high school baseball team. After looking over your team in a couple of practice sessions, you soon realize that there is a great deal of potential on the team. However, at this point the team members are individually and collectively making too many errors in fielding the ball and making too many basic mistakes at the plate (for example, not stepping into the ball and swinging at bad pitches) to win many games in this league. You have decided that your coaching can make a difference between success and failure of this team, and you want to be a winner.

1 What concepts and principles of behavior modification could be used by you in coaching this softball team? How would these be applied?
2 What are some potential reinforcers that you could use?
3 Do you think coaching and management are similar? Why or why not?

Questions for Review and Discussion

1 What is the definition of learning? Summarize the two major theoretical approaches to learning.
2 What is the difference between classical and operant conditioning?
3 What is positive reinforcement? Summarize the four major schedules for administering reinforcement.
4 What is punishment? How does it differ from extinction?
5 Explain the meaning and application of generalization and discrimination.

References

Bass, Bernard M., and James A. Vaughan: *Training in Industry: The Management of Learning,* Wadsworth, Belmont, Calif., 1966.

Child, John: "Strategies of Control and Organizational Behavior," *Administrative Science Quarterly,* March 1973, pp. 1–17.

Deci, Edward L.: "Paying People Doesn't Always Work the Way You Expect It To," *Human Resource Management,* Summer 1973, pp. 28–32.

Dowling, William F.: "Conversation with B. F. Skinner," *Organizational Dynamics,* Winter 1973, pp. 31–40.

Hill, Winfred F.: *Learning: A Survey of Psychological Interpretations,* Chandler, Scranton, Pa., 1971.

Jablonsky, Stephen F., and David DeVries: "Operant Conditioning Principles Extrapolated to the Theory of Management," *Organizational Behavior and Human Performance,* April 1972, pp. 340–358.

Kagan, Jerome, and Ernest Havemann: *Psychology,* Harcourt, Brace & World, New York, 1968.

Keller, Fred S.: *Learning: Reinforcement Theory,* Random House, New York, 1969.

Kendler, Howard H.: *Basic Psychology,* 2d ed., Appleton-Century-Crofts, New York, 1968.

Kimble, Gregory A., Norman Garmezy, and Edward Zigler: *Principles of General Psychology,* 4th ed., Ronald, New York, 1974.

Lawson, Tom E.: "Gagne's Learning Theory Applied to Technical Instruction," *Training and Development Journal,* April 1974, pp. 32–40.

Luthans, Fred, and Donald D. White, Jr.: "Behavior Modification: Application to Manpower Management," *Personnel Administration,* July–August 1971, pp. 41–47.

——— **and David Lyman:** "Training Supervisors to Use Organizational Behavior Modification," *Personnel,* September–October 1973, pp. 38–44.

——— **and Robert Kreitner:** *Organizational Behavior Modification,* Scott, Foresman, Glenview, Ill., 1975.

——— **and** ———: "The Role of Punishment in Organizational Behavior Modification," *Public Personnel Management,* May–June 1973, pp. 159–160.

——— **and** ———: "The Management of Behavioral Contingencies," *Personnel,* July–August 1974, pp. 7–16.

Schneier, Craig Eric: "Behavior Modification in Management: A Review and Critique," *Academy of Management Journal,* September 1974, pp. 528–548.

———: "Training and Development Programs: What Learning Theory and Research Have to Offer," *Personnel Journal,* April 1974, pp. 288–293.

Skinner, B. F.: *Science and Human Behavior,* Free Press, New York, 1953.

Staats, Arthur W., and Carolyn K. Staats: *Complex Human Behavior,* Holt, New York, 1963.

This, Leslie E., and Gordon L. Lippitt: "Learning Theories and Training," *Training and Development Journal,* May 1966, pp. 10–18.

Wiard, Harry: "Why Manage Behavior? A Case for Positive Reinforcement," *Human Resource Management,* Summer 1972, pp. 15–20.

Chapter 13

The Process
and Content
of Motivation

The theoretical bases for motivating people in organizations have dramatically changed in the last few years and are still in a state of transition. The simplistic motivational assumptions of the past are no longer applicable to present or future human resource management. The motivational process is quite complex, and the content is extremely diverse. The purpose of this chapter is to explain the motivation process through the basic need-drive-goal cycle and then add the dimensions provided by the Vroom, Porter and Lawler, and Smith and Cranny expectancy models of motivation. The last part of the chapter is devoted to the content of motivation. The content theories of Maslow and Herzberg provide the framework for discussing specific money, security, status, power, competence, and achievement motives of human beings in modern organizations.

The Basic Motivational Process

Everybody thinks they understand motivation. It is commonly expressed in words such as *desires, wants, wishes, aims, goals, needs, drives, motives,* and *incentives.* Technically, the term *motivation* can be traced to the Latin word *movere,* which means "to move." This Latin meaning is evidenced by the formal definition of motivation given by Berelson and Steiner, "A motive is an inner state that energizes, activates, or moves (hence 'motivation'), and that directs or channels behavior toward goals."[1]

In a less formal sense, Sanford and Wrightsman describe a motive as follows: "A motive is a restlessness, a lack, a yen, a force. Once in the grip of a motive, the organism does something. It most generally does something to reduce the restlessness, to remedy the lack, to alleviate the yen, to mitigate the force."[2] The best way to gain an understanding of motivation is to recognize that it is a process and break it down into the basic component parts of needs, drives, and goals.

---

[1] Bernard Berelson and Gary A. Steiner, *Human Behavior,* Harcourt, Brace & World, New York, 1964, p. 240.
[2] Fillmore H. Sanford and Lawrence S. Wrightsman, Jr., *Psychology,* 3d ed., Brooks/Cole, Belmont, Calif., 1970, p. 189.

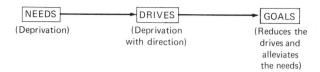

Figure 13-1 The Basic Motivational Process.

Figure 13-1 graphically depicts the basic motivation process. Needs set up drives to accomplish goals. This process depicts what motivation is all about. The following briefly summarizes the three elements:

1 *Needs* The best one-word definition of a motivational need is *deficiency*. Needs are created whenever there is a physiological *or* psychological imbalance. For example, a need exists when a cell or body is deprived of food or water, and a need develops when a high achiever is deprived of opportunities for achievement-oriented activities.

2 *Drives* In almost all cases drives or motives (the two terms are used interchangeably in this chapter) are set up to alleviate needs. A drive can be simply defined as a deficiency with direction. Drives are action-oriented and provide an energizing thrust toward goal accomplishment. They represent the behavior in the motivational process. The examples of the needs for food and water are translated into the hunger and thirst drives, which are action-oriented, and the need for achievement-related activities becomes a drive for achievement.

3 *Goals* At the end of the basic motivational process is the goal. Such a goal can be defined as anything which will alleviate a need and reduce the intensity of a drive. Thus, attaining a goal will tend to restore physiological or psychological balance and will reduce or cut off the drive. Eating food, drinking water, and working on achievement-oriented tasks balance and reduce the corresponding drives. Food, water, and achievement-oriented tasks are the goals in these examples.

It should be remembered that the basic motivational process is a hypothetical construct or intervening variable. No one has actually observed motivation or isolated it under a microscope. Only the behavioral manifestations of drives are observable, and these behaviors take three forms:[3]

1 *Consummatory Behavior* This is the most obvious type of motivated behavior because it directly satisfies the need in question. Examples of consummatory behavior with the corresponding drives include eating (hunger), drinking (thirst), joining a lunch group (affiliation or status), and running for union steward (power).

2 *Instrumental Behavior* Similar to its meaning in learning, this type of motivated behavior is instrumental in satisfying the need in question. Walking to the water fountain or

[3] Gregory A. Kimble and Norman Garmezy, *General Psychology*, 3d ed., Ronald, New York, 1968, pp. 378–379.

joining the company softball team are behavioral expressions of the thirst and affiliation motives. But this behavior is only instrumental in obtaining water or friends. The instrumental behavior does not directly satisfy the need as does consummatory behavior. A complicating factor is that the same behavior may be instrumental for one person but consummatory for another.

3 *Substitute Behavior*   This type of motivated behavior is the most complex and difficult to explain. The reason is that it is indirect or substitutive in nature and on the surface seems to have little relevance to the need in question. An example is the worker who has a strong need for affiliation but is a "rate buster" (produces above the group norm). In a way, substitute behavior is a "black box" concept; it is known to be motivated behavior but the reasons cannot be fully explained.

The existence of instrumental and substitute behavior points out the difficulty in trying to understand motivation. The process of motivation is extremely complex, and there is certainly not a simple relationship between motivation and behavior. Yet, despite this complexity, much can be gained by examining various aspects of the process. So far just the basic need-drive-goal process has been examined. Recently, more complex expectancy models of motivation have greatly improved understanding of the motivation process.

Expectancy Models of Motivation

Two distinct approaches to work motivation have evolved in recent years. On the one hand are the content theories that attempt to determine what it is that motivates behavior (i.e., money or responsibility) and on the other hand are the more process-oriented expectancy theories that attempt to determine how motivation is translated into action. The content theories are given attention in the last part of the chapter. The expectancy theories depict the multiplicative interaction between variables in the motivation process. Such an approach is not new. However, the application to work motivation is relatively new. The expectancy model of Victor Vroom started the trend which has now been refined in models by Porter and Lawler and Smith and Cranny.

The Vroom Expectancy Model

The work of Victor Vroom is the most widely known expectancy theory of work motivation. Figure 13-2 shows that the model is built around the concepts of valence, expectancy, and force; the basic assumption is that "the choices made by a person among alternative courses of action are lawfully related to psychological events occurring contemporaneously with the behavior."[4] Vroom's concept of force is basically equivalent to motivation and is shown to be the algebraic sum of the product of valence times expectancy.

[4] Victor Vroom, *Work and Motivation,* Wiley, New York, 1964, pp. 14–15.

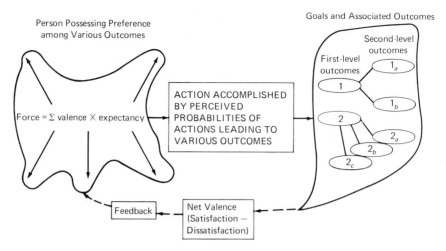

Figure 13-2 Vroom's Motivation Model. *Source:* Adapted from Marvin D. Dunnette, "The Motives of Indus-trial Managers," *Organizational Behavior and Human Performance,* May 1967, p. 178. Dunnette developed the model from Victor H. Vroom, *Work and Motivation,* John Wiley & Sons, Inc., New York, 1964. Used with permission.

Valence is the strength of an individual's preference for a particular outcome, and in order to be positive, the individual would prefer attaining the outcome to not attaining it. A valence of zero occurs when the individual is indifferent toward the outcome, and a negative valence occurs when the individual prefers not attaining the outcome to attaining it. Another major input into valence is the instrumentality that the first-level outcome has in obtaining a desired second-level outcome.

Besides valence, the other major variable is expectancy. This expectancy is the probabil-ity (ranging from 0 to 1) that a particular action or effort will lead to a particular *first-level* outcome. Instrumentality, on the other hand, refers to the degree to which a first-level outcome will lead to a desired second-level outcome. To reiterate, the Vroom model states that the strength of the motivation to perform a certain act will depend on the algebraic sum of the products of the valences for the outcomes (which includes instru-mentality) times the expectancies.

Although the Vroom theory does not directly contribute to techniques of motivating per-sonnel in an organization, it is of value in understanding the process of motivation and thus improves human resource management. For example, suppose a worker is given a certain standard for production. By measuring the worker's outputs, management can determine how important are the various personal goals (second-level outcomes such as money, security, and recognition), the instrumentality of the organizational goal (the first-level outcome such as the production standard) for the attainment of the personal goals, and the worker's expectancies that effort and ability will accomplish the organizational goal. If output is below standard, it may be that the worker does not place a high value on the second-level outcomes, or the worker may not feel that the first-level outcome is

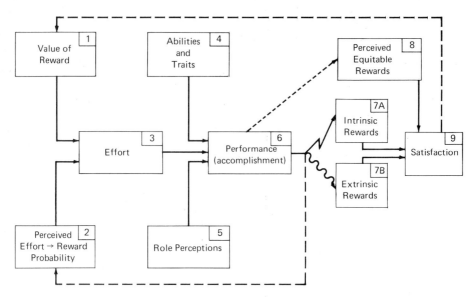

Figure 13-3 Porter and Lawler Motivation Model. Reproduced with permission from Lyman W. Porter and Edward E. Lawler, III, *Managerial Attitudes and Performance*, Homewood, Ill.: Richard D. Irwin, Inc., © 1968.

instrumental in obtaining the second-level outcomes, or the worker may feel that his or her efforts will not be able to accomplish the first-level outcome. Any one or a combination of these possibilities will result in a low level of motivation to produce. The Vroom model is designed to help management analyze the worker's motivation and identify some of the relevant variables; it does not provide specific solutions.

The Porter and Lawler Expectancy Model

In an extension of the Vroom model, Lyman Porter and Edward Lawler propose the multivariable model in Figure 13-3 to explain the complex relationship between job attitudes and job performance. Their model counters some of the simplistic traditional assumptions made about the positive relationship between satisfaction and performance and is expectancy-based. A future-oriented model, it emphasizes the anticipation of response-outcome connections. Porter and Lawler explain the reason for their approach as follows:

The emphasis in expectancy theory on rationality and expectations seems to us to describe best the kinds of cognitions that influence managerial performance. We assume that managers operate on the basis of some sort of expectancies which, although based upon previous experience, are forward-oriented in a way that does not seem to be as easily handled by the concept of habit strength.[5]

[5] Lyman W. Porter and Edward E. Lawler, III, *Managerial Attitudes and Performance*, Irwin, Homewood, Ill., 1968, pp. 12–13.

Thus, expectancy provides the theoretical foundation for this model of the motivational process. The main variables in the process are effort, performance, reward, and satisfaction.

1 *Effort* Effort is the amount of energy exerted by an individual on a given task. However, contrary to common usage, effort is not the same as performance in the Porter and Lawler model. Effort is more closely associated with motivation than with performance. The amount of effort depends upon the interaction between the value that the person places on the reward and his or her perceived effort-reward probability. The value depends on its degree of attractiveness and desirability. In an organization, friendship, promotion, pay, recognition, and praise have different values for different employees. For example, one employee may place a high value on promotion while another may place a low value on it because it would make him or her feel threatened and insecure. The perceived effort-reward probability refers to the employee's perception of the probability that a given amount of effort will in fact lead to a given reward. In other words, will working as hard as possible lead to a promotion? Based on experience and intuition, the employee would assign a probability to this happening. The interaction between the value of reward and this effort-reward probability would result in the amount of effort put forth by the employee.

2 *Performance* Performance can be objectively measured. It results from effort but cannot be equated with effort. There may be a difference between effort and performance because of abilities and traits and/or role perceptions. In other words, performance depends not only upon the amount of effort exerted, but also on the person's abilities (e.g., job knowledge and skill) and the way the person perceives the role he or she should take. How the job is defined, the direction efforts take, and the level of effort perceived to be necessary for effective performance all go into role perception. This explains how an employee exerting a great amount of effort, but with little ability and/or an inaccurate role perception, could end up with ineffective performance.

3 *Rewards* Initially Porter and Lawler included only a single reward variable in their model. However, empirical testing showed that it should more accurately be divided into extrinsic and intrinsic categories. Both the extrinsic and intrinsic rewards are desirable, but the intrinsic ones are more likely to produce satisfaction that affects performance. In addition, the perceived equitable rewards vitally affect the performance-satisfaction relationship. The perceived equitable rewards reflect the fair level of rewards that the individual feels should be granted for a given level of performance. The perception of equitable rewards can be directly affected by self-rated performance, as indicated by the short arrows in the model.

4 *Satisfaction* Satisfaction is derived from the extent to which actual rewards fall short, meet, or exceed the person's perceived equitable level of rewards. In other words, if actual rewards meet or exceed perceived equitable rewards, then the individual will be satisfied, but if actual rewards are below what is perceived to be equitable, then the individual will be dissatisfied. This explanation of satisfaction makes two important departures from traditional thinking about satisfaction. First, the model recognizes that satisfaction is only in part determined by actual rewards received. It also depends on what a person feels the organization *should* reward for a given level of performance.

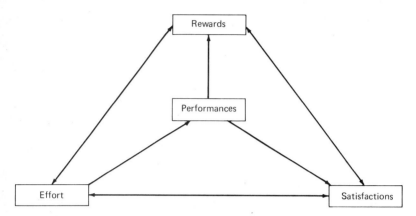

Figure 13-4 Smith and Cranny Motivation Model. *Source:* Patricia Cain Smith and C. J. Cranny, "Psychology of Men at Work," *Annual Review of Psychology,* vol. 19, p. 469, 1968.

Second, and of greater importance, the model recognizes satisfaction to be more dependent on performance than performance is on satisfaction. Only through indirect feedback will satisfaction affect performance. This represents a marked departure from the traditional analysis of the satisfaction-performance relationship.

There has been a deluge of research and theorizing concerning the performance-satisfaction relationship. With some slight modifications, most researchers generally support the Porter and Lawler expectancy model of motivation.[6] Yet, the evidence is not conclusive and a controversy still exists.[7] In addition, even though the Porter and Lawler model is more applications-oriented than the Vroom model, it is still quite complex and may prove difficult to bridge the gap to actual management practice.

The Smith and Cranny Expectancy Model

In contrast to the relatively complex Vroom and Porter and Lawler models, Patricia Smith and C. J. Cranny propose a simpler three-way relationship among effort, satisfaction, and reward. Each variable in the corners of the triangle in Figure 13-4 has causal effects on the others, either individually or in combination. In other words, praise from a supervisor (reward) may lead to increased satisfaction or a satisfied, cooperative worker may lead to

[6] For example, see David G. Kuhn, John W. Slocum, Jr., and Richard B. Chase, "Does Job Performance Affect Employee Satisfaction?" *Personnel Journal,* June 1971, pp. 455–459, 485; Jay R. Schuster, Barbara Clark, and Miles Rogers, "Testing Portions of the Porter and Lawler Model Regarding the Motivational Role of Pay," *Journal of Applied Psychology,* June 1971, pp. 187–195; and H. Heneman and D. P. Schwab, "Evaluation of Research on Expectancy Theory Predictions of Employee Performance," *Psychological Bulletin,* vol. 78, pp. 1–9, 1972.

[7] See Charles N. Greene, "The Satisfaction-Performance Controversy," *Business Horizons,* October 1972, pp. 31–41; and Orlando Behling and Frederick Starke, "The Postulates of Expectancy Theory," *Academy of Management Journal,* September 1973, pp. 373–388.

praise from the supervisor. However, as in the Porter and Lawler scheme, the real key to the Smith and Cranny model lies in the concept of effort. Performance is affected *only* by effort, not by reward or satisfaction. As depicted in Figure 13-4, performance is at the heart of the model and can influence rewards and satisfactions but can itself be influenced only by effort.

Whereas the Vroom and Porter and Lawler models can be criticized for using technical jargon and making application difficult for the practitioner, the Smith and Cranny model overcomes some of this problem. Recognizing the complexity of work motivation and incorporating some of the same concepts as Vroom and Porter and Lawler, the Smith and Cranny model is easy to understand and apply. The model stresses that management's job is to administer rewards but recognizes that this alone does not have a direct impact on performance. Taking a systems viewpoint, Smith and Cranny's model emphasizes the interrelationships and interdependencies among effort, satisfaction, and reward. Yet, it is effort, not reward or satisfaction, that directly affects performance. Most of the research that has been conducted so far on work motivation plus the basic psychological research done on the impact that intention or expectancies have on task performance lend support to the model.[8]

Although the expectancy models effectively relate the important variables of the motivation process and have some practical implications for management, they generally fall short of the theoretical goals of prediction and control. The models can help practicing managers focus on the relevant variables and their relationships and thus lead to better understanding of motivation, but they do not provide ready answers as to what types or techniques of reward produce the most effort for performance. The next part of the chapter will concentrate on these content variables of work motivation.

Content Models of Motivation

Traditionally, management has approached motivation from the perspective of its content. Almost exclusive attention was devoted to the search for what it was that motivated workers and managers. In the human relations movement of the 1940s and 1950s, money, working conditions, and security were thought to be the answer to work motivation. It was assumed that providing personnel with good wages and salaries, excellent working conditions, and security would make them happy and that happy employees were productive employees. Such a simplistic approach to motivation did not work out in practice. Although no harm was done and some good actually occurred in the early stages of organizational development, it soon became painfully clear that this human relations approach fell far short of providing a meaningful solution to the complex motivational problems facing management.

[8] Patricia Cain Smith and C. J. Cranny, "Psychology of Men at Work," *Annual Review of Psychology*, vol. 19, pp. 469–477, 1968.

The major fault of the traditional approach is that the assumptions are much too simplistic. As the expectancy models point out, human motivation is more complex and diverse than is suggested by the narrow content approach. Moreover, happiness or morale turned out to be a very elusive concept. Seldom operationally defined, morale became a catch-all word and scapegoat for all the human problems facing management. If management could not explain a problem, it was a morale problem. Finally, as systematic research began to accumulate, the relationship between morale and productivity became less clear. The positive correlation between morale and productivity became more of an issue rather than an automatic assumption. The Porter and Lawler approach is representative of the new thinking.

As the human problems facing management began to mount, the limitations of the traditional human relations approach to motivation began to surface. Starting at the beginning of the 1960s, the behavioral approach to management started to earnestly search for a new theoretical framework for the content of work motivation. The theories of Abraham Maslow and Frederick Herzberg were the result.

Maslow's Content Model of Motivation

Abraham Maslow, in a classic paper published in 1943, outlined the basic elements of his motivation model. Drawing primarily from his clinical experience, Maslow felt that man's motivational needs could be arranged in the hierarchical manner of Figure 13-5. In essence, he believed that once a given level of need became satisfied, it no longer served

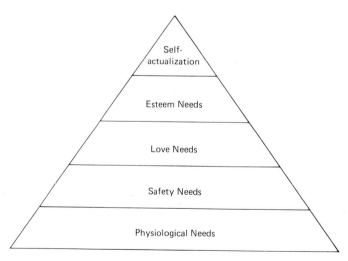

Figure 13-5   Maslow's Hierarchy of Needs.

to motivate. The next higher level of need had to be activated in order to motivate the individual. In terms of content, he identified the following:

1 *Physiological Needs*   The most basic things that motivate are the needs for hunger, thirst, sleep, and sex. According to his theory, once these basic needs are satisfied, they no longer motivate. For instance, a hungry man will be motivated by a carrot held out in front of him. However, after he eats his fill of carrots and another carrot is held out, he will no longer strive for a carrot. Only the next higher level of needs will motivate him. In other words, if there is a need for carrots, then they will be motivating; if there is no need, then they will not be motivating. Maslow's model would say that managers cannot continually hold out the same carrots and expect employees to be motivated by them.

2 *Safety Needs*   This second type of need identified by Maslow is roughly equivalent to security. Maslow stressed emotional as well as physical safety. The whole organism may become a safety-seeking mechanism. Yet, like the physiological needs, once these safety needs are satisfied, they no longer motivate. Security is given further attention toward the end of the chapter.

3 *Love Needs*   This third content area in the hierarchy corresponds to affection and affiliation. Like Sigmund Freud, Maslow seems guilty of poor choice of wording to identify his motives. The word *love* has many misleading connotations such as sex, which is actually a physiological need. Perhaps a more appropriate word describing this level would be *belongingness*, for example, being an accepted member in an informal work group.

4 *Esteem Needs*   The esteem motives are at the higher level of human motivation. Power, achievement, and status could be considered to be part of this content level. Maslow carefully pointed out that this esteem motive contains both self-esteem and esteem from others.

5 *Need for Self-Actualization*   This content area of motivation represents the culmination of all the lower, intermediate, and higher needs of human beings. A person who has become self-actualized is self-fulfilled and has realized all his or her potential. Self-actualization is closely related to the self-concept of personality. In effect, self-actualization is the person's motivation to make real the perception of self.

Maslow did not intend that his need-hierarchy be directly applied to work motivation. In fact he did not delve into the motivating aspects of human beings in organizations until about 20 years after he originally proposed his theory.[9] Despite this lack of intent on the part of Maslow himself, others, such as Douglas McGregor, popularized his theory in management literature. Figure 13-6 shows how the need hierarchy can be translated to the content factors available in management practice. This need hierarchy has had a tremendous impact on the modern content approach to motivation.

[9] A. H. Maslow, *Eupsychian Management*, Dorsey-Irwin, Homewood, Ill., 1965.

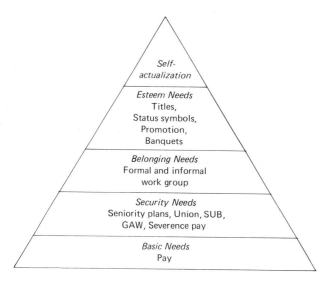

Figure 13-6 A Hierarchy of Work Motivation.

Herzberg's Content Model of Motivation

In the 1950s, Frederick Herzberg conducted a motivational study on about 200 account-ants and engineers employed by firms in and around Pittsburgh. He used the critical incident method of obtaining data for analysis. The professional subjects in the study were given the following directions by an interviewer: "Think of a time when you felt exceptionally good or exceptionally bad about your job, either your present job or any other job you have had. This can be either the 'long-range' or the 'short-range' kind of situation, as I have just described it. Tell me what happened."[10] Responses obtained from this critical incident method were interesting and fairly consistent. Reported good feelings were generally associated with job experiences and job content. An example was the accounting supervisor who felt good about being given the job of installing new computer equipment. He took pride and was gratified knowing that the new equipment made a big difference in the overall functioning of his department. Reported bad feelings, on the other hand, were generally associated with the surrounding or peripheral aspects of the job, the job context. An example of this latter feeling was related by an engineer whose first job was to keep tabulation sheets and manage the office when the boss was gone. It turned out that his boss was always too busy to train him and became annoyed when he tried to ask questions. The engineer said that he felt frustrated in this type of job context and that he felt like a "flunky" in a dead-end job. Tabulating these reported good and bad

[10] Frederick Herzberg, Bernard Mausner, and Barbara Bloch Snyderman, *The Motivation to Work,* 2d ed., Wiley, New York, 1959, p. 141.

feelings, Herzberg concluded that job satisfiers were related to job content and job dissatisfiers were related to job context. The satisfiers were labeled *motivators* and the dissatisfiers were called *hygiene factors*. Taken together, they became known as Herzberg's two-factor theory of motivation and are shown in Figure 13-7.

Herzberg's theory is closely related to Maslow's need hierarchy. Herzberg reduced Maslow's five levels to two levels. The hygiene factors, as the term suggests, are preventive and environmental in nature and are roughly equivalent to Maslow's lower-level needs. These hygiene factors prevent dissatisfaction; they do not lead to satisfaction. In effect, they bring motivation up to a theoretical zero level and are a necessary "floor" to prevent a "negative" type of motivation. However, by themselves the hygiene factors do not motivate. Only the motivators (see Figure 13-7) motivate human beings on the job. These motivators are roughly equivalent to Maslow's higher-level needs. According to the Herzberg theory, an individual must have a job with a challenging content in order to be truly motivated. This content included achievement, recognition, responsibility, and advancement.

Content Models in Perspective

The Maslow and Herzberg models cast a new light on work motivation. Up to this point, management had generally concentrated only on money, working conditions, and security, i.e., Maslow's lower levels or Herzberg's hygiene factors. The typical solution to a "morale problem" was higher pay, more fringe benefits, and better conditions. However, as was pointed out earlier, this simplistic solution did not work. Managers often complained, "We have the highest wages and salaries, the best fringe benefit package, and the plushest conditions of any organization in the area, but these ungrateful guys are still not motivated." Maslow and Herzberg offered a logical explanation for this dilemma. By concentrating on only the lower-level or hygiene factors, management was plainly not motivating personnel.

Although both the Maslow and Herzberg approaches are widely accepted by practitioners, they have come under heavy attack by most academicians. Research has not generally upheld the content theories of motivation. Maslow himself provided no research backup, and the few studies that have attempted to test the model come up with inconclu-

Figure 13-7 Herzberg's Two-Factor Theory

Hygiene Factors	Motivators
Company policy and administration	Achievement
Supervision—technical	Recognition
Salary	Work itself
Interpersonal relations—supervisor	Responsibility
Working conditions	Advancement

sive results.[11] The same holds true with Herzberg's model. Whenever researchers depart from the critical incident method used by Herzberg, they generally obtain results which are quite different from what the two-factor theory would predict. These studies find that there is not always a clear distinction between factors that lead to satisfaction and those that lead to dissatisfaction. One study even used Herzberg's same methodology and obtained results different from what the two-factor theory would predict.[12] There seem to be job factors that lead to both satisfaction and dissatisfaction. The research findings tend to invalidate a strict interpretation of either the Maslow or Herzberg content models of motivation.

In spite of the seemingly legitimate criticism, few would question that Maslow and Herzberg made important contributions to work motivation. They extended the simplistic human relations approach. They drew attention to important job content factors in work motivation which had been badly neglected and often totally overlooked by the human relations approach.

Specific Content Factors in Motivation

The Maslow and Herzberg models contribute to the understanding of motivation but even more than the expectancy models fall short of prediction and control. The process-oriented expectancy models probably accurately depict what motivation is all about, but the content models are more applicable to the practice of human resource management. In particular, the traditional content factors of money, security, and status and the more nontraditional content factors such as power, competence, and especially achievement should be given specific attention in trying to improve the understanding and practice of human resource management.

Money as a Motivator

In the past money has played the most important role in work motivation. In fact, practicing managers tended consciously or unconsciously to equate money with motivation itself. There is now a tendency to downgrade its importance. The new trend is a result of the Maslow and Herzberg influence plus the publicity from surveys which consistently place wages near the middle of the list of employment factors that are important to workers. Although money was undoubtedly overemphasized as a motivator in the past,

---

[11] Michael Beer, *Leadership, Employee Needs, and Motivation*, Bureau of Business Research, Monograph 129, College of Commerce and Administration, Ohio State University, Columbus, Ohio, 1966, p. 68; D. T. Hall and K. E. Nougaim, "An Examination of Maslow's Need Hierarchy in an Organizational Setting," *Organizational Behavior and Human Performance*, vol. 23, 1968, pp. 12–35; and E. E. Lawler and J. L. Suttle, "A Causal Correlational Test of the Need Hierarchy Concept," *Organizational Behavior and Human Performance*, vol. 7, 1972, pp. 265–287.

[12] Donald P. Schwab, H. William DeVitt, and Larry L. Cummings, "A Test of the Adequacy of the Two-Factor Theory as a Predictor of Self-Report Performance Effects," *Personnel Psychology*, Summer 1971, pp. 293–303.

the pendulum now seems to have swung too far in the opposite direction. Money remains a very important but admittedly complex motivator.

In terms of Maslow's hierarchy, money is often equated with the lowest level of needs. It is viewed in the material sense of buying food, clothing, and shelter to satisfy the physiological needs. Yet, money has a definite symbolic as well as economic material meaning. It can provide security, power, and status and can be used to measure achievement. Thus, in this latter sense, money can be used to help an individual satisfy the higher- as well as the lower-level motives in the Maslow hierarchy.

In relation to Herzberg's two-factor theory of motivation, money plays an important but often overlooked role. It is the most important hygiene factor and is an absolute necessity to prevent dissatisfaction. Vroom's expectancy approach would say that money has a direct impact on satisfaction as well. In an extensive review of the research on the role money plays in motivating workers and managers, Vroom concludes, "Considering the labor force as a whole, job satisfaction is positively related to level of wages. A similar relationship has been obtained in studies conducted solely on managers. The more income a manager receives from his job, the more likely he is to report that he is satisfied with his job."[13] This kind of evidence indicates that the Maslow and Herzberg models have probably wrongly had a dampening effect on the role of money as a motivator. This interpretation can also explain why workers place money in the middle of the list of factors that motivate them. Workers may be satisfied with the amount of money they are receiving, but that does not mean that it is not extremely important to them. Moreover, workers probably assume that their wages will be taken care of by the union or the labor market, and thus, they rate higher the factors that affect them directly.

Security Motive
Security is a very intense motive in a fast-paced, highly technological society such as is found in modern America. The typical American can be insecure in a number of areas of everyday living—being able to make the payments on the car or house; keeping a lover's or spouse's affections; staying in school, getting into graduate, law, or medical school; obtaining and/or keeping a good job. Job insecurity, in particular, has a great effect on the motivation of most employees in modern organizations.

On the surface, security is much simpler than other motives, for it is based largely on fear and is avoidance-oriented. Morgan and King note that security "involves being able to hold on to what one has, being sure that one will be able to fare as well in the future as in the past. Conversely, insecurity is a haunting fear that 'things may not last,' that one may lose what he now has."[14] Simply stated, human beings have a learned security

---

[13] Victor H. Vroom, *Motivation in Management,* American Foundation for Management Research, New York, 1965, pp. 51–52.
[14] Clifford T. Morgan and Richard A. King, *Introduction to Psychology,* 3d ed., McGraw-Hill, New York, 1966, p. 234.

motive to protect themselves from the problems of everyday living and actively try to avoid situations which would prevent them from satisfying their other important needs. However, there are also some complexities of security. For example, Gellerman notes that a more complex drive for security is largely unconscious, but greatly influences the behavior of many people. He explains, "the hazards against which they seek to protect themselves are vague, pervasive, and fearsome; usually they have an underlying conviction that the environment is at best capricious and at worst malicious."[15] The simple, conscious security motive of employees is typically taken care of in modern organizations by insurance programs and personal savings plans. On the other hand, the more complex, unconscious security motive is not so easily taken care of but may have a greater and more intense impact on human behavior in organizations. Although much attention has been given to the simple security motive, much more understanding is needed of the role of the unconscious, more complex security motive.

Status Motive
Along with security, the status or prestige motive is especially relevant to a dynamic society. The affluent person is often pictured as a "status seeker" or "pyramid climber." People are accused of being more concerned with external symbols of status—the right clothes, the right car, the right address, and a swimming pool or an executive sandbox— than with the more basic, human-oriented values in life. Stories about the corporate "pecking order" are widely recognized. Although the symbols of status are inferred to be a unique by-product of modern society, the fact is that status has been in existence since there have been two or more persons on the earth.

Status can be simply defined as the *relative* ranking that a person holds in a group, organization, or society. Thus any time two or more persons are together, a status hierarchy, or "pecking order," will evolve. The symbols of status help identify the relative ranking. Both the relative position a person has and the accompanying symbols depend on the prevailing cultural values and societal roles. An example of the impact of cultural values would be the number of spouses that a person has. In some cultures, the more wives a man has, the higher is his status. However, in Western cultures, a person who has more than one spouse is labeled a bigamist and is considered to be an undesirable, low-status character who may even be sent to jail. It must be remembered that such cultural values are highly volatile and change with the time and circumstance. There are also many subcultures in a given society which may have values different from the prevailing values and correspondingly different statuses and accompanying symbols.

Besides values, cultural roles also have a big impact on status determination. A role represents expectations that societal members have of a given position. A level of status is accorded to each such role in the society. Status is inferred from roles such as those of parent and child, student and teacher, and general and private. Related to organizations, the roles of manager and worker have different statuses, as do specific roles within

---

[15] Saul W. Gellerman, *Motivation and Productivity,* American Management Association, New York, 1963, p. 156.

the management and worker ranks. For example, in a manufacturing organization the production manager has more prestige than the personnel manager. However, as societal values place more emphasis on the human being, the status rankings of production and personnel may be reversed. Salary, office furniture and location, and parking privileges are just a few of the accompanying status symbols found among management ranks. Although the symbols are often scoffed at and ridiculed, most workers or managers in all types of organizations are intensely motivated by status.

Power Motive

The power motive has not traditionally been associated with the content of motivating human beings in organizations. Yet, in the behavioral sciences, it is recognized as one of the most important human motives. In 1911, Alfred Adler officially broke his close ties with Sigmund Freud and proposed a theoretical position based on power instead of sex. He felt that human motivation was based on an overwhelming drive for superiority or power and in his own words stated,

Now I began to see clearly in every psychical phenomenon the *striving for superiority*. . . . All our functions follow its direction; rightly or wrongly they strive for conquest, surety, increase. . . . Whatever premises all our philosophers and psychologists dream of—self preservation, pleasure principle, equalization—all these are but vague representations, attempts to express the great upward drive . . . *the fundamental fact of our life.*[16]

To explain the power motive, Adler developed the concepts of inferiority complex and compensation. He felt that every person growing up experienced a sense of inferiority which together with an inborn need for superiority ruled all behavior. The person's life style was characterized by striving to compensate for the feelings of inferiority which were combined with the drive for power.

Although modern behavioral scientists do not generally accept that the power motive is inborn or so dominating, the events of recent years have prompted renewed interest. The quest for power is readily observable in many areas of modern society. The Senate Watergate hearings brought this into the homes of the American public. Although the politician is probably the best example, anyone in a responsible position in business, government, education, or the military typically possesses an intense power motive. The problem for generalizing the importance of the power motive is the notable absence of any significant research back-up. Yet, for understanding human behavior in organizations it must be recognized as a motivating force.

Competence Motive

Like power, competence has been neglected in work motivation. Robert W. White is most closely associated with the competence motive. He questioned the approaches to motivation that were based solely on unlearned, primary drives. For example, the traditional

---

[16] Alfred Adler, "Individual Psychology," in C. Murchison (ed.), *Psychologies of 1930,* translated by Susanne Langer, Clark University Press, Worcester, Mass., 1930, pp. 398–399.

primary drives could not explain curiosity, manipulation, and activity. White proposed a new conceptualization based on the assumption that human beings have the capacity to interact effectively with their environment. He called this capacity competence and stated, "It receives substantial contributions from activities which, though playful and exploratory in character, at the same time show direction, selectivity, and persistence in interacting with the environment."[17] Thus defined, competence is obviously an all-encompassing motive. The important needs of curiosity, manipulation, and activity that all human beings (children and adults) have, are part of the competence motive.

The competence motive points out that people strive to have control or competence over their environment. An individual needs to know what he or she is doing and be able to make things happen. White found that the critical age for competence development is between six and nine years. During this age period, children cut the apron strings and venture out into the world on their own. Children are very curious and need to be active. Although these drives often get the child into trouble, when carried forward to adulthood, they become very important. If they are stifled or inhibited, the total society could become stagnant. The same is true on an organizational level. If employees are not allowed to express their competence motives in their jobs, the organization as a whole will definitely suffer the consequences.

Achievement Motive

Achievement is one of the most important but overlooked motives in work motivation. Herzberg recognized it but did not follow through. Yet, in the behavioral sciences more is known about achievement than any other motive. David McClelland, a Harvard psychologist, has done the most research on achievement. Beginning in 1947, McClelland has thoroughly investigated and written about all aspects of *n Ach* (need for achievement). Out of this extensive research has emerged a clear profile of the high achiever. The following summarizes some of the high achiever's characteristics:[18]

1 *Moderate Risks* Taking moderate risks is probably the single most descriptive characteristic of the person possessing high n Ach. Common sense would probably say that a high achiever would take high risks. However, once again research proves to discredit common sense about human behavior. The simple ring toss game can be used to demonstrate risk-taking behavior of high achievers. It has been shown that when instructions are given to the ring tosser that he or she can stand anywhere to toss the rings at the peg, low and high achievers behave quite differently. The low achiever will either stand very close and just drop the rings over the peg or stand very far away and wildly throw the rings at the peg. In contrast, the high achiever will almost always carefully calculate the exact distance from the peg that will give maximum

---

[17] Robert W. White, "Motivation Reconsidered: The Concept of Competence," *Psychological Review,* September 1959, p. 329.

[18] For an expanded summary of the characteristics of the high achiever see Gellerman, op. cit., chap. 12.

challenge. In other words, the low achiever takes either a high or a low risk and the high achiever takes a moderate risk. This seems to hold true in the simple children's game and for important adult decisions or activities.

2 *Immediate Feedback*   Closely connected to the high achiever's taking moderate risks is his or her desire for immediate feedback. People with high n Ach prefer activities which provide immediate and precise feedback information on how they are progressing toward a goal. Some hobbies and vocations offer such feedback and others do not. High achievers generally prefer hobbies such as woodworking or mechanics which provide prompt, exact feedback and shy away from the coin-collecting type of hobby which takes years to develop. Likewise, the high achievers tend to gravitate or are at least more satisfied in job careers such as sales or certain management positions which are frequently evaluated by specific performance criteria. On the other side of the coin, high n Ach persons will generally not be found or will tend to be frustrated in research and development jobs where performance feedback is very imprecise, vague, and long range.

3 *Accomplishment*   The high achiever finds accomplishing a task intrinsically satisfying. Accomplishing a goal in and of itself is rewarding to high n Ach people and they do not expect nor necessarily want the accompanying material rewards. A good illustration of this characteristic is the high achiever's attitude toward money. Achievers definitely like to earn a lot of money, but not for the usual reasons. The high n Ach person does not strive to earn money for its own sake or for the material benefits that it can buy. Rather, the high achiever looks at money as a form of feedback or measurement of how he or she is doing. Given the choice between a simple task with a good payoff for accomplishment and a challenging task with the same or even lower payoff for accomplishment, other things being equal, the high achiever will generally choose the latter.

4 *Preoccupation with the Task*   Once high achievers select a goal, they tend to be completely preoccupied with the task until it is successfully completed. High achievers cannot stand to leave a job half completed and are not satisfied with themselves until they have given maximum effort. This type of dedicated commitment often reflects on the high achiever's outward personality, which often has a negative effect on those who come in contact with him or her. The high achiever often strikes others as being unfriendly and a "loner." High achievers may be very quiet and seldom brag about their accomplishments. The high achiever tends to be very realistic about his or her abilities and does not allow other people to get in the way of goal accomplishment. Obviously, with this type of approach the high achiever does not always get along well with other people. As a result, high achievers often make excellent salespersons but seldom good sales managers.

The full impact of the research findings on the achievement motive is yet to be felt. Probably the most basic question is whether a high degree of achievement motivation is always of beneficial value to the individual or the organization. Traditionally, the high achiever has been portrayed as an American folk hero. Yet, from a "normal" personality standpoint, some of the characteristics are of questionable desirability. Certainly employees need a degree of achievement motivation, but how much? The answer must be forthcoming for effective management of human resources.

Summary

This chapter describes and analyzes the motivational process and some of its content factors. First, the basic process is broken down into needs (deprivations) that set up drives (deprivations with direction) to accomplish goals (reduction of drives and alleviation of the needs). This basic process is then extended by the more complex expectancy models of Vroom, Porter and Lawler, and Smith and Cranny. Vroom states that motivation is the result of the algebraic sum of the product of valence (value of the first-level outcome) times expectancy (probability that effort will lead to a particular outcome). Porter and Lawler extend the Vroom model. They emphasize not only what goes into motivation (value of reward and perceived effort-reward probability) but also what impact this has on performance and satisfaction. Their model states that motivation does not automatically lead to performance but instead is mediated by the individual's abilities, traits, and role perceptions. In addition, Porter and Lawler feel that performance leads to satisfaction rather than vice versa. Performance leads to rewards which are compared with perceived equitable rewards. The result of this comparison is satisfaction or dissatisfaction. Whereas both the Vroom and the Porter and Lawler models are relatively complex, the Smith and Cranny model simply relates in systems interaction the variables of reward, satisfaction, and effort (motivation). Rewards affect satisfaction and vice versa, and rewards affect effort and vice versa. However, only effort directly affects performance, which in turn may affect satisfaction and rewards. This latter model by Smith and Cranny accounts for the important variables in the motivational process and relates them in a very understandable manner. Knowledge of the basic need-drive-goal cycle and refinements added by the expectancy models lead to a thorough understanding of the motivation process for human resource management.

The last half of the chapter dealt with some of the content factors of motivation. Traditionally, motivation took on the narrow perspective of money, working conditions, and security. The process theories dispel this simplistic approach to motivation. Yet, when applied to the practice of human resource management, content factors are still important. The content theories of Maslow and Herzberg give a needed framework for the content factors of work motivation. Maslow proposes a hierarchy of needs (physiological, safety, love, esteem, and self-actualization) and Herzberg derived two factors which he called hygiene (money, conditions, security) and motivators (achievement, recognition, responsibility, advancement). The hygiene factors were the ones traditionally given emphasis in management of people. The motivators were traditionally ignored. Yet, Herzberg is careful to point out that the hygiene factors do not motivate; they only prevent dissatisfaction if fulfilled.

Although there is criticism of and lack of research support for both the Maslow and Herzberg theories, knowledge of content factors such as money, security, status, power, competence, and achievement will lead to more effective human resource management. Money will always be an important motive—not necessarily in the materialistic sense but for all the other things that money stands for and can bring the individual. Security, both conscious and unconscious, is an intense motive for most organization participants. Status, the relative position one has in a group, organization, or society, along with its accompanying symbols is also a powerful motive for personnel in modern organizations. Whereas money, security, and status have been given a great deal of attention, motives such as power, competence, and achievement have been generally ignored in human resource management. These latter motives are equivalent to Maslow's higher-level needs and Herzberg's motivators. Power is the motive to manipulate others and is very intense in those holding positions of authority and leadership. Competence is the motive to control one's environment and includes curiosity, manipulation, and activity. Achievement is well researched by behavioral scientists. The high achiever is one who takes moderate risks, needs immediate feedback, strives to accomplish goals, and is preoccupied with the task. Another important motive, affiliation, with its ramifications and implications through group dynamics, is the subject of the next chapter.

☐ **Critical Incident**

The general manager of a large manufacturing firm called in his personnel manager, Jim James, and said, "Jim, we are faced with a real people problem around here. Our employees don't seem to care about anything but getting a big, fat paycheck every 2 weeks. Absenteeism and turnover are higher than they should be, but the worst problem of all is that most of our people, hourly and salaried people, have retired but have many years remaining on the job. They just aren't motivated. What can we do?"

1 What answer would you give the boss?
2 Analyze the statement, "They just aren't motivated."
3 Did the general manager call in the right person to solve the problem? Whose responsibility is motivating the organization's human resources? Explain.

Questions for Review and Discussion

1 Define the components of the basic motivational process.
2 Briefly summarize the Vroom expectancy model of motivation. How does the Porter and Lawler model differ? What contribution can the expectancy models make to the understanding, prediction, and control of organizational behavior?
3 Summarize the content models of motivation proposed by Maslow and Herzberg. How do they differ from the expectancy models?
4 What are some of the major dimensions of money, security, status, power, competence, and achievement as motives? How would you rank their importance in motivating people in today's organizations?

References

Annas, John W.: "Profiles of Motivation," *Personnel Journal,* March 1973, pp. 205–208.

Behling, Orlando, and Frederick A. Starke: "The Postulates of Expectancy Theory," *Academy of Management Journal,* September 1973, pp. 373–388.

————— **and Mitchell B. Shapiro:** "Motivation Theory: Source of Solution or Part of Problem?" *Business Horizons,* February 1974, pp. 59–66.

Bockman, Valerie M.: "The Herzberg Controversy," *Personnel Psychology,* Summer 1971, pp. 155–189.

Davis, Louis E.: "Job Satisfaction Research: The Post-Industrial View," *Industrial Relations Review,* May 1971, pp. 176–193.

DeLeo, Phillip J., and Robert D. Pritchard: "An Examination of Some Methodological Problems in Testing Expectance-Valence Models with Survey Techniques," *Organizational Behavior and Human Performance,* August 1974, pp. 143–148.

Gellerman, Saul W.: *Motivation and Productivity,* American Management Association, New York, 1963, part II.

Golightly, Henry O.: "Needed: Decision Makers for Today's Business Environment," *S.A.M. Advanced Management Journal,* April 1974, pp. 4–9.

Graen, George: "Instrumentality Theory of Work Motivation: Some Experimental Results and Suggested Modifications," *Journal of Applied Psychology Monograph,* April 1969.

Greene, Charles N.: "The Satisfaction-Performance Controversy," *Business Horizons,* October 1973, pp. 31–41.

Gyllenhammar, Pehr: "Volvo's Solution to the Blue Collar Blues," *Business and Society Review/Innovation,* Autumn 1973, pp. 50–53.

Heneman, H., and D. P. Schwab: "Evaluation of Research on Expectancy Theory Predictions of Employee Performance," *Psychological Bulletin,* 1972, pp. 1–9.

Hunt, J. G., and J. W. Hill: "The New Look in Motivation Theory for Organizational Research," *Human Organization,* Summer 1969, pp. 100–109.

Kaplan, H. Roy, Curt Tausky, and Bhopinder S. Bolaria: "The Human Relations View of Motivation: Fact or Fantasy?" *Organizational Dynamics,* Autumn 1972, pp. 68–80.

Kesselman, Gerald A., Michael T. Wood, and Eileen L. Hagen: "Relationships between Performance and Satisfaction under Contingent and Noncontingent Reward Systems," *Journal of Applied Psychology,* June 1974, pp. 374–376.

Kimble, Gregory A., Norman Garmezy, and Edward Zigler: *General Psychology,* 4th ed., Ronald, New York, 1974.

Klein, Stuart M.: "Pay Factors as Predictors to Satisfaction: A Comparison of Reinforcement, Equity, and Expectancy," *Academy of Management Journal,* December 1973, pp. 598–610.

Kuhn, David G., John W. Slocum, Jr., and Richard B. Chase: "Does Job Performance Affect Employee Satisfaction," *Personnel Journal,* June 1971, pp. 455–459.

Lawler, Edward E., III: "Compensating the New-Life-Style Worker," *Personnel,* June 1971, pp. 19–25.

————— : "Job Design and Employee Motivation," *Personnel Psychology,* Winter 1969, pp. 426–435.

Leidecker, Joel K., and James J. Hall: "Motivation: Good Theory—Poor Application," *Training and Development Journal,* June 1974, pp. 3–7.

Luthans, Fred, and Edward Knod: "Critical Factors in Job Enrichment," *Atlanta Economic Review,* May–June 1974, pp. 6–11.

————— **and Robert Ottemann:** "Motivation vs. Learning Approaches to Organizational Behavior," *Business Horizons,* December 1973, pp. 55–62.

————— **and William E. Reif:** "Job Enrichment: Long on Theory, Short on Practice," *Organizational Dynamics,* Winter 1974, pp. 31–38.

Porter, Lyman W., and Edward E. Lawler, III: *Managerial Attitudes and Performance,* Irwin, Homewood, Ill., 1968.

Prybil, Lawrence D.: "Job Satisfaction in Relation to Job Performance and Occupational Level," *Personnel Journal,* February 1973, pp. 94–100.

Roberts, Karlene H., Gordon A. Walter, and Raymond E. Miles: "A Factor Analytic Study of Job Satisfaction Items Designed to Measure Maslow Need Categories," *Personnel Psychology,* Summer 1971, pp. 205–220.

Schuster, Jay R., Barbara Clark, and Miles Rogers: "Testing Portions of the Porter and Lawler Model Regarding the Motivational Role of Pay," *Journal of Applied Psychology,* June 1971, pp. 187–195.

Schwab, Donald P., and Larry L. Cummings: "Theories of Performance and Satisfaction: A Review," *Industrial Relations,* October 1970, pp. 408–430.

—————, **H. William DeVitt, and Larry L. Cummings:** "A Test of the Adequacy of the Two-Factor Theory as a Predictor of Self-Report Performance Effects," *Personnel Psychology,* Summer 1971, pp. 293–303.

Sheridan, John E., Max D. Richards, and John W. Slocum, Jr.: "The Descriptive Power of Vroom's Expectancy Model of Motivation," *Academy of Management Proceedings,* August 1973, pp. 414–421.

Smith, Patricia Cain, and C. J. Cranny: "Psychology of Men at Work," *Annual Review of Psychology,* vol. 19, pp. 469–477, 1968.

Vroom, Victor H.: *Work and Motivation,* Wiley, New York, 1964.

Wahba, Mahmoud A., and Lawrence G. Bridwell: "Maslow Reconsidered: A Review of Research on the Need Hierarchy Theory," *Academy of Management Proceedings,* August 1973, pp. 514–520.

Group
Dynamics

The behavioral variables studied so far have been primarily individual in nature. Learning and motivation focus on individual human behavior. However, another important behavioral variable in contingency management is that of groups. Group behavior is not necessarily the sum of the individual behaviors in the group. The interactive effects and the dynamics make group behavior different from individual behavior.

There is no universal definition of what a group is, but the following two definitions pretty well depict what a group is and what it is not. George Homans, in his classic book *The Human Group,* describes a group as "a number of persons who communicate with one another often over a span of time, and who are few enough so that each person is able to communicate with all the others, not at secondhand, through other people, but face-to-face."[1] In other words, according to Homans a group is made up of persons who are able to have direct, face-to-face communication. Edgar Schein gives three specific dimensions when defining a group as made up of any number of persons who "(1) interact with one another, (2) are psychologically aware of one another, and (3) perceive themselves to be a group."[2] Thus, besides being *able* to communicate on a face-to-face basis, the group members must have mutual interactions and awareness. This mutual interaction and awareness is what group dynamics is all about. This chapter will take a group dynamics perspective by examining why groups form from a theoretical and practical standpoint; the various types of groups, including primary groups, formal and informal groups, and groups as communication networks; and some of the specific dynamic behaviors within and between groups. The latter concentrates on role conflicts, laboratory training, instrumented and sociometric analysis, intergroup conflict, and the management of conflict.

Group Formation

There are many reasons why people form into groups. Behavioral scientists have studied

[1] George C. Homans, *The Human Group,* Harcourt, Brace & World, New York, 1950, p. 1.
[2] Edgar H. Schein, *Organizational Psychology,* 2d ed., Prentice-Hall, Englewood Cliffs, N.J., 1970, p. 81.

need to be with other people is inborn. Some anthropological studies and the psychologist Harry Harlow's studies with primates at the University of Wisconsin tend to lend support to this position. Yet, most behavioral scientists maintain that the need to affiliate with others, to be part of a group, is a learned but very intense human motive. The plain fact is that people need other people. Isolation is intolerable even when other needs are provided for. People form into groups to satisfy their intense need to be with other people.

In addition to the affiliation need that all human beings possess, there are more theoretical and very practical reasons for group formation. The next two sections explore these reasons.

Theoretical Explanations for Groups
In social psychology there are many theories of group formation. Most have been supported by research findings and are additive rather than mutually exclusive. These theories can be summarized as follows:

1 *Propinquity Theory*   This is perhaps the most basic theory for explaining group formation. This interesting word *propinquity* simply means that individuals join together because of spatial, geographical, or physical proximity. The theory would predict that students sitting next to one another in class, for example, are more likely to form into a group than students sitting at opposite ends of the room. In an organization, employees who work in the same area of the plant or office or managers with offices close to one another would more probably form into groups than those who are not physically located together. There is some research evidence to support the propinquity theory, and on the surface it has a great deal of logic for explaining group formation. The drawback is that it is descriptive rather than analytical and is inadequate to explain some of the complexities of group formation.

2 *Interaction Theory*   A more comprehensive theory of group formation comes from George Homans. His theory is based on activities, interactions, and sentiments. These three elements are directly related to one another. The more activities persons share, the greater will be their interactions and sentiments; the more interactions between persons, the greater will be their shared activities and sentiments; and the more sentiments persons have for one another, the greater will be their shared activities and interactions. This interaction theory lends a great deal to the understanding of group formation and process. Persons in a group interact with one another, not just in the physical propinquity sense, but also to make decisions, communicate, support one another, coordinate, and attain goals. Participants in organizations who interact in this manner tend to form into powerful groups.

3 *Balance Theory*   A very comprehensive theory of group formation is proposed by Theodore Newcomb. His balance theory states that persons are attracted to one another on the basis of similar attitudes toward commonly relevant objects and goals. Once a relationship is formed, it strives to maintain a symmetrical balance between the attraction and the common attitudes. If an imbalance occurs, an attempt is made to

restore the balance. If the balance cannot be restored, the relationship dissolves. Both propinquity and interaction play a role in balance theory.

4 *Exchange Theory* The approach to group formation receiving the most recent emphasis is exchange theory. Mentioned in the Chapter 5 discussion of organization theories, it is based upon reward/cost outcomes of interaction. A minimum positive level (rewards greater than costs) of an outcome must exist in order for attraction or affiliation to take place. Rewards from interactions gratify needs, while costs incur anxiety, frustration, embarrassment, or fatigue. Propinquity, interaction, and balance all have an input into the exchange theory of group formation.

Practical Explanations of Groups
Besides the theoretical explanations for group formation, there are some very practical reasons for joining and/or forming a group. For instance, employees in an organization may form a group for economic, security, or social reasons. Economically, workers may form a group to work on a project that is paid for on a group-incentive plan or form a union to demand higher wages. For security, joining a group provides the individual with a united front in combating indiscriminate, unilateral treatment. The adage that there is strength in numbers applies in this case. Schein also suggests that joining a group is a means of establishing and testing reality. He explains,

Through developing consensus among group members, uncertain parts of the social environment can be made "real" and stable, as when several workers agree that their boss is a slave-driver or when, by mutual agreement, they establish the reality that if they work harder, management will cut the piece rate of whatever they are making.[3]

Through joining a group, an individual can compare his or her view of reality with the views of the rest of the members of the group.

Joining and/or forming a group also helps satisfy the upper-level needs identified by Maslow that were discussed in the last chapter. Certain groups are very prestigious. For example, in an organization, certain functional departments are more prestigious than others. Becoming a member of a high-status department would help satisfy a person's esteem needs. The same holds true in the informal groups that exist in an organization. To become a member of the Tuesday evening bowling group, the "trouble-making" group, or the Friday afternoon drinking group may be highly prestigious in certain situations and thus help satisfy the esteem needs. The pinnacle of Maslow's hierarchy of needs, self-actualization, can also be facilitated by group membership. Realizing one's potential and growing psychologically can often be enhanced by joining and/or forming a group. Professionals, in particular, are extremely concerned about how they are viewed by their peers. For many, self-actualization can occur only if they become accepted by a small informal group of their colleagues, for example, a group that goes to lunch together, or a more formalized group, for example, a learned society or a special task force. Group

3 Ibid., pp. 84–85.

membership may have the same kind of appeal to self-actualization needs for skilled workers or line managers in an organization. However, similar to the other theoretical and practical explanations for group formation, self-actualization depends on certain situational factors in order for it to serve as a reason for group formation.

Types of Groups

There are many different types of groups. The theories of group formation mainly relate to the attraction between two persons—the simple dyad group. Of course, in the real world groups are usually much more complex than the dyad. Different types of groups have different impacts on the members. For example, a reference group serves as a dominating influence on the members' attitudes and values, while in a membership group the person belongs but is not necessarily influenced. The same distinction can be made on in- and out-groups. An in-group is composed of members with values similar to the prevailing societal values, and an out-group is made up of members with values that are different from the prevailing cultural values. The major types of groups relevant to the study of group dynamics in an organizational context are primary groups, formal and informal groups, and groups as communication networks.

Primary Groups

Charles H. Cooley was the first to define and analyze a primary group in his book *Social Organization,* first published in 1909. He wrote, "By primary groups I mean those characterized by intimate, face-to-face association and cooperation. They are primary in several senses, but chiefly in that they are fundamental in forming the social nature and ideals of the individual."[4] Thus, a primary group is small, but technically, there is a difference between small groups and primary groups. A small group has to meet only the criterion of small size. Usually no attempt is made to assign precise numbers, but the accepted rule of thumb is that it must be small enough for face-to-face interaction and communication to occur. In addition to being small, a primary group must also have a feeling of comradeship, loyalty, and a common sense of values among its members. Thus, all primary groups are small groups but not all small groups are primary. The primary group is more relevant to the study of group dynamics.

Two examples of a primary group are the family and the work group found in organizations. Initially, the primary group was limited to socializing groups like the family, but from results such as the Hawthorne studies, work groups were also given primary group status. Later, equally famous studies—*Street Corner Society* by William F. Whyte and *The American Soldier* by Samuel Stouffer et al.—further expanded the concept of the primary

---

[4] Charles H. Cooley, *Social Organization,* Scribner, New York, 1911, p. 23. The book was originally published in 1909.

group. These and many recent studies all point to the tremendous impact that the primary group has on human behavior.

Formal Groups in Organizations

The formal organization structure discussed in Chapter 5 is composed almost entirely of formalized groups. The various functional departments in a business organization (marketing, finance, production, and personnel) are formally designated groups of people. A more conceptual breakdown in organizations would be command and task groups.[5] A command group consists of a superior and his or her direct subordinates. The membership and structure of command groups are formally determined and are represented on the organization chart. The superior is granted formal authority over the other members of the command group. The task group is formally designed to work on a specific project or job. Its interactions and structure are formally designed to accomplish the task.

Besides command and task breakdowns, any discussion of formal groups in an organization must give major attention to committees. They are a prevalent and important type of formally designated group found in today's organizations. Unfortunately, such committee groups are often described as follows:

> A camel is a horse designed by a committee.
> The best committee is a five-man committee with four members absent.
> In a committee, minutes are taken but hours are wasted.
> A committee is a collection of the unfit appointed by the unwilling to perform the unnecessary.

Although these remarks are jokes, they represent the widespread negativism attached to committee groups. Yet, despite the attacks, all indications are that the use and perceived value of committees in organizations is on the increase.

NATURE AND FUNCTIONS OF COMMITTEES   There are many definitions of committees. The definitions stress the idea that committees consist of groups that are formed to accomplish specific objectives. They are formally designated but can be conducted in either a formal or an informal manner. Most often, committees have specified duties and authority. Some committees meet on an ad hoc basis to solve some specialized problem and then disband. Committees may be referred to as teams, commissions, boards, groups, or task forces and are found in governmental, educational, religious, health, and business organizations. For example, the board of directors is a type of committee present in all corporate forms of organization. Other prevalent types in business organizations are the finance, executive, operations, bonus, audit, and grievance committees. Although they are more common at the top of the pyramid, there is usually some type of formal committee on every level of the organization.

---

[5] See Leonard R. Sayles, "Work Group Behavior and the Larger Organization," in *Research in Industrial Human Relations*, Industrial Relations Research Association, Publication 17, Harper, New York, 1957, pp. 131–145.

Committee groups perform many different functions in an organization. They may act in a service, advisory, coordinating, informational, or final decision-making capacity. In the decision-making function, a committee may act in a line capacity and is then termed a plural executive. Many organizations are moving toward the plural-executive concept rather than the single executive.

POSITIVE ATTRIBUTES OF COMMITTEES Committee group action has many advantages over individual action. Perhaps the greatest attribute of the committee group is the combined and integrated judgment which it can offer. It supports the adage that two heads are better than one. Committee members often bring with them a wide range of experience, knowledge, ability, and personality characteristics. This conglomeration lends itself to the tremendous amount of diverse knowledge that is required to solve modern organizational problems. For example, a committee group can help reduce conflict and promote coordination between departments and specialized subunits. Through committee discussion, each member can empathize with the other members' purposes and problems and facilitate horizontal communication. In a typical interdepartmental meeting each member receives information and insights about the others' departments. The production department is informed of delivery dates being promised by sales, and sales gets a first-hand look at the problems it may be creating for production scheduling and inventory.

From a human standpoint, the biggest advantage of committees is the increased motivation and commitment derived from participation. By being involved in the analysis and solution of committee problems, individual members will more readily accept and try to implement what has been decided. A committee can also be instrumental in human development and growth. Group members, especially the young and inexperienced, can take advantage of observing and learning from other members with more experience or with different viewpoints and knowledge. This type of group interaction provides the opportunity for personal development that the individual would never receive.

NEGATIVE ATTRIBUTES OF COMMITTEES Traditionally, the negative aspects were given major attention. In fact, classical writers such as Luther Gulick or Lyndall Urwick had very few good things to say about committees. Today, advantages are recognized, but the negative attributes still dominate.

Some very practical disadvantages involve time and cost. The nature of a committee is that everyone has an equal chance to speak out, but this takes a great deal of time, and time costs money. A $20,000-per-year executive costs in the neighborhood of $10 per hour. Therefore, a five-member committee of this caliber costs the organization $50 per hour. Added to this figure may be indirect costs such as transportation, lodging, and staff back-up costs. On the other side of the coin, it can be argued that committees are actually *less* expensive when compared with a series of repetitious two-person conferences. In terms of worker-hours, a committee meeting where an executive meets with five others for 1 hour represents 6 worker-hours. On the other hand, if the same executive meets for 1 hour with each of the five individually, the expended time turns out to be 10 worker-hours. Assume that the six individuals average $20,000 ($10 per hour). For the 1-hour committee meeting the cost would be $60, but for the five individual conferences the total cost would be $100, almost twice as much. The point of this elementary cost analysis is that one cannot automatically condemn all committees as being excessively expensive. The nature and purpose must be considered when assessing cost. Furthermore, it is difficult, if not impossible, to quantify for cost purposes the advantages of a committee that were discussed in the last section.

From an organizational standpoint, there are some potential problems inherent in committee groups. The most obvious disadvantage is divided responsibility. Urwick made the analogy that a committee is like a corporation with "neither a soul to be damned nor a body to be kicked."[6] This is saying that, in a committee, there is group or corporate, but no individual, responsibility or accountability. Thus the committee in reality turns out to have no responsibility or accountability. In fact, individuals may use the committee as a shield to avoid personal responsibility for bad decisions or mistakes. One solution to this problem is to make all committee members responsible, and another is to hold the chairperson responsible. Both approaches have many obvious difficulties. For example, if the entire committee is held responsible for a wrong decision, what about the individual members who voted against the majority? Holding them accountable for the committee's decision could have disastrous effects on their morale, but holding only those who voted for a particular decision responsible would create an inhibiting effect that would destroy the value of committee action.

Besides being time-consuming, costly, and having divided responsibility, committees may reach decisions that are products of excessive compromise, logrolling, and one-person or minority domination. Where unanimity is either formally required or an informal group norm, the difficulties are compounded. The final decision may be extremely watered down or "compromised to death." The strength of committee action comes through a synthesis and integration of divergent viewpoints, not through a compromise of the least common denominator. One way to avoid the problem is to limit the committee to serving as a forum for the exchange of information and ideas. Another possibility is to let the chairperson have the final decision-making prerogative. Yet, these solutions are not always satisfactory because when the committee is charged with making a decision, considerable social skill and a willingness to cooperate fully must exist if good-quality decisions are to evolve.

Informal Groups in the Organization

Just as there are many types of formally designated groups, there are also numerous informal groups in the organization. Interest and friendship groups are common examples.[7] Although interest groups may also be formally designated, generally they are es-

---

[6] Lyndall Urwick, *The Elements of Administration*, Harper & Row, New York, 1943, p. 72.
[7] Sayles, op. cit.

tablished on an informal basis according to common interests or attitudes in the manner described by Newcomb's balance theory. Common interests range from sports (an informal group gets together to bet on sports events) to hatred of management (an informal group unites to restrict output). Friendship groups are a more common kind of informal group. Persons join this type of group in the manner described by exchange theory—the rewards of the friendship group outweigh the costs. Organizational participants join and form friendship groups in order to satisfy their needs for affiliation. Most often, formal organizational arrangements do not satisfy the important social needs.

The major difference between the formal and informal groups in the organization is that the formal groups have officially prescribed goals and relationships while the informal ones do not. Yet, it is a mistake to think of the formal and informal groups as two distinctly separate organizational entities. The two coexist and often are inseparable. Every formal group in the organization has an informal structure, and every informal group eventually evolves into some degree of formal structuring.

Informal groups in the organization have both functional and dysfunctional consequences. Only the dysfunctional aspects were generally examined in the traditional management literature. For example, Frederick Taylor felt that informal work groups would inevitably restrict output. He advocated breaking the group up. Modern analysis recognizes the functional aspects of informal groups as well. For example, Keith Davis notes the following very practical benefits that can be derived from informal groups in the organization[8]:

1 They blend with the formal organization to make a workable system for getting the work done.
2 They lighten the workload of formal managers and fill in some of the gaps of their abilities.
3 They give satisfaction and stability to formal work groups.
4 They are very useful channels of communication in the organization.
5 Their presence encourages managers to plan and act more carefully than they would otherwise.

Because of the inevitability and power of informal groups, the functions should be exploited in the attainment of objectives rather than futilely combated by management. This is especially true in regard to the communication networks of an organization.

Groups as Communication Networks

Both formal and informal groups serve as important communication networks for an organization. The system of communication channels, which can be thought of as the interactions of members of a group (face-to-face oral and nonverbal and/or written trans-

---

[8] Keith Davis, *Human Behavior at Work,* 4th ed., McGraw-Hill, New York 1972, pp. 257–259.

fer of information), makes up a communication network. A thorough understanding of group dynamics should incorporate an analysis of communication networks.

For the past 25 years, behavioral scientists have systematically researched communication networks. In highly controlled experiments, the networks serve as the independent variable; performance and satisfaction are generally the dependent variables; and the task performed, conditions, and personal characteristics of the group members of the network are controlled. The typical experimental setup is to have each group assigned a specific task which calls for a solution to a problem. The individual members of the group are seated around a large table but are separated from each other by wooden partitions. Members can pass (or not pass) notes containing information about the problem task through slots in the partitions according to a prearranged communication network. Figure 14-1 shows the most frequently used networks. Through this experimental procedure, the effect that the independent variable (network) has on the dependent variables (performance and satisfaction) can be accurately observed and measured. With these experimental procedures, researchers can conclude with assurance that it is the network which is affecting performance and satisfaction because everything else is held constant.

Although the numerous network studies do not have wholly consistent results, the general conclusion for performance is that, at least for simple tasks, the wheel is the most effective and the all-channel network the least effective. The order goes e, d, c, b, a. However, it must be emphasized that some studies have different results, and in fact, for difficult tasks, the order of effectiveness seems to be reversed. With the same caution that there is not universal agreement among all studies, in terms of the satisfaction of individual group members, the all-channel network is usually considered to contain the highest degree of satisfaction among members, with the descending order of b, c, d, and e. The peripheral members of the wheel are the least satisfied, but the hub of the wheel is very satisfied.

Network research has provided some interesting insights into the effect that group patterns have on performance and satisfaction. On the other hand, as most behavioral scientists now acknowledge, a highly simplified analysis of the effects of group networks on performance and satisfaction has reached a point of diminishing returns. Although a simple analogy can be made between the networks shown in Figure 14-1 and an organi-

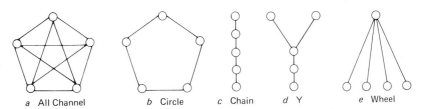

    a All Channel   *b* Circle   *c* Chain   *d* Y   *e* Wheel

Figure 14-1 Common Communication Networks.

zation chart, a more comprehensive analysis stressing the direct implications that communication networks have on group structure and functioning is desirable. Sweeping generalizations from this research are not justified. It is a long way from five students in a group sitting around a partitioned table attempting to find a common symbol on a card to the modern, complex organization. Yet, network research has provided many interesting insights and has made a historical contribution to the study of groups in organizations.

The Dynamics within Groups

There are many dynamics or forces occurring within a group. Conflict is perhaps the most dominating force. An understanding of the concept and ramifications of conflict has become a vital part of the study of group dynamics. Conflict can mean many different things to many different people and can range in intensity from a minor difference of opinion between a boss and a subordinate to war between nations. From a group dynamics perspective, conflict occurs when the group faces a novel problem or task, when new values are imported from the social environment into the group, or when a member's extragroup role is different from his or her intragroup role.[9] Yet, even though these and many other examples indicate the inherent problems conflict can cause in groups, its presence does not necessarily imply a negative impact for goal attainment. Citing George Simmel's classic essay called "Conflict," Lewis Coser explains that "groups require disharmony as well as harmony, dissociation as well as association; and conflicts within them are by no means altogether disruptive factors. Group formation is the result of both types of processes. Far from being necessarily dysfunctional, a certain degree of conflict is an essential."[10]

The next section examines the role conflicts that occur within groups. This is followed by an examination of the dynamics within groups from the perspective of laboratory training and instrumented and sociometric analysis. These latter approaches attempt to understand and resolve intragroup conflict.

Role Conflicts within Groups

Perhaps the best way to analyze intragroup conflict is from the perspective of roles. The concept of role is a basic unit of analysis in the study of groups. Closely related to the concept of norms (the "oughts" of behavior), a role can be best defined as a position that has expectations evolving from established norms. Persons living in a contemporary Western society assume a succession of roles throughout life. A typical sequence of social roles is that of child, son or daughter, teenager, college student, boyfriend or

---

[9] Joe Kelly, *Organizational Behaviour,* 2d ed., Dorsey-Irwin, Homewood, Ill., 1974, p. 565.
[10] Lewis Coser, *The Functions of Social Conflict,* Free Press, Glencoe, Ill., 1956, p. 31.

girlfriend, husband or wife, father or mother, and grandfather or grandmother. Each of these roles has recognized expectations which are acted out like a role in a play.

Besides progressing through a succession of roles such as those just mentioned, the adult in modern society fills numerous roles at the same time. It is not uncommon for the adult middle-class male to be simultaneously playing the roles of husband, father, provider, son (to elderly parents), worker or manager, student (in a night program), coach of a Little League baseball team, church member, member of a social club, bridge partner, poker club member, officer of a community group, and weekend golfer. The person brings many roles into a group with him or her. The result is often conflict between these roles. A classic case is the first-line supervisor in industry.

The first-line supervisor is often described as the person in the middle. One set of expectations of this role is that the supervisor is part of the management group and should have the corresponding values and attitudes. A second set of expectations is that the supervisor came from, and is still part of, the workers' group and should have their values and attitudes. Still a third set of expectations comes from the supervisor's group of peers. Conflict arises because the supervisor, like the workers and managers, does not know which set of expectations to follow.

The first-line supervisor in organizations obviously represents the extreme case of role conflict. Yet, to degrees varying with the individual and the situation, every other position in various types of groups also experiences role conflict. It cannot be wished or completely planned away. One technique that is widely used to reduce intragroup conflict is laboratory or sensitivity training.

Laboratory Training of Groups

Laboratory or sensitivity training of groups evolved from the group dynamics work of Kurt Lewin. The first specific laboratory training session was held in 1946 on the campus of the State Teachers College in New Britain, Connecticut. The more widely recognized beginning was in 1947 at the National Training Laboratory in Bethel, Maine. Beside Lewin, who is the recognized father of group dynamics, Kenneth Benne, Leland Bradford, and Ronald Lippitt played major roles in the early sensitivity training effort.

Since the beginning at Bethel, sensitivity training has become a widely used technique to train group members. Psychotherapists, counselors, educators, nurses, social workers, religious workers, and organizational trainers and consultants aim their efforts at six major target populations:

1 Professional helpers with educational and consultative responsibilities (workers in religion, wives of corporation presidents, school superintendents, classroom teachers, juvenile court judges, and youth workers).
2 Middle and top management.
3 Total membership of a given organization (Red Cross executives, a family, or a business organization).

4 Laymen and/or professionals in a heterogenous occupational group.

5 Children, youth, and college students.

6 Persons with different cultural and/or national backgrounds.[11]

This list points out the diverse applications of laboratory training.

Just as there are many applications, there are also many different goals of laboratory training. However, in general, training sessions stress either the personal development aspects of group members or how to become a more effective group member or both. Overall, the goals can be summarized in the following manner:

1 To make the participant increasingly aware of, and sensitive to, the emotional reactions and expressions in himself and others.

2 To increase the ability of the participant to perceive, and to learn from, the consequences of his actions through attention to his or her own and others' feelings.

3 To stimulate the clarification and development of personal values and goals consonant with a democratic and scientific approach to problems of social and personal decision and action.

4 To develop concepts and theoretical insights which will serve as tools in linking personal values, goals, and intentions to actions consistent with these inner factors and with the requirements of the situation.

5 To foster the achievement of behavioral effectiveness in transactions with the participant's environments.[12]

Because of the rapid growth in popularity of laboratory training and the tremendous impact, both pro and con, that it seems to have on those who have undergone training, it has become highly controversial. To clarify the many misconceptions that have evolved and at the same time gain a better understanding of what laboratory training is all about, Chris Argyris gives the following list of things which sensitivity training is not:

1 Sensitivity training is not a set of hidden, manipulative processes by which individuals can be brainwashed into thinking, believing, and feeling the way someone might want them to without realizing what is happening to them.

2 Sensitivity training is not an educational process guided by a staff leader who is covertly in control and who by some magic hides this fact from the participants.

3 The objective of sensitivity training is not to suppress conflict and to get everyone to like one another.

4 Sensitivity training does not attempt to teach people to be callous and disrespectful of society and to dislike those who live a less-open life.

5 Sensitivity training is neither psychoanalysis nor intensive group therapy.

6 Sensitivity training is not necessarily dangerous, but it must focus on feelings.

7 Sensitivity training is not education for authoritarian leadership. Its objective is to develop effective, reality-centered leaders. The most sensitivity training can do is help the individual to see certain unintended consequences and costs of his leadership and to develop other leadership styles if he wishes.

8 Sensitivity training does not guarantee change as a result of attendance at the training sessions.[13]

---

[11] Kenneth Benne, Leland Bradford, and Ronald Lippitt, "The Laboratory Method," in Leland Bradford, Jack R. Gibb, and Kenneth Benne (eds.), *T-Group Theory and Laboratory Method,* Wiley, New York, 1964, pp. 19–22.

[12] Ibid., pp. 16–17.

[13] Chris Argyris, "T-Groups for Organizational Effectiveness," *Harvard Business Review,* March–April 1964, pp. 68–70.

THE DESIGN AND CONDUCT OF LABORATORIES   The training may be designed as a stranger-lab, a cousin-lab, or a family-lab. In the stranger-labs the group members do not know one another. The sequence of events may run something like the following:

1 In the beginning, there is a purposeful lack of directive leadership, formal agenda and recognized power and status. This creates a behavioral vacuum which the participants fill with enormously rich projections of traditional behavior.
2 In the second phase, the trainer becomes open, non-defensive and empathetic, and he expresses his own feelings in a minimally evaluative way. However, the major impact on each participant comes from the feedback received from the here-and-now behavior of the other group members.
3 In the third phase, interpersonal relationships develop. The members serve as resources to one another and facilitate experimentation with new personal, interpersonal, and collaborative behavior.
4 The last phase attempts to explore the relevance of the experience in terms of "back-home" situations and problems. [14]

In the cousin-labs the group members may know one another but not intimately. Cousin-labs may be made up of persons from the same organization but not the same department. In family-labs the group members all know one another fairly well, i.e., are members of the same department in an organization. The cousin- and family-labs may be conducted in the same way as the stranger-lab described above, but greater attention is usually given to intergroup linkages. Typically in the cousin- and family-labs there is much more confrontation of real data between group members. They come to grips with real problems, decisions, or interpersonal or personality problems which they face on a day-to-day basis.

EVALUATION OF LABORATORY TRAINING   Both the critics and advocates of laboratory training emotionally defend their position. George Odiorne, one of the leading critics, reports that he has incurred personal attacks from the other side. He complains that personalized rebuttals to his position typically state, "The very fact that you attack sensitivity training indicates that you are in favor of autocratic management and therefore *need* sensitivity training to straighten out your personal inadequacies." [15] Odiorne feels that this type of argument, which sets itself above and immune to attacks, is a sure sign of weakness. The heated debate still continues. To date, although research evidence is beginning to accumulate, neither side can be fully supported by the facts. For example, Robert House concluded after an extensive review of sensitivity training literature that it had a measurable effect on supervisory behavior which in turn resulted in observable changes in on-the-job behavior. [16] In another extensive review, Mangham and Cooper concluded that sensitivity training did change behaviors of participants such as improved skills in diagnosing individual and group behaviors, clearer communication, and greater tolerance and consideration, but these changes tended to not be permanent. [17]

[14] Andre Delbecq, "Sensitivity Training," *Training and Development Journal,* January 1970, p. 33.
[15] George S. Odiorne, *Training by Objectives,* Macmillan, New York, 1970, p. 51.
[16] R. J. House, "T-Group Education and Leadership Effectiveness: A Review of the Empirical Literature and a Critical Evaluation," *Personnel Psychology,* Spring 1967, pp. 1–32.
[17] I. Mangham and C. L. Cooper, "The Impact of T-Groups on Managerial Behavior," *Journal of Management Studies,* vol. 6, no. 1, 1969, pp. 53–72.

The general conclusion from research evidence so far seems to be that sensitivity training does change behaviors, at least temporarily, but does not necessarily improve organizational effectiveness.[18] Although those who have gone through sensitivity training seem to be more open, have better understanding of themselves and how they affect others, and show improved communication and leadership skills, it has not been fully proved by scientific research. In addition, there are many other important aspects of sensitivity training in which there has been practically no research indicating that it is good or bad. Much remains to be done on showing the impact that laboratory training has on reducing intragroup conflict and whether the training improves individual and group organizational effectiveness and whether the training is temporary or permanent.

Team Building

A currently popular organization development technique called team building is an extension of family sensitivity training. Margulies and Wallace writing about team building note the following:

The process of team development is not unlike the general change process formulated by Kurt Lewin. The process uses a three-step procedure:

Unfreezing—the awareness and development of the need to change.

Moving—a diagnosis of the situation and the establishment of action elements.

Refreezing—the evaluation and stabilization of the change.[19]

From this beginning, team building as a specific method of organization development follows certain prescribed steps. Although there is some variation, the following represents a sequence for implementing team building in an organization development process:

1 Team skills training

2 Data collection

3 Data confrontation

4 Action planning

5 Team building

6 Intergroup building[20]

In other words, team building attempts to improve the effectiveness of the group and in turn the total organization.

---

[18] See: Marvin D. Dunnette and John P. Campbell, "Laboratory Education: Impact on People and Organizations," *Industrial Relations,* October 1968, pp. 1–45.

[19] Newton Margulies and John Wallace, *Organizational Change,* Scott, Foresman, Glenview, Ill., 1973, p. 103.

[20] Warren R. Nielsen and John R. Kimberly, "The Impact of Organizational Development on the Quality of Organizational Output," *Academy of Management Proceedings,* 1974, pp. 528–529.

Instrumented Analysis of Groups

Like team building, instrumented analysis of groups is also an extension of laboratory training. Benne explains the nature of the instrumented approach as follows:

In the instrumented T-group, the trainer is removed from direct participation in the group. In his place, a series of self-administered instruments are introduced. The feedback provided by the compilation and analysis of the data provided by all members in responding to these instruments serves as a principal steering mechanism in the group's development and in the learning which members achieve.[21]

This instrumented approach is usually attributed to the work of Robert R. Blake and Jane S. Mouton of the Southwest Human Relations Laboratory. The principal instrument they developed was a two-dimensional grid. Figure 14-2 shows that this grid contains a concern for people and production that ranges in degree from 1 to 9. A 9,9 position on the grid indicates a maximum concern for people and production and is the goal of this form of instrumented training.

Blake and Mouton's managerial grid is a comprehensive approach to improve individual and group effectiveness. They explain,

The Grid helps to give businessmen a language system for describing their current managerial preferences. It also involves classroom materials and an educational program for designing more productive problem-solving relationships. Even more important, the program is meant to be taught and applied by line managers over a time span involving six overlapping phases.[22]

Briefly summarized, the six phases of instrumented training of groups are the following:

1 *Laboratory-Seminar Training* The purpose of this first phase is to introduce the participants to the overall concepts and materials used in grid training. The seminars that are held are not like therapeutic sensitivity training. There is more structure and concentration on leadership styles rather than on developing self-insights and group insights.

2 *Team Development* This is an extension of the first phase. Members of the same department are brought together to chart out how they are going to attain a 9,9 position on the grid. In this stage, what was learned in the orientation stage is applied to the actual organizational situation.

3 *Intergroup Development* Whereas the first two phases are aimed at managerial development, this phase marks the beginning of overall organization development. There is a shift from the microlevel of individual and group development to a macrolevel group-to-group organization development. Conflict situations between groups are identified and analyzed.

4 *Organizational Goal Setting* In the manner of management by objectives, this phase has the participants contribute to and agree upon the important goals for the organization. A sense of commitment and self-control is instilled in the participants.

---

[21] Kenneth D. Benne, "History of the T-group in the Laboratory Setting," in Bradford et al., op. cit., p. 129.
[22] Robert R. Blake, Jane S. Mouton, Louis B. Barnes, and Larry E. Greiner, "Break-through in Organization Development," *Harvard Business Review*, November–December 1964, p. 134.

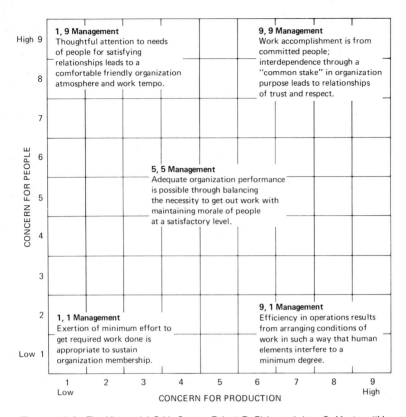

Figure 14-2 The Managerial Grid. *Source:* Robert R. Blake and Jane S. Mouton, "Managerial Facades," *Advanced Management Journal,* July 1966, p. 31. Used with permission.

5 *Goal Attainment*   In this phase the participants attempt to accomplish the goals which they set in the last phase. As in the first phase, the participants get together, but this time they are discussing major organizational issues and the stakes are for real.

6 *Stabilization*   In this final phase, support is marshaled for earlier changes, and an evaluation of the overall program is conducted. [23]

These six phases of instrumented training of groups may take from 3 to 5 years to implement but, in some cases, may be compressed into a shorter period of time.

More recently, William Reddin has added an effectiveness dimension to the two dimen-

---

[23] Ibid., pp. 137–138.

sions (people and productivity) emphasized by Blake and Mouton. Reddin has developed an interesting test to show managers what style they are using in his 3-D theory of managerial effectiveness. His approach has a strong situational emphasis, and Figure 14-3 briefly summarizes the eight major styles of management. The four on the right are more effective than the four on the left.

Like laboratory training, the instrumented approach is gaining in popularity but needs more research to validate its effectiveness in either reducing intragroup conflict or improving the attainment of group or organizational goals. However, it is currently playing a major role in organization development.

Sociometric Analysis of Groups

Sociometric methods of group analysis are used to measure, analyze, and predict group structure and behavior. Jacob Moreno, who at one time was a colleague of Sigmund Freud, is the founder of this technique. Specific research tools in sociometry are sociometric tests and sociograms. For therapy purposes, Moreno also developed role playing and psychodrama. Role playing has become an effective technique for supervisory training. It allows the participants to empathize the role they are playing, thus gaining insights into how subordinates or union leaders may feel about particular issues.

Sociometric tests determine the structure of groups and the interactions between group members. The technique involves asking all group members to list their preferred choices according to criteria such as friendship or task accomplishment. The data resulting from the sociometric test can then be graphically presented in a sociogram. Interpretations of the sociogram lead to many insights and conclusions about social processes. Group leaders (stars) and least-accepted members (isolates) can be easily identified. Analyses of cliques, cohesiveness, patterns of communication, status, and social distance are also aided by the use of sociometric analysis of groups.

The Dynamics between Groups

So far, intragroup analysis has been given the major emphasis. Now attention turns to the dynamics between groups. Once again, conflict is the major vehicle for discussion. In an organization setting, there is a great deal of intergroup conflict. Litterer suggests four causes of this intergroup conflict: (1) an incompatible goals situation, (2) the existence of incompatible means or incompatible resource allocations, (3) a problem of status incongruities, and (4) a difference in perceptions.[24] These sources of conflict result largely from the dynamics of intergroup interactions.

---

[24] Joseph A. Litterer, "Managing Conflict in Organizations," *Proceedings of the 8th Annual Midwest Management Conference,* Southern Illinois University, Business Research Bureau, 1965. Reprinted in Max S. Wortman and Fred Luthans, *Emerging Concepts in Management,* Macmillan, 1969, pp. 192–194.

Figure 14-3 Reddin's 3-D Management Styles

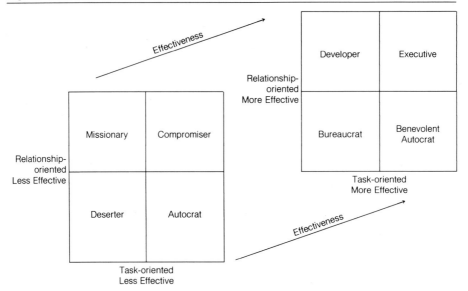

1 *Executive:* A manager who is using a high task orientation and high relationships orientation in a situation where such behavior is appropriate and who is therefore more effective. Seen as a good motivator who sets high standards, who treats everyone differently, and who prefers team management.

2 *Compromiser:* A manager who is using a high task orientation and a high relationships orientation in a situation that requires a high orientation to only one or neither and who is therefore less effective. Seen as being a poor decision maker and as one who allows various pressures in the situation to influence him or her too much. Seen as minimizing immediate pressures and problems rather than maximizing long-term production.

3 *Benevolent Autocrat:* A manager who is using a high task orientation and a low relationships orientation in a situation where such behavior is appropriate and who is therefore more effective. Seen as knowing what he or she wants and how to get it without creating resentment.

4 *Autocrat:* A manager who is using a high task orientation and a low relationships orientation in a situation where such behavior is inappropriate and who is therefore less effective. Seen as having no confidence in others, as unpleasant, and as being interested only in the immediate job.

5 *Developer:* A manager who is using a high relationships orientation and a low task orientation in a situation where such behavior is appropriate and who is therefore more effective. Seen as having implicit trust in people and as being primarily concerned with developing them as individuals.

6 *Missionary:* A manager who is using a high relationships orientation and a low task orientation in a situation where such behavior is inappropriate and who is therefore less effective. Seen as being primarily interested in harmony.

7 *Bureaucrat:* A manager who is using a low task orientation and a low relationships orientation in a situation where such behavior is appropriate and who is therefore more effective. Seen as being primarily interested in rules and procedures for their own sake, and as wanting to maintain and control the situation by their use. Often seen as conscientious.

8 *Deserter:* A manager who is using a low task orientation and a low relationships orientation in a situation where such behavior is inappropriate and who is therefore less effective. Seen as uninvolved and passive

Source: Adapted from William J. Reddin, *Managerial Effectiveness*, McGraw-Hill, New York, 1970.

Types of Intergroup Conflict in Organizations

In an organization there are four major areas of intergroup conflict:

1 *Hierarchical Conflict*   There may be conflict between the various levels of the organization. The board of directors may be in conflict with top management; middle management may be in conflict with supervisory personnel; or there may be general conflict between management and the workers in a large corporation. The same type of conflict may exist between waiters and cooks in a restaurant or officers and enlisted persons in the military.

2 *Functional Conflict*   There may be conflict between the various functional departments of an organization. Conflict between the production and marketing departments and between maintenance and engineering in an industrial organization are examples. There may also be conflict between salad and dessert employees in the kitchen of a large restaurant or between the infantry and artillery of an army unit.

3 *Line-Staff Conflict*   There may be conflict between line and staff groups. It often results from situations where pure staff personnel do not formally possess authority over line personnel. The classic case of conflict in an industrial organization is between line supervisors and staff engineers. The supervisors typically have a great number of years with the company and a wealth of experience. They do not have much formal education but are very confident and even "bull-headed" about the way they are conducting their jobs. The other combatants in the classic line-staff battle are the staff engineers. With one exception, they generally have essentially the opposite backgrounds and characteristics from the supervisors. Staff engineers are typically fresh out of college and have little or no company or job experience. The only thing they have in common with the line supervisors is their degree of confidence and "bullheadedness." The opposite and same characteristics of these two groups chart an obvious collision course. When the staff engineers start telling line supervisors how to do their job, the result is easily imagined. The same type of conflict can occur in a restaurant between the bookkeeper (staff) and the manager (line) and in the military between an intelligence staff officer and a company commander in a line unit.

4 *Formal-Informal Conflict*   There may be conflict between the formal and informal groups in an organization. For example, the informal organization's norms for performance may be incompatible with the formal organization's norms for performance. This was documented in the bank wiring room phase of the Hawthorne studies. The industrial engineers arrived at a production standard of 2½ equipments per day. The informal work groups established a different norm for production. They decided that two equipments represented a "proper" day's work for the group. The difference between formal and informal norms such as that found in the bank wiring room study at Hawthorne is common in all organizations. In a restaurant, the dishwashers' standard for output may be much lower than management's, and the informal group of a military unit has many ways of getting around what the "book" says.

The Management of Intergroup Conflict

Traditionally, the approach to the management of intergroup conflict was very simple and optimistic. It was based upon assumptions such as:

1 Conflict can be avoided.
2 Conflict primarily comes from personality problems in the organization.
3 Conflict causes inappropriate reactions by the persons involved.
4 Conflict results in polarization of perception, sentiments, and behavior.[25]

Management relied on formal authority and restructuring to solve the "conflict problem." Individual managers often became hypocritical in order to avoid conflicts from groups above or below. They developed blind spots to the existence of conflict, created ingenious delaying tactics to avoid conflict, and reverted to the extensive use of defense mechanisms as pseudosolutions to conflict.[26]

Starting with the wide acceptance of behavioral theories of organization, management theorists and practitioners began to reexamine their assumptions about intergroup conflict. This recent concern has, at least indirectly, been caused by the overall societal concern for conflict on national, organizational, group, and individual bases. The outcome has been a new set of assumptions about intergroup conflict which are almost exactly opposite the traditional assumptions:

1 Conflict is inevitable.
2 The causes of conflict can be found only in the total situation.
3 Conflict is a vital element in change.
4 Conflict may be good for the organization.[27]

Based on the above assumptions, the management of intergroup conflict has taken a new approach. Representative are Litterer's three basic strategies to reduce conflict.[28] First, buffers can be erected between conflicting groups. The classic example of this strategy was described by William F. Whyte in his study of the restaurant industry. To reduce the conflict between the cooks and runners which was caused by status incongruency—the runners were giving orders to the higher-status chefs—the runners were told to place their order slips on a hook. This hook created a buffer between the conflicting parties, and the conflict was reduced. A second strategy is to help group members in the conflicting situation develop better insights into themselves and how they affect others. A major technique used to implement this strategy is the laboratory training discussed earlier. A third strategy is to redesign the organization structure in order to reduce the intergroup conflict. This, of course, was the major strategy taken by the traditional approach to the management conflict.

---

[25] Joe Kelly, *Organizational Behaviour,* Dorsey-Irwin, Homewood, Ill., 1969, pp. 500–501.
[26] Bernard M. Bass, *Organizational Psychology,* Allyn and Bacon, Boston, 1965, pp. 326–327.
[27] Kelly, op. cit., pp. 503–505.
[28] Litterer, op. cit., p. 195.

Intra- and intergroup dynamics can be functional or dysfunctional. Some functional aspects include the forces for change, motivation, and competition. The goal of modern management should be to harness these group dynamics to work for rather than against individual, group, and organizational goal attainment.

Summary

Group dynamics is concerned with group rather than individual behavior. There are many reasons why groups form. Some theoretical explanations include propinquity (physical proximity), interactions, balance of similar attitudes toward commonly relevant objects and goals, and positive exchange of rewards over costs. These theoretical explanations are additive rather than mutually exclusive. There are also many practical reasons why people join and/or form into groups. Individuals form groups for security, to test reality (comparative purposes), and to satisfy their social needs. Many types of groups were discussed. The most basic was the primary group, which permits face-to-face interaction and a feeling of comradeship, loyalty, and a common sense of values among its members. Formal types of groups existing in the organization structure were also discussed. Formal groups may be of a command or task variety. However, committees are probably the most prevalent type of formal group in organizations. Committees can give combined and integrated judgment, allow participation leading to motivated commitment, and permit members to develop and grow. On the negative side, committees can also be costly, have divided responsibility, and be plagued by excessive compromise, logrolling, and one-person or minority domination. Most of these disadvantages can be eliminated by careful planning and logical procedures. Besides the formal groups, informal groups in the organization were given attention. Similar to the formal groups, the informal groups can be functional or dysfunctional. Good management must capitalize on the functional aspects. Both the formal and informal groups serve as communication networks. These networks can take several forms and have an impact of task performance and member satisfaction. For example, the all-channel network is typically low on simple task performance but high on member satisfaction, and the wheel is effective for simple task performance but has low satisfaction for peripheral members. Many insights can be derived, but overgeneralization from network research can be dangerous.

The last part of the chapter was concerned with dynamics within and between groups. Conflict was used as the main vehicle for discussing these dynamics. Role conflict is an especially important dynamic within groups. Laboratory or sensitivity training, team building, instrumented analysis, and sociometric analysis of groups help in identifying and understanding some of the dynamics and resolving the dysfunctional conflict. The dynamics between groups was also discussed from a conflict perspective. Intergroup conflict in organizations can take the form of hierarchical, functional, line-staff, and/or formal-informal conflict. To manage this conflict, new assumptions and strategies are needed. The new assumptions are basically that intergroup conflict is inevitable and can be good for the organization. Some effective management strategies are to erect buffers between the conflicting groups, improve the group members' understanding of themselves and how they affect other groups, and reorganize to reduce the intergroup conflict. Strategies such as these can take advantage of rather than fight the dynamics of intergroup relations.

☐ Critical Incident

You are a newly hired management trainee in the home office of a large insurance company. After you have gone through a week of orientation where you met with each of the major department heads and received numerous audio-visual presentations on various facets of the company, your coworker at the next desk waves you over one day and says: "I would guess that after getting the full treatment last week you think you know this company pretty well. I certainly did when I went through the orientation. Well, I'll give you some friendly advice. You have only half the picture. They introduced you to the department heads and showed you the organization chart, but what they didn't show you was the informal chart. In this company it's not what you know but whom you know. The powerful people in this company, the ones you go to in order to get something done, do not necessarily show up on the charts they showed you in the orientation. My advice to you is to get to know who these people are as quickly as possible. Be part of the 'in' group rather than an outsider looking in."

1 Do you think this is an accurate assessment in this organization? Are you receiving good advice? What role do informal organizations play?
2 Analyze the statement, "It's not what you know but whom you know."
3 What are some of the dynamics of the "in" group described in the incident? How are they formed? What are some possible conflicts?

Questions for Review and Discussion

1 What is a group? What are some theoretical explanations of group formation? What are some very practical reasons for group formation?
2 A committee is a major type of formal group found in modern organizations. What is the definition of a committee and how do committees function? What are some of the positive and negative attributes of committees?
3 What are the major findings from communication network research?
4 Intragroup conflict is an important facet of group dynamics. Explain how role conflict occurs. How can laboratory or sensitivity training reduce conflict? Briefly explain the goals, design, and conduct of the laboratories.
5 How does team building differ from laboratory training? What are some examples of instrumented training of groups?
6 What are some examples of intergroup conflict? How can this conflict be managed?

References

Allen, Louis A.: "The T-Group: Short Cut or Short Circuit?" *Business Horizons,* August 1973, pp. 54-64.

Back, Kurt W.: "Sensitivity Training: Questions and Quest," *Personnel Administration,* January–February 1971, pp. 22-26.

Bell, Cecil, John Cheney, and Clara Mayo: "Structural and Subject Variation in Communication Networks," *Human Relations,* February 1972, pp. 1-8.

Bennis, Warren G., David E. Berlew, Edgar Schein, and Fred I. Steele: *Interpersonal Dynamics,* 3d ed., Dorsey, Homewood, Ill., 1973.

Blake, Robert R., and Jane Srygley Mouton: *Building a Dynamic Corporation through Grid Organization Development,* Addison-Wesley, Reading, Mass., 1969.

Bradford, Leland P., Jack R. Gibb, and Kenneth D. Benne (eds.): *T-Group Theory and Laboratory Method,* Wiley, New York, 1964.

Cartwright, Darwin, and Alvin Zander: *Group Dynamics,* 2d ed., Row, Peterson, Evanston, Ill., 1962.

Davis, Keith: "Grapevine Analysis for Organizational Communication," *Arizona Business Bulletin,* August–September 1971, pp. 10-14.

Filley, A. C.: "Committee Management: Guidelines from Social Science Research," *California Management Review,* Fall 1970, pp. 13-20.

Golembiewski, Robert T., and Arthur Blumbery: "The Laboratory Approach to Organization Change: 'Confrontation Design,'" *Academy of Management Journal,* June 1968, pp. 199-210.

———— **and Stokes B. Carrigan:** "Planned Change through Laboratory Methods," *Training and Development Journal,* March 1973, pp. 18-27.

Homans, George C.: *The Human Group,* Harcourt, Brace & World, New York, 1950.

House, R. J.: "T-Group Education and Leadership Effectiveness: A Review of the Empirical Literature and a Critical Evaluation," *Personnel Psychology,* Spring 1967, pp. 1-32.

Mangham, I., and C. L. Cooper: "The Impact of T-Groups on Managerial Behavior," *Journal of Management Studies,* vol. 12, 1969, pp. 53-72.

Margulies, Newton, and John Wallace: *Organizational Change,* Scott, Foresman, Glenview, Ill., 1973.

Nielsen, Warren R., and John R. Kimberly: "The Impact of Organizational Development on the Quality of Organizational Output," *Academy of Management Proceedings,* 1974, pp. 528-529.

Rush, Francis M., and Victor E. Phillips, Jr.: "Getting the Most out of Meetings," *Business Horizons,* October 1974, pp. 55-61.

Schein, Edgar H.: *Organizational Psychology,* Prentice-Hall, Englewood Cliffs, N.J., 1970.

Sims, Henry P., Jr.: "The Business Organization, Environment and T-Group Training: New Viewpoint," *Management Personnel Quarterly,* Winter 1970, pp. 21-27.

Thibaut, John W., and Harold H. Kelley: *The Social Psychology of Groups,* Wiley, New York, 1959.

Van de Ven, Andrew, and Andre L. Delbecq: "Nominal versus Interacting Group Processes for Committee Decision-making Effectiveness," *Academy of Management Journal,* June 1971, pp. 203-212.

Weiss, Alan: "Conflict: It's What You Make It," *Supervisory Management,* June 1974, pp. 29-36.

Wessman, Fred: "The Group Construct: A Model for OD Interventions," *Personnel,* September–October 1973, pp. 19-29.

Chapter 15

Behavioral Variables and Contingency Management

In contrast to the other management variables discussed in this book, the contingency concept has played a vital role in the understanding and practical applications concerning human behavior. As Chapter 12 pointed out, an operant-based approach to learning theory and behavior modification greatly depends on the contingency concept. It was pointed out that there is a contingent relationship between the antecedent, the behavior, and the consequence. The first part of this chapter takes this behavioral contingency idea and adapts it to the management of human resources through an organizational behavior modification technique called behavioral contingency management, or simply BCM. The background and specific steps of BCM are given detailed attention.

The second half of the chapter deals with organization development, or OD. The applied aspects of the behavioral approach to management are embodied in OD. Any OD technique must recognize the influence of the contingent environment. As Lawrence and Lorsch note with regard to a contingency approach to OD, "The key developmental problem in this area, however, is not just initial strategy formulation at the time of organizational birth, but also continuing evaluation of the constant changes in the organization's relevant environment and the effect of these changes on the quality of transactions between the organization and its environment."[1] Unfortunately, the most widely used OD techniques have generally ignored this perspective. If-then contingencies for the environment and the specific OD technique that would lead to effective, planned change have not generally been established. An exception is the work that is just getting under way with job enrichment. The contingent application of this OD technique is discussed in the last section of the chapter. The case which follows this chapter gives the reader the opportunity to make a contingency analysis of behavioral problems in a real organizational situation.

Behavioral Contingencies

Traditionally, the behavioral approach to management has been very vague and nonscientific. Attempts were made to look "inside" the organizational participant for explana-

[1] Paul R. Lawrence and Jay W. Lorsch, *Developing Organizations,* Addison-Wesley, Reading, Mass., 1969, p. 5.

tions of behavior. "Attitudes," "desires," "feelings," and, especially, "motives" were typically used to explain human behavior in organizations. Such an internal perspective depended mostly upon the study of motivation to determine the causes of behavior. However, no one has ever really seen motivation. All anyone can observe and measure are behaviors. Whether a process or content explanation of motivation is used, motives can only be *inferred* from the behaviors that are observed. For example, if a supervisor observes a subordinate working diligently at a task, the supervisor may infer that the employee is achievement-motivated. In actuality the employee may not be achievement-motivated at all. He may be working diligently on the task for fear of losing his job or to impress a coworker or for numerous other reasons. However, this does not imply that he is not motivated. The point is that the internal explanation for his behavior is unobservable and thus is very difficult if not impossible for a practicing manager to deal with. It is for this very reason that many behavioral scientists (at least those with a background in behaviorism) have turned to an external approach to human behavior.

An External O.B. Mod. Approach

The external behavioristic approach to human behavior is much more scientific than the inner psychoanalytic and humanistic approaches. The founding of the external approach is attributed to John B. Watson in the early 1900s. He rejected the methods of introspection which had dominated psychology up to that time and stressed the need for scientific measurement of observable behavior. Based on the classical conditioning experiments discussed in Chapter 12, the stimulus-response, or S-R, analysis of human behavior was formed. A stimulus (S) elicits a response (R). Such an approach, of course, was very simplistic and almost mechanistic in nature. Watsonian behaviorism depended upon physical reflexes (jumping when stuck by a pin or extending the lower leg when tapped below the knee cap) and emotional reactions (crying when subjected to a loud noise) to analyze and explain human behavior. The inference was that the stimulus caused the behavior.

Watsonian behaviorism, because of its oversimplification and dependence on respondent behavior, soon faded as a widely held view of human behavior. Starting in the 1930s B. F. Skinner made the important distinction between respondent and operant behavior and advocated operant conditioning as being a better explanation of human behavior. In operant conditioning there is less interest in the preceding stimulus and more interest in the consequences of the response. Obviously, both classical and operant approaches help explain human behavior, but the operant-conditioning approach is much more applicable to the understanding, prediction, and control of organizational behavior. Whereas the strict mechanistic S-R approach is limited to explaining respondent or reflexive behavior, operant conditioning explains more complex behavior, which, of course, is more applicable to human behavior in organizations.

After making the distinction between respondent and operant behavior, Skinner then went on to develop the behavioral contingency. He made the very significant observation that "An adequate formulation of the interaction between an organism and its environment must always specify three things: (1) the occasion upon which a response occurs, (2) the response itself, and (3) the . . . consequences. The interrelationships among them are the contingencies.''[2] In other words, Skinner stated that there was a behavioral contingency consisting of the antecedent, the behavior, and the consequence. This behavioral contingency can be observed and thus managed. When applied to the management of human resources, the approach becomes known as organizational behavior modification, or simply O.B. Mod.[3] This O.B. Mod. approach takes an external perspective and combines learning theory and the management field of organizational behavior in the manner of Figure 15-1.

The Role of Behavioral Contingencies in O.B. Mod.

The basic premise of O.B. Mod. is that organizational behavior depends on its consequences. The contingency relationship between antecedents, organizational behaviors, and consequences is vital to both the theory and practice of O.B. Mod. For example, suppose a production supervisor is having a problem with an employee taking too many unscheduled breaks. At about 9:30 every day the employee wanders off from his task. The supervisor observes that the worker usually meets a friend from another department at this time. They talk awhile, have a cigarette, and then go back to the job. This example can be neatly placed into a behavioral contingency framework. The clock serves as the antecedent cue, walking over and having a cigarette is the behavior, and the consequence is socializing with a friend. There is a contingent relationship between antecedent cue (clock), behavior (walking away from the task and puffing a cigarette), and consequence (socializing with a friend). Importantly, it must be remembered that the clock being at 9:30 did not cause the behavior. It only set the occasion and was a cue for the employee to emit the behavior.

If the supervisor wanted to change the worker's behavior in the above example, she must change either the antecedent or the consequence. Obviously, in this case she cannot change the antecedent; she cannot change time. At present, the employee is being reinforced for walking away from the task and meeting a friend at 9:30. In terms of an if-then contingency, if he walks away, then he can talk with a friend and have a cigarette. As Chapter 12 pointed out, this positive consequence will tend to strengthen the behavior and increase its subsequent frequency. If the supervisor wanted to change this behavior, she would have to change the consequence. In other words, she would have to change the contingent consequence upon which this unscheduled break behavior is based. She may punish the worker when leaving the task or, more appropriately, she can provide positive social reinforcement for staying at the job.

Using behavioral contingencies to more effectively manage human resources is basically the same conceptual framework as is used for contingency management as a whole. Both approaches are concerned with managing environmental contingencies—in the behavioral case, relating the environment to organizational behavior, and in overall con-

---

[2] B. F. Skinner, *Contingencies of Reinforcement*, Appleton-Century-Crofts, New York, 1969, p. 7.
[3] See Fred Luthans and Robert Kreitner, *Organizational Behavior Modification*, Scott, Foresman, Glenview, Ill., 1975, for a comprehensive treatment of all aspects of O.B. Mod.

tingency management, relating the environment to the various management concepts and techniques.

The Behavioral Contingency Management Technique

O.B. Mod. represents an overall operant-based approach to human resource management. A specific problem-solving technique that has evolved from O.B. Mod. is called

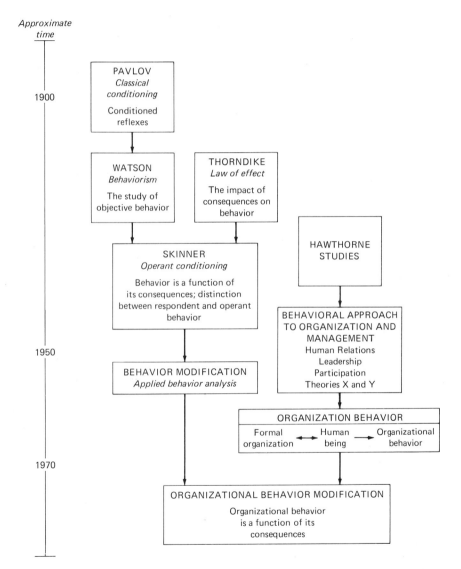

Figure 15-1 Historical Development of Organization Behavior Modification. *Source: Organizational Behavior Modification,* by Fred Luthans and Robert Kreitner. Copyright © 1975 by Scott, Foresman and Company. Reprinted by permission of the publisher.

behavioral contingency management or BCM.[4] Like job enrichment, which is discussed at the end of the chapter, BCM can be thought of as an organizational development technique.[5] The BCM model is shown in its entirety in Figure 15-2. The five steps are to identify, measure, analyze, intervene, and evaluate. The following discussion brings out what is involved in each of these steps.

IDENTIFY PERFORMANCE-RELATED BEHAVIORAL EVENTS   The first step in any problem-solving process is to identify the problem. In BCM, a specific performance-related behavioral problem must be identified. Only behaviors that are observable and measurable are appropriate. This, of course, takes an external approach and eliminates the tendency of managers to deal with feelings, attitudes, motives, and other inner states. Only objective behavioral events are appropriate for behavioral contingency management.

There are countless behavioral events occurring in any work situation. Some of these behaviors are related to performance and some of them are not. The manager using BCM must deal only with behaviors that are related to performance. For example, suppose a particular file clerk in a large office is known as a gossip. This office gossip tells one story after another as she gathers materials for filing. The supervisor may focus on this gossiping behavior as being a problem. However, it may not be. She may be an oustanding performer but have a "wagging tongue." On the other hand, if this gossiping behavior detracts from her or others' work, in other words is disruptive and counterproductive, then it would be appropriate for the supervisor to apply BCM to this gossiping behavior.

The manager can also work from the other direction in selecting appropriate behaviors applicable to BCM. Managers could select a particular performance problem such as productivity or quality and track it back to a particular behavioral event. However, just as not all behaviors are related to performance, not all performance problems are behaviorally based. The most obvious example would be some type of technological difficulty. The reason production is low or quality standards are not being met is that the machines are deficient or the procedures are wrong. This would be a technology problem, not a behavioral problem. The same could be said for standards being set wrong. Maybe the standards for performance or quality are set unrealistically high and there is no performance problem at all. Finally, it could be that there is an ability problem. Maybe the worker is not capable of producing any higher or attaining quality because he or she lacks the necessary ability. This is also not a behavioral problem appropriate for BCM. An ability problem is more of a selection problem. To reiterate, only specific behavioral events that are related to performance are identified in this first step of BCM.

---

[4] See Fred Luthans and Robert Kreitner, "The Management of Behavioral Contingencies," *Personnel*, July–August 1974, pp. 7–16; Fred Luthans and Robert Kreitner, *Organizational Behavior Modification*, op. cit., chap. 4; and Fred Luthans and David Lyman, "Training Supervisors to Use Organizational Behavior Modification," *Personnel*, September–October 1973, pp. 38–44.

[5] Fred Luthans, "An Organizational Behavior Modification (O.B. Mod.) Approach to O.D." Thirty-fourth Annual Meeting of the Academy of Management, Seattle, Wash., Aug. 20, 1974.

MEASURE THE BEHAVIORAL FREQUENCY   Measurement is vital to any scientific approach. Once an appropriate performance-related behavioral event is identified in step 1, then its frequency is measured. This is called a baseline measure; it answers the question of how often the behavior is now occurring. This baseline measure itself is often very

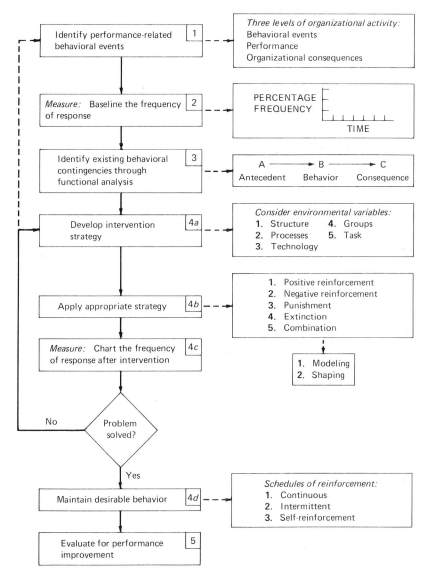

Figure 15-2 Behavioral Contingency Management. *Source:* Fred Luthans and Robert Kreitner, "The Management of Behavioral Contingencies," *Personnel,* July/August 1974, p. 13. Used with permission.

revealing to the manager. The manager may think a particular behavior problem is happening more or less often than it actually is. For example, a manager may feel that an employee is "never" attending to his job, that he is always goofing off someplace. However, when the manager measures how often the employee is not at his job station, he may actually be gone only 5 percent of the time. This measurement certainly reveals that the employee is gone much less than the boss thought. With the data in hand, the boss may now determine that this is actually not a problem. However, the opposite may also occur. The problem behavior may be occurring much more often than the manager had thought. In either case, only objective measurement will provide an answer. There is no place for subjective opinions or impressions in BCM.

A tally sheet is tailor-made to measure the exact response frequency. This tally is designed so that a yes or no count can be made according to predetermined criteria. Using the example above, what constitutes being away from the job must be clearly established before the measurement is taken. If the employee is away to obtain materials, on a break, or to work on another task, this would normally not be counted as being away from the job. Such criteria would be consistently applied, and the observer could record the behavior with a check of yes the employee was at the job or no he was not.

Another mechanical aspect of measuring is the use of time-sampling techniques. There are no human resource managers who have enough time to observe every occurrence of the behavioral event. Therefore, the tally sheet is set up so that only certain random time periods during a given day are observed. Similar to common work-sampling techniques used by industrial engineering, the time sampling may consist of observing some 5-minute period during each hour of the 8-hour working period. The important point is to arrange the time sample so that it is representative of the whole. Figure 15-3a shows a typical tally sheet for measuring the behavior of attending to the assigned task. However, it must be remembered that each tally is tailor-made for the particular behavior identified in step 1 and what the individual manager using BCM feels is the most appropriate criteria and time sample.

Once the data have been collected on the tally, they are then transferred to a frequency chart, as shown in Figure 15-3b. The chart has percentage frequency on the vertical axis and time on the horizontal. The reason percentage frequency is used is to allow for any missed observations. For example, if the manager doing the measuring had to attend a committee meeting or the employee he or she was measuring was absent, the missed observations would not throw the data out of line. What is being measured is the percentage, not the absolute number of occurrences of the behavioral event. The resulting chart gives the manager a visual indication of the baseline measure of the behavioral frequency identified in the first step. This measurement is continued in the subsequent steps of BCM.

FUNCTIONALLY ANALYZE THE BEHAVIOR This third step of BCM is most directly related to the contingency concept. After the appropriate performance-related behavior has been identified and a baseline measure obtained, then the manager using BCM analyzes the behavior in terms of the antecedent cues and the contingent consequences. For simplicity, this functional analysis follows an A→B→C approach. The manager is interested in analyzing the antecedent (A)→behavior (B)→consequence (C) contingency. The manager must first know what A's are serving as cues for the behavior to be emitted and what C's are maintaining the behavior. Both the A's and C's are environmental contingencies of the behavior. If the manager wants to change the behavior, he or she must change either the A or the C or both. As in the example cited earlier of the employee taking unscheduled breaks, it is often difficult to change the A (the clock in this case) and more feasible to manage the environmental consequences. However, for a more comprehensive approach to contingency management both the A and C environment must be

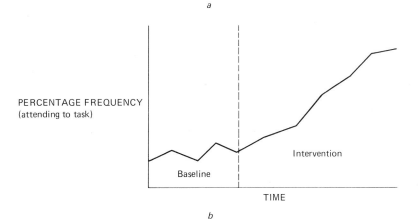

Employee: *Joe Doe*   Behavior: *Attending to task*
Position: *Machine operator*   Supervisor: *Russ Jones*

Sample Times	Monday		Tuesday		Wednesday		Thursday		Friday	
	Yes	No	Yes	No	Yes	No	Yes	No	Yes	No
8:15										
9:25										
10:40										
11:10										
1:50										
2:30										
3:10										

a

PERCENTAGE FREQUENCY
(attending to task)

Baseline

Intervention

TIME

b

Figure 15-3 Sample Tally Sheet for BCM Measurement.

managed. The manager can manage the environmental contingencies to make the more desirable behaviors probable of being emitted. This third step of BCM gives the manager an understanding and objective examination of the behavioral contingency that is needed for the next step.

INTERVENTION STRATEGY FOR BEHAVIORAL CHANGE   This fourth step is the first action taken by the manager using BCM. In this step, a reinforcement, punishment, or extinction strategy is developed and applied by the manager. Remember that reinforcement (positive or negative) increases the frequency of the behavior and that punishment and extinction decrease the frequency of the behavior. So, if the manager wants to decelerate the behavior that has been identified and measured in the first two steps, he or she will have to apply a punishment or extinction strategy. If the behavior is to be increased or the desirable alternative to the behavior is to be increased, then a reinforcement strategy must be used.

There are two important aspects of the intervention strategy. First is to determine what is reinforcing or punishing. The manager should try to use a positive reinforcement strategy whenever possible, but the question becomes ''What is a positive reinforcer?'' The operational answer, of course, is anything that will strengthen the behavior. But pragmatically the manager must try something before he or she can determine through continued measurement after the intervention whether the behavioral frequency increased or decreased.

BCM attempts to utilize only natural reinforcers: those currently available to the manager under existing policies and practices which cost nothing extra. This, of course, generally rules out potential reinforcers such as more money, fringe benefits, time off, or on-the-spot promotions. Many may say, ''Well, what else is there?'' The answer is mainly the extremely important social reinforcers available to any manager. Compliments, attention, recognition, and even a smile are potentially very potent reinforcers. The other ''natural'' reinforcers available to any manager are feedback and scheduling. Feedback to the individual employee of how he or she is doing can be very reinforcing. The management information systems of most organizations are providing voluminous data about performance but very little is provided to individual employees, at any level, of how they personally are performing on any dimension. If the manager supplies this information to the individual, it can be very reinforcing. As far as scheduling goes, almost every manager has some latitude. A behavioral science principle named after David Premack states that a more desirable behavior can be reinforcing to a less desirable behavior.[6] Applied to scheduling work, if an employee has two tasks to do, A and B, and likes to do A better than B, the Premack principle would say that the manager should schedule the tasks so that B must first be completed before the employee is allowed to do the more desirable A. In this manner, A will reinforce the completion of B. This relatively simple principle allows the manager to find natural reinforcers in merely the way tasks are scheduled for people.

---

[6] See Fred Luthans and Robert Ottemann, ''Motivation vs. Learning Approaches to Organizational Behavior,'' *Business Horizons,* December 1973, pp. 60–61, for further discussion of the application of the Premack principle.

As a rule of thumb, positive reinforcement is the most preferred BCM intervention strategy. Negative reinforcement (the withdrawal of an aversive or noxious stimulus) gets to be very complicated, and punishment has the undesirable side effects discussed in Chapter 12 (the behavior is only temporarily suppressed, the person being punished becomes anxious and upset, and it is hard for a punisher to turn around and be a reinforcer as well). Therefore, unless the behavior must be decreased relatively quickly, such as an unsafe behavior, it is preferable to use an extinction rather than a punishment strategy to decelerate undesirable behaviors. If the manager feels he or she must use punishment, then the desirable alternative behavior must be pointed out and reinforced. In the extinction strategy, reinforcement is withheld. The functional contingency analysis of step 3 should have identified the reinforcing consequences that were currently maintaining the undesirable behavior. Under an extinction strategy, these reinforcers would be withheld or eliminated and the undesirable behavior would decrease in subsequent frequency.

Besides determining what is reinforcing or punishing, the other important aspect of the intervention is in the administration of the appropriate strategy. How reinforcement or punishment is administered can be even more important to behavioral change than the actual content of the reinforcement or punishment strategies. First of all, the reinforcer or punisher must always be made contingent on the behavior. In other words, the reinforcers or punishers are not given randomly or indiscriminately, but only contingent upon the behavior that is being changed. This contingency application is what separates BCM from more humanistically based OD techniques. For example, the manager using BCM only gives social reinforcers (compliments, attention, and recognition) contingent upon emitting desirable responses. Humanistic approaches advocate giving compliments, attention, and recognition in a noncontingent manner. The person must be able to determine that there is a contingent relationship between his or her behavior and the consequence of that behavior. For example, the worker would view the contingency: if I produce at 90 percent or above of standard, then my boss will compliment me and pay attention to me; and if I produce below 90 percent, then my boss will ignore me. In other words, viewing the if-then contingency is as important as or even more important than the reinforcer or punisher.

The other important aspect of administering the intervention strategy is the timing that is used. The proper use of the continuous and intermittent schedules discussed in Chapter 12 is extremely important to a successful intervention. The preferable strategy would be to start off administering the reinforcers on a continuous basis and then move to an intermittent schedule. The continuous schedule would get the behavior moving in the desired direction, and then the switch to an intermittent schedule would tend to strengthen the behavior and make it more resistant to extinction. Pragmatically, of course, the intermittent schedule is much more realistic for the busy practicing manager. Managers just do not have the time to reinforce every desirable response of their subordinates. The ultimate goal of the BCM strategy is to have a self-reinforcing participant in the pursuit of organizational objectives.

Once the practicing manager becomes comfortable with basic reinforcement, punishment, and extinction strategies, more sophisticated shaping and modeling procedures may also be used. In shaping, the manager would reinforce successive approximations toward the desired level of performance. For example, a worker may be performing at 85 percent of standard. The goal may be to reach 100 percent. There are very few instances where the behavior would leap to the desired level in one intervention. But reinforcing any improvement, such as 87, and then withholding until 89 is reached before reinforcing again, and so forth, could shape the employee to the desired level of performance over a period of time. The same is true of modeling. The manager could serve as a model, or an outstanding subordinate could be placed in the contingent environment to serve as a model for desirable performance. For example, the best performer could be placed across from the worst performer. The outstanding performer could serve as a model for the low performer. In some cases, however, this strategy could backfire. To avoid the potential opposite affects, there is continual measurement following any intervention strategy. As shown in the BCM model of Figure 15-3, if measurement reveals that a particular strategy is not having the desired affects, then another strategy must be employed. The frequency chart shows at a glance whether the intervention is working or not. In exceptional cases where nothing seems to work, the manager using BCM may have to return to the original step and give more thought to the problem and identification of a behavioral event that is adaptable to effective behavioral contingency management.

EVALUATE FOR PERFORMANCE IMPROVEMENT   The preceding steps of BCM are geared to one overriding goal—performance improvement, or simply PI. This fifth and final step is designed to assure the attainment of this PI goal. In the past, other human resource management approaches and specific OD techniques have failed to make careful, systematic evaluations. Reaction is about the only evaluation consistently attempted. In other words, a questionnaire survey or subjective impressions by the personnel or training director of whether the program is liked or not is about the only evaluation that is made. Whether anything was learned, whether any behavioral changes took place, and, most importantly, whether there was any positive impact on objective, "bottom-line" performance are generally not evaluated. For example, the results of a comprehensive survey of 154 selected companies concluded that "most organizations are measuring *reaction* to training programs. As we consider the more important and difficult steps in the evaluation process (i.e., *learning, behavior,* and *results*) we find less and less being done, and many of these efforts are superficial and subjective."[7] Evaluation of BCM accounts for all four levels: reaction, learning, behavior, and, mainly, results.

The four-level evaluation is made of all BCM efforts. The reaction of the personnel, both those using the technique and those having the technique used on them, is one factor that goes into the evaluation. So is whether the personnel trained in the use of BCM learned anything. The ability of the technique to change specific behaviors is of course also vital to the evaluation. But the overriding consideration is the impact on objectively measured performance. If a production department increases productivity or quality, a

---

[7] Ralph F. Catalanello and Donald L. Kirkpatrick, "Evaluating Training Programs—The State of the Art," *Training and Development Journal,* May 1968, p. 9.

retail store department increases sales or decreases customer returns, a hospital dietetic department reduces food-handling costs or decreases the number of complaints about food at check-out time, or a government welfare department increases the quality of service to clients or reduces the number of ineligible recipients of welfare, then the BCM technique is deemed to be effective in these respective examples. Performance improvement is what BCM is all about.

The Experience Using Behavioral Contingency Management

So far, there have been some very successful applications of BCM. Some of the underlying concepts and principles of BCM were successfully applied at Emery Air Freight. Under the direction of Edward J. Feeney, a program of feedback and positive reinforcement was implemented. The approach was to first conduct a performance audit (similar to step 1 of BCM). For example, being a major freight forwarder, Emery must attempt to maximize the use of large freight containers. Both supervisors and warehouse workers thought that the containers were being used 90 percent of the time. However, Feeney and his five-person performance audit team found these containers were actually only being used about 45 percent (this is similar to the measurement step of BCM). The intervention (similar to step 4 of BCM) consisted of providing feedback about performance and positive reinforcement for any improvements. In the case of the containers, the dock workers kept a checklist to provide self-feedback. Accurate record keeping was reinforced, and improvements in container utilization were reinforced mainly by praise and attention. As far as results were concerned (step 5 of BCM), Emery estimates a savings of $520,000 in the first year of the program applied to container utilization and reports over $2 million saved over a 3-year period using the feedback/positive reinforcement program at Emery.[8]

Although the Emery experience has received the most publicity, *Business Week* reported a few years ago that many other companies, such as Michigan Bell Telephone, are currently using the approach and many other large companies are beginning to investigate the use of behavior modification techniques.[9] The author has also had first-hand experience, both directly and indirectly, in applying behavioral contingency management. In one small manufacturing plant, absenteeism was reduced significantly by using an intermittent schedule of reinforcement contingent upon attendance behavior.

The most comprehensive direct application of BCM was recently completed at two different Midwestern manufacturing concerns, one medium sized and one large. Using a field experimental design in both cases, the experimental group of first-line supervisors in the operating divisions who were trained in the BCM technique were able to more effectively manage their departments than the control group who did not receive the BCM training.

---

[8] See "Performance Audit, Feedback and Positive Reinforcement," *Training and Development Journal*, November 1972, pp. 8–13; and "At Emery Air Freight: Positive Reinforcement Boosts Performance," *Organizational Dynamics*, Winter 1973, pp. 41–50.
[9] "Where Skinner's Theories Work," *Business Week*, Dec. 2, 1972, pp. 64–65.

Systematic analysis indicated that the reaction to the program was very favorable at both companies; a before-and-after test administered at the large company indicated that the supervisors had learned many of the concepts and principles inherent in BCM (no such test was used to evaluate learning in the medium-sized company); in both companies, almost without exception, the supervisors were able to change individual and in some cases group behaviors through the BCM process. Here are a few of the examples from both plants. The supervisors using BCM were able to:

Obtain a significant decrease in a worker leaving a work station unnecessarily

Increase the performance of a worker from 80.3 (average percent of standard over a 6-month baseline period) to 93

Significantly decrease the group scrap rate

Obtain the quality standard for the group for the first time in 3 years

Rapidly decrease the number of complaints of one subordinate

Have 100 percent attendance after a baseline period of 92 percent

Although not all supervisors were able to obtain as clear-cut results as indicated above because of the nature of the problem they were working on, the above is representative of what all the supervisors were able to accomplish with BCM. Last, and most important, there seems to be a definite, lasting positive impact on objective performance in the respective supervisor's departments. In both studies, completed statistical analysis reveals that department production rates of BCM-trained supervisors increased significantly more than rates in the departments of the control supervisors. The statistical analysis (based on before, during, and after the training intervention) clearly shows the impact of BCM on performance improvement. Figure 15–4 shows this impact in the medium-sized firm.

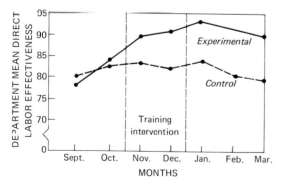

Figure 15-4 Performance Results of Experimental (those who received BCM training) and Control Groups. *Source:* Robert Ottemann and Fred Luthans, "An Experimental Analysis of the Effectiveness of an Organizational Behavior Modification Program in Industry," *Academy of Management Proceedings,* 1975. Used with permission of the authors.

The positive impact on total performance as found in these two studies is the real test of the future value of BCM. Of course, other applications and more research are needed before any significant claims of the value of BCM can be made. However, the current evidence indicates that this contingency approach to the management of human resources is very promising. Although some people are undoubtedly troubled by the apparent manipulative aspects of BCM, it must be remembered that the manager is manipulating the environmental contingencies, not the individual employee per se.[10] In addition, since behavior depends on its consequences, all people, in whatever system, for whatever reason, are being "manipulated." All BCM attempts to do is systematically manage the environmental contingencies of employees' behavior so that there can be more effective goal attainment.

Contingency Management and Organization Development

So far the chapter has dealt with the concept of behavioral contingency and a specific O.B. Mod. technique of behavioral contingency management. BCM can also be thought of as an OD technique because the goal is to change individual and group behaviors that will lead to organizational performance improvement. However, BCM is primarily concerned with the consequences in the behavioral contingency. The antecedents are not given as much emphasis in a BCM approach. Total OD, though, is more concerned with the antecedent side of the behavioral contingency. The total organization system must be structured and developed to increase the emission of desirable, productive behaviors of organizational participants at every level. Thus, the goal of OD is the planned change of the antecedent environment. This approach, of course, is very closely related to overall contingency management—relating the environment to the specific concepts and techniques.

There are numerous OD techniques available to the modern manager. Figure 15-5 summarizes the essence of most of these techniques. They represent ways of applying the theoretical and conceptual ideas discussed in the previous three chapters on learning, motivation, and group dynamics. Not all these OD techniques directly attempt to systematically change the environmental contingencies in the manner of BCM. For example, some try to change the person, not the organizational environment. In addition, very few systematic attempts have been made to isolate if-then contingencies for successful application of specific OD techniques. In other words, conditions where one technique would be more effective than another have generally not been identified.

The Contingent Application of Job Enrichment

Job enrichment, or JE, can be thought of as a motivationally based OD technique. It is directly derived from Herzberg's two-factor theory of motivation that was discussed in

---

[10] See Luthans and Kreitner, *Organizational Behavior Modification, op. cit.*, chap. 9, for a full discussion of the ethical implications. This book also contains other applications of BCM.

Figure 15-5 Modern OD Techniques

OD Technique	Definition	Focus	Basic Assumptions	Goals	Advantages	Disadvantages
1. Differentiation and integration	A diagnostic approach which gathers information about the interdepartmental and intergroup differences of orientation with respect to time, interpersonal relations, goals, and structure. It also identifies the integrative mechanisms for dealing with those differences in order to achieve collaboration within the total organization.	Each group, department, or unit is studied in terms of its needs and methods of meeting those needs in order to best accomplish its task. Intergroup interfaces and methods of dealing with differences are also of major interest.	Different areas of assignment within an organization need to be structured differently in order to best accomplish their purposes. Integrative mechanisms must be designed to bridge the differences and provide effective collaboration.	Identify differentiation needs, integrative mechanisms, and methods of conflict resolution. Redesign to better fit the environmental demands upon the various groups.	Helps in identifying possible intergroup problems. Very effective as a diagnostic tool. Focuses on task, structure, goals, etc., rather than personality dimensions. Useful in identifying environmental demands. Takes into account system interdependencies. Adaptable in a consistent manner to local conditions and problems. Written diagnosis is usually provided.	Extensive complex diagnosis is necessary. Minimum focus on individual problems. Depends heavily on other techniques for implementation of change. Relatively less used presently than other more common approaches.

2. Life planning— career development	A process for identifying personal strengths and successes in order to establish a base for accomplishing personal, career, and organizational goals.	Personal development and increased contribution to organizational goals. Career opportunities. More creative use of individual and organizational resources.	Identifying strengths and providing relevant training does lead to a more productive use of individual resources. The organization exists for the benefit of all members. Individual fulfillment brings increased organizational effectiveness and optimizes use of member skills. Individual and organizational goals can complement each other.	Improve individual resources. Match tasks with individual strengths and resources and desires. Increase personal growth and fulfillment. Harmonize organizational and individual goals.	Career conflicts faced and resolved. Especially useful in mergers; rapid growth; acquisitions, etc. Actualization of potential of all members. Clarification of roles and expectations. Identification of personal goals and organizational goals. Team-building device for an already cohesive group. Happy, dedicated, contributing, self-actualizing employees.	May not survive change in top management. Dissatisfaction if work styles cannot be altered. Possible incongruency between reality and what one would like work to be. Conflicts between individuals' career goals. Requires great amount of flexibility on the part of management.
3. Management by objectives	A process whereby the superior and the subordinate members of an enterprise jointly analyze their assignments in terms of reason for existence and contribution to the mission of the organization. Mutually they identify expected results and establish measures as guides for evaluation of performance. A special effort is made to focus on the desired *results*, not on the methods of achieving the results.	Primarily "end results," hence on "task." Key to success is when groups and individuals mesh goals and efforts to succeed in the "situation." It can apply to any manager or individual no matter what level of function, and to any organization, regardless of size.	Organization and/or individuals have, or can be given, elements of "planning" and "control" as well as the function of "doing." Reasonable and normal control over activities and results is desirable. Theory Y beliefs about people, if maximum potential of MBO as an OD strategy is to be achieved.	Improved performance of organization and of individuals. Coordination of resources. Increased ownership in decisions and goals. Improved measurement of results. Clarification of responsibilities and goals.	Focuses on measurable results. Contains in its processes the traditionally recognized management structure. Gives participant responsibility for decision making. Does not limit methods—only end results.	Results focus tends to obscure process and climate issues. The tendency to "simulate" shared decision making when in reality the decisions are unilateral. Diverse misconceptions about what MBO is or is not.

Figure 15-5 Continued

OD Technique	Definition	Focus	Basic Assumptions	Goals	Advantages	Disadvantages
4. Open-systems planning	A method of studying an organization by identifying its "mission" and analyzing all relevant variables *without* as well as *within* the organization.	All aspects of the internal and external environmental systems. The organizational processes that need to be modified in order to best adapt to environmental demands.	System has right and responsibility to make itself the way it wants to be. Organizations can to a great degree control their internal and external operations and environment. The complex organization is a set of interdependent parts which together make up a whole because each contributes something and receives something from the whole, which in turn is interdependent with some larger environment. Understanding organizations involves much more than understanding goals and the arrangements that are developed for their accomplishment. Organizations are affected by what comes into them in the form of input, by what transpires inside the organization, and by the nature of the environmental acceptance of the organization and its output.	Clarify organization's mission. Make explicit the demands from other systems. Look at present organizational response to demands. Redesign of system to be more active in meeting its environment and accomplishing its mission. Directly specifying those elements important for organizational analysis. Survival of the system.	Useful when major changes are to be made such as mergers, new top management, etc. Useful when things seem *too good*. Useful when ability to perform is impaired by other outside groups. Useful when a group is just forming or coming into existence. Useful at regular intervals of approximately 5 years. Especially useful for organizations with "service" type technologies. Useful when organization receives undue criticism. Useful to unite total organization to accomplish its mission. When well done, it resolves some of the organization's most difficult problems. Establishes a representative "core group."	A complex and demanding procedure which entails some risk of negative outcome. Typically requires much effort in follow-through. Requires careful planning, management, and commitment. Usually requires a fairly high time commitment especially on the part of top management. Relatively new and undeveloped at present.

| 5. Process consultation | PC is a set of activities on the part of the consultant which help the client to perceive, understand, and act upon process events which occur in the client's environment.

This process consultant seeks to give the clients "insight" into what is going on around them, within them, and between them and other people. The events to be observed and learned from are primarily the various human actions which occur in the normal flow of work, in the conduct of meetings, and in formal or informal encounters between members of the organization. Of particular relevance are the client's own actions and their impact on other people. | All interpersonal processes within the organization. All (or at least primary) relationships and procedures. | The process model starts with the assumption that the organization knows how to solve its particular problems or knows how to get help in solving them, but that it often does not know how to *use its own resources effectively* either in initial problem solution or in implementation of solutions. The process model further assumes that inadequate use of internal resources or ineffective implementation results from process problems, i.e., that people fail to communicate effectively with each other, or develop mistrust, or engage in destructive competition, or punish those who they mean to reward and vice versa, or fail to give feedback, and so on. | The goal of the process consultant is to help the organization to solve its own problems by making it aware of organizational processes and of the consequences of these processes and the organization to learn from self-diagnosis and self-intervention. The ultimate concern of the process consultant is the organization's capacity to do for itself what he or she has done for it. Where the standard consultant is more concerned about passing on knowledge, the process consultant is concerned about passing on skills and values. | Goes hand in hand with team and interpersonal relations training.
Conducted on the job in the normal work setting.
Effective solution of interpersonal, individual, and intergroup problems.
Intended to build the needed skill in the participants to carry on, with little external contact.
Participants assume full responsibility for change efforts.
Change tends to be relatively permanent.
Organic in nature.
Contributes toward effective solutions in any and all areas involving human beings. | Does not afford the intensive involvement offered by various forms of interpersonal relations training or team building.
Takes into account only the process issues.
Requires sustained involvement over a 2- or 3-year period. |

Figure 15-5 Continued

OD Technique	Definition	Focus	Basic Assumptions	Goals	Advantages	Disadvantages
6. Survey-feedback-action planning	A process of gathering data usually by interview, observation, or questionnaire about important organizational or group concerns. The data are summarized and fed back to the group members and used as impetus for discussion of needed changes. Plans for action are then made and in most cases a resurvey is taken to provide a comparative measure of change before and after discussion.	Getting information flowing within the system. Work groups and their work-related concerns. Relevant issues as defined by consultant or client. Organizational climate and/or management.	Data alone will provide an impetus for discussion and solution of problems. Decision makers will accept the implications of scientifically valid data. Data-gathering methods have no disagreeable significant intervention impact upon the organization.	Providing the necessary accurate information for proper decision making to those responsible for decisions. Increasing the participation of a greater number of resource people in management decisions.	Can be adapted to any area of interest or issue relevant to organization members. Can be organizationwide or used only by those groups most interested. Provides for easy measurement and comparison of before and after any chosen intervention. Validated, reliable questionnaires already available for use in several areas of concern. May be an effective way of changing hard data indicators as well as less objective measures.	Often requires computer for analysis of data. Ownership of data is often difficult to achieve. Requires extensive preparation for feedback sessions in order to ensure effectiveness. Time lag between data collection and feedback minimizes effectiveness.

7. Team and interpersonal relations	A method of learning and planning for change in which the participants are helped to diagnose and experience their own behavior, culture, and relationships. Skill exercises, simulations, theoretical discussions, and real work analysis and planning are done in a specially designed environment.	Interpersonal and group skills. Group expectations and goals. Intensive problem solving. Expression of feelings—emotional behavior.	The amount of work carried out by workers is determined not by their physical capacities but by their social capacities; noneconomic rewards are most important in the motivation and satisfaction of workers, who react to their work situations as groups and not as individuals; the leader is not necessarily the person appointed to be in charge; informal leaders can develop who have more power; the effective supervisor is "employee-centered" and "job-centered"; that is, he or she regards his or her job as dealing with human beings as well as with the work; communication and participation in decision making are some of the most significant rewards which can be offered to obtain the commitment of the individuals.	Increased trust, openness, and team work. Joint planning and commitment to action. Improved work climate. Improved individual and group interaction and communication skills.	Cultural and environmental change. Improved conflict resolution skills. Improved data flow within organizations. Especially useful for individual growth and interpersonal skill development. Useful in establishing effective working teams. Provides opportunity for interpersonal feedback analysis of interpersonal processes. Provide opportunity for examination of the social impact and consequences of one's behavior. Builds democratic and participative norms.	Payoffs sometimes individually rather than organizationally oriented. Possible tendencies toward extremism on the part of some participants. Relatively high emotional demands required. Often seen as subjective rather than objective in terms of measurable results. Possible misuse as "therapy" for unstable or unproductive members in the organization.

Figure 15-5 Continued

OD Technique	Definition	Focus	Basic Assumptions	Goals	Advantages	Disadvantages
8. Third-party consultation	A process of diagnosing recurrent conflict between persons or groups. Then on the basis of our understanding of the dynamics of the dynamics of interpersonal conflict episodes, performing a number of strategic functions which facilitate a constructive confrontation of the conflict.	"Interpersonal conflict in organizational settings," such as differences between fellow members of a governing committee, heads of interrelated departments, a manager and his or her boss. Interpersonal conflict is defined broadly to include both (1) interpersonal disagreement over substantive issues, such as differences over organizational structures, policies, and practices, and (2) interpersonal antagonisms, that is, the more personal and emotional differences which arise between interdependent human beings.	The innumerable interdependencies inherent in organizations make interpersonal conflicts inevitable. Even if it were thought to be desirable, it would not be possible to create organizations free from interpersonal conflicts. The amount of emotional energy necessary to confront a conflict and resolve it is often less in the long run than the amount of energy necessary to suppress it. Indirect conflicts, have the longest life expectancy and have the most costs that cannot be charged back against the original conflict.	To develop the interpersonal skills and to create an open confrontive organizational climate conducive to effective conflict resolution. To develop capacities within or available to organizations that make it possible to resolve more of the interpersonal conflicts and lessen the costs of those which cannot readily be resolved. To increase the authenticity of the relationships and the personal integrity experienced in the relationships.	Useful on the job in the "real" work setting. Provides resolution of problems so that energies can be used for productive purposes rather than to protect or defend. Provides a balance of power for the disadvantaged. Provides a third ("objective") view of otherwise polarized issues. Provides for the "referee" function in interpersonal conflict issues. Can provide a constructive amount of anxiety; i.e., a certain pressure is sometimes necessary for resolution or confrontation of problems.	Deals with only one of many development areas. Requires a highly skilled consultant. If they are not well managed, confrontations can further polarize the individuals, increase the costs of the conflict, or discourage the principals from further efforts. As in all areas of possible high return, the risks can also be high if the proper precautions are not taken.

Source: Adapted from *Typical O.D. Intervention Models for Planned Change,* © 1975 by Robert A. Baird. Reprinted with permission.

Chapter 13. JE has become quite controversial because on the one hand the advocates claim that it is *the* solution to all human resource management problems and on the other hand there are highly critical accounts of its empirical validity. As Chapter 13 indicated, part of the problem is due to the "shaky" two-factor theory foundation of JE. The two-factor theory appears to be too simplistic an explanation for complex human motivation. However, an even bigger problem than the theoretical base has been the "all-or-nothing" perspective taken on the application of JE. The proponents extol the virtues of JE and imply it has universal applicability to all types of jobs at all levels of any organization. The critics, on the other hand, take the opposite extreme. They feel that JE will not work under any conditions. This all-or-nothing approach seems unjustified by the evidence. Research to date shows that JE is successful under some conditions and unsuccessful under others. Thus, JE is especially adaptable to a contingency approach. The goal of contingency management is to identify those environmental conditions where behavioral techniques such as JE can be used successfully and those conditions where it will tend to be unsuccessful.

A comprehensive definition of JE would be the following:

Job enrichment is concerned with designing jobs that include a greater variety of work content; require a higher level of knowledge and skill; give the worker more autonomy and responsibility for planning, directing, and controlling his or her own performance; and provide the opportunity for personal growth and meaningful work experience.

A recent survey found that only 5 of 125 firms have made any formal, systematic attempt to enrich jobs this way.[11] One reason for this limited application of JE has been the lack of any specific guidelines of how and where JE can be successfully implemented. An extensive review of related JE research literature uncovers three critical variables for job enrichment to help successfully implement JE. Figure 15-6 shows these three variables to be the job(s) to be enriched, the employee on the enriched job, and the organization impact on the job enrichment program.

Based on research findings to date,[12] ten specific contingency relationships relating to the three critical factors can be confidently stated:

1 If the job is a relatively high-level job, then JE seems to be more successful.
2 If the work module is capable of being vertically loaded (defines responsibility and gives the opportunity for recognition for completed tasks), then JE seems to be successful.
3 If the employee has control over the job, then the more successful the JE program tends to be.
4 If the job permits performance feedback, then JE has a better chance for success.
5 If the employee is skilled, semiskilled, or professional, then there is a better chance for successful JE.

---

[11] Fred Luthans and William E. Reif, "Job Enrichment: Long on Theory, Short on Practice," *Organizational Dynamics,* Winter 1974, p. 31.
[12] See Fred Luthans and Edward Knod, "Critical Factors in Job Enrichment," *Atlanta Economic Review,* May–June 1974, pp. 6–11, for a review of this literature.

Figure 15-6 Critical Variables for Job Enrichment

The *Job(s)* to be enriched
   Organizational level
   Autonomous work unit
   Job control
   Performance feedback

The *Employee* on the enriched job
   Skill level
   Personal values
   Need for "motivators"

The *Organization* impact of the job enrichment program
   Approval and support
   Costs
   Evaluation

Source: Fred Luthans and Edward Knod, "Critical Factors in Job Enrichment," *Atlanta Economic Review,* May–June 1974, p. 9.

6 If employees have Protestant ethic types of personal values (hard workers striving to get ahead), then they are better candidates for successful JE.

7 If the employees have "motivator" types of needs (for example, high achievement needs), then they tend to be more successful on job enrichment programs.

8 If there is approval and support from top management, then there is a better chance of success for JE.

9 If the cost is reasonable in implementing a JE program, then there is better chance of success.

10 If objective evaluation is an inherent part of the JE program, then there is a better chance for long-run success.

Generally, the opposites of each of these ten statements hold for unsuccessful JE programs. For example, enriching low-level jobs tends to be unsuccessful, and employees with a high need for affiliation (not a "motivator" need) tend to be unsuccessful candidates for a job enrichment program. Obviously, there are exceptions to each of the if-then contingency statements and more research needs to be done. But, these spelled-out contingency relationships for JE represent how contingency management can incorporate the behavioral concepts and techniques. The same type of contingency relationships should be determined for other behavioral concepts and techniques.

The *if*'s in the above ten statements were mainly concerned with internal organizational environment and individual variables. A more comprehensive JE contingency model which incorporates the external environment as well has recently been developed. Figure 15-7 shows this model. The environmental forces identified in this model are similar to the general environment factors discussed in Chapter 3, and the box identified as resource inputs is similar to the specific environmental variables of Chapter 3. This type of model can serve as a prototype for the contingency approach to the other behavioral concepts and techniques.

THE ORGANIZATION

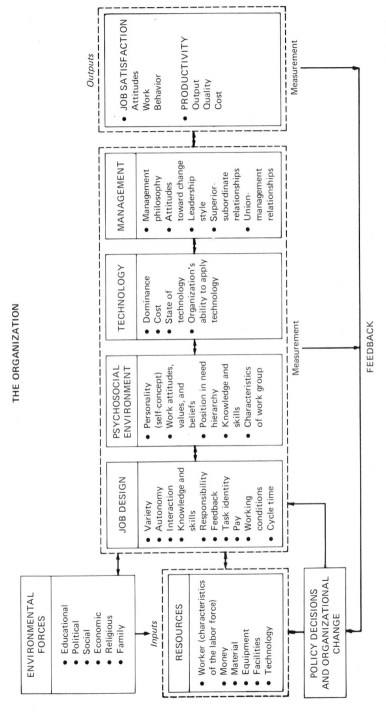

Figure 15-7 A Contingency Model of Job Enrichment. *Source:* Robert M. Monczka and William E. Reif, "A Contingency Approach to Job Enrichment Design," *Human Resource Management,* Winter 1973, p. 11. Used with permission.

Summary

This chapter attempts to analyze from a contingency perspective some of the behavioral variables discussed in the preceding three chapters. The first part gives detailed attention to behavioral contingencies. A behavioral contingency consists of the antecedent, the behavior, and the consequence. Based on this behavioral contingency and an external, as opposed to an internal, perspective, organizational behavior modification or simply O.B. Mod. is proposed as a contingency approach to human resource management. O.B. Mod. has the overriding premise that organizational behavior is a function of its consequences. The specific problem-solving technique of behavior contingency management (BCM) is derived from O.B. Mod. BCM involves the basic steps of identification, measurement, analysis, intervention, and evaluation. So far, the experience of using the BCM technique has been very promising. Although O.B. Mod. in general and BCM in particular do not establish a contingency relationship with the external environment, like Fiedler's leadership model and Lawrence and Lorsch's organization design model discussed in Chapter 8, this behavioral approach is important to overall contingency management. O.B. Mod. is directly concerned with managing the environmental contingencies of complex organizational behavior.

The second part of the chapter dealt specifically with the contingency implications of currently popular organization development techniques. The goals and applications of OD are very compatible with contingency management. However, to date, there have been very few systematic attempts to determine specific if-then contingency relationships for OD techniques. Yet, the work that has begun on the contingent application of job enrichment shows that it can be done with good results. As in the other areas of management, much more work remains in contingently relating the environment to behavioral concepts and techniques that lead to effective goal attainment.

Questions for Review and Discussion

1 Analyze the internal versus external approaches to organizational behavior. Explain what is meant by behavioral contingency.

2 Briefly summarize the steps of behavioral contingency management. Give examples where appropriate.

3 What is the purpose of organization development? Give examples of OD techniques.

4 What is job enrichment? How can it be placed into the contingency framework? Give some specific examples of the contingent application of JE.

References

Adam, Everett E., Jr., and William E. Scott, Jr.: "The Application of Behavioral Conditioning Procedures to the Problems of Quality Control," *Academy of Management Journal,* June 1971, pp. 175–193.

Adams, John D.: *Theory and Method in Organization Development: An Evolutionary Process,* NTL Institute for Applied Behavioral Science, Arlington, Va., 1974.

Beckhard, Richard: *Organization Development: Strategies and Models,* Addison-Wesley, Reading, Mass., 1969.

Bennis, Warren G.: *Organization Development: Its Nature, Origins and Prospects,* Addison-Wesley, Reading, Mass., 1969.

Bobbitt, H. Randolph, Jr., Robert H. Breinholt, Robert H. Doktor, and James P. McNaul: *Organizational Behavior: Understanding and Prediction,* Prentice-Hall, Englewood Cliffs, N.J., 1974.

Deci, Edward L.: "The Effects of Contingent and Noncontingent Rewards and Controls on Intrinsic Motivation," *Organizational Behavior and Human Performance,* October 1972, pp. 217–229.

Dunahee, Michael H., and Lawrence A. Wangler: "The Psychological Contract: A Conceptual Structure for Management-Employee Relations," *Personnel Journal,* July 1974, pp. 518–526.

French, Wendell: "Organization Development: Objectives, Assumptions and Strategies," *California Management Review,* Winter 1969, pp. 23–32.

―――― **and Cecil H. Bell, Jr.:** *Organization Development,* Prentice-Hall, Englewood Cliffs, N.J., 1973.

Fry, Fred L.: "Operant Conditioning in Organizational Settings: Of Mice and Men?" *Personnel,* July–August 1974, pp. 17–24.

Goldstein, Arnold P., and Melvin Sorcher: "Changing Managerial Behavior by Applied Learning Techniques," *Training and Development Journal,* March 1973, pp. 36–39.

Greiner, Larry E.: "Red Flags in Organization Development," *Business Horizons,* June 1972, pp. 17–24.

Grote, Richard C.: "Implementing Job Enrichment," *California Management Review,* Fall 1972, pp. 16–21.

Hersey, Paul, and Kenneth H. Blanchard: "The Management of Change: Part 2—Change through Behavior Modification," *Training and Development Journal,* February 1972, pp. 20–24.

Katz, Daniel, and Robert L. Kahn: *The Social Psychology of Organizations,* Wiley, New York, 1966.

Lawrence, Paul R., and Jay W. Lorsch: *Developing Organizations,* Addison-Wesley, Reading, Mass., 1969.

Lee, James A.: "Behavioral Theory vs. Reality," *Harvard Business Review,* March–April 1971, pp. 20–28, 157–159.

Lippert, Frederick G.: "Toward Flexibility in Application of Behavioral Science Research," *Journal of the Academy of Management,* June 1971, pp. 195–201.

Luthans, Fred, and David Lyman: "Training Supervisors to Use Organizational Behavior Modification," *Personnel,* September–October 1973, pp. 38–44.

―――― **and Edward Knod:** "Critical Factors in Job Enrichment," *Atlanta Economic Review,* May–June 1974, pp. 6–11.

―――― **and Robert Kreitner:** "The Management of Behavioral Contingencies," *Personnel,* July–August 1974, pp. 7–16.

―――― **and ――――:** *Organizational Behavior Modification,* Scott, Foresman, Glenview, Ill., 1975.

―――― **and ――――:** "The Role of Punishment in Organizational Behavior Modification (O.B. Mod.)," *Public Personnel Management,* May–June 1973, pp. 156–161.

―――― **and Robert Ottemann:** "Motivation vs. Learning Approaches to Organizational Behavior," *Business Horizons,* December 1973, pp. 55–62.

Margerison, Charles J.: "Organization Development—A Managerial Problem Solving Approach," *Management Decision Monograph,* Summer 1973, pp. 205–236.

Margulies, Newton, and John Wallace: *Organizational Change,* Scott, Foresman, Glenview, Ill., 1973.

Mockler, Robert J.: *Management Decision Making and Action in Behavioral Situations,* Austin Press, Educational Division of Shoal Creek Publishers, Austin, Tex., 1973.

Monczka, Robert M., and William E. Reif: "A Contingency Approach to Job Enrichment Design," *Human Resource Management,* Winter 1973, pp. 9–17.

Morse, John J.: "A Contingency Look at Job Design," *California Management Review,* Fall 1973, pp. 67–75.

―――― **and Jay W. Lorsch:** "Beyond Theory Y," *Harvard Business Review,* May–June 1970, pp. 61–68.

Ottemann, Robert, and Fred Luthans: "An Experimental Analysis of the Effectiveness of an Organizational Behavior Modification Program in Industry," *Academy of Management Proceedings,* 1975.

Raia, Anthony P.: "Organizational Development—Some Issues and Challenges," *California Management Review,* Summer 1972, pp. 13–20.

Reif, William E., and Fred Luthans: "Does Job Enrichment Really Pay Off?" *California Management Review,* Fall 1972, pp. 30–37.

―――― **and Ronald C. Tinnell:** "A Diagnostic Approach to Job Enrichment," *MSU Business Topics,* Autumn 1973, pp. 29–37.

Rice, Linda E., and Terence R. Mitchell: "Structural Determinants of Individual Behavior in Organizations," *Administrative Science Quarterly,* March 1973, pp. 56–70.

Schneier, Craig Eric: "Behavior Modification in Management: A Review and Critique," *Academy of Management Journal,* September 1974, pp. 528–548.

Sielaff, Theodore J.: "Modification of Work Behavior," *Personnel Journal,* July 1974, pp. 513–517.

Skinner, B. F.: *Contingencies of Reinforcement,* Appleton-Century-Crofts, New York, 1969.

Tosi, Henry L., and W. Clay Hamner: *Organizational Behavior and Management: A Contingency Approach,* St. Clair Press, Chicago, 1974.

Yorks, Lyle: "Key Elements in Implementing Job Enrichment," *Personnel,* September–October 1973, pp. 45–52.

Case Study for Part Four
"How Are They Gonna Treat 'Em in South Dakota after They've Been to Detroit"

Jackson Company is a small, light manufacturing firm located in a South Dakota community with a population of 4,200. The nearest big city is Sioux Falls, which is 73 miles away. During World War II, the company, which was founded and operated by Henry Jackson, switched from farm implement parts manufacturing to the manufacture of armament parts for the war effort. The company achieved its highest level of employment of 350 just before the end of the war. Today, there are 210 employees who work on missile parts under defense contracts. Three years ago, Ted Lowe purchased the Jackson Company from the estate of Henry Jackson, who had died 3 months earlier of a heart attack while at work. Ted had financial backing from the community's leading banker, physician, and lawyer. These three were long-time friends of the family. They had put up 49 percent of the purchase price, and Ted, with the help of his wealthy, retired father, had put up the rest. When Ted took over, he was thirty-one years of age. He had graduated from State University with a mechanical engineering degree and had worked in quality control for one of the "Big Three" auto companies in Detroit in the years from his graduation to the time of taking over Jackson Company.

While working in the auto industry in Detroit, Ted had formulated some very definite ideas on how to most effectively manage human resources. Since his engineering education had not included any courses in the behavioral sciences or human resource management, most of these ideas came from observation and practical experience. Ted used to enjoy telling his South Dakota friends about some of the quality problems his department had to deal with back in Detroit. Dealers from across the country used to write back to the home office complaining about lunch bags and pop bottles inside the door panels, but the best one was the story from a dealer that had one of his former best customers return a new car with a very strange "tinkling" sound in the door. It seemed that every time the proud car owner turned a corner, there was this tinkling sound, and when the car was straightened out, there was the tinkling sound again. The dealer had one of his mechanics undo the door panel, and there, welded into the door frame, was a little steel rod with several washers on it. The rod had been welded on at exactly the right angle so that every time the driver turned the corner, the washers slid down to one end and when the car was straightened out the washers all slid to the other end. Ted would then go on to say that one of the biggest problems he had had as a quality control engineer was finding space to park the rejected automobiles coming off the assembly line.

Ted was convinced that workers were all basically the same. Sure, the union was much stronger in the big cities and in the auto industry, but the guy wearing a blue collar had basically the same attitude regardless of where he worked: "Work as little as possible" and "Try to beat the system before it beats you." Ted had seen this attitude time after time in his years in Detroit. The problems his quality control operation faced were human, not technological problems. Ted felt that the reason for the human problems in the auto company was that top management had bought that "goodie-goodie" human relations stuff. Ted felt that the only way to deal with employees was to "let them know who's boss and fire them if they don't like it." In Ted's opinion, the idea of trying to motivate and reinforce people only led to the problems he had personally observed in his years in Detroit. For example, he often said, "Why in the world should management reinforce employees with compliments for something they are supposed to be doing and, in fact, are being paid good money to do." It just didn't make any sense to Ted. It was the same when he used to bale hay in the summers on farms around home when he was growing up; workers only understood threats that they would be fired if they didn't "toe the mark" and "get the job done as it is supposed to be done." "This human relations stuff just doesn't work," Ted frequently said. While working in Detroit, Ted had made a vow that if he was ever in the position to make policy and directly influence human resource management, things would be different. Three years ago, after taking over Jackson Company, he carried out this vow.

The first thing Ted did when he took over Jackson Company was to create a new organization climate from top to bottom. Under old Mr. Jackson things had been pretty loose. Ted straightened things out very quickly. He implemented a set of personnel policies and procedures that were very demanding. For example, any unexcused absence or tardiness was grounds for immediate dismissal, and if an employee was judged by his or her immediate supervisor to have a bad attitude about his or her work, the immediate supervisor, or the company in general, it would be brought to Ted's personal attention, and if talking with the person didn't help, the employee would be fired. Ted fired seventeen employees the first year and twenty-three the second under this procedure. In the third year, Ted complained to the lawyer, who was part owner, that he was not as rough as he used to be on this policy because replacements were not as easy to find as they had been. Ted was concerned that the labor market in the area was drying up. He had fired only twelve the third year.

The lawyer and banker had initially been very upset with Ted's personnel policies. They tried to tell him that his home town was different from Detroit. Sure, the workers in the big cities were no good and needed more discipline, but back home this wasn't the case. Jackson had been very successful being nice to his people. They doubted whether Ted's approach would work and felt that it might even backfire. The doctor, however, convinced them that they really knew nothing about a modern manufacturing operation and that they should give Ted a free hand to manage as he saw fit. All they were interested in were "bottom-line" results. If Ted could attain a good return on their investment, this is all they should be concerned about. How Ted ran the company was up to him.

For the first 2½ years things were going great. The investors couldn't have asked for better bottom-line results, and the lawyer and banker told Ted after the second year they were sure happy he had not listened to them about how to manage people. However, in the last 6 months the company has run into some very serious problems. They have lost two major contracts and have none coming up. Ted blames the problem on the end of the Vietnam war and the state of the economy. The doctor, however, has been told by one of his patients, who is a maintenance worker at Jackson Company, that the company is not meeting the necessary quality standards for the defense contracts. This is why the company lost the contracts and have none coming up. He also said that morale at the plant is unbelievably low and that there is talk of a union organization drive. The doctor relayed this information to the banker and lawyer. They decided to meet with Ted to air the issues and to withdraw their financial backing as soon as they could unless he could come up with some logical solutions to the company's problems.

Questions for Analysis:

1 What environmental factors did Ted Lowe ignore in formulating his human resource policies and procedures for Jackson Company?

2 Comment on Ted Lowe's feeling that all workers have basically the same attitude of "work as little as possible" and "try to beat the system before it beats you."

3 Analyze Ted's comment that management should not reinforce employees with social rewards for something they should be doing and are getting well paid for doing.

4 What, if anything, would you have done differently 3 years ago if you had taken over the company under identical conditions? What would you do now if you replaced Ted as the head of this company?

Part Five

Systems
Variables

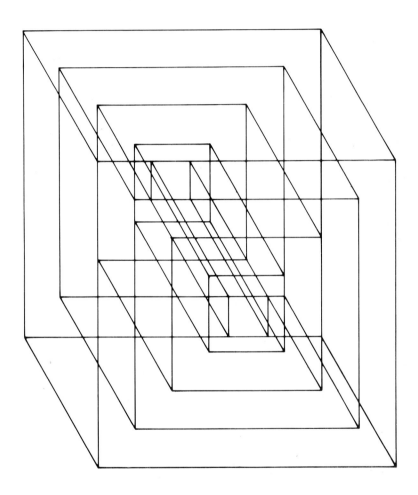

General Systems Theory and the Systems Approach to Management

The systems approach is most closely related conceptually and practically to the contingency approach to management. In fact, Kast and Rosenzweig note, "The contingency view of organizations and their management suggests that an organization is a system composed of subsystems and delineated by identifiable boundaries from its environmental suprasystem."[1] As this quote and Chapter 2 pointed out, systems variables and the contingency approach are very closely related.

This initial chapter in the systems part of the book lays down the basic ideas of systems thinking from the perspective of general systems theory (GST) and the systems approach to management. The first section discusses the reasons for and scope of the general systems movement. The next section is concerned with GST from a closed or cybernetic perspective and from an open perspective. The last part of the chapter deals specifically with the systems approach to management. The management of objectives, decisions, and information is given attention. Finally, some of the limitations and criticisms of the systems approach are explored.

The General Systems Movement

In the old days an educated person was steeped in the classics, was able to read and converse in Latin, and was knowledgeable in the physical and biological sciences. Today, this standardized education has long since passed. The modern Shakespearean scholar may know little of Byron, and the Byronic scholar little of Shakespeare. Similarly, in the social sciences, psychologists generally know little if any economics or political science and vice versa. Narrowing still further, within business administration the specialist in marketing or personnel may know little about basic accounting, and in the factory or office, training is specialized to the point where one employee may know only how to insert bolts or open letters while a different worker turns nuts or separates letters into piles. Chapter 5 pointed out that such degrees of specialization may be dysfunctional. For

---

[1] Fremont E. Kast and James E. Rosenzweig, "General Systems Theory: Applications for Organization and Management," *Academy of Management Journal,* December 1972, p. 460.

example, specialists have their own jargons and cannot communicate well with one another. This hurts coordination and efficiency, which is the very reason for specialization in the first place. Even worse is the fact that specialization may create conflict to the detriment of overall goal attainment.

In this modern era of specialization and wide divergence there is a crying need for unification of philosophical and scientific thought on an upper plane as well as on the more practical operational level. General systems theory, or GST, is beginning to fill this need at the upper levels. GST identifies and provides common patterns in the divergent philosophies and sciences but is not necessarily concerned with the operational level. However, a related concept which may be viewed as a subelement or subsystem of GST is more concerned with the integration of parts at the operating level. This latter approach is known as the systems approach to management. GST, on the other hand, is more of an overall philosophy and/or science, while the systems approach is directly concerned with application and can be used in the practice of management or psychology or biology or economics or philosophy or any other field of endeavor. This application of the systems approach to management is given detailed attention in the last part of this chapter and in the next two chapters.

Meaning and Scope of GST

There is a relatively high degree of confusion and controversy surrounding the meaning of GST. A recent issue of the *Academy of Management Journal* was entirely devoted to GST.[2] A reading of these articles and reference to GST in other books and articles does not give a common meaning or use of the term. For the purpose of this book, GST will simply mean the philosophical and practical assumption of interrelatedness and interdependency of the parts to the whole. Its roots can be traced as far back as the ancient Greek philosopher Aristotle, who stated a holistic systems idea that "the whole is greater than the sum of its parts." The Aristotelian view, focusing on wholes and their purposes, waned somewhat in the succeeding years with the rise of a narrower mathematical-mechanistic approach emerging from the work of Galileo. Under this latter influence, most of the sciences (physical, biological, and social) became more and more mechanistic and reductionist (reducing everything down to molecules and atoms, cells and genes, reflexes and roles, and so forth).

Ludwig von Bertalanffy, who is considered to be the father of modern GST, in the 1930s and 1940s initiated the movement back to Aristotelian thinking. He labeled his approach general systems theory or GST. Von Bertalanffy, a biologist, was led into general systems thinking through his study of metabolism, steady states, growth, and open systems. Especially in the study of steady states and open systems, he found himself delving into concepts found in physical chemistry, kinetics, and thermodynamics. From this broaden-

---

[2] See *Academy of Management Journal*, December 1972.

ing, von Bertalanffy was able to see the generality of the systems concepts he was using, and GST was conceived.

In 1954, von Bertalanffy, the economist Kenneth Boulding, the biomathematician Anatol Rapoport, and the physiologist Ralph Gerard founded the Society for General Systems Research, which is an affiliate of the American Association for the Advancement of Science. These scholars are all closely associated with GST and the *General Systems Year-book*, the society's official journal. Rapoport once said that "General systems theory is best described not as a theory" at all, that it is more of a "direction in the contemporary philosophy of science" aimed at "the integration of diverse content areas by means of a unified methodology of conceptualization or of research."[3]

In 1956, Kenneth Boulding wrote a now famous article entitled "General Systems Theory: The Skeleton of Science."[4] The article described the general nature, purpose, and needs for a systems approach to all scientific phenomena. He stressed the need for a systematic, theoretical framework which would describe general relationships of the empirical world. He carefully pointed out that the purpose of GST is *not* "to establish a single, self-contained 'general theory of practically everything' which will replace all the special theories of particular disciplines."[5] Rather, his purpose was to reach a happy medium between the "specific that has no meaning and the general that has no content. . . . It is the contention of the General Systems Theorists that this optimum degree of generality in theory is not always reached by the particular sciences."[6] He then went on to describe a hierarchy of systems. Going from the simplest to the most complex, Boulding classified nine such systems levels:

1 The most basic level is the static structure. It could be termed the level of *frameworks*. An example would be the anatomy of the universe.

2 The second level is the simple dynamic system. It incorporates necessary predetermined motions. This could be termed the level of *clockworks*.

3 The next level is a cybernetic system characterized by automatic feedback control mechanisms. This could be thought of as the level of the *thermostat*.

4 The fourth level is the open-system level. It is a self-maintaining structure and is the level where life begins to differentiate from nonlife. This is the level of the *cell*.

5 The fifth level is the genetic-societal level. It is typified by the *plant* and preoccupies the empirical world of the botanist.

6 The next is the *animal* level, which is characterized by increased mobility, teleological behavior, and self-awareness.

---

[3] Anatol Rapoport, "General Systems Theory," in David Sills, (ed.), *International Encyclopedia of the Social Sciences*, Vol. 15, Macmillan, New York, 1968, p. 452.

[4] Kenneth Boulding, "General Systems Theory: The Skeleton of Science," *Management Science,* April 1956, pp. 197–208.

[5] Ibid., p. 197.

[6] Ibid.

7 The seventh level is the *human* level. The major difference between the human level and the animal level is the possession of self-consciousness by human beings.

8 The next level is that of *social and human organizations*. The important unit in social organization is not the human being per se but rather the organizational role that the person assumes.

9 The ninth and last level is reserved for *transcendental systems*. This allows for ultimates, absolutes, and the inescapable unknowables.[7]

At present, varying degrees of knowledge exist at each of Boulding's levels. For example, much knowledge exists at the static level; most academic disciplines have very good descriptive static models. However, even this first level is not completely developed (e.g., the theory of cataloging and indexing is still not complete). In each succeeding level in the hierarchy there is more and more incompleteness. In fact, beyond the second level, comprehensive theoretical models are very rare. At the very complex human and social organization levels, Boulding does not feel that there are even the rudiments of meaningful theoretical systems. However, this observation does not entirely rule out the applicability of general systems theory to management. As will be pointed out in this chapter and the two succeeding chapters, systems thinking can and does make a valuable contribution to management.

In its simplest terms, GST is somewhat like a set of carpenter's tools, equipment, skills, and concepts. The elements are known, but the purpose of carpentry is not. A few things may be known about the environment of carpentry, such as that wood and nails are involved. Substituting the term *general systems* for *carpentry* and *system and organization* for *wood and nails* gives a fairly accurate picture of the present status of GST's contribution to management. The tools and skills of GST are identifiable, and it is concerned with systems and organizations, but the purpose is still being developed. Figure 16-1 summarizes some of the major tools of GST. All those listed in the figure are useful in explaining, analyzing, or synthesizing certain kinds of system behaviors. Boulding's levels and the "tools" listed in Figure 16-1 give some idea of the tremendous scope of GST.

GST and System Organization

The above discussion infers that general systems theory is developing in sort of a reverse manner. Many GST subsystems, subconcepts, and tools are identified and available, but GST is still searching for an overriding theoretical base. The precise nature of such a theory is not yet known. However, early development of a GST base has been aimed at system organization. As von Bertalanffy states, "A basic problem posed to modern science is a general theory of organization. General system theory is, in principle, capable of giving exact definitions for such concepts and, in suitable cases, of putting them to

---

[7] Ibid., pp. 202–205.

Figure 16-1 The "Tools" of GST

Classical systems theory—principles of kinetics, diffusion, steady state and statistical mechanics, and allometric analysis

Computerization and simulation

Compartment theory—uses Laplace transforms

Set theory—mathematical sets

Graph theory—investigates system structure or topology

Net theory—study of networks, e.g., nervous system networks

Cybernetics—theory of control systems based on communications

Information theory—information used as a measure of degree of organization

Theory of automata—concerns the Turing machine or algorithmic machines in general

Game theory—systems in competition

Decision theory—concerns choices among alternatives

Queuing theory—or waiting-line theory

Factor analysis—for example, multivariate analysis of sociopsychological phenomena

Source: Adapted from Ludwig von Bertalanffy, *General Systems Theory: Foundations, Development, Applications,* George Braziller, New York, 1968, pp. 19–23 and 90–91.

quantitative analysis."[8] This quote points out that the central problem of science, and the primary problem to which GST should address itself, is the formulation of universal laws of system organization. To be sure there are other GST problems such as system dynamics, but at the present stage of development system organization takes priority. For example, there are upper limits to organization size. Organizations form (cells unite, machines are linked, people hierarchically relate themselves) in order to gain the efficiencies of cooperative endeavor. But when an organization becomes too large, it may become less efficient. Economists propose economies of scale to explain this phenomenon, and at a macrosystem level the Club of Rome commissioned a study of life systems on the planet Earth using empirical-simulation methods to demonstrate the limits of the growth of population, food supply, natural resources, material goods, and so forth.[9]

Boulding discussed the matter of system organization in terms of what he calls "iron laws" of organization.[10] Foremost of these laws is the thesis proposed by the pioneering economist Thomas Malthus that if there are no checks on the growth of population except starvation and misery, then the population will grow until the people are miserable and starved. The supply of food increases at an arithmetic rate, but the population grows at a geometric rate. This Malthusian thesis had fallen into neglect and some disfavor until recently, when it was revitalized by findings such as those of the Club of Rome and the emphasis given population growth by the ecology movement. Similar to Malthus, Bould-

---

[8] Ludwig von Bertalanffy, *General System Theory: Foundations, Development Applications,* George Braziller, New York, 1968, p. 34.

[9] See Donella Meadows, Dennis L. Meadows, Jorgen Randers, and William W. Behrens, III, *The Limits to Growth,* Universe Books, New York, 1972.

[10] Kenneth E. Boulding, *The Organizational Revolution: A Study in the Ethics of Economic Organization,* Quadrangle, Chicago, 1968, pp. 77–80. The book was originally published by Harper, New York, 1953.

emphasis given population growth by the ecology movement. Similar to Malthus, Boulding proposes an iron law of size: any given organization has an optimum size. The situation determines the optimum size. If the optimum is exceeded, executive and communication systems break down and equality and brotherhood become impossible. There may also be an iron law of instability which arises because of uncontrolled interaction of a large number of organizations. The large number of organizations could be different coalitions (economic, ethnic, class, etc.) within a society or suborganizations within a single large organization.

As described by Boulding, the law of instability appears to be an extension of the law of size. Though size is an important factor, complexity is probably more important. For example, a sizable organization (or group of organizations) that is not very complex may be quite stable and manageable. On the other hand, the same size organization with very complex information and communication linkages may be much more difficult to manage and be more susceptible to instability and failure.

One of the most vexing problems facing modern management is to design complex systems that prevent instability and failure. Massive instability and failure have already occured in electric power systems. These systems' large size is part of the problem, but the greater problem is the extreme complexity of the system. The electric power system has warning and communication devices, redundant capability, elaborate switching, energy conversion, back-up systems, and on, and on. Other examples of complex systems in our society include, but are not limited to, various governmental activities (defense, internal revenue service, justice, etc.), transportation (freight and passenger service), and mail delivery. These systems are becoming more and more complex and more and more subject to serious instability and breakdown.

In a similar manner, organizational complexity may also lead to biological systems deteriorating and breaking down. Evolution has created highly organized and complex biological systems. These life forms compete for available sustenance, with the higher forms having a distinct advantage. Today, there is a mounting list of endangered biological species. Organizational evolution has created the diversity and complexity of biological systems, but it could end them as well. Whether physical or biological, system organization to handle increasing complexity is a challenge facing GST.

GST: Closed and Open
GST is concerned both with static, unchanging two-variable cause-and-effect "closed" systems and with multivariable, dynamic systems that are "open" to change, reorganization, and evolution. General systems theory is most closely associated with open systems, but closed or cybernetic systems are actually a restrictive case within GST. Open systems are not necessarily more important than closed systems, but in the final analysis all systems tend to be open. However, for ease of discussion, Figure 16-2 makes some distinctions between open and closed systems.

Figure 16-2   Distinctions between Open and Closed Systems

Open Systems	Closed Systems
Needs net import of information, energy, and materials to offset losses (or entropy) and thereby survive	Relies on information feedback to achieve control (cybernetics)
	Can input and output information, energy, and materials but will have a net loss of these commodities over time
Can acquire negentropy and evolve to higher form	Acquires entropy and disintegrates (obeys second law of thermodynamics)
May reach steady state (e.g., of growth)	Reaches equilibrium
Irreversible over time	May be reversible
Based on complex nonlinear interaction of components	Based on linear causal trains

Cybernetic Systems

The first item under closed systems in Figure 16-2 is roughly a definition of cybernetics. It can be simply defined as automatic feedback control systems, one step beyond automation where machines run and control other machines. Typically systems engineers are concerned with cybernetics in designing closed-loop electromechanical processes. The simplest cybernetic system is the thermostat in the home. In the thermostatic system, feedback concerns the temperature of the environment in which the system operates. This feedback information goes to a comparator. Here the feedback is compared with the system's temperature setting or objective. Information then goes from the comparator to the effector, which in the case of the home is the furnace or air conditioner where appropriate control action is taken.

An analogy between thermostatic control of the home and managerial cybernetic control in a modern complex organization can be made. A good portion of the work of managers and staff professionals is devoted to designing and operating control systems in which feedback information is compared with goals and standards. Examples include quality control, budgetary control, inventory control, tool control, quantity control, and worker-hour control systems. As more and more repetitive control processes depend upon electronic high-speed computers and other automatic machines, the managerial cybernetic control systems come to act more and more like the thermostat in the home. Cybernetic, closed systems are becoming increasingly important in managing complex organizations, but it should be remembered that they are also somewhat restricted. For example, closed systems have difficulty adjusting to growth and change. Of more relevance to the modern environment is an open-systems approach to organization and management.

Open-Systems Theory

The cybernetic closed-system model appears to be suitable for explaining and operating static organizations in the short run but not for dynamic organizations depending on longer-run strategic considerations such as growth, new products, technological improvement, and changes in key personnel. For such dynamic, strategic considerations, an open-system model is more appropriate for both understanding and operating a modern organization.

Although not normally identified as such, two pioneering management and organization theorists, Chester Barnard and Herbert Simon, took an open-systems approach. Their inducements-contributions model is an excellent example of an open-systems approach. They emphasized that an organization is by no means autonomous; it is highly dependent upon offering sufficient inducements to gain needed contributions from its members. The organization's membership was viewed as including not only the employees and officers (managers) but also stockholders, customers, creditors, suppliers, community citizenry and services (police and firefighters, for example), and regulatory agencies. The organization must provide all these members with proper inducements—money, products, labor, services, goodwill, or other intangibles—in exchange for their contributions—money, product, labor, services, goodwill, or other intangibles. This analysis is from an open-systems perspective.

More widely recognized in connection with modern applied open-systems analysis is the work of Daniel Katz and Robert Kahn and the Tavistock Institute of Human Relations in London. The work of Katz and Kahn was discussed in Chapter 5. They identified the characteristics (input, throughput, exporting, reenergizing, negative entropy, feedback, differentiation, and equifinality) of an open system of organization. The Tavistock group, especially F. E. Emery and E. L. Trist, developed the concept of the open sociotechnical system. They stressed the importance of technology and were able to classify environmental variables. These were given attention in Chapters 2 and 3.

The Systems Approach to Management

GST serves as the foundation for the more specific and operational systems approach to management. However, there is a fine line between GST and the systems approach to management, and the terms are often used interchangeably. Figure 16-3 clarifies the relationships between different systems approaches. GST is the broadest category, and the systems approach to management is one step below. The rest of this chapter is concerned with this second level, and the next two chapters are more directly concerned with the narrow or more applications-oriented aspects of systems.

As the figure shows, the systems approach to management should not be equated with computers, yet, the following dialogue is typical:

Professor: *What is there about the systems approach to management that makes it unique?*

Student: *Why, the computer, of course.*

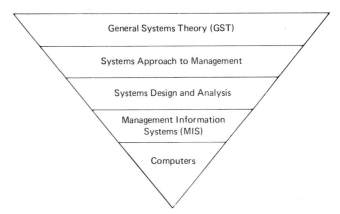

Figure 16-3 Relationships in Systems Thinking.

Professor: *Wrong! As those of us in the systems field are fond of saying, the computer is only a tool of systems management. The systems approach is more of an overall approach—an attitude, viewpoint, or concept—which has become associated with various techniques, some of which employ the computer as a tool.*

The professor in this example should then go on to explain that only some information used in management decision making is computer-processed. In fact, in very small organizations information may still not be computer-processed at all. Studies show that managers in larger organizations spend a large portion of their time writing and reading memos and letters, attending conferences and committee meetings, and conversing with others either by telephone or face to face. These noncomputerized activities constitute a major part of any organization's information system. The professor should stress again that the systems approach to management is essentially a way of thinking about organization and management. He should explain that the systems approach is concerned with the interrelateness and interdependency of the parts to the whole and should give reasons such as the following for moving toward a systems approach to management:

1 *Growth* Many organizations have grown so large that managers literally have difficulty keeping track of them.
2 *Complexity* Many organizational entanglements and communications flows cannot be understood, nor can the products and production processes for which organizations exist.
3 *Rapid Change and Diversity* Many organizations are experiencing shortened product life cycles and product and service proliferations.
4 *Uncertainty* Chapter 9 pointed out the decision-making conditions of certainty, risk, or uncertainty. Small, repetitive types of managerial problems are placed in the cer-

tainty category. Problems with limited experience are classed under risk. However, today with large, complex, diverse, and rapidly changing (dynamic) organizations, managers are forced to make many decisions under conditions of uncertainty.

Thus, the systems approach to management is generally misunderstood and has many precipitating causes. To further the understanding of the systems approach and to distinguish it from other closely related approaches to management, the following section traces its evolutionary development.

Evolutionary Development of the Systems Approach to Management

Some may argue that the systems approach to mangement is nothing more than good old-fashioned scientific management started by Frederick W. Taylor at the turn of the century. There is no doubt that scientific management is a systematic approach, but it is quite different from a systems approach. One early view of scientific management hinted at systems thinking by saying that measured units of work be "so combined that the entire work of the enterprise is thoroughly integrated and organized."[11] Yet, even this view is contrary to the systems approach because it is going from the bottom upward instead of focusing on overall system objectives at the outset and then developing downward.

Traditional scientific management is primarily concerned with the improvement of methods and the measurement of work units at the lowest level of the organization (at the workbench or for the work crew). This focus on improvement at the basic operational level is rather the opposite of the systems approach. On the other hand, scientific management did incorporate some systems thinking in a limited way. For example, Frank Gilbreth and Henry Gantt were concerned about larger problems of coordinating work flow between work stations. As a tool for analyzing this systems-type problem, Gilbreth developed a process flowchart and Gantt developed the chart discussed in Chapters 4 and 7.

Prior to the twentieth century internal organizational communication was mostly by word of mouth. Then came the paperwork explosion. Harrington Emerson, another of the pioneers of scientific management, directed much of his effort to applying work measurement and improvement techniques in the clerical, paperwork areas. By the 1940s, the paperwork specialist became commonplace. The Systems and Procedures Society of America was formed to promote and improve paperwork management. The systems and procedures specialist used flowcharts to follow and improve paperwork flows as Gantt had done with production flows in an earlier era. But just as Gantt's approach was not a top-down systems approach, neither was that of the systems and procedures specialist.

The systems and procedures field first evolved into punched-card processing and then, with more difficulty, into computerization. In 1968 the Systems and Procedures Society changed its name to the Association for Systems Management, with major emphasis

---

[11] E. H. Anderson and G. T. Schwenning, *The Science of Production Organization,* Wiley, New York, 1938, p. 83.

given to computer systems analysis. The computer systems analyst, like the earlier systems and procedures specialist, generally has little decision-making authority. The analyst is limited to the study and improvement of information flows. Thus, this computer systems analysis also falls short of being a systems approach to management.

If scientific management and systems and procedures analysis fall short of a systems approach to management, where did the approach originate? As with many other areas of modern management, the origin can be traced back to the work of Chester Barnard. Not only did Barnard propose the broad open-systems idea of inducements for contributions discussed earlier but he also maintained that one of the three primary functions of the executive is to provide for purpose through an organizationwide effort to formulate mutually beneficial goals. This is definitely systems thinking on a theoretical plane. However, the applied origins of the systems approach to management can be traced to two separate movements, the organizational revolution and operations research.

The importance of the organizational revolution has not been properly recognized by most systems theorists. This revolution began in nationally prominent firms such as General Motors, Du Pont, Standard Oil, and Sears. These firms had grown in size and complexity in the early part of this century to the point where their chief executives could no longer manage on a highly personal, centralized basis. Thus, they reorganized toward some form of decentralization, as discussed in Chapter 5. Most other large organizations soon followed suit. For these organizations, decentralization involved far more than changing a few lines on the organization chart. The matter of system objectives had to be thought through, because each subsystem or division in the new decentralized structure had to now be assigned its own particular set of goals or objectives. This, of course, required a systems approach to management.

Another and probably more important step in the development of the systems approach to management was operations research. As Chapter 10 pointed out, OR had its beginnings in World War II. Interdisciplinary OR teams were formed to solve complex military planning and control problems. The quantitative OR models, especially linear programming and queuing, were used to attain optimal solutions. After the war ended, the specialists began to apply OR to civilian management problems. The all-important initial step taken by the OR approach was to determine objectives or goals at a reasonably high system level. Complementing this systems-level objective setting was the strong interdisciplinary emphasis. Unfortunately, as operations research matured, much of this interdisciplinary flavor was lost. The emphasis shifted away from a broad systems approach toward a narrower mathematical and computerized modeling approach. Yet, the OR approach was an important initial impetus to the systems approach to management. As the introductory chapter of the book pointed out, in the last couple of years OR seems to be returning to a broader-based systems type of orientation.

The modern systems approach to management integrates and draws from the three major historical roots (systems and procedures analysis of information flows, the organizational revolution emphasizing systems objectives, and operations research utilizing decision models). Figure 16-4 shows that the systems approach to management is made up

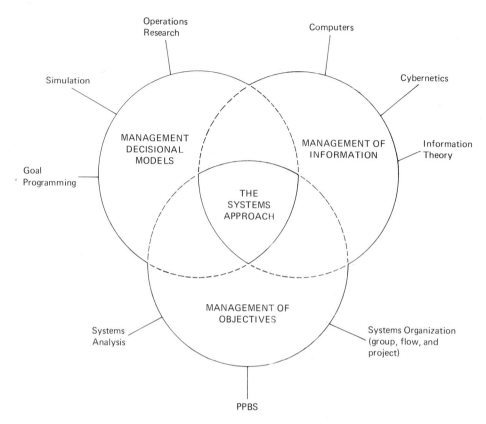

Figure 16-4 The Systems Approach to Management. *Source:* Adapted from Richard J. Schonberger, "A Taxonomy of Systems Management," *Nebraska Journal of Economics and Business,* Spring 1973, p. 36. Rapoport and Horvath propose a similar idea in a discussion of organization theory. They state that the three elements of organization theory are theory of decisions, cybernetics, and topology (these are analogous to management decision models, management of information, and management of objectives in the figure given here). See: Anatol Rapoport and William J. Horvath, "Thoughts on Organization Theory," in Walter Buckley (ed.), *Modern Systems Research for the Behavior Scientist,* Aldine, Chicago, 1968, p. 75.

of the combination of the management of information, objectives, and decision models. Effective systems management depends on focusing on overall system *objectives* using proven *decision models* fed by accurate *information*. Thus, objectives, models, and information are the key elements of the systems approach to management. The following sections discuss these three key elements in a general way as, of course, do many of the earlier and later chapters of the book.

Management of Objectives

Management of objectives in the systems approach should not be confused with or equated with management by objectives (MBO). The latter is a specific planning and control technique but, of course, incorporates systems thinking and application. However, this section is dealing with objectives on a more theoretical, conceptual level in the overall systems approach to management. Attention is given to general organizational considerations and systems analysis of objectives.

GROUP MANAGEMENT   As has been pointed out, organizationally, many modern systems have become very large, complex, and unwieldy. Group management techniques such as interfunctional teams or committees (plural executives) have been utilized to handle systemwide matters. General Electric's and Union Carbide's office of the president, General Motor's executive committee, and McCormick's multiple management are all ways of combating system disintegration and gaining systemwide focus on a single set of goals and objectives. These are alternatives to strict bureaucratically structured organizations. For example, Union Carbide's office of the president consists of the president and three executive vice-presidents. Every Monday morning this group meets to discuss overall company strategy on the systems level.

FLOW ORGANIZATIONS   As Chapters 5 and 6 indicated, the bureaucratic structure facilitates vertical (at least downward) information flows. But in this era of rapid change, the responsive organization must also have effective communications horizontally between subsystems. To rely strictly on vertical communication is simply too slow. Successful bureaucratically structured organizations often circumvent the formal communication channels and rely on the informal organization in order to get things done. Today, probably more information flows horizontally—across the organization from subsystem to subsystem—than vertically. So, the systems approach has increasingly turned away from bureaucratically structured organization designs. The hierarchical structure is replaced by horizontal flows of information and materials. This flow type of structure works fine where the product flow lines and information flow lines are simple and predictable. However, with the complexity of modern organizations this is usually not the case. A modern organization seldom has just one line of flow (for example, a lumber firm does not have the simple flow of land to forest to logs to cutting mill to finish mill to wholesaler to retailer to carpenter to final user). Instead, there are usually multiple-flow problems. To date, many organizations, like those in the lumber industry, still largely depend on traditional hierarchical structures similar to those discussed in Chapter 5 because multiple-flow structures have not been fully developed.

PRODUCT AND PROJECT MANAGEMENT   In repetitive manufacturing types of organizations another systems form of structuring objectives called product management is used. Procter and Gamble originated the product-manager (or brand-manager) concept about 50 years ago. Procter and Gamble's organization structure has the traditional functional departments (marketing, manufacturing, finance, and personnel), but then has various product managers superimposed over many of the departments. *Business Week* recently described the product manager as

. . . a middle-management coordinator who focuses on a single product or small family of products. Drawing on specialists within his company, he orchestrates everything from market research and manufacturing to sales, package design, and advertising. In some companies, he has broad deci-sion-making powers. More often, he is a junior executive in his mid- or late-20s who makes recom-mendations to a marketing vice-president or some other higher level executive.[12]

An extension of the product-manager concept is project management. Whereas product or brand management is a more or less "permanent" organizational arrangement, project management is more temporary in nature. The various types of project structures were given detailed attention in Chapter 5. Generally, project managers and their small staff determine *what* (specifications and performance goals) and *when* (planned due dates for all developmental phases) but leave the *how* to the traditional functional organization structure heads.

Project managers may have a few design and quality engineers, contracting agents, and personnel specialists who help them plan and control, but not execute. The personnel who execute the plans are generally from the permanent functional organization. They may be in the middle of a matrix (vertical and horizontal) organizational structure in which they have two bosses, their permanent functional head and one or more temporary project managers. Such a structure was shown in Chapter 5. This confusing and poten-tially explosive two-boss situation is tolerated to simply get things done fast. For example, if an important project is assigned to the normal functional organization for development and implementation, it may take a very long time. However, when assigned to a project manager, whose job is to act as a strong focal point, cut red tape, circumvent formal chains of command and otherwise apply intensive management, the time may be reduced significantly with little, if any, sacrifice in terms of quality or cost.

The experience of the Department of Defense with project management points to the advantages but also potential problems. DOD's first experiences with project manage-ment were massive undertakings involving hundreds of thousands of agencies and civil-ian contractors. The major projects of Polaris, Atlas, Minuteman, BMEWS (ballistic missle early warning system), and Titan are familiar to those who have experienced the cold war years. The projects were all accomplished in 4 to 6 years in the late 1950s and early 1960s. This represents an amazing managerial feat because 10 to 15 years was the normal development period for far less complex weapons systems prior to the use of project management. Because of this success, DOD made project management manda-tory for all large and urgent weapon and equipment system undertakings. Supporting civilian contractors in the aerospace, electronics, and automotive industries followed suit. Today, project management is an important form of organization in these industries.

Despite the importance of project management to defense work, it should be pointed out that the greatest quantity of developmental work in DOD and supporting civilian industry is not under project management. For example, at the height of the Vietnam conflict there were about 170 project managers in DOD, but there were also tens of thousands of smaller and less urgent weapon systems that were assigned to the permanent functional organization for normal, i.e., slow, development. In retrospect, the 170 project managers

---

[12] *Business Week*, June 9, 1973, p. 58.

may have been too many.[13] In 1968 a consulting group studied all 67 of the army's project managers and found that most were not very effective in achieving their main purpose, which was speedy project development. When there were only five project managers in the entire DOD in the late 1950s, they had credibility with the functional personnel; their urgency was believable. By 1968, project management had proliferated to the point where project managers' demands for urgent service (from design engineers, contract officers, testing labs, etc.) were doubling up. By sheer volume, the project managers had cried "wolf" too many times for the functional people to listen anymore. Like the other concepts and techniques discussed in this book, project management must be applied contingently to be successful. Chapters 8 and 19 discuss some actual contingency relationships applicable to project management.

PPBS AND SYSTEMS ANALYSIS   Barnard emphasized the formulation of unifying purpose for organizations. Planning-programming-budgeting systems or PPBS and systems analysis are aimed at maintaining focus on the purpose, objectives, and goals of organizations. Whereas group management, flows, and project management are structural in nature, PPBS and systems analysis are more developmental. PPBS was given specific attention in Chapter 7, and systems analysis is covered in the next chapter. They are just mentioned here to show that they are part of management of objectives.

Management Decision Models

Whereas management of objectives is concerned with the formulation, maintenance, and development of purpose, objectives, and goals, i.e., with systems ends or the "what's," management decision models are concerned with means, or the answer to the question of "how." Management decision models and operations research were given specific attention in Chapter 10. Most of the models discussed there are directly applicable to complex systems problems. For example, simulation models are especially promising in complex systems management. Simulation is applicable to systems problems that are too complicated to be economically reduced to a simple mathematical relationship. Whole firms and/or economies may be simulated. Econometric and input/output models and Jay Forrester's industrial dynamics, urban dynamics, and world dynamics are some specific simulation approaches that are applicable to complex systems.[14] In Stafford Beer's colorful parlance, simulation is experimenting "on the model instead of on the firm. If the model of the company goes bankrupt, nobody cares—except the scientist. He is delighted, because he knows the limit of the effectiveness of the policy he has been studying."[15]

---

[13] For example, see "AMC Project Management: An Assessment of Seven Years Field Testing of the Concept," United States Army Management Engineering Training Agency, Rock Island, Ill., July 15, 1969.

[14] See Jay Forrester, "Industrial Dynamics—After the First Decade," *Management Science*, March 1968, pp. 398–414.

[15] Stafford Beer, *Management Science: The Business Use of Operations Research*, Doubleday, Garden City, N.Y., 1968, p. 82.

A recent development in management science that is especially useful in systems problems is goal programming. The rationale for goal programming is that linear programming is too restrictive in that it requires numerical solution to a problem in which there is but a single goal or objective function. Goal programming builds upon and extends the more limited linear programming technique by allowing ordinal (rank-ordering) solutions in systems of complex multiple goals. Goal programming potentially can get away from the mundane operational level of an organization by being applicable to matters involving the highest objectives, in the realm of management of objectives. However, to date, the many examples of uses of goal programming have been restricted to low-level operational objectives instead of global system objectives.[16] Yet, it is this type of decision model that should prove to be most useful to the systems approach to management in the future.

Management of Information

The quantitative aspects of systems management tend to be preoccupied with modeling concepts and often neglect the information systems that are vital in providing the data for building and testing the model. However, by the same token there is the equally parochial tendency in dealing with information systems to concentrate on means and neglect ends—the problems, models, and decisions. Unfortunately, in management practice there often is a tendency for computer systems analysis and electronic data processing to dominate rather than to serve. This can prove to be a very costly problem. There must be a middle ground to emphasize both means and ends. Maybe a term like *information-decision system,* as suggested by some writers in the field, may suggest the appropriate dimensions to which information systems should address itself.[17] The next two chapters will show that in systems design and analysis and in management information systems, the ends or objectives must dictate and that proper application of the systems approach to management requires balanced consideration of objectives, decision models, and supporting information.

Critical Analysis of the Systems Approach

GST and the systems approach to management have not been without criticism. Two of the most comprehensive critical analyses come from the separate works of C. West Churchman and Robert Boguslaw.[18] Both Churchman and Boguslaw posit, under different terminology, four separate approaches that can be taken to problem solving in general. In analyzing the four approaches, they relate various criticisms of the systems approach. The four problem-solving approaches and their descriptions are summarized in Figure 16-5.

---

[16] See Sang M. Lee, *Goal Programming for Decision Analysis,* Auerbach Publishers, Philadelphia, 1972.

[17] See Richard A. Johnson, Fremont E. Kast, and James E. Rosenzweig, *The Theory and Management of Systems,* 3d ed., McGraw-Hill, New York, 1973, pp. 107–109.

[18] C. West Churchman, *The Systems Approach,* Dell Books, New York, 1968; and Robert Boguslaw, *The New Utopians: A Study of System Design and Social Change,* Prentice-Hall, Englewood Cliffs, N.J., 1965.

Figure 16-5 Approaches to Problem Solving

Churchman's Terms	Boguslaw's Terms	Explanation
Science approach	Formalist approach	This is an approach based on the premise that we can solve our problems through grander designs and larger models encompassing more variables.
Efficiency approach	Operating unit approach	This is a reductionist approach—breaking down into smallest systems and system elements and improving the pieces; it is characteristic of scientific management, psychology, and microeconomics.
Humanist approach	Heuristic approach	The humanist approach says that systems are human beings and that system design should be guided by humanistic principles or heuristics such as privacy, dignity, and freedom.
Antiplanning approach	Ad hoc approach	The antiplanner, be he religious or merely a skeptic, believes that planning is uncertain (or preordained) in a world that is foolish and maybe dangerous. A day-to-day ad hoc "muddling through" process is prescribed.

Source: Adapted from C. West Churchman, *The Systems Approach,* Dell Books, New York, 1968; and Robert Boguslaw, *The New Utopians: A Study of System Design and Social Change,* Prentice-Hall, Englewood Cliffs, N.J., 1965.

Approaches to Problem Solving

Boguslaw faults the formalist or science approach to problem solving because existing formal models (e.g., operations research models) are limited and work well only under certain restrictive conditions. He is implying that with more sophisticated modeling techniques the formalist approach would be ideal, but he is doubtful that better models will be forthcoming.[19] Churchman, on the other hand, faults the science or formalist approach because its purveyors are not the decision makers and often cannot even get close to the decision makers. The creator of the model—operations researcher, management scientist, or systems analyst—may recommend but rarely makes the decision. Final decisions are often in the hands of executives, stockholders, legislators, unions, the courts, consumers, and the general public. Systems scientists are rarely able to influence the decision makers' thinking, so Churchman feels systems scientists either speak to the wind or scale down their studies to suboptimal sizes.[20]

The second efficiency or operating-unit approach to problem solving also has obvious limitations. It is far from, indeed nearly opposite to, the systems approach. In regard to this second approach, Churchman notes that idle inventories (of any resource) may appear inefficient but may still enable the whole system to be more flexible, responsive, and effective.[21] Boguslaw cites the behaviorism of B. F. Skinner as exemplifying the operating-unit approach. In Skinner's book *Walden Two,* the community produced through behavioral engineering the kind of individuals (operating units) that it desired.

[19] Boguslaw, ibid., pp. 47–70.
[20] Churchman, op. cit., pp. 28–176.
[21] Ibid., pp. 16–27.

However, from a systems perspective, the matter of determining what behaviors are appropriate is a problem that goes beyond the operating-unit level. Consensus is needed, and consensus may be marshaled only at the overall level.

The humanist or heuristic problem-solving approach can also be criticized. Critics of humanism soon get into the realm of philosophy. One line of criticism centers around the problems of determining human values and ethics. What is good or bad, right or wrong? Who is to say? Who is to make this decision? The answers to these questions are in the realm of philosophy, not science.

Finally, there is the ad hoc or antiplanning approach to problem solving. According to Boguslaw, this approach would include mercantilism, laissez faire, evolution or "survival of the fittest," and existentialism.[22] Churchman states that an antiplanning philosophy is traditional in America. The citizenry has been loath to commission broad planning activities in the various social and economic realms. Instead, the idea "is to get somebody to manage it."[23] The manager uses brilliance, perception, experience, leadership, and the results of some quick staff studies to make the needed decisions.

Problem Solving and Systems

Churchman feels that the science, efficiency, humanist, and antiplanning approaches all should be accounted for or have a place in a true systems approach. However, with the criticisms just cited, a true systems approach may be impossible. The problems with limited models, suboptimal efficiencies, elusive human values, and effective planning in an awesomely complex (or preordained) world may be impossible to overcome. For example, the antiplanning approach at first glance seems to be a know-nothing viewpoint. It actually warrants serious consideration. It could be thought of as an alternative, but perhaps better as a complement, to the systems approach.

Herbert Simon's view that managers are content to "satisfice" because they lack the wits to maximize may be accurate.[24] The modern administrative world may be too complicated to understand and define in the systems sense, so the best one can do is search for workable, pragmatic answers. The lexicon of search behaviors and search models has sprung forth from these basic beliefs. Simulation, artificial intelligence, suboptimizing heuristics, and trial-and-error management are symptomatic of the limitations of the more rational approaches.

In an analysis similar to that of Simon, Charles E. Lindblom proposes "The Science of 'Muddling Through.'"[25] Economists Lindblom and Albert O. Hirschman felt that traditional theories and models, which presume to understand and to prescribe long-term solutions, are unrealistically optimistic. They offer what they feel is a more realistic approach

[22] Boguslaw, op. cit., pp. 127–159.

[23] Churchman, op. cit., p. 215.

[24] Herbert A. Simon, *Administrative Behavior*, 2d ed., Macmillan, New York, 1957, p. xxiv.

[25] Charles E. Lindblom, "The Science of 'Muddling Through,'" *Public Administration Review*, Spring 1959, pp. 79–88.

to problem solving under conditions of complexity and uncertainty. The ten assumptions of what they call "disjointed incrementalism" are as follows:

1 Attempt at understanding is limited to policies that differ only incrementally from existing policy.
2 Instead of simply adjusting means to ends, ends are chosen that are appropriate to available or nearly available means.
3 A relatively small number of means (alternative possible policies) is considered, as follows from 1.
4 Instead of comparing alternative means or policies in the light of postulated ends or objectives, alternative ends or objectives are also compared in the light of postulated means or policies and their consequences.
5 Ends and means are chosen simultaneously; the choice of means does not follow the choice of ends.
6 Ends are indefinitely explored, reconsidered, discovered, rather than relatively fixed.
7 At any given analytical point ("point" refers to any one individual, group, agency, or institution), analysis and policy making are serial or successive; that is, problems are not "solved" but are repeatedly attacked.
8 Analysis and policy making are remedial; they move *away* from ills rather than *toward* known objectives.
9 At any one analytical point, the analysis of consequences is quite incomplete.
10 Analysis and policy making are socially fragmented; they go on at a very large number of separate points simultaneously. [26]

Both Simon and Lindblom point out that complexity may indeed prevent a science of systems management and the more "satisficing," nonrational approaches should be given attention. Most systems theorists would agree that a degree of caution should be used. Even von Bertalanffy stated, "Systems science, centered in computer technology, cybernetics, automation and systems engineering, appears to make the systems idea another—and indeed the ultimate—technique to shape men and society ever more into the 'megamachine' which Mumford has so impressively described in its advance through history." [27] GST and the systems approach to management are certainly a unifying theme, but "go-go," "can-do" enthusiasm should be tempered by the realization that system complexity and uncertainty will limit its wholesale application to management theory and practice for the foreseeable future.

Summary

This chapter lays down the theoretical foundation for the systems approach to management. There is not universal agreement on either the definition or scope of general systems theory. One thing is certain, however; GST is concerned with very broad-based "wholes." GST is concerned with interrelatedness and interdependencies of parts to

---

[26] Albert O. Hirschman and Charles E. Lindblom, "Economic Development, Research and Development, Policy Making: Some Converging Views," *Behavioral Science,* April 1962, pp. 215–216.
[27] von Bertalanffy, op. cit., pp. vii–viii.

wholes. The levels (frameworks, clockworks, thermostat, cell, plant, animal, human, organization, and transcendental system) and tools of GST are fairly well identified, but the overriding theory is not. Areas of special concern for GST are system organization and closed- versus open-systems thinking. The challenge of organization size and complexity must be met, and more open-system as opposed to closed- (cybernetic) system thinking must be incorporated into GST.

The systems approach to management is one step below overall GST but is not and should not be equated with computers. The systems approach to management has its roots in scientific management, paperwork systems and procedures analysis, the organizational revolution, and the operations research movement. By themselves, each of these falls short of a systems approach. However, by extending and integrating these concepts, the systems approach can be viewed from the perspective of management of information, management of objectives, and management decision models. In the systems approach to management, the portion concerned with management of objectives incorporates new system organization concepts (group, flow, and project management), planning-programming-budgeting systems, and systems analysis. The management decision models aspect of systems management is more concerned with the questions of "how." All the operations research models (e.g., linear programming and queuing) but especially simulation and goal programming are relevant. The management of information is where the computer makes the biggest, but not the only, input into systems management.

GST and the systems approach to management are certainly the closest conceptually and practically to contingency management. The systems approach, however, is not without criticism. The four approaches to problem solving identified by Churchman and Boguslaw (science or formalist, efficiency or operating unit, humanist or heuristic, and antiplanning or ad hoc) point out some of the limitations of the systems approach. Although some management theorists would argue the reverse, the position taken in this book is that the contingency approach takes up where the systems approach leaves off. This does not deny that there is a great deal of similarity between the two approaches, especially when open-system thinking is stressed, or does not intend to downgrade the importance of GST and the systems approach to management. The systems variables are extremely important to contingency management and are given more detailed attention in the next two chapters.

☐ Critical Incident

You have been selected and placed in the position of house coordinator for a large general hospital. This position has traditionally been staffed by a registered nurse, but the administrator of the hospital feels that a person with management education and experience would be more appropriate. The job of the house coordinator is to represent administration in all matters, including making decisions, in off-duty hours. In other words, from 7 A.M. to 3 P.M. the regular administrator and staff are in their offices and make the necessary decisions in running the hospital. But from 3 P.M. to 11 P.M. and from 11 P.M.

to 7 A.M. the house coordinator on duty represents administration. Since many things that need immediate response happen in a hospital in the off-duty hours, the house coordinator must make some very important decisions. You are convinced that the job can be done better than it has been performed in the past, and the systems approach seems to be the best way to go.

1 What is the systems approach to management, and how could it be applied in this house coordinator's job?

2 Is a hospital an open or closed system? Support your position. What about other organizations in modern society? Are they open or closed? Give examples.

Questions for Review and Discussion

1 Trace through some of the background, meaning, and scope of general systems theory.

2 What are the definitions and major differences between open and closed systems?

3 Describe and analyze the different relationships and levels of systems thinking found in management. What is meant by the systems approach to management? What are the major components of the systems approach to management?

4 Critically analyze the systems approach to management. Incorporate the role of problem solving into your answer.

References

Ackoff, Russell L.: "Towards a System of Systems Concepts," *Management Science,* July 1971, pp. 661–671.

Baker, Frank: *Organizational Systems: General Systems Approaches to Complex Organizations,* Irwin, Homewood, Ill., 1973.

Beckett, John A.: *Management Dynamics: The New Synthesis,* McGraw-Hill, New York, 1971.

Beer, Stafford: *Cybernetics and Management,* Wiley, New York, 1959.

Boguslaw, Robert: *The New Utopians: A Study of System Design and Social Change,* Prentice-Hall, Englewood Cliffs, N.J., 1965.

Boulding, Kenneth: "General Systems Theory: The Skelton of Science," *Management Science,* April 1956, pp. 197–208.

———: *The Organizational Revolution: A Study in the Ethics of Economic Organization,* Harper, New York, 1953.

Buckley, Walter (ed.): *Modern Systems Research for the Behavioral Scientist: A Sourcebook,* Aldine, Chicago, 1968.

Churchman, C. West: *The Systems Approach,* Dell Books, New York, 1968.

Cleland, David I., and William R. King: *Management: A Systems Approach,* McGraw-Hill, New York, 1972.

Coleman, Charles J., and David D. Palmer: "Organizational Application of System Theory," *Business Horizons,* December 1973, pp. 77–84.

Emery, R. E. (ed.): *Systems Thinking,* Penquin Books, Baltimore, 1969.

Forrester, Jay: "Industrial Dynamics—After the First Decade," *Management Science,* March 1968, pp. 398–414.

Fox, William M.: "The Systems Approach to Organizational Effectiveness," *S.A.M. Advanced Management Journal,* April 1974, pp. 34–40.

Hoos, Ida Russakoff: *Systems Analysis in Social Policy: A Critical Review,* Institute of Economic Affairs, London, 1969.

Johnson, Richard A., Fremont E. Kast, and James E. Rosenzweig: *The Theory and Management of Systems,* 3d ed., McGraw-Hill, New York, 1973.

Kast, Fremont E., and James E. Rosenzweig: "General Systems Theory: Applications for Organization and Management," *Academy of Management Journal,* December 1972, pp. 447–465.

Katz, D., and R. L. Kahn: *The Social Psychology of Organizations,* Wiley, New York, 1966.

Kelly, William F.: *Management through Systems and Procedures: The Total Systems Concept,* Wiley, New York, 1969.

Lee, Sang M.: *Goal Programming for Decision Analysis,* Auerbach Publishers, Philadelphia, 1972.

Lyden, Fremont J., and Ernest G. Miller: *Planning Program Budgeting: A Systems Approach to Management,* Markham Publishing, Chicago, 1968.

Petit, Thomas A.: "Systems Approach to Management Theory," *Journal of Systems Management,* July 1972, pp. 32–34.

Quade, E. S., and W. I. Boucher (eds.): *Systems Analysis and Policy Planning Applications in Defense,* American Elsevier New York, 1968.

Rudwick, Bernard H.: *Systems Analysis for Effective Planning: Principles and Cases,* Wiley, New York, 1969.

Schonberger, Richard J.: "A Taxonomy of Systems Management," *Nebraska Journal of Economics and Business,* Spring 1973, pp. 35–44.

Tersine, Richard J.: "Systems Theory in Modern Organizations," *Managerial Planning,* November/December 1973, pp. 32–40.

van Gigch, John P.: *Applied General Systems Theory,* Harper & Row, New York, 1974.

von Bertalanffy, Ludwig: *General Systems Theory: Foundations, Development, Applications,* George Braziller, New York, 1968.

————: "The History and Status of General Systems Theory," *Academy of Management Journal,* December 1972, pp. 407–426.

Woodside, Arch G.: "Analysis of General Systems Theory," *Marquette Business Review,* Summer 1969, pp. 45–64.

Young, Stanley D.: *Management: A Systems Analysis,* Scott, Foresman, Glenview, Ill., 1966.

Systems Design and Analysis

The last chapter laid down a broad philosophical and theoretical base for systems. General systems theory and the overall systems approach to management (management of objectives, decisions, and information) was given attention. This chapter goes one step down the ladder toward management application by looking at systems design and analysis. In essence, the chapter takes a systems approach to planning and control of complex organizations. Many of the topics were discussed from a process (Chapter 4 on planning and Chapter 7 on controlling) or quantitative (Chapter 10 on decision models and operations research) perspective in earlier chapters. After discussing the meaning and scope of systems design and analysis, planning-programming-budgeting systems, benefit/cost and cost-effectiveness analysis, computer systems design and analysis, simulation, and network (PERT/CPM) analysis are given specific attention.

The Scope of Systems Design and Analysis

The world with all its myriad parts and manifestations is extremely complex. To gain some appreciation of this complexity, consider the problem faced by a social scientist in attempting to analyze the effects of various population distributions in a square land mass.

Figure 17-1a shows a square land mass divided into 400 separate lots, with each lot occupied by a family household. Each of these units could be analyzed in depth, in which case there would be 400 single-family studies, one for each possible geographical site. Figure 17b shows one of the 400 possibilities. However, for better understanding, an analysis of two families, located successively in each possible pair of locations, or 159,600 more studies should be conducted. One such study is shown in Figure 17c. If successive numbers of families at a time (three, four, and so forth), are analyzed, the number of possible studies becomes 2^{400}, or about 10^{120}. Ideally, to gain an in-depth understanding of the effects of population distributions in the example above, 10^{120} studies should be made. Obviously, this is impossible. To give some idea of how big this number is, there are about 10^{76} total atoms in the known universe. The social scientist, of course, is not alone in this world of complexity. The geneticist, for example, is faced with the problem of DNA molecules, which transmit genetic characteristics, theoretically combining in about $10^{2,400,000,000}$ ways.

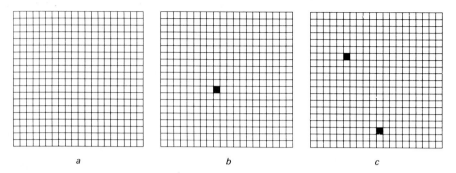

Figure 17-1 Hypothetical Study of Population Distributions in a 400-Lot Land Mass.

This world of tremendous complexity carries over into the organizations of modern society. The possible combinations of variables in any modern organization are as awesome as the figures cited above. The allocation of physical resources in an organization may be of sufficiently restricted scope to apply the decision models of Chapter 10. However, because of the behavioral variables (discussed in Part Four) in every organization, the problem becomes much more complex. Organizational systems are human-machine, cybernetic, and open systems, not purely physical systems. An enormous number of complicating variables are introduced with the inclusion of even a single person in a physical system, let alone the environmental input suggested by open systems. Because of this complexity, the systems designer or analyst cannot possibly explore all the combinations of variables any more than the social scientist can examine all the combinations of population distribution or the geneticist the DNA combinations.

Systems design and analysis begins by simplifying and abstracting from the total realm of combinations. The goal is to concentrate on the problems that are most important and reasonably amenable to available analysis and solution procedures. For example, optimization techniques such as linear programming, queuing, and other decision models are available for design and analysis situations that have been highly simplified. Human variability is usually abstracted out in these cases. On the other hand, much of systems design and analysis operates at more complex levels. It attempts to account for human variability, organizational dynamics, and environmental factors. Acceptable rather than optimal solutions become the goal of this approach to systems design and analysis.

Design or Analysis?
There is often confusion over the terms *systems design* and *systems analysis*. It should be remembered that the two are very close and overlap. There is essentially a "chicken or egg" problem in differentiating between the two. Are systems designed and then analyzed or are existing systems analyzed for the purpose of redesign? The answer is

that both approaches are taken. Design is best defined as putting together or creating, i.e., synthesis. Analysis, on the other hand, is taking apart to test, evaluate, and study. Originally, the system is designed, but analysis also goes into the design. Design implies some degree of permanence or finality. Analysis, on the other hand, is a more continuous process. The systems analyst's job is to test the existing systems design and to diagnose and solve problems. Figure 17-2 shows a suggested problem-solving process for systems analysis. Frequently such a problem-solving process results in recommendations for

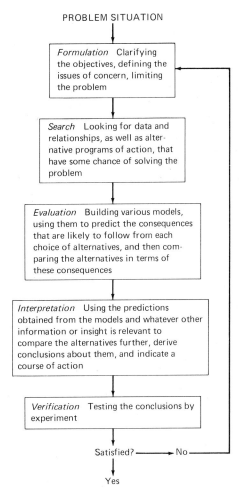

PROBLEM SITUATION

Formulation Clarifying the objectives, defining the issues of concern, limiting the problem

Search Looking for data and relationships, as well as alternative programs of action, that have some chance of solving the problem

Evaluation Building various models, using them to predict the consequences that are likely to follow from each choice of alternatives, and then comparing the alternatives in terms of these consequences

Interpretation Using the predictions obtained from the models and whatever other information or insight is relevant to compare the alternatives further, derive conclusions about them, and indicate a course of action

Verification Testing the conclusions by experiment

Satisfied? ———— No

Yes

Figure 17-2 Problem-solving Process in Systems Analysis. *Source:* Adapted from E. S. Quade, "Principles and Procedures of Systems Analysis," in E. S. Quade and W. I. Boucher (eds.), *Systems Analysis and Policy Planning*, American Elsevier, New York, 1968, pp. 33, 35.

some degree of systems redesign. Since there is such a fine line between systems design and analysis, the terms can be used together or interchangeably. This is how the terms will be used in the following discussion.

Levels of Design and Analysis

The last chapter pointed out that management of objectives is an important aspect of the systems approach to management. The techniques used in systems design and analysis can best be explained in terms of the objectives they serve. Although there is considerable ambiguity among terms like *objectives, purposes, goals, missions, programs, plans,* and *ends,* there are certain high-level objectives (or purposes or goals, etc.), second-level objectives, third-level objectives, and so forth in an organization. The various techniques and functions of systems design and analysis can be classified according to these different levels of objectives. Figure 17-3 shows such a classification scheme.

The first level of systems design and analysis shown in Figure 17-3 involves techniques such as entrepreneurship and the democratic process. These global types of techniques are used to obtain some measure of consensus among organization members about its overall purpose. This type of thinking is in the realm of management of objectives discussed in the last chapter. The second through fifth levels are more directly applicable to systems design and analysis. The remainder of the chapter will examine, corresponding to the descending levels of objectives, the techniques of planning-programming-budgeting, benefit/cost, cost-effectiveness, and computer, simulation, and network analyses. These are the major techniques of systems design and analysis of modern organizations.

Planning-Programming-Budgeting Systems

The second-level function shown in Figure 17-3 involves the translation of organization purpose into major, usually long-range, programs or product lines. Programs are usually more closely associated with organizations in the public sector, while products are more related to private industry. The difference is that in the private sector the product is a tangible physical entity, generally produced uniformly and repetitively at a rather invariable rate of resource expenditure; in the public sector the program is likely to be more intangible, nonuniform, and irregularly accomplished. Thus, programs are usually more

Figure 17-3 Levels of Systems Design and Analysis

Levels of Organizational Objectives	Systems Design and Analysis Functions	Systems Design and Analysis Techniques
First (highest)	Formulation of purpose	Entrepreneurship and/or the democratic process
Second	Program or product planning	Planning-programming-budgeting systems
Third	Resource allocation	Benefit/cost analysis
Fourth	Product design	Cost-effectiveness study
Fifth (lowest)	Operational design	Simulation, computer, and network analysis

complex and adaptable to systems techniques like planning-programming-budgeting systems. Public-sector examples will mainly be used in the ensuing discussion, but the reader should realize that the concepts and techniques apply equally to the private sector.

Approaches to Budgeting

The PPBS approach is to plan, manage, and control resources or funds by desired outcomes or programs. In other words, programs justify expenditures. Traditional budgeting, on the other hand, is not oriented to the outcome or program. Instead, especially in public budgeting, budgets are oriented toward expenditure categories or line items such as wages, rent, supplies, and utilities. These budgets are time-bound or periodic, generally on an annual or biennial basis. The traditional budgeting process requires each major department or organizational unit to estimate its forthcoming expenditures for each line item (like wages) and line-item subcategory (for example, regular wages, overtime wages, FICA, and bonuses). These estimates then go to higher authority for modification, consolidation, and approval. The relationship to outcome objectives and long-range plans is incidental.

Dissatisfaction with periodic, line-item budgeting goes way back. As early as 1915, the New York City Bureau of Municipal Research recommended that three different budgets for three different purposes be developed:[1]

1 Ordinary object-class or line-item budgeting by organizational units. This type of budget provides ongoing control.
2 A functional or performance budget, which aids in the management of services rendered.
3 A work program budget, which is based on planned outcomes or outputs.

Even though the city's administrators and politicians turned down the three-budget proposal and stayed with the traditional line-item method, it marked the beginning of what was to come. In 1949, the Hoover Commission called for performance budgeting in the federal government, and as Chapter 7 mentioned, a planning-programming-budgeting-system was adopted by the Department of Defense in 1961. Thus, three types of budgets are used in the public sector today: traditional periodic line-item, performance, and program. Figure 17-4 differentiates these three approaches to budgeting. Program budgeting or PPBS is most closely associated with a systems approach.

The PPBS Approach

As Chapter 7 brought out, the largest-scale application of PPBS is in the Department of Defense. Major programs in DOD include strategic forces, general-purpose forces, airlift and sealift, research and development, and central supply and maintenance. All these

---

[1] New York Bureau of Municipal Research, "Next Steps in the Development of a Budget Procedure for the City of Greater New York," *Municipal Research*, vol. 57, p. 30, 1915.

Figure 17-4 Approaches to Budgeting

Type of Public Budgeting	Administrative Function	Time Orientation	Budget Purpose	Similar Concepts in Private Sector	Examples of Budget Categories
Line-item budgeting	Control	Present and past	To gain organizational controls over expenditures	Financial accounting	Salaries Wages Rent Materials Supplies Utilities Equipment
Performance budgeting	Control	Present and past	To keep expenditures for ongoing activities in line with spending goals or standards	Profit-center or responsibility accounting Cost accounting Work measurement	Research and development Procurement Operations Maintenance Supply Construction
Program budgeting	Planning	Future	To tie proposed expenditures to high-level planned outcomes or objectives	Departmentation by product line (in repetitive industry) Project management (in the project industry)	Crime control Occupational health and safety Housing Recreation Food and drug supply Transportation

programs transcend and in some cases conflict with the traditional organizational breakdown into army, navy, and air force. One way to resolve the conflict attending program budgeting in DOD would be to disband the army, navy, and air force organizational arrangements and reconstitute the elements into such departments as the Strategic Forces Department, composed of B-52 forces, Polaris/Trident submarine forces, and Nike-Hercules missile forces. This restructuring would redirect the forces toward a major program. However, Arthur Smithies of Rand Corporation gives five reasons why this will probably never happen:

1 The traditional structure has deep historical roots that no President or Congress would deign to disturb.

2 There may be some virtues in competition between the services.

3 Some program overlap problems are inevitable if for no other reason than geographical segmentation.

4 Such organizations as the Corps of Engineers are vital to defense programs but in peacetime are more in harmony with Interior Department programs.

5 Good programming is sometimes inconsistent with good administration. For example, research and development is most easily administered in a single department even though separate R&D projects may fit into different programs.[2]

[2] Arthur Smithies, "A Conceptual Framework for the Program Budget," RM-4271-RC, The Rand Corporation, Santa Monica, Calif., September 1964. Reprinted in David I. Cleland and William R. King (eds.), *Systems, Organizations, Analysis, Management: A Book of Readings*, McGraw-Hill, New York, 1969, p. 178.

At the state level of government the inconsistencies between programs and organizational units are not as great as would be found at the federal level. For example, states may have an education program and an education department. At the subprogram level a state education program might be divided into pre-school, elementary, high school, college, graduate school, vocational, and special education. Fortunately, the programs generally correspond to traditional organizational units usually found in state government, and the program budgets and the traditional line-item budgets are not in conflict. However, this is not always the case. For example, a state crime-control program could be broken down two ways:

1 *State Crime-Control Programs*
   Law enforcement
   Courts

2 *State Crime-Control Programs*
   Violent crimes
   Victimless crimes

The first list (not necessarily complete) corresponds with usual organizational units and therefore with the line-item budgets. Upon close examination, however, the items in the first list are process-oriented rather than outcome-oriented. The second list is more program-oriented and more adaptable to PPBS by getting spending plans and desired outcomes together. The second list has the advantage of giving state lawmakers some concrete choices regarding the purposes for which state money is to be spent. If an elected official campaigns for reduction of violent crime, then his priorities are clear when appropriations are made to various types of crime control.

The problem is that the second list is not in line with existing organizational structures. Since altering organizations to fit programs is difficult if not impossible in many cases, an acceptable rather than an optimum application of PPBS is often made.

Cost/Benefit and Cost-Effectiveness Analysis

Cost/benefit and cost-effectiveness analysis are applied to the third (resource allocation) and fourth (product design) levels of objectives of an organization. The approach is in some ways similar to more traditional techniques such as feasibility study, operations research, engineering economy (or capital budgeting), and work measurement. However, as the continuum in Figure 17-5 shows, cost/benefit and cost effectiveness are more applicable to complex, systems types of problems. Examples of applying these techniques to varying degrees of problem complexity would include cost/benefit analysis made of sea or space exploration; cost-effectiveness analysis made of building a manned

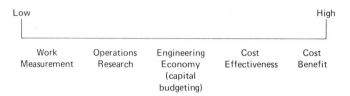

PROBLEM COMPLEXITY

Figure 17-5 Relationship of Cost/Benefit and Cost-Effectiveness Analysis to Traditional Techniques.

space craft; engineering economy/capital budgeting made of building a factory or adding equipment; operations research used to determine locations and numbers of regional warehouses; and work measurement used to determine whether to buy paintbrushes or spray guns. Obviously, cost/benefit and cost effectiveness are systems analysis techniques whereas the others are not.

The Cost/Benefit Approach to Systems Analysis

In cost/benefit analysis, total cost is expressed in dollars and is the denominator of the cost/benefit ratio:

$$Ratio = \frac{\text{dollars of benefits}}{\text{dollars of costs}}$$

To obtain the dollar costs, any future resource allocations for a given alternative must be discounted back to the present and be added to the initial cost allocations for the alternative. This present-value technique was discussed in Chapter 9. Of more difficulty is calculating the benefits. These are usually very speculative and difficult to quantify. For example, the benefits of sea exploration might be the discovery of scientific knowledge, natural resources, food supply, recreational possibilities, health and safety benefits, and sunken treasure. But it is difficult to meaningfully put these benefits into dollar terms. On the other hand, in some areas like water resources there is considerable experience in estimating dollar benefits of improved flood control, barge commerce, and irrigation—but even here recreational benefits are difficult to measure. The problems are compounded because, just as future costs must be discounted back to the present, so must future benefits. In most cases the bulk of the estimated benefits are in future years. Thus, the discount rate (or interest rate) becomes critical. For example, if $1 million is to be allocated to an exploration proposal having projected annual benefits of $100,000 for 15 years, the cost/benefit ratio, at a 4 percent discount rate, would be:

$$\frac{\text{Benefit}}{\text{Cost}} = \frac{\$100,000 \times 11.118}{\$1,000,000} = \frac{1,111,800}{1,000,000} = 1.11 \qquad \text{(11.118 is the present value for a 4 percent discount rate for 15 years)}$$

This would be a favorable cost/benefit ratio—a $1.11 return for every $1 spent. However, with the same example except for a 10 percent discount rate the result is quite

$$\frac{\text{Benefit}}{\text{Cost}} = \frac{\$100,000 \times 7.606}{\$1,000,000} = \frac{760,600}{1,000,000} = 0.76$$

(7.606 is the present value for a 10 percent discount rate for 15 years)

Now, the cost/benefit ratio is decidedly unfavorable. Choice of the discount rate becomes critical to cost/benefit analysis.

The Cost-Effectiveness Approach to Systems Analysis

Once a project is determined to be cost-beneficial, the next step is to evaluate feasible alternatives for specific accomplishment. Because of the magnitude of most projects, comparing the alternatives becomes a formidable task. The cost-effectiveness technique can help. It involves comparing alternatives according to cost and a number of carefully established criteria of effectiveness. Examples of effectiveness criteria might be economy, safety, growth potential, versatility, service life, maintainability, and prestige. Generally, the effectiveness must be compared criterion by criterion and a ranking attached. If one of the alternatives ranks first with respect to all the effectiveness criteria, then the evaluation may cease. Usually, however, the ranking offers less definite conclusions, and considerable judgmental analysis is necessary. A further refinement in the form of sensitivity analysis may be added. The purpose is to see what the impact on a particular alternative would be if the basic assumptions were altered. For example, suppose that a petroleum-fueled alternative powering a sewage treatment facility was determined to be most cost-effective. Other alternatives included are, in descending order of cost effectiveness, nuclear fuel, garbage burning, and a gravity system. Perhaps the high level of cost effectiveness of the preferred alternative was based on the assumption of an inexhaustible supply of petroleum fuel. That is, its cost effectiveness is sensitive to petroleum fuel availability. Sensitivity analysis would reveal the risk in accepting an alternative that might be rendered inoperable by a petroleum fuel shortage. If sensitivity analysis showed similar risks over fuel supply for the nuclear and garbage alternatives, then the gravity system could emerge as most cost-effective under the new assumptions.

To date, DOD has been a major user of cost-effectiveness analysis. The Department of Defense is concerned with such problems as whether strategic capability can be better obtained by B-1 bombers or Trident submarines. Cost effectiveness can give an answer. However, it may be that cost-effectiveness analysis may actually be better suited to areas like social welfare. One writer, in comparing the application to defense and the application to welfare notes:

1 Welfare is easier to measure than deterrence. Improvement of people's income and other variables can be measured and has been measured for thirty years or more. To really measure deterrence capability requires a war.

2 The "game" in welfare is played against a neutral adversary: nature. In defense the adversary is a wily and much less predictable "enemy."[3]

Both cost/benefit and cost-effectiveness systems analysis should have wider application in the future.

Computer Systems Analysis

Computer systems analysis is applied at the lowest level of objectives to the operational design of an organization. Contrary to common belief, most administrative systems are still not computerized. There is a vast unexplored territory for computer systems analysis in modern organizations. For example, computerization of the actual decision to allocate resources to undersea exploration, to develop a new product, or to dam a river is not yet done today. Yet, it should be understood that computers are routinely used today to help make these kinds of decisions. The computer helps in storing, manipulating, and formatting; these can be and often are done manually, but computers are a tremendous aid to modern decision makers. Most of this work is concerned with management information systems (MIS), which is the subject of the next chapter. The discussion here is more directly concerned with computer systems analysis.

Feasibility of Computer Systems

Feasible means possible and reasonable, and designing a computer system should proceed only after an initial feasibility study has indicated that the project is both possible and reasonable. There are four types of participants having major involvement in a computer feasibility study. Top management and users are concerned with reasonability, whereas data processing managers and systems analysts are more concerned with possibility.

There are three general types of feasibility:

1 *Technical Feasibility* Is the proposed computer system possible with available technology and capability?
2 *Economic Feasibility* Does the proposed computer system promise a favorable rate of return on investment?
3 *Operational Feasibility* Will the proposed computer system be accepted and understood by the users, and will it operate properly?

Generally, sufficient attention is given to technical feasibility of computer systems. The systems analysts and data processing managers know their capabilities and the technological requirements. Economic feasibility, on the other hand, tends to be assessed too casually. The costs are readily determined, but estimating the return on the investment is

---

[3] Robert A. Levine, "Systems Analysis in the War on Poverty," in Cleland and King, op. cit., p. 235.

more difficult. Because of this difficulty, top management should normally participate in evaluation of the returns. Operational feasibility tends to be even more neglected for several reasons. Operational considerations are rather remote at the outset of designing the computer system. The designer often takes the attitude, "We'll design it; it's up to the user to make it work." Systems designers also often underestimate the degree of human resistance to change and fear of the computer. Finally, computer system developers tend to be preoccupied with the design and give too little concern to availability of accurate and complete input data to make the system meaningfully operate.

Failure to assure economic and operational feasibility has been the downfall of many computer systems. The next chapter gives further attention to MIS feasibility.

Analysis and Design of Computer Systems

Once the feasibility study gives the go-ahead, the analysis and design can begin. Keeping with the systems approach, this effort begins with the ends or outputs, for example, computer printouts or master files. Determining the computer system outputs involves designing prototype printout formats, cathode ray tube (CRT) displays, punched documents, general formats for master files, and so forth. The systems analysts and the users should work together very closely on these outputs. The users' needs have to be translated into various output formats.

Once the desired output formats have been determined, the system flowchart or run diagram is designed. Figure 17-6 gives examples of such system flowcharts. It is a schematic diagram of the flow of input data through processing to become desired outputs. The American National Standards Institute (ANSI) developed the standard flowcharting symbols. Figure 17-6a shows the system design using only the two basic ANSI symbols: the leaning parallelogram representing any input or output step and the rectangle representing any processing step. Figure 17-6b shows the same flow but uses the specialized optional ANSI symbols. These and some other symbols are identified in Figure 17-7.

Programming the Computer System

The actual detailed processing of the computer system is not the responsibility of the analysts but instead is the job of the programmers. Whereas the system flowchart serves a communications purpose, the program flowchart does not. The symbols are not even the same. Since program flowcharts indicate only the detailed process within the computer, there need be no special symbols. Some essential symbols often used in a program flowchart are shown in Figure 17-8. Figure 17-9 shows a simple program flowchart for the primary subprogram of a payroll system. Note that the predefined process symbol is used for the "end-subroutine," which is a standard process that could be written once and called upon to end any program. The "error routine," which would be flowcharted on a separate page, is special for this program and thus is not shown as a predefined process. Note also that a distinctive feature of the program flowchart is the decision symbol which represents the basic kinds of comparison that computers are able to per-

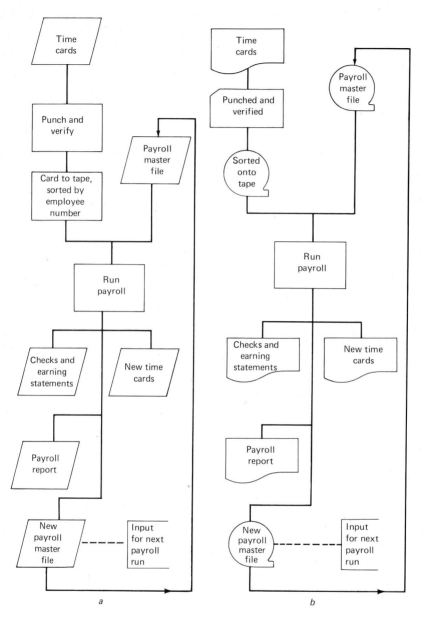

Figure 17-6 System Flowcharts.

form. Computers can compare any two variables or values and take action based on whether one is greater than, less than, or equal to the other. This capability represents much of the potential decision-making power of the computer, since it permits the repetition of processing steps if, for example, the card being processed is not "equal to" the end-of-file card. Such repetition or looping occurs without the processing instruction set being written over and over again. Thus, a relatively short computer program can control the repetitive processing of thousands of data records.

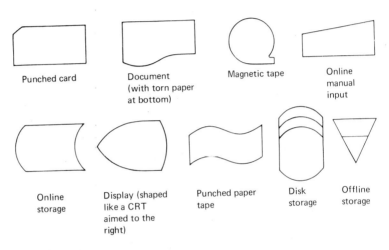

Punched card   Document   Magnetic tape   Online
                (with torn paper   manual
                at bottom)   input

Online   Display (shaped   Punched paper   Disk   Offline
storage   like a CRT   tape   storage storage
          aimed to the
          right)

Figure 17-7 ANSI Symbols.

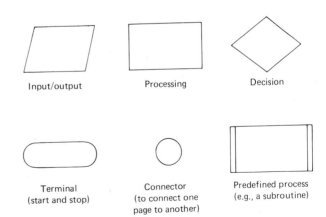

Input/output   Processing   Decision

Terminal   Connector   Predefined process
(start and stop) (to connect one   (e.g., a subroutine)
                 page to another)

Figure 17-8 Symbols for Program Flowchart.

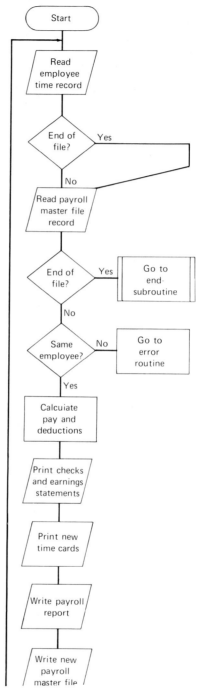

Figure 17-9 Program Flowchart for Payroll Subprogram.

Testing, Operating, and Maintaining Computer Systems

The testing, operating, and maintaining phases of computer systems analysis involve pilot tests, parallel runs, and system and program revisions. Pilot testing, which may be tried after the program has been debugged, consists of running input data from previous months through the new program and comparing outputs with known outputs from the earlier periods. Sometimes pilot testing may even be performed on the computer vendor's equipment prior to arrival of the permanent equipment.

Parallel runs involve running current input data through the new system and through the existing or old system as well. Dual operations may continue for several periods in order to get the new system fully operational and fully accepted by users. One problem frequently noted by data processing experts is that the parallel-run period all too often continues indefinitely because of indecisiveness or lingering doubts about the new system.

System and program maintenance primarily involves updating to incorporate new routines or extra features and to improve routines that are not working properly. A major requisite of effective maintenance is good documentation. A file containing complete correspondence, minutes of meetings, systems and program flowcharts, sample program listings and sample data, and records of program changes should all be kept. Because programmers and analysts are usually pressed to develop systems quickly, they tend to skimp on this documentation. This lack of documentation causes no end of difficulties for analysts and programmers who are trying to maintain and update systems. But with the state of rapid change faced by modern organizations, maintaining and updating computer systems is a major challenge that must be met for successful systems management in the future.

System Simulation

Management science as a whole could be divided into two opposing camps: optimization and simulation. In optimization, certain desirable outcomes are maximized and undesirable outcomes are minimized. In some cases, outcomes may be clearly defined like those discussed in the quantitative chapters, Chapters 9 and 10, and optimization reached. In many other cases, however, where complexity and variability exists to the extent that desirable and undesirable outcomes are not obvious or clearly definable, it becomes necessary to simulate rather than optimize. Where the possible outcomes are rather complex sets, simulation can generate a full range of such sets of outcomes by trying out different reasonable sets of inputs. This simulation process leads to "What might happen if . . ." types of thinking and systems analysis.

Deterministic and Probabilistic Simulation Models

Simulation of a management system may focus on such factors as average (or perhaps maximum and minimum) work flow times inventory build-ups or delays and shortages.

The simulation model consists of a set of decision rules or algorithms that closely approximate an actual management system. The model could use one or more equations, but algorithms are more realistic since they call for sequential steps over time. Enough past or projected input data are introduced into the algorithm(s) to simulate a realistically complete range of input alternatives and are of two types: deterministic and probabalistic.

Deterministic input data are those which exhibit little variability under real operating conditions. For example, assume that a state prison garment shop has only one work contract: to produce uniforms for the state patrol. Assume further that, because the state patrol has extremely narrow standards for height and weight, all uniforms may be made the same size. Size is therefore a deterministic factor and would make it that much simpler to simulate the work flow.

A probabalistic input data item in the same problem would be arrivals of work orders. Orders may arrive on an average of two per week, which equals the mean rate of new inductions into the patrol. Realistically, the arrival rate of work orders is more likely to be quite variable, and using two per week in the work flow simulation would yield grossly erroneous results. To be more accurate, the simulation should consider the full range of variability of likely arrivals of work orders. The range of variability could be fitted into a probability curve, or Monte Carlo numbers could be used for the simulation.

If both the size of the uniform is invariable and the order arrivals per week is invariable (the patrol hired precisely two officers each week), then there is no frequency distribution, no sets of Monte Carlo numbers, and, in fact, no simulation problem at all. The garment shop administration has no tactical decisions to make regarding mix or number of uniforms to be produced because these are constant. The only problems remaining are human ones.

Human Behavior Simulation Models

Human simulations are very difficult but not impossible. In one case, a behavioral simulation was made of a unit in a department store.[4] Simulation models in the form of decision rules, algorithms, flowcharts, and, derivatively, computer programs of six kinds of managerial decision behaviors were designed. Three of the models concerned output (sales estimation, advance orders, and reorders), and the other three concerned pricing (markups, sale pricing, and markdowns). For example, the sales estimation model was based on a general 6-month rule and four specific rules for certain months by product class. The general rule was that the department estimated its total sales for the next 6 months to be the same as for that period the year before, less one-half of the sales of the last month of that 6-month period. That this rule expresses simulated behavior rather than explicit department policy is clarified as follows: "We do not mean to imply that the department

[4] Richard M. Cyert, James G. March, and Charles G. Moore, Jr., "Price and Output Determination in a Retail Department Store," in John M. Dutton and William H. Starbuck (eds.), *Computer Simulation of Human Behavior*, Wiley, New York, 1971, pp. 194–217.

uses such a rule. Although the rule was inferred from a study of actual behavior, the head of the department did not describe his estimation rule in these terms."[5] The four estimation rules for specific months and product class generally equated this year's prediction with last year's actual sales for the given months. An exception was the rule for January and July: this year's estimate equals one-half of last year's actual, rounded to the nearest one hundred dollars.

The retail department store was estimating somewhat less sales than the previous year. This was probably the manager's conscious or unconscious way of getting sales targets that could usually be exceeded. The low estimates for January and July perhaps reflect the idea that since the department management cannot look good in these two slow months on a total volume basis, it should at least make sure it is able to exceed the sales target.

The sales estimation simulation model in this example was tested using 2 years of actual data and found to be accurate within about 5 percent. The model designers felt they could, if necessary, refine the rules and achieve even greater accuracy. The two other output models in this retail store case are similarly uncomplicated. The three pricing models are more involved and require elaborate decision rules and flowcharts for expressing the logic and computer programs for testing the models. The process of sale pricing, for example, is composed of four major subroutines: regular price determination, approximate sale price adjustment, price-rounding routine, and internal price consistency routine. The last and simplest internal price consistency routine or subroutine is shown in Figure 17-10. To verify this particular empirical model of the department's sales-pricing behavior, the flowcharts for each routing were converted to computer programs and tested using a random sample of fifty-eight sales items from past records. The criterion for correctness was that the price predicted by the computer output match the actual price to the penny.

Markup behavior and markdown behavior were similarly simulated and tested. Of 197 predicted markups, 95 percent were correct to the penny, and 88 percent of predicted markdowns were correct to the penny.

This retail store example and other such simulations of human behaviors constitute synergistic exploitation of methods and concepts in the behavior sciences, quantitative analysis, and computer technology. The potential applications of such simulations are many and varied. At one extreme is the esoteric realm of developing artificial intelligence or artificially intelligent machines. Nearer at hand are uses of these simulation results as a means of analyzing and improving goal-oriented human behavior, of revealing inconsistent dysfunctional behaviors, and of identifying behaviors that are incongruent with objectives of the organization.

[5] Ibid., p. 198.

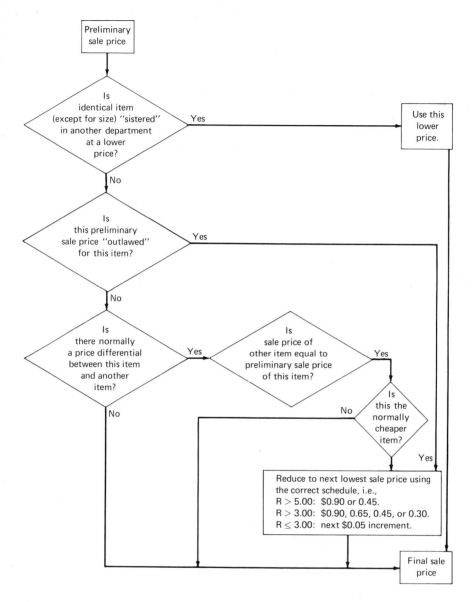

Figure 17-10 Internal Price Consistency Simulation. *Source:* Adapted from Richard M. Cyert, James G. March, and Charles G. Moore, Jr., "Price and Output Determination in a Retail Department Store," in John M. Dutton and William H. Starbuck (eds.), *Computer Simulation of Human Behavior*, Wiley, New York, 1971, p. 203.

Network Analysis (PERT/CPM)

Computer system design and analysis is often limited to repetitive processes. Network analysis uses the techniques of PERT (Program-Evaluation-Review-Technique) and CPM (Critical-Path-Method) which are useful in large-scale nonrepetitive endeavors such as construction and research and development projects.

Network analysis is not a single indivisible management approach but instead is a multi-faceted approach. PERT/CPM (a distinction is often not made between PERT and CPM; see Chapter 7 for a discussion of the difference) has four major facets: (1) goal planning and sequencing, (2) time planning, (3) scheduling, and (4) control. These four aspects of PERT/CPM are discussed in turn.

Goal Planning and Sequencing

In keeping with the overall systems approach to management, the way to initiate PERT/CPM analysis is to define the project in terms of output-oriented (product- or project-oriented) goals. A schematic model called a work breakdown structure (WBS) can be used for this purpose. WBS was not an original part of PERT/CPM and is not yet mentioned in most of the PERT/CPM literature or widely applied in practice. However, because of its potential usefulness to network analysis, it is given specific attention here. Figure 17-11 demonstrates how WBS can be applied. Actually, building a house is such a relatively routine and standardized procedure that it approximates mass production rather than project production and is only used here for illustrative purposes. A larger-

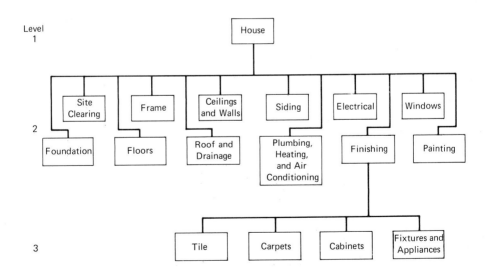

Figure 17-11 WBS for House-building Project. (Note: for simplicity, only one of the second-level components, finishing, is broken down into the third level.)

scope project would break down into more than the three levels shown in the example in Figure 17-11.

The WBS is project- or product-oriented. Its purpose is to focus on major integral subsystems of the total system. This allows the various subsystems (pieces, components, or stages) to be assigned to different managers for better project planning and control. Conversely, a function- or process-oriented WBS in the house construction example would show the project broken down into processes such as landscaping, masonry, carpentry, and painting. This latter fractionated approach is more usual; it does not provide cohesive time-oriented work packages that may be easily managed. Carpentry, for example, is done at various points in the project (building forms for concrete footings, building the frame, laying the floor and roof, and finishing work). Painting, landscaping, and masonry would similarly be interspersed throughout the project. In this approach when the project is delayed or resources are idled or anything goes wrong, there is a strong tendency for the painters to blame the carpenters, and vice versa, and so forth. If a manager is appointed to "honcho" a particular product-oriented (as opposed to functional) stage of the project (for example, site clearing, foundation, frame, roof, flooring, walls, etc.), that manager may work to secure cooperation from the various crafts and thereby save time and cut costs of idle resources.

Once a project has been broken down into manageable components or stages as determined by a WBS, tasks for accomplishing each component may be identified and arranged in a particular kind of sequence flowchart called a PERT or CPM network (sometimes called a PERT chart or arrow diagram). The way that the WBS relates to network development is shown in Figure 17-12. The carpeting activities are independent of cabinets, fixtures, appliances, and tile; thus they are shown as a separate network segment. The two segments in Figure 17-12 would combine with other segments to produce a single network for the whole construction project. All arrows lead from a single starting event and connect by various paths to arrive at a single end event. The end events (circles) together with all intervening events and activities (activities or tasks are represented by arrows) constitute a sequential network model for a given project or subproject.

The point of drawing a PERT network is not that the project will be accomplished in that exact task sequence indicated. There will always be deviations from the plan. The point is that the PERT network, along with the preceding WBS, explicitly shows everything that must be done and the best sequence for doing it. The people concerned may see approximately when they are expected to do their parts. Without such a network to guide the course of work tasks in a complex project, it is all too easy to fail to be ready to do necessary tasks at the right time.

Time Planning for Network Analysis

The first step in the time-planning phase of network analysis is to obtain a time estimate for every activity. Normally projects are different enough that one cannot simply go to the files to see how long the activity took last time. Historical and/or carefully engineered

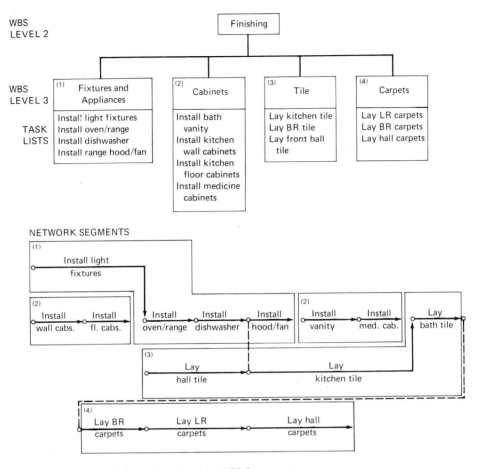

Figure 17-12 Network Segments as Related to WBS Components.

time standard data are usually not available. Therefore, the time-estimating procedure involves going to the managers and technicians who are most familiar with the task and requesting their time estimates. Obviously, this is a very inexact, subjective procedure, and as a result actual activity times seldom correspond to the estimates. The time plan tries to compensate over the span of a 2-week or 1-month reporting period by having the high and low estimates cancel each other. There was also an attempt in the formative years of PERT (late 1950s and early 1960s) to make time estimating more accurate by giving three rather than one time estimate for each activity: an optimistic, a most likely, and a pessimistic estimate. Three estimates rather than one provided a range of variability which in turn was translated into statistical probabilities. The statistics were valid, but the

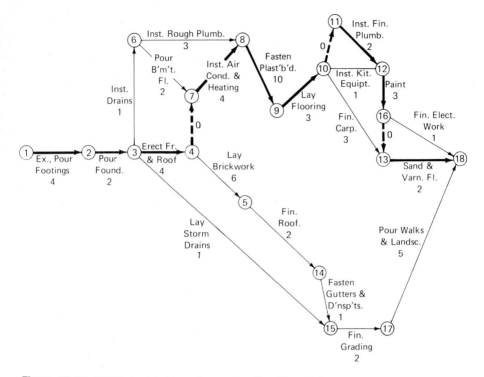

Figure 17-13 PERT Network for House Construction. (Note: The critical path is designated by the heavy lines.)

problem was getting people to give three good time estimates; it was hard enough to get people to commit themselves to one estimate, much less three. The three-time estimating procedure has generally failed in practice to improve accuracy, but the approach continues to be discussed in the literature.[6]

Once the time estimates for all activities have been determined, the next step in network analysis is to calculate critical and slack paths. The critical path means the *time*-critical path. It is the path that consumes the most time in the project from first to last event. This critical path becomes the constraining path, the path that determines how long the project is expected to take. Other paths taking less time contain some "slack" or "float" and thus need not be managed so closely.

Figure 17-13 shows a house construction project network with the critical (1-2-3-4-7-8-9-10-11-12-16-13-18) and next most critical paths (1-2-3-6-7-8-9-10-12-16-18) identified. It shows that the length of the critical path—the estimated project completion time of 34

---

[6] Originally, PERT used three time estimates per activity, but CPM has always used just one. Today, in practice both networks normally use just one; hence PERT and CPM have become virtually the same.

weeks—is simply the sum of all the activity times in that path. All other routines through the network take less time. A path from 1 to 18 (the whole project) encompassing any of the following activities takes 1 week less than the critical path: 3-6-7 instead of 3-4-7, 10-12 instead of 10-11-12, and 10-13 instead of 10-12-16-13. These nearly critical path segments are said to have slack (or float) time, which in these cases amounts to 1 week. These slack activities may be delayed by 1 week without affecting the expected completion time for the project as a whole. Since they have some slack or flexibility, they need not be subject to as intensive mangerial scrutiny as the critical-path activities.

Note that the critical path also goes through what are called dummy activities (represented by dashed lines) 4-7, 10-11, and 16-13. Dummy activities take no time and are not real tasks at all but are necessary for sequence logic.

In a project larger than the example (some PERT charts cover a whole wall), the computer would normally be used to calculate the critical and slack paths. The required inputs would be put into punched cards for each activity. The cards would identify the predecessor and successor event numbers and the activity time estimates. The computer would be programmed to simply add the activity times from one event number to the next.

For most projects, but especially those that are large, complex, and time-critical, it is extremely valuable to project management to know the critical path. The project manager can intensively manage the activities on that path. The project manager can call for frequent progress reports, assign expeditors or special assistants to help assure that steps are not delayed, be prepared to offer extra resources, and so forth. By averting delay on the critical path(s), the project manager is averting delay on the total project and thus can more successfully complete the project.

Scheduling in Network Analysis

The need for network analysis in scheduling project activities depends on having a project that is at least of medium size and complexity and that is highly time-critical. Much large construction work is of this type. For example, many large construction projects (large buildings, dams, bridges, and highways) contain a contract clause calling for lateness penalties, thus making them highly time-critical. Most such projects would normally be medium-sized (as opposed to really large-sized construction like the John Hancock building in Chicago or the Aswan High Dam in Egypt) and moderately complex (having, for example, only ten to twenty major subcontractors).

The scheduling of PERT/CPM is enhanced by a simulation procedure known as the time-cost tradeoff. As the name implies, it requires cost data as well as time estimates. Figure 17-14 shows a simplified network and gives the related time and cost data needed for demonstrating a time-cost tradeoff simulation. The critical path designated by a double line is B-D-E and is 8 days long. Path A-C-E at 7 days has 1 day of slack, and path B-F at 6 days has 2 days of slack. The data at the bottom of Figure 17-14 give the normal time estimates and costs as taken from the network. In other words, for activity A, the estimated normal time is 3 days at a cost of $50; activity B is estimated to take 1 day at a cost of $40; etc. The whole six-activity project is estimated to take 8 days (the critical-path

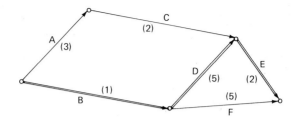

| Activities | Normal | | "Crash" | | Cost per Day of |
	Time	Cost	Time	Cost	"Crashing" the Project
A	3	$ 50	1	$100	$25
B	1	40	1	40	—
C	2	40	1	80	40
D	5	100	3	280	90
E	2	70	1	100	30
F	5	90	2	300	70
		$390		$900	$255

Figure 17-14 Simplified Network and Time-Cost Tradeoff Simulation.

time shown in the network) and cost $390. However, this plan need not be accepted. There is always the possibility of spending more money—for extra shifts, overtime, air freight, etc.—to reduce the time. This is called "crashing" the schedule or putting the project on a crash basis.

The crash data shown in Figure 17-14 permit calculation of the least expensive way to cut project time. The right-hand column shows these calculations. For example, the cost per day to reduce A's time is $25, calculated as follows:

$$\text{Cost per day} = \frac{\text{crash cost} - \text{normal cost}}{\text{normal time} - \text{crash time}} = \frac{100 - 50}{3 - 1} = \frac{50}{2} = \$25 \text{ per day to crash the project}$$

This means that activity A costs $50 to do in 3 days (normal time), $75 to do in 2 days (perhaps paying for overtime), and $100 to do in 1 day (paying still more, perhaps for extra shifts). The linear assumption ($25 for each day reduced) is somewhat unrealistic but is generally accurate enough for most projects.

The question now becomes, "If it costs $390 to do the project in the normal 8 days, how much would it cost to do it in 7?" One cannot simply take the lowest total in the cost-per-day column, for example, $25 for A, to crash the project. Spending $25 more on A would reduce A from 3 to 2 days but it would not affect the 8-day project time. The only way to reduce the project time is to crash one of the critical-path activities, B, D, or E. B is out because its crash time is no better than its normal time. The choice between D or E favors

D at an additional cost of $30 as opposed to $90 for E. Thus, to do the project in 7 days requires $30 more, for a total cost of $420 for the project.

Having simulated the tradeoff of extra cost for 1 day's reduction in project time, the next step is to try 2 days. Under this case, there are now two critical 7-day paths, B-D-E and A-C-E. Reducing the project to 6 days is possible either by crashing A and D together at a cost of $115 or by crashing D and C together at a cost of $130. The former is cheaper and thus would be selected. No further crashing is possible in this example because B, D, and E, one path through the project, have been crashed to their maximum. The time-cost alternatives for the decision are the following:

Alternative	Time, days	Cost
1	8	$390
2	7	$420
3	6	$535

This time-cost simulation procedure was originally developed in connection with CPM and the construction industry. However, it can be applied to other areas, such as research and development projects, and use PERT terminology just as well. The main reason that it has been of special interest to construction is the frequent use of the late penalties so that the time column may be translated into dollars of penalty payments and added to construction costs to give a total. Thus, in the example, if the penalty is $100 for every day beyond 6, then alternative 2 is shown to be most desirable in terms of total project cost:

Alternative	Time, days	Construction Cost	Penalty Cost	Total Project Cost
1	8	$390	$200	$590
2	7	$420	$100	$520 ←
3	6	$535	$ 0	$535

The entire time-cost tradeoff simulation process is easily computerized. Most computer vendors offer "canned" programs that will translate a network plus the normal and crash time and cost data into the type of listing shown in Figure 17-14 and will also summarize the time-cost alternatives as shown above.

The final step after a time-cost alternative has been selected is to put dates on each event in the final network. These dates are based on the final activity times and allow for appropriate holiday and weekend time off. This dating may also be done by a computer, with the output being a complete listing of scheduled events.

Control in Network Analysis

The control aspect of PERT/CPM analysis is characteristically very expensive. The procedure almost always involves a computer, and the periodic punched-card inputs and printed outputs require the direct attention of the highly paid management team involved with the project. Because of this large expense, such control is recommended for only very large projects that are highly complex and time-critical. Some construction examples that would require such controls are a world's fair site, facilities for the Olympic Games, a space center, a major hydroelectric dam, or a project like the New York World Trade Center. Equivalent major research and development projects might include a major weapon system, a major space project, or major domestic projects such as development of peaceful uses of the atom and development of new mass-transit systems.

Computerized PERT/CPM control involves simple data manipulations by the computer to produce periodic (every 2 weeks or once a month) printed reports on project status. The input data for producing the PERT/CPM control reports are by no means fixed. New or improved activity time estimates may be submitted at any time as conditions change or as more is learned about the activities to be performed. Furthermore, the network may be easily changed: activities may be added if the scope of the project expands, and activities may be dropped, perhaps in order to have a better chance of meeting the project schedule. All that needs to be done to effect any of these changes is to substitute or withdraw a few punched cards and run the data deck through the computer to produce a report showing the revised project status.

These kinds of corrective action in the control process may be supplemented with managerial pressures to force people to follow the plan as is. For example, managers getting a copy of the periodic control report may be asked for a written explanation of any variance from the scheduled date that is greater than 10 percent.

If the expensive, computerized PERT/CPM control is not used, this does not mean there is no project control or should not be any. It merely means that less formalized managerial control techniques must be employed. More dependence would be made on the traditional control techniques discussed in Chapter 7.

Summary

This chapter goes a step toward management application from the last chapter on GST by getting into actual systems design and application. The chapter is broken down into various systems design and analysis functions according to descending levels of objectives (formulation of purpose, program or product planning, resource allocation, product design, and operational design). The major systems analysis techniques directly applicable to these levels of objectives problems are given attention in this chapter.

The first systems technique examined was planning-programming-budgeting systems. This approach reverses the traditional budgeting process by emphasizing desired outcomes or programs rather than line-item expenditures. The PPBS approach is compatible with a systems organization design and has been extensively applied in the public sector. Cost/benefit and cost-effectiveness techniques were discussed next. Cost/benefit analysis is expressed in terms of a ratio of benefits (numerator) to costs (denominator). There are problems of accurately estimating the dollar values of the benefits and costs, but the ratio can be helpful in resource allocation decisions. Cost effectiveness is valuable in comparing alternatives by cost and effectiveness criteria such as economy, safety, growth potential, versatility, service life, maintainability, and prestige. Computer systems analysis was the third approach examined. This approach is usually applied to the lowest level of objectives in systems, the operational design. The first step in computer systems analysis is to determine feasibility. Technical feasibility is usually given sufficient attention, but economic and operational feasibility is not. Once the feasibility study indicates the desirability, then output formats are determined and the system flowchart is designed. The analysts then turn the job over to the programmers, who put the system into operational terms. The computer system is then tested, put into operation, and maintained.

Besides computer systems analysis, system simulation and network analysis are used for systems analysis at the operational level. Simulation is especially applicable where possible outcomes are rather complex sets. The simulation model is a set of decision rules or algorithms that approximate as closely as possible the actual system being analyzed. Inputs can be either deterministic (little variability) or probabalistic (variability is fitted to a probability curve or Monte Carlo techniques are used). Even human decision-making behaviors are adaptable to simulation models for analysis. The last part of the chapter discussed network analysis. This approach is especially applicable to nonrepetitive endeavors. There are four major facets of PERT/CPM: goal planning and sequencing, time planning, scheduling, and control. As a whole the chapter was very technique-oriented but it must be remembered that the purpose of these techniques is to make systems design and analysis more effective for goal attainment.

□ Critical Incident

Jim Stanley has been social services director for the State Welfare Department for three years. Jim knows what programs are needed to service the welfare clients of the state, but it seems that his job is getting more complicated every day. The biggest problem is the countless number of federal, state, and local regulations regarding eligibility, amount of payments, and timeliness of payments. Lately, there has been a push for quality control of the eligibility for social services. The federal guidelines suggest that there should be only a 3 percent error rate in eligibility. A spot check indicates that Jim's department is probably serving close to 25 percent who are not eligible according to federal requirements. Although the state does not have to abide by the federal guidelines in determining eligibility or error rate, it stands to lose up to half of the social service budget for noncompliance. Jim has been reading about systems design and analysis in the management course he is taking Tuesday evenings at the university. He wonders if it could somehow be applied to his problems in the social services department.

1 Could the concept of systems design and analysis be applied to Jim's department? How?

2 Could PPBS, benefit/cost, cost-effectiveness, computer systems design, simulation, and/or network analysis be applied to the eligibility problem described in the incident? Discuss some of the possible variables and try to give hypothetical examples.

Questions for Review and Discussion

1 What is meant by systems design and analysis? Is there any difference between design and analysis? Give examples of the various levels of design and analysis.

2 Briefly describe the PPBS approach. Give examples of how it can be applied.

3 What is the cost/benefit ratio? After a project is determined to be cost-beneficial, how is it determined to be cost-effective?

4 What would be some considerations in determining the feasibility and design of computer systems?

5 Make the distinction between and give examples of deterministic and probabilistic simulation models.

6 What are the major facets of network analysis? Comment on each.

References

Aldrick, Howard: "Organizational Boundaries and Inter-Organizational Conflict," *Human Relations,* August 1971, pp. 279–293.

Eckman, Donald P. (ed.): *Systems: Research and Design,* Wiley, New York, 1961.

Emery, James C.: *Organizational Planning and Control Systems,* Macmillan, New York, 1969.

Galbraith, Jay: *Designing Complex Organizations,* Addison-Wesley, Reading, Mass., 1973.

Hay, Leon E.: "What Is an Information System?" *Business Horizons,* February 1971, pp. 65–72.

Hebden, J. E.: "The Importance of Organizational Variables in the Computerization of Management Information Systems," *The Journal of Management Studies,* May 1971, pp. 179–198.

Kast, Fremont E., and James E. Rosenzweig: *Contingency Views of Organization and Management,* Science Research, Chicago, 1973.

Melly, Francis J.: "Report on the Computer Backlash," *S.A.M. Advanced Management Journal,* April 1974, pp. 10–14.

Moan, Floyd E.: "Does Management Practice Lag behind Theory in the Computer Environment?" *Academy of Management Journal,* March 1973, pp. 7–23.

Quade, E. S., and W. I. Boucher (eds.): *Systems Analysis and Policy Planning Applications in Defense,* American Elsevier, New York, 1968.

Management
Information
Systems

Whereas the first chapter in this systems part of the book presented a broad theoretical foundation (GST and the systems approach to management) and the last chapter was more applications-oriented in terms of actual systems design and analysis, this chapter gets right down to the "nitty gritty" of systems, management information systems or, more commonly, MIS. The first section of the chapter gives the meaning and scope of MIS. It is pointed out that MIS means more than just electronic computers. In fact, there is a hierarchy of MIS applications going from formulation of purpose down through medium-range decision making, and, finally, short-range decision making done by the MIS. The second major section of the chapter examines this hierarchical application of MIS. The next major section looks at some MIS myths and dysfunctional applications that have been made of MIS. Finally, the chapter ends on a philosophical note by analyzing the present capacity of computers and the role of computers in society at large.

The Meaning and Scope of MIS

There are few concepts in the field of management as misunderstood as management information systems. A few years ago one researcher found no less than 2,000 different definitions of MIS.[1] Today, MIS experts are in general agreement on what is meant by MIS, but the layperson and many practicing managers are still confused. This confusion is a serious problem because many managers who have only partial or no knowledge are in positions that require them to fund, authorize, direct, or design management information systems. The result has been considerable misdirected effort in MIS design and practice. MIS should be precisely defined, and the goal of quality information should be stressed.

MIS Defined

Probably the two biggest misconceptions about MIS are that the information must be computer-processed and that the purpose is limited to telling management about re-

[1] Robert V. Head, "The Elusive MIS," *Datamation*, Sept. 1, 1970, p. 29.

source capacities and utilizations. These are only partially true. Some parts of an MIS may be computerized, but other parts certainly will not be, and only one purpose of an MIS concerns resources (inputs); its greater purpose is to report on outcomes, i.e., the attainments of objectives and missions for which the organization exists.

Best defined, *MIS can be said to be a system of regular or irregular information collection, reduction, storage, and dissemination.* Like the levels of systems design and analysis discussed in the last chapter, MIS is also aimed at different levels of the organization. Regardless of whether they are computerized or not, all organizations have an information system. In some cases it is very sophisticated and effective, and in other cases it is very naïve and ineffective. For example, as has been mentioned, one common inadequacy is that the MIS provides only information on means, i.e., on resources or inputs. A good MIS, on the other hand, provides not only information on means but also information on ends or outcomes (profit, growth, and goodwill in the private sector or service in the public sector).

A distinction should also be made between a system that provides information for managerial decision making and a system that actually executes decisions itself. The latter decision-making systems might be found in a highly automated manufacturing process or in a routine information-producing system like payroll, inventory, or invoicing. These latter operational systems are part of MIS because they involve information for decision making analogous to managerial decision making.

Quality Information

The goal of any MIS is to provide *quality* information to make more effective management decisions. Donald Sanders feels that the information should ideally be accurate, timely, complete, concise, and relevant.[2] The accuracy of information could be measured by the ratio of correct information to the total amount of information produced over a period of time. What is an acceptable ratio depends on the situation. In manned space flights the information must be extremely accurate with no room for error, while in another type of operation (for example, the quality control on shipping boxes for fruit) the ratio of accuracy has much more latitude.

The timeliness of information may take precedence over accuracy. If the information is not available when it is needed, then the accuracy does not matter. All decision makers have deadlines to meet, and they need information at the appropriate time. Completeness also contributes to quality information. The most famous case of the devastating effects of incomplete information occurred on December 7, 1941. United States intelligence sources had generated bits and pieces of information that the Japanese were "up to something." Unfortunately, the information was not complete, and the result was the disastrous Pearl Harbor attack. If the decision makers (military and government leaders)

[2] Donald H. Sanders, *Computers in Business*, 3d ed., McGraw-Hill, New York, 1975, pp. 19–23.

had had complete information, the disaster could have been avoided. The information was timely and accurate, but it was not put together into a complete or unitary whole.

Seemingly opposite from completeness, but instead a complementary requirement of quality information, is conciseness. Most of today's managers spend a great deal of time reading reports, attending committee meetings and briefings, and, if they have a computerized MIS, receiving reams of printouts. A problem is to sift through the voluminous data to get to the information that is needed for a particular decision. This is where conciseness comes to play an important role. A closely related variable of quality information is relevancy. It stresses the difference between "need to know" types of information from "nice to know" types of information. Relevant information should receive major attention in the decision-making process.

MIS Hierarchy

An MIS hierarchy is given in Figure 18-1. The executing systems, referred to in the figure as routine (programmable) operational decision-making systems, occupy the bottom rung of the hierarchy. They are the initial product of what Norbert Wiener labeled the "second industrial revolution." The first industrial revolution amplified force or the muscle power, the second amplified logical and communicative powers.[3]

Figure 18-1 indicates that the long-range decisions on purpose are the basis for the medium-range MIS decisions on the kinds of products, services, and resources which in turn are inputs to the lowest short-range resource planning, heuristic, and routine level. Designs, plans, schedules, and assignments are inputs for the lower levels. They result in producing products and performing services. While the flow of decisions is generally downward from long-range to short-range, some of the informational by-products are fed back to facilitate decision making in an upward direction. The following discussion will analyze these levels in such an upward direction.

Routine or Programmed Decision Making in MIS

The meaning of routine or programmable decision making listed last in Figure 18-1 is decision making that is routine enough and recurring sufficiently often to develop preestablished decision rules. They are essentially the decisions under certainty that were discussed in Chapter 9. Any set of standard instructions, such as those the Internal Revenue Service provides for determining income tax, would be an example. Mass-produced instructions become a program. They attempt to be logical and communicative. The use of mechanical and electronic means of handling these programmed sets of instructions is common. Thus, today one may send the appropriate personal and financial data to the IRS people, who enter it into a computer which contains the stored program of

---

[3] See Norbert Wiener, *The Human Use of Human Beings,* Avon Books, New York, 1950, pp. 185–221.

Figure 18-1 MIS Hierarchy

Decision-making Level	Information Needed for the Decision	Information Generated
(Top) 1 *Long-Range Decision Making* What is the purpose? Sensing and acting on environmental stimuli.	*Measures of environmental changes and trends* The organization's demonstrated capabilities to exert controls over its environment and to react to environment change	Information on the role of the organization in its environment (society) passes to that environment
(Middle) 2 *Medium-Range Decision Making* What kinds of products, services, and resources?	*Projected demand data* Measures of past performance; i.e., degree of attainment of desired outcomes (quality, quantity, growth, survival, satisfaction, profit, etc.)	Gross aggregated outcome measures may aid in formulating purpose
(Lower) 3 *Short-Range Decision Making* a *Resource* planning: Product or service design, operations planning and scheduling, resource assignment.	*"Customer order" data (tasks to be done)* Typical "data bank" information: on resources available, resources busy, and resource utilization and efficiency rates; files of designs, operating plans, and task/customer records	Data bank information on costs, on existing resources, and on operational capacities and capabilities is useful in strategic planning
b *Heuristic* decision making: Supervisory decisions, nonrecurring operator decisions, staff decisions (e.g., a purchasing agent buys something).	*Temporal data on the problem itself— sometimes not recorded and retained until after decision has been made* Policies or heuristics (principles) as guides to decisions	The data, if recorded, may be formulated in a way that will facilitate their aggregation into statistics useful in resource or operations planning
c *Routine* (programmable) decision making: Producing goods, providing services, printing paychecks, reports, and invoices.	*Data on the task itself* Programmed decision rules and algorithms; job tickets and plans (e.g., blueprints and route sheets)	Enrollment reports; inventories; expenditure reports, etc.; useful in operational decision making

instructions for calculating the income tax. The computer eliminates the need for separate steps in the program to be communicated to and acted on by a human being. In Wiener's words, "The parts of the machine must speak to one another through an appropriate language, without speaking to any person or listening to any person, except in the terminal and initial stages of the process."[4] Such cybernetic processes are usually computer-controlled, but slower devices like simple mechanical or electrical punched-card and paper-tape equipment can also be used.

More advanced examples of programmed operations can be found in the processing industries such as glass and steel making, petroleum and sugar refining, and grain processing. These are all capital-intensive industries, which simply means that human operators or workers play a minor role in the productive process. People are replaced by

[4] Ibid., p. 206.

highly automated machines (capital equipment) programmed with blueprints, specifications, dimensions, and operational sequence information. The information for decisions is contained in internal storage or on external devices such as punched cards or magnetic tapes and is under the control of analog or digital computers. Minicomputers have created an increasing impetus for this type of automation.[5]

Heuristic Decision Making in MIS

Besides the routine, programmable operational decisions, there are also certain nonrecurring or heuristic types of decisions made at the operational, short-range level. This heuristic approach occurs among more highly skilled operators—generalists assigned custom work or special projects or programs. An example is a maintenance tradesperson who applies the principles (heuristics) of his or her trade to handle each unique job. In addition to executing the task, the person acts as his or her own manager, making certain basic decisions about the job.

The degree of automation of nonrecurring, heuristic operations is small but growing. The growth is mainly concentrated in the area of numerically controlled (NC) machines. Until recently, NC equipment was run by punched paper tape or other such indirect or "off-line" media and controlled by human operators. Today DNC (direct numerical control) machines, which are NC machines directly controlled by a computer or minicomputer, are growing in use.

Heuristic operational decision making also involves activities that directly support primary operations. First-line supervisory activities are of this type. So are purchasing needed materials and hiring employees. The second industrial revolution is having a small but growing impact in this area of heuristic operational decision making as well. There are now computerized personnel systems that assist workforce planning and matching applicants with vacancies. There are inventory systems that include a subsystem that actually supplants the purchasing agent; i.e., the subsystem writes purchase orders under computer control. Yet, despite these advances, most computer-assisted decisions still tend to remain at a low-value or low-impact level. However, there is considerable interest and a move toward developing artificially intelligent computers that can evaluate data and make decisions based on certain benchmarks or heuristics. The computer is presently capable of making logical choices and learning on its own. The last part of the chapter covers this in more depth.

Resource Planning and the Data Bank in MIS

Figure 18-1 shows that along with routine and heuristic decision making is resource planning in the short-range category of the MIS hierarchy. This resource planning includes designing the product or service, planning and scheduling the operations, and

---

[5] See "Minicomputers That Run the Factory," *Business Week,* Dec. 8, 1973, pp. 68–78.

assigning or allocating resources (people, equipment, space, materials, tools, information, and money). This approach requires, first of all, knowledge of the organization's own capacities and demonstrated capabilities to accomplish given tasks. The capacities of the organization are its resources on hand, and the capabilities include past resource utilization rates (time in use divided by time available for a machine, a person, a building, or other resource) and past resource efficiency rates (standard time divided by actual time, standard cost divided by actual cost, and standard material allotment divided by actual material used).

The term *data bank* is closely associated with this resource planning aspect of MIS. Unfortunately, there is not general agreement about what data a data bank is supposed to contain nor what it is used for. However, a data bank is generally used as a repository for data on resource capacities and capabilities. These data are necessary for effectively planning and scheduling operations and assigning resources to operations and to functional areas. Secondary data, which in some cases would be the primary data, may also be included in a data bank. Examples of secondary data are aggregate figures on tasks performed or kinds of customers served. Such data can help the planners and schedulers to develop better processes and procedures (including better decision rules for any routine decision making) and to preassign resources in a way that matches task and customer distribution patterns. Creating aggregate data on tasks and customers requires having records on individual cases. For example, a psychiatric data bank serving a medical association would need, as inputs, individual patient records from which aggregate statistics, such as incidence of schizophrenia among various age groups, could be computed. The privacy and freedom issues involved in such personal data banks are very controversial and will be given specific attention in the last part of the chapter.

Other data needed for resource planning are past design data. Blueprints, specifications, dimensions, prescriptions, formulas, recipes, assembly sequences, machine speeds and feeds, and time standards for standard tasks are examples. These data were discussed earlier in connection with their primary purpose, routine decision making. They are also useful in planning new designs. For example, computer-aided design (CAD) and computer graphics are readily used in the electronics industry. The necessary input for CAD and computer graphics comes from a computer data bank containing design modules, formulas, blueprint-drawing routines, and so forth. Computer-aided manufacturing planning and scheduling, also growing in use, requires a computer data bank containing data on standard times and resource requirements for standard manufacturing operations. The planner may create manufacturing plans (work orders, job tickets, route sheets, warehouse material releases, tool orders, and schedules) by using a computer terminal. The planner draws on the data bank to evaluate alternative methods and then combines his or her choices to form a cohesive and economical plan. In some respects this MIS approach completes the full circle back to something resembling the pre-industrial revolution era of the craftsworkers. The craftsworkers were their own product and process designers, schedulers, supervisors, and operators. In an analogous manner the computer-assisted MIS permits an engineer (who is at a terminal interacting with a computer and data bank) to design a product, plan an economical method of producing it, and control automatic delivery of necessary materials and the equipment to produce it. Figure 18-2 depicts this circle.

Besides industry, many other types of organizations depend on data banks. For example, dietetics, health care, the legal profession, scientific research, and instructional design all make extensive use of data banks. It is feasible for a dietician to design, plan, produce, and deliver meals with computer assistance and for a chemist to design and execute an experiment while seated at a computer terminal. As Figure 18-2 shows, the age of crafts-workers, as opposed to narrowly trained specialists, may be returning. The difference, of course, is the computer, which can do the jobs formerly done by specialists.

Medium-Range Decision Making in MIS

So far, only short-range decisions in the MIS have been given attention. Figure 18-1 showed that the medium-range MIS is more concerned with answering the question of

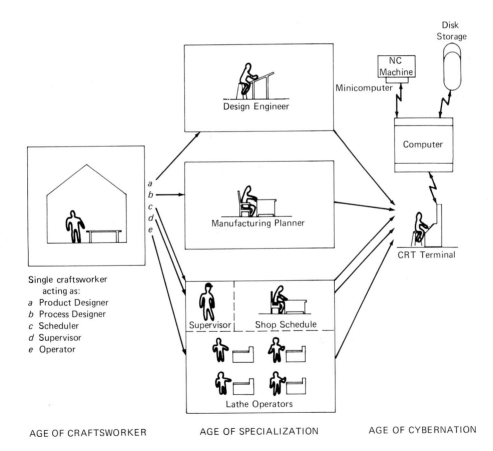

Figure 18-2 The Full Circle of Technology.

what kinds of products, services, and resources the organization should concentrate on. Projected demand data and measures of past performance are vital information for this purpose. In other words, at this level of decision making there must be good information on outcomes, which is basically a problem of measurement. For example, it is not hard to measure profit, if profit is the primary desired outcome for the organization. However, the problem is that profit is a gross measure, a measure based on certain accounting, time, and tax-oriented expediencies, and a measure that can overlook mismanagement and hide long-run mistakes while focusing on the short run. Besides, most organizations today have other desired outcomes, such as growth and social responsibility, which are not covered in the "bottom line" profit outcome.

During the 1960s the "go-go" firms were not those producing steady and high profits as much as they were those trying to grow, sometimes at the expense of profit. This was the era of the conglomerates. Growth was the key factor to be measured for these firms, and the measures of past, present, and projected growth were of key importance to them. They needed information on growth in order to plan for their products, services, and resources. The same is true of companies concerned with social responsibility outcomes. The questions of what the company is doing about poverty, equal rights, environmental protection, and consumerism must be answered by firms concerned with social responsibility outcomes.

In addition to profit, growth, and social responsibility, many individual employees, who do most of the measuring and designing of the information systems, are often interested in other outcomes such as pay, advancement, recognition, variety, self-actualization, or social satisfaction. The MIS should provide information on all these desired outcomes. Ideally, the MIS should attempt to reconcile the conflicting objectives of the diverse interests of the organization.

MEASUREMENT PROBLEMS   Providing good information on outcomes has more to do with measurement than with data processing. This fact has caused many problems because of the tendency to assign electronic data processing-oriented people, who generally are not experts in measuring outcomes, to design the MIS. Their talents are appropriate for the shorter-range MIS functions discussed in the last section but not for the medium- and longer-range decisions. The next major section on the myths of MIS examines some of these types of problems in more detail.

The problem of measurement of outcomes is multifaceted and is illustrated by the two examples shown in Figure 18-3. Two extremely different kinds of organizations are exemplified: the tuna boat fleet is profit-oriented and produces a tangible, countable product, while the symphony orchestra is service-oriented and produces an intangible, noncountable, artistic product. The management decisions for the tuna boat fleet on types and quantities of boats, fishing grounds, kinds of employee talent needed, and outlets for the catch greatly depend on objective measures such as pounds of tuna per day per boat, rate of return on investment, and growth rate. The decision makers for the symphony orchestra have no such objective measures to go by. However, although the orchestra's measures—critics' opinions—are entirely subjective, they can provide a basis for decisions on the director, the kinds of music performed, the soloists, the concert hall, and the traveling schedule. Although no single critic's judgment is conclusive, the collective judgment of all the leading critics can be as important to decision making about the orchestra as pounds of tuna are for the tuna fleet. Also, both the tuna fleet and the symphony orchestra are concerned about certain outcomes that can only be measured by partially objective and partially subjective criteria. A number index of employee satisfaction, obtained by quantifying the results of an attitude survey, is an example. Charitable performances (for the symphony orchestra) and protection of tuna spawning areas (for the tuna fleet) are other measurements.

MEASURING NONPROFIT ORGANIZATIONS   There are problems in all three categories of measurement shown in Figure 18-3. Countable outputs, such as pounds of tuna, may be deliberately or nondeliberately misrepresented by employees. As industrial engineers of an earlier era discovered when attempting to set production standards, employees can find a way to "beat the system." In addition to the problems with "objective" measures, there are numerous difficulties with the middle category, part objective and part subjective measurement. For some organizations, notably nonprofit organizations such as hospitals, educational institutions, and governmental agencies, virtually all their desired outcomes must be measured by part objective and part subjective criteria. Hospitals typically do not measure their degree of success in treating patients, educational institutions do not measure how well they disseminate knowledge and generate research, and governmental agencies do not measure how well they serve the public. It is not that these obviously prime outcomes cannot be measured. If the quality of a symphony orchestra, bottle of wine, or a dramatic performance can be measured, then any outcome can be measured. Yet, measuring performance outcomes is often viewed as a threat. Tuna fleets and symphony orchestras are put to the test of measurement or they cease to grow; their budgets and resources will dry up if they are not able to demonstrate some measures of success. On the other hand, hospitals, educational institutions, and governmental agencies have managed to survive and in some cases even grow and prosper without subject-

Figure 18-3   The Measurement Problem in MIS

Criteria	Tuna Boat Fleet	Symphony Orchestra
Objective performance criteria (measured by counting)	Pounds of tuna per day per boat Pounds of tuna per running foot of boat Pounds of tuna per dollar of cost Percent of high-grade tuna in catch Rate of return on investment (ROI) Rate of growth	
Objective/subjective criteria	Index of employee satisfaction Protection of tuna spawning areas	Index of employee satisfaction Charity performances given Number in audience
Subjective performance criteria (measured by opinion)		Critics' opinions

ing themselves to performance measurement and evaluation. Ironically, the nonprofit organizations' large investments in punched-card and computing equipment have permitted these institutions to forestall such measurement. As mentioned before, this is true because EDP personnel are often not interested or qualified to measure outcomes. The MIS efforts of nonprofit organizations have largely been in the routine data processing and data bank areas. Thus, the typical hospital, educational, or public administrator will respond to how his or her organization is doing in terms of input data, such as efficiencies, expenditures, and numbers of patients, students, cases, or worker-hours, and not about outcomes, such as quality, satisfaction, units of outputs per dollar of cost, accessibility, responsiveness, patient care, education of students, and service to the public. Calling this approach "The Grand Shaman," Amitai Etzioni notes, "Instead of hearing how many persons have stopped smoking, we learn how many antismoking clinics have opened. Or, instead of reading about a decline of pollutants in the air, water and land, we find a fuss over a rise in expenditures on depollution."[6]

The public at large must share the responsibility for misdirected MIS approaches to measurement along with administrators and data processing personnel. Only recently has pressure been brought to bear on accountability of nonprofit organizations for their performance.

Formulation of Purpose in MIS
The long-range decision-making aspect of MIS shown in Figure 18-1, formulation of purpose, draws upon diverse kinds of information unlikely to be processed by or stored in a computer. The kinds of information needed are assessments of environmental changes and the organization's ability to cope with these changes. The information is nonstandardized and often abstract, and the information sources are generally difficult to capture and are unstable.

The ideal information system to support the long-range decision making for purpose would be, as one author put it, "one with all a company's or society's resources contained on it, with input from the environment, and output to it, where the high-priest controller stood in front of the console adjusting the environment as he saw fit."[7] Essentially, what is asked at this level is that the open system discussed in Chapter 16 be put into a MIS. This, of course, is almost an impossible task. A major impediment is the high cost of capturing the necessary environmental input. "With present computer systems, humans participate in *translating* their event into an *input model* of that event—onto a piece of paper that will be key punched, read by an optical scanner, by keying in what they are doing, or have done, onto a terminal keyboard, and so on. The drawback is that this is very expensive."[8]

---

[6] Amitai Etzioni, "The Grand Shaman," *Psychology Today,* November 1972, p. 91.
[7] Brian Rothery, *The Myth of the Computer,* Business Books, London, 1971, p. 67.
[8] Ibid., p. 68.

There would be almost an infinite number of environmental inputs into the MIS, making the cost prohibitive. Even if technological advances brought the costs down to a tolerable level, there are doubts about how comprehensive an automated environmental sensing system could become. Because of environmental changes, a computerized sensing system that works at one point in time may be obsolete a short time later. Thus, unless the rapid rate of environmental change slows down, which is highly unlikely, accurate environmental sensing systems would be extremely difficult to design.

The primary sensory components currently available in the typical organization for determining purpose are top management. The chief operating executive generally spends large amounts of time, but most would argue not enough time, interacting with influential outsiders who dominate the organization's environment (suppliers, customers, competitors, regulatory officials, community leaders, labor leaders, bankers, politicians, and the public at large). For example, the reason for having a conference or lunch with one of the outsiders may be to discuss a short-range problem, but their exchanges also provide the chief executive with a better awareness of the outside or exogenous trends affecting the organization. Board members can serve the same function. Most directors sit on several boards, serve on governmental commissions, or perhaps serve as regents for a university. Such broad environmental exposure of board members can make valuable contributions to the MIS of the organization.

Besides top management and board members, most modern organizations can draw upon other highly educated and trained employees who have considerable knowledge about the outside environment. These employees can and should serve as sensory inputs for the MIS to keep up with the changing environment. The organization can encourage this process by a participative, open, upward communication system and by encouraging employee participation in professional organizations, community affairs, and continuing education.

Besides these human inputs, there is little else that the organization can do to systemize the collection and coding of environmental information. Yet, to improve MIS at this top level, an organization can identify (1) what its environment is, (2) which aspects of the environment are most critical to its success, and (3) what the organization is doing about sensing those critical aspects. Done on a systematic basis, these simple steps can improve MIS at the long-range, purpose level. Following the concepts of strategic planning discussed in Chapter 4 would help in this effort.

MIS Myths and Dysfunctional Applications

The "bandwagon" days of unchecked and unquestioned expansion of computer systems and electronic data processing in general have ended. In recent years, it has almost become the rule rather than the exception to find articles in the journals titled "The Myths of MIS," "Bad Decisions on Computer Use," and "MIS Is a Mirage." In *The Myth of the Computer* the author notes that "professional computer advisors all over the world are packing lecture halls hammering the same stern message home: " 'more than half,' 'more than 60 per cent,' and in some cases, 'more than 80 per cent of all computer installations are failures.' ''[9]

There are obviously a multitude of deficiencies in information systems and misdirected efforts by computer users. The major problems and pitfalls, however, seem to fit into three areas: (1) misassigned design responsibility, (2) misunderstood human factors, and (3) poor selection of projects. The following discussion is concerned with these three problem areas of MIS.

Problems in MIS Design

The head of the information systems department of a large manufacturer bluntly stated that every computer system developed in his otherwise successful company had been a failure—and there had been hundreds. They were failures, he reasoned, because they were worth less to the using departments than they cost. The major reason for this startling discovery was that the using departments had not played enough of a role in the system design. Instead, as is typical, the system design projects were always assigned to computer systems analysts who were knowledgeable in their specialty but knew virtually nothing about the problems confronting the using departments. In this case the company adopted a drastic but effective approach. System design was completely turned over to teams of users who were assembled for a period of up to 6 months at corporate head-quarters. For example, a marketing system team was formed of marketing managers from the company's plants and branches all over the country. They all moved temporarily to corporate headquarters and met on a daily basis to define their problems and decide how to solve them. When computer assistance seemed necessary and desirable, a computer systems analyst was called in to offer advice and help develop the appropriate informa-tion systems.

Bearing out the importance of user-manager involvement in computer operations are the results of an extensive survey conducted by the consulting firm McKinsey and Company. The sample in the study was composed of eighteen large firms that had proven them-selves to be "more successful" computer users and eighteen "less successful" users. Over 80 percent of the more successful users reported that their operating managers were usually involved in planning, staffing, and managing computer system design proj-ects; only a third of the less successful users reported this involvement.[10] It would seem that an effective MIS must involve users at the design stage.

Human Problems in MIS

Recently, a small team of university administrators and professors spent 6 months devel-oping a 5-year master plan for their computer system. A group of computer experts studying the completed 5-year projection was particularly disturbed over the lack of

[9] Ibid., p. 1.

[10] "Unlocking the Computer's Profit Potential," McKinsey, New York, 1968, p. 30.

coordination between the university's system and various other systems (state government, state colleges, and other universities in the area). The team director responded to the criticism by noting that although such interconnections are technologically simple today (to say nothing of 5 years from now), the administration of such linkages is extremely difficult. He explained that his team had recognized the problem and studied it carefully. However, they concluded that the intersystem management problems with budgets, staffing (programmers, installers, maintenance personnel, and managers), supplies, and equipment would prove to be almost insurmountable. The administrative problems of such a system would be much more difficult than the technical problems. This was true despite the genuine desire of the participating institutions to cooperate.

Another type of human problem, this one within the system itself, was brought out by Henry Mintzberg. He noted that informal channels of information are heavily relied upon by managers but are not incorporated into computerized MIS. While the formal computerized system is good at providing aggregated, precise, historical information, the modern manager generally needs rapid, speculative, and more current information. "Getting information *rapidly* appears to be more important to the manager than getting it absolutely *right*. This means that gossip, hearsay, and speculation constitute a large part of the manager's information diet. 'I have to sift about forty rumors every day,' said one manager."[11]

It should be noted that Mintzberg is not advocating seat-of-the-pants management. His prescription is for "an inbetween system, a formal MIS which will systematically process the information that the computer cannot now handle but that the manager now needs."[12] Ideally, all informal sources of information should be gleaned in a systematic fashion so that the information can become part of the MIS. In essence, MIS should be consistent with the human as well as the technical needs of managers.

Low- versus High-Payoff Projects for MIS
Even before the wide use of computers, punched-card equipment and other information-handling projects were aimed almost solely at routine payroll, invoicing, billing, and accounting projects. Since the computer, these types of projects have increased. The previously mentioned study by McKinsey and Company on computer usage suggested that it may be a mistake to computerize only these kinds of applications. One reason is that they generally are not troublesome problem areas needing computer assistance. In contrast, the logistics area of a typical film is likely to be much more troublesome and has a potential for high payoffs through computerization. This is also true of some of the marketing, shipping, purchasing, operations, and scheduling functions.

Emphasizing the other applications of computers does not imply that payroll and the other routine systems should not be computerized and will not pay off. In fact, there are two possible advantages of developing these systems early. First, the routine systems are easy to computerize because the decision rules are known and operations are generally

---

[11] Henry Mintzberg, "The Myths of MIS," *California Management Review,* Fall 1972, p. 95.
[12] Ibid., p. 97.

simple and highly repetitive. Second, they may be good projects—quick and easy—on which a newly assembled staff of analysts and programmers can gain valuable experience for more sophisticated systems.

The cost/benefit and cost-effectiveness analyses discussed in the last chapter can apply to MIS, but the following two general guidelines can also be helpful in determining the kind of MIS project that promises the higher payoff:

1 In the MIS hierarchy of Figure 18-1 in the first part of the chapter, the longer-range decisional functions are generally more vital and thus have a greater potential for a high payoff. Thus, resource planning has potentially a higher payoff from computerization than does computerizing routine areas like payroll. Computers used on the routine areas sometimes turn out to be very expensive typewriters.

2 On the other hand, there is a simpleminded adage in the computer field that "if you automate a poor system, you will have a poor automated system." Higher-order, longer-range systems tend to be poorer risks for computerization than the routine and repetitive lower-order systems.

The above two guidelines can be illustrated by a recently developed on-line computerized social service system of client referrals. This system represents automation of information processing at the lowest level, that of client and caseworker. According to the first guideline above, the welfare function might have gained a higher payoff for its money by developing a system at a higher level. For example, money could have been spent to develop a social service appraisal system using survey techniques to show how well each agency was serving the community and thereby show what social programs and agencies need more funding and support and which warrant less.

The on-line referral system perhaps did—or perhaps did not—violate the second guideline. The safest way to develop an automated system that works is to develop a manual system first and get the bugs out of it and then automate later. For the social services system, the precomputerization steps might have been to establish committees for interagency cooperation which in turn could have developed information packets for caseworkers and/or clients on types of services needed for different classes of clients. They also could have developed good manual files and telephone referral procedures and a radio-dispatched transportation service. All this could become the on-line computer system if and when the manual version proved to be working properly and if the payoff from automation appeared to significantly exceed the cost.

The guidelines can help an organization proceed along a cautious and fiscally responsible path toward effective computer MIS design. Such an approach is necessary to avoid the myths of MIS and the frequent dysfunctional applications of computer-based information systems.

Capacity of Computers and Their Role in the Future
So far the discussion of MIS has deliberately avoided direct background or comment on computers. MIS is much more than computers, but realistically no one can ignore their

importance to MIS, management, and society as a whole. Thus, this last part of the chapter is specifically devoted to the computer and its future role.

Development of Computers

The electronic digital computer has been commercially available for only about 20 years. However, its origin can be traced back to the work of the British mathematician Charles Babbage in the 1800s. He labored unsuccessfully some 40 years to build an analytical engine. The next major landmark in computer development was Herman Hollerith's tabulation device that was used in the 1890 United States census. His punched-card data processing device proved to be much easier and faster than manual methods. However, it was not until the 1940s that the first electronic computer was developed. The Electronic Numerical Integrator and Calculator or ENIAC was drawn from the genius of many men but was primarily designed by J. Presper Eckert and John W. Mauchly at the University of Pennsylvania. Dedicated in February 1946, the ENIAC consisted of forty-seven panels, each 9 feet high, 2 feet wide, and 1 foot thick. The story goes that the lights in West Philadelphia would dim when it was turned on. It was closely followed in 1951 by the UNIVAC, which was the first commercial electronic computer. Eckert and Mauchly were also responsible for this computer.

There have been three generally recognized generations of computers.[13] The first generation took place in the decade of the 1950s. These early computers were dominated by vacuum tube technology and depended upon punched-card and paper-tape inputs and had very limited memories. There were many growing pains with these early computers. Errors were relatively common, there was much downtime (ENIAC was down 30 percent of the time), and programming was very inflexible and tedious. The technological breakthrough which provided the impetus for second generation computers was the transistor. Around the beginning of the 1960s solid-state transistorized components replaced vacuum tubes in computer hardware. This greatly reduced the size of computers and resulted in much greater speeds. Magnetic tapes were also used much more with second-generation machines. In terms of software, new languages such as FORTRAN and CO-BOL simplified programming and led to many diverse applications. In the middle and late sixties, third-generation computers came on the market with hardware consisting of miniature, integrated circuits which further reduced the size of the computer and greatly increased the operating speed. Computer speeds are commonly measured in a billionth or even a trillionth of a second. The memory capacity of third-generation machines is much greater, and more flexibility is possible in programming and in expansion and conversion. Perhaps the most important capability of the third-generation computer is time sharing from remote terminals in real time. As noted by Hopeman, "Both card I/O [Input-Output] and magnetic tape I/O became unnecessary where these terminals were remote typewriters tied into the CPU [Central Processing Unit]. In such cases programs could be loaded on discs and recalled for use at any time by typing in the program name."[14]

---

[13] See Richard J. Hopeman, *Production,* 2d ed., Merrill, Columbus, Ohio, 1971, pp. 300–301.
[14] Ibid., p. 301.

Current Capacity of Computers

The fourth generation of computers has started to appear. These newest machines emphasize software (programming) rather than hardware. Through new software techniques such as heuristic programming and responding to ordinary voice and written English, the electronic computer is starting to take over activities formerly reserved for the human brain. For example, at MIT a computer can be told in written English to do a task normally performed by human beings and actually learn and improve its performance with each task. Cameron Hall observes, "Whereas up to now technology has extended or even taken over what men do with their physical equipment—their hands and eyes and legs—with our generation for the first time the computer is providing brain power."[15]

There are many pro and con arguments about the computer's capability to think. Albers after reviewing both sides, concludes the following:

Present-day computers can "think" in the sense that they have the capacity to make such logical choices. The programmer provides the instructions as to when and how a choice is to be made; the computer then automatically makes these choices as information is processed. . . . There would appear to be no absolute barrier to the development of computers that simulate the human thinking apparatus.[16]

Herbert Simon, the foremost researcher on artificial intelligence, is quoted in a recent *Wall Street Journal* article as saying, "I think you can say that the computer is now showing intuition and the ability to think for itself. Some of us don't see any principle or reason that would prevent machines from becoming more intelligent than man."[17]

The latest machines can see, hear, speak, and even sing. At Stanford University researchers have instructed a computer to assemble a water pump made up of three parts and six screws. Based on a television camera sending images of the pieces to the computer's memory, the computer directs a mechanical arm to grasp the pieces of the pump, assemble them, and screw them together. Bell Laboratory researchers have told computers to calculate job instructions and then speak them directly to an automatic recorder. Such computer job instructions have been effectively used on an assembly line in a large factory. These representative examples are only the beginning. The future capacity of computers seems almost unlimited.

Impact of Computers on Society

Although computers have had and will continue to have a tremendous impact on management, pehaps the greater impact will be on society itself. Many people are fearful that a "thinking" computer can damage society and even take over the world. At present, this possibility seems more like science fiction than reality. Computers like HAL 9000 in Stanley Kubrick's movie *2001—A Space Odyssey* are theoretically possible but not prob-

---

[15] Cameron P. Hall, *Technology and People,* Judson Press, Valley Forge, Pa., 1969, p. 27.

[16] Henry H. Albers, *Principles of Management,* 4th ed., Wiley, New York, 1974, pp. 283–284, 286.

[17] "I Am a Computer," *The Wall Street Journal,* June 28, 1973, p. 1.

able. The catch is that computers will never be capable of making a value decision (determine what is ethically right or wrong) unless human beings choose to live in a computer culture. It is hoped that the choice will be to live in a human rather than a computer culture. Society must ask itself not whether computers can do something but instead whether computers should be allowed to do something. This choice is up to human beings, not computers. The role of computers is becoming more a question of human values and morality than of technological feasibility.

A humanist viewpoint is very concerned with values such as freedom, individuality, and privacy. It is no wonder that computers with their accompanying data banks and automation are a societal concern. This concern carries over into modern organizations. Many managers are fearful of being replaced by a computer, and the recent Equity Funding Life Insurance Company scandal, referred to by the *Wall Street Journal* as the "first great computer fraud," deepens the fear and mistrust. Many managers fear that they are losing control to computers. This fear is certain to become more acute in the future as the potential efficiencies of computer system linkages become more visible and feasible.

Intersystem Computer Linkages

In the private sector a much-discussed use of computer linkages is that between supplier and user. The supplier-user interface typically occurs many times between raw material extraction (or growth) and ultimate purchase of products by consumers. Large organizations often have computerized inventory systems which print purchase orders when stocks are low. In a vertically integrated firm, such as a lumber company which owns everything from land and trees to wholesale and retail outlets, linking the supplier-user subsystems together can result in more efficient operations. Many of the delays and other dysfunctions can be eliminated. Nonvertically integrated competitors are at a distinct disadvantage. Obviously the suppliers and users would like to link their computers together.

A major impediment to intersystem linkages is antitrust laws. An intersystem linkage is similar to an actual merger between independent supplier and user firms. Thus, intersystem linkages violate antitrust laws which attempt to maintain a relatively free and competitive commercial environment.

Besides the issue of economic freedom and competition, there is the equally vital issue in the design of intersystem linkages of personal freedom and privacy. The following examples focus on this controversial issue of computerization. The issues revolve around technical feasibility and efficiency versus human values and ethics.

1 *Social Services* Various types of integrated computerized information systems are being considered, developed, or used by municipalities across the country to support the delivery of social services. One of the more advanced systems coordinates 600 social service facilities (schools, hospitals, welfare offices, and housing offices; voluntary organizations such as Lions' clubs and Boy and Girl Scouts; and even private physicians, attorneys, and business firms). Ninety-five of these service facilities are

connected by an on-line computer input and referral system, and the rest are handled by manual and batch data processing. A client who visits any of the ninety-five facilities on the computer is asked, regardless of the problem, for a standard twelve items of information. This personal information is typed at a visual display computer terminal. A data bank is searched, and the screen almost instantaneously displays whether or not the client has been served before; what services he or she has received; and a priority-ordered list of what services the client now needs to help move him or her toward nondependency. Radio-dispatched vehicles are available to take the client to the next facility after he or she is served by the admitting agency. Each client is surveyed 30 days later on the treatment received and how it changed the client's well-being. Computer printouts of survey results then go to caseworkers in the serving agencies.

2 *Banking* A bank wanted to cross-reference all the different accounts held by each customer. The management of the bank reasoned that if this could be done the bank would know things like whether a customer has funds in, say, a savings account when he or she is in arrears on payments in another account, such as a personal loan. Also, the bank could improve services to customers by offering automatic payments and transfers from account to account. It was decided to try to obtain Social Security numbers as the common data link from account to account (names were deemed to be undependable because of duplications). A problem, however, was that the management felt it did not dare to tell account holders why it wanted their Social Security numbers. The management felt that customers would consider the request an infringement on their personal privacy. It was finally decided to send, along with monthly statements, a stamped card to checking account holders asking them to verify account balances and to write in their Social Security numbers with no further explanation. A small number of account holders saw through the scheme and wrote indignant letters of refusal. However, most complied, and the bank was able to integrate most computerized accounts.

3 *Health* A large number of hospitals nationwide subscribe to the PAS–MAP (Professional Activity Study–Medical Audit Program). It is a computerized patient record processing system (there are other such systems) which is operated by the Commission on Professional and Hospital Activities. A very strong element in the public relations and promotional efforts of PAS–MAP is the assurance that individual patient data will never be reported and are protected against access. The system is intended to offer each hospital subscriber statistics on its costs of care, length of stay, usage of various services, etc., as compared with other subscribers within the same state and for the nation.

Although certain parts of the above three examples can be questioned from a humanistic, personal privacy, or ethical standpoint, there are some examples of more controversial misuses of computer systems. One that recently came to light was the U.S. Army's use of a data bank on certain nonmilitary people. The public outcry was not universal but was loud enough to force a halt to the practice. Another recent example was the proposed national credit bureau data bank. Many people were outraged because of the possibility of erroneous information, possible misuse, inaccessibility to affected citizens, and infringement of personal privacy.

Besides these obvious kinds of objections by the public at large, there is also an intellectual argument against data banks, information systems, and integrated computerization. The argument centers around the potential for computerization to make George Orwell's ominous book *1984* become a reality. The book itself is a fictional account of a futuristic society in which all citizens were under constant surveillance by telescreens, computers, and "thought police." Victor Zorza, a British expert on the communist world, wrote the following about the trends in national computer network development in the Soviet Union:

Already there is talk of a cable television system which could, with the aid of computers, switch into each home the kind of advertising message to which the particular recipient would be more likely to respond—like the mail advertising that is now differentiated according to what the advertiser knows of the consumer's needs. . . .

The new totalitarianism—the total control of the individual and of society—would have nothing of the Stalinist terror system about it. It would be more like Aldous Huxley's "Brave New World," whose benevolent rulers exerted themselves to ensure that the masses had all the consumer satisfaction, and spiritual fare, that should keep them contented—and compliant. [18]

There is little doubt that unless human beings make the appropriate value decisions, intersystem linkages could curb individual freedom and privacy as they are known today. By the same token, if the appropriate human value judgments are made, computers can be used to benefit and actually increase the freedom of human society.

Computer Efficiency versus Individual Privacy and Freedom

After years of trying to cope with society's miseries—poverty, crime, premature death, disease, illiteracy, degradation—it is frustrating to many people to see so few results. Brainpower, sympathy, technology, money—nothing seems to work. However, the arguments given by advocates of computerized referral systems for welfare or social service like the one cited in the last section are convincing. As one proponent noted,

The benefits that a system of this kind offers its clients are . . . obvious: guaranteed access to all services, vastly fewer problems with referral red tape, transportation and waiting rooms, and the accountability of a system being publicly judged by measurable criteria on whether or not it is actually changing clients' lives for the better.

The social benefits of a system of this kind are also obvious: reduced costs to taxpayers through significant increases in efficiency, and—for the first time—an online, instantly up-datable social indicator system for an entire city. [19]

Although such an argument has a lot of pragmatic logic, there is still the issue of efficiency versus individual privacy and freedom. The right to privacy and freedom is as valid

[18] Victor Zorza, "Computerizing Soviet Society," *Current,* September 1971, p. 29.
[19] From report presented to conference on Comprehensive Social Data Bank, Lincoln, Nebraska, November 14, 1973.

for those in need as for anyone else. But poverty, crime, and other social problems are very real as well.

On the other hand, as the earlier section on "myths" pointed out, computer systems are probably less efficient than is generally thought. In addition, some studies, such as a large-scale one sponsored by the National Science Foundation (NSF), indicate that computers have not yet endangered personal liberties to any significant extent in this country.[20] The study's conclusions are based on detailed on-site visits and follow-up contacts to fifty-five leading organizations of all kinds. Fourteen of the organizations are profiled in detail for the study report.[21]

Most of the organizations in the NSF study had instituted rather extensive procedures for protecting data bank records from loss or misuse. The Bank of America, for example, has a data security program that it estimates to cost a million dollars annually. When the Isla Vista branch bank was burned, the Bank of America was able to reconstruct customer accounts the next day from backup tapes that were updated to the last posting day and transported to remote off-premises storage locations.

Perhaps the best example of protecting privacy and freedom is the measures taken by the American Council on Education (ACE) to protect its extensive "behavioral research" data bank from unauthorized use. ACE has for many years been surveying attitudes, opinions, behavioral practices, etc., of over 200,000 college freshmen annually in about 300 participating colleges. The stored data are kept on magnetic tape and include names and addresses so that longitudinal research is possible. The students are surveyed at different points in their later lives to provide insight into the effects of early college experiences on later achievements and activities. Threatened by the possibility that the House Un-American Activities Committee (HUAC) would subpoena its records on certain student activists in the turbulent student revolts of the 1960s, ACE staffers developed the LINK data protection system. The purpose of this system was not necessarily to flout investigators but instead was to protect ACE's credibility with cooperating institutions and students. In the LINK system the magnetic tapes used in this country for producing statistically aggregated data contain identification numbers that can only be matched to names of surveyed students by use of a special LINK tape. The safety factor is that this tape is stored abroad. The ACE contract with a foreign research institution provides that not even ACE may automatically obtain the LINK tape. Some of the processing of new longitudinal survey data is actually done out of the country to protect it from subpoena.

---

[20] Alan F. Westin and Michael A. Baker, *Databanks in a Free Society: Computers, Record-Keeping and Privacy*, Report of the Project on Computer Databanks of the Computer Science and Engineering Board of the National Academy of Sciences, Quadrangle, New York, 1972.

[21] These organizations include Social Security Administration; FBI's National Crime Information Center; New York State Department of Motor Vehicles; Kansas City Police Department; the city of New Haven, Connecticut; Santa Clara County, California; Bank of America; TRW Credit Data Corporation; Mutual of Omaha; R. L. Polk and Company; Massachusetts Institute of Technology; American Council on Education; Church of the Latter-Day Saints; and Kaiser-Permanente Medical Care Program.

One of the more significant conclusions from the NSF study is that while "computerization has proceeded with great speed in the past decade, there has *not* been a similar acceleration in the development of new legal rules responding to demands for greater rights of citizen access to records, specification of limits on data collection, and rules controlling the sharing of personal data among organizational entities."[22] The report emphasizes that legislation and legal actions are overdue in these three areas and urges that further attention be given to improving technological safeguards, to gaining congressional attention to proper use of Social Security numbers as national citizen identifiers, and to the creation of information trust agencies whose function it would be to manage certain bodies of particularly sensitive personal data.[23]

Some of the proposals suggested by the NSF study have already been adopted in Sweden. This Scandinavian country has a new data bank control law, the world's first, which creates an information trust agency. The Swedish law provides for a nine-person data inspection board headed by a prominent jurist. The board has broad authority to rule on the appropriateness of government retention of personal records on private citizens and on establishment of private data banks as well.[24]

In the final analysis, there is little question that the computer will have more rather than less impact on individuals, organizations, and society as a whole. It is hoped that the proper safeguards will be established and that human decisions will be made to have the computer help achieve rather than deter achieving a fuller life for every human. Perhaps the best way to summarize the future impact of computers is the astute observation by one businessman who noted, "The greatest danger in modern technology isn't that machines will begin to think like men, but that men will begin to think like machines."[25]

Summary

This chapter narrowed down systems to the application of management information systems or MIS. Although an MIS does not have to be computerized, the electronic computer nevertheless plays the most significant role. MIS can be simply defined as regular or irregular information collection, reduction, storage, and dissemination. There is a hierarchy of application in every organization. From top to bottom there are long-, medium-, and short-range decision-making applications. The MIS applied in the long-range area attempts to help determine purpose, and the medium-range application is to help determine what kinds of products, services, and resources the organization should strive to attain. The short-range application of MIS is more directly concerned with the actual operations of the organization. The MIS at this operational level includes routine (pro-

---

[22] Westin and Baker, op. cit., p. 347.

[23] Ibid., p. 400.

[24] "Sweden Regulates Those Snooping Data Banks," *Business Week,* Oct. 6, 1973, pp. 93–95.

[25] Edward H. Weiss, quoted in "Care and Feeding of the Idea," *Printers' Ink,* June 14, 1963, p. 105.

grammable) and heuristic decision making and resource planning. Each of these applications has many functions for goal attainment but also many problems and dysfunctional applications. There are design problems (no involvement of users), human problems (lack of coordination and administration), and payoff problems. Besides the myths and dysfunctional applications of MIS, there is the whole question of the role of computers now and in the future. The present capacity of computers is almost unbelievable. Now going into the fourth generation, computers can see, hear, speak, and even sing. Although it is still controversial whether computers can actually think in the human sense, if thinking is defined as logical choice, most would agree that computers can indeed think. What the computer cannot do is make a human value judgment. The questions of intersystem linkages and computer efficiency versus individual privacy and freedom must still be scrutinized. However, the major challenge ahead is to make certain that computers are used to help and improve rather than hinder or replace human society.

☐ **Critical Incident**

Tom Nix is the head of the electronic data processing (EDP) section of a small insurance firm. Tom and his assistant, Jerry Peters, along with four keypunch operators and two secretaries make up the section. Tom has been the head of the section since it originated 17 years ago. Tom at first tried to keep up with the fast-growing computer field by attending short courses sponsored by computer manufacturers. He has not attended any of these for the past 5 years and is now waiting out retirement for 2 more years. Tom has mainly used the EDP section to send out premium notices. Jerry, his assistant, graduated from the university last year. Jerry had been a business adminstration major. Jerry was very disturbed that the EDP section was being underutilized. He could no longer hold back his concern, and so one day he said to the boss, "Tom, I think our computers are being used as very expensive typewriters. We should attempt to use our computers to provide more and better information to all managers in the home office and our salespeople in the field. This is what the purpose of our section should be, a management information system, not just a billing department." Tom slowly shook his head and replied, "Son, I've been in this computer game from the beginning. I know what they tell you in school and what the books say, but believe me it just doesn't work that way in practice. As far as I'm concerned, the computer has been and still is a big, dumb counting machine. It will only do what it is told to do. I'm afraid all this new talk about management information systems still falls under the category of GIGO—garbage in, garbage out."

1 How would you reply to the boss? Could you convince him of the need for a management information system approach after hearing his argument? How?

2 Analyze the statement, "The computer has been and still is a big, dumb counting machine. It will only do what it is told to do."

3 What do you think the role of the computer will be in management in the near future? What impact will the computer have upon society as a whole in the near future?

Questions for Review and Discussion

1 Define management information systems. What would be the characteristics of quality information provided by the MIS?

2 Summarize the MIS hierarchy. Analyze the contributions MIS can make to the various levels in the hierarchy.

3 What are some of the major myths and dysfunctional applications of MIS?

4 Briefly trace the development of computers and comment on their current capacity. What does the future hold for computers? What are some of the controversial issues surrounding computers now and in the future?

References

Adams, Carl R., and Roger G. Schroeder: "Managers and MIS: 'They Get What They Want, '" *Business Horizons,* December 1973, pp. 63–68.

Albers, Henry H.: *Principles of Management,* 4th ed., Wiley, New York, 1974.

Argyris, Chris: "Management Information Systems: The Challenge to Rationality and Emotionality," *Management Science,* February 1971, pp. B275–B292.

Berkeley, Edmund C.: "Barriers in Applying Computers," *Computers and Automation,* July 1972, pp. 24–25, 28–29.

Buckley, John W.: "The Empirical Approach to MIS Design," *Organizational Dynamics,* Autumn 1972, pp. 19–30.

Dearden, John: "MIS Is a Mirage," *Harvard Business Review,* January–February 1972, pp. 90–99.

Dobelis, M. C.: "Bridging the Gap between Computer Technicians and Users," *Management Review,* July 1974, pp. 28–33.

Emery, James C.: "An Overview of Management Information Systems," *Management Review,* July 1974, pp. 44–47.

Gallagher, Charles A.: "Perceptions of the Value of a Management Information System," *Academy of Management Journal,* March 1974, pp. 46–55.

Hall, Cameron P.: *Technology and People,* Judson Press, Valley Forge, Pa., 1969.

Hay, Leon E.: "What Is an Information System?" *Business Horizons,* February 1971, pp. 65–72.

Head, Robert V.: "The Elusive MIS," *Datamation,* Sept. 1, 1970, p. 29.

Kaufman, Felix: "On Understanding the Computer," *The Conference Board Record,* October 1974, pp. 52–58.

Kelly, W. E.: "Computer Systems: Slaves or Masters," *Management Accounting,* October 1971, pp. 9–11.

King, William R.: "The Intelligent MIS—A Management Helper," *Business Horizons,* October 1973, pp. 5–12.

Mintzberg, Henry: "The Myths of MIS," *California Management Review,* Fall 1972, pp. 92–97.

Nolan, Richard L.: "Computer Data Bases: The Future Is Now," *Harvard Business Review,* September–October 1973, pp. 98–114.

Peery, Newman S., Jr.: "General Systems Theory: An Inquiry into Its Social Philosophy," *Academy of Management Journal,* December 1972, pp. 495–510.

Plummer, John: "A Human Model for Computer Systems," *Business Horizons,* April 1971, pp. 35–43.

Powers, Richard F., and Gary W. Dickson: "MIS Project Management: Myths, Opinions, and Reality," *California Management Review,* Spring 1973, pp. 147–156.

Ross, Joel E.: "Computers: Their Use and Misuse," *Business Horizons,* April 1972, pp. 55–60.

Rothery, Brian: *The Myth of the Computer,* Business Books, London 1971.

Sanders, Donald H.: *Computers in Business,* 2d ed., McGraw-Hill, New York, 1972.

Weizenbaum, Joseph: "The Impact of the Computer on Society—Some Comments," *Computers and Automation,* July 1972, pp. 18–23.

Westin, Alan F.: "The Problem of Privacy and Security with Computerized Data Collection," *The Conference Board Record,* March 1974, pp. 31–34.

———— **and Michael A. Baker:** *Databanks in a Free Society: Computers, Record-Keeping and Privacy,* Quadrangle, New York, 1972.

Withington, Frederic G.: "Five Generations of Computers," *Harvard Business Review,* July–August 1974, pp. 99–108.

Chapter 19

Systems Variables and Contingency Management

In this last major chapter in the book, the full circle is completed. After the introductory chapters laid down the contingency framework, process, quantitative, behavioral, and systems variables in contingency management were presented. The concluding chapter in each major part attempted to contingently relate the environment to the management variables. Because contingency management is just getting underway, this task has proved to be relatively difficult. With some important exceptions, only surface; sketchy attempts can be made to functionally relate external and internal environment variables with management variables. This is especially the case in the systems area.

As pointed out in Chapter 2, there is a very fine line between the contingency and systems approach to management theory and practice. Yet, as Chapter 2 also pointed out, the contingency approach is more pragmatic than the systems approach. The systems approach merely recognizes the input of the environment and the interrelatedness and interdependency of the parts to the whole. The contingency approach, on the other hand, attempts to develop specific functional relationships between independent environmental variables and dependent process, quantitative, behavioral, and systems variables. The purpose of this chapter is to specifically as possible relate environmental variables with systems variables that were discussed in the three previous chapters.

The first two-thirds of the chapter analyzes the three most important and common aspects of all systems (complexity, interaction, and boundaries) from a contingency perspective. The last third of the chapter examines some specific contingency relationships for more effective management. As in the concluding chapters in the other major parts of the book, a realistic case is included for the reader to analyze and discuss systems variables in a contingency management framework.

Systems Complexity

Most systems that management must deal with are extremely complex. An academic department in a university, an advertising department in a large retail chain, social services in a welfare agency, and inventory control in a manufacturing plant are all complex systems. Because of this complexity, the systems approach to management faces a dilemma. GST emphasizes the importance of studying the whole. Yet, GST also recognizes that the whole is made up of interacting and interdependent subsystems. Systems experts such as Russell Ackoff suggest that each of these interacting subsystems requires study in its own right.[1] But when a complex system is broken down into its subsystems for study and analysis, the whole is sometimes lost sight of. Thus, a dilemma results. On the one hand, systems are generally too complex to study and meaningfully analyze as a whole; on the other hand, if the system is broken down into more manageable subsystems, the perspective of the total system is often sacrificed.

Fragmenting Complex Systems

The solution to the dilemma posed above is not simple. However, a contingency approach can help. First of all, despite the ideal of GST concentrating only on the whole, pragmatically there seems little doubt that most systems must be broken down into subsystems for analysis. The process of breaking down complex systems is called fragmentation in systems analysis.[2]

An example of systems fragmentation is a computerized inventory control system. It soon becomes evident that this target system is too complex to analyze as a whole, and so it must be fragmented. The computerized inventory control system must be broken down into its elementary tasks for meaningful analysis. The analyst may break the system down into such elementary tasks as counting stock on hand by making the appropriate entries into the data base, making entries into the data base to record sales or orders, developing data collection forms for use in data processing, and even dusting off the boxes of computer printout paper before placing them into the computer room. By fragmenting the inventory control system in this manner, the analyst is attempting to identify all the subsystems.

One of the biggest problems facing systems analysis is that there may be too much fragmentation. In the inventory control example, dusting off the computer printout paper may be unnecessary fragmentation. All systems can be broken down into excessively minute parts. For example, a system can be subdivided all the way down into atoms or even electrons or protons. But for most management systems, the fragmentation does not need to be so fine. If there is too much fragmentation, the *total* system perspective is lost.

A goal for contingency management is to identify the environmental conditions which would indicate the amount of system fragmentation that should take place for more effective goal attainment. Such a contingency relationship (environmental variables which would be the independent variables and the degree of system fragmentation which would be the dependent variable) would help solve the systems complexity dilemma.

---

[1] Russell L. Ackoff, "Systems, Organizations, and Interdisciplinary Research," in Donald P. Eckman (ed.), *Systems: Research and Design,* Wiley, New York, 1961, p. 28.

[2] James C. Emery, *Organizational Planning and Control Systems: Theory and Technology,* Macmillan, New York, 1969, pp. 9–10.

Contingency Management Applied to a Complex System

In the inventory control system cited above, suppose that the technological environment was such that computerization dictated that only third-level fragmentation was necessary for effective goal attainment (improved inventory control leading to lower costs and higher profits for a manufacturing plant). The established contingency relationship would be: if there is computerized technology, then third-level system fragmentation will lead to the most effective analysis for inventory control. Once this contingency relationship is determined, then the analysis of the complex system could proceed as follows:

1 The data entry tasks of counting stock and recording sales and orders could be combined into one subsystem-data entry at the third level.
2 Minute tasks like dusting the computer paper could become a subsystem (third level) of a second-level subsystem called maintenance.
3 The contingency relationship would indicate that fourth-level fragmentation would not be necessary for effective analysis.
4 If the analysis determined that the strategic subsystem was data entry, then the other subsystems such as maintenance could be treated as "black boxes." (A "black box" in systems analysis recognizes the existence of the subsystem but does not explain its inner workings; it is left untouched by the systems analyst.)
5 In the future, the environmental contingencies could be identified that would help pinpoint the data entry problem of the inventory control system.

Figure 19-1 illustrates the fragmentation of the inventory control system into the various levels. The contingency framework is suggested as being helpful in predicting the appro-

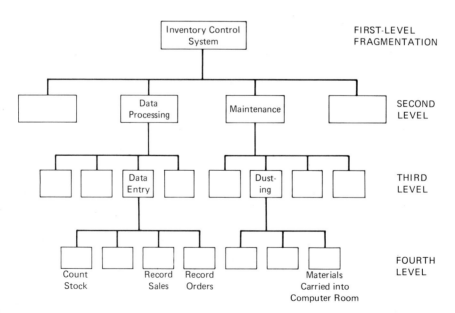

Figure 19-1 Levels of Systems Fragmentation.

priate degree of system fragmentation. By identifying the environmental contingencies (technological in the inventory control example), the dilemma facing complex systems analysis (the whole versus fragmentation) can begin to be solved.

Systems Interaction

Interaction is one of the most vital aspects of GST and plays an important role in systems analysis and management information systems. Emery explains that systems interactions are the result of *coupling* between units through their inputs and outputs.[3] Each subsystem, as it performs its own function, generally must depend on other subsystems to perform their specific functions in some designated manner. For example, the dietetic department of a hospital must depend on other subsystems such as purchasing and nursing service to perform its function properly. The coupling takes place when the output from one subsystem becomes the input into another subsystem.

Major Types of Couplings

There are three major types of interaction or coupling that take place in most systems. Figure 19-2 summarizes the serial, parallel, and feedback couplings. In serial coupling, subsystem A interacts with B and B in turn interacts with C. In other words, A is coupled serially with B and B is coupled serially with C. In the parallel form, A is directly coupled with two or more subsystems (B and C in the figure). Feedback coupling can be either immediate or indirect. In immediate feedback, A is coupled with B, which is then coupled back to A. In the indirect case, A interacts or is coupled with B, which in turn interacts with C and is fed back to A. In a sense, B is ultimately coupled back to A through C.

Systems in practicing organizations involve all three types of couplings. The couplings of the numerous subsystems become a very complex pattern of interdependence. Typically the activities and functioning of any one subsystem have a great impact on the activities and functioning of many other subsystems. Important from a contingency standpoint is the fact that not all couplings are internal to the organization. For example, Emery carefully points out that interactions may be transmitted through a common environment.

In other words, all coupling need not be internal to the system. For example, one product department of a decentralized company may engage in practices that harm the reputation of the entire company, affecting the sales of all other departments. External agents such as customers, labor unions, competitors, and the government can all serve as channels for transmitting interactions among organizational units.[4]

Determining the interactions between operating subsystems and both the external and internal environment should be a major goal of contingency management.

[3] Ibid., p. 22.
[4] Ibid., pp. 22–23.

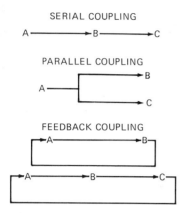

SERIAL COUPLING

PARALLEL COUPLING

FEEDBACK COUPLING

Figure 19-2 Types of Couplings in Systems. *Source:* James C. Emery, *Organizational Planning and Control Systems,* Macmillan, New York, 1969, p. 22.

Coordinating Systems Interactions

To improve managerial effectiveness, the coordination between interacting subsystems and the relationship to external environmental influences must be accomplished. The management process variables of planning, organizing, communicating, directing, and controlling play a major role in such a coordination effort. For example, a functional organization structure can reduce the problem of coordinating interacting subsystems by grouping together all those using a common resource. A project organization structure, on the other hand, would be more appropriate for an autonomous operation that does not require coordinated activities with functional units in other projects. The contingency framework could be used to determine the environmental variables that would functionally relate to the appropriate structural arrangements. By determining if-then relationships between the environment and the management process variables, the coordination problem between subsystem couplings can be minimized. Chapter 8 suggested some contingency relationships that could help in such an effort.

Systems Boundaries

The systems concept of boundaries, like systems complexity and interactions, can be discussed in terms of the contingency approach. The boundary concept is used to separate the system from its external environment. Contingency management attempts to relate the environment to the appropriate management variables for effective goal attainment; systems boundaries are merely used to *separate* and *distinguish* the environment from the system in question. However, by identifying the systems boundaries, both contingency and systems management can benefit.

Boundaries for Open and Closed Systems

The concept of systems boundaries is important to the distinction between open and closed systems. A closed system operates totally within precise boundaries, and these boundaries are impenetrable. The external environment does not affect the workings of the closed system. The open system, on the other hand, has unclear boundaries and receives much input from the external environment and transmits outputs back into the environment. The open-system boundaries are permeable; they can be penetrated. However, it should be remembered that *open* and *closed* are only conceptual terms. In reality, at least in management, systems are relatively open or closed. There are no absolutes.

In the past, closed-system thinking dominated management theory and practice. The external environment was given little if any attention. However, as Chapter 2 pointed out, open-systems thinking and analysis is very closely related to contingency management. Both recognize the important role that the external environment plays in management. The difference is that the open-systems approach merely recognizes environmental input and, at best, attempts to identify and describe; the contingency approach determines functional if-then relationships between the environment and the inner workings of the system.

Boundary Analysis

Open systems with permeable boundaries are obviously much more complex and difficult to analyze than closed systems with impenetrable boundaries. The uncertainties of environmental inputs make the separation and identification of open-system variables difficult if not impossible. This is where the determination of contingent relationships could greatly improve open-systems analysis. The establishment of if-then relationships could provide the bridge between nebulous recognition of environmental input and effective open-system analysis leading to more effective management.

Environmental Suprasystem

Management must recognize that systems boundaries can be penetrated. There are few, if any, completely closed systems in modern organizations. In systems terminology, the general and specific external environments identified in Chapter 3 are known as the environmental suprasystem. Figure 19-3 identifies the boundaries for subsystems, systems, and suprasystems.

In the figure, A and B represent subsystems of C, and D and E are subsystems of F. Thus, C could be thought of as the suprasystem of A and B, and F as the suprasystem of D and E. A more representative suprasystem though would be G for the systems C and F. For example, suppose C and F are two industrial organizations. A may be the production department and B the marketing department in plant C. In plant F, D may be the finance department and E the personnel department. The suprasystem for the functional departments is the plant organization as a whole. This would be equivalent to the internal environment discussed in Chapter 3. In other words, the suprasystem outside the bound-

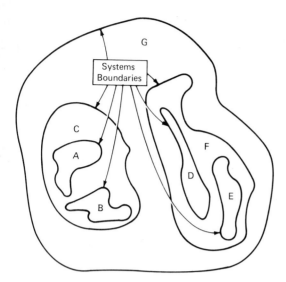

Figure 19-3 Subsystems, Systems, and Suprasystems.

aries of the functional departments would consist of structure, processes, and technology. However, the external environment is generally more closely associated with suprasystems. Thus, outside the plant boundaries would be both the general (social, economic, political/legal, and technological) and specific (customers, suppliers, and competitors) environments.

If the functional departments and plants were closed systems, the boundaries shown in Figure 19-3 would be impregnable. But the fact is that both the functional and plant systems boundaries are penetrable. The internal environment affects the functional departments of an organization, and the general and especially the specific environment influence and have an input into the organizational system. The systems can be viewed as closed for ease of analysis, but the challenge for modern management is to recognize and cope with the organization and its major subsystems as open systems. The contingency approach can give some order and direction to open-systems analysis.

Specific Contingency Relationships

The discussion so far has only dealt with a contingency approach to broad systems characteristics of complexity, interactions, and boundaries. Now attention turns to specific contingency relationships between environmental variables and systems variables. Similar to the contingency relationships for process, quantitative, and behavioral variables, there are very few empirically determined if-then statements for systems variables.

Only a few attempts have been made to establish functional relationships between environmental *if*'s and systems *then*'s.

Contingency Relationships with Practicing Systems

One approach in determining contingency relationships would be to relate changes in the environment with changes in practicing management systems in modern organizations. Such an approach does not follow the contingency model of Chapter 2 because the dependent variables are systems changes rather than systems concepts and techniques leading to effective goal attainment. Nevertheless, giving examples of the impact general and specific external environmental changes have on practicing systems can provide useful insights for modern management.

Figure 19-4 gives examples of systems adjustments to each of the general and specific external environmental factors that were identified in Chapter 3. The examples do not represent if-then statements for more effective management but rather are intended to illustrate systems reaction and adjustment to the external environment. To date, very little

Figure 19-4 Systems Adjustments to the External Environment

External Environment	Example	System Adjustment
General		
Shift in societal values	Movie studio shifts from shooting epic pictures in Hollywood to art movies filmed on location	Size of production function reduced and move toward project structures
Economic recession	An automobile manufacturer moves from semiluxurious cars to low-priced economy cars	The marketing function now stresses economy rather than luxury
A legal decision	Paper company forced to purify water discharged into a lake	Purification equipment is installed, and the processing system is redesigned
Technological innovation	A firm switches from vacuum tubes and hand wiring to transistors and printed circuit boards	The quality control system moves from visual inspection to automatic feedback (cybernation)
Specific		
Changes in supply	Razor blade company is cut off from Rhodesian chrome suppliers and must use lower-grade Turkish chrome	Added metal processing and more quality control
Change in customer demand	Furniture manufacturer experiences high demand for low-cost stereo cabinets and little demand for custom cabinets	Production system moves from process layout to product layout
Change in competition	Newspaper publisher's subscriptions increase due to a competitor going out of business	Increase in plant, equipment, and labor force

Source: Adapted from Richard B. Chase and Nicholas J. Aquilano, *Production and Operations Management,* Irwin, Homewood, Ill., 1973, p. 627.

has been done to empirically relate environmental conditions with appropriate systems concepts and techniques that lead to goal attainment. The remainder of the chapter suggests some possible contingency relationships that do or may exist with GST, systems design and analysis, and MIS concepts and techniques.

Contingency Approach to GST

GST is applicable to accomplishing the goal of a common, unified philosophy of science. GST can pull together what the diverse scientific disciplines have in common. As the complexity of the environment increases, GST concepts stressing the interrelatedness and interdependency of the parts to the whole become increasing important to management. In contingency terms, if the environment is extremely complex, then GST perspectives of organization and management should be utilized.

Some of the indirect aspects of GST in relation to a contingency approach were already discussed under system complexity, interactions, and boundaries. However, in specific if-then terms it could be stated that if there is a definite external environmental impact on the system, then open-systems concepts should be used. A more specific example would be that if there is a service type of technology (has much influence from the external environment), then open-systems planning should be used.[5] On the other hand, if the environment plays a minimal role in a system, then closed-system concepts should be used. More precisely, if there is a highly automated, computerized technology, then a cybernated control system is appropriate.

Contingency Approach to Systems Design and Analysis

More specific applications of contingency management can be made to systems design and analysis than can be made to GST. In systems organization designs, several if-then relationships have been fairly well established. For example, if there is an advanced-technology, large and complex operation with a definite closure, then a project or matrix organization design is most appropriate. An example using specific systems techniques would be: if environmental complexity lends itself to the need for integration of organizational goals with financial controls, then the planning-programming-budgeting system is appropriate. Other possible contingency relationships in the systems design and analysis area could include:

1 If there is a complex and unique environment, then cost-effectiveness analysis would be appropriate.

2 If there is a unique but relatively noncomplex environment, then capital budgeting would be appropriate.

3 If there is a complex but familiar environment where desired outcomes are not clearly definable, then systems simulation techniques are desirable.

---

[5] Open-systems planning was identified in Chapter 15 as a specific technique that is used in modern organization development.

4 If there is a noncomplex and familiar environment, then work measurement techniques would be effective.

This list is not intended to be exhaustive, and the general and specific environment is stated in only very broad terms of complexity, uniqueness, and familiarity. The goal of contingency management in the future will be to develop more precise, empirically derived relationships between more specific environmental variables and systems design and analysis concepts and techniques.

Contingency Approach to Management Information Systems

Contingently relating environmental conditions with MIS concepts and techniques has been given relatively more attention than either GST or systems design and analysis. For example, Jay Galbraith noted that "the greater the task uncertainty, the greater amount of information that must be processed among decision makers during task execution in order to achieve a given level of performance."[6] He carefully points out that it is not uncertainty per se that is important to effective management but rather information processing during task execution. He cites the problem in an automobile assembly line as follows:

Here the work is divided into thousands of highly interdependent subtasks. The line produces many diverse models and sizes, and it runs at a high level of efficiency. The result is that when decisions are made about rate of production or model mix, the impact of that decision on every job must be taken into account. This is a complicated decision known as the assembly line balancing problem. However, if customer demand, labor skills, and technology are predictable, there is little information to be processed after the line has been balanced.[7]

The last sentence in Galbraith's example has important contingency implications for MIS.

Besides the sophisticated analysis of the contingency aspects of MIS provided by organization theorists such as Galbraith, more specific if-then statements can also be determined. For example, if there is a complex environment requiring a very comprehensive MIS, then attention should be given to measuring outputs (adaptability, profit, service, quality, satisfaction, or growth) as opposed to inputs (the needed resources). However, like the other areas of systems as well as the other areas of management in general, considerable work is needed in the future to develop specific contingency relationships between environmental conditions and MIS concepts and techniques.

Summary

Similar to the concluding chapters in the other major parts of the book, this chapter attempted to relate the systems variables discussed in the preceding chapters in this last part of the book to contingency management. Because systems management and contin-

---

[6] Jay Galbraith, *Designing Complex Organizations,* Addison-Wesley, Reading, Mass., 1973, p. 4.
[7] Ibid, p. 5.

gency management are so close conceptually and because of the lack of empirical research linking the external environment with systems concepts and techniques, the chapter is limited to only a fairly general discussion.

The first two-thirds of the chapter discussed the contingency implications of systems complexity, interrelatedness, and boundaries. These three aspects were selected not only because they are vital to the systems approach but also because they can be put into a contingency framework. For instance, contingency management was suggested for helping solve the systems complexity dilemma. Contingency relationships could be developed that determine the degree of system fragmentation necessary for effective goal attainment. The same is true of systems interaction or coupling. The determination of the couplings (serial, parallel, or feedback) between operating subsystems of an organization and both internal and external environments falls right in line with a contingency management approach. Systems boundaries were discussed primarily with reference to open and closed systems. If the boundary can be penetrated by the external environment, then the system becomes open. Such "openness," of course, is a major assumption made by contingency management. Determining if-then contingency relationships can lend scientific direction to accumulating meaningful insights into more effective management of open systems.

The last third of the chapter suggested some actual if-then statements that could be made about systems variables. One approach was to specify, by way of realistic examples, the impact that external environment (both general and specific) had on practicing systems. Such an approach provides insights but is not part of the contingency management approach per se. The dependent variables are not systems concepts and techniques leading to effective goal attainment but instead are merely reactions and adjustments to the external environment. More direct contingency approaches to GST, systems design and analysis, and MIS yielded at least some tentative if-then statements. Independent environmental variables are functionally related to dependent systems concepts and techniques. The need for the future is to develop more if-then relationships in the systems area and all other management areas discussed in the book. The next chapter specifically pinpoints these challenges.

Questions for Review and Discussion

1 What is a major dilemma facing the systems approach? How can a contingency approach help solve this dilemma?

2 What is meant by the concept of coupling in systems? What are the major types of couplings that can take place in a system?

3 Explain the concept of systems boundaries. How does the concept relate to open and closed systems? How does the concept relate to contingency management?

4 Briefly summarize and analyze how the contingency approach can be applied to GST, systems design and analysis, and MIS.

References

Cleland, David I., and William R. King (eds.): *Systems, Organizations, Analysis, Management: A Book of Readings,* McGraw-Hill, New York, 1969.

Dutton, John M., and William H. Starbuck (eds.): *Computer Simulation of Human Behavior,* Wiley, New York, 1971.

English, J. Morley: *Cost-Effectiveness: The Economic Evaluation of Engineered Systems,* Wiley, New York, 1968.

Fertakis, John, and John Moss: "An Introduction to PERT and PERT/Cost Systems," *Managerial Planning,* January–February 1971, pp. 24–31.

Hare, Van Court: *Systems Analysis: A Diagnostic Approach,* Harcourt, Brace & World, New York, 1967.

Levin, Richard I., and Charles A. Kirkpatrick: *Planning and Control with PERT/CPM,* McGraw-Hill, New York, 1966.

Li, David H. (ed.): *Design and Management of Information Systems,* Science Research, Chicago, 1972.

McMillan, Claude, and Richard F. Gonzales: *Systems Analysis: A Computer Approach to Decision Models,* 3d ed., Irwin, Homewood, Ill., 1973.

Michaels, Andrew J.: "Establishing a PERT System," *Management Accounting,* October 1971, pp. 26–32.

Novick, David: *Program Budgeting,* Holt, New York, 1969.

Quade, E. S.: "Principles and Procedures of Systems Analysis," in E. S. Quade and W. I. Boucher (eds.), *Systems Analysis and Policy Planning,* American Elsevier, New York, 1968.

Roy, Herbert J. H.: "Using Computer-based Control Systems for Decision Making," *S.A.M. Advanced Management Journal,* January 1971, pp. 57–62.

Schonberger, Richard J.: "Custom-tailored PERT/CPM Systems," *Business Horizons,* December 1972, pp. 64–66.

Shell, Richard L., and David F. Stelzer: "Systems Analysis: Aid to Decision Making," *Business Horizons,* December 1971, pp. 67–72.

Case Study for Part Five
"Read All about It"

In Lake City the *Capital Journal* is the only surviving newspaper in town. One competitor went under 17 years ago, and the other succumbed last year. Despite the fact that Lake City is the capital of the state and one of the region's largest urban centers (175,000 population), the *Journal* is also in trouble. The president of the paper, Jacob Harwood, comes from a well-known publishing family. His great grandfather founded the *Journal* over a hundred years ago. The Harwoods are one of the most prominent families in Lake City and the entire state.

Jacob had started at the *Journal* as a reporter fresh out of college with a journalism major and at the age of 47 became president and executive head of the paper. When he took over, the operation was very profitable and in good financial condition. Now 10 years later the paper is facing a financial crisis. Jacob's father, Harold, who is seventy-two years old, was the preceding president and now serves in the capacity of chairman of the board. Harold and his second wife, Marie, winter in Florida, and about his only involvement with the running of the paper is his attendance at the four board meetings held every year. However, after reading the latest financial report, he became extremely upset with his son. For the life of him, Harold couldn't understand why the paper was in such bad shape. The old man reasoned that the *Journal* obtained a virtual monopoly when the only competitor went under last year and that Lake City was a growing city with one of the highest per capita incomes in the nation. The only conclusion he could draw was that the paper was being mismanaged.

After listening to his father's angry words, Jacob was both hurt and puzzled. Maybe the problem was mismanagement. He had always followed a practice of decentralized management with the staff of the *Journal*. The major functional areas did pretty much their "own thing." He devoted most of his efforts to community service. He was president of the chamber of commerce and served on numerous civic committees. Maybe he had not been "tending the store," as his dad was now accusing him. Jacob resolved to turn over a new leaf and get to the bottom of the problem as quickly as possible. He was not going to let something that had taken the family nearly a century to build go down the drain.

Jacob called an emergency meeting of his top staff (the editor, controller, production manager, advertising manager, and circulation manager). Jacob started off the meeting with a stern tone that he had not used before. "Gentlemen, as you know, or at least I hope you know, the paper is in very bad shape. I have had a financial analysis made of costs and revenues by our public accounting firm, and the alarming results are in the report that Alice is handing out to you now. Frankly, after going over this report last night, I have concluded that if we don't come up with some solutions to our problems pretty quick, I don't see how we can avoid shutting our doors within 1 year to 18 months. We are in pretty bad shape. What I am going to ask you is to take this report, study the facts, and meet again in 2 weeks. At that time, I want each of you to be prepared to discuss what the problems really are and, more important, what the solutions are. I hope I don't have to emphasize the importance of this effort. We must work this thing out for the sake of the community, our employees, our families, and ourselves."

After 2 weeks had passed, Jacob called the meeting to order. Jacob started off the meeting by saying, "Well gentlemen, I trust you have studied the report. What is the problem and what are the solutions?"

The production manager was the first to speak. "I would like to start off by saying that the report shows our production costs are way too high. I agree, but I truly believe it is not our fault. How in the world can I be expected to do adequate plannning and run a more efficient operation when I can't get the supplies I need? The newsprint problem is the best example. I can't get a firm commitment from our major supplier, and the other suppliers won't even talk to me. This past month we received only 85 percent of our order, and next month they indicate we're going to be lucky to get 75 percent. When I complain, they tell me to be careful or I won't get any. They also tell me to expect higher prices on the next order. The only alternative I have is to go to the local print shops and buy some of their inventory. I have worn out my welcome with them, and their prices are skyrocketing. With such a supply problem the only solution I see is to cut back on the amount of newsprint we are using. I know this will hurt, but I don't see that there is any other choice."

The editor spoke next. "I have studied the report also and realize that there are rising costs of production. But we just can't cut back on the size of the newspaper. For example, I feel to keep up the demand for our newspaper we need more, not fewer, feature stories. When we drop anything, there are all kinds of complaints, and we are constantly bombarded with suggestions for new features. The same goes for news; the TV stations are already offering stiff competition. If we cut back on our features or our news coverage, we could end up with a paper that no one wants to buy. Then where would we be? I don't have a solution to the production cost problem, but it is not to cut back on features and news."

The advertising manager then broke in and said, "The same is true of advertising. We couldn't possibly cut back on our advertising space. As the report clearly indicated, the majority of our revenues are currently coming from advertising. Obviously, we need more revenue. The only way I can see to get it is to have more advertising accounts, which of course takes more newsprint. We have our present advertisers backed up against a wall. They won't stand for another increase in rates. A couple have already closed their accounts and have gone to radio and TV."

Next came the circulation manager, who said, "Let me get in my two cents. Speaking of revenues, I'd like to remind everyone that it is the number of paid subscribers which attracts our advertisers, and of course our subscribers' payments have a significant impact on total revenues. If we lose subscribers by dropping features and skimping on news coverage, we might as well close down next month instead of next year. We could charge higher subscription rates, but I am convinced that our readers wouldn't stand for it; they would cancel their subscriptions. Besides, we may have a big drop in subscription anyway because of the recent Interstate Commerce Commission ruling. The ICC allowed the railroad to discontinue service to the Brighter area. The Postal Service uses that run to carry the *Journal* to 3,775 of our subscribers. The Postal Service is going to have to use trucks to distribute the mail in that area, and I've heard through the grapevine that an efficiency study revealed that the Postal Service could make considerable cost savings by going to the small towns only two or three times a week. If this comes about, our daily paper loses its appeal to these surrounding towns, and they will switch to their local weeklies. I think our only solution is to buy some more trucks and make the daily deliveries ourselves."

Jacob scratched his head and with a concerned look on his face said, "Why in the world didn't you guys tell me some of these problems before. My door has always been open to you! I just hope it is not too late to save the newspaper."

Questions for Analysis:

1 Is it too late to save the newspaper? What do you think the major problems are? What are your solutions?

2 Describe some of the GST, systems design and analysis, and MIS implications in this case.

3 Describe some of the external (general and specific) environmental impacts on this newspaper company. Is this an open or closed system? Why?

4 How could contingency management be applied to this case? What would be some possible if-then relationships using external environment *if*'s and systems concepts and techniques *then*'s?

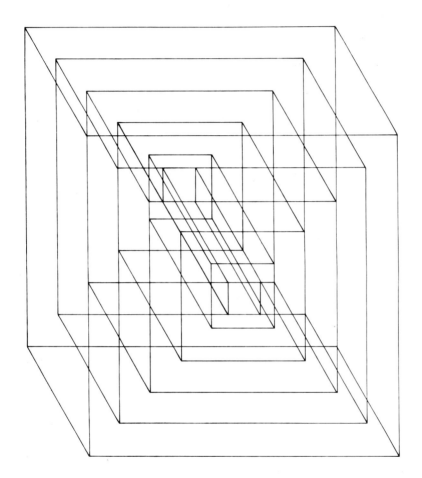

Chapter 20

Summary and the Future Development of Contingency Management

The preceding chapters have attempted to take the best from the past and present so that it can be projected into the future. Many will argue that a contingency approach has merit but is a bit ahead of its time. This type of criticism would seem to be very good for the future prospects of contingency management. A major goal of the book is to contribute to and perhaps change the future course of management. The opening paragraph of Alvin Toffler's book *The Futurists* provides the reasoning for striving for such a goal. He states, "If we do not learn from history, we shall be compelled to relive it. True. But if we do not change the future, we shall be compelled to endure it. And that could be worse."[1]

Toffler's observation seems to apply especially to the field of management. Its future development cannot afford to ignore the past. Much can be learned from the process, quantitative, behavioral, and systems approaches to management. They all have contributed and will definitely continue to contribute to the advancement of management theory and practice. However, with the increasing environmental influence on management theory and practice, the field can no longer afford to just endure the future. It seems imperative to change the future course of management by conceptually integrating the environment and by providing empirically derived, pragmatic guidelines for the more effective practice of management. The contingency approach can learn from the past and can benefit from the further development of the other approaches, but, at the same time, can accomplish the very real needs for the future.

The first half of this final chapter gives a very brief overview of contingency management as presented in this book. The last half identifies and analyzes some of the critical challenges for the future development of contingency management. In other words, the first half attempts to give the "big picture," and the second half states some challenges that need to be met for further development of the contingency approach.

An Overview of Contingency Management

Contingency management was presented in this book in five major parts. The first part gave the historical background, presented the conceptual framework for contingency

[1] Alvin Toffler (ed.), *The Futurists*, Random House, New York, 1972, p. 3.

management, and summarized the major categories of the general and specific environments affecting the management of today's organizations. The second through fifth parts of the book presented the major concepts and techniques from the process, quantitative, behavioral, and systems approaches to management. The concluding chapter in each of these parts attempted to place the concepts and techniques that were discussed into the contingency framework. Specific if-then relationships were formulated where possible.

Historical Perspective

A historical foundation is a necessity for understanding and applying contingency management. As the opening comments in this chapter suggested, there is much that can be learned from studying the history of management. The practice of management, of course, has been in existence as long as human beings have attempted to attain goals through organized effort. There are numerous examples of effective management practice in antiquity. For example, the success of the ancient Egyptian, Hebrew, Chinese, and Greek civilizations was in large part due to effective management. However, although the practice of management has been around since the beginning of civilization, the theory of management had its beginnings in feudalism, preindustrialized commerce, and most importantly, industrialization.

The schools of theoretical thought can be summarized into the process, quantitative, behavioral, and systems approaches. These approaches represent theoretical conceptualizations of what management is all about. Numerous concepts and techniques are associated with each approach. However, with the important exception of the relatively recent open-systems approach, these theoretical approaches either ignored or assumed away the environment. Furthermore, in recent times, these theoretical approaches have been moving further and further away from the practice of management. By making universal assumptions, the advocates of each approach have in many cases lost touch with reality. In this regard, Joseph McGuire has observed that in recent years many management scholars have become deeply involved with methodology rather than content. "Many modern professors, oriented toward mathematics, computers, and the behavioral sciences, abandoned the study of management *per se,* and many of them came to believe that their mission, even indirectly, had little to do with the preparation of students for a managerial career."[2]

Up to the last few years, the omission of the environment in management theory was tolerable. However, now with a new professionalism emerging in management, the expanding scope of management, and, most significantly, the sheer impact that the environment itself is having on management, there is a definite need to incorporate the environment into management theory. The same holds true for bringing management theory back to management practice. Especially the older process approach gave very few empirically validated guidelines for the practice of management. However, as indicated by

[2] Joseph W. McGuire (ed.), *Contemporary Management,* Prentice-Hall, Englewood Cliffs, N.J., 1974, p. 640.

the quote from McGuire, the same holds true of the newer approaches. The quantitative, behavioral, and systems approaches in recent years have moved further and further away from management practice. The current situation is that the process approach, because of the universal assumptions, is no longer adequate for modern practice and the newer quantitative, behavioral, and systems theories are making very little attempt whatsoever to relate to practice. The time is ripe for integrating the environment into management theory and bringing management theory back to management practice. The contingency approach to theory and practice can accomplish these two important objectives.

The Conceptual Framework for Contingency Management

The essence of the contingency approach is that the environment is functionally related to management. Specifically, contingency management is concerned with the relationship between relevant environmental variables and appropriate management concepts and techniques that lead to effective goal attainment. The contingency is simply a functional relationship between environment *if*'s and management *then*'s. Normally, the environmental *if*'s are independent variables and the management *then*'s are dependent variables. Contingency management differs from situational management in that situational management stresses diagnosing the situation and adapting to it, while contingency management strives to identify specific if-then relationships between environmental variables and management variables that lead to effective goal attainment.

A matrix with environmental *if*'s on the horizontal axis and management *then*'s on the vertical axis serves as the conceptual framework for contingency management. It is this conceptual framework that is of special importance to both management theory and practice. Past management knowledge from all the theoretical approaches (process, quantitative, behavioral, and systems) can be placed into the contingency framework. The framework can also give direction and order to the future theoretical development of the field. Although the two-dimensional matrix must sometimes rely upon the cascading-matrices concept introduced in Chapter 2 to reduce the environment-management contingency down to a practical level, the result can be a very specific guideline for the improved practice of management. Thus, the conceptual framework for contingency management can be utilized for both the theoretical development and actual practice of management.

The Role of the Environment

The impact of the environment on management has been the major impetus for the development of a contingency approach. Management does not operate in a vacuum. In systems terminology, management operates in an *open,* not *closed,* sense. The direct impact that the environment has on all aspects of management has become an accepted, irrefutable fact. In the future, the environment will play an even bigger role in management than it has in the recent past. All predictions of the future of management emphasize environmental impact. For example, Kast and Rosenzweig, after reviewing various experts' predictions of the future, summarize that organizations and factors influencing them will be as follows:

1 Organizations will be operating in a turbulent environment which requires continual change and adjustment.
2 They will have to adapt to an increasing diversity of cultural values in the social environment.
3 Greater emphasis will be placed on technological and social forecasting.
4 Organizations will continue to expand their boundaries and domains. They will increase in size and complexity.
5 Organizations will continue to differentiate their activities, causing increased problems of integration and coordination.
6 Organizations will continue to have major problems in the accumulation and utilization of knowledge. Intellectual activities will be stressed.
7 Greater emphasis will be focused on suggestion and persuasion rather than coercion based on authoritarian power as the means for coordinating the activities of the participants and functions within the organization.
8 Participants at all levels in organizations will have more influence. Organizations of the future will adopt a power-equalization rather than power-differentiation model.
9 There will be greater diversity in values and life styles among people and groups in organizations. A mosaic psychosocial system will be normal.
10 Problems of interface between organizations will increase. New means for effective interorganizational coordination will be developed.
11 Computerized information-decision systems will have an increasing impact upon organizations.
12 The number of professionals and scientists and their influence within organizations will increase. There will also be a decline in the proportion of independent professionals with many more salaried professionals.
13 Goals of complex organizations will diversify. Emphasis will be upon satisficing a number of goals rather than maximizing any one.
14 Evaluation of organizational performance will be difficult. Many new administrative techniques will be developed for evaluation of performance in all spheres of activity.[3]

The current scene plus predictions such as those above practically demand that the environment play a vital, integral role in management theory and practice.

The contingency conceptual framework, as presented in this book, classifies the external environment into general and specific categories. The general environment includes social, technical, economic, and political/legal forces. The specific environment consists of competitors, customers, and suppliers. Obviously, there are numerous possible environmental factors that can affect management. This is why classification schemes of the environment are necessary for a conceptual framework. The content of the classification will be constantly changing, but the categories themselves should not. Once again, this is why a sound *conceptual framework* is so important to contingency management.

[3] Fremont E. Kast and James E. Rosenzweig, *Organization and Management,* 2d ed., McGraw-Hill, New York, 1974, pp. 617–618.

The Management Concepts and Techniques

The major portion of the book was devoted to presenting the concepts and techniques from the process, quantitative, behavioral, and systems approaches. The format was to first present the best and most modern concepts and techniques from each of the respective approaches and then in the concluding chapter of each part contingently relate them to the environment.

The process concepts and techniques that were given specific attention included planning (forecasting and strategic and tactical plans), organizing (classical, neoclassical, behavioral, and modern structures), directing (leadership styles), communicating (interpersonal and organizational), and controlling (feedforward and feedback and modern techniques). The quantitative part emphasized the concept of quantitative decision making and the techniques of breakeven analysis, present value, linear programming, economic order quantity, queuing, and simulation. The major behavioral concepts and techniques included learning (classical and operant), behavior modification (reinforcement and punishment), motivation (expectancy and content), group dynamics (formation, conflict, and sensitivity training), and organization development (behavioral contingency management and job enrichment). The systems approach was presented in terms of general systems theory (closed and open), systems design and analysis (PPBS, cost/benefit and cost-effectiveness analysis, computer systems design, simulation, and network analysis), and management information systems (hierarchy of applications and the role of the computer).

The concluding chapter for each part was not intended to be an all-inclusive summary of the known environment-management contingency relationships. Instead, the concluding chapters, and the case that followed each, attempted to demonstrate how the particular management approach being considered could be placed into the contingency framework. The if-then statements were illustrative and representative of contingency management. To date, as was readily discernable from the contingency chapters themselves, the process and behavioral approaches are way ahead of the quantitative and systems approaches in their adaptability to contingency management. Much more attention and research has been devoted to contingently relating the environment to process and behavioral concepts and techniques than has been the case for the quantitative and systems areas. A major challenge for management in the future will be to continue and extend the contingency work that has gotten off to a good start in the process and behavioral areas and begin to develop needed contingency approaches in the quantitative and systems areas. The remainder of the chapter will examine and analyze in more detail some of the specific areas of needed development.

Future Development of Contingency Management

Besides the problem areas that have been directly or indirectly discussed in the preceding chapters and so far in this final chapter, there are several high-priority challenges that need attention for the future development of contingency management. Specifically, the problems associated with change, complexity, goals, measurement, and field research must be dealt with in the coming years.

The Challenge of Change

Contingency management does not escape the universal problem of change. Yet, it is because of the dynamic, turbulent nature of the environment that the contingency approach has emerged. The conceptual framework is designed to handle change, but the problem evolves from the specific if-then relationships that are identified for the more effective practice of management. Because of omnipresent change, the empirically validated if-then relationships may become obsolete relatively fast. A related problem is that an independent variable in a contingency relationship at one point in time may become dependent at a later point in time.

A major challenge for contingency management will be to remember that the conceptual framework is relatively stable, but the specific contingency relationships are subject to change. The practice of contingency management should maintain the perspective of flexibility and ability to cope with and adapt to change. Even though the squares of the conceptual matrix (the if-then statements) are based upon empirical research, they are subject to change. The contingency statements are in no way meant to be substitutes for the principles of management. In other words, the contingency statements are not universal across time. They are simply empirically determined *guidelines* for more effective practice. Such static (one point in time) guidelines are certainly better than what currently exists, which is essentially no guidelines for practice at all. However, it must be remembered, as the environment changes and as management changes, and they inevitably will, then it is expected that the contingency relationships will change. The conceptual framework, on the other hand, should remain the same. In other words, the conceptual framework for contingency management is constant, but the content will change over time.

The Challenge of Complexity

Closely related to the problem of change is that of complexity. The two tend to go hand in hand. As with change, contingency management does not solve the complexity problem. Yet, it does provide the conceptual framework to deal with the problem head on. One of the major reasons why the traditional approaches have been so popular and why they will continue to be popular in the coming years is that they greatly simplify management and ignore the extremely complex relationship with the environment. Although contingency management can also be criticized for its simplicity, at least it recognizes and provides the conceptual framework for dealing with the complexity.

The cascading-submatrices concept presented in Chapter 2 demonstrates how some of the complexity problems can be handled. Mathematical techniques such as factor analysis can also help solve some of the complexity problems. Yet, the very real problems of the interdependencies within and between the environment and management variables cannot and are not minimized in contingency management. The systems approach, of course, recognizes the interdependencies of the parts to the whole on a conceptual but not practical level. Contingency management also recognizes complex interdependencies conceptually but, unlike the systems approach, has already suggested some ways of dealing with this on a practical level and is committed to giving further attention to it in the future.

The Challenge of Goals

Contingency management is aimed at more effective goal attainment. However, like other scientific endeavors, there is the success criterion problem. A major thrust of contingency management is to establish empirically validated if-then relationships that lead to effective goal attainment. An unanswered question is, "What is effective goal attainment?" Contingency management will have to deal more directly with this question in the future.

It is not sufficient to point the finger at other academic disciplines such as economics and the behavioral sciences that have also not satisfactorily dealt with the success criterion problem. Both the content of goals and the degree of effectiveness of goal attainment must be given attention by contingency management in the future. Merely assuming goals such as profit, service, satisfaction, or social responsibility is not enough. For example, a contingent relationship that is established under the assumption that the goal is profit may not hold up for a goal that is actually social responsibility. The same is true of the degree of effectiveness. An assumption of a maximizing criterion may lead to a different set of contingencies than does a "satisficing" criterion. As indicated, these problems are not unique to contingency management. As the organizational sociologist James Price has noted,

Ideally, a standardized measure of effectiveness should be developed and applied to all types of organizations. Only in this way is it possible to classify organizations on a continuum from high to low effectiveness. However, relatively few studies of organizations have dealt explicitly with effectiveness, and, even where the problem is explicitly treated, diverse measures of effectiveness have been used. [4]

A major challenge for the future of contingency management will be to develop measurement approaches to both goals and effectiveness.

The Challenge of Measurement

Besides developing measures for goals and effectiveness, there is the whole problem of quantification and measurement of the contingency variables in general. Accurate measurement and quantification of the variables is a major goal of any scientific pursuit.

---

[4] James L. Price, *Organizational Effectiveness*, Irwin, Homewood, Ill., 1968, p. 5.

Although it is not absolutely required that quantification be used in measurement (for example, agreed-upon observations could be used to measure), quantification, especially of the environmental variables, would contribute to the future development of contingency management.

One reason quantifiable measures are so important to contingency management is that there may be differing intensities of environmental variables. A future goal may be to actually assign appropriate quantified weights to relevant environmental variables in establishing contingency relationships. The economic factors in the environment have already largely accomplished this quantifiable measurement through national income accounting methods. To relate this to contingency management, an example might be that if the GNP was at a certain level, then a certain organization structure should be used; or if the cost of living index was at a certain level, then a certain motivational technique should be used. These are only illustrative and may be unrealistic at the present time, but there seems little doubt of the need for more quantification of technological, political/legal, and especially, social factors in the environment.

Improved measurement and quantification of the variables can help fight the complexity problem discussed earlier. In addition, with quantification, computerization could begin to play an important role in contingency management. For instance, environmental input data could be fed into the computer, which would then search through its memory of empirically derived research findings and print out specific recommendations on the appropriate process, quantitative, behavioral, and systems concepts and techniques for effective management practice. Such use of the computer is very much within the realm of possibility, but, of course, at this point in time the output is only as good as the input and stored information. A major challenge for the future will be to develop more and better input data, which is largely a measurement problem, and expand the stored information, which is largely a problem of more and better field research.

The Challenge of Field Research

Management is long overdue for more good, rigorous empirical research. Only through scientifically derived research findings can a truly meaningful body of contingency management be built. The if-then relationships that directly relate to contingency management practice must be empirically validated.

A research base is one of the major ways that contingency management can differ from the traditional approaches to management. In the past, the other approaches, especially the process approach, have lacked a research tradition. The absence of any meaningful research back-up was very comfortable for those who advocated universal application of their respective approach. The proselytizers (advocates) repeatedly cited a few old studies to verify their approach. Leonard Sayles describes this prevailing situation as follows:

Lacking an accepted research tradition, the field of management and all its branches (human relations, organization theory, and organization behavior) often rest on proselytizing. In both the regular and the executive development classroom the emphasis is on a narrow range of interpersonal and rationalistic skills (for example, communicating trust and thinking in policy terms). A group of essentially unvalidated but remarkable demonstration studies are most frequently emphasized—described, lectured about, and repeated *ad nauseum*.[5]

Contingency management will have to avoid the problem pinpointed by Sayles. On the other hand, it is important that the right kind of research be performed. Both basic research and applied field research are needed in contingency management. Basic research is certainly needed to further develop the theoretical aspects of contingency management, but of greater importance and priority is the need for applied field research.

Although there is little agreement on the terminology that is used to differentiate the various types of research methods, basic research is used here to mean the systematic investigation of theoretical problems (such as the goals problem cited earlier) inherent in contingency management. The more needed field research is applied and includes both field studies and field experiments. A field study would systematically investigate environment-management relationships as they exist in a real, field setting without attempting to influence the variables. In this way, meaningful contingency relationships could be identified for management practice. One major advantage of a field study is that there is little or no disruption and hence no "Hawthorne effect" problem with the results. Secondly, because the study is conducted in the actual setting, the problems of generalization are minimized. The results of a field study can be directly applied to management practice. The major disadvantages are controlling the variables and drawing any generalizations about cause and effect. The field experiment, on the other hand, overcomes these disadvantages but has the problem of disrupting the situation, and generalizations are less confident. In a field experiment changes are introduced in order to test a hypothesis or evaluate the effectiveness of some intervention. For example, the environmental situation may be changed to see what impact this will have on the effectiveness of various management concepts and techniques. In the future, existing contingency relationships must be continually tested and new contingency relationships must be determined through such field research techniques.

A Final Word

This book has attempted to present a new conceptual framework for management that incorporates the environment; to present the modern management concepts and techniques in an eclectic manner from the process, quantitative, behavioral, and systems approaches; and to show how the environment and management can be contingently related to lead to more effective management practice. This all comes under what is broadly called contingency management. It must carefully avoid the trap that is characteristic of the other approaches—that there is one best way to manage. In seemingly contradictory logic, this book suggests that contingency management is the one best approach

---

[5] Leonard Sayles, "Whatever Happened to Management?" *Business Horizons*, April 1970, p. 32.

to theory and practice, but by the very essence of contingency management this simply means that there is *no one best way to manage.* If attention is given to the challenges outlined in this chapter, then the contingency approach may serve as a unifying force for more meaningful management theory and more effective management practice.

Questions for Review and Discussion

1 In your own words, give an overview of contingency management as presented in this book. Include the historical background, conceptual framework, role of the environment, and management concepts and techniques.

2 Identify and analyze the challenges for the future development of contingency management.

3 What is the relative ranking of the challenges for the future development? Defend your answer.

4 Critically analyze the concluding statement of the book that there is "no one best way to manage."

References

Bearinger, Van W.: "Emerging Technologies and Their Impacts," *S.A.M. Advanced Management Journal,* January 1974, pp. 25–28.

Conrad, Robert B.: "The Antithetical Manager and Why He Succeeds," *S.A.M. Advanced Management Journal,* January 1974, pp. 7–15.

Douglas, Jack D. (ed.): *The Technological Threat,* Prentice-Hall, Englewood Cliffs, N.J., 1971.

Greenwood, William T.: "Future Management Theory: A Comparative Evolution to a General Theory," *Academy of Management Journal,* September 1974, pp. 503–513.

Hunt, J. G., and P. F. Newell: "Management in the 1980's Revisited," *Personnel Journal,* January 1971, pp. 35–43, 71.

Katz, Daniel, and Basil S. Georgopoulus: "Organizations in a Changing World," *Journal of Applied Behavioral Science,* May–June 1971, pp. 342–370.

Luthans, Fred: "Contingency Theory of Management: A Path out of the Jungle," *Business Horizons,* June 1973, pp. 67–72.

Reddin, W. J.: "Management Effectiveness in the 1980's," *Business Horizons,* August 1974, pp. 5–12.

Toffler, Alvin (ed.): *The Futurists,* Random House, New York, 1972.

Name Index

Subject Index